WORLD FOOD

— **Volume 1** —

WORLD FOOD

An Encyclopedia of
History, Culture, and
Social Influence from
Hunter-Gatherers to the
Age of Globalization

—— Volume 1 ——

Mary Ellen Snodgrass

SHARPE REFERENCE
an imprint of M.E. Sharpe, Inc.

SHARPE REFERENCE

Sharpe Reference is an imprint of M.E. Sharpe, Inc.

M.E. Sharpe, Inc.
80 Business Park Drive
Armonk, NY 10504

Cover images (clockwise from top left) provided by: De Agostini/Getty Images; Stringer/AFP/Getty Images; The Granger Collection, New York; Bachrach/Getty Images; Vincent Thian/Associated Press.

Library of Congress Cataloging-in-Publication Data

Snodgrass, Mary Ellen.
World food: an encyclopedia of history, culture, and social influence from hunter-gatherers to the age of globalization / Mary Ellen Snodgrass.
      p. cm.
Includes bibliographical references and index.
ISBN 978-0-7656-8278-9 (cloth: alk. paper)
1. Food—History—Encyclopedias. 2. Cooking—History—Encyclopedias. I. Title.

TX349.S66 2013
641.303—dc23

2012014375

Printed and bound in the United States

SP (c) 10 9 8 7 6 5 4 3

Publisher: Myron E. Sharpe
Vice President and Director of New Product Development: Donna Sanzone
Vice President and Production Director: Carmen Chetti
Executive Development Editor: Jeff Hacker
Project Manager: Laura Brengelman
Program Coordinator: Cathleen Prisco
Editorial Assistant: Lauren LoPinto
Text Design and Cover Design: Jesse Sanchez

Every social gathering and holiday is
With a feast begun and terminated;
And before our heads can have their say,
Our bellies must be fully sated.

Pellegrino Artusi
La Scienza in Cucina e l'Arte di Mangiar Bene, 1891

Contents

x   Contents

Recipes

Topic Finder

Wheat
Yeast

Health, Medicine, Nutrition
Allergies, Food
Curative Foods
Disease, Food-Borne
Hormones in Food
Malnutrition
Nutrition
Obesity
Plant Disease and Prevention
Poisonous Foods
Sanitation
Trans Fat

Meals and Courses
Appetizers and Hors d'Oeuvres
Breakfast
Dinner
Feasting
Finger Food
Holiday Dishes and Festival Foods
Lunch
Salad and Salad Bars
Snack Food
Soups

Preservation and Storage
Caching
Canning
Curing
Dried Food
Fermented Foods
Packaging
Pemmican
Pickling
Refrigeration
Seaman's Diet and Cuisine
Smoked Food
Storage, Food
Travel Food

Science and Technology
Additives, Food
Adulterated Food
Agroecology
Aquaponics
Blenders and Food Processors
Cookware
Coprolites
Desalination
Dye, Food
Freeze-Drying

Genetically Modified Food
Hormones in Food
Hybridization
Industrial Food Processing
Inspection and Safety, Food
Irrigation
Middens
Milling
Refrigeration
Trans Fat

Social Issues and Government Programs
Airlifts, Food
Biopiracy
Commodity Regulation
Commodity Riots
Consumer Protection Laws
Endangered Species
Famine
Famine Relief
Farm Subsidies and Government Agricultural
    Programs
Inspection and Safety, Food
International Food Aid
Malnutrition
Obesity
Prohibition
Rationing
Sanitation
Soup Kitchens
Whaling

Sources and Acquisition
(See also "Foodstuffs"; "Trade, Commerce,
    Distribution")
Agriculture
Animal Husbandry
Cannibalism
Dairy Food
Fish and Fishing
Free-Range Foods
Fructarianism
Hunter-Gatherers
Paleolithic Diet
Wild Food

Trade, Commerce, Distribution
African Food Trade
Agribusiness
Airlifts, Food
Asian Food Trade
Australian Food Trade
Barter

British East India Company
Caravans
Clipper Ships
Commodity Regulation
Cooperatives, Food
Currency, Food as
Danish East India Company
Danish West India Company
Dutch East India Company
Exotic Food Clubs
Famine Relief
French East India Company
French West India Company
House of India
Hudson's Bay Company
International Food Aid
London Virginia Company
Mail-Order Food
Maritime Trade Routes
Markets and Marketing
McDonald's
Mozambique Company
North Borneo Company
Packaging
Portuguese East India Company
Restaurants
Royal Greenland Trade Department
Seed Trade
Sierra Leone Company

Silk Road
Supermarkets
Swedish East India Company
Swedish West India Company
Trade Routes
Trading Vessels
Virginia Company of Plymouth
World Trade

Trends and Movements, Modern

Cooperatives, Food
Ecofeminism
Exotic Food Clubs
Fads
Fast Food
Free-Range Foods
Fructarianism
Fusion Cuisine
Genetically Modified Food
Heirloom Plants
Local Food Movement
Nouvelle Cuisine
Organic Foods
Paleolithic Diet
Slow Food
Veganism
Vegetarianism
Wild Food

Preface

World Food examines the spectrum of comestibles as they apply to history, politics, economics, medicine, nutrition, ethnicity, worship, and invention. For the convenience and edification of the teacher, student, researcher, chef, and food faddist, the text summarizes specifics of eating history—the development of humankind from hunter-gatherers to Turkish herders and German vintners, the marketing of foodstuffs at the produce stalls of Nice and the canal boats of Bangkok, and the exploitation of valuable edibles by Sri Lankan planters and Spanish conquerors. The issues of the present—improvements in the packaging, sanitation, and transportation of perishables—forecast the future of nontoxic, nourishing food for both the privileged and the have-nots.

The list of entries covers travel writers (Ibn Battuta, Herodotus, Marco Polo), growers (Thomas Jefferson, Jethro Tull), preparers (Huou, Apicius, Pierre La Varenne, Julia Child), marketers (Agnes Marshall, Luther Burbank), scientists (James Lind, Nicholas Culpeper, Carolus Linnaeus), and corporations (Swedish East India Company, Virginia Company of Plymouth, McDonald's). National tastes figure in entries on specific examples of diet and cuisine—Russian, Inca, Indonesian, Portuguese, Byzantine—and in the preparation of such ethnic specialties as tofu, bushmeat, chowder, kebabs, dal, and condiments.

Essays particularize flora and fauna that impact world events—beef and corn and maize in the settlement of North America, einkorn and emmer wheats in the evolution of bread, the buffalo in the gastronomy of Plains Indians, and tea in the socialization of Japan and China. Food processing attests to the ingenuity of cooks and industrialists and its importance in world history, notably pasta in the industrialization of Sicily, tortillas in Latin America, chutney in India, pemmican in the success of the Hudson's Bay Company, whiskey in the struggle between imbibers and abstainers, salt and vinegar to early miners and vegetable preservers, biscuits and bouillon to expeditions and military provisioners, and baby food and infant formulas for child nutritionists.

In addition to kitchen staff and grocery dealers, gastronomy overlaps the concerns of altruists and activists, including ecofeminists, the battlefield cookery of Mary Jane Seacole during the Crimean War, the relief kitchens of Alexis Soyer to mitigate the Irish Potato Famine, rationing during world wars, soup kitchen cooks, and U.S. supply airlifts to the Burma Road and war-ravaged Berlin in the 1940s. The ethical sale and consumption of food permeates entries on food taboos, halal, biopiracy, prohibition, peyote, kosher food, alcoholic beverages, and vegetarianism. Some of the most serious issues emerge under the headings of commodity riots, famine relief, and endangered species.

The role of exploration in acquainting consumers with new possibilities in table fare elevates the importance of Christopher Columbus, Captain James Cook, Amédée François Frézier, Giovanni da Verrazzano, and Hernán de Cortés. Entries on trade routes and trading vessels, caravans, clipper ships, and world trade summarize the successful conveyance of such perishables as yams, strawberries, and birch beer. From the transporters' holds, crates and bags pass to the operators of food inspection and safety, commodity regulation, public markets, food cooperatives, cooking schools, and farm subsidies and government agricultural programs. More technological matters fill essays on freeze-drying, refrigeration, monoculture, food storage, hormones in food, Count Rumford, and seed trade.

Peripheral issues stress the crucial nature of food intake to well-being, the focus of articles on obesity, nutrition, food allergies, curative foods, fads, adulterated and poisonous foods, and additives and dyes. An overview of the food preparer in grilling, barbecue, saucing, pickling, cook-offs, espaliering, animal husbandry, and milling emphasizes the continued importance of the individual in feeding the world. A thorough survey of world food would not be complete without the evolution of agriculture into agribusiness, the rise of barter as a means of negotiation, foods used as currency, garbage disposal in middens, the selection of recipes for cookbooks, the invention of cookware and blenders and food processors, the representation of dining in the arts and film, and future concerns for traditions, customs, and food in the afterlife.

Research involved delvings into a range of literature, beginning with retrospects on the Paleolithic diet, the Fertile Crescent, the Silk Road, the tea ceremony, and the fare of the Crusaders. In addition to the biographies of Charlemagne and Catherine de' Médici, food critiques derived from chronicler Garcilaso de la Vega, sugar refiner Jules Paul Benjamin Delessert, esthete Jean Anthelme Brillat-Savarin, environmentalist Rachel Carson, ethnographer Bernardino da Sahagún, horticulturist Antoine Nicholas Duchesne, folklorist and columnist Linda West Eckhardt, encyclopedist Pliny the Elder, and infantryman Bernal Díaz. The best in pantry and dining histories came from the works of Ken Albala, Sidney C.H. Cheung, Linda Civitello, Andrew Dalby, Alan Davidson, Yiu H. Hui, Michael Krondl, Andrew F. Smith, and Maguelonne Toussaint-Samat as well as articles from *Archaeology, History, Mother Earth News, National Geographic, Saudi Aramco World, The New York Times,* and *Vegetarian Times.*

Rounding out the text, additional study aids and special sections elucidate individual foods, events, and concepts:

Topic Finder classifies the encyclopedia's more than 350 articles into general subject categories.

Chronology covers events from the origin of cooked food to the twenty-first century. Entries recognize the importance of the natural changes that coagulated yogurt and fermented grape juice and the marches and voyages that generated awareness of world cuisines and customs. Landmarks note the transplanting of New World breadfruit, publication of cookbooks, and environmental research into adulterated food and pollutants. Within events are the achievements of notable figures in related fields.

Appendix of Herbal Foods and Uses reveals the multiple applications of native flora to recipes, wellness, and alternative medical treatments. Sources include chaparral, a Mexican and South African heath plant that flavors a tea and cure for cough; ginseng, an age-old Chinese nostrum used in candy and for treating malaise and poor appetite; bergamot, an Ojibwa salad green valuable for relieving insomnia; and scurvy grass, a British salad and potherb that supplies the body with vitamin C to combat loose teeth and bleeding caused by a nutrient deficiency. The listings mention slippery elm and yarrow, two favorites of Australasians and the Cheyenne for skin disease and infected wounds, and willow, a food for beekeeping in China and a multinational ingredient in an analgesic tea once prescribed in Assyria, Egypt, Greece, and Sumer.

Glossary of terms defines the use of tagines and mandolines, invention of the bain-marie and *shaduf,* philosophies of macrobiotics and the frugivore, treatment of zoonosis and imbalance in the four humors, creation of forcemeat and gene banks, and differences among the gastronome, gourmand, epicure, and gourmet. Perspectives on food history explain value judgments concerning heritage foods, national dishes, and idiocuisine. Key terms—*terroir, fermentation, agribusiness, curing, food justice*—lend insight to such issues as where and how to grow, preserve, and market comestibles for the benefit of all.

Acknowledgments

I could not have completed this text without advice from a long list, which follows, of researchers, chemists, archivists, chefs, travelers, gourmands, farmers, and especially reference librarians, the backbone of scholarship. Historical societies, university libraries, the Library of Congress, book and film reviewers, and specialists in food preparation and marketing elucidated various details. Charity workers and church and ethnic authorities suggested variant points of view on famine in East Africa, the agricultural advances of Norman Borlaug, child malnutrition along the Sahel, and the dietary compromises between faith groups in India and China. I found particularly helpful the databases of the Alexandria Street Press, UNICEF advisories, and the additions of Laura Brengelman concerning endangered flora and fauna.

Special thanks to Martin Otts and Mark Schumacher for running down sources and bibliography information and to Eileen Lawrence and Stephen Rhind-Tutt for the use of Anthropology Online and Women and Social Movements, International, two databases hosted by Alexandria Street Press. Blessings on Mary Canrobert for answering my myriad questions about Chinese grocery stores and hot shops. As always, I rely on editor Jeff Hacker and my publicist, Joan Lail, for dissuading me from folly.

Jason Achiu, reference, Hawaii State Archives, Honolulu, Hawaii

Belk Library, Appalachian State University, Boone, North Carolina

Beth Bradshaw and Martin Otts, reference librarians, and Mary Sizemore, Patrick Beaver Library, Hickory, North Carolina

Brown University Library, Providence, Rhode Island

Burton Library, George Mason University, Fairfax, Virginia

Julie Byrd and Terri Cain, Catawba County Social Services, Hickory, North Carolina

Mark and Mary Canrobert, former residents of Souzhou, China

Bonnie Chandler, reference, Columbus Public Library, Columbus, Ohio

Sergei Demchenko, restaurateur, Odessa, Ukraine

A. Asa Eger, history professor, University of North Carolina at Greensboro, North Carolina

Miguel Gonzales and Ernesto Hernandez, Mexico City, Mexico

Ken Ho, industrialist, Hong Kong, China

Virginia Iubio, resident of Gualajara, Mexico

Jackson Library, University of North Carolina, Greensboro, North Carolina

J.D. Williams Library, University of Mississippi, Oxford, Mississippi

Joyner Library, East Carolina University, Greenville, North Carolina

Eleanor Kleiber, Dore Minatodani, and James Cartwright, archivists, University of Hawaii at Manoa Library, Honolulu, Hawaii

Kristin McCormick, reference, Reynoldsburg Public Library, Reynoldsburg, Ohio

Brian Mierau, industrialist, Souzhou, China

Nicole Mones, author of *The Last Chinese Chef,* Portland, Oregon

Susan Nahwoosky, administrative assistant to the president, Comanche Nation College, Lawton, Oklahoma

Diana Norman, novelist, Stevenage, England

Hannah Owen, children's librarian emerita, Patrick Beaver Library, Hickory, North Carolina

Lotsee Patterson, professor emerita, University of Oklahoma, Norman, Oklahoma

Juan Manuel Perez, Hispanic reference librarian, Library of Congress, Washington, D.C.

Mark Schumacher, reference, University of North Carolina at Greensboro, North Carolina

Texas A&M University Libraries, College Station, Texas

Introduction

Food history refuses to stay in the market basket. Eating is too important to humankind for its story to boil down to tidy pantry lists and shortbread recipes. The best in dining ranges from Charlemagne's Easter feasts and exotic food club banquets to soul food pig pickins' and the *pièces montées* of nineteenth-century French master chef and author Marie-Antoine Carême. An overview of how people choose, prepare, and consume edibles strays into camel caravans, Christmas Eve, ships' galleys, potato chip factories, Aztec mano and metate, and Ramadan.

A comprehensive history of human sustenance looks back many millennia for glimpses of roasting chestnuts at the fireside of Belgian Celts and pressing wild plums for juice along the Fertile Crescent. Preceding the skills of the Halifax sea captain and Alexandrian grocer, the instincts for paddy patterns and the best weather for combining ensure ample harvests of rice and wheat. The knowledge of provisioners, meat carvers, and bakers incorporates the finer points of coopering barrels for stowing Norwegian dried cod, impaling agave and beef heart for pit roasting, and creaming lard and castor sugar for icing hot cross buns and stollen.

Tucked deep into prehistory lie the menus of Hopi, Australian Aborigines, Berbers, and Greenlanders. Stirring moments in the culinary past juxtapose the first fermentation of Greek yogurt and the clubbing of wild rice into Cree canoes with the establishment of Chinese restaurants along the path of the Union Pacific Railroad and the pioneer squeeze tubes that extruded fruit for early space crews. Improvements to oyster trading on Southeast Asian sampans parallel the development of Carnation canned milk and the debut of containerized pineapples lifted by gantry aboard Dole's transoceanic steamers. Awards for innovation extend credit to salt rinds on Dutch cheese, Ball's improved canning jar, Japan's first rice-winnowing basket, and upgraded shrink-wrap to protect Irish salmon.

Overall, the story of food consumption reveals the rudiments of human life. Like breathing and sleeping, eating sequences the regular satisfaction of needs that connects appetites to nature. The urge to sip and chew explains teatime and the coffee or *yerba buena* break and justifies the search for newer titillations of the taste buds with sashimi, passion fruit, Kaffir lime, hummus, near beer, vitamin water, deep-fried pickles—anything new or unusual. So long as the drive persists to delight in aroma and mouthfeel, the consumer will scan grocery shelves and restaurant menus and pay the price.

WORLD FOOD

— Volume 1 —

Abreu, António de (ca. 1480–ca. 1514), and Francisco Serrao (?–1521)

Explorer António de Abreu, an experienced sea voyager, and his second-in-command, Francisco Serrao, introduced the Portuguese to a monopoly on cloves and nutmeg in Indonesia that broke the Arab and Venetian control of luxury spices in the early sixteenth century.

Intrigued by adventurer Ludovico de Varthema's tales of Bandanese nutmegs and Moluccan cloves in 1502, Afonso de Albuquerque, Portugal's viceroy to India at Goa, dispatched a three-ship fleet from the Bay of Bengal to Malacca in December 1511. He instructed the crew to reconnoiter the Spice Islands, where clove and nutmeg trees flourished on the five-island cluster. Buyers in London, Paris, and Rotterdam paid princely amounts for nutmeg, a preservative for meat, tranquilizer, sleep inducer, and alleged deterrent of bubonic plague. In the flagship *Santa Catarina,* de Abreu, serving as the ambassador of commerce, hired three Javanese pilots and 120 men to crew the two caravels and an Indian supply ship from the Strait of Malacca east through uncharted seas toward Java.

The fleet reached Gresik, Java, in sight of terraced rice fields and exotic fruits. The first Europeans to discover Banda and the Pacific Ocean, de Abreu's crew advanced directly to the heart of a global bonanza, spices bought cheap and sold with a 30,000 percent markup. The Portuguese sailors encountered a lively sea emporium that had drawn Chinese merchants in junks for centuries. De Abreu exchanged bells, bracelets, and trinkets for cloves, the sepals of red tubular flowers that dotted 40-foot (12-meter) trees.

Nutmeg trees grew to 50 feet (15 meters) and produced a quince-shaped fruit. Covering the nut at the center, mace had its own distinctive flavor from the kernel, which users grated for its spicy scent and tangy taste. The wholesale cost was so low that de Abreu anticipated a tenfold profit in Lisbon. De Abreu raised a stele acknowledging Portugal's annexation of the Banda Islands. He died in the Azores on his return trip to Portugal.

Before the voyage to the Portuguese home port in India in December 1512, greed inspired de Abreu to overtax his vessels. Francisco Serrao, skipper of the second caravel, the aged *Sabaia,* burned the leaky hull and purchased a junk, on which he loaded cloves, mace, and nutmegs. Another product of the islands, dead flycatchers, honeyeaters, kingfishers, and pigeons covered in elegant plumage, brought high prices on the fashion market.

On the return journey to Malacca, winds beached Serrao's junk off the island of Pude. He and his crew commandeered a pirate outrigger and sailed to Hitu, where a tribal chief treated the Portuguese to attractive women and a banquet of fowl and goat meat, cups of arak (anise liquor), and dishes of sago, the main food of the Malay people. They encountered bamboo as thick as a man's leg, a source of pure, refreshing water.

To increase their power and income, the islanders sought reliable trading partners. Clove growers on Ternate and Tidore arrived by outrigger canoes to court potential purchasers of cloves. Serrao remained in the islands as prime minister to the king of Ternate, which became the center of the Portuguese spice trade. Ferdinand Magellan, a friend and cousin who had accompanied him on the voyage, parted ways and continued sailing, eventually leading the first expedition (1519–1522) to circumnavigate the globe.

After a follow-up expedition arrived in the Moluccas in 1514, Portuguese merchants set up regular voyages between outposts in Molucca and India and collaborated with the Dutch in distributing spice to sellers along the Rhine River valley. Serrao died in Ternate in 1521 a short time before Philippine natives killed Magellan in a skirmish.

See also: House of India.

Further Reading

Bernstein, William J. *A Splendid Exchange: How Trade Shaped the World.* New York: Atlantic Monthly, 2008.

Headrick, Daniel R. *Power over Peoples: Technology, Environments, and Western Imperialism, 1400 to the Present.* Princeton, NJ: Princeton University Press, 2010.

Mercene, Floro L. *Manila Men in the New World: Filipino Migration to Mexico and the Americas from the Sixteenth Century.* Diliman, Quezon City: University of the Philippines Press, 2007.

Additives, Food

The adjustment of taste, aroma, texture, and longevity in modern food derives from some 2,800 additives. Since the seventeenth century, processors of food have relied primarily on natural additives—salt, smoke, sugar, and vinegar—to enhance the flavor and shelf life of beef, century eggs (preserved eggs), ham, herring, hominy, *kimchi,* lutefisk, salmon, and sauerkraut. The Industrial Revolution increased reliance on other modifications. A common example, carbon dioxide, a harmless gas, creates effervescence in beer, mineral water, and whipped topping. A safe and effective thickener, cellulose from cotton lint or wood pulp congeals diet food and pie filling. Casein, a milk protein, thickens sherbet. Corn syrup has the same effect in marshmallows, much as various food starches condense baby food. Citric acid flavors instant potatoes; chicory root sweetens granola. Malt ferments beer; quinine enlivens tonic water.

Some additives alter appearance, such as bleaches (chlorine), glazers (paraffin), humectants (urea), and anticaking (talc), defoaming (silicone oil), and bulking agents (nuts and arrowroot). Algae, egg yolk, kelp, pectin, whey, and other emulsifiers maintain the smooth blend of coffee creamers, cranberry sauce, jam, and mayonnaise. The beeswax that glazes cheese rounds and melons and the paraffin coating on apples, chocolates, and cucumbers prevent deterioration from the action of air, bacteria, fungi, and light. Soybeans and tapioca provide the texture in imitation meats, such as veggie burgers, faux crabmeat, and tempeh. Flavorants increase the smell and taste of familiar processed foods—apple acid in iced tea mix, esters in Juicy Fruit gum, lactic acid in cheese, and phosphoric acid in Coca-Cola.

Food dyes, a common food additive, contribute the natural shades of alfalfa, algae, blueberries, caramel, carrots, elderberries, grapes, mushrooms, peas, and turmeric to enhance the eye appeal of products such as Kool-Aid, M&Ms, popcorn, and wine. Consumers associate annatto yellow with margarine; ascorbic acid with canned peaches; beet red with icings, puddings, and yogurt; dextrose with brown bread crust; paprika with salad dressing and tomato soup; saffron yellow with rice; and strawberry red with jelly.

Carmine, the red dye in cider and chewing gum and on hot dog and sausage casings, differs from vegetable dye in that it derives from the *Dactylopius coccus,* an insect that infests the opuntia cactus in Central and North America. Because of its animal source, vegans and vegetarians avoid it. Orthodox Jews ban carmine from kosher foods. Hindus, Jains, and Muslims also demand oversight of food enhancement to restrict animal by-products, particularly rennet from the stomachs of ruminants and gelatin obtained from animal bones, hides, and hooves.

For binding and texture, packagers of ready-to-eat foods into the early twentieth century added potato and rice flour, oat fiber, and soybean products, the standard thickeners that gave authentic mouthfeel to ice cream and tomato ketchup. When a new wave of synthetics compromised food quality, the Pure Food and Drug Act of 1906 approved orange dye, the first synthetic tint. The law also allowed six other artificial colorants, ranging from red, pink, and yellow to indigo and black. Also deemed safe were dyes on orange peels and maraschino cherries and in butter and red velvet cake. In 1938, the Federal Food, Drug, and Cosmetic Act enumerated food tints such as amaranth, labeled Red No. 2.

On January 1, 1958, the Food Additives Amendment identified 700 safe food substances and banned such carcinogens as cyclamate and lead and halogenated compounds. New regulations required specific clearances for questionable additives, including binders, enzymes, gelatin thickeners, stabilizers, and texturizers. In 1960, the Color Additives Amendments delisted some of the colors previously classified as safe for use in food, notably, blue 2, green 3, orange B, red 3, and yellow 5 and 6. Thereafter, the United Kingdom reduced its approved food dyes to 16, and Canadian health officials banned azo compounds, the source of nearly 70 percent of all dyes. Norway and Sweden proscribed all colorants as health hazards. In March 2011, China forbade millers from bleaching wheat flour.

Worldwide, biochemists investigate the effects of antinutritional additives on internal organs, as well as on diabetics, hemophiliacs, and pregnant women and fetuses. Nutritional watch lists continue to question the antioxidant butylated hydroxyanisole (BHA) in cereal and oil, caffeine in cocoa and energy drinks, potassium bromate in bread and rolls, diacetyl in butter-flavored popcorn and sour cream, caramel coloring in soy sauce, and aspartame and other artificial sweeteners in diet products. All of these chemicals increase cancer risks.

In 2010, the United Nations published the findings of a global consortium on specific food additives. The group, consisting of members of the Food and Agriculture Organization and the World Health Organization, found acceptable cassia gum in cream cheese and lycopene food color from tomatoes in sauces. The consortium required more study of gum arabic and nitrous oxide in bread and recommended limited consumption of cyclamates in energy drinks, especially for children.

More recent concerns target guar gum in cottage cheese, nitrates and nitrites in cured meats such as bacon and salami, propyl gallate in chicken soup, and the use of antibiotics in cattle.

See also: Adulterated Food; Allergies, Food; Guar; Hormones in Food; Monosodium Glutamate; Organic Foods.

Further Reading

Branen, A. Larry, P. Michael Davidson, Seppo Salminen, and John H. Thorngate, eds. *Food Additives.* 2nd ed. New York: Marcel Dekker, 2002.

Greenfield, Amy Butler. *A Perfect Red: Empire, Espionage, and the Quest for the Color of Desire.* New York: HarperCollins, 2005.

Joint FAO/WHO Expert Committee on Food Additives. Meeting. *Evaluation of Certain Food Additives.* Geneva, Switzerland: World Health Organization, 2010.

Sun, Da-wen, ed. *Modern Techniques for Food Authentication.* Boston: Elsevier, 2008.

Adulterated Food

Corrupt and bogus foods have threatened the well-being of the human community since prehistory. Adulterants derive from natural deterioration, domestic and industrial contamination, and extenders introduced during processing, packaging, and storage.

As a business and public relations measure, early commodities sellers recognized standards that protected consumers from spurious additives, such as the blending of fresh goods with stale or spoiled stock and the masking of foul odors. Book four of the Indian Kautilya's *Arthashastra* (*Statecraft,* ca. 300 B.C.E.), an economic advisement to the first Maurya emperor, authorized the penalizing of market cheats for adding filler to alkali, grain, oil, and salt, watering milk, or stretching flour with ground alum, bone, chalk, plaster, or stones. As described in the Confucian ritual text *Zhouli* (*Chou-li, Rites of Chou,* compiled ca. 1116 B.C.E.), similar oversight in Chinese markets confirmed the quality of goods from food processors, public kitchens, and wineries.

For the average consumer, warnings about adulterated food traditionally required more education than most possessed. Greco-Roman officials inspected wholesale goods and fined vendors for applying gypsum, lead, and lime as sweeteners in wine and soft white silt to bread. During the fifth decade of the Roman Empire, encyclopedist Pliny the Elder warned in his *Historia Naturae* (*Natural History,* ca. 77 C.E.) of grain adulteration in Tunisia, where dealers added 25 percent gypsum to emmer grain, the basis of common porridge.

Florentine merchant Francesco Balducci Pegolotti, a late medieval consumer advocate, composed *Pratica della Mercatura* (*Merchant's Handbook,* ca. 1343), a guide to measures and standards for fruit, honey, loaf and granular sugar, molasses, potash, salt fish, and wine. He warned of irregularities in packaging and weights and measures as well as the length of time goods traveled over known routes. In London, sellers of putrid meat and spice vendors who padded their stocks with extenders suffered pillorying over a fire of offensive goods. In Nuremberg, Germany, conspiracy to defraud consumers could result in defrauders suffering exile, lashing, lopping of ears or nose, blinding, poisoning, drowning, burning, or being buried alive.

Fraudulent Food

Merchants shared ill fame with professional cooks. Caterers adulterated food through menu substitutions, sup-planting boar with pig, caviar with fish roe, stag with beef, veal with sturgeon, even imitation meat from almond paste and dried fruit grilled on a spit. In fifteenth-century Sicily, bakers color-coded bread quality—pure white loaves for the rich, dark to black loaves for the poor. In times of famine, the wealthy continued to eat well, but the lowest class ate loaves permeated with grain substitutes—bean husks, berries, grass, leaves, nuts, parsnips, sawdust, seeds, squash, and wild radish and asparagus. In *Historia General de las Cosas de Nueva España* (*General History of the Things of New Spain,* 1540–1585), culinary historian Bernardino de Sahagún encountered a swindler in Mexico who concocted amaranth seeds, chalk, and wax into dough and sold it as cacao beans.

Honey offered the dishonest opportunities to sell rancid or spiked goods. In England, a lawsuit over sulphurated honey set buyer against seller in 1457, with damages assessed at 40 shillings. Elizabeth I fought such faulty commodities by proclaiming a purity act of 1580 requiring bona fide labeling of honey. Those selling counterfeit produce risked a penalty of 6 shillings 8 pence. The following year, similar stringent regulations forbade the contamination of beeswax with resin, tallow, or turpentine. European standards appear to have dropped in the mid-1700s, when apothecary John Hill reported honey contaminated during collection and laced with flour. To ensure quality goods, he recommended buying only thin, transparent stock.

Worldwide, the adulteration of foodstuffs has involved innovative addition of almond oil, alum, elderberry juice, limewater, sugar, sulphuric acid, tartar salts, and turpentine to foodstuffs. Domestic manuals, including *The School of Arts,* a handbook published in 1754 by the Royal Society of Arts, suggested testing for chalk in flour by mixing a sample with vinegar or lemon juice, which generates bubbles in calcium carbonate (though an absence of bubbles does not ensure purity). When taoism influenced food selection and preparation, poet Yuan Mei, author of *Shih Tan* (*The Menu,* 1796), advocated inspection of pigs and chickens for disease. For bird's nest soup, he declared that no feathers should mar the broth. On the subject of sea slugs and sharks, he urged rinsing out sand and mud, which inflated the cost and threatened teeth with grit.

Early Food Analysis

In 1820, mineralogist and analytic chemist Friedrich Christian Accum, apothecary to George III, issued *A Treatise on the Adulterations of Food and Culinary Poisons.* The jeremiad, subtitled "There is Death in the Pot," exposed sham Chinese tea consisting of dried thorn leaves dyed with toxic verdigris and also warned of blancmange laced with copper arsenite, a deadly food dye. Because he named names, angry food adulterers forced him to flee to Berlin. Corroborating Accum's identification of lethal commodities, the *Edinburgh Magistrates Minute Book* from

September 7, 1847, warned that a Dalkeith veterinarian observed provisioners salting, slicing into roasts, making into pies, or grinding into sausage the carcasses of cattle felled by disease. In this same period, John Marius Wilson's *The Rural Cyclopaedia* (1849) exposed Edinburgh dairies that removed cream from milk and thickened and whitened skim milk with magnesium carbonate or rice or wheat flour. Additional milk camouflage involved adding ground almonds or hemp seed and egg whites to simulate a creamy consistency.

In the 1850s, when the Industrial Revolution made laborers more dependent on processed foods than on home gardens, Arthur Hill Hassall, another British consumer advocate, found nearly half of arrowroot in London markets to be blended with potato flour. With a microscope, Hassall identified chicory in coffee, a substitution that kept the cost low in a highly competitive market. He also uncovered irregularities in name brands—Frys and Cadbury cocoa, Crosse & Blackwell condiments, Fortnum & Mason's sauces, and J. & J. Coleman mustard. His crusade disclosed red earth in French tomato sauce and burned treacle in Indian soy. Hassall's praise for Borden's Patent Meat Biscuit so improved sales that firms sought his certification on food labels. An American contemporary, commercial beekeeper Moses Quinby of New York, complained that food tainters pumped glucose and maple syrup into honey to inflate profits and extend shelf life. Consumers rashly blamed exporters of foreign goods for polluting packaged foods, but investigators found most deception among conspirators closer to home.

During the rise of home economics to a profession in the mid-nineteenth century, the media published warnings about wheat flour adulterated with plaster of paris, copper salts in pickles and bottled fruits and vegetables, oil of vitriol in vinegar, and red lead in cayenne pepper. In 1850, Thomas Wakley, editor of *The Lancet*, England's primary medical journal, established the Analytical and Sanitary Commission, which vilified chemical enhancement of 2,500 foodstuffs. Commissioners impugned cider passed off as wine, copper and lead salts in candy, iron compounds in fish and potted meat, poisons in beer, potash lining in bottles, rancid butter, red lead in cheese, and turmeric in mustard.

Within five years of empanelment, analysts, aided by London medical officer Henry Letheby, prompted the English parliament to halt food fraud by passing the Food Adulteration Act of 1860. The commission noted that the lower class suffered from purchase of the most polluted and least authentic foods and palliatives, such as caffeine, cocaine, and opium in soda fountain drinks and morphine-laced soothing syrups for babies. The Adulteration of Food, Drink, and Drugs Act of 1872 put more bite into enforcement. By the 1890s, English market goods were purer and safer.

Pure Food Movement

Americans demanded similar strictures. As early as 1641, the Massachusetts Bay Colony protected meat and pork from impurity and appointed a bread inspector. In 1876, industrialist Henry J. Heinz guaranteed customers wholesome tomato ketchup rather than tomato sauce adulterated with turnips or wood fiber. He sold his spicy blend in glass bottles but his candor failed to protect the public from the most debased goods. In 1882, inspectors in New York City published tampering rates in the least dependable goods: coffee (90.5 percent), candy (70.0 percent), brandy (64.0 percent), and spices (62.2 percent). To alert Congress and the Federation of Women's Clubs to the danger of additives, author Ella Hoes Neville stated the difference between cheating and poisoning the public: "Give us short measure and we lose; give us adulterated food and we die."

Before the U.S. Congress authorized the federal government to inspect, test, and approve foods and food additives in 1883, Harvey Washington Wiley, chief forensic chemist of the U.S. Department of Agriculture, led a 30-year crusade for food safety and purity standards. A subsequent campaign begun by the Michigan Women's Christian Temperance Union attacked impure comestibles and drugs. Led by dietitian Ella Eaton Kellogg, author of *Science in the Kitchen* (1892), the women challenged dangerous and unhygienic foodstuffs. Echoing her concerns, the Department of Agriculture found that additives and fillers were an industry standard in processed foods.

In *Air, Water, and Food: From a Sanitary Standpoint* (1901), a classic study of the human need for safe life-giving elements, authors Ellen Swallow Richards and Alpheus Grant Woodman devoted much of their text to adulterated food. They warned of unscrupulous dealers and specified the dangers of baking powder containing alum, ginger mixed with turmeric and redwood sawdust, wood ash in rancid pork, and watered milk colored with coal tar and preserved with benzoic acid, borax, formaldehyde, or potassium chromate. Whereas they found flour and rice usually pure, ginger, mustard, pepper, and wine tended toward heavy defilement. The authors also suspected currant, grape, and raspberry jellies, which sometimes contained only processed, sugared, and colored apple cores and peelings.

In part, Richards and Woodman blamed the public for such unrealistic demands as oysters and summer fruit and vegetables out of season. They encouraged readers to be skeptical of abnormally bright colors in canned foods, such as green canned peas and pickles brightly colored by copper salt dye. An editorial in the *New England Kitchen Magazine* concurred that dishonesty would thrive as long as the consumer remained naive and unsuspecting. At the height of social activism, feminist Charlotte Perkins Gilman's *The Home: Its Work and Influence* (1903) declared that bad food found its way into homes because the housewife was untrained in identifying additives.

On June 30, 1906, at the urging of President Theodore Roosevelt, the U.S. Congress passed the Pure Food and Drug Act, which launched an interstate watchdog on fraudulent, mislabeled goods. A stronger version in 1938 opposed unwholesome food by authorizing factory inspection and seizure of proscribed goods.

Renewed Vigilance

When a new wave of synthetics compromised American foodstuffs in the post–World War II era, a congressional committee investigated for 21 months. Impaneled in June 1950 and chaired by Representative James Joseph Delaney (D-NY), the group heard testimony on chemical additives and noxious substances in food. Although the committee issued four volumes covering unwholesome foods and fluoridated water, Congress ignored the committee's recommendations for seven years. In 1958, the Food Additives Amendment banned such carcinogens as lead and halogenated compounds and required clearance of questionable additives, including binders, enzymes, gelatin thickeners, stabilizers, and texturizers.

Early in 2001, a new product for identifying dangerous levels of lead set consumers' minds at rest on the subject of toxic metals in food cans and water. Homax Products in Bellingham, Washington, began distributing LeadCheck, which identified lead in dishes, a problem that the U.S. government estimated occurred at the rate of one in seven sets. The product was the invention of chemical engineer Marcia J. Stone at Hybrivet in Reading, Pennsylvania, a diagnostician for DuPont and New England Nuclear. The kit offered test swabs and reagents that turned pink or red if they came in contact with leachable lead, which could damage brain tissue in the unborn.

See also: Disease, Food-Borne; Hormones in Food; Inspection and Safety, Food; Plant Disease and Prevention; Poisonous Foods.

Further Reading

Satin, Morton. *Death in the Pot: The Impact of Food Poisoning on History.* New York: Prometheus, 2007.

Sun, Da-Wen, ed. *Modern Techniques for Food Authentication.* Boston: Elsevier, 2008.

Trentmann, Frank. *The Making of the Consumer: Knowledge, Power and Identity in the Modern World.* New York: Berg, 2005.

African Diet and Cuisine, Sub-Saharan

Tropical and southern African gastronomy incorporates varied tribal and language groups, each following its own culinary methods of preparing local ingredients. Because 60 percent of the area is agrarian, sub-Saharan Africa produces homegrown food and supplements fruit and vegetables with fish netted from local waterways. A model recipe for *maafé* (rice stew) with peanut, spinach, and tomato sauce derives input for each variation by Angolan, Gambian, Ivory Coast, and Wolof cooks. Ghanaians contribute pierced boiled eggs, which soak up juices; Ivory Coast preparers stress tomatoes and tomato paste; Senegalese add cabbage and eggplant; the Bambara of Mali accentuate sweet potatoes and turnips. In the centuries after the slave diaspora, African American versions of maafé supplanted peanuts with peanut butter.

After 6000 B.C.E., continental nomads based meals on meat from cattle, goats, and sheep. Wanderers benefited from trading stock with disparate groups, thus acquiring more culinary diversity in dried fish, fruits, greens, and tubers. Unique combinations anchored societies to regions and defined ritual feast cycles, such as the yam festival that ended the Ashanti hungry time and marked the annual Ibo thanksgiving. Simple kitchen arrangement involved the balancing of a single pot on three stones over a fire. A sedentary lifestyle made possible melon patches and lettuce and nettle crops and the gathering of wild jackfruit and passionfruit.

During the slave trade in the 1800s, the importation of cassava, peanuts, and peppers made the first impact of outsiders on Congo rain forest dishes of *fonio* (millet), griddle breads, millet, and native rice. Despite the drain of human bondage on the citizenry and the introduction of European diseases, the boost to food security increased the West African population. Arab, Indian, and Portuguese traders carried hot pepper pods as handy pocket currency and a kitchen garden curiosity for buyers in São Tomé and Zanzibar. The cuisine of Africa's long shoreline profited from the long-distance swap, which added pungency to bland dishes.

Culinary Blossoming

Cassava, cocoyams, and yams added sweetness to Nigerian *patten doya* (yam pottage) and greens to *kuka* (baobab leaf stew), a heritage dish made by the mother of Sundiata, the thirteenth-century epic hero of the Mali Empire. In Ghana, cassava provided starchy roots for pounding into *fufu,* a national dish served with dried or smoked fish, guinea fowl, and *suya* (shish kebabs), a spicy Hausan grilled meat in Niger and Nigeria. Coconut, guinea pepper, néré seeds, palm oil, peanuts, and shea butter flavored sauces for chicken, corn and pea fritters, okra and pumpkin seed soup, rice, and wild bushmeat from antelopes, bush rats, crocodiles, giant snails, simians, and warthogs.

Plantain supplied a staple food crop in East Africa, but its nutritional deficiency resulted in disease and death among pregnant women and an infant mortality rate of more than 30 percent. As a result of shortened female life spans, polygynous men accumulated multiple wives. In Mozambique, a more nutritious kitchen preparation involved quartering green plantains for grating into coconut milk and lemon juice.

The cooks at a street restaurant in Dakar, Senegal, prepare a traditional dish of seasoned fish and white rice with vegetables. Fish is a dietary staple in coastal West Africa. Starchy tubers and root vegetables, peanuts, tomatoes, and palm nut oil are also common. *(Georges Gobet/AFP/ Getty Images)*

Mixtures of black-eyed or field peas, eggplant, locust beans, okra, pumpkin, and squash wrapped in banana, cabbage, plantain, or roselle (hibiscus) leaves fed families with handheld portions. The tight bundles, spiced with coriander and ginger, steamed fish and root vegetables while retaining aroma and savor. The Yoruba washed down their servings with sweet roselle juice.

The arrival of New World chili pepper and tomatoes in the sixteenth century altered recipes for dried and flaked fish and goat, the dominant meats, and steamed *moimoi,* a Nigerian bean pudding. The additions presaged the basic colors and flavors of Brazilian, Cajun, and Creole cookery. An open-ended recipe for one-pot Gambian *jollof* rice, a parallel of Arab pilaf, Iberian paella, and Louisiana jambalaya, invited the cook to improvise in apportioning the flavors of onion, pepper, and tomato. For these spicy meals, West Africans drank millet beer and palm wine as table beverages.

To the east, herders sold cattle, goats, and sheep, keeping only blood and milk for their own meals. Heavy reliance on coconut, grains, and rice anchored meals to carbohydrates, such as Ugandan *matoke,* steamed green bananas. Around 1000 C.E., when Arab traders settled among Swahili speakers, bland African fare acquired Persian flavors from cinnamon, cloves, pomegranate juice, and saffron. The introduction of Peruvian corn in the 1500s supplied the ingredient for *ugali,* a staple starch similar to fufu and eaten with meat and vegetable stews. During the diaspora, Africans bore recipes for corn mush to the West Indies.

In the early sixteenth century, fields of Mesoamerican corn along the Gold Coast attested to a continent-to-continent food transfer and stimulation of population growth. Only the coastal Axumites and residents of the Volta River delta clung to rice as the dominant cereal. Portuguese traders demonstrated pudding making and the marination, basting, and spit-roasting of pork joints in fragrant sauces. Iberian marinades relied on chilies, citrus juice, pineapples, and tomatoes, uncommon ingredients in African entrées. British influence transported Indian specialties to African colonies. By incorporating chapatis, chutney, curry, lentil soup, and pickles to gastronomy, East Africans developed indigenous flavors to new heights.

Fusion Cuisine

Farther north in Eritrea, Ethiopia, and Somalia, communal dining centered on finger food and bread as both a carbohydrate and utensil. Diners relied on *injera,* a spongy sourdough flatbread made into convenient rounds from barley, corn, sorghum, teff, or wheat. The regional complement, *hilbet,* involved the creaming of fava beans and lentils into a paste. Because of Coptic Orthodox Christian, Islamic, and Jewish food taboos, families avoided alcohol, horsemeat, pork, reptiles, shellfish, and wild birds and game. Peasants preferred dried peas, noodles, and oat porridge with honey to fresh vegetables. The more sophisticated Somali spiced basmati rice with cardamom, cinnamon, cloves, cumin, and sage and drank spiced tea Arab style.

The centrality of South Africa to world trade brought the food of outsiders to the local Sotho, Xhosa, and Zulu, an agrarian and pastoral tribal network that overran the aboriginal Khoi herders around 1000 C.E. To Khoi brewing, spit-roasting impala and ostrich, and biltong (jerky), colonists from Britain, France, Germany, Holland, and Portugal added the traditions of barbecuing, *boerewors* (sausage), and pig's feet with beans. Complementary dishes of corn mush, onion and tomato sauce, and yogurt supplied energy and vitamins. To the northeast in Zambia, the rural Bemba maintained a peasant diet of fish, game, insects, and wild fruit as additives to kitchen garden greens, gourds, and cowpeas. They farmed by the swidden system and cooked by methods passed from mother to daughter.

From the mid-eighteenth century, South African recipes displayed the venturesome combinations of innovators, especially *bobotie,* a Malaysian meatloaf with bananas, coconut, and raisins, and *isidudu,* a gruel of cabbage, liver, and pumpkin served with a milk dressing. Indian restaurateurs added bunny chow, a quarter loaf of bread hollowed and stuffed with curried vegetables. Beach communities developed recipes for fish stew and broiled and steamed crayfish, lobster, mackerel, mussels, octopus, oysters, shrimp, and tuna.

See also: African Food Trade; African Slave Diet; Bushmeat; Malnutrition; Soul Food; Swiddens; Taro.

Further Reading

Collins, Geneva. "Where Settlers, Slaves and Natives Converged, a Way of Eating Was Born." *Washington Post,* May 9, 2007.

McCann, James. *Stirring the Pot: A History of African Cuisine.* Athens: Ohio University Press, 2009.

Page, Willie F. *Encyclopedia of African History and Culture.* New York: Facts on File, 2001.

African Food Trade

Referred to by archaeologists as "the cradle of humanity," Africa abounds in natural resources and the age-old agropastoral wisdom of food producers. Across the Sahara and the Nile River valley beginning in 6000 B.C.E., trade in cattle, donkeys, and goats built sophistication in raising animals for sale. Informal barter enabled breeders to diversify mammals and poultry and to select the best egg, meat, and milk producers.

Serious drought in 4000 B.C.E. forced farmers south from the Sahel grasslands into the tropical lake and river territory of the Ashanti and Yoruba. Homesteaders adapted to the bushmeat and wild food to the south in Mali. In addition to hunting the gazelle and oryx, seminomadic growers domesticated guinea fowl and grew African spinach, black-eyed peas, *fonio* (a type of millet), groundnuts (peanuts), millet, okra, pigeon peas, plantains, rice, sorghum, taro, and yams. Swiddens and applied animal and green manure upgraded soil fertility and halted erosion. Gradually, journeymen ventured into promising bazaars to the north to sell fruit, tubers, and vegetables. In 2000 B.C.E., enterprising Africans exported food plants across the Indian Ocean to semiarid Asian lands.

Precolonial Africa slowly realized its economic promise as a food provider for Europe and Asia. After 200 B.C.E., Roman buyers solved their national wheat crises by looking to Berbers in Numidia for emergency provender. To accommodate the grain trade, transporters established the Nubian river corridor from Aksum (Ethiopia) to Egypt and smaller overland routes that are still in use today. By 350 C.E., Red Sea ports developed international commerce so active that it fostered a vigorous pirate culture, which preyed on African wealth. The agricultural yield declined in the sixth century from drought, overfarming, and shifts in the Nile's annual overflow.

Early Commercial Success

From the late Middle Ages into the 1870s, waystations at Gao, Jenne, and Timbuktu controlled trans-Saharan traffic in cotton, salt, and kola nuts, a sacred item from the Cameroon and Gabon. As far south as the Congo River basin, West Africans valued the kola pod as a stimulant, diviner's tool, and holy offering at Igbo and Kanuri ancestor worship and funerals. Lagos, Nigeria, on the Atlantic coast, developed into the export center for the kola nut, valued as an aphrodisiac and in the drug industry to treat migraine and neuralgia. The growth of Islam spread demand for the nut for chewing by Muslims, to whom the Koran forbade alcohol. Conveyors traversing the Upper Niger and Upper Senegal by canoe accessed Moorish kola markets in Morocco and Tripoli.

At the end of the eighteenth century, Europeans viewed Africa as a vulnerable fortress of agricultural wealth. Much of the region's unique produce traveled by canoe fleet to anchorage on the Bight of Benin to provision the transatlantic slave trade. By shipping a taste of African food to slave markets in Europe and the Americas, enslavers unwittingly introduced the Dark Continent to world food commerce in bananas, eggplant, guinea squash, manioc, melons, sesame, and taro. In 1670, planters in Barbados and Jamaica established the first New World growth of Africa's green wealth.

The transport of Bengalese, blacks, and West Indians from Nova Scotia to Sierra Leone after 1792 enabled British investors to reap proceeds from the grain trade. Bambara, Fula, Hausa, Mandinka, Soso, Wolof, and Yoruba middlemen converged on Freetown to sell bananas, cashews, castor oil, cocoa, corn, eddoes, kola nuts, millet, okra, palm wine, peanuts, plantain, potatoes, rice, sweet potatoes, and yams. The group netted immediate profits from merchandizing arrowroot, coffee, cotton, ginger, honey, nutmeg, palm oil, and pepper. Upon gaining freedom, the West African nexus built on past success. In the 1820s, Freetown flourished from connections with caravans arriving from the Sahel with food goods for global trade.

Farther south of the Congo estuary, British and German merchants exploited profits in kernel and palm oil. The Fang, who migrated from Cameroon into the forest zone, brokered the kola nut and palm oil trade as well as a complex business in guns, ivory, and slaves. As the predatory slave trade came to an end in the mid-1860s, cotton enjoyed a temporary boom along the Congo and Ubangi rivers because of the dearth of agriculture during the American Civil War.

A brisk business in cassava, coffee, gum, salt, and whitebait drew central Africans into a permanent symbiosis with free-spending European colonists. Because of lack of education and financial backing, blacks remained passive trade partners with white Europeans. The memoirs of Danish planter Karen Blixen, captured in the biographical film *Out of Africa* (1985), characterize the racial suppression and land theft from such indigenous laborers and coffee pickers as the stateless Kikuyu of Kenya.

Empire Builders

From Zanzibar, British, French, German, Indian, and U.S. exploiters who traded in cloves, copal, cotton, and gum erected export bans, quotas, and taxes that protected their interests. Arab merchants contributed to the international fervor by offering dates in exchange for salt and spices, which they transported down the Nile to Cairo and Khartoum. In Angola in the late 1860s, Brazilian and Portuguese moguls operated press gangs to grow coffee and sugar, both dependable plantation crops. By playing one Bantu faction against the other, empire builders perpetuated political intrigue as a method of spurring profits. Gunrunners and mercenaries fostered central Africa's reputation for thuggery and violence.

By the 1870s, the hegemony of Britain in Egypt, France in Algeria, and Afrikaner (Boer) and British settlers and railroad builders of South Africa south of the Kalahari absorbed greater control of precapitalist agricultural and pastoral produce. Western technology developed uses for corn as a source of fodder and oil, thereby displacing millet and sorghum as major cash crops. European dominance of wholesale mutton and wine exports from Cape Town and Natal ensured steady returns but little reward for Swazi and Zulu producers. Overall, British deal makers undersold African competitors and used sea power to tyrannize free trade.

In 1888, the Mozambique Company, a Portuguese investment in 60,000 square miles (155,000 square kilometers) of farmland, benefited from the export of a variety of East African goods—agave, cashews, cassava, copra, corn, fruit, peanuts (groundnuts), potatoes, rice, sugar, wax, and wheat. The promising stock appealed to importers in England, France, Germany, and North America. At the beginning of the twentieth century, the peanut offered more protein for the money than any other sustainable crop in Burkina Faso, Cameroon, Congo, Mali, Zambia, or Zimbabwe and advanced to millionaire status Alhassan Dantata, a Nigerian broker. Industrialization fostered trade in flour, liquor, meat, milk, peanuts, rice, and sugar in the 1920s until the Mozambique Company's downfall in 1941.

After World War II, the rise in urbanization increased demands for fresh produce and grain. The independence of sub-Saharan Africa in 1961 buoyed population so rapidly that the continent shifted from a cereal exporter to a food importer in just four decades. Employment figures into the late 1960s varied from 33 percent in Mombasa to 60 percent in Lusaka, an indication that large numbers of

central Africans continued to rely on agriculture and pastoralism for their livelihood.

Into the 1990s, world economists awaited a green revolution of the magnitude of the Chinese and Southeast Asian food markets, which based their success on government investment in small farms. Contributing to Africa's rise as a trading partner, the dismantling of commercial restrictions and trade barriers allowed new competitors to export surplus goods. Meanwhile, African farmers offered testing grounds for genetically modified cotton and other crops in Burkina Faso, Egypt, Kenya, Morocco, Senegal, Tanzania, Zambia, and Zimbabwe.

In 2004, an increase in irrigation of rice lands in Cameroon, Kenya, Mauritania, and Niger augmented Africa's ability to compete against an entrenched Asian monopoly. By 2010, however, ecologists warned that African hydrology remained dangerously unpredictable in grain fields and pasturage along the Sahel and throughout northern and southern regions. To offset shortages, urban horticulturalists planted high-value commodities—cucumbers, melons, peppers, strawberries, tomatoes—on marginal and peripheral land to heighten food security.

Recent Import-Export Trends

In 2011, global financiers noted that half of the world's ten fastest-growing economies—Algeria, Angola, Ghana, Mauritius, and Nigeria—were African. Since 2005, agricultural commerce had increased by 92 percent. More than Latin American and Pacific Rim buyers, both Canada and China courted small African markets in Burkina Faso, Ethiopia, and Malawi. To stabilize income, farmers replaced corn with drought-tolerant cassava. At the same time, Kenyan, Tanzanian, and Ugandan fishermen expanded their fresh water catch beyond Nile perch, the most seriously overharvested species; however, sabotaging regional efforts, health and pollution regulations passed by the European Union increased overhead, notably the cost of analyzing and inspecting seafood, maintaining quality control, removing pesticide residues, and tracing aflatoxins. U.S. border rejections of African foods tended toward the ridding of cereals, dried fruit, nuts, and vegetables of foreign matter and pathogens, especially botulism in canned goods.

Zambia, a landlocked entity once absorbed with the copper trade, hovers on the edge of enlarging subsistence farming into commerce in grain and diversified food staples appealing to urbanites. Like other poor countries—Kenya, Malawi, Tanzania, and Zimbabwe—Zambia has begun venturing into agribusiness by developing markets for beef, chicken, corn, eggs, fish, oil, pork, and vegetables. Government controls assist financiers in stabilizing income and protecting smallholders from the impacts of border regulations and unpredictable vicissitudes in weather and harvests.

The Islamic Food Council oversees imports of dairy products, frozen food, meat and poultry, and processed goods, such as beef and chicken from Brazil to African markets. To meet the demand for halal meat specified by Muslims, McDonalds, Nestlé, and Tesco have expanded their offerings, especially among affluent Muslims in Burkina Faso, Egypt, Guinea, Morocco, Niger, Senegal, Somalia, and Tunisia.

Niche marketing nets a smaller exchange, such as the sale of American and Canadian mead—cyser, melomel, and metheglin—in Ethiopia and South Africa, where honey wine outsells grape wines. Despite a large Muslim population, Egypt markets Canadian ice wine, a dessert beverage pressed from frozen grapes. Exporters anticipated higher wine sales in Egypt, Morocco, and South Africa but reduced expectations for North Africa after the turmoil of the "Arab spring," especially in Libya.

Farmers in Angola, like those in South Africa, produce enough subsistence crops to import beans, meat, and wine and to supply the rest of the world with bananas, beer, coffee, corn, cotton, fish, and sugarcane. On a higher economic level, Algeria tops demand for imported groceries, convenience and luxury foods for the hotel trade, diet foods, and grains and legumes, namely corn, lentils, peas, and wheat. The imports sustain Algeria's main industries, which include food processing.

Nigeria, like Algeria, offers new markets for grapes, potatoes, processed food, and wheat flour for supermarkets and convenience stores. Nigerian farmers balance trade with their output of cocoa beans and sesame seeds. Generating a high employment rate, the country's dynamic income can afford imports of baby food, beverages, and breakfast cereal.

In Accra, the financial heart of Ghana, a vibrant young population supports imports of beer, canned goods, fruit juice, ice cream, pastry, potato chips, powdered milk, sauces and seasonings, and wine. Outgoing shipments of cocoa beans and cocoa powder help satisfy the world demand for chocolate. Additional profit from arrowroot, cashews, coconuts, coffee, flour, pineapples, spice, and sweet potatoes enables a growing nation to flourish. Projections for future exports of tuna and other fish species raised in aquaculture increase interest in investments on Africa's western coast.

At a faster rate, Mauritius, off the east coast, exerts the greatest claim on dairy products, eggs, fresh and frozen foods, lentils, oil, peas, pork, rice, and soybeans. From ports on the Indian Ocean, Mauritians deal in bananas, corn, potatoes, pulses, sugarcane, and tea. In a competitive environment, entrepreneurs intend to increase the Mauritian processing of seafood and to import luxury beef cuts to feed the tourist trade.

See also: African Diet and Cuisine, Sub-Saharan; Mozambique Company; Sierra Leone Company.

Further Reading

Aksoy, M. Ataman, and John C. Beghin. *Global Agricultural Trade and Developing Countries.* Washington, DC: World Bank, 2005.

Carney, Judith Ann, and Richard Nicholas Rosomoff. *In the Shadow of Slavery: Africa's Botanical Legacy in the Atlantic World.* Berkeley: University of California Press, 2009.

Djurfeldt, Göran, ed. *The African Food Crisis: Lessons from the Asian Green Revolution.* Cambridge, MA: CABI, 2005.

Hassan, Rashid M., R.J. Scholes, and Neville Ash. *Ecosystems and Human Well-Being: Current State and Trends.* Washington, DC: Island Press, 2005.

Sarris, Alexander, and Jamie Morrison. *Food Security in Africa: Market and Trade Policy for Staple Foods in Eastern and Southern Africa.* Northampton, MA: Edward Elgar, 2010.

African Slave Diet

In the late 1600s, West Africans favored a largely vegetarian diet augmented with dried fish, goat, iguana, marrow bones, poultry, and shark. Women cultivated small plots and created call-and-response field chants, the music of female cooperatives. Their kitchen gardens contained indigenous plants as well as imports.

Arabs introduced onions, rice, sorghum, sugarcane, and wheat to Sierra Leone. As late as 1455, the Senegalese grew kidney beans and sesame, but no barley, corn, rye, spelt, or vine crops. From India and Malaya through Madagascar and Kenya came the banana, cocoyam, and millet. Pineapples flourished at the Gold Coast. Angola and the Congo received fruit and vegetable strains from the Americas, and New World foods—chili peppers, dasheen, tomatoes—more than doubled supplies of staples. The hybrid cuisine included molasses beer to wash down peanuts and pawpaws that the Portuguese first planted in Gambia, coconut palms and herbs that the explorers planted in Sierra Leone, and cassava and maize, imported by Portuguese traders around 1550 to Benin, Gambia, and Ghana. West African vendors propagated produce to sell to trading vessels at Cape Verde.

The new varieties supported a burgeoning African population despite losses to disease and enslavement. Transport by coffle overland or up to 30 to a canoe weakened the youngest and oldest of captives. Many died of tainted food in coastal barracoons (temporary barracks); others succumbed to contagious diseases or seasickness.

To maintain the vigor of Africans seized in the rain forest and to lessen mortality rates during the Middle Passage of transport to the New World, sea captains of British slave ships belonging to the South Sea Company and the London-based Royal African Company of England, a project begun by King William III, emulated the African diet. With ships' surgeons superintending food service, the mortality rate for transported slaves fell from as high as one-third to 13 percent by 1720.

A Familiar Diet

Key to health during slave transport were citrus fruits, coconut, millet bread, and medicinal herbs at meals, lime and water beverages throughout the day, kola nuts to combat thirst, and cleansings of the hold with vinegar. In hopes of suppressing slave revolts and hunger strikes, suppliers at Whydah on the Bight of Benin stocked corn, malagueta pepper, palm oil, and yams from Lower Guinea. Aboard the *Hannibal* in 1693, the galley crew cooked a ground slurry into porridge called *dabbadabb* (corn dumplings), varied three times a week by horse beans, which controlled the flux (dysentery). In 1707 at Cape Coast, Ghana, ships' cooks chose beans, corn, and rum as a wholesome and familiar diet. Above grain from farther west at El Mina, ships' mess staffs favored hominy, maize grown by the Fanti, red rice from Senegambia, and palm oil. The oil doubled as a skin emollient to heighten the appeal of captives to slave brokers. For the sick, the addition of sago, sugar, and wine to mutton soup roused some from malaise. Even serving an African diet, over an eight-year period the Royal African Company lost more than one-quarter of its abductees, who were buried at sea before the ships reached the Chesapeake Bay.

The importation of African slaves to the Western Hemisphere introduced a third cuisine to Indian and Iberian fare in Colombia and Brazil. Additions altered the cooking styles and foodstuffs favored by Spanish colonists and saved lives. At Cartagena, Colombia, Jesuits stopped feeding slaves heavy cereal, eggs, and salt fish, a diet that killed off the weak who awaited sale to buyers at the docks. Other slaves, exhausted by dysentery and fevers, died on the trail during transport to Lima, Peru. From 1610 to 1650, religious worker Pedro Claver Corberó, the patron saint of slaves, visited slave hospitals and pens and treated dehydration, hunger, psychological shock, and scurvy in newcomers with brandy, bread, lemons, preserves, and sweets. At San Lazaro, he fed a special diet to lepers.

European opinions about the value of slaves changed as the fame of West African farmers and herders spread among planters, particularly in Bermuda, the first island to import black slaves. Along the coastal Carolinas, West African slaves rotated cattle pasturage with rice plantings, a method of restoring soil nitrates to improve the yield. To ensure working strength and stamina, overseers allotted a daily diet of 2,500 to 3,000 calories for each slave. African field hands cooked their own breakfast and dinner. For the afternoon meal, they rebelled against the feeding of slaves at a common trough like swine.

Typical fare in Maryland at the 2 P.M. serving included beans, buttermilk, cornmeal, molasses, and poke greens, a springtime delicacy valued as a tonic. Salt herring dominated meat servings along with discarded ham hocks, hog jowls and maw, chitterlings (animal intestines boiled in vinegar and water), fatback, organ meats, and pigs' feet. In New Orleans, crawfish and shrimp produced a rich, vivid Creole cuisine. Hunting, fishing, and trapping added carp, catfish, opossums, rabbits, turtles, and wild turkeys. When masters wanted to encourage harder work during planting and harvest, they augmented slave cuisine with food gifts and rum and whiskey from the big house.

Roots of Soul Food

To combat humiliation, coercion, and homesickness, slaves craved food common to their home countries. They grew gourds and made ceramic colanders and dishes for slow-cooking rice, fanning baskets for winnowing, hoes for baking corn cakes, reed and sedge baskets for gathering root crops, and wood utensils for food cultivation and preparation of *cala* (sweet rice cakes), *jollof* (red rice), and gunger cake (molasses cookies). Women joined in the pounding of rice with mortars and pestles, a perpetuation of African sisterhood.

At Barbuda, agropastoralists staked out animals in vegetable plots and spread the drying manure to nourish plantings of dasheen, a South American famine food adaptable to many cooking needs. Amaranth and manioc leaves, collards, dasheen, mustard greens, and sorrel served as salads, nutrient-rich steamed side dishes, and extenders and thickeners of meat soup and stew. Island farmers boiled callaloo and yam, eddo, and plantain, which they flavored with salt and cayenne or red pepper. Around 1730, Virginia slaves raised watermelons to eat out of the hand like pome fruit and added African specialties to plantation menus.

Additional slave favorites—black-eyed and pigeon peas, broad beans, kola nuts, cowpeas, grits, millet, peanuts, okra, red rice—became Southern staples. Slaves adapted culinary styles and tastes from memory, including deep-fat frying of chicken and fish in peanut oil. Along the Guinea shore, cooks had anchored meals to root crops. In Cameroon, Ghana, and Nigeria, pureed potatoes and yams produced *fufu*, a basis for complex toppings and condiments that slaves duplicated in Brazil, Cuba, the Dominican Republic, and Puerto Rico. Diaspora dishes featured cornmeal for fish fries, grated ginger and pumpkin in soup, greens and mackerel in pepper pot, okra in gumbo, peas and rice in hoppin' John, peanuts in pralines, pepper in barbecue sauce, rice in meatball pilau, and later, kola nuts in Coca-Cola. At Monticello, Thomas Jefferson's Virginia home, slave farmers grew guinea corn (also called benne or sorghum), which they ate in broth, bread, greens, salads, and toasted as a soup topping.

Weekend markets held by slaves in Antigua, the Bahamas, Barbados, Jamaica, and St. John featured lima beans, cabbage, corn, ginger, mustard greens, and pumpkins. Savvy marketing raised cash to enhance the African American diet. Slaves from Nigeria protected their investment by digging cellars to protect root crops over the winter. Using their horticultural skills at fertilizing fields, intercropping corn with peas, and weeding and topping plants, they enriched cotton, sugar, and tobacco tycoons.

See also: African Diet and Cuisine, Sub-Saharan; Language, Food; Manioc; Sierra Leone Company; Vinegar.

Further Reading

Bower, Anne L., ed. *African American Foodways: Explorations of History and Culture.* Urbana: University of Illinois Press, 2007.

Brooks, George E. *Eurafricans in Western Africa: Commerce, Social Status, Gender, and Religious Observance from the Sixteenth to the Eighteenth Century.* Athens: Ohio University Press, 2003.

Knight, Frederick C. *Working the Diaspora: The Impact of African Labor on the Anglo-American World, 1650–1850.* New York: New York University Press, 2010.

Zahediah, Nuala. *The Capital and the Colonies: London and the Atlantic Economy, 1660–1700.* Cambridge, UK: Cambridge University Press, 2010.

Afterlife and Food

To allay the grief of death and bodily atrophy, mourners throughout history have supplied their dead with food and drinks. As early as 100,000 B.C.E., Neanderthal mourners supplied meals for the dead as nourishment for a netherworld. In contrast, the Sumerians envisioned a more austere afterlife lived in a dark, silent cave surrounded by dust. In a more uplifting philosophy, Japanese Shintoists and Koreans celebrating Chuseok offered favorite dishes to ancestors as a way of strengthening family ties.

Edible grave goods, such as the libations of milk and wine in Homer's *Odyssey* (800 B.C.E.) and Sophocles's *Antigone* (441 B.C.E.), were believed to have magical powers over the soul's destiny. Among Polynesians, the tasting of burial foods sealed the fate of the spirit, which, like the mythic Greek victim Persephone, belonged forever to the land of the dead. To the Buddhist, Hindu, and Norse, the act of eating sustained the journeyer on the road to a final destination. According to the twentieth-century Hindu swami Prabhavananda, soul hunger readies the newly deceased for the great change from human to spirit. The newcomer fasts for three days without water or sleep until the King of Death extends welcome to the world beyond.

Food as Propitiation

In the Middle East, from around 4000 B.C.E., the gift of meals to the deceased ensured reciprocity—food in exchange for guidance and protection. At Gezer, an archaeological site between Jerusalem and Tel Aviv, Canaanites poked hollow feeding tubes into headstones to guide sustenance into the mouths of the dead. At Megiddo, north of Syria, Israelites delivered liquid sustenance to burial chambers through funnels. The custom came under attack in Ecclesiasticus 30:18 around 200 B.C.E., when poet Ben Sirach mocked the waste of meals piled on sepulchres. After the evolution of shivah, a consolatory meal for mourners, family members chose round foods—bagels, eggs, lentils—as symbols of the life cycle. Modern shivah gifts shift the emphasis from the inevitability of death to reminders of earthly sweetness, such as brownies, cheesecake, fruit, rugelach (nut rolls), and wine.

Egyptians protected agrarianism by burying the dead within sight of productive fields. Families stocked funeral chambers with plows and tools for growing grain and harvesting figs and dates. After opening the mouth of the deceased to ensure speech and eating, they assembled edible grave goods to feed the remains on a boat voyage to judgment in the afterlife. Coffin paintings glimpsed a full pantry of figs and lotus, duck and ibis, gazelle and oryx, flatbread, and seafood and jars of staples alongside cooking utensils and seats at a banquet table. To ensure a vigorous sex life, the painters added lettuce, an aphrodisiac.

A hieroglyphic list from after 2600 B.C.E. at Dahshur, south of Cairo, depicts uniformed maidservants delivering appealing meals to the dead on trays. On tomb walls, menus reminded servants in the afterlife of the foods enjoyed by the deceased. Drawings of foods allegedly shapeshifted into real servings. On the fortieth day after the burial, survivors brought provisions to the cemetery. After prayers, the living distributed the edibles to the needy, a gesture propitiating favor from Horus, Maat, and Thoth, the judges of earthly behaviors.

Foods of Paradise

Scripture, sagas, and art since prehistory have illustrated visions of heavenly dining. Bas-relief and grave goods of Viking funerals depicted the dead warrior on a sea voyage. In his burial boat, provisioners placed a well-rounded diet—apples, beer, cress, hazelnuts, horseradish, mustard, oats, oxen, and wheat. Because Finns and Swedes believed that the dead remained on Earth until their bodies decayed completely, visitors offered grave foods to long-dead ancestors. Among Balto-Finns and the Sami, a ritual meal of animal hearts accompanied by magic incantations sung by a female chorus strengthened the resolve of the journeyer. As described in the Finnish epic *Kalevala* (1881), the ceremony concluded with a banquet, at which a fortune-teller predicted the destiny of each mourner.

In some societies, mock foods take the place of real dishes. In 141 B.C.E., clay models of sheep and pigs suggest meaty meals for the Chinese Emperor Jing of the Han dynasty. Around 1450 C.E., Chinese artists in Shaanxi Province made model foodstuffs on ceremonial plates. The offering of fish, goat, goose, pork, and rabbit and fresh servings of peaches, persimmons, pomegranates, steamed bread, and water chestnuts represented the common diet of the period.

World religions have typically endowed funereal meals with power and sanctity. Even though Jews believed that the dead had no need of sustenance, the Kabbala, mystical writings compiled between 100 and 1200 C.E., pictured a symbolic meal of fish, meat, and wine served in the Garden of Eden. The divine food contained "sparks of holiness," the magical power that elevated the spirit to heaven.

Pagan Rites

The living worldwide went to great lengths to honor the elite dead by accepting the cost of sacrifice. After 668 B.C.E., Ashurbanipal, the Assyrian monarch at Nineveh, acknowledged his piety with an inscription crediting him with reviving old customs of libations and meals for royal spirits. In a similar gesture to the privileged class, the Aztec ensured convivial meals of familiar foods by sacrificing cooks to accompany the noble dead to the next world. Among the Lenni Lenape of North America, women pounded corn and made unsalted loaves in outdoor ovens. Zoroastrian women spread communal food offerings to the deceased on *sufras* (funeral cloths).

For Amerindians, tobacco generated visual prayers for the dead. Plains and Pacific Coast Indians sprinkled *kinni-kinnick* (herbed tobacco) or unadulterated tobacco over remains as a holy gift and propitiation of the gods while the spirit crossed over the star path from Earth to sky. The Winnebago extended the tobacco pipe to the deceased as though including them in the feasting and pleasures. At an Algonquin funeral in October 1647 in Nonanetum, Massachusetts, the corpse bore the calumet (pipe) of peace during his journey as a gesture of nonviolence to the spirit world.

African religions favored killing a goat or ox at the burial. According to the pastoral Nguni of southern Africa around 1400 C.E., the slaughtered beast made two journeys—following the deceased to the netherworld and, on Earth, feeding the bereaved who remained behind. On a more upbeat note, the Arawak of the Caribbean anticipated joy in Coyaba, a land of dancing and endless banquets, a concept they shared with the Celts. The Inca interred their dead sitting upright amid pots of food, symbols of abundance. As proof that the afterlife liberated the spirit from want, the Papago and Pima pictured their ancestors living free from hunger and thirst.

Islamic Funeral Food

Muslims observed the same sharing of food and celebration as a form of friendship and condolence. Unlike the ancient Jews, Egyptians, Greeks, Japanese, and Chinese, Islamic families directed gift meals toward the community rather than to the deceased. In the style of Cushites, the bereaved ended the day with a feast, which required slaughter of camels, cattle, and sheep to feed a large gathering. As a form of ritual almsgiving, one of the Five Pillars of Muslim worship, family mourners shared the bounty with children, the hungry, neighbors, and strangers.

Meanwhile, the Muslim dead earned their rewards in paradise, where sumptuous tables bore a perpetual supply of food and drink served on gold and silver tableware by handsome young men and women. The Koran (650 C.E.) specified the luxuries awaiting those who died in a state of grace. Lush gated gardens, angels, and streams of honey, milk, water, and wine surrounded the righteous, who won favor with God by eating only halal (permissible) food on Earth. Permeating the air were the appetizing scents of camphor, ginger, and musk and the mist of fountains.

Uniting Past and Present

Food today maintains its role as an element of life's goodness, from the Inuit vision of a warm land of plenty to the beneficent comforts of the Baha'i and Cree "good land." For Wiccans, dancing, singing, and partaking of cake and wine honor the soul as it makes its way to Summerland. Practitioners of Santeria, a pantheistic faith that originated in West Africa, offer sacrifices to spirits to maintain a reciprocal relationship with the world beyond. By feeding the deceased with artistic patterns of cornmeal and the blood of sacrificial chickens and goats, the living receive health and shielding from harm.

The peasant holiday of Día de los Muertos (Day of the Dead), celebrated on November 1 and 2, involves Roman Catholics in Ecuador, Guatemala, Mexico, and the Philippines as well as Arizona and California. In addition to candles and marigold petals, mourners honor their deceased with photographs, aniseed bread, tamales, and liquor. Like the ancient Maya, communities bury sustenance to feed the spirits on their way to the afterlife, which they entered through caves to eat wild birds, which were no long taboo. Home altars bear heaps of *atole,* cocoa, egg bread, fruit, peanuts, sugarcane, tortillas, and turkey mole. A folk art confection introduced during the colonial period, sugar skulls release the sweetness that death fails to conquer. All-night vigils bring celebrants together in an effort to direct souls home again.

See also: Breadfruit; Jerky; Pasta.

Further Reading

Bingham, Ann, and Jeremy Roberts. *South and Meso-American Mythology A to Z.* New York: Chelsea House, 2010.

Bryant, Clifton D., and Dennis L. Peck. *Encyclopedia of Death and the Human Experience.* Los Angeles: Sage, 2009.

Campo, Juan Eduardo. *Encyclopedia of Islam.* New York: Facts on File, 2009.

Janer, Zilkia. *Latino Food Culture.* Westport, CT: Greenwood, 2008.

Raphael, Simcha Paull. *Jewish Views of the Afterlife.* Lanham, MD: Rowman & Littlefield, 2009.

Agribusiness

The totality of buying and selling involved in bringing food crops to the table, agribusiness forms a vast network of farmers and herders, financiers, equipment manufacturers, seed suppliers, livestock marketers, and food processors, advertisers, and distributors. In the mid-1800s, the mechanization of plowing by Cyrus McCormick and John Deere preceded a U.S. refrigerated rail network that sped grain, citrus fruit, potatoes, and meat to emerging processors, notably, Armour, Campbell's, Del Monte, Heinz, and Swift. After establishment of the U.S. Department of Agriculture in 1862 and the building of land grant colleges, contract farming replaced subsistence farms with more advantageous methods of sharing risk.

An American model, contract poultry began in 1929 at the collapse of post–Civil War sharecropping and tenancy. Rural sociologist Rupert Vance surveyed agribusiness at the onset of the Great Depression when Georgia cotton growers abandoned their traditional monocrop for chicken coops. Educated by the federal home demonstration service and guided by county agents, poultry growers supported a food industry based on hatcheries, feed mills, and chicken-processing plants.

During World War II, demand for eggs and meat solidified the fate of the American small farm with reciprocal contracts and indebtedness to the poultry speculator. In 1955, John H. Davis, a Harvard professor of agriculture and marketing, created the term *agribusiness* to describe the evolution of subsistence farming into a business complex.

Efforts to curb corporate power mongering involved growers as well as laborers and truckers. In 1960, journalist Edward R. Murrow presented the television documentary *Harvest of Shame,* a graphic view of the bottom rung of the agrifood hierarchy. In the 1970s, César Chávez and Dolores Huerta organized the United Farm Workers, the first effort of migrant labor to battle U.S. exploitation of the disempowered. The set-to between union members and illegal immigrant strikebreakers revealed to consumers the cost in human terms of cheap grapes and lettuce from corporate farms.

To supply the growing demand for convenience foods, such as powdered eggs and ready-to-fry chicken, transnational corporations in the 1980s stepped up involvement in world agriculture. The era's low commodity prices spurred land speculation and rising property taxes, which strapped family farms, ranches, and rural communities. A complex interaction, agribusiness coordinated the efforts of genetic seed modification to increase yields and food transportability and the addition of corn ethanol and palm oil to tractor fuels to stretch the costly supply of fossil energy. Entrepreneurs and seed patenters targeted fruit, vegetables, and seafood from Third World producers for financial exploitation. To the dismay of smallholders, corporate farming placed huge markets under the control of micromanagers and biotechnologists. The top earners for agrifood—bananas, cocoa, coffee, grain, oil—remained chiefly in the purview of a handful of companies, including Bunge, Cargill, Carrefour, ConAgra, Danone, Dole, General Foods, Huanong, Kraft, Nabisco, Nestlé, Parmalot, Ralston-Purina, and Tesco.

In 2007, Brazil flexed its agrarian muscle as an emerging producer of citrus fruit, corn, cotton, soybeans, and sugar, and cattle, pork, and poultry. Rated third in corporate clout behind China and India, Brazil competed against China's food moguls at a vulnerable point in food security following the adulteration of Chinese baby food, soy products, and pet food with melamine. The mounting threat of farm takeovers increased following the formulation of international food purity and safety standards. Costs lay beyond the grasp of smallholders, such as producers of leafy greens, Mexican tomatoes, and organic grapes and strawberries.

Beside purity concerns, a variety of global issues impact agribusiness and agrofinance today, including control of pesticide-resistant insects, buyout attempts between European food giants, and the growing power of women in microfinance and corporate farming. Layered situations create a domino effect: The Australian investment outlook remains cautiously optimistic, depending on the U.S. settlement of its debt ceiling and Indonesia's postcyclone cattle imports from Queensland.

The collapse of Soviet Communism allowed some nations to regain traction in the world food market. In July 2011, farmers formed a customs union of Belarus, Kazakhstan, and Russia. Simultaneously, after the "Arab spring" of 2011, Egypt, the most populous Arab nation and a major player in the wheat market, fielded a record crop. With political control still unpredictable and the Middle East teetering on upheaval, farmers projected growth into 2015 in dairying and the cultivation of beets, which reduce the natural salinity of Egyptian fields.

See also: Commodity Regulation; Farm Subsidies and Government Agricultural Programs; Genetically Modified Food; Greenhouse Horticulture; Hanna, Gordie C.

Further Reading

Allen, Gary, and Ken Albala. *The Business of Food: Encyclopedia of the Food and Drink Industries.* Westport, CT: Greenwood, 2007.

Hamilton, Shane. *Trucking Country: The Road to America's Wal-Mart Economy.* Princeton, NJ: Princeton University Press, 2008.

Hurt, Ray Douglas. *Problems of Plenty: The American Farmer in the Twentieth Century.* Chicago: Ivan R. Dee, 2002.

Jansen, Kees, and Sietze Vellema, eds. *Agribusiness and Society: Corporate Responses to Environmentalism, Market Opportunities, and Public Regulation.* New York: Zed, 2004.

Agriculture

A basis for civilization, agrarianism tied the support of a clan or tribe to the output of herding, orchardry, seed and tuber planting, and viticulture (the cultivation of grapes), all sources of portable trade commodities. During the Neolithic revolution around 12,000 B.C.E., hunter-gatherers embraced a settled life by planting wild einkorn wheat, an annual hulled grain that thrived at the western end of the Fertile Crescent. Threshers collected the hulled seeds to roast at campfires into digestible, satisfying grains. Low yielding, but protein rich, einkorn wheat cooked into a low-fiber gruel suitable for invalid and weaning meals.

After the establishment of Abu Hureyra and Mureybit, east of Aleppo in western Mesopotamia (Syria), in 11,050 B.C.E., a thousand-year drought forced early Palestinians to irrigate plantings of comestibles and water sheep herds. To feed the most people, workers selected animal and grain traits, particularly dependable milking from cows and sheep and sturdy grain heads on slender stalks for the largest crop. Growers planted seeds in fertile fields and cached harvests. In the Neolithic Levant, Natufian villagers fenced out gazelles and broadcast seeds in open spots among wild almond, pistachio, and plum groves and berry bushes. Because of the ease of threshing wild wheat stands growing 36 inches (91 centimeters) tall, in three weeks, a clan could garner a year's supply of grain.

As farms thrived, population density rose from one to 15 persons per square mile. To feed all, protofarmers across the east-west Fertile Crescent naturalized self-pollinating, early-maturing founder crops—barley, bitter vetch, chickpeas, einkorn and emmer wheat, flax, lentils, and peas. Blacksmiths tempered blades for cutting grain; stonemasons nested grinding stones and mortars and pestles for reducing grain into a fine grist for flatbread and beer. Cultivation in Jordan, North Africa, and the Taurus and Zagros valleys of Turkey spread across the Balkans to Serbia, the Danube River delta, the mouth of the Rhine as far as northern Italy and Valencia, Spain, and north to proto-Celtic enclaves.

Grain-Based Diet

The acceptance of grain as a daily staple paralleled the cultivation of wild figs and the domestication of dogs, goats, pigs, and sheep for fiber, meat, and milk. In southeastern Turkey in 9000 B.C.E. and Jericho in 8000 B.C.E, innovations of Neolithic, or New Stone Age, cuisine shifted focus from a meat-only diet to cooked legumes. Herders in India raised zebu for meat and evolved dairy foods from cows. Cooks chose from barley, corn, millet, oats, rice, sorghum, and wheat the appropriate grains for bread, flour, noodles, and pasta. In the Chihuahua Desert on the Tex-Mex border around 7500 B.C.E., paleo-Indian farmers hunted less and consumed more domesticated cheese, grain, meat, and milk.

From this era, agriculture evolved formalized methods and strategies. Syrian agrarianism flourished at Damascus, where planned cultivation rapidly replaced the more rigorous and hazardous hunting-and-gathering lifestyle. In Papua, practical farmers raised root crops and sugarcane alongside pigs, useful recyclers of green wastes. The seeding of barley and wheat spread to the Aegean isles, Egypt, the Harappan culture of the Indus Valley, Kurdistan, and Pakistan in 7000 B.C.E. and to Argissa, Greece, Germany, Iberia, and Crete in 6000 B.C.E. India's farmers domesticated the jujube (date) for drying and pickling, trained elephants for heavy lifting, and penned chickens to supply eggs and meat. Harappans also drained bogs and diverted sewage from irrigation water. Growers gained sophistication at seed selection by choosing emmer wheat and barley for cultivation in clay and marl soils. Meanwhile, in the Far East, Chinese and Indonesian crop tenders developed a more integrated diet of adzuki beans, rice, soy, and taro as accompaniments to chicken and the fish they netted from rivers. The broad-based diet fueled a population explosion.

At the same time that proto-Americans were reaping arrowroot, corn, and manioc around 5500 B.C.E., Irish growers at Céide Fields became the first to raze forests and surround permanent croplands with rock walls. Agrarianism reached Macedonia, Thessaly, and Thrace after 5200 B.C.E., when food control began to generate exciting possibilities. Sumerians, the empire builders at the Tigris and Euphrates delta, bred cattle and sheep and irrigated fields after 5000 B.C.E. The advances coincided with the growing of oranges in the Indus Valley, where farmers gradually added apples, barley, cotton, grapes, mangos, peas, plums, rice, and sesame seeds to their harvests and butter and cheese from their herds. In the Ukraine in about 4500 B.C.E., herders tamed the horse, a major contribution to streamlined sod breaking.

Agrarianism and Civilization

The improvement of nutrition and farm yield aided cities in recruiting and maintaining standing armies on grain and vegetable surpluses. The nourishment of soldiers allowed the Egyptians to found a 3,000-year series of dynasties, to advance in architecture and technology, and to triple their territory through conquest via a standing army fed by farms along the Nile. The Sumerians reached a height of urbanization at Ur, where farmers produced enough food crops to sustain the world's first bureaucracy. The city employed granary workers and accountants, overseers, and harvest foremen, who supervised the harnessing of onagers and oxen to plows. Also around 4000 B.C.E., the Chinese tamed the water buffalo, Arabians herded dromedaries, and Eurasians bred the dray horse. Simultaneously, beekeeping produced a new dimension in raising flowering plants to yield nectar for honey and wax.

In this same period, the Andean Inca terraced vegetable gardens to produce beans, coca, pepper, potatoes,

A mural from the tomb of Sennedjem, an ancient Egyptian artisan of the Nineteenth Dynasty (ca. 1298–1187 B.C.E.), depicts the harvesting of wheat along the banks of the Nile. Egyptian civilization was one of the first to practice agriculture on a large scale. *(De Agostini/ Getty Images)*

squash, and tomatoes. For meat, they stocked their farms with alpacas, guinea pigs, and llamas. Farther north, Central Americans turned cocoa into a dominant crop and domesticated the wild turkey, a bird found only in the Western Hemisphere. Northeastern Americans made their own agricultural strides by grooming maple groves for sugar sap collection and harvesting pecans, strawberries, sunflowers, wild grapes, and wild rice, a specialty of the Anishinabe, Menominee, Ojibwa, and Winnebago of the Great Lakes region.

Not until 3,300 B.C.E., on the slopes of the Alps, did northeastern Europeans evolve a three-grain cultivation of barley and einkorn and emmer wheat. In another burst of agrarian innovation, the mid-fourth millennium B.C.E. saw rapid improvements in agricultural technology, followed by formal poultry farming in India and Pakistan and the domestication of ducks, geese, and rock pigeons in China. The ard or frame plow replaced the dibble, a simple pointed digging stick. The buffalo, camel, and donkey took the lead in carving furrows and trampling weeds in moist subsoil. British and Scandinavian plowmen organized their efforts by heaping dislodged stones in clearance cairns, evidence of farm ownership and cyclical tillage of land.

The taming of more animals for proto-ranching required securing winter fodder and raising and trading excess stock for slaughter. In Russia in 3000 B.C.E., reindeer herds provided both milk and meat as well as hides for clothing and shelters. In Egypt, the goose became a specialty food and layer of protein-rich eggs. By 2500 B.C.E., central Asians had added both the Bactrian camel and the yak to agrarian investments. Southeast Asians in Borneo, Burma, and Java raised two distinct relatives of oxen, the banteng and gayal. Adventurers later relayed the animals to Arnhem Land in northern Australia to procreate feral herds.

In 161 B.C.E., Romans evaded the Lex Fannia, an anti-gluttony law, by colonizing rabbits and castrating roosters to produce capons, a meatier form of poultry. The *latifundia* (plantation) employed slave labor and tenant farming to grow edibles for a densely populated empire. Artisanal training readied specialized laborers to press olive oil and ferment *garum* (fish pickle) and wine. All three products traveled by two-wheeled cart to ports for loading on cargo vessels bound for Marseilles, Iberia, North Africa, Egypt, and the Middle East.

Medieval Farming

The Middle Ages advanced less labor-intensive watering systems employing dams and weirs, norias, waterwheels, windmills, and shadoofs, the pole-and-dipper method that irrigated vegetable plots along the Nile, the world's original ecosystem. Roman texts reveal the refinements of the classical era, in which vineyards and orchards coordinated with apiculture and the gathering of honey and beeswax for use and export.

Agroecologist Jia Sixie, a governor in Shandong Province, compiled an indexed guide to progressive Chinese farming, *Qimin Yaoshu* (Skills for Peasants, 534 C.E.), one of the world's oldest agricultural monographs. Out of pity for poor yeomen, Jia traveled to Hebei, Henan, and Shanxi provinces to record up-to-date methods of soil cultivation and list 86 varieties of millet according to insect and wind resistance and early ripening. He took notes on monoculture for export, crop rotation, green manures, caching, animal husbandry, and selective breeding. He also summarized yam cultivation and cited the leading farm treatises of his day on orchardry, thinning bottle gourds, drying and pickling pomegranates, fermenting soybeans, and raising fish in rice paddies. Jia divided rice into mucilaginous and dry types. Among 31 common vegetables, he focused on calabashes, cucumbers, dropwort (meadowsweet), eggplant, garlic and onion, Japanese pepper, mallow, muskmelon, mustard, radish, and rutabagas. For grafting pears onto crab apple trees, he recommended an upward limb thrust to allow orchards to thrive near buildings. His text, which recommended methods of selecting and cooking farm produce and making vinegar and yogurt, remained in print for six centuries in Chinese and Japanese editions.

In the tropics and subtropics, crop rotation and swidden agriculture reformed food production. The Olmec and Maya and the slaves of the British Caribbean torched underbrush, roots and stumps, and diseased vegetation as a quick method of denuding cropland. Seedlings, slips, and suckers from earlier swiddens at least two years old supplied transplants of select species, such as coconut palms or paper mulberry, which growers fertilized with human excrement and livestock manure.

Farmers modernized soil preparation with the invention of the horseshoe and halters for draft horses and the moldboard plow for inverting weedy clods and exposing the roots to the sun. A heavier metal-faced plow crafted around 600 C.E. improved yield and fostered a population spurt.

Exchanges and Improvements

The greatest revolution in farming occurred with the Spanish exploration of the New World after 1492. From transatlantic voyagers, European growers acquired a treasure of plant species—corn, peppers, potatoes, red beans, and sunflower oil and the titillating flavors of avocados, bergamot, blueberries, cashews, cocoa, cranberries, guavas, mangos, papayas, pecans, persimmons, pineapple, and tarragon. Exotic crops invigorated the diet with the mouthfeel and taste sensations of indigenous products. The Western Hemisphere received its share of the Columbian Exchange in coffee, spices, sugarcane, and wheat.

For the New World farmer, the arrival of the horse and hunting hound offered methods of pulling plows and travois (skin drags). In the temperate zone around 1600, rabbitries became a source of delectable fryers and roasters and older stock for stewing. In the Canadian Maritimes, marshland mixed agriculture increased pasturage and truck farming along with fish processing for export.

In 1701, English agronomist Jethro Tull invented a seed drill—a hopper and cylinder that turned against a spring-loaded tongue to sow pasture grass. By directing beans and peas through grooves into a funnel, the device regulated distribution over three rows at a time, leaving space for tillage. Tull promoted the use of horses to replace oxen as draft animals and adapted his drill for the planting of potatoes and turnips, two popular tubers of his era. He engineered a four-coultered disk plow and a horse-drawn hoe to pulverize dirt clods to release minerals into wheat and forage plants. In *The New Horse-Hoeing Husbandry* (1731), Tull proposed contour plowing to terrace the soil, retain water runoff, and limit soil erosion. A century later, the introduction of steam plows by English inventor John Fowler reduced demand for draft animals and the need to grow fodder and straw for stalls.

North American Innovations

During the agrarian phase of North American development, farmers broke more virgin land than ever in the course of history. Over half the population of Canada and the United States worked on farms. On ranches, the hybridization of the buffalo and cow in 1749 encouraged ranchers to breed hardy stock capable of weathering droughts and blizzards. For citrus and vegetable growers in Orange County, California, support of railways in the nineteenth century boosted profits from the rapid distribution of perishable lemons and oranges, apricots, beets, celery, grapes, lima beans, and walnuts.

An independent U.S. Bureau of Agriculture, established in 1862, salvaged heritage seeds and preserved plants and seeds. Agents purchased seeds from foreign countries and compiled statistics concerning the terroir in which crops grew best and under what climatic conditions. The new department took shape at an agrarian flash point—the death of slavery and the Southern plantation system, the expansion of greenhouse propagation, and the birth of frontier farms, orchards, vineyards, and cattle and sheep ranches. As former slaves migrated from the Carolinas and Georgia to farm the rich silt of the lower Mississippi River valley, agronomists debated the use of powdered and liquid fertilizers to revitalize depleted fields, a concept still new to farmers. The staff of 30 bureau scientists analyzed soil, introduced resilient varieties and livestock, tested farm implements, answered citizens' questions, and forecast farm needs.

North and South American ranching methods allowed calves to forage the grassland outside of villages and settlements, particularly in Argentina. Science and technology assisted the postwar agrarians with drought and other cyclical obstacles. In Hawaii in 1861, King Kamehameha IV imported honeybees, experimented with new hybrid rice seed, and added a waterworks to ensure even distribution of fresh water. On the truck farms of Dayton, Nevada, horticulturists stored water in ponds and underground and earned top dollar for fresh vegetables sold in railroad camps and mining communities. In New Mexico, the construction of log flumes channeled irrigation water to cornfields, enriching the San Juan River valley from the sale of forage and stock. Russian Mennonites purchased 100,000 acres (405,000 hectares) around Topeka and initiated the planting of "Turkey Red" wheat, the hardy winter variety that turned Kansas into America's breadbasket.

Abraham Lincoln's progressivism fostered both livestock and farming throughout the rapidly growing West. On July 2, 1862, congressional ratification of the Morrill Land Grant Act authorized federal distribution of 17.4 million acres (7.0 million hectares) of public land at the prorated acreage of 30,000 (12,150 hectares) per legislator. The Civil War threatened grain farming by raising the price of implements and seed and by reducing the acreage farmable by cash-strapped smallholders. The decimation of South Carolina and Louisiana rice plantations shifted cultivation to California's Sacramento River valley, the nation's new rice bowl, propagated by immigrants from Guangdong Province, China. Wisconsin farmers experimented with alfalfa, a digestible fiber for stock; the Dakotas and Minnesota dominated trade in flaxseed, a source of linseed oil. Sonoma, California, produced hops for brewing beer. By 1879, as corn developed into the world's top feed grain, American yields reached 1 million bushels. After passage of the Dominion Land Act of 1872 in Canada, North America led the world in the increase of alfalfa, canola, oats, and wheat harvests. In 1873, U.S. corn cultivation expanded to more than 34 million acres (13.8 million hectares).

During the Indian Wars, the U.S. military's need for beef increased the profitability for stockmen and homesteaders. On the northern Texas border at Guthrie in 1870, Samuel Burk Burnett of the Four Sixes Ranch interbred longhorns with Durhams and Herefords. Captain Richard King of Corpus Christi bought up the King Ranch, which grew to 860,000 acres (348,000 hectares), the world's largest ranch. Burnett and King plotted drives to East Coast cities, where hotels and restaurants increased the demand for beef.

Large-Scale Farming

Ambitious Oregon ranchers took advantage of the Desert Land Act, passed on March 3, 1877, to promote the irrigation and cultivation of 640-acre (260-hectare) plots of semiarid public land at a cost of $1.25 per acre ($3.09 per hectare). Agronomists in Nevada guarded turf and waterways as the life-or-death resources to support grasslands and livestock. The fencing of free prairies led to protracted range wars over independent foraging rights. Overgrazing plus a disastrous blizzard in 1886 drove some ranchers out of business and forced others to diversify. Those reduced to subsistence farming gained a labor advantage in 1892 with the advent of the gasoline-powered tractor.

With the Great Plains of Canada and the United States thoroughly settled by 1920, agronomists heightened yields by breeding more productive animal varieties, developing cattle vaccines, and growing disease-resistant plant species, notably, durum and marquis wheat. Farm cooperatives lowered costs from the purchase of balers and pickers. Colombia and Panama developed resilient sheep herds; Saskatchewan produced half of Canada's wheat. In 1926, hybrid corn seed suited individual varieties to climate and soil. Long-distance refrigerated trucking linked consumers with dairy and vegetable perishables. By 1930, Americans exported $2 billion per year in farm goods. Pre–World War II collaboration with South American agronomists enhanced diversity throughout the hemisphere.

Exigencies of World War II in Europe and the Pacific forced American and European farmers to develop new technologies, such as the harvesting of kelp as a military foodstuff. Enhancing the demand for contract staples, food stamps and the 1946 National School Lunch Act guaranteed markets for agrarian commerce. Keeping pace with conventional farming, such innovations as the growing of mussels, oysters, and salmon by New Zealand aquaculturists broadened the definition of farming to include hydroponics and controlled pisciculture.

With liquid fertilizers, chelated plant nutrients, herbicides, and pesticides, agriculture boosted yields into the 1970s. The quick-freezing of edibles for transportation on cargo planes and trains maintained affordability of produce and citrus juices in inner cities and increased the outsourcing of surplus crops to the Soviet Union, Jamaica, the Dominican Republic, and other parts of Latin America. In the 1990s, charitable outreaches diverted infant formula and dried milk to the needy in developing nations.

Tomorrow's Food Supply

By the twenty-first century, farming dynamics raised controversies about world food security. Advanced farming strategies—selective breeding, satellite weather tracking, biotech crops and livestock, Internet agriculture courses, and patented seeds—augmented yields. China, the world's most populous nation, enhanced traditional farm crops by harvesting 33.7 million tons (30.6 million metric tons) of fish from aquaculture in 2004. Mariculture added algae, cobia, oysters, prawns, and seaweed to exports in Australia, Chile, China, France, Ireland, Italy, Japan, Mexico, and Norway. Theories of "sea ranching" proposed controlled methods of salvaging endangered species of seafood. At the same time, global warming foretokened flooding and disastrous storms that displaced topsoil and destroyed family farms, pastures, and orchards.

Other issues infringed on the traditional farming model. Monoculture threatened food diversity by earmarking large parcels of farmland for the top staples— corn, soybeans, and wheat. Hive beetles and viruses reduced bee colonies. Government aid to farmers reached 9 percent in the United States and 4 percent in Australia, compared with 52 percent in Korea and 61 percent in Norway, the most subsidized national agriculture. Surprisingly, global crop choices remained similar to those of Neolithic farms. Cereals and pulses far outranked vegetables and tubers in importance; grains outpaced sugar sources, with Saskatchewan producing 77 percent of the world's poultry feed. Dairy products held first place, preceding sales of fruit and meat.

Ironically, the dominance of agribusiness slumped in the public's estimation following revelations of unjust farm subsidies, burgeoning greenhouse gases, and pollution of groundwater with pesticides, veterinary antibiotics, and chemical fertilizers. Grassroots actions by locavores reclaimed the farmers' market and popularized heirloom varieties and Slow Food, a resurgence in artisanal cheeses, eggs from free-range hens, herb blends, pastries, and wines. Health warnings about the cumulative effects of additives and dyes in processed foods called for a re-evaluation of purity standards, the regulations begun in the Middle Ages.

On the eve of fossil fuel collapse, venturesome farmers increased their incomes by jettisoning scientific wizardry and embracing organic produce, intercropping, and biomass crops—corn, fruit wood, sorghum, palm, and sugarcane, the sources of ethanol and hybrid fuels. In a model of agrarian cooperation, Australian farmers upped farm sustainability to 88 percent and bolstered environmental protection by 75 percent. Nonetheless, Greenpeace foresaw abandonment of capitalistic excesses as the only means of restoring healthful food to local markets. Irish agrarians predicted that agrifood was the "sleeping giant" of investment potential. International financiers looked to microponics (backyard farming) and distribution of farm surpluses among the have-not nations as two means of reducing poverty and elevating wellness worldwide.

In 2011, the United Nations (UN) envisioned restored interest in the food supply, especially in Ghana, Rwanda, and Tanzania. According to the UN Food and Agriculture Organization, Africa may hold the key to world food security. Forecasts of the continent's role as food grower for the world pictured a profound shift toward modernization and a reversal of cyclical famine in Ethiopia, Somalia, and Sudan, where desertification and drought have defeated field agriculture. According to population projections for 2050, the 986 million people in industrialized nations will face huge political and economic challenges in raising food security for the 7.987 billion who will populate developing countries, the locales that generate an average hunger rate of 6 percent.

The UN set as an interim goal the halving of hunger by 2015 and the reduction of child mortality by 66.6 percent. By 2030, poor nations will have to engineer a 20 percent boost in arable land and installation of aquaponics in Third World deserts, notably, sub-Saharan Africa. Desertification, erosion, salinization, trade deficits, and water shortages will worsen, as will the undernourishment of the most vulnerable. Hopeful indicators in Benin, Burkina Faso, Ghana, Mali, Mauritania, and Nigeria foretell rapid increases in the cultivation of cereals, roots, and tubers as the underclasses raise self-sufficiency.

See also: Agribusiness; Aquaponics; Einkorn Wheat; Emmer Wheat; Fertile Crescent Diet and Food Trade; Greenhouse Horticulture; Irrigation; Monoculture; New World Commodities; Organic Foods; Sicilian Diet and Cuisine; Slow Food; Swiddens; Vegetarianism.

Further Reading

Bruinsma, Jelle, ed. *World Agriculture: Towards 2015/2030: An FAO Perspective.* London: Earthscan, 2003.

Mazoyer, Marcel, and Laurence Roudart. *A History of World Agriculture: From the Neolithic Age to the Current Crisis.* Trans. James H. Membrez. London: Earthscan, 2006.

Sherow, James Earl. *The Grasslands of the United States: An Environmental History.* Santa Barbara, CA: ABC-Clio, 2007.

Tauger, Mark. *Agriculture in World History.* New York: Taylor & Francis, 2009.

Agroecology

By allying scientific knowledge of natural systems with farming, herding, and orchardry methods, agroecology integrates food production into a sustainable whole. Unlike dogmatic philosophies of monoculture, organic farming, and technological harvesting, agroecology balances all methods to ensure a stable, equitable distribution of food worldwide without damaging nature.

The task of agroecologists begins with the management of both traditional and innovative approaches within the land and water resources of communities, such as the use of farmer's markets and urban vegetable beds to supply Cubans in Havana. Among modern-day priorities, specialists name halting the replanting of Amazonian rain forests with herd pasturage, diverting fresh water to drought-stricken regions of northeastern Africa, overcoming poverty in Guatemala and Haiti with cheaper cereals and grains, engineering new power sources to replace nonrenewable fossil fuels, and preventing China's industrial complex from poisoning air, earth, and waterways with chemicals and heavy metals.

Since 1911, farming pioneers have analyzed the best locales and methods for saving seeds and growing crops. In 1961, 34 countries convened the Organisation of Economic Co-operation and Development (OECD) as a means of stimulating world trade and global prosperity. Inspired by the Marshall Plan, which rebuilt Europe after World War II, the consortium defined areas of concern, particularly maximizing coffee harvests in India, Indonesia, and Vietnam and stemming bribery and graft at distribution points, a major source of starvation in Afghanistan, Bosnia, Ethiopia, Rwanda, Somalia, and Sudan. Jolting members to action, conservationist Rachel Carson's book *Silent Spring* (1962) warned that humankind had a limited time to reverse the damage that industrial agriculture did to the environment.

The OECD resolved to raise standards of health and nutrition by furthering democratic market economies. Target areas included the least developed areas of Africa, Eastern Europe, Indonesia, the Middle East, and much of Central and South America. Methods began with educating farmers on rotating crops for maximum food diversity and planting legumes under fruit trees to upgrade soil fertility. Educators taught smallholders to make full use of land by interplanting lentils with sorghum and by developing complementary herding and horticulture— for example, raising chickens and guinea fowl alongside melon patches as a natural pest control. Demonstrators presented methods of mulching and nutrient recycling, soil aeration, and no-till field preparation to lower costs of producing corn and soybeans. Geneticists proposed new sources of rice seeds for farms in Bohol, the Philippines, and Ghats, India.

Early in the twenty-first century, rural sociologist Frederick H. Buttel, a professor at Cornell University and editor of *Society and Natural Resources,* promoted agricultural activism as a means of shielding the environment while ensuring fair distribution of the world's food supply. By applying ethical and political fairness to modern agriculture, his disciples intend to monitor population growth and the use of air, land, and water to satisfy the needs of remote indigenous peoples. The task of feeding the world's people requires cooperation among specialties—agronomy, biology, demography, genetics, and geochemistry. The immediate goal is to maintain the well-being of nature, animal and human populations, and soil.

See also: Aquaponics; Ecofeminism.

Further Reading

Gliessman, Stephen R. *Agroecology: The Ecology of Sustainable Food Systems.* Boca Raton, FL: CRC, 2007.

Lockie, Stewart, and David Carpenter. *Agriculture, Biodiversity and Markets: Livelihoods and Agroecology in Comparative Perspective.* Sterling, VA: Earthscan, 2010.

Uphoff, Norman Thomas, ed. *Agroecological Innovations: Increasing Food Production with Participatory Development.* Sterling, VA: Earthscan, 2002.

Warner, Keith. *Agroecology in Action: Extending Alternative Agriculture Through Social Networks.* Cambridge, MA: MIT Press, 2007.

Wojtkowski, Paul Anthony. *Landscape Agroecology.* Binghamton, NY: Food Products, 2004.

Airlifts, Food

Since the advent of long-range air transportation in the 1920s, the deployment of cargo planes and helicopters to world catastrophes has relieved hunger in situations approaching starvation and genocide.

In April 1942, the U.S. Air Force, at the command of President Franklin Delano Roosevelt, launched air relief over the eastern Himalayas to supply Chiang Kai-shek's troops. After the Japanese halted supply trains along the Burma Road, American planes began a 43-month rescue operation delivering 650,000 tons (590,000 metric tons) of goods over 500 miles (800 kilometers) from Assam, India, to Chinese Nationalists in Yunnan Province. Navigating the perils of mountain updrafts, ice, and bombing and strafing by the Japanese, the cargo planes ferried weapons, medical supplies to treat dysentery and malaria, tons of beer, cigarettes, iodine for water purification, and C rations in tins. Each tin contained biscuits, chocolate, instant coffee, and sugar cubes.

Berlin Airlift

In the aftermath of World War II, the Berlin Airlift overcame a Soviet blockade of barge, rail, and road traffic into Germany's divided capital. The effort began with the resolve of U.S. President Harry S. Truman to halt the advance of Communism into a war-devastated city. On June 24, 1948, lacking coal, food, and electricity, 2 million Berliners looked to the skies for aid from the same military forces that had supplied Chiang Kai-shek. American radio lifted spirits by guaranteeing rations. Until help arrived, families snared songbirds for fresh meat. Truckers from the west delivered loads of oranges along the autobahn and tossed them to children on the roadside. Black marketers smuggled in edibles to Potsdammerplatz.

Although the Allies had scaled back their occupation forces, in the face of 1.5 million Russian troops primed for attack, General Curtis LeMay, assisted by Major General William Henry Tunner, organized a rescue dubbed Operation Vittles. On June 28, the first sortie of 32 Douglas C-47 Skytrains delivered 80 tons (73 metric tons) of flour, medicine, and milk, along with CARE (Cooperative for Assistance and Relief Everywhere) packages. Children named the four-prop transport planes "raisin bombers." The choice of dehydrated foodstuffs eased the burden for deliveries made by Douglas C-54 Skymasters, additional transports that rendezvoused at Rhein-Maine Air Base every four minutes for a half hour's unloading. On return flights, the planes carried a total of 1,113 malnourished children to aid stations.

With the aid of Australian, British, Canadian, and French crews and planes, American fliers pledged to supply 1,700 calories per person each day. In a gesture of forgiveness to Germans for causing world war, the Allies ferried tons of wheat, dried potatoes and sugar, dehydrated vegetables, cereal, oil, milk, and coffee. To fend off cold, the C-47 Skytrains flew 3,475 tons (3,152 metrics tons) of coal and gasoline to the makeshift depot at Tempelhof Airport, where Mayor Ernst Reuter and aide Willy Brandt superintended distribution. Each plane bore 3.5 tons (3.2 metric tons) of needed goods, including cheese, cod liver oil, deboned meat, oatmeal, powdered eggs, sausage, vitamin C tablets, and yeast. Compassionate specialty hauls brought kosher food to Jews, saccharine to diabetics, and vegetable seeds to gardeners. The total shipments per day of 750 tons (680 metric tons) required rapid reinforcements of bigger, newer planes.

As the rotation advanced to 1,500 flights per day and 5,000 tons (4,500 metric tons) of goods, canteen trucks dished up coffee, doughnuts, hamburgers, hot chocolate, and sandwiches to crews. The uplift to children brought relief from anemia, dwarfism, rickets, and tuberculosis. Pilot Gail Halvorsen, the "Chocolate Uncle," treated German children to handkerchief parachute drops of chocolates and gum, dubbed Operation Little Vittles. With donations from confectioners, additional gifts of 3 tons (2.7 metric tons) of candy to children boosted morale and quashed tyrant Josef Stalin's plan to sweep Berlin into his empire.

On August 1, Soviet propagandists tried to lure Berliners to the eastern sector with offers of free rations. In another ploy to overrun the capital, Russian harassment began with antiaircraft guns and escalated to bomb and rocket attacks on Allied planes. A half million Berliners massed at the Brandenburg Gate to express thanks to their deliverers and to plead for further assistance against the Soviet siege.

Winter increased the demand for coal and the exhaustion of pilots and ground crews. In a logistical miracle, ex-Luftwaffe repair crews kept the heavy schedule on time; civilian volunteers repaired overtaxed runways with asphalt. Female laborers completed a new airport in the French sector. The upgraded airdrop enabled the Allies to sustain a daily caloric intake of 1,880 per person. By outflanking the Soviets, the Allies maintained the airlift until September 30, 1949, at a total cost of $224 million.

Later Efforts

The Berlin Airlift set a precedent for subsequent humanitarian relief efforts. Altruistic aid produced mixed success in Biafra, Nigeria, in 1969. Although Nigerian officials banned Red Cross deliveries, an efficient mix of corn, soybeans, and powdered milk along with canned milk and dried fish arrived from Caritas and the World Council of Churches, which maintained warehouses on the Portuguese island of São Tomé. Despite food drops, 1 million people died from combat or starvation. In 1975, loads of rice relieved embattled defenders of Phnom Penh, Cambodia, the blockaded capital of the Khmer Republic, a holdout against Communism in Southeast Asia. Daily mercy flights in November 1990 to Asmara, Eritrea, at-

tempted to relieve those suffering from the drought cycle in the Horn of Africa. A parallel effort in Somalia in winter 1992–1993 involved U.S. military planes in extending a food lifeline to East Africa.

From July 3, 1992, to January 9, 1996, a multinational effort supplied 180,000 tons (163,000 metric tons) of goods from Ancona, Italy, and Frankfurt, Germany, to tens of thousands of war-beleaguered residents in Sarajevo, Bosnia. In 1993, the addition of airdrops in besieged Muslim enclaves dispatched 20,000 tons (18,000 metric tons) of food to the hungry. United Nations (UN) supervisors, led by Major General Lewis W. MacKenzie of Canada, offered hope to Sarajevans. Victims cowered beneath artillery, mortar, and sniper fire and surface-to-air missiles, too terrified to venture into local markets. At the end of the feeding project, UN officials proclaimed the effort the longest humanitarian air bridge in history. The success prefaced renewed flights of food, water, and cholera treatments to central Africa in July 1994, when U.S. forces aided refugees from genocide in Goma, Zaire.

Further taxing international aid networks, on July 29, 2005, the UN began a 23,000-ton (21,000-metric-ton) food airlift to Maradi, Niger. Flown from Italy to Niamey, goods required a truck convoy to convey supplies to some 80,000 starving people who were victims of drought and locust invasion of pastures. Survivors scoured the bush for edible grass and leaves. Even with the intervention of Médecins Sans Frontières (Doctors Without Borders) and gifts of thousands of tons of food and $512 million in financial aid from the World Bank, cholera and malaria limited the chances for survival. The crisis threatened to spill over into Burkina Faso, Ethiopia, Kenya, Mali, Mauritania, and Uganda.

The next half decade saw Lockheed Martin C-130 Hercules transport planes and Boeing CH-47 Chinook helicopters bound for airdrops to war-torn Katanga, Congo, in 2007; for flood relief in Bihar, India, in 2008; for war relief in Sri Lanka in 2009; and for earthquake relief in Haiti and posthurricane aid in Guatemala in 2010. On July 11, 2011, news of a lethal food and water crisis in Nairobi and Turkana, Kenya, described the plight of 380,000 refugees of drought on the Horn of Africa. Some 12 million victims in Ethiopia and Somalia faced parched fields and no food. At camps in Dadaab, Kenya, child deaths multiplied sixfold from a malnutrition rate of 30 percent. On July 18, UNICEF (the United Nation's Children's Fund) began shipping nutrition and water to Baidoa, Somalia; on July 21, Kuwait Red Crescent Society dispatched two planeloads of medicine, tents, and 20 tons (18 metric tons) of food.

Within the week, the UN urged donors to send immediate relief. Aid workers scrambled to serve nourishing Unimix porridge to preschoolers and beans, corn, and millet to adults arriving over "roads of death." On July 25, a world airlift began importing emergency rations to Mogadishu, Somalia, and to border airports in Dolo, Ethiopia, and Wajir, Kenya. An Islamic backlash against Western charities—CARE and the World Food Program—blocked efforts to transport aid to endangered Africans.

See also: Famine Relief; International Food Aid.

Further Reading

Rutherford, Ken. *Humanitarianism under Fire: The US and UN Intervention in Somalia.* Sterling, VA: Kumarian, 2008.

Slayton, Robert A. *Master of the Air: William Tunner and the Success of Military Airlift.* Tuscaloosa: University of Alabama Press, 2010.

Sutherland, Jonathan, and Diane Canwell. *Berlin Airlift: The Salvation of a City.* Gretna, LA: Pelican, 2008.

Weiss, Thomas George. *Military-Civilian Interactions: Humanitarian Crises and the Responsibility to Protect.* Lanham, MD: Rowman & Littlefield, 2005.

Alcoholic Beverages

From the Stone Age to the present, alcoholic drinks have increased conviviality at social gatherings and promoted euphoria and spirituality at festivals and rituals. By definition, ethanol is more drug than nourishment. By suppressing psychological controls on behavior, foods containing ethanol have freed interaction to include ecstatic dance and singing and enjoyment of card playing, dining, and sports. Yet, nations enjoying the release of intoxication have acknowledged the liabilities of "ardent spirits."

The sources of intoxication range from fermented agave hearts in Mesoamerican tequila and gentian root in the Angostura Bitters made in Tobago and Trinidad to sugarcane in Indian and Malay rum and fruit must and peppermint in European akquavit or schnapps. Ingredients have seemed as innocuous as molasses in Caribbean rum, lemon peel in Italian limoncello, pear pulp in English perry, antimalarial quinine in Dubonnet, and rice, hawthorn, and honey for drinks in Jiahu in Henan, China, in 7000 B.C.E. More complex drinks incorporated spice in Old English metheglin and vinegar in oxymel, beets and bitter oranges in Cointreau, coconut in Japanese and Sri Lankan arrack and Filipino vodka, and agave in mescal, a specialty in Oaxaca, Mexico.

Early Innovations

Alcohol originally served consumers as curatives. In 2100 B.C.E., Egyptian, Hindu, and Sumerian physicians advised patients on dosages. The Sanskrit Rig Veda (ca. 1200 B.C.E.) and epic *Ramayana* (ca. 400 B.C.E.) affirmed the fermenting of honey into Indian mead and refining ephedra into soma, a Zoroastrian hallucinogen. After 300 B.C.E., Turkish physicians at Cnidus listed hydromel, mulsum, and oxymel as cures of acute ailments.

Since 200 C.E., the Aztec served *aguamiel* (sweet water), which they fermented from thick, frothy agave sap. Collectors siphoned juice and scrapings from the leaves through a gourd tube. Fermentation for 10–15 days resulted in *pulque,* a ritualistic forerunner of tequila reserved for the clergy and royalty. During the colonial era, Spanish authorities licensed *pulquerias* and forbade consumption by mixed assemblies of men and women. Jesuit priests usurped distilleries and used the proceeds to build Catholic academies.

In the 800s, Slavic distillers turned grain into vodka, a bracing hard liquor that encouraged trade between Poland and Russia for service in Polish pubs. Healers recommended vodka as an aphrodisiac and cure for infertility. In 1386, Genoan legates introduced a grape drink in Russia. Trade relations between Krakow and Poznan bottlers and Silesian importers spread to Austria, Bulgaria, Germany, Hungary, Romania, and the Ukraine. The introduction of potato vodka in the 1810s increased demand, which by 2003 had risen to 5.3 million gallons (2 billion liters), one-quarter of the world's distilled spirits.

Gin emerged at Monte Cassino near Salerno in 1100, when Benedictine monks, instructed by translations of Arabic and Greek medical texts by Avicenna and Galen, distilled the juice of juniper berries. Across Europe during the Black Death in the 1300s, the fearful turned to gin as a remedy. Sold in pharmacies, the drink reputedly lessened the pain of arthritis, gallstones, gastric ills, gout, and kidney stones. Bootleg hooch inflicted debauchery and dependence on the Dutch and English, who besotted themselves with *jenever* and gin in the 1660s. By 1727, when consumption grew over the previous 37 years from 500,000 gallons (1.9 million liters) annually to 3.5 million gallons (13.2 million liters), crime waves ensued. Colonial authorities invented the gin and tonic, an effervescent mixer laced with quinine to prevent malaria.

In the 1200s, Europeans avoided cholera epidemics by drinking fermented grape pulp, small beer, and spirits. Monasteries produced floral and herbal bitters, digestives, and tonics, the bases of aperitifs and liqueurs such as Bénédictine from Normandy and Chartreuse, a Carthusian concoction from Vauvert, France, containing 130 herbs. Aromatics and flavorings included artemisia (wormwood) leaves in absinthe, a heady curative and intoxicant called "the green fairy" for its psychogenic effects. Opponents of absinthe claimed it turned men into bruisers and caused consumption and fits. Louche, the milky emulsion in Greek ouzo, a liqueur distilled from anise, extended into an adjective used to describe debauched, risqué behavior.

Simultaneous with the gin, pulque, and vodka industries, in the 1620s, Barbadian slaves at Holetown turned molasses into rum, a source of summery drinks. Healers used rum as a treatment for smallpox and a cleanser for corpses. Along with sugar, bottled rum boosted profits, with 102,000 gallons (386,000 liters) exported to Great

Britain in 1884. In literature, rum fueled scenes of male debauchery and bar ditties in Robert Louis Stevenson's pirate classic *Treasure Island* (1883).

On a more genteel scale, cream liqueurs, including Chambord raspberry liqueur, crème de cacao, and crème de menthe, concentrated the sugar content to produce syrups for flavoring ice or cakes. Additional cream liqueurs took their fundamental aroma and taste from almonds, apricots, bananas, cherries, citrus fruits, coconuts, currants, goji berries, lotus, lychees, melons, prickly pears, sloes, and strawberries as well as the blossoms of elder, roses, and violets. Jamaican Tia Maria and Mexican Kahlúa, two coffee-infused liqueurs, added savor to cheesecakes, eggnog, and mixed drinks.

Society and the Imbiber

Much as they had in classical Athens, Rome, and Pompeii, village taverns anchored social life in colonial North America. Binge drinking burgeoned in the urban United States in 1829, among reservation Indians in the 1860s–1880s, and in the Russian military in the 1940s. Spirits dehydrated the body and depleted stores of vitamin B1, causing beri-beri, the source of cardiac arrhythmia and numb lips and tongue. Globally, drunkenness posed new dangers for drivers and pedestrians and influenced the outcomes of elections until cities closed saloons during voting hours. Teen overconsumption resulted in alcohol poisoning from episodes of "chugging" (gulping) spirits.

Long-term effects of overconsumption include alimentary and throat cancers, diabetes, gastritis, heart disease, impotence, mental illness, and pancreatitis. Because some 90 percent of alcohol metabolism occurs in the liver, heavy drinkers incur alcohol hepatitis, cirrhotic liver, and hepatic jaundice. The unborn children of alcoholic mothers may suffer fetal alcohol syndrome, an irreversible destruction of brain neurons and cause of behavior impairment. Because of liabilities of drinking hard liquor, tippling dropped after 1980 except in Japan, where consumption increased. As of early 2012, "white drinks"— gin, rum, tequila, and vodka—outdistanced brown whiskies in sales.

See also: Beer; Cider; Honey; Potatoes; Prohibition; Rice; Soft Drinks and Juices; Temperance; Vegetarianism; Whiskey; Wine; Yeast.

Further Reading

Buglass, Alan J., ed. *Handbook of Alcoholic Beverages: Technical, Analytical and Nutritional Aspects.* Hoboken, NJ: John Wiley & Sons, 2011.
Gately, Iain. *Drink: A Cultural History of Alcohol.* New York: Gotham, 2008.
Holt, Mack P. *Alcohol: A Social and Cultural History.* New York: Berg, 2006.
Katsigris, Costas, and Chris Thomas. *The Bar and Beverage Book.* Hoboken, NJ: John Wiley & Sons, 2007.
McGovern, Patrick E. *Uncorking the Past: The Quest for Wine, Beer, and Other Alcoholic Beverages.* Berkeley: University of California Press, 2009.

Allergies, Food

An adverse physiological reaction to food, a food allergy results from an autoimmune response to a harmless protein that antibodies identify as toxic. From prehistory, a simple feeding of infants with breast milk bolstered immunity and reduced health risk from allergies. Around 400 B.C.E., Hippocrates, the Greek "Father of Medicine," recognized mealtime reactions as a human incompatibility with common foods.

In 1905, Francis Hare, an Australian psychiatrist at Brisbane Hospital, developed theories of headache treatment in his two-volume treatise *The Food Factor in Disease,* which blamed the inability to metabolize starches and sugars for acute and chronic ailments. By extension, he cited food as the source of asthma, dyspepsia, eczema, gout, and nerve disorders. A year later, pioneer immunologist Clemens Freiherr von Pirquet of Vienna, Austria, named these hypersensitivities "allergies."

Allergies to such common food components as gliadin in wheat, ovalbumin in egg white, parvalbumin in cod, and ripening agents in strawberries currently strike an estimated 6–8 percent of children under age three and 2 percent of adults. Abnormal reactions can be as mild as burning on the tongue, flatulence, itching eyes, tingling, and urticaria (skin eruptions or hives). More serious hyperactivity in the body may produce bloating and swelling, diarrhea, fainting, migraines, panic attacks, and wheezing. Sudden death is rare.

Dermatologists and immunologists attempt to isolate the cause of unidentified anaphylaxis. Clinicians test individuals by skin pricks and blood tests that re-create the physiological response. More exacting tests for life-threatening allergies that trigger heart arrhythmia and shock may involve feeding the patient a capsule of the suspected ingredient. A doctor monitors evidence of anaphylaxis, particularly celiac disease, irritable bowel syndrome, throat constriction, and vomiting.

Treatment for food intolerance may require desensitization or eliminating harmful ingredients from the diet. The most common culprits include chocolate, eggs, milk, peanuts, shellfish, tree nuts (almonds, cashews, hazelnuts, pecans, pine nuts, pistachios, walnuts), and yeast. The allergens in cow's milk, casein and whey protein, may vary from the makeup of goat's and sheep's milk, two possible substitutes. Infant food formulators have attempted a similar protection of babies by making hypoallergenic infant formula from predigested hydrolyzed protein. For adults, treatment with antihistamines, epinephrine, and steroid creams and nasal sprays seeks to restore breathing and heart rate to normal levels and reduce inflammation in eyes, mucus membranes, and skin.

In 1975, Seattle gastroenterologist Walter Lyle Voegtlin, author of *The Stone Age Diet,* promoted the foods eaten by caveman as ideal sustenance for human wellness and stamina. He researched the Stone Age diet as a source of relief from alcoholism, allergies, and autoimmune disease. Because the Neolithic intake consisted of unprocessed foods, consumers lowered the risk of triggering responses to additives, including artificial flavorings, benzoate and sulfite preservatives in salad bars and white wines, and food dyes—Brilliant Black BN, Brown HT, Fast Yellow AB, Lithol Rubine BK, Orange B, Para Red, Sunset Yellow, Tetrazine, and Yellow 2G. In 2002, Loren Cordain, an expert in health and physiology at Colorado State University, promoted an evolutionary diet to rid humans of chronic afflictions from allergies.

Additives to processed foods generated concerns for allergies, resulting in serious reactions from monosodium glutamate, nut residue, poppy and sesame seeds, and red and yellow dyes. Because nuts can subvert the immune system, concern for lethal nut allergies demanded the monitoring of ingredients in public venues. School cafeterias shielded susceptible children from ingesting nut products. Food processors introduced voluntary labeling to alert consumers to nuts in multi-ingredient products as well as to foods produced in facilities that process nuts. In September 2006, Ronald van Ree, a researcher at Amsterdam University, predicted that genetic engineering would produce an immunotherapy vaccine for allergy sufferers within the decade.

See also: Additives, Food; Honey; Monosodium Glutamate; Nuts and Seeds; Shellfish.

Further Reading

Brostoff, Jonathan, and Linda Gamlin. *Food Allergies and Food Intolerance.* Rochester, VT: Healing Arts, 2000.

Lipkowitz, Myron A., and Tova Navarra. *Encyclopedia of Allergies.* New York: Facts on File, 2001.

Maleki, Soheila J. *Food Allergy.* Washington, DC: ASM, 2006.

Metcalfe, Dean D., Hugh A. Sampson, and Ronald A. Simon. *Food Allergy: Adverse Reactions to Food and Food Additives.* Malden, MA: Blackwell Science, 2003.

Amerindian Diet

For millennia, Amerindians survived uncertain times through the wise processing, distribution, and storage of local foods. The holistic philosophy of first peoples revered reciprocity in nature and the human place in the food chain.

During high productivity, food preparers prevented famine by dehydrating and smoking fish and venison, packing jerky with mint to discourage vermin, brining salmon and fermenting herring and salmon roe, leaching acorns for grinding into flour, and drying fruit leather on wood slabs or birch bark trays. Sedentary tribes froze salmon and cached camassia, Jerusalem artichoke, and yucca tubers in grass-lined pits. North Atlantic tribes tapped birch and maple trees for sap, which they crystallized into sugar cakes. The Haida, Nootka, and Tlingit of Vancouver Island submerged the eulachon (or candlefish) in oil to protect from insect infestation, mold, and rot and also to add fish oil to the diet.

Beans, maize (corn), and squash—the "three sisters" of Amerindian agriculture—grew interdependently. The bean vines climbed up the corn stalks and provided essential soil nitrogen. The squash plants spread along the ground to shade and protect the root system. *(North Wind Picture Archives/Associated Press)*

Pre-Columbian Native American Diets

People	Place	Staple Foods
Algonquin	Quebec	bear, bird, corn, eggs, deer, rabbit, and wild rice
Anasazi	American Southwest	amaranth greens, piñon nut, prickly pear fruit, and prairie dog
Aztec	Mexico	bee, cochineal insects, dog, duck, monkey, opossum, rodent, and turkey
Carib	Lesser Antilles	cassava, fish, lime, lobster, and pepper
Inca	Colombia and Peru	lima bean, pepper, potato, and tomato
Inuit	Alaska	beluga whale, ringed seal, seaweed, and walrus
Pawnee	Great Plains	buffalo, camassia root, chokecherry, elk, and turnip
Taíno Arawak	Greater Antilles	fish, iguana, parrot, and pepper
Tlingit	Northwestern Pacific	berries, chicory, salmon, trout, and wild celery
Tuolumne	California	clam, duck, geese, mussel, pine nut, salmon, sea otter, seal, smelt, trout, and whale
Tupi and Guaraní	Amazon River	cacao, cassava, termite, and wild boar
Warao	Guyana	cassava, caiman, dasheen, eddo, and waterfowl
Yaghan	Tierra del Fuego	cranberry, guanaco, limpet, mussel, and wild celery

Some preservation methods required special tools and containers, particularly crocks and jars for burying soapberries and smoked salmon in sand, cedar boxes holding bound berry cakes, and underwater skin bags to fill with cloudberries, cranberries, crab apples, and lingonberries. The Cherokee, Hopi, and Navajo excelled at cultivating corn and beans and storing them in baskets.

The pre-Columbian diet of Native Americans focused on indigenous fauna. Specialties indicate the adaptation of human tastes to the locale and the number and variety of staples. For instance, the Aztec ate from a full range of animal life—armadillos, frogs, iguanas, rattlesnakes, salamanders, and tadpoles. Historian Bernardino de Sahagún issued the *Historia General de las Cosas de Nueva España* (*General History of the Things of New Spain*, 1540–1569), also known as the *Florentine Codex,* a multivolume overview of Aztec life that describes their use of a variety of chilies, peppers, and corn served in tamales and tortillas. In the Andes, cooks favored the meat of llama and guinea pig. Among Arctic Greenlanders and the Inuit of Nunavut in northern Canada, narwhal and *maktaaq* (whale skin) dominated the menu with a fat-rich cuisine that provided energy for life in subzero temperatures.

Food and Wellness

European observers admired the well-being of the Western Hemisphere's hunter-gatherers, such as the Yupik of Alaska, who proportioned seal blubber and blood to maintain the balance between body and spirit, and the Inca, who kept their soldiers healthy on dried bonito and shark, animal fat, and quinoa, a common cereal grain. In the tropics in 1527, Spanish explorer Álvar Núñez Cabeza de Vaca admired the handsome Florida natives, whose diet produced a strong but spare build as well as strength and speed for running. Explorer Jacques Cartier learned from the Algonquin of Montreal how to cure scurvy. During the winter of 1534–1535, native healers provided an evergreen drink made from the white cedar, which relieved French sailors of painful joints and loose teeth resulting from a deficiency of vitamin C.

George Catlin, the nineteenth-century American painter of the Crow of the Great Plains, described sixfooters endowed with well-formed frames and graceful musculature. In 1864, French explorer René Laudonnière summarized the ability of Timucua women of eastern Florida to climb trees and swim rivers while carrying their children. Even elderly females loved dancing at feasts. With the initiation of anthropological surveys, gastroethnographers revisited foodways in Machu Picchu and Chichén Itzá and restructured the kitchen gardening and cookery of the Anasazi, a people of the American Southwest who, from 1200 B.C.E. to 1300 C.E., evolved the dietary culture of the "three sisters": beans, corn, and squash, three crops that thrived when planted together.

Food studies of desert lands characterize a lifestyle devoted to survival. After service in Baja California from 1751 to 1768, Johann Jakob Baegert, a Jesuit missionary and author of *Observations in Lower California* (1771), compiled eyewitness accounts of the diet of Guaycura hunter-gatherers. He complimented them on their wellness and hardihood, despite a spartan intake of agave, fish, grubs and insects, mesquite beans, reed roots, turtles, and yucca washed down with water. They made forays every three days to areas offering more prolific scavenging and bow hunting. When hunger overwhelmed them, they sliced rawhide shoes and hides and devoured them. To relish meat flavor, they tied a piece with string, chewed and swallowed, then pulled the meat back into the mouth a dozen times for more savoring. They retrieved any seed of the pitahaya fruit that passed in the feces in a process the Spanish ridiculed as a "second harvest." Because of their primitive culture, the Guaycura charred whole bats, birds, snakes, and voles in the flame rather than boiling or roasting them, which took too long. They quick-fried inedible pods in turtle shells; the fibrous agave required roasting in coals for half a day. Guaycura lives revolved so tightly around sustenance that their language contained little more than terms for scavenging, cooking, and eating.

Pragmatism and Syncretism

The recipes of first peoples demonstrated pragmatism toward what was available. The Blackfoot exhibited reverence for the whole animal by boiling wild onions with hooves, tongues, and udders and by consuming buffalo intestines along with the contents of semi-digested grass. They valued creamy marrow straight from cracked femurs and turned mammal intestines into casings for blood or meat sausages for roasting over coals. The Ojibwa added sassafras to boiling water for tea, poured broth over snow for a cold dish, and thickened soup with corn silk and pumpkin blossoms. The Cherokee made *sofkee* from soaked cornmeal and wrapped *nixtamal* dough in corn shucks to ferment before baking. The Narragansett one-dish meal called succotash, a bean and corn mixture, blended well with sunflower seeds, chopped pepper, pine nuts, or chunks of dog, fish, or venison. The Lakota devised *wojape* (fruit pudding) from pureed blueberries thickened with any kind of flour and water. To enhance wild rice, the Menominee boiled the grains in the broth of birds or fish and added such ingredients as cattail buds, cranberries, unfurled fern tips, honey, and wild sage.

Before contact with Europeans, the Amerindian low-fat diet produced sturdy organs and skeletons, little arthritis or dental decay, and no tuberculosis. The addition of colonial cookery to Amerindian food staples and recipes created a syncretic cuisine. For example, hominy, pumpkin seed tacos, and piki bread increased creative applications of corn; Indian pudding, a creamy corn dish, took on an Old World flavor with the addition of molasses.

At the same time, the introduction of beef, pork, pomegranates, and radishes teased the palate of first peoples. Spanish colonists added to the largely vegetarian Aztec regimen more dairy products and meat. From Basque and Portuguese settlers of the Maritime provinces, the Beothuk and Micmac learned to pack cod, venison, and oysters in barrels with generous sprinklings of rock salt. The increased sodium in the diet introduced Indians to cardiac ailments and high blood pressure.

With the displacement of tribes from traditional habitats, European colonists encouraged commercializa-tion of plant and animal harvests and the elevation of profits above the sustenance and longevity of indigenous peoples.

See also: Aztec Diet and Cuisine; Barbecue; Cacti; Chicle and Chewing Gum; Columbus, Christopher; Curative Foods; Díaz, Bernal; Hudson's Bay Company; Hunter-Gatherers; Inca Diet and Cuisine; Jerky; Jiménez de Quesada, Gonzalo; Lapérouse, Jean François Galaup; Las Casas, Bartolomé de; London Virginia Company; Manioc; Mexican Diet and Cuisine; Pemmican; Peyote; Pit Cookery; Religion and Food; Royal Greenland Trade Department; Sauces and Saucing; Seaweed; Shellfish; Soft Drinks and Juices; Tortillas; Trade Routes; Travel Food; Vanilla; Verrazzano, Giovanni da.

Further Reading

Fussell, Betty Harper. *The Story of Corn.* Albuquerque: University of New Mexico Press, 2004.

Hamilton, Cherie Y. *Brazil: A Culinary Journey.* New York: Hippocrene, 2005.

Janer, Zilkia. *Latino Food Culture.* Westport, CT: Greenwood, 2008.

Parrish, Christopher C., Nancy J. Turner, and Shirley M. Solberg, eds. *Resetting the Kitchen Table: Food Security, Culture, Health and Resilience in Coastal Communities.* New York: Nova Science, 2008.

Animal Husbandry

A parallel to plant agriculture in civilized states, animal husbandry sustained a clan or community from the output of herds and poultry flocks. After 25,000 B.C.E., a time when over half the human diet derived from wild bison, caribou, horses, and mammoths, evidence suggests that feral mammals adapted to human presence as a source of protection from wild predators. Because of the contiguity of beast and humankind, hunting parties no longer had to track wild animals far from home.

In Africa, the Americas, Eurasia, and Australia, honeybees generated a sweetener and wax, a malleable repair material for pottery, and a commodity for sale or trade. Tame mammals provided dependable dairy goods and reliable sources of eggs and meat, tallow for lighting, and hides for rugs and shoes. Cooking advanced from innovations in technique and tools for grinding, pit baking, pounding, roasting, and scraping. Because of predictable flock and herd growth, the human population density rose from one to 15 persons per square mile (9 persons per square kilometer).

Prehistoric Food Sources

Before the agrarian revolution, in the Tigris River basin from 13,000 B.C.E., humans managed wild boars, an available source of meat, fat, and useful bone, bristle, hide, and intestines for food storage. During the Neolithic revolution around 12,000 B.C.E., hunter-gatherers tamed those animals with a temperament amenable to flocking and herding and an ability to adapt to pens and barns, breed in captivity, and follow a human leader. To feed the most people during the transitional Mesolithic Age, early stockmen observed nature and selected animal traits, particularly for beekeeping, the earliest form of animal colonization. By revering nature as a beneficent source of nourishment, magico-religious ritual venerated food sources, such as bird eggs, fish, and yams.

After the formation of Abu Hureyra, Syria, in 11,050 B.C.E., a 1,000-year drought forced Natufians (early Palestinians) to settle near streams to pasture sheep, which converted grass to the first staple protein to feed human omnivores. In lieu of currency, sheep served as a medium of exchange in barter. From experimentation with ewe's milk, herders evolved highly nutritious feta and ricotta cheeses, blocks of pecorino and Roquefort hard cheeses, and *labneh* (strained yogurt), a basis of savory and sweet entrées eaten with bread, cucumbers, olives, olive oil, and onions.

Omnivores balanced their diet with foods from multiple sources. From 10,000 B.C.E., the Nordic Sami followed reindeer herds, which appeared on petroglyphs and on bone etchings as producers of milk and venison cooked over pit fires. The acceptance of grain as a daily staple paralleled the domestication of dogs, goats and ibexes, pigs, and sheep for fiber, meat, and milk. In the Zagros region of Anatolia, herders first domesticated the goat from the Bezoar strain, herbivores that lived on bark, berries, grass, and leaves. Herding clans profited from goat's milk and meat as well as dung for cooking and heating fuel, hair for fabric, hide for carafes, and sinew for sewing. Goat herding spread to Iran and Israel, where graziers developed milking and meat cutting, fiber weaving, and leatherwork as specialized crafts.

In Germany, Iraq, and southeastern Turkey in 9000 B.C.E. and Iran in 8000 B.C.E, innovations of Neolithic, or New Stone Age, cuisine advanced the taming of goats as dairy animals and the penning of pigs as a four-legged pantry. Studies of year-old animals in bone heaps attested to the sophisticated taste of meat eaters.

In this same period, North American Athabascans tamed the camp dog from the feral wolf as their only domesticated beast. The dog earned its keep as hunter, guardian, dray animal, and rodent and snake controller. The eating of dog meat paralleled similar consumption of small canids in China, Korea, and Vietnam.

Wild and cultivated beef consumption also dates to prehistory. Cave paintings at Lascaux, France, pictured the hunting of the aurochs, the ancestor of modern cattle, which flourished from sub-Saharan Africa throughout India and the Middle East. Herders in India raised another scion, the zebu, for wagon pulling and meat and evolved dairy foods from cows. In the Chihuahua Desert on the Tex-Mex border, around 7500 B.C.E., Paleo-Indian

settlers grew grains and consumed quantities of milk, cheese, and meat from domesticated animals.

Husbandry as Survival Skill

Around 7000 B.C.E., during an era that saw depletion of the wild gazelle from overhunting, food growers evolved formalized methods and strategies. In Papua, practical farmers raised root crops and sugarcane alongside pigs, eager recyclers of otherwise wasted greens and stalks. In 6000 B.C.E., Indian, Iranian, Pakistani, and Thai farmers tamed elephants for lifting and pulling chores and domesticated chickens, offspring of the red jungle fowl, a tropical pheasant. In the Far East, Chinese and Indonesian crop tenders integrated the vegetable and grain diet with chicken and fish netted from rivers. The broadbased diet fueled a population explosion.

After 5200 B.C.E., animal rearing began to generate a sedentary lifestyle that prefaced the rise of city-states. Sumerians, the empire builders at the Tigris and Euphrates delta, bred cattle and sheep after 5000 B.C.E. At Ur, state-run agriculture systematized staffing, which migrated according to seasonal demands to cut grain for fodder and reeds for barn bedding. Farm foremen supervised the harnessing of onagers and oxen to plows, the caching of forage for winter feed, and professional butchery. Secondary products from cattle added 5 quarts (4.7 liters) of butter and 7.5 quarts (7.1 liters) of cheese per cow to income. In the Indus Valley, farmers enhanced their diet with butter and cheese from their herds, two sources of interregional trade. In the Ukraine about 4500 B.C.E., herders tamed the horse, a major contribution to streamlined labor and transport for warriors. Scythians milked mares to produce koumiss, a staple drink as far north as Mongolia. Europeans ate horsemeat and revered the dish as the focus of a religious propitiation of the Germanic god Odin.

Around 4000 B.C.E., the swan entered waterfowl culture in Britain, Ireland, Italy, and Portugal. Simultaneously, the Chinese tamed the duck and water buffalo, a source of mozzarella cheese and curd, while Eurasians moved plows and sledges with the aid of a pony later named Przewalski's horse. Arab nomads herded dromedaries for milk to make butter and yogurt. Persians later roasted whole camels for feasts and reserved hump meat for special occasions; Armenians wind-dried the meat for *pastirma*, a spiced travel food. In this same period, the Andean Inca raised alpacas, guinea pigs, and llamas for meat. Farther north, residents of Yucatán tamed the wild turkey, a bird found only in the Western Hemisphere.

In another burst of agrarian innovation, the midfourth millennium B.C.E. saw rapid improvements in farming technology, followed by the domestication of geese and rock pigeons in China, poultry farming in India and Pakistan, and the taming of the wild ass on the Black and Caspian seas. As animal power for pulling the ard or frame plow, the buffalo, camel, and donkey overturned surface crust to access moist subsoil for seeding. In Great Britain and Scandinavia, plowmen amassed stones into barriers and markers of property lines. Pork production took prominence among stockers because pigs converted 35 percent of plant energy—acorns, beechnuts, and chestnuts—to meat, as contrasted with sheep at 13 percent and cattle at 6.5 percent. South of the Alps, religious taboos declared swine too dirty for human consumption.

Animal domestication made demands on the farmer for wintertime feed and barn straw, but provided beasts for meat during the thinning of herds. Among the Nenet, the indigenous people of the Russian tundra, in 3000 B.C.E., semidomesticated reindeer herds produced both milk and meat as well as hides for clothing and shelters. In Crete, Egypt, Israel, and Knossos, skeps (domed hives of straw) held honeycomb. The squab, a domestic pigeon, yielded succulent meat; the goose became a specialty food and layer of protein-rich eggs. Hebrews fancied the tame dove. By 2500 B.C.E., Central Asians in the Tibetan Plateau, Mongolia, and Russia added both the double-humped Bactrian camel and the yak to agrarian investments as meat animals and sources of dung for fuel and strength for caravanning. From Burma east to Borneo and Java, stockmen kept peafowl in pens and bred banteng and gayal, ox-like dray animals.

The domestication and breeding of livestock improved the human diet with nutritious cheese, meat, and milk. Among the Inca of Altiplano, Peru, alpacas and llamas provided meat deemed special to the gods. About 2000 B.C.E., stockmen domesticated the guinea pig, a fast-multiplying meat source that thrived on vegetation. Andeans cooked guinea pigs by stuffing heated stones in the carcass. They valued the entrails for flavoring gravy or sauce and for adding to potato soup.

Classical and Medieval Husbandry

In the classical era and early Middle Ages, North Africans introduced the barbary, or ringneck, dove to pen fowl. Roman texts by Columella, Hyginus, Varro, and Virgil revealed the refinements of the classical era, in which apiculture (beekeeping) and the gathering of honey and wax produced goods for the table and for export. In 200 B.C.E., Cato compiled veterinary treatments for sheep that combined lupine extract, olive oil dregs, and wine. The colonizing of rabbits on islands stocked meat for ships' larders. In 162 B.C.E., the castration of the capon produced a plumper bird than the hen or peafowl for roasting. Roman Spain produced squabs (pigeons) for meat markets. Umbrian herders bred Chianina oxen, a valuable draft and beef animal.

The propagation of animals in the first century B.C.E. increased animal diversity. On the march of Roman legions into Gaul in 52 B.C.E., provisioners took along the pheasant, a source of eggs and meat. In attempts to strengthen farmyard investments, Asian stockers practiced animal acupuncture as early as 10 C.E.

Parallel to high market-quality ox breeding, the Japanese brought Wagyu cattle from the Korea Peninsula to cultivate rice fields and supply marbled beef prized for its juicy tenderness. In Peru, the Moche tamed the alpaca, llama, and vicuña, three producers of meat and soft wool. The use of llama dung as fertilizer increased the yield of Peru's green revolution.

In 534 C.E., agro-encyclopedist Jia Sixie, the prefecture of Gaoyang County in Shandong Province, compiled *Qimin Yaoshu* (*Skills for Peasants*), one of the world's oldest farming treatises. Out of concern for the underclass, Jia observed tillage techniques in Hebei, Henan, and Shanxi and summarized animal herding and feeding and methods of selective breeding and vinegar and wine fermentation. He also published an overview of contemporary monographs on fish raising in rice paddies and making yogurt.

Over the next five centuries, husbandry techniques focused on small details of food production. Medieval hunters trained falcons, ferrets, and hawks to flush rabbits from warrens into nets. Regular stalking yielded little meat but prevented leporids from overrunning gardens and devouring vegetables. By maintaining dovecotes at manor houses, stockmen kept poultry at hand to supplement pantry staples and for sale at village markets. The Japanese domesticated quail in 1100 as a source of attractive entrées and tiny eggs for exotic plate adornments and street food.

Stockers evolved more food diversity based on climate and terroir. Around 1200, Christian monks in Yorkshire and the Rhineland turned eel weirs and pond tending into a form of pisciculture that yielded bream, carp, eels, and fish milt, a nonred meat source during Lent and other meatless holy days. During the same era, because of a short growing period, the settlement of Iceland rated the tending of stock above other areas of agriculture. After deforestation, goats thrived on the underbrush, while cattle and pigs fended for themselves, often freezing in the bitter clime.

European farmers raised the peafowl for meat and ornamental feathers and followed the advice of fourteenth-century French naturalist Gaston Phoebus on the treatment of animal bites and wounds with raw wool soaked in olive oil, a source of natural anesthesia and antisepsis.

In post-Columbian Mesoamerica, European explorers introduced horses and hunting hounds. For the indigenous farmer, the new mammals pulled plows and travois, a wheelless drag useful for ferrying light loads. By the late 1500s, stockers built rabbit hutches and sold the meat for frying, roasting, and stewing.

North American Experiments

During the agrarian phase of North American development, graziers broke more virgin prairie than ever in the course of history and armed themselves against rustlers. More than half the population of Canada and the United States worked livestock by branding, neutering, and worming their animals. On ranches after 1749, the cross-breeding of the cow and buffalo resulted in resilient herds of beefalo. Importation of Merino sheep from Britain created new opportunities for New England graziers to raise a more adaptable ruminant. Three more imports, the early maturing Berkshire, the compact Spanish Duroc, and weighty Poland-China swine, intensified North American pig breeding and raised prices for more flavorful, moist pork suited to longer cooking at high temperatures.

Cattle breeding entered a scientific phrase in 1840 after Americans imported vigorous British Ayrshire and meaty Galloway and Hereford cattle for ranches and Dutch Holstein-Friesian and Jersey milkers for dairies. Stockers began consulting husbandry manuals and displaying prize scions at county fairs and stock exhibitions. After the emancipation of slaves in 1863 and the subsequent collapse of the Southern plantation system, an independent U.S. Bureau of Agriculture oversaw the expansion of frontier cattle and sheep ranches. The staff of 30 bureau scientists introduced hardy livestock and answered questions about mad cow and other zoonotic diseases. The last half of the century saw the manufacture of the Langstroth beekeeping frame to streamline honeycomb collection and the addition of the ostrich to exotic poultry farming and the sale of feathers to decorators.

North and South American ranching methods allowed calves to forage the grassland outside of villages and settlements, particularly in Argentina, the world's third-largest beef exporter. Hollywood later romanticized the task of the cowboy, gaucho, and vaquero, the mounted wranglers of the Western Hemisphere who ensured herd safety. Science and technology assisted postwar agrarians with drought and other cyclical obstacles. The manufacture of chick incubators and farrowing pens lowered mortality rates in the young. Stampede and wildfire alarms and windmills reduced the chances of losing animals to common hazards. Navajo sheepherding in the San Juan River valley, New Mexico, ensured independence for the nation's most prosperous Amerindians.

Abraham Lincoln harbored prospects for a secure food supply from frontier ranching. On July 2, 1862, congressional ratification of the Morrill Land Grant Act authorized federal distribution of 17.4 million acres (7 million hectares) of public land. During the Indian Wars, the military increased consumption of beef, raising the profitability for stocking and homesteading on the Great Plains.

On the northern Texas border at Guthrie in 1870, Samuel Burk Burnett of the Four Sixes Ranch interbred longhorns with British shorthorns, which gained popularity in Australia, Canada, Ireland, New Zealand, South Africa, Uruguay, and Zimbabwe. Captain Richard King of Corpus Christi bought up the 860,000-acre (348,000-hectare) King Ranch, the world's largest. Under protection of Texas Rangers, Burnett and King plotted cattle drives to Kansas railheads for transfer to Chicago stockyards. Carcasses of King's American-bred Santa Ger-

trudis steers traveled by rail to meet the demands for beef at Atlantic Coast inns and restaurants.

Profitable Ranching

After passage of the Desert Land Act on March 3, 1877, Oregon livestock required the cultivation and watering of 640-acre (260-hectare) plots of semiarid public land at a cost of $1.25 per acre ($3.09 per hectare). Agronomists in Nevada guarded turf and waterways as the life-or-death resources to support grasslands and livestock, which generated food as well as horn for tools, hooves for glue, and blood and bone for fertilizer. Fearing ruin from quarantines, breeders agitated for cures for hog cholera, pleuropneumonia, and tick fever. Barbed wire fencing of free prairies led to protracted range wars over independent pasturing rights. Overgrazing plus a disastrous blizzard in 1886 drove some ranchers out of business and forced others to diversify. In one experiment with scaled-back stock, North Americans raised the pigeon for squab meat, a specialty market item.

In the 1900s, science professionalized animal husbandry to predict and manipulate the value of tame animals. Tuberculin tests isolated sick cattle in 35 states. With the Great Plains of Canada and the United States thoroughly settled by 1920, agronomists turned to heightened yield by breeding more productive animal varieties, cattle vaccines, and species resistant to the hoof-and-mouth virus, spread by air and fodder. Colombia and Panama, meanwhile, developed resilient sheep herds.

In 1926, long-distance refrigerated trucking linked consumers with fresh beef, chicken, pork, veal, eggs, and milk. The importation of New Zealand targhee sheep, a source of tender lamb, and British landrace hogs, producers of flavorful bacon, further diversified meat sources. In the 1940s, the addition of French Charolais cattle to North American herds raised standards for tender beef. Pre–World War II collaboration with South American agronomists enhanced diversity throughout the hemisphere and heightened surveillance against zoonotic disease. Wartime food rationing in England and northwestern Europe returned the dove, pigeon, and horse to favor as supplements to the meatless table.

Enhancing the demand for contract staples, food stamps and the 1946 National School Lunch Act guaranteed markets for eggs, meat, and milk. Keeping pace with conventional farming, such innovations as the growing of mussels, oysters, and salmon by New Zealand aquaculturists broadened the definition of farming to include hydroponics and controlled catfish and tilapia pisciculture. Electric fencing protected investments by stopping strays and warding off coyotes, hyenas, wild dingo and dog packs, and wolves. From advances in artificial insemination for genetic diversity, cloning, and embryo transfer from quality breed stock to surrogate females, animal husbandry amplified herd quality and profitability. In the 1990s, People for the Ethical Treatment of Animals (PETA) and other animal rights groups stepped up protests of inhumane treatment of farm animals—small pens for calves and pullets, stunning devices to control bulls, and the absence of water and space during transport of animals to abattoirs and poultry processors.

Herding and Mechanization

By the twenty-first century, technology had advanced selective breeding and biotech crops and livestock, such as squab bred for breast meat in France, Italy, the Middle East, Nigeria, North Africa, and the United States. Chefs in China and global Chinatowns reserved the squab for New Year's banquets. Print and electronic advertisement prompted the health conscious to demand pigeon over chicken because of lowered microbe count. In defiance of factory farming, organic husbandry evaluated the placement of livestock on the land near flowing water to reduce pollution and animal stress while producing for sale healthful eggs, cheese, milk, and meat. Managers oversaw sanitary feedlots and housing and scheduled seasonal diet and vaccines to protect the food supply from such microbes and parasites as brucellosis, trichinosis, and tuberculosis.

Future intervention in faulty livestock management anticipated a cleaner, more sustainable universe. At Penn State University, dairy nutritionist Alexander Hristov proposed a diet to control bovine gut microbes and limit the emission of greenhouse gas. The reputation of agribusiness deteriorated in the public's esteem following revelations of unjust farm subsidies and veterinary antibiotics and growth hormones in meat. Grassroots actions by locavores reclaimed the farmer's market and popularized heirloom varieties and Slow Food, a resurgence in artisanal sausage, goat cheese and milk, and eggs from free-range hens.

By 2050, according to a 2006 United Nations Food and Agriculture Organization report, the world will risk ecosystem collapse from "Livestock's Long Shadow." Analysts itemized greenhouse and methane gases as causes of global warming and condemned deforestation and land and water damage generated by the overgrazing of livestock and the penning of poultry. A comparison of water use cited graziers for needing 21,877 cubic yards (16,726 cubic meters) of water to produce a ton of beef in contrast with potatoes, which required only 174 cubic yards (133 cubic meters). Vegans and vegetarians enlarged on lopsided use of natural resources as justification for condemning meat consumption.

See also: Agriculture; Buffalo; Hormones in Food; Manioc; Organic Foods; Slow Food.

Further Reading

Damron, W. Stephen. *Introduction to Animal Science: Global, Biological, Social, and Industry Perspectives.* 4th ed. Upper Saddle River, NJ: Pearson Prentice Hall, 2009.

Field, Thomas G. *Scientific Farm Animal Production: An Introduction to Animal Science.* 10th ed. Boston: Prentice Hall, 2012.

Shaler, Nathaniel Southgate. *Domesticated Animals: Their Relation to Man and to His Advancement in Civilization.* New York: Charles Scribner's Sons, 1895.

Shapiro, Leland S. *Introduction to Animal Science.* Upper Saddle River, NJ: Prentice Hall, 2001.

Aphrodisiacs

Since ancient times, consumers have classified as aphrodisiacs any food that enhances sexual pleasure and potency. To heighten fertility and performance, Phoenicians added saffron to moon cakes, which honored Ashtoreth (Astarte), the goddess of fertility and sexuality. In Mesopotamia, the hot, spicy taste of asafetida in food contributed an aromatic stimulus to romance. For Arabs, the chewing of nutmeg increased fecundity over a three-day period; in Yemen, the same effect came from eating walnuts.

Vitality from liquids and solids, such as those listed by the ancient Greek encyclopedist Theophrastus, became the source of carnal appetite and satisfaction. For strength, the Chinese preferred caterpillar fungus, ginseng tea, and bird's nest and shark fin soups. In the early 1400s, Huou (Hu Szu-hui), the chef of Kublai Khan's imperial kitchen, chose eggs and onions, the tried-and-true dish, for a self-indulgent master who had to satisfy a sizable harem. The secret to bursts of Greek energy, honey cakes bristled with poppy seeds, a source of potassium and sugar. The Greeks heightened desire by chewing thyme or mint, a stimulant that Alexander the Great denied his Macedonian army to deflect their interest from women toward war.

The Romans invented a variety of priapic aids, including chervil infusions to reduce prebedtime tension. A presex punch, hippomane, blended herbs with genital secretions from colts to lengthen male staying power. For unflagging libido, the Roman poet Ovid recommended shallots. The Emperor Tiberius preferred skirret, a tuber similar to salsify; he imported the roots from Germania to serve with vegetables to boost his lust. The satirist Martial relied on onions, a cheaper, locally available tonic crop also recommended by the gourmet Apicius and the physician Galen for its restorative juice.

Throughout the late Middle Ages and Renaissance, mystic love potions inspired aphorism, song, and verse, with ingredients varying as widely as the turtle eggs admired in Borneo and wild thyme tea steeped by the Alaskan Inuit. The Moroccan scholar and traveler Ibn Battuta relied on coconuts for marital success with multiple wives; Marco Polo returned from China with advice to warm women's hearts with mandarin duck soup. For Catherine de' Médici, artichokes spurred passion.

English herbalist William Langham's *The Garden of Health* (1579) recommended aromatic rosemary as a goad to lust. The English also revered coriander, which they added to hippocras, a wine cordial heated with a hot poker. Henry VIII preferred bedtime sherry warmed with pungent caraway seed. His daughter, Elizabeth I, added fragrant vanilla to marzipan, a stiff candy shaped into human body parts for table decorations and nuptial gifts. Sarsaparilla-flavored drinks, the first European food fad from the New World, reputedly cured impotence. In the eighteenth century, Prussian King Frederick the Great aroused his passions with a mustard concoction from his secret recipe.

Through the centuries, erogenous dishes reputedly stimulated blood to the genitals and affected coital function and conception in a variety of ways:

boost fertility: basil, bull testicles, caviar, coriander, ginger, grain, honey, kola nuts, leeks, mandrake, mustard greens, papayas, parsley, pomegranate, sage, tansy, walnuts

enhance performance: cactus flowers, cardamom, chili pepper, coconut, ginseng, honey, maple syrup, nettles, pineapple, pine nuts, purslane, shrimp, tea, turkey, yohimbe bark

inspire fantasies: artichokes, asparagus, avocado, cinnamon, cucumbers, figs, fugu (pufferfish), ginkgo, nutmeg, raspberries, strawberries, tomatoes, whipped cream

lower inhibitions: absinthe, celery, champagne, cherries, damiana tea, lavender, marijuana, pepper, pumpkin, saffron, salted peanuts, wine

stimulate passion: anise, arugula, asafetida, betel nut, celery, chocolate, coffee, fennel, garlic, gentian, licorice, *quat* (Abyssinian tea), sage, tobacco, truffles, vanilla

Foods associated with love deities, such as the Greek love icon Aphrodite's scallops and sparrows, the Greek wine god Bacchus's grapes, and the West African sky power Min and the Egyptian chaos god Seth's preference for lettuce, bore an erotic mystique. As antidotes to the over-ardent lover, chefs served beans, dill, lentils, marjoram, rue, soy, watercress, and water lily root and offered tobacco and whiskey at the end of the meal to dampen desire. Small doses of a chancy food additive, nightshade, a hallucinogen and alkaloid poison, reputedly increased sexual energy.

Foods visually associated with ova, phalli, and semen, such as almonds, bananas, carrots and parsnips, cucumbers, eels, eggs, orchid bulbs, radishes, rhinoceros horn, and river snails, engendered erotic mythology. The Aztecs

viewed the avocado as a scrotal-shaped stimulant to male sensuality. Widespread global lore lauded oysters because they resembled female labia and vulva; similarly, apricot and melon halves looked like breasts. The all-purpose mandrake suggested the human groin in full stride.

See also: Ibn Battuta; Medieval Diet and Cuisine; Pliny the Elder.

Further Reading

Albertson, Ellen, and Michael Albertson. *Temptations: Igniting the Pleasure and Power of Aphrodisiacs.* New York: Simon & Schuster, 2002.

Dalby, Andrew. *Food in the Ancient World from A to Z.* London: Routledge, 2003.

Ricotti, Eugenia Salza Prina. *Meals and Recipes from Ancient Greece.* Los Angeles: Getty, 2007.

Svoboda, Robert. *Ayurveda for Women: A Guide to Vitality and Health.* Rochester, VT: Healing Arts, 2000.

Watts, Donald. *Elsevier's Dictionary of Plant Lore.* Oxford, UK: Academic Press, 2007.

Apicius (fl. 25–45 C.E.)

The wealthy Roman gourmet and cookbook author Marcus Gavius Apicius compiled recipes from the kitchens of ancient Rome, Greece, and Egypt. A native of the Campania region in southern Italy, he flourished during the reign of the Emperor Tiberius. He earned his cognomen from Caelius Apicius, a gourmand living in 90 B.C.E. Historians surmise that the nickname may have been a generic term meaning "professional chef."

Because of Apicius's composition of an illustrated recipe book, *De Re Coquinaria* (*On Cookery,* ca. 35 C.E.), Rome became one of the few ancient cities to have codified its cuisine. Perhaps drawing on the experience of professional cooks, Apicius organized entries into ten books, beginning with a description of the chef's job and advancing to meat, garden produce, varied entrées, legumes, poultry, gourmet specialties, mammals, seafood, and fish. Missing from the compilation are chapters on pastries and desserts. For his gluttony, he earned sneers from Juvenal and Martial, imperial Rome's chief satirists.

Apicius's writing style detailed the meticulous care of a professional cook who handled sautéing, stirring, and seasoning personally, rather than supervising slave helpers. His language, the mundane Latin of the streets, lacked elegance but bristled with exact terms for forcemeat, mincing, mortaring, and trussing. His tone suggested a man intent on his work, such as whisking egg batter for pancakes, pureeing lettuce with onions, twisting heads and sinews off wild birds, skewering a sow's udder, and cooling chicken salad with snow. He advocated boiling wild boar in seawater and shaping gingered dolphin or rabbit into meatballs and touted the blending of eight leafy greens with pulses and barley for a vegetable ragout.

Master Chef

Apicius was a hands-on cook who apparently evolved recipes by trial and error. He appeared to abjure garlic as peasant food and specified beans only from Baiae, which he served with celery, *caroenum* (wine concentrate), and *liquamen* (fermented fish sauce). His instructions avoided exact amounts. Instead of measuring spoons, he depended on the educated mouth, by which he tested sauces for balance and proper flavoring as well as for texture. His dishes earned him the regard of encyclopedist Pliny the Elder, who proclaimed Apicius "the greatest and most prodigal gourmand of all."

The writer's knowledge of flavorings extended from the usual—almonds, basil, coriander, cumin, dill, fennel, leeks, mint, and pine nuts—to the lesser known, such as fleabane, grape hyacinth bulbs, laser root (a relative of fennel), lovage, nettles, and origanum (wild marjoram). Of his 470 recipes, 349 contained pepper. He specified dried, fresh, leafy, or seed rue to flavor olives, pickles, or wine. To ensure quality ingredients, he sailed to Libya to sample North African shrimp, then rejected them as too ordinary for purchase. For everyday fare, he outlined the creaming of hot mayonnaise and the preparation of *mulsum* (honeyed wine) for travel.

Apicius favored the elitist palate. Among his extravagances, he advocated marinating red mullet to make the most expensive *garum* (fish sauce). He recommended sauces featuring sweet and sour turnips and imported Armenian plums and Jericho dates and endorsed feeding swine on figs and a final meal of *mulsum* (sherry). His stuffing for chicken and fish included cabbage and mustard, fish sauce, and tender black bryony, which resembled asparagus shoots.

His gourmet recipes and dinner arrangements earned him cash gifts from the imperial family. Although biographical details are limited, he reputedly used his professional fortune to endow a culinary training center.

Legacy

To disguise the basic flavor of fish, meat, and vegetables, Apicius compiled 270 recipes for entrées and 200 recipes for sauces. His balance of simple staples and layerings of complex flavors resulted in such recipes as lentils cooked in coriander and rue, fish sauce, honey, leeks, raisins, and vinegar. He promoted use of the cucumber with bread steeped in vinegar and the dressing of cucumber salad with honey and fish sauce.

In an aside to the thrifty, he proposed preserving quince in grape must, a sweet aperitif made from three parts grape pulp reconstituted with ten parts honey, and keeping asafetida in a container of pine nuts to extend the use of the expensive herb. In an early form of aromatherapy, his beverages featured citrus leaves and the petals of

Recipe: Sweet-and-Sour Fried Fish Fillets

Parboil four large fish fillets and save the stock. Boil six peeled parsnips or turnips and mash to a pulp. Stir-fry 1 tablespoon of flour in 1 tablespoon of olive oil. Add 1/2 cup of fish stock to the roux. Stir in 1/4 cup of white wine, 1 teaspoon of honey, 1/2 teaspoon of cumin, 1/8 teaspoon of saffron powder, and four crushed laurel berries. Bring to a slow boil, then simmer the sauce for 30 minutes. Roll the fish fillets in the vegetable pulp and fry in olive oil. Remove to a heated platter and top with the sweet-and-sour sauce and a sprinkle of red wine vinegar.

roses and violets. He favored the wealthy with cheesecakes, rice starch gruel, and exotica such as five-course meals featuring flamingo tongues, oversized prawns, and squid while demeaning such plebeian fare as cabbage.

The extant text of *On Cookery* contains anachronisms introduced later, such as description of the imperial bulimia of Apicius's disciple Vitellius, who ruled the empire briefly in 69 C.E. The emperor stuffed himself four times a day with heavy meals, then drank emetics and disgorged the excess. At one banquet, the emperor's brother Lucius served 7,000 birds and 2,000 fish. Vitellius reciprocated by dispatching battleships east to the Aegean and west to Hispania to collect ingredients for the Shield of Minerva, a complex salad of charfish liver, eel entrails, flamingo tongues, and peacock and pheasant brains. Another disciple, the epicure emperor Heliogabalus, admired Apician curiosities and acquired his own—camel heels, cockscombs, nightingale tongues, parrot heads, and partridge eggs.

These irregularities in *De Re Coquinaria* suggest that posthumous additions continued altering Apicius's original recipe collection into the fourth century C.E. Nonetheless, the fragmented text, written at Rome's height, remained a favorite at medieval monasteries and Renaissance palace kitchens.

See also: Cookbooks; Grilling; Medieval Diet and Cuisine; Pliny the Elder; Pulses; Sausage; Shellfish.

Further Reading

Alcock, Joan Pilsbury. *Food in the Ancient World.* Westport, CT: Greenwood, 2006.

Faas, Patrick. *Around the Roman Table: Food and Feasting in Ancient Rome.* Trans. Shaun Whiteside. Chicago: University of Chicago Press, 2005.

Grainger, Sally. *Cooking Apicius: Roman Recipes for Today.* Illus. Andras Kaldor. Totnes, UK: Prospect, 2006.

Appetizers and Hors d'Oeuvres

The service of appetizers, or starters, has a long history as a preface to the eating and digestion of a satisfying meal. In Egypt around 1450 B.C.E., tomb art depicted hand washing in aromatic unguents preceding hors d'oeuvres and grand banquets. The implied purpose, contrast of aroma, taste, texture, and appearance, encouraged chefs to import unusual foods for their color and mouthfeel.

The Greeks introduced the appetizer buffet. To encourage fellowship, they passed a loving cup, a two-handled drinking bowl, for sharing an aperitif of hippocras (spiced wine), mead, or vermouth (wine fortified with aromatic herbs). For Greek cuisine, Cypriot capers and marinated hyacinth bulbs provided savory tight buds for pickling with onions. Zingy vinegars and olive tapenade added pizzazz to rural dinners of beans and peas, lentil soup, and cups of goat's milk.

Among the Romans, the *gustatio* (salad course) consisted of platters of eggs, lettuce, mushrooms, and radishes. For more sumptuous feasts, slaves offered salvers of boiled fungus, clams, dormice, jellyfish, mussels, onions, oysters, and prawns. Hosts passed trays of such rich, bemusing tidbits as pickled fern shoots and sea urchins with *mulsum* (sherry), a sweet aperitif made from three parts sour grape must reconstituted with ten parts honey. The conversation stimulators became a prelude to six or seven courses, which filled a three-hour evening of *gustus* (tasty pleasure).

Middle Ages

For the table of Byzantine Emperor Justinian the Great in the early sixth century, the Empress Theodora aimed for dining ambience. She hired Greek, Indian, Persian, and Syrian specialists to plan an impressive variety of cold appetizers—creamed eggplant, hummus, and garlic paste on bread triangles—to complement grilled sea bass and sturgeon or roasted suckling pig. Dishes of caviar gave evidence of the host's willingness to pay for the best in seafood.

Around 900 C.E., Arab insurgents in Iberia introduced the Spanish to food sampling in the style of Jordanian and Lebanese *mezes* (appetizers) of baby spinach, melon cubes, olive paste, pickled turnips, and sardines. The charming presentation developed into tapas (Spanish for "lids"), small portions of free bar munchies set on top of glasses of beer and enjoyed in Seville and spread throughout Andalusia. The reduction of entrées to samplers of chorizo, cheese tarts, and mussels grew into a national flare for serving satisfying bites with drinks of Manzanilla sherry or sangria.

In the 1500s, the English adopted the "antepast" as a true appetite titillation, similar in panache to the French *amuse-bouche* (mouth teaser), an arty display of the chef's talent. The introduction of the term *hors d'oeuvre* (apart from the main work) in 1691 in Paris by François Massialot, premier chef of Louis XIV, indicated the passing of entremets, light extras such as artichoke hearts, served on oval trays or footed compotes to complement a main course. Beribboned baskets of table favors, such as almonds and marzipan, marked place settings. Open-faced sandwiches contrasted make-your-own service in Chile, China, and Ethiopia, where guests chose a relish to roll up hot dog– or taco-style in *injera* (flatbread).

Modern Era

In *Il Cuoco Piemontese Perfezionato a Parigi* (*The Piedmont Cook Perfected in Paris*, 1766), an anonymous testimonial to Italo-French cookery, the term *antipasto* defined a first course rather than a preliminary warm-up. Savories arrived small enough to eat in one bite without the help of a knife and fork, such as a small chunk of melon wrapped in prosciutto or a phyllo nest filled with blackberry jam. Each emphasizes a three-dimensional quality of food and the geometrics of, for example, square crackers or round vegetable patties topped with aioli, a garlicky mayonnaise.

Spanish tapas, bite-size appetizers served cold or hot at bars and social gatherings, evolved from early Arab fare. Local ingredients and cooking methods have made tapas a varied and sophisticated cuisine in their own right. *(Gallo Images/Rex Features/Associated Press)*

Nineteenth-century Europe developed the appetizer into a culinary masterstroke. In 1891, Pellegrino Artusi, the Bolognese author of *La Scienza in Cucina e l'Arte di Mangiar Bene* (*Kitchen Science and the Art of Eating Well*), characterized appetizers as "delicious trifles," a taste sensation on *crostini* (bread crusts) preceding the service of pasta. In Sweden, the smorgasbord moved away from tempting trays to a full buffet piled several layers high with butter balls and cracker and bread baskets to accompany frittatas, gravlax, hard-cooked eggs piped with creamed fish, meatballs, pots of beans, apple cake and lingonberries, carafes of aquavit and *jenever* (gin), and urns of coffee. Swedish hostesses showcased their relishes on china and crystal pedestals and silver chafing dishes. The star of the show, pickled herring, has a long history in European diet, down the coast from Finland to Portugal and inland to Polish Jews.

Worldwide, from Chinese pickled turnips, Korean *gujeolpan* (decorated pancakes), Japanese daikon radish slices, and Hausa groundnut balls in Nigeria to Cantonese dim sums (dumplings) and Hawaiian pupu platters, starters prepare the taste buds for vegetable entrées, fish stews, soups, or roast meats. In Russia, *zakuski* names the profusion of black bread, duck tartare, and marinated mushrooms and plums, a buffet array that precedes formal table service. Sicilians arrange the most visually appealing morsels—anchovies, cured ham and pecorino, figs, and preserved lemons—on an antipasto tray to lure guests from conversation toward a place at the table.

High-toned dining rooms distribute whimsical appetizers as a signature gift from the chef and a test run for a proposed entrée, such as a taste of Tahitian crab muffins, Pennsylvania Dutch cabbage rolls, or Bajun flying fish and christophene in Barbados. The sharing of finger fritters, hot crab puffs, marinated shrimp, nut nibbles, a shot glass of pepper confit, and quail eggs, such as those served on transoceanic voyages or at ambassadorial gatherings, ready the palate for the meal to come. Tiny cups of corn chowder

Recipe: Pickled Pinwheels

Soften one block of cream cheese and blend in 2 tablespoons of dill weed, 2 tablespoons of chopped pimiento or roasted red peppers, and 1 tablespoon each of chopped celery leaves and minced bread and butter pickles. Spread a counter with slices of chipped beef or thin Danish ham. Top each slice with a heavy smear of the cheese spread. At the center of each meat slice, place a pickle spear. Roll each slice over the pickle. Place in the freezer for an hour. Remove and slice each roll into 1/2-inch pinwheels. Top each pinwheel with a dab of olive mayonnaise and secure to a snow pea or endive leaf with a cocktail pick.

and Gruyère puffs served by wait staff encourage relaxation and informality among friends and strangers. Venetian *cicchetti,* miniature sandwiches served with relishes, encourage bar traffic in the afternoon, a version of the American happy hour.

For residential guests, hosts circulate delicate canapés and roasted baby vegetables on trays along with flutes of champagne. At the Brown Palace in Denver, Colorado, an array of chocolate bites accompanies cups of herb or fruit tea. For televised football games and election nights, heartier fare declines in daintiness from predinner wisps of food to hearty snacks—marinated wienies on toothpicks, buffalo wings, and chips and dip.

See also: Crackers; Feasting; Finger Food; Snack Food.

Further Reading
Civitello, Linda. *Cuisine and Culture: A History of Food and People.* 3rd ed. Hoboken, NJ: John Wiley & Sons, 2011.
Clark, Melissa. "Tiny Come-Ons, Plain and Fancy." *The New York Times,* August 30, 2006.
Meyer, Arthur L., and Jon M. Vann. *The Appetizer Atlas: A World of Small Bites.* Hoboken, NJ: John Wiley & Sons, 2003.
Nunez, David G. *The Appetizer Is the Meal.* Bloomington, IN: AuthorHouse, 2011.
Scully, D. Eleanor, and Terence Scully. *Early French Cookery: Sources, History, Original Recipes, and Modern Adaptations.* Ann Arbor: University of Michigan Press, 2002.

Aquaponics

The method of raising fish and growing plants in a sustainable, integrated system, aquaponics applies a simulated habitat to the controlled cultivation of organic fruit, herbs, meat, and vegetables. A combination of aquaculture (cultivation of aquatic organisms) and hydroponics (cultivation in water), aquaponics gained interest in the 1970s as a form of green farming. The system constantly filters through sand and recirculates fluids that contain clean metabolites. Extension horticulture updates Chinese and Thai paddy gardening as adjuncts to carp, eel, and pond snail gardens and emulates the planting of reed mat gardens in Inle, Burma.

To reclaim wetlands, the Aztec cultivated *chinampas,* floating gardens that farmers anchored in lake bottoms as early as 1150 B.C.E. The Mexican reach-in beds produced amaranth, beans, corn, peppers, squash, and tomatoes, along with medicinal herbs, maguey for beer, and grasses for weaving baskets and mats. The root systems of beds reaching 4 meters (13 feet) by 40 meters (130 feet) fed on sediment and sewage and flourished from constant soil moisture. When food plants matured, gardeners poled the artificial island to market at Tenochtitlán.

Essential to a life-sustaining aquaponic environment are added oxygen and the removal of slimy biofilm and particulates, which pollute and acidify the effluent. Within the biofilter, bacteria convert toxic ammonia and nitrites from algae and fish feces into nitrates, an organic plant food. Treatment with calcium hydroxide or potassium hydroxide neutralizes the acidity. Worms liquefy solid organic wastes into humus for use by fauna and flora. Gardeners can assess needs and inject fertigation—irrigation water containing soluble fertilizer—directly into the cycle.

Aquaponics contributes to the food web such ordinary edibles as fresh water perch and bass, saltwater char and tilapia, crayfish and prawns, and bibb and leaf lettuce, chard, and basil, all grown on rafts or platforms without pesticides. In addition to common garden vegetables—cabbage, cantaloupe, cucumbers, okra, onions, peppers, sweet potatoes, strawberries, tomatoes—the systems also intercrop ornamentals, particularly portulaca and roses. Plants that do poorly include carrots and potatoes, which evolve into unwieldy shapes without soil to guide their development. Specialty greens—basil, chives, spinach, taro, and watercress—adapt well to the flowing water garden. Application of ladybugs and wasps offsets the threat of aphids and whiteflies.

Polyculture and water reuse systems increase the variety and economy of truck gardens and lower the cost of fresh foods in winter months. Because of the efficiency of a closed-loop nitrogen cycle, aquaponic gardens use 2 percent of the water necessary to grow crops in soil and avoid the waste of nondissolvable nutrients. The method also suits communities that recycle treated sewage wastewater.

Aquaculture wins converts because of its economical space needs. One acre (0.4 hectare) of space can yield 25 tons (23 metric tons) of fish and 50 tons (45 metric tons) of vegetables annually. By contrast, a steer raised for two years on 8 acres (3.2 hectares) of pasture yields only 75 pounds (34 kilograms) of marketable beef.

The concept of soilless indoor gardening shows promise for development in parched sub-Saharan Africa and in Barbados and the Virgin Islands, where crop space and irrigation water are scarce. In Australia and Canada, urban farming via aquaponics reduces the mileage that such crops as barramundi and cod travel to market, making local produce both cheaper and fresher. Gourmands question the flavor and texture of foods harvested from a closed environment. Another complaint, the rapid spoilage of aquaponic tomatoes, suggests a lack of vigor from vines grown in liquid rather than soil.

See also: African Food Trade; Fish and Fishing; Seaweed; Shellfish; Taro.

Further Reading

Cooke, Elise. *The Grocery Garden: How Busy People Can Grow Cheap Food.* Denver, CO: Outskirts, 2009.

McWilliams, James E. *Just Food: Where Locavores Get It Wrong and How We Can Truly Eat Responsibly.* New York: Little, Brown, 2009.
Parker, Rick. *Plant and Soil Science: Fundamentals and Applications.* Clifton Park, NY: Delmar Cengage Learning, 2010.
Rakocy, James E., Michael P. Masser, and Thomas M. Losordo. "Recirculation Aquaculture Tank Production Systems: Aquaponics—Integrating Fish and Plant Culture." *SRAC Publication* 454 (November 2006): 1–15.
Tracey, David. *Urban Agriculture: Ideas and Designs for the New Food Revolution.* Gabriola, British Columbia, Canada: New Society, 2011.

Arab Diet and Cuisine

Spanning the Arab world from the Arabian Peninsula west to Turkey, Syria, Jordan, Egypt, Somalia, Yemen, and the Umayyad Maghreb, Arab diet and cuisine consists of a lively, palate-pleasing blend of textures, aromas, and flavors. Religious cookbooks from Mesopotamia dating to 8000 B.C.E. exhibited local enthusiasm for refined cookery of dugong, fish, shellfish, and turtles. Hospitality, a Koranic requirement, formed the bedrock of interpersonal relations.

Among the Bedouin, Berber influences coexisted with Arab cuisine. The roasting of thin sheets of dough over a convex metal griddle yielded a brittle bread, used as a utensil for scooping up dips and sauces. Loaves, broken by hand, accompanied sheep tail fat and curdled buttermilk with dates and toasted locusts for snacks. Large metal pans held several sheep carcasses for roasting whole. Cooks served festive fare to a group from a common dish.

Archaeological digs at Al-Zubara on the Qatari coast revealed a heavy meat and seafood diet prepared at low hearths from 4000 B.C.E. by pearl fishermen. At nearby Ruwayqa, date presses produced syrup for export. In Baghdad, the Muslim capital, red meat kebabs and spitted whole lamb spiced with garlic simmered over charcoal. The Persian *biryani*, a rice-based fricassee, combined spiced meat and vegetables with boiled eggs. The Indian influence added dressings of chutney and curry.

In the Middle Ages, dhow and caravan carried over sea and land the Ceylonese tea, Indonesian pepper, saffron, and sultanas sold in Persian Gulf *souks* (open-air markets). At the heart of the Arabian Gulf spice routes, emirs of Oman dipped hands in perfumed waters before seating themselves at low tables. Over incense, they conversed informally while eating olives or dates with the thumb and first two fingers of the right hand.

Meals began casually with Jordanian and Lebanese *mezes* (appetizers), consisting of baby spinach, melon cubes, olive paste, pickled turnips, sardines, and walnuts. A national dish, *masgouf,* a butterflied carp marinated with tamarind and turmeric, required a firebox and an upright roasting grill, on which the cook burned out the fish fat. For the freshest carp, diners ate picnic style on riverbanks with lemon and salt for seasoning. Since 2007, Arabs have rejected carp from the Euphrates or Tigris rivers because of wartime pollution.

Today, the basic entrées of camel, chicken, and lamb gain variety and nutrition from combinations of goat's milk yogurt, olive oil and lemon juice, parsley with mint, garlic, and blends of cinnamon, clove, coriander, cumin, nutmeg, and paprika. Tunisians prefer *harissa,* a table condiment of caraway and coriander seeds pounded with garlic, hot pepper, olive oil, and salt. Yemeni condiments add cilantro, fenugreek seed, and green chilies. Cooks sauce red snapper with a red splash—pomegranate mixed with tomato. Iraqi meat pies feature leavened dough and celery and scallions as complements to lamb or mutton.

Consumed with hot coffee or Yemeni cardamom tea, meals frequently begin with a base of bulgur or rice or

Recipe: Desert Salad (Tabbouleh)

Combine 1/2 cup each of chopped lemon mint and parsley. Soften 1/2 cup bulgur by covering it with 1 cup boiling water and letting it sit for about 20 minutes—then drain and press out any excess water. Add one large tomato cut into small cubes, one minced spring onion, and one chopped cucumber. Dress the mixture with 3 tablespoons each of olive oil and lemon juice. Season with pepper and sea salt and serve with pita triangles.

North African couscous and *samoons* (wheat flatbread). Moroccans serve couscous, the national dish, with thick *harira* (chicken soup) flavored with cinnamon and saffron. Lavish menus combine medleys of chickpeas and fava beans with eggplant or zucchini and salads of cucumbers and onions or of sauteed dandelion greens or purslane.

Breakfast varies from light yogurt cream, dill, and olives with Somali *canjeero* (pancake bread) to lentil soup or chickpea stew, a Tunisian specialty. Palestinians set their morning tables with a shaker of *zaatar,* a staple seasoning of oregano, sesame, sumac, and thyme that accompanies foods served with sage tea. Following noon prayers, Palestinian diners favor mixed appetizers preceding basmati rice and lentils with meat and tomato sauce and a carrot salad. A dessert of baklava (paper-thin pastry with nuts and honey) or *basbousa* (a Carthaginian semolina tart) and frothy yogurt drinks refresh and round out the meal. After dinner, a fruit course features fresh peaches or oranges, an Algerian preference, or decorative Qatari cupcakes.

Palestinian snacks revolve around hummus (chickpea paste) and chili sauce. Desserts feature dates, figs, and pomegranates as well as green almonds and pistachios served with fruit juice and goat's milk or Algerian mint tea and *halwa* (hard jelly) cookies from the Maghreb. Palestinian fruit trays include apples and carob pods with Jerusalem cheeses. In Bahrain, fruit choices include bananas and mangoes; Tunisians offer apricots, cherries, and prunes. Yemenis prefer rice pudding. Dinner in open-air shops concludes with *sheesha* (sweet flavored tobaccos) smoked in hookahs, or water pipes.

See also: Cereal; Crusaders' Diet and Cuisine; Halal; Ibn Battuta; Ice Cream; Pasta; Street Food; Taboos, Food.

Algerian Muslims gather in the courtyard of a mosque to share couscous after prayer. Traditional Berber couscous—steamed semolina pasta covered with an aromatic meat or vegetable stew—has been a mainstay of North African cuisine since the 800s C.E. *(Thierry Zoccolan/AFP/Getty Images)*

Further Reading

Basan, Ghillie. *The Middle Eastern Kitchen.* New York: Hippocrene, 2006.

Brennan, Georgeanne. *The Mediterranean Herb Cookbook.* San Francisco: Chronicle, 2000.

Bsisu, May. *The Arab Table: Recipes and Culinary Traditions.* New York: HarperCollins, 2005.

Campo, Juan Eduardo. *Encyclopedia of Islam.* New York: Facts on File, 2009.

Potter, Lawrence G. *The Persian Gulf in History.* New York: Macmillan, 2009.

Arctic Diet and Cuisine

On terrain where agriculture is impossible, Arctic dwellers rely on hunting and gathering for a well-rounded diet that suits their cultural and metabolic needs. For the Inuit of North America, the world's purest hunting society, a protein- and fat-focused regimen ranges from dried capelin and ptarmigan and kittiwake eggs to smoked bowhead whale and reindeer tongue. To transport fresh meat to camp, hunters rely on a backpack or a tumpline, a headband and dragline to pull the carcass through snow. An ulu, a semicircular carving knife, makes short work of skinning and dressing haunches.

A land-based meat from the musk-ox arrives at the table *tartare* (chopped raw). For vegetables, families save the stomach contents of browsing mammals and gather tubers and grasses as well as seasonal berries and seaweed, both sources of vitamin C. In the Arctic wetlands, evergreen rhododendron provides leaves for Labrador tea, a favorite Athabascan drink. In Greenland, brewers turn angelica and crowberries into ale.

The circumpolar staple from the marine food web comes from the ringed seal and the seasonal harp seal and walrus. After harpooning a seal or narwhal, hunters secure a stock of food that lasts for months by preserving blubber and meat as well as edible skin for raw *muktuk*. In Greenland, cooks turn sea mammal meat into *suaasat*, a soup thickened with barley or rice and flavored with bay leaves and onions. The consumption of a marine-based diet heavy in omega-3 acids and selenium protects indigenous peoples from prostate cancer.

Arctic cuisine is surprisingly varied. Ice fishing among the Siberian Nenet and the Alaskan Aleut yields char and polar cod and lake trout, which they prepare with mouse food, the tundra roots such as cottongrass that voles store in their burrows. For the Pribilof Islanders on the Bering Sea, dried salmon and eider ducks provide winter subsistence. The traditional consumption of seal blood and organ meats reputedly fortifies the body against cold weather. Diners share the kill by status, according male hunters first choice and women and children the remains. Inuit and Mackenzie River Inuvialuit villagers, including the elderly and disabled, receive an allotment, which they consume with fireweed greens and bannocks or frybread.

The fermentation of summer kill butchered into steaks requires one year for the meat to decompose in the ground, a dangerous preparation method that causes more than ten deaths per year from botulism. Called *igu-naq,* cached mammal meat contributes a treat to everyday foodstuffs. In Greenland, Inuit food preservers stuff a seal carcass with up to 500 auks and press the treat under a boulder for months until the birds decay into a thick gel, a popular entrée for birthday and wedding parties. The northern Swedish *surströmming,* a rotted herring dish, served with crisp bread and chopped onion, releases so putrid a smell that people eat it outdoors.

The Yupik of the Yukon-Kuskokwim delta west of Anchorage, Alaska, fill barrels with salmon entrails and heads and bury them for a week to make a delicacy. An Icelandic equivalent, *hákarl,* requires the pressing in sand and the hang-drying of a basking shark for up to 20 weeks to cure. A masculine repast, hákarl smells of ammonia. It pairs with *akavit* (literally "water of life"), a strong liqueur made from caraway and spices.

Berries add a fruity savor to meat and fish entrées. A favorite dessert, *agutak,* or "Eskimo ice cream," blends the flavor of whipped fat or tallow with blueberries, cloudberries, cranberries, crowberries, or salmonberries. Around Kamchatka in northeastern Russia, Chukchi reindeer herders, like the Nenet of Siberia, pound into reindeer fat a similar dessert concocted from fish roe and bilberries or crowberries. In Labrador and Newfoundland, cloudberries are the basis of a wine for drinking with sweets and blue cheese.

After World War II, Icelanders popularized festivals of country fare called *thorramatur* (winter foods). A buffet of native dishes and sour specialties includes pressed rams' testicles and singed sheep heads, as well as smoked lamb and seal flippers fermented in whey to heighten the tang. The spread features blood pudding and liver sausage as well as wind-dried cod and haddock with rye bread. Dishes come to the buffet in wooden *trogs* (troughs), an antique touch.

The cuisine of some 50,000 Northern Sami of Norway and Sweden as well as Canadian menus feature lutefisk, a gelatinous entrée of cod or pollock softened and cured with lye leached from birch ash. Dating to the Renaissance, the aromatic dish requires spices or butter to enhance the mild taste. Scandinavians celebrate Christmas and Easter with servings of lutefisk. For everyday eating, salt-fermented gravlax (buried salmon), a medieval recipe, offers a mix of dill and sugar flavors in thin slices served on crackers with capers and lemon. The marine diet appears to protect the Sami as well as northern lumberjack families from ischemic heart and vascular diseases.

A threat to Arctic survival, the environmental buildup of the pesticide dichlorodiphenyltrichloroethane (DDT) and polychlorinated biphenyls (PCBs) flows north on current and wind to infiltrate the habitats of crustaceans and squid. Within the food web, refuse from industrialized Asia, Europe, and North America has destroyed birds and mutated sex hormones and immune systems. Seabird eggs carry the world's highest concentrations of the neurotoxin dichlorodiphenyldichloroethylene (DDE), a contributor to Alzheimer's disease, breast cancer, and Parkinson's disease. Studies of human breast milk at Baffin Island and Nunavik, Canada, in 1988 and in the Faeroe Islands, northwest of Scotland, in the 1990s revealed methylmercury in seal, walrus, and whale blubber.

Compounding the danger, the role of fermentation in sand and gravel introduces ground and water contaminants during fermentation. Among some 13,000 Chukchi on the Russian shores of the Bering Sea, anatomical studies find one of the highest hexachlorobenzene (HCB) and hexachlorocyclohexane (HCH) rates in the Northern Hemisphere. To save themselves from chemical poisons, Arctic dwellers turn more and more to a diet of land-raised beef, poultry, fruit, grains, and vegetables.

See also: Caching; Whaling.

Further Reading

Cone, Marla. *Silent Snow: The Slow Poisoning of the Arctic.* New York: Grove, 2005.

Ferguson, Steven H., Lisa L. Loseto, and Mark L. Mallory, eds. *A Little Less Arctic: Top Predators in the World's Largest Northern Inland Sea, Hudson Bay.* New York: Springer, 2010.

Nuttall, Mark. *Encyclopedia of the Arctic.* New York: Routledge, 2005.

Taylor, Alan. *American Colonies.* New York: Penguin, 2002.

Taylor, Colin F. *The American Indian.* Philadelphia: Courage, 2002.

Art, Food in

Kitchen work in art has furnished culinary historians with a glimpse of kitchen gardening and cooking style and method from early times to the present. The pictures of a bride offering chocolate to the Mixtec king in the *Codex Zouche-Nuttall* (1051 C.E.) and the late-sixteenth-century *Codex Tudela* demonstrate how Aztec servers generated foam on ritual pots of chocolate by twirling swizzles in the liquid. Egyptian tomb art subtly praises the fruitful Nile culture by depicting bakers at the oven and wait staff carrying baskets and heaped trays to the table. Hellenistic vase art displays the various stages of cutting and winnowing wheat, trampling grapes, and harvesting and preserving olives, the three fundamental foods of the Mediterranean diet.

Medieval wall art features monks splitting wood for the fireplace and filling bowls with stew, an embodiment of the Benedictine rule requiring daily work and domestic chores that welcomed wayfarers to the monastery table. Miniaturist Jean Pucelle honored a full calendar of peasant home labors in *Le Livre d'Heures de Jeanne d'Evreux* (*The Book of Hours of Jeanne d'Evreux,* ca. 1327), a 209-page prayer book illustrated for King Charles IV of France. Medieval stained glass art bears similar imagery of Christian virtues, daily labor and supervision, the essentials of tending to family sustenance.

From the Renaissance, artists Lubin Baugin of France, Juan Sánchez Cotán of Spain, the brothers Isaac and Jan Soreau in Germany, and Dutch master Cornelius van Ryck began spotlighting cooks in their milieu as artists of the culinary trade. As explained by food historians, these coded canvases contain the ingredients and implements needed for preparing a recipe or feast. In an ebullient woodcut by Italian scenarist Christoforo di Messisburgo-Ferrara from 1549, the glorification of entrées presented to a table set for nine captures the anticipation of diners and the pride of cooks in their profession.

Artistic Close-Ups

In precise period elements, art gives the viewer a detailed glimpse of preparing and consuming an era's gastronomy, such as Caravaggio's *Supper at Emmaus* (1601). An unidentified sketch of the industry of an orderly Tudor kitchen establishes a clear separation by gender of hearth cookery. While men loll and converse at table, three aproned kitchen maids clean game birds, skewer them on spits, and baste the carcasses as they roast on andirons over the fire. At the far edge of the scenario, a plate of fruit and a basket of carrots and greens draw little attention in a setting where meat and masculinity dominate the menu.

Hands-on work at stoves, hearths, and tables offers historians a picture of utensils, serving sizes, and accompaniments. An appealing display of sixteenth-century abundance, Vincenzo Campi's *The Fruit Vendor* (1580) presents a woman surrounded by crockery bowls of berries, baskets of fruits and legumes, plates of figs and nuts, an apron of peaches, and a piggin of grapes, from which she extracts a likely bunch. Around the outer edge, a cabbage, a bunch of asparagus, and artichokes and a woman in the distance lifting a basket of nuts extend the image of plenty.

In Annibale Carracci's *The Bean-Eater* (ca. 1585), a rustic diner leans toward an unadorned, long-handled spoon for a bite of black-eyed peas, an African import to Italy that he consumes with crusty rolls, scallions, a plate of greens, and a glass of wine. A contemporary, Paolo Veronese, painter of lavish, life-affirming historical and biblical scenes, outraged ecclesiastical purists with *The Feast in the House of Levi* (ca. 1573), a high Renaissance tableau of table riches. A decade earlier, he had adapted Christ's first miracle into a Mediterranean event for *Marriage at Cana* (ca. 1563), a food festival bustling with shared dishes, servants refreshing wine pitchers, and a complex gabble exchanged from table to table among well-dressed guests.

Food pictures articulated an era's culinary sensibilities. Influenced by naturalism, Carthusian layman Juan Sánchez Cotán's *Still Life with Game Fowl, Fruit, and Vegetables* (1602) accents shadings, light, and color as well as texture and shape, elements of menus that delighted and satisfied diners. Like the camera's eye, the artist's hand captures the normalcy of foodstuffs in profusion. His mélange of humble but nourishing edibles in pleasing juxtaposition presages Spain's baroque realism.

One of the pervasive subjects of late Renaissance art, the still life accentuates a passive arrangement of produce on a table or window sill, along a kitchen counter, suspended from ceiling beams, or arranged in baskets, in cauldrons, or on platters. Diego Rodríguez de Silva y Velázquez's *Old Woman Cooking Eggs* (1618) overlays labor-intensive cookery with a subdued domestic tension common to seventeenth-century portraiture. The spare scene and strained profile of the cook particularize the act of brazier cookery in a peasant setting limited to common farm foods. Displayed in bold chiaroscuro, her use of mortar and pestle and stirring spoon require limited motions from a seated position. Velázquez's *bambochdas* (drinking scenes) and *badegones* (kitchen pictures), such as *The Water Carriers of Seville* (ca. 1620), highlight dignified, contented individuals set against somber earth tones of olive, silvery-gray, yellow, burnt umber, and black. He ennobles the humble with a mystery and drama that prefigure the impressionism of Claude Monet's *Luncheon at Argenteuil* (1873) and Anna Ancher's *The Maid in the Kitchen* (ca. 1883).

In *Kitchen Scene with Christ in the House of Martha and Mary* (1620), Velázquez excels at contrast, another side of drama and mystery. Drawing on the biographical details of Jesus' ministry from Luke 10:38–42, the painter illustrates the difference between sisters. The housewifely Martha pounds food in a brass mortar in preparation for cooking eggs and fish; Mary, in the inset at right, rivets her attention on the evangelist while allowing her sister to shoulder the kitchen work. The pairing illustrates the need of Christians for spiritual sustenance as well as earthly food.

Pieter Cornelisz van Ryck of Ghent produced *The Cook* (1628), a kitchen spread in chiaroscuro. As the rather generous light travels from the lower left-hand corner to the upper right, it backlights a jumble of carrots, apples, grapes, and pumpkin and a braid of onions. At the cook's level lies a haunch of meat with cut side facing out; she bears grapes and cabbage in her hands. Above her shoulder, poultry hangs from hooks. The profusion of fish on a platter, a tub at the cook's elbow, and a plated ham to the rear attest to the household's prosperity and access to a broad menu, but the noncommittal expression on the subject's face leaves open to interpretation her opinion of the job.

A view of kitchen work from the servant's vantage point appears on Jean-Siméon Chardin's canvas *Scullery Maid* (1738). A deliberately bare-walled environment strewn with a heavy-bailed copper cauldron, warming pan, cylindrical crock, and short-handled bean pot frames a single gesture by a serving woman gazing absently at the scene. Neatly dressed in white cap, wide-sleeved tunic, wide skirts, and apron, she reaches into a cask for fruit or vegetables to fill a long-handled skillet. The absence of clear food shapes and the distant focus of her eye suggest a blur of tedium. A blue ribbon dangles a gold medallion from her neck, a symbol of validation of her repetitive chores.

Food Commerce

From a commercial perspective, an illustration in Denis Diderot's *Encyclopédie* (1745) captures the labor and teamwork of an eighteenth-century pastry shop. Division of labor placed each man at a particular post. To the left, the shop boy bears a basket of fruit. At the open oven, the baker extends a wooden peel toward items surrounded by flame. At the back wall, a laborer kneads dough at a wood dresser top. The most complex part of baking occurs at the center of the picture, where racks of game birds and a haunch of meat hang over the central workstation and a servant pots a huge meat pie. In the foreground, an ax lies beneath a chopping block draped with the lifeless body of a hare. More activity at a huge pestle and counter to the right indicates that professional baking in the eighteenth century required heavy effort from all involved.

In 1770, Huguenot painter Daniel Chadowiecki sketched an anecdotal street view of a Polish market. Amid pushcarts selling stringed instruments, dolls, and wooden horses, the butcher offers splayed pig carcasses and loops of sausage and salami. The folk spirit of market day mixes strolling aristocrats among bumptious children and out-at-elbows fishmongers lifting their wares from four-legged tubs. Beyond women with market baskets and bonneted fruit sellers, the implement seller sits in the shade under a row of iron trivets amid tankards, bowls carved from layered wood, and huge wicker urns, the practical cooking equipment of every kitchen.

Late in the eighteenth century, English painter and engraver Francis Wheatley characterized the vigor of grocery sales on London streets. His popular series of folk etchings *Cryes of London* (1795), exhibited at the Royal Academy, originally carried the title *The Itinerant Traders of London.* At the core of his vision labored the cooks, hawkers, and milkmaids of rural and domestic England. In one market scene, a basket of peas lies in the foreground, admired by an urban crowd after its early morning arrival by cart from the country. The juxtaposition reflects the dependence of city folk on imported produce.

Vasili Perov's *Tea-Drinking in Mytishchi, near Moscow* (1862) uses food to make grim social commentary overblown with prerevolutionary melodrama. While a fat Russian orthodox prelate stretches grandly at an outdoor table and stuffs his rounded gut with dainties and tea from an ample samovar, an attendant sips from a saucer behind him while a maid refills the pot from a ceramic jar and pushes beggars aside. Two ragged figures dominate the right side of the canvas with humbly inclined heads and outstretched palms. A barefoot child accompanies the taller figure, a blind, peg legged veteran of the Crimean War, two of Russia's down-and-out in the decades preceding the fall of the Romanov dynasty.

French impressionist Edouard Manet turned wholeheartedly to kitchen and table still life in the 1880s. Vital and evocative in their details, his *Bunch of Asparagus* (1880) and *Still Life with Brioche* (1880) reprise the tender contours of vegetables bound with grocer's twine and awaiting the pot. Under a fluted brioche, the sparkling blue plate balances a single pink rose in full bloom and the perky ears and whiskers of the kitchen tabby. More dramatic, *Still Life with Salmon* (1880) produces delight in disorder with yellow lemons, raffia-clad wine carafe, and an imposing slab of fish on a bed of greens. Manet's works conveyed promise in the fragility of fresh food, provisions for the sturdy, sense-pleasing meals on which his European contemporaries fed.

See also: Afterlife and Food; Egyptian Diet and Cuisine, Ancient; Medieval Diet and Cuisine.

Further Reading

Baumbusch, Brigitte. *Food in Art.* Milwaukee, WI: Gareth Stevens, 2005.

Bendiner, Kenneth. *Food in Painting: From the Renaissance to the Present.* London: Reaktion, 2005.

Malaguzzi, Silvia. *Food and Feasting in Art.* Los Angeles: J. Paul Getty Museum, 2008.

Asian Food Trade

The Asian food exchange coordinated a series of multiethnic handoffs of goods as foodstuffs made their way to other nations. From the 400s B.C.E., the Scythians maintained two centuries of trade with Greek markets selling cheese, mutton, and wheat. Cambodians supplied India with rice and livestock, which increased Indian Ocean exports from 100 B.C.E. China maintained a similar relationship with Mongolia by bartering in dairy products and livestock for resale. From the late 600s C.E., as Islam fanned out from its Arabian origins, commodities of aromatics, black pepper, horses, and sugar turned port cities into world markets. Safe conduct through lands and waters evolved through sharing of profits with pirates and savvy merchants in Aden, Calcutta, Canton, Hormuz, and Malacca.

From the Bay of Bengal, Coromandel, Gujarat, Malabar, and Sri Lanka, Indian maritime commerce distributed candied fruit, dried fish, ginger, pickles, salt meat, spices, sugar, and tea across the Indian Ocean to the east through Malaysian middlemen. By land and sea, Asian trade involved power brokers in Constantinople, Venice, and Iberia. Redistribution in Portugal and Spain sped coffee and tea north to France and to the northern seas to the Hanseatic League, which formed at Lübeck, Germany, in 1159 to trade in rye, salt fish, and wheat. As European cuisine moved away from heavy medieval spicing toward sugary foods, the Polish and Russians replaced the Dutch and French as customers for Asian cinnamon, ginger, and nutmeg.

On the way to England and France, alcoholic drinks, allspice, bay leaf, cardamom, ginger, rice, sesame seed, tea, and white pepper traveled by speedy caravel and camel caravans from southern China through the Middle East and the Baltic Sea to Poland and Russia. Merging goods from India, the Philippines, Thailand, and Vietnam, another avenue arrived at the Malay Peninsula and continued east to the Spice Islands and southwest to Borneo, Mindanao, and Sumatra. The fluid exchange of Vietnamese goods came under stricter control after 1471, when loose federations of river merchants along the Jiaozhi Ocean collapsed under tyranny by Dai Viet conquerors. To the east, Chinese trade with Luzon in the Philippines in the early 1500s extended commerce in birds' nests for soup, cinnamon, ginger, and honey.

Primary Sea-Lanes

In the age of voyagers, the encounters between Eastern and Western traders extended a lively inter-Asian commerce to the rest of the world. In the 1500s, on the shortest run between Calcutta and Macau, Portuguese explorers reported steady seagoing traffic in cardamom, oil, rice, tamarind, and wine to Malacca. On a smaller scale, consumers rallied to exotica—areca nuts, durian, *jagra, maja,* and tampoy.

In 1633, the Dutch usurped Portuguese shipping and operated 4,785 vessels at dividends as high as 40 percent from cocoa, coffee, macassar oil, and rice. What Asian commerce lacked in sophisticated merchant capitalism, it made up for in manpower, its primary asset. The Strait of Malacca, the primary Asian emporium, formed a coastal "cosmopolis" of shared Java-based authorities over the sale of dried fish, pepper, rice, salt, and spices. In 1720, the Dutch lost commercial control of Bengal, Malabar, Persia, and Surat in northwestern India.

Through cyclical booms and depressions, piracy, and wars, local potentates at the Banda Islands capitalized on alum, bananas, camphor, mace, nutmeg, pepper, and sago cakes, a multi-use palm starch. A consortium set rates of exchange and weights and measures and expedited port traffic and duty levying. Foreign dealers maintained year-round quarters and warehouses, which protected shipments during monsoons. Purchases from the Philippines added to the accumulated stock of betel nuts, coconuts, copra, dried meat, lard, rice, and sesame seeds.

Technological Advances

Beginning in the 1770s, clipper ships increased the speed of east-west trade from Malayan entrepôts to distant ports at the rate of 400 miles (640 kilometers) per day. The sleek schooners carried apples and ice to Asia and returned with allspice, cinnamon, cloves, coffee, ginger, mustard, pepper, rice, and tea. At Singapore, speculators dickered for betel nuts, cardamom, and red cane sugar, sold from Chinese and Siamese junks.

On August 29, 1842, the Treaty of Nanking opened Amoy, Canton, Fouchou, Ningpo, and Shanghai to entrepreneurs from Great Britain. The agreement gave the British a monopoly over half of global transactions in coffee, pickles, salt, tea, and wine. Lighters and sampans delivered tea chests around the clock for careful stowage away from salt air and sea water.

By the 1860s, the steel fleet of the U.S. merchant marine unseated Great Britain's hold on global commerce. In New York Harbor, the Great American Tea Company sold cut-rate Chinese and Japanese tea straight from the cargo holds. After the opening of the Suez Canal on November 17, 1869, food carriers lopped 36 days from the ocean route between London and Calcutta, metaphorically shrinking the globe and speeding Indian wheat to England at low prices.

The emergence of technological advances in milling, refrigeration, and food processing brought students from Asia to the Americas. With scientific advancement in canning, packaging, and crane lifting of goods stacked on pallets, Asian bottlers of flavorings and sauces and canners of seaweed and smoked oysters energized the food industry with new trends. After the agricultural lapses of World War II, the dissolution of European colonies increased opportunities for Asian growers of black and brown rice, melons, pineapples, and soybeans for tofu.

Jet travel introduced tourists to Indian curry and Mongolian hot pots; soldiers returning from postings in Japan, Korea, Vietnam, and Iraq developed a taste for sake, imitation crab, soy sauce, bamboo shoots, *kimchi, belachan* (shrimp spread), hummus, and *tagine* lamb pilaf. Long-distance commerce provided Asians more social mobility and gave female farmers opportunities for expanded agricultural markets, especially in postwar Vietnam. The expectations of consumers in industrialized nations increased demands for food security, genetic modification of crops, and the use of growth hormones, matters settled after 1948 by the World Trade Organization.

In October 2011, the 21-nation Asia-Pacific Economic Cooperation pledged to create the world's largest free-trade area. Members promised to fight protectionism and support green industries. The agreement focused on beef, dairy, eggs, grain, pork, soybeans, and turkeys and on competition by domestic catfish farmers with Vietnam marketing of the pangasius, which supplies 2 percent of the nation's income. By promoting seamless regional commerce, 600 CEOs from the region sought to overcome financial lapses caused by natural disasters. Specifics of their consensus included welcoming China to a stronger position in trade governance and a reduction of tariffs by 5 percent.

See also: Caravans; Clipper Ships; Coffee; Gama, Vasco da; Spices; Tea; Trading Vessels; World Trade.

Further Reading

Hall, Kenneth R. *A History of Early Southeast Asia: Maritime Trade and Societal Development, 100–1500.* Lanham, MD: Rowman & Littlefield, 2011.

Martin, Laura C. *Tea: The Drink That Changed the World.* Rutland, VT: Tuttle, 2007.

Paine, Lincoln P. *Ships of Discovery and Exploration.* New York: Houghton Mifflin, 2002.

Stursberg, Peter. *No Foreign Bones in China: Memoirs of Imperialism and Its Ending.* Edmonton, Canada: University of Alberta Press, 2002.

Athenaeus (ca. 170–ca. 230)

A Greek living in Egypt, Athenaeus of Naucratis gained fame as an observant writer on diet, health, leisure, and wellness. He was a product of Naucratis, a trading center in the Egyptian delta between Alexandria and Memphis. Like physicians Celsus, Galen, Rufus of Ephesus, Oribasius, Scribonius Largus, Asclepiades, and Anthimus, in response to public carousing, Athenaeus issued a treatise on more sensible lifestyles.

His 15-volume *Deipnosophistae (The Banquet Philosophers,* ca. 190 C.E.) ignored Roman food fads and covered the Greek love of luxury and table camaraderie, which separated dining from the *symposion* (drinking). Athenaeus divided his text into topics: a book on food in Homer's epics and other literature, two books on bread and hors d'oeuvres, a chapter on dinner courses and music, a chapter on indulgence, another on flatterers and gate-crashers, two books on fish, another on meat and poultry, a book on gluttony and wine, another on cups, a treatise on behavior and courtesies, a book on romance and women, a chapter on desserts and music, and a concluding commentary on perfumes and wreaths. Permeating the text, citations from 1,000 authors attest to the author's meticulous research of primary sources, commentaries, and glossaries. He defended table courtesy by rejecting salacious jokes in favor of wit and riddles.

In a fictional dialogue with Timocrates set between the death of Galen in 199 C.E. and the death of Ulpian in 223 C.E., Athenaeus speaks in the first person of a feast at the home of the Roman arts patron Larensius. The text describes the *andreion* (men's house) as a place for communal meals where educated guests discuss varied topics, such as the plain fare consumed by Homeric heroes. For themes, the author draws from stage comedy and from public sexual mores, hedonism, and the use of aphrodisiacs, such as *kandaulos,* a hearty collation of stewed meat, grated cheese, and bread crumbs in gravy flavored with anise. Philosophically, the diners acknowledge the civilizing aspect of cereal, by which Demeter socialized bestial meat eaters and introduced table decorum and the sharing of communal platters. The speakers honor gastronomy and refer to a cook as a free man, never a slave or a woman, who achieves professional status as a food artist.

Among gustatory concerns, Athenaeus differentiated the types of food suited to social classes, such as palm fruit for domestic slaves as opposed to the select hearts of palm presented to the slave owner. He classified 72 types of bread and introduced rare produce, including the arbutus fruit and the medlar. In references to regional cuisine, he enlarged on the breads of Sardis, lotus wine in Libya, Attic figs and small fry, and the seaside cookshops in Alexandria that sold sausage and sweetbreads. He referred to cooking contests in Sybaris, Italy, in 500 B.C.E. Under a food patent law, the winner gained commercial control of his entrée for a year.

Discussions bandied about individual responses to food as mundane as a plowman's lunch of bread and cheese and as foreign to Greek menus as dog meat and cicadas and grasshoppers as appetizers. As a symbol of luxury foods, Athenaeus named the Samian cheesecake. He had no respect for the gobbler who polished off the dishes of almond appetizers, and he demeaned the glutton as a "potbelly."

The tension between the Greek ideal of Achilles and Agamemnon and the effete gourmand infused discussion with the range of deviations from the norm. Athenaeus had to admit that macho men such as Ajax would lose stature if they valorized dainty dishes such as those admired by the Persians and Sicilians.

Athenaeus's subject matter never strays far from issues of masculinity. As his fictional discussion ebbs and flows, at a risk of seeming obsessed with dining, gastronomes of the privileged class display a passion for cooking and banqueting. They discuss obesity, health, food prices, and the service of condiments, pilafs, prized fish, and sauces. As models, the author mentions numerous recipe compendia, one on breads by Chrysippus of Tyana, another on salt fish by Euthydemus of Athens, Greco-

Syracusan poet Archestratus's *Hedypatheia* (*Life of Luxury,* ca. 350 B.C.E.), and a collection by Mithaecus, the first Greek to compile a cookbook.

Athenaeus's recipes vary from stuffed grape leaves to cheesecake and Coan wine fermented in seawater, but he focused on meat cookery. He explained a concept of religious cookery in the stewing of meat for a sacrifice to the seasons. Unlike spit-roasting, stewing tenderized the entrée and brought out the best flavors. In another recipe, he explained the making of *muma,* a meat stew that began with minced meat cooked in animal blood and entrails and flavored with coriander, cumin, honey, pomegranate, poppy seeds, raisins, scallions, silphium, toasted cheese, and vinegar.

See also: Fermented Foods; Pork; Shellfish.

Further Reading

Braund, David, and John Wilkins, eds. *Athenaeus and His World: Reading Greek Culture in the Roman Empire.* Exeter, UK: University of Exeter Press, 2000.
Dalby, Andrew. *Food in the Ancient World from A to Z.* London: Routledge, 2003.
Wilkins, John M., and Shaun Hill. *Food in the Ancient World.* Malden, MA: Wiley-Blackwell, 2006.

Australian Diet and Cuisine

Australian diet and cuisine confirms the success of adaptation to a unique environment. Upon arrival to the island continent on January 26, 1788, the first English soldiers and transportees from jails and workhouses found Aborigines surviving on hunting and gathering. The nation's first peoples preferred a diet dominated by honey and nectars, wild spinach, and such found protein as crocodiles, snakes, and witchetties, a large white grub easily grilled into finger food. For health, the bush people inhaled eucalyptus and tea tree oils and drank rock fuchsia tea to cure respiratory ailments.

From the highly romanticized bush tucker (bush food), the kakadu plum (*Terminalia ferdinandiana*) ranked as the world's richest source of vitamin C, ahead of quandong (wild peach) and muntry berries. Additional nutrients came from gathering abalone, beefsteak fungi, limpets, and macadamia nuts. Aborigines also snared albatross and muttonbirds, robbed their nests of eggs, and caught crayfish, fish, goannas (monitor lizards), penguins, rats, and seals.

Aborigines collected paperbark for wrapping seed bread and meat portions for roasting in ground ovens. For food preservation, in Queensland, Aborigines air-dried tropical water lily roots and yams. They cached wild grain in hollow woodbins or tied *bunya-bunya* pine nuts in skin bags coated in muddy straw. Gatherers of

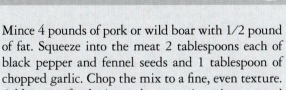

Recipe: Greek Sausage

Mince 4 pounds of pork or wild boar with 1/2 pound of fat. Squeeze into the meat 2 tablespoons each of black pepper and fennel seeds and 1 tablespoon of chopped garlic. Chop the mix to a fine, even texture. Add 1 cup of red wine and squeeze into the seasoned meat. Force the mix into casings and tie the ends. Suspend sausages to air-dry for three hours. Fry in light oil, turning frequently. Serve with a sprinkle of vinegar.

cycad nuts, one of the world's most ancient tropical and subtropical foods, wrapped them in tea tree bark stacked in grass-lined trenches.

In a world apart from Aborigines, the English fed themselves temporarily on a two-year stock of cheese, dried beef, flour, oatmeal, and tea. Meanwhile, they accustomed themselves to apple berries (*Billardiera scandens*), emu and kangaroo meat, *kutjera* (desert raisins), parrot pie, reef fish, wattleseed, and wild raspberries and plums. When traditional farming floundered under extreme weather conditions, the pioneers developed expertise at raising cattle and sheep, two sources of a heavy dairy and meat diet. The importation of Chinese laborers for cotton plantations and gold mines in 1851 introduced Asian vegetables, particularly Asian greens, bean shoots, bitter melon, and bok choy, a brassica plant related to cabbage and turnips.

By raising apples, grapes, sugarcane, and wheat, colonists reverted to foods from the motherland, notably ale and beer, wine, and traditional sweets, such as apple tart, for which the English were famous. From experiences in the two world wars, bakers evolved a recipe for ANZAC biscuits, a mailable oatmeal cookie intended for the Australian and New Zealand Army Corps.

In the 1950s, Australia slipped its tether to England and became Americanized, the beginning of a cosmopolitan cuisine based on the U.S. passion for Chinese food. From the influence of Asia and Oceania, Australians balanced the standard roast-and-potato menu to include lamb kebabs, stir-fried leeks and mushrooms, river finfish and ocean trout, Malaysian pork rolls, and sliced cucumbers and onion in yogurt, a Middle Eastern favorite.

Aussies embraced *yum cha,* a dumpling feast from South China, and advertised a local food craze, farmhouse cheese from Gippsland, Victoria. Pack and snack foods favored jerky, fried flake fish (shark), meat pies, native wines, and Vegemite, a bottled yeast spread that required no preparation. For bread, stockmen and trekkers baked damper, a flat soda bread cooked on hot embers or in a billy (camp oven) and eaten with tinned treacle (corn syrup).

History bore out the palatability of Australian wild foods. In the 1970s, the back-to-nature movement popularized local foods, a revocation of Victorian era snobbery about European edibles and outback inedibles. After a hasty dismissal of aboriginal wild food in 1788, islanders rediscovered such indigenous plants as Chinese yams, finger limes, lotus, saltbush, warrigal greens, and Australian cashews and gooseberries. Restaurants returned kangaroo tail soup to menus and reclaimed gourmet recipes of local produce and seafood, notably, mud crabs, stuffed emu, and crocodile tail with pepperleaf.

From the clear waters off New South Wales, one of the world's least polluted stretches of ocean, Australian gourmands reclaimed less familiar delicacies, Balmain

Recipe: Rissoles on Buns

Mix 1 pound of ground sirloin with two eggs, 1/2 teaspoon of black pepper, and 3/4 cup of Italian bread crumbs. Shape the meat into bun-sized patties. Dust with granulated flour or powdered gravy mix. Fry or grill the patties over medium heat until they are crusty and the juices run clear. Serve on burger buns with fried eggs or pickle relish.

bugs (fan lobster), yabbies (crayfish), and baked latchet (sea robin) with mussels and olives. In 2004, the television series *Dining Downunder,* hosted by innovators Benjamin Christie and Vic Cherikoff, introduced grilled plank salmon flavored with lemon myrtle sprinkle and paperbark smoke oil, two distinct native savors.

Australian outdoor cookery and shore meals, especially at Christmas, lean toward barbecuing prawns and steak. In place of the stereotypical ham or turkey, cooks serve cold cuts and gherkins, curried rice, and pasta salad. Carpetbagger steak is a Sydney specialty dating to the 1950s, a beefsteak stuffed with oysters and served with fried eggs and Worcestershire sauce. For a simple lunch, shepherd's pie (ground lamb covered in mashed potatoes mixed with other vegetables) varies the usual beef entrée.

Yule dessert tables exhibit fruitcake, peach Melba, and plum pudding, a favorite holiday treat derived from England. Lamington cube cakes combine cream or jam filling with a topping of chocolate and coconut, best enjoyed with gourmet coffees. At Easter, cooks display the pavlova, or "pav," a passionfruit and kiwi dessert built on a bed of egg white and sugar meringue and named for Anna Pavlova, an early twentieth-century Russian ballerina.

See also: Barbecue; Cheese; Dried Food; Grilling; Insects; Nutrition.

Further Reading

Germaine, Elizabeth, and Ann Burckhardt. *Cooking the Australian Way.* Minneapolis, MN: Lerner, 2004.

Kittler, Pamela Goyan, and Kathryn Sucher. *Food and Culture.* Belmont, CA: Wadsworth/Thomson Learning, 2004.

O'Brien, Charmaine. *Flavours of Melbourne: A Culinary Biography.* Kent Town, South Australia: Wakefield, 2008.

Ver Berkmoes, Ryan. *East Coast Australia.* Oakland, CA: Lonely Planet, 2008.

Australian Food Trade

Because of Australia's varied terrain and climates, the island continent markets a wide range of foodstuffs to world tables. When the English populated coastal Australia with convicts and soldiers in January 1788, the newcomers faced a constant struggle for subsistence. Cornish felon James Ruse of Parramatta claimed agricultural prominence in Campbelltown with his epitaph, "I sowd the Forst Grain," a source of subsequent colonial trade wealth. By 1795, flour milling of oats and wheat became the first source of island exports, followed by the sale of biscuit.

Immigrant brewers, butter and cheese makers, and meat salters at Parramatta and Sydney sustained planting styles and foodways from the motherland. In 1819, the first 1,000 agrarians adapted a stubborn terrain to herding rather than farming and opened canneries to cure game birds and rabbit in brine. To feed themselves salt pork, Australians established a triangular trade, shipping salt from Hawaii to pork farmers in Tahiti, who sent salt pork to the pioneers. Following failures with distilling, investors made their first advance in 1830 with the export of salt beef to England, followed late in the decade with cheese and potted butter sales in California.

Success with cotton in 1842 added vegetable oil to Australian food products. In September 1846, food processor Staddon and Price led the island market in banana conserves and guava and leptoma (blue fungus) jelly. Dried apple slices from Tasmania in 1850 increased the export of pome fruit. A burst of pioneering in the 1850s by some 600,000 immigrants demanded more food farming from the province of Victoria. To feed them, George Peacock, a Hobart grocer, became the first to can jam from apples, berries, and pears.

Before the decline in the salt beef trade in the 1860s, industrialist Sizar Elliott anticipated a demand for tinned meat from his factory in Sydney. By 1869, the Clarence, New South Wales, meat shippers alone marketed 14,331 cases of canned beef and processed gelatin, meat extract, and tallow for export. Simultaneously, Robert McCracken's Victoria Meat Preserving Company of Melbourne filled orders for canned meat in Japan and in England for the Royal Navy and for Jewish kosher markets.

The Industrial Revolution in New South Wales extended opportunities for processing crocodile and kangaroo bushmeat as well as mutton, plum pudding, and fresh apples and pears, which W.D. Peacock transported from Hobart, Tasmania, by sea in cold storage. On February 2, 1880, the freighter *Strathleven* brought the first frozen meat from Melbourne and Sydney to London. That November, the SS *Protos* carried frozen mutton and refrigerated butter and cheddar cheese, colored with yellow-orange annatto (*Bixa orellana*), a food dye also used in ice cream.

Colonial imports became indispensable to England, particularly frozen berries and apples and chilled meats. For the safety of families, Australian firms distributed instructions on the correct methods of thawing and cooking of raw meat. The success of Queensland meat markets resulted in competition with Argentine beef producers and a lowering of prices for the consumer.

As British agriculture declined, the working class profited from low-cost pickled and smoked beef, butter, cheese, mutton, and tinned fruit and fruit and tomato juices, which arrived in port from Australia and New Zealand in greater quantities than produce from Ireland or France. From 1890 to 1894, when Chinese laborers increased Australian food harvests, fruit and vegetables and butter imports to London alone rose in quantity from 643 tons (583 metric tons) to 11,070 tons (10,040 metric tons).

With refinements to Michael Faraday's ammonia compressor system, processing plants boosted the output of food in 1892 by adding fish to exports. In 1895, total exports of preserved meat to the United Kingdom reached 23,325 tons (21,156 metric tons), much of it directed to orphanages, schools, and workhouses. Loosening ties to the United Kingdom, Australia extended its clout in world food commerce by dealing directly with other nations rather than through London middlemen.

In 1901, with Australia providing nearly 50 percent of British commodities, the island nation became a federal commonwealth. The twentieth century saw the rise of agro-markets for abalone, Asian herbs, lychees, nashi pears, olives, potatoes, poultry, and farm-raised salmon and tuna. The promotion of Asian vegetables added bitter melon, bok choi, Chinese celery, flat cabbage, garlic chives, and mizuna (peppergrass).

In 1908, the British Board of Trade appointed four commissioners to live in Australia and promote commercial opportunities, such as the tunnel dehydration of eggs, minced mutton, and raisins. Trade with India in 1910 produced an amicable swap of wheat for tea and jute, a source of Australian gunnysacks. Bags cycled back to the United Kingdom from 1909 to 1913 bearing 2.46 million tons (2.23 million metric tons) of wheat.

By 1925, after a drop of 15 percent in farm and herd labor during World War I, 95 percent of Australian exports consisted of produce. To hold a place among other advanced economies, the Australians raised standards and policy on food safety from allergens and chemical and microbial hazards, such as widespread spraying of apple, pear, and quince orchards with toxic Paris green (copper arsenate) to control codling moth.

By 2010, the Australian economy depended on some 2,000 companies in the food and wine industries for nearly half its retail sales. At Sydney in September 2011, food purveyors displayed their goods at Fine Food Australia, the nation's largest trade show. The chief buyers, Arab and Pacific Rim nations, purchased baby food, baked goods, candied fruit, chutney and pickles, custard and milk pudding, dairy foods, desserts, honey, meats, milk, poultry, powdered drinks, sauces and soup, vegetables, and wine and cordials.

See also: Aquaponics; Markets and Marketing; Milling; Refrigeration.

Further Reading

Clarke, Francis G. *The History of Australia.* Westport, CT: Greenwood, 2002.

Cole, Martin B. "Trends in Food Safety Management." *Microbiology Australia* 25:3 (July 2004): 6–9.

Farrer, Keith Thomas Henry. *To Feed a Nation: A History of Australian Food Science and Technology.* Collingwood, Australia: CSIRO, 2005.

West, Barbara A., and Frances T. Murphy. *A Brief History of Australia.* New York: Facts on File, 2010.

Aztec Diet and Cuisine

The foodways of the Aztec, viewed through the eyes of Spanish conquistadors, imbedded native culture with outlets for worship and the appreciation of savory native flora and fauna. The Renaissance encyclopedist, linguist, and Spanish friar Bernardino de Sahagún, the father of ethnography and culinary history, detailed for Europeans the lifestyle of the Aztec, including cooking utensils, beverages, and foods. In 1529, under orders of Charles V, Holy Roman Emperor, Sahagún posted to Tlalmanalco at

A drawing from the *Florentine Codex,* compiled in the sixteenth century by Spanish missionary and ethnographer Bernardo de Sahagún, shows the Aztecs eating tamales for the midday meal. The dough was made with maize (corn), the staple Aztec crop. *(The Granger Collection, New York)*

Xochimilco in south-central Mexico. While cataloging language and food customs in the Nahua language, he compiled specific vocabulary for pantries, hearth cookery, kitchenware, and therapeutic herbs, which he listed in his Nahuatl dictionary and grammar book.

Aztec bloodletting impacted their values and customs, including food gifts of eggs and turkey sprinkled with human blood. They made ritual stews from the hearts of slaughtered criminals or prisoners of war. Beyond cannibalism, they adopted the word tortilla, Spanish for "omelet," to name the staple bread.

At the Tenochtitlán food market, street cooks prepared entrées; *curanderos* (herbalists) linked eating with curative nutrition. Sahagún's encyclopedia, the 12-volume *Historia General de las Cosas de Nueva España* (*General History of the Things of New Spain,* 1540–1569), also known as the *Florentine Codex,* compiled details in parallel columns of Nahuatl and Spanish. Concerning favorite dinners, he incorporated spiced shrimp dishes, his preference for turkey wing tips, and the visions and dreams experienced by diners on honey and psychedelic black mushrooms, a common aphrodisiac. He remarked on the fattening of the wild peccary with stall feedings of acorns, cherries, corn, and roots.

A People's Diet

For the Spanish, foodways became a basis for understanding the Aztec. At court, staff set the emperor's table with 2,000 dishes. Entrées made for the emperor alone included whipped chocolate sweetened with wild honey, avocados and cactus fruit, and the *moles* (sauces) that flavored caiman, crayfish, dog, jackrabbit, quail, and lake and sea fish. Unlike the privileged aristocracy, peasants favored raw fruits and vegetables, a contrast to the meat-heavy, alcohol-rich Spanish diet. In the Tenochtitlán market, some 50,000 people came to examine baskets and gourd dippers, cutting tools made from volcanic glass, and the griddles and *ollas* (cooking jars) displayed and sold by potters.

Aztec dietary lore contained unique elements, such as the casting of bits of food and drops of *octli* or pulque, an alcoholic drink fermented from agave sap, onto the hearth before each meal to propitiate the gods. Crafters molded and painted idols from food. At the end of a ritual, worshippers ate the images. For Xiuhtecuhtli, the fire deity, and Huitzilopochtli, the war god, the Aztec made pastries and consumed them in the god's honor, a sacrament that paralleled the Christian Eucharist. A similar obeisance to a dead monarch required a four-day presentation of flowers, food, and tobacco. On the fifth day, Aztec subjects feasted and made speeches.

In times of famine, a prophet warned the people that those with plenty must tolerate seizure of their stores of amaranth, cacao beans, corn, and seeds to share with the poor. Out of compassion for the hungry, the ruler stopped collecting taxes. In fealty to the gods, the Aztec carried their families up the mountains and sacrificed their children to solicit rain and to make the prickly pears and amaranth greens grow, the grasshoppers return, and the gardens produce once more.

The *Florentine Codex* incorporated 1,800 illustrations drawn by Aztec scribes to capture the importance of sustenance to a culture bedeviled by attackers and drought. Central to native festivals and worship, corn in all its forms demanded reverence, sacraments, and hymn-singing to the earth mother, the giver of life. Vast storage facilities operated by food accountants and *pochteca* (distributors) mediated between urban consumers and outlying farms, where peasants used cacao beans as a medium of exchange. Book 10 summarized the bean-chili-and-corn-based diet by describing the purchase of corn in city markets for making popcorn, tortillas, and a variety of tamales flavored with beans, eggs, fruit, and honey.

Kitchen Specifics

Although the Spanish demeaned the Aztec diet as crude and pagan, kitchen masterworks—frothy cacao and vanilla drinks, poultry stew, chayote and jicama, opuntia cactus pads, and duck egg and squash dishes—displayed expertise. One example of harmonic baking began with the kneading of amaranth seed into a loaf called *alegría* (joy). The *moles* featured chili and spices, a symphony of flavors still dominant in Mexican cookery. At the heart of table service, cooks poured cups of *atole,* a beverage made of parched cornmeal and chia, a gelatinous seed so valuable that the Aztec used it as currency to pay their taxes. More than taste or nutrition, their national foods imparted feelings of patriotism, heritage, and family.

Aztec cuisine figured in major life passages, particularly funerals and weddings. As part of the cult of the dead, the devout enshrined images and proffered tamales and turkey or dog stew to feed the spirit on its journey from earth. The ritual concluded with songs and toasts of pulque. As Sahagún's illustrations showed, girls of mar-

riageable age learned from their mothers how to soak corn kernels in ash and water to remove hulls. Grinding involved kneeling at a stone metate and pressing the mano (roller) over dried corn until it broke into meal. By adding water to the flour and shaping into a palm-sized ball, the cook readied dough to pat out a thin cake for heating on a *comal* (stone griddle).

At the heart of Aztec cooking lay distinct flavorings—green, red, and yellow peppers and the cooking of frogs, grubs, lizards, and termites with chilies, tomatoes, squash seed, and savory herbs. The food sellers at the market stalls identified peppers by color and pungency and by use as pickles or with fish, newts, tadpoles, turkey, and smoked meats. To Aztec cookery, the Spanish newcomers added black pepper, cinnamon, coriander, olive oil, oregano, and parsley as well as almonds, bananas, barley, chickpeas, eggplant, garlic, grapes, lettuce, onions, rice, sugar, and wheat. From the blending of flavors emerged Mesoamerican cuisine, a previously vegetable-rich cuisine broadened with the addition of beef, lamb, lard, milk, rice, and wheat and the blending of butter and cheese into rich cream sauces.

See also: Chicle and Chewing Gum; Díaz, Bernal; Insects; Las Casas, Bartolomé de; Peyote; Prohibition; Religion and Food; Sauces and Saucing; Tortillas; Yeast.

Further Reading

Cantú, Norma Elia, ed. *Moctezuma's Table: Rolando Briseño's Mexican and Chicano Tablescapes.* College Station: Texas A&M University Press, 2010.

Janer, Zilkia. *Latino Food Culture.* Westport, CT: Greenwood, 2008.

León-Portilla, Miguel. *Bernardino de Sahagún, First Anthropologist.* Trans. Mauricio J. Mixco. Norman: University of Oklahoma Press, 2002.

Staller, John Edward, and Michael Carrasco, eds. *Pre-Columbian Foodways: Interdisciplinary Approaches to Food, Culture, and Markets in Ancient Mesoamerica.* New York: Springer, 2010.

Baby Food and Infant Feeding

Globally, the nourishment of infants and toddlers reflects the attitudes and means of individual cultures. The breast feeding of infants currently lowers the risk of dying in the first 12 months by 20 percent. Typically the decision of mothers, newborn feeding relied for eons on the birth parent or a wet nurse. The job of surrogate breast feeder rewarded donors with a serene life and abundant food.

Either the mother or the donor fed the child every two hours. In past ages, the first postpartum secretion, called colostrum or beestings, held such mystic powers that herders saved the colostrum from lactating animals for special needs. Human milk bolstered immunity and reduced health risks, particularly allergies, diabetes, and obesity.

For mothers of stillborn or deceased children, nursing another baby solaced the sorrow of losing a child. Among Native Americans, the sharing of breast feeding of community infants created a parental bond with all the tribe's children. In Malaysia and the Philippines, the employ of a wet nurse symbolized luxury and status. For whatever reason, the insistence on human sustenance strengthened the suckling babe through a diet of high-quality fluids that adapt naturally to the baby's needs and maturation.

For families choosing surrogate mammalian milk or supplementing breast milk for fretful or sickly babies, hard-spouted clay containers such as miniature Cypriot wine jugs from 2000 B.C.E. simplified infant feeding. A terra-cotta nurser shaped like a piglet from 450 B.C.E. suited a Greek mother, who filled it with a formula of honeyed wine. The Egyptians and Romans in 300 B.C.E. used blown glass for shaping feeding vessels. In the thirteenth century in northwestern Europe, a cow's horn capped with a chamois leather nipple served as an infant flask.

Solid Foods

Other nations standardized infant solids, the meals that sufficed for teething infants. In eastern Asia, homemakers first introduced rice gruel, followed by mashed vegetables and tofu as teeth emerged from infant gums. Japanese mothers extended weaning meals to bonito flakes, miso (soy paste), and seaweed. In India, Hindus and Parsis made a food ritual of Annaprashana, the introduction of rice porridge or a mix of milk, ghee, and honey to a baby at age six months.

In some cultures, the mother's chewing of solids macerated food for shifting to the child's mouth, often from tongue to tongue. Examples include the banana pulp that Ugandan mothers fed their babies and the chewed fish and heated water that Eskimo mothers passed to their infants from mouth to mouth. Choices of flavors affected the growing child, who established preferences as early as age two for indigenous plants, such as avocado, coconut, and pomegranate.

According to Thomas Phaire's *Boke of Chyldren* (1544), the first pediatric treatise in English, evil traits and an ugly complexion dated back to the "gyver of the mylke" who fed the individual in infancy. Renaissance mothers worried that substitution of goat's and sheep's milk could introduce coarse animal elements to the baby's hair and skin. For weaning, families made digestible, nutritious pap from barley, oats, or rice mixed with egg for spoon-feeding. In the 1700s, the addition of broth, butter, or oil produced panada (bread soup), a specialty in northern Italy.

Nature vs. Science

By the Industrial Revolution, mass production of infant food applied the scientific knowledge of nutritionists, who formulated feedings based on the analysis of mother's milk. Cookbooks outlined complex formulas from cream and milk, sugar, and water and listed pablum alongside menus for invalids. In 1845, New York inventor Elijah Pratt patented the vulcanized rubber teat. The concept replaced hard glass and metal nipples, yet doctors warned of the difficulty of sterilizing the inner channel.

For weanlings, American mothers ventured into cereal and meat, in part because of a pervasive suspicion of fruit and vegetables as a source of cholera. In 1854, Bostonian writer Sarah Josepha Hale, author of *The New Household Receipt-Book,* advocated "gruel alone, or mixed with cow's milk; mutton broth, or beef tea; stale bread, rusks or biscuits, boiled in water to a proper consistence, and a little sugar added." For a sickly child, she prescribed arrowroot or sago boiled in milk and flavorings of cinnamon, nutmeg, sugar, and wine. Her varied list of sickbed meals included cornmeal or egg gruel, oatmeal, rice jelly, and stewed prunes, a treatment for fever.

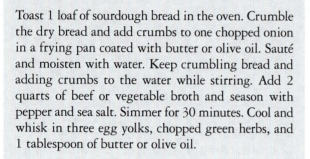

Recipe: Panada

Toast 1 loaf of sourdough bread in the oven. Crumble the dry bread and add crumbs to one chopped onion in a frying pan coated with butter or olive oil. Sauté and moisten with water. Keep crumbling bread and adding crumbs to the water while stirring. Add 2 quarts of beef or vegetable broth and season with pepper and sea salt. Simmer for 30 minutes. Cool and whisk in three egg yolks, chopped green herbs, and 1 tablespoon of butter or olive oil.

Massachusetts natives Joseph Bardwell Lyman and Laura Elizabeth Baker Lyman's *The Philosophy of Housekeeping: A Scientific and Practical Manual* (1859) corroborated Hale's prescription. In a summary of the best "tissue-making" infant foods, they highlighted "Flesh, milk, eggs, and wheat bread." Additional lists named fat-free servings of barley, cabbage, oatmeal, onions, and potatoes. Ironically, doubts about beans and fresh greens overlooked the most pernicious source of pathogens, the water supply.

The nineteenth-century German organic chemist Justus von Liebig emulated breast milk with proportional blends of carbohydrates, fats, and protein in a farinaceous food called Liebig's Soluble Food for Babies. Historians have called his introduction of artificial milk the world's largest uncontrolled experiment on humans. In 1867, his Registered Concentrated Milk Company in London shipped artificial mother's milk to American and European markets. He followed the liquid version with a powder of dried cow's milk, malt and wheat flour, and potassium bicarbonate for reconstitution with milk and water. A letter to the *Medical Times and Gazette* in 1877 proclaimed the formulation "a panacea to little children from birth, and in every rank of society."

A Blow to Tradition

Simultaneously with the medicalization of birthing and the revolution in liquid formula and solid baby food, mothers abandoned centuries-old concepts of pureeing food at home in favor of scientific regimens. In 1867, for babies for whom cow's, goat's, or sheep's milk proved unpalatable, German-born pharmacist Henri Nestlé of Vevey, Switzerland, formulated Farine Lactée (milk cereal), a powder of sweetened condensed milk and malted wheat rusks. In the 1870s, he marketed it in the United States as a weaning formula under the logo "Best for Babies."

In London, Danish chemist Gustav Mellin improved on Liebig's food in 1874 by inventing a portable, easily mixed powder that required no boiling or straining for dissolving in hot water and mixing with cold milk. Rich in grape sugar, the dry food received accolades from the *Boston Daily Globe.* Booklets accompanied the product to impress on women two adjectives, *scientific* and *modern.* In 1887, Mellin began marketing his breakthrough in Burma, Ceylon, and India as a scientific substitute for mother's milk.

Traditionalists rejected liquid formula and fortified pablum out of fear of contaminants. Mediators insisted that the weakness of boxed formula and cereals or canned fruits and vegetables lay in the addition of polluted water or milk. Aggressive advertisement massaged fears of early childhood death, which spiked to 20 percent in the 1890s in Europe during epidemics of cholera, diphtheria, enteritis, malaria, measles, pertussis, pneumonia, scarlet fever, and typhoid. Such verbal manipulations failed to pinpoint a common endangerment, a bottle or pap boat that became septic because the feeding channels were too narrow for thorough washing. By 1900, the reversible rubber nipple made it easier to sterilize nursers.

In 1896, Dutch industrialist Martinus van der Hagen's Nutricia foods first commercialized prepared infant foods resembling mother's milk. In Brunei, China, France, Malaysia, Singapore, Thailand, and Vietnam, he turned spin-off brands Dumex and Sari Husada, Bambix cereals, and Olvarit organic mixed fruit and entrées into top international sellers. Advertisers depicted evaporated milk and ready-to-eat baby food as a convenience to the modern mother based on science rather than home preparations.

Selling Wholesomeness

Concern for purity drove the baby food industry, which got its start before World War I. Knowledge of sepsis caused families to demand milk from herds tested for staphylococcal and tuberculin pathogens. Shoppers also watched for signs of watering milk and additions of borax and formaldehyde, pernicious dairy preservatives.

In *L'Alimentation des Enfants Malades (Feeding Sick Infants,* 1908), French nutritionist Maurice Péhu, a physician at the University of Lyons, advised mothers to adopt the slow simmering of beets, carrots, and spinach and straining the pulp into one quart of water. When similar manufactured food arrived in grocery stores, it was the brainchild of Daniel and Dorothy Gerber of Fremont, Michigan. The couple introduced jarred strained beef and vegetables soup, carrots, peas, prunes, and spinach in 1928 at six cans for a dollar. The popular canned food outsold Harold Clapp's formula, shipped from Rochester, New York, and distributed only by druggists since 1921. Sketches of the Gerber Baby in *Good Housekeeping* and *Ladies' Home Journal* increased the brand's market share. In one generation, the company turned *Gerber's* into a synonym for solid baby food.

Families began buying prepared foods in glass jars, a see-through container introduced by Beech-Nut featuring 13 varieties in 1931. The entrance of Heinz and Libby's foods into the infant market in 1935 did not lessen Gerber's dominance, which it still maintains. The market leaders added salt, starch, sugar, and preservatives with impunity until the 1990s, when the Food and Drug Administration mandated the listing of additives by percentage. As of 1998, Gerber topped all U.S. brands in customer loyalty. Heinz continues to dominate the market in Australia, Canada, Great Britain, Italy, and New Zealand.

Advances in Bottle Feeding

During the quarter century preceding World War II, breast feeding declined in the United States from 80 percent to 38 percent. Baby bottle kits offered the all-in-one convenience of a metal sterilizer and nesting basket for stovetop boiling. Mothers could clean bottles and nipples and prepare and store a whole day's feedings, poured into either round or hexagonal bottles. The lidded carryalls made by Therma Products of Toledo, Ohio, also held baby food packed with ice for outings and travel.

By 1956, when more than 50 percent of American infants drank home-mixed evaporated milk formulas, the La Leche League encouraged mothers to return to natural breast feeding for at least a year. The grassroots effort spread to Canada, France, Mexico, and New Zealand. By 1972, breast feeding began to advance at an average of 3 percent annually. The United Nations supported the effort in 32 nations.

Parents worried less about impure food after the introduction of boilable Pyrex nursers. The marketing of sterilized ready-to-eat formula in disposable glass bottles improved convenience. Fortification with iron and an adjusted calcium and phosphorus ratio bolstered nutrients in a basis of soy protein. Mead Johnson's Enfamil and Abbott Laboratories' Similac and other soy formulas solved some of the problems with animal milk and lactose intolerance and gained the trust of vegetarian families and women incapable of nursing their young.

Back-to-Nature Movement

The 1970s produced a revolt against industrialized, overprocessed food and wasteful packaging. In March 1974, journalist Mike Muller of the British nonprofit War on Want issued "The Baby Killer: A War on Want," an exposé of the deception of developing world mothers, such as the women of rural San Salvador, where infants died at the rate of 50 out of 1,000. In the opening paragraph, Muller charged that the children who survived remained mentally and physically stunted.

A global uprising on July 4, 1977, against Nestlé's unethical merchandizing of Lactogen to nursing mothers shamed a respectable company for misleading mothers in have-not nations. By dispatching 200 saleswomen dressed in nurses' uniforms, the company influenced women to switch from breast milk to the commercial formulas popular in industrialized nations. The missing link, literacy, made the campaign incomprehensible to the preliterate and semiliterate of Brazil, Chile, Jamaica, Jordan, India, Israel, Nigeria, Pakistan, and Sierra Leone. Subsequently, the faulty preparation of commercial foods and lack of refrigeration resulted in higher infant mortality rates from enteritis and ear and respiratory infection.

In a rebellion against overcooking and flavoring with salt and sugar and thickening with starch, mothers returned to breast feeding and to blending organic produce into baby food with food mills and processors. The World Health Organization (WHO) legitimized their concerns in 1981 by adopting the International Code of Marketing of Breast-Milk Substitutes. To increase income, baby food companies directed advertising toward African and Latino shoppers. In an effort to enhance breast feeding, Brazil in 1988 issued guidelines for marketing infant food.

Fortifying the Pantry

Because of inadequate formula mixing and contaminated water supplies worldwide, some 1.5 million infants died in 2001 alone. To save lives, WHO continued to advise mothers to breastfeed their infants for the first six months. As a substitute for human milk when the mother is weak or taking drugs for herpes, human immunodeficiency virus/acquired immune deficiency syndrome (HIV/AIDS), or tuberculosis, communities formed human milk banks to collect and dispense breast milk. Heifer International, a nonprofit poverty relief agency begun in Little Rock, Arkansas, gained support for combating malnutrition by giving poor families milk-producing animals—dairy cows, goats, sheep, and water buffalo—as well as chickens, ducks, geese, llamas, pigs, and rabbits as sustainable livestock.

Under the Child Nutrition Act of 1966, the U.S. Department of Agriculture established the Women, Infants, and Children (WIC) Program in 1972. The third-largest national food aid program, WIC distributed iron-fortified infant formula and cereal to some 88,000 applicants in the United States. By 2010, the number of recipients exceeded 9.1 million, with a per-person average of $41.45 per month in food assistance. Parents received more sustainable infant diet from jarred produce and meat and from milk formulas that provided complex fatty acids from egg yolk and fish for the development of brain and vision.

Alternatives to standard jarred food include the organic meals from Earth's Best, which appeared on grocery shelves in the 1980s. Designer entrées, available fresh or frozen from Bohemian Baby and Whole Foods after 2005, replaced savorless jarred baby food with such gourmet entrées as asparagus risotto and Tex-Mex beans and rice. In a $3.6 billion annual industry, the creative pairing of fruit with rice pudding and meat stew with bay leaf enhanced a discriminating palate in infants. Multicultural choices introduced dal with cinnamon and lentils with coriander. Babies learned early to recognize celeriac and to appreciate the addition of ginger and shallots to dishes.

Globally, the baby food industry remains in its infancy. Russian mothers, especially rural peasants, spend more than 80 percent of their infant food allowance on imported jarred foods. Tanzania's Lisha brand imitates nineteenth-century creative efforts by selling local corn and soy beans blended with milk and supplemental nutrients. Farmers in Costa Rica and Honduras seized the wave of interest in more natural baby feeding by marketing pureed organic bananas and tubers to sell to African immigrants to the United States.

At the same time, disparities mock the advances in infant nutrition. Angola leads the world with more than 180 deaths per 1,000 live births, compared with Singapore, with the lowest ratio of 2.31 per 1,000 live births. For the Central and South American outback peasant, such as the Yanomami of the rain forest, baby food retains the age-old simplicity of fruit or meat mashed by hand and diluted with water.

See also: Allergies, Food; Cereal; Crackers; Liebig, Justus von; Sloane, Hans.

Further Reading

Belasco, Warren James, and Philip Scranton. *Food Nations: Selling Taste in Consumer Societies.* New York: Routledge, 2002.

Greene, Alan R. *Feeding Baby Green: The Earth-Friendly Program for Healthy, Safe Nutrition During Pregnancy, Childhood, and Beyond.* San Francisco: Jossey-Bass, 2009.

Lauwers, Judith, and Anna Swisher. *Counseling the Nursing Mother: A Lactation Consultant's Guide.* Sudbury, MA: Jones and Bartlett, 2005.

Smith, Andrew F., ed. *The Oxford Companion to American Food and Drink.* New York: Oxford University Press, 2007.

Bamboo

A treelike member of the grass family common to the Caribbean, East and Southeast Asia, Pacific Islands, and the Americas, bamboo impacts world cuisine as a food and a versatile raw material for making cooking and eating utensils. A miraculous perennial that can grow as much as 39 inches (100 centimeters) per day, bamboo comes in 1,400 varieties.

In prehistory, Asians used bamboo leaves as food wrappers and strips to bind raw foods together for spit roasting. Aborigines of India collected sugar crystals from the stems for trade. Koreans roasted sea salt in sections of bamboo to leach out impurities. In the 1300s, Mongol nomads taught the Chinese their *kao* cuisine, toasting meat on bamboo skewers over charcoal grills. Cooks

Recipe: Vegetable Pork Rolls

Sauté 1/2 pound of ground pork in 1/4 cup of sesame oil. Rinse and sliver 2 cups of bamboo shoots and 1/2 cup each of chopped carrots and water chestnuts and add to the pork. Top with 1 teaspoon each of rice vinegar and soy sauce and lower heat to medium. Stir-fry for five minutes. Sprinkle on 1/4 cup of chopped curly parsley. Allow the mixture to cool and divide it into five portions. Spoon each portion onto an egg roll wrapper and roll the filled wrappers into cigar shapes. Brush with one beaten egg and bake for half an hour.

placed individual grills on tables, offering informal diners the opportunity to roast morsels to the desired level of doneness.

Bamboo is a cheap, lightweight, renewable resource. In Cambodia and New Guinea, kitchen staff heat greens and yams in bamboo tubes over fires; in Kerala, India, designers modify the tubes with baffles and use them to control steam arising from woks. At Vietnamese food markets, vendors of fishball soup draw customers by clapping *tok toks,* bamboo sticks that emit a hollow sound. Bamboo easily shapes into baskets for air-drying mushrooms and rice, beer carafes, brushes and scrubbers, canisters, chopsticks, cups and scoops, filters and mats, napkin rings, shelving, sieves, vegetable steamers, and winnowing trays. As a fiber, bamboo weaves into a soft, antimicrobial fabric for curtains and table linens.

On farms and in courtyards, bamboo conforms to geometric shapes and arches to support espaliered and vining plants. In the mid-1900s, Kudo Kazuyoshi, a Japanese master of bamboo implement manufacture, designed creels for draining seaweed, transporting salt for pickling eels, and trapping and storing live fish in water.

One of the world's major food sources, bamboo produces edible sap and shoots that can be baked into rice pancakes, cooked in broths, grated over salads, mixed with other vegetables, pickled into a condiment, or fermented into wine. Shoots are available fresh or canned. Fresh stalks impart a distinct savor to rice, soup, or tea.

See also: Cantonese Diet and Cuisine; Dried Food; Hearth Cookery.

Further Reading

Bess, Nancy Moore, and Bibi Wein. *Bamboo in Japan.* New York: Kodansha International, 2001.

Chapman, Geoffrey P. *The Bamboos.* London: Academic Press, 1997.

Farrelly, David. *The Book of Bamboo.* San Francisco: Sierra Club, 1984.

Barbecue

An indigenous New World cooking method, barbecuing slow-cooks meat, usually a whole deer or hog, over a smoky fire.

On November 7, 1504, Christopher Columbus arrived back in Spain with details of Jamaican-style barbecuing. In 1542, Hernando de Soto's expedition along the St. Johns River, Europe's longest foray into native America, introduced Castillians to a Timucuan culinary specialty, barbecued hens. In the Caribbean in the seventeenth century, food writer Gonzalo Fernández de Oviedo observed the Arawak, Carib, and Taíno cooking alligator and fish on racks of bearded fig wood raised on saplings. During slow grilling, smoke from the wood fire drove off insects and halted putrefaction. On Hispaniola, pitmasters adapted grate grilling to whole cattle and pigs, dressed and split for maximum contact with heat. In Central America and southeastern Mexico, the Maya developed their own grilling method for iguana and turkey. A similar framework in Argentina called a *parrilla* accommodated haunches, tongue, tripe, and whole carcasses over radiant heat. Filipinos popularized the barbecuing of *criadillo* (bull's testicles) and the large intestines of pigs.

The first commercial U.S. barbecue, opened in Ayden, North Carolina, in 1830, sold smoked meat from a chuck wagon. In her epic Civil War novel, *Gone with the Wind* (1936), author Margaret Mitchell prefaced war and destruction with the barbecue at the Wilkes family's Twelve Oaks plantation, a symbolic outdoor repast that welcomed the county gentry to the cookery of Georgia domestic slaves. Before reaching the Wilkes veranda, the heroine, Scarlett O'Hara, spies barbecue pits that "had been slowly burning since last night . . . long troughs of rose-red embers, with the meats turning on spits above them and the juices trickling down and hissing into the coals." From political talk over plates of meat burst the announcement of war between North and South, a cataclysm fought over the nearly invisible slaves who cooked and served meals to Southern gentry.

After emancipation, black cooks migrating north and west took Southern barbecue styles with them and ate " 'que" on Juneteenth, a celebration of the news of slave emancipation on June 19, 1863. In 1907, Henry Perry, a Tennessee-born steamboat cook, introduced the cooking style in Kansas City. Because of the availability of cattle at railheads, barbecuers in Kansas, Missouri, Oklahoma, and Texas favored beef over pork. After barbecuing over a mesquite fire, Texas-style steers fed large parties, such as the one featured in the film *Giant* (1956). Brisket arrived at the table in tender slices rather than chopped. Use of a closed pit produced a pinkish ring on the meat, evidence of a chemical change wrought by smoke. Side dishes included roasting ears of corn, baked beans, and thick slices of Texas toast.

Europeans developed a male-dominated cooking method of barbecuing meat and vegetables on a gridiron over hot coals or charcoal. In the late 1940s, Australians and New Zealanders embraced barbecuing for special occasions by grilling game or skewered chicken or lamb and sausages. The popular nationalistic gathering rejected the prim English diet of a Sunday beef roast and boiled potatoes.

A North Carolina pitmaster checks one of the whole hogs smoking in his barbecue grill. A slow-cooking method indigenous to the Caribbean and North America, barbecuing constitutes a diverse—and often competitive—subculture across the American South. *(Richard Drew/Associated Press)*

In other European colonies, cooks in Botswana, Lesotho, Namibia, South Africa, Zambia, and Zimbabwe developed the *braai,* a barbecue over a gas or wood flame of Dutch-style *boerewors* (sausages), rock lobster, and skewered *sosaties* (the Afrikaans term for spiced kebabs). Diners preferred their barbecue with cornmeal mush, *chakalaka* (hot sauce), and chutney, called "monkeygland" sauce. The regional meal acquired its own holiday, National Braai Day, which it shared with Heritage Day every September 24.

Current North American tastes favor the backyard barbecue, popularly known as 'que. The method is relaxed, especially in warm weather, when outdoor cookery directs heat and odors away from the kitchen. At a traditional "pig-pickin'" in the Pork Belt, Southeastern Americans observe regional preferences for ribs or chopped fatty pork butt or shoulder.

The melting of fat into the flames gives the barbecue its distinctive aroma and succulence. Coarse chopping breaks down tough collagen fibers and produces a satisfying mouthfeel. For its homey appeal, barbecue became a focus of county fairs and political rallies. In 1991, producer Jon Avnet filmed Fannie Flagg's *Fried Green Tomatoes at the Whistle Stop Cafe,* a Gothic comedy that depicts barbecuing of the villain as a way to hide the corpse.

All-male aficionados in the Piedmont Carolinas and Georgia construct barbecue pits from scratch or recycle fuel drums into hinged basin and lid. A natural competition emerges between "loggers" and "gassers" over the best fuel for authentic 'que. At church socials and Fourth of July community picnics, pitmasters slather a peppery, vinegar-based tomato sauce over pulled pork or chicken with a long-handled marinade mop. The sauce also seasons cabbage cole slaw, a standard accompaniment along with hush puppies (corn fritters), pickles, and sweet tea. South Carolinians add mustard to their sauce. Nearer the Atlantic Coast, cooks flavor marinade with brown sugar and molasses. Kentuckians massage seasonings directly into mutton for a presmoking dry rub.

Friendly competition, cook-offs at Kansas City, Missouri, Lynchburg and Memphis, Tennessee, and elsewhere in America feature the best regional recipes and techniques for the juiciest meat. Vying over the choice of hickory or oak hardwood or mesquite generates factions among grilling sportsmen. From these challenge meets have come a spate of barbecue cookbooks, most compiled by men.

See also: Amerindian Diet; Columbus, Christopher; Sauces and Saucing.

Further Reading

Elie, Lolis Eric, ed. *Cornbread Nation 2: The United States of Barbecue.* Chapel Hill: University of North Carolina Press, 2004.

Lovegren, Sylvia. "Barbecue." *American Heritage* 54 (June 1, 2003): 36–44.

Moss, Robert F. *Barbecue: The History of an American Institution.* Montgomery: University of Alabama Press, 2010.

Suddath, Claire. "A Brief History of Barbecue." *Time,* July 3, 2009.

Walsh, Robb. *Legends of Texas Barbecue Cookbook: Recipes and Recollections from the Pit Bosses.* San Francisco: Chronicle, 2002.

Barter

A direct method of exchanging goods and services in a cooperative milieu, barter bypasses the use of currency as a medium of change. Bartering follows a number of patterns depending on location, need, and time factors. These may include:

Pure bilateral exchange of goods.

Pure bilateral exchange of goods and services.

Offset of debt or obligation with a pledge of goods.

Exchange of goods for a promissory note.

Debt swap canceling obligations bilaterally.

In a simultaneous face-to-face swap, individuals or clans set the value of one commodity in units equal to an offering that differs in kind, such as a basket of camassia tubers for a swordfish or the skin and meat of three rabbits. In times of calamity, such as the collapse of monetary systems during depressions or war, only the trading partners can establish the fairness of a swap.

In a climate of distrust, the exchange may progress in silence, with one group leaving, for example, a stack of herbs or wax for examination. A potential customer may then leave an offering, such as bananas or sea bass. The first group may accept the offering or remove the herbs or wax from the site. This type of one-to-one deal suits soldiers on the march, such as the Macedonians under Alexander the Great, who bartered for grapes and bread loaves with Bactrians who spoke no Greek nor recognized Greek coins. The invaders were more likely to receive fresh goods that had not yet gone to market. Unscrupulous Bactrians, on the other hand, could cheat soldiers by selling stale or mixed-quality foods to men who moved on to new bivouacs before examining the exchange medium for trickery.

More complex exchanges involve multiple commodities, for example, huckleberries and barley swapped for clay pots and obsidian knives. Among most North American Indians, trade in surplus corn and dried fish increased supplies of food for winter storage when red meat was scarce. The Cherokee fermented corn liquor, a valuable food or medicinal commodity on a par with Aztec cacao beans or Guatemalan *chicha.*

When the first white traders entered Plains Indian territory, they demonstrated the use of items unknown to their trading partners, such as fishing gear or work gloves to protect the hands from blisters. The Comanche rejected the gloves as well as lines and hooks, the Western world's method of catching fish one at a time. The ultimate good to both parties derived from mutual satisfaction. Thus the Comanche found use for imported grain baskets, which they paid for with deer pelts.

In modern markets, for the sale of goods and such services as plowing fields and bailing winter oats, non-monetary transactions avoid the paper trails of banks and tax accounting. By reducing an item to its base value, such as the use of a prize bull for freshening dairy herds, reciprocity avoids inflating yearly farm income or incurring a luxury or value-added tax such as that of Bosnia, Ireland, or New Zealand. For agrarian communities, deals arranged between relatives or fellow farmers enhance long-standing relationships and offer opportunities to lower overhead costs, for example, the seasonal use of a neighbor's corn picker in exchange for the shared trucking of soybeans to a grain elevator.

A downside of barter stems from the length of time required to establish worth and to negotiate conditions of transport and delivery, a major concern in Barcelona, Spain, in deals involving herd animals and perishable fruit and seafood. If the trading partners engage a third party or broker, involvement of an outsider lessens the savings by requiring payment for arbitration. Throughout history, dickering and haggling, such as the deal-making in the bible between Laban and his son-in-law Jacob over white and black sheep, has resulted in resentment and grudges that sometimes escalated into personal and tribal vendettas.

See also: Animal Husbandry; Currency, Food as; Local Food Movement; Silk Road.

Further Reading

Carrier, James G. *A Handbook of Economic Anthropology.* Cheltenham, UK: Elgar, 2005.

Fisher, Bart S., and Kathleen M. Harte, eds. *Barter in the World Economy.* New York: Praeger, 1985.

Hann, Chris, and Keith Hart. *Economic Anthropology.* Malden, MA: Polity, 2011.

Humphrey, Caroline, and Stephen Hugh-Jones. *Barter, Exchange and Value: An Anthropological Approach.* New York: Cambridge University Press, 1992.

Beans and Legumes

Beans and legumes, the world's first cultivated plants, have fed humankind since prehistory on complex carbohydrates, dietary fiber, and vegetable protein. Until the refinement of breads, dishes of bean, lentil, and pea porridge sustained much of the Mediterranean world and the Middle East. Culinary bean innovations began in Afghanistan and central Asia with wild crops and spread to Georgia, Pakistan, and India. In Africa, the viny hyacinth bean promoted rural welfare and land reclamation; Indonesians cultivated the winged bean, a trellised annual that yielded edible flowers, leaves, and tubers containing 50 percent protein.

During the Paleolithic era, milling separated kernels from pods and augmented the taste and digestibility of beans and grains for use in flatbreads and loaves. After 10,000 B.C.E., the Olmec and Maya balanced a corn-heavy diet with amaranth and beans, sources of complete proteins. Improvements in Neolithic or New Stone Age cuisine in southeastern Turkey in 9000 B.C.E. and Jericho in 8000 B.C.E. shifted focus from meat to cooked grains and legumes, which required clay pots for cooking. In Iraq as well as Chile and Peru, the bean diet altered lifestyles from nomadic herding to settled agriculture. Egyptians so reverenced legume nutrition that they chose beans as grave goods to nourish the dead in the afterlife.

Nutritional diversity placed beans at the center of global food intake. In 6000 B.C.E., Thai hunter-gatherers profited from fields of wild beans; by 5500 B.C.E., chickpeas nourished the Middle East. In the Far East, Chinese and Indonesian growers integrated a diet of fish and poultry with adzuki beans, rice, soybeans, and taro. The broad-based cuisine yielded a population spike as well as health benefits.

By 4000 B.C.E., the Andean Inca terraced vegetable gardens to produce beans and complementary flavorings from pepper and tomatoes. Around 2000 B.C.E., the grower in central China added soybeans to vital grain crops; a similar dietary advance in 1500 B.C.E. placed the pigeon pea at the disposal of cooks in Orissa, India. On the Fertile Crescent, the Akkadians dug canals to water bean fields. Around 950 B.C.E., Arabic author ibn Sayyar al-Warraq of Baghdad collected innovative recipes for beans cooked with grain and vegetables and for stews of lentils, rice, and white beans.

Staples

The incorporation of beans into basic diet stripped the legume of its cachet. Around 800 B.C.E., Hindus validated a standard diet of barley, beans, legumes, and lentils as adjuncts to rice, sesame, vetches, and wheat. For Greek farmers, dinners of beans, lupins, and pea and lentil soup featured vinegars and olive tapenade as table dressings. When legumes fell in prestige, only the poor in classical Greece served them in *etnos* (bean soup) dressed with vinegar and baked bean meal into loaves and sold split pea soup on the streets of Athens. Virgil's *Georgics* (29 B.C.E.) corroborates the ranking of kidney beans as a peasant crop.

Classic dietary advice ignored patrician trends and connected Roman staples—beans and lentils, bread, oil, olives, and wine—with sensible regimens and with noble clans: Cicero (chickpea), the Fabii (fava), Lentuli (lentils), and Pisos (peas). Families in Crete, Greece, Italy, the Levant, and Magna Graecia (lower Italy and Sicily) relied on whole grains, legumes, and vegetables for meals and roasted *erebinthos* (chickpeas) for snacks. Roman legionaries packed chickpeas on marches to Germania. Nine days after a funeral, mourners spared the dead bellyaches by leaving bowls of broadbeans and chickpeas at grave sites. To avoid vindictive ghosts, impressionable Romans spit fava beans.

In the late fourth century B.C.E., encyclopedist Theophrastus of Lesbos, the "Father of Botany," indicated the centrality of legumes to the Mediterranean diet and analyzed the nitrogen process by which legumes enrich soil. He evaluated potage made from fava beans and lentils and named chickpeas and lupines as famine food. In the next century, the poet Theocritus's *Idylls* (ca. 270 B.C.E.) extolled the freshness of rural produce, including dinners of beans. Apicius, a Roman cook around 40 C.E., advised cleaning and soaking legumes, a means of tenderizing the thiamine-rich outer coat. He purchased beans only from Baiae and served them with celery, fermented fish sauce, and wine concentrate. His love of peas is obvious in nine recipes featuring peas seasoned with herbs and spices.

New World Beans

In the Western Hemisphere, Indians revered the "three sisters" of gardening, beans, corn, and squash, a xeric vegetable culture the Anasazi developed in the American Southwest from 1200 B.C.E. to 1300 C.E. South of the Equator, the Inca spread their tables with a healthful variety of amaranth, corn, lima and red beans, lupins, peppers, tomatoes, and tubers. For flavor, cooks served beans in oil and vinegar. On Dominica, Grenada, St. Vincent, and Tobago, the Carib shared with the Taíno the growing of lima beans, pumpkins, squashes, and starchy tubers in a single mound.

In Mesoamerica from the 500s C.E., the Aztec of Tenochtitlán toasted bean pods on a comal and simmered crushed beans to a paste in a clay *olla* (pottery cooking jar). Intercropping on *chinampas* (floating gardens) boosted yields of wild herbs, which flavored dishes of corn and beans. The *Florentine Codex* incorporated 1,800 illustrations drawn by Aztec scribes to capture the importance of beans and corn to the diet. From Spanish voyagers, European growers acquired an enduring recipe of red beans and rice as the basis for Cajun and Creole hoppin' John.

The fall of the Roman Empire left behind a regard for legumes in cuisine. During the rise of Constantinople, fragrant grain cereals and legumes filled the communal pot much as they had during Roman times. Because Christian dietitians from Egypt to Ireland dominated period nutritional research, monastery libraries contained up-to-date information on fava beans. Missionaries to China may have introduced *hu tou* (pod peas) in the 600s.

During the Nara era of the eighth century, when Japan turned to Buddhism, citizens embraced vegetarianism and cultivated rice along with grains and legumes. In Beijing, dealers traded in beans and dried fish, staples of China's extensive catering businesses. Shipping routes from Denzhou bore yellow beans farther east over the Yellow Sea to Japan and Korea. Simultaneously, in Western Europe, Charlemagne built the reputation of his kitchen at Aachen on a huge pantry of beans and chickpeas and homegrown peas. To ensure plenty, his accountants tallied provisions in the *Inventaire des Domaines* (*Domestic Inventory*, 810).

Protoscientific theories validated the worth of beans. A layman's perception of complex bean chemistry in 1000 led to crop rotation, an agrarian technique that enriched soil with the rhizobial bacteria of legumes. In India, a detailed recipe in the *Lokopakara* (*For the People's Benefit*, ca. 1025), a Sanskrit encyclopedia, described the soaking of urad dal (black beans) in buttermilk, providing a tenderizing application of lactic acid. In 1096 at the beginning of the First Crusade, Christian supply trains from Europe ensured military preparedness by transporting barley, beans, chickpeas, and lentils over 3,000 miles (4,800 kilometers) to the Middle East.

During the late Middle Ages, beans and grains continued to monopolize peasant fare. Society's bottom rung ate their legumes and rye crusts from wooden bowls, while the moneyed class bought tiny fresh peas in the pod rather than cheaper dried peas. In 1455, Europeans reported that the Senegalese grew kidney beans as the anchor of their West African diet.

The age of discovery rapidly spread bean varieties worldwide, introducing Europe to the black bean, butter bean, kidney bean, lima bean, navy bean, and pinto bean and initiating the growing of chickpeas and fava beans in the West Indies. In 1514, Spanish explorer Hernán de Cortés observed Mesoamerican reverence for legumes when 50 Tlaxcalans offered them as gifts. He discovered that citizens paid their taxes in beans, corn, and sage. He marveled at idols shaped from ground legumes and seeds mixed with the heart blood of Aztec victims. North of the Mexican border, monoculture farmers coated slatted bins in clay to secure acorns, mesquite beans, and nuts, the basics of their daily intake. Trading in small and large beans from Lima, Peru, earned the name "lima bean" for a family of beans, including the baby lima and butter bean.

The Cherokee, Hopi, and Navajo excelled at cultivating corn and beans and storing them in baskets for use in bean bread and soup. Drought-resistant mesquite and tepary beans centered the cookery of Arizona Pueblos and natives as far south as Costa Rica. Plains Indians recommended cooking beans with honey, the forerunner of American baked beans. Algonquin succotash wed butter beans to corn and bear fat. The Narragansett varied ingredients with kidney beans. The Hidatsa of Montana cooked *mapee nakapah* (pounded mush) from beans and corn kernels.

In 1643, the Lenni Lenape moved closer to trading posts along the Schuylkill River to tend subsistence gardens of beans and cucurbits. For marketing, they stored beans and corn in woven sacks in caverns and subterranean caches. After 1670, the spread of Hudson's Bay Company trading posts among the Inuit expanded their knowledge of European legumes, which Florentine newcomer Catherine de' Médici had introduced to France in 1533. In France, the popularity of peas continued to grow, making a late-night pea pudding snack a preface to bedtime.

Beans in Kitchen History

Essential to bean cuisine is the versatility of cooking and serving. In East Africa, mixtures of black-eyed or field peas wrapped in banana, cabbage, plantain, or roselle leaves fed families on handheld portions requiring no utensils. The tight bundles retained aroma and savor while steaming fillings. Farther north in Eritrea, Ethiopia, and Somalia, communal dining featured *injera,* a spongy sourdough flatbread, paired with *hilbet,* a creamy paste of fava beans and lentils, eaten taco style.

Throughout the Atlantic slave trade, legumes kept abductees alive. Aboard the slave ship *Hannibal* in 1693, the galley crew cooked *dabbadabb* (corn dumplings), varied three times a week by horse beans (*Vicia faba*), which relieved chronic dysentery. In 1707 at Cape Coast, Ghana, ships' cooks chose a familiar diet of beans, corn, and rum, which staved off seasickness. After slave sales, the typical fare in Maryland at the 2 P.M. feeding featured beans with buttermilk, cornmeal, molasses, and poke greens, the basics of Southern cuisine. Additional slave favorites—black-eyed and pigeon peas, broad beans, cowpeas, millet, and peanuts—became soul food staples. Weekend markets held by slaves in Antigua, the Bahamas, Barbados, Jamaica, and St. John offered lima beans, spices, and vegetables as fund-raisers to enhance island laborers' diet.

Research and technology advanced the bean business. In 1701, farmers abandoned broadcast sowing after English agronomist Jethro Tull invented a drill that directed beans and peas into three evenly spaced rows. At Monticello, Virginia, amateur agronomist Thomas Jefferson instructed his gardener to plant Ravenscroft peas, one of the 30 varieties the former president enjoyed.

For vegetable growers of Orange County, California, in the 1850s, support of railways elevated profits from the rapid distribution of fresh green and lima beans. For bulk in chili, prison and ranch cooks added black beans, black-eyed peas, great northern beans, and navy or pink beans. In Boston and New York, home economics classes enlightened immigrants on the cheap, nourishing protein available from dried beans. A nineteenth-century high-fiber favorite among Germans, three-bean salad in a sweet-and-sour sauce contrasted green beans and kidney beans with chickpeas.

During World War I, beans earned their reputation as food for the impoverished. Austrian social reformers Sophie Grünfeld and Hermine Kadisch opened kosher soup kitchens featuring menus of beans and soup to feed displaced persons, orphans, and refugees. Throughout the Harlem Renaissance, music lured whites to "speakeasies," where black bootleggers plied customers with a soul food combo of pinto beans and corn bread to soak up pot liquor. World War II airlifts set a precedent for subsequent humanitarian relief, which relied on beans as a lightweight and sanitary staple that most people eat.

Modern Uses

At present, more than 4,000 species of beans, lentils, and peas support peasant agriculture and supply 8 percent of the world's protein, usually in single-pot dishes. In the Philippines, the Hanunóo of southern Mindoro Island intercrop beans with betel, corn, and sugarcane. Eroded farmland in Kenya and Tanzania generates gullies in which wild legumes sprout and enrich the soil. Farmers in Angola, like those in South Africa, produce enough subsistence crops to import beans. Mauritius does a brisk business in lentils and soybeans from outside sources. On a higher economic level, Algeria tops Africa's demand for imported grain, lentils, and peas.

Restaurant cooks retail legumes as traditional ingredients. Satisfying Arab dishes combine chickpeas and fava beans with eggplant or zucchini. To achieve a sweet-and-sour savor, Szechuan cooks parboil tofu cubes with douban jiang paste, a spread of fermented and spiced broad beans. Raw food diners encourage meals of beans and grains, fruits and vegetables. For vegetarians, soybeans and tapioca mimic meat texture in faux crabmeat, tofu, and veggie burgers.

In Eritrea, Ethiopia, and Sudan, two affordable pulses, the chickpea and split pea, contain less protein than other legumes but suit infant and invalid needs for their digestibility, especially in bean mush. Unlike the poor of Africa's Horn and Bangladesh, consumers in Kenya, Malawi, Tanzania, Uganda, and Zimbabwe are less eager to add the chickpea to their traditional cuisine. In South Asia, fried chickpeas add crunch and salt to snacks while bolstering nutrition. In central and western India, the drought-resistant moth bean generates sweet sprouts for salad and pairs well with pearl millet and sorghum.

The lima bean of Madagascar and the United States and the Mexican tepary make excellent meal extenders, as do the climbing scarlet runner, pole beans, and sugar snap peas. Caribbean consumers prefer haricot beans and pickled pigeon peas. Along the Sahel, the fringe of the Sahara Desert, beans sustain subsistence farmers; Tanzanians terrace their fields and market crops as mixed beans, a common source of soup.

Most legumes suit varied recipes, such as the mix of mung or soya beans with foxtail millet or noodles in China and Hawaiian jack beans baked in sugar and pineapple chunks. Southeast Asians sprout soybeans and sell bean crops to commercial processors of bean cheese, curd, milk, sauce, and tofu. In Bulgaria and other parts of southeastern Europe, broad beans, dumplings, and cabbage accompany poultry and pork. To facilitate the breakdown of the outer legume coat in the stomach, cooks parboil and cook beans in fresh water or tenderize them with baking soda.

See also: New World Commodities; Pulses.

Further Reading

Albala, Ken. *Beans: A History.* New York: Berg, 2007.

Dalby, Andrew. *Food in the Ancient World from A to Z.* London: Routledge, 2003.

Prance, Ghillean T., and Mark Nesbitt. *The Cultural History of Plants.* New York: Taylor & Francis, 2005.

Smith, Andrew F. *Eating History: 30 Turning Points in the Making of American Cuisine.* New York: Columbia University Press, 2009.

Beard, James (1903–1985)

American culinary columnist, teacher, and cultural connoisseur, James Andrew Beard elevated North American heritage foods to gourmet status.

A native of Portland, Oregon, Beard was born on May 3, 1903. A chubby, energetic, and fun-loving child, he grew up under the influence of his English mother, Elizabeth Jones Brennan Beard, the innkeeper of the Gladstone Hotel, and her Chinese cook, Jue Let. In defiance of the gastronomic barbarities of Prohibition, he learned complex French cuisine made with raw artichokes and wine vinegar as well as recipes for Pacific Coast asparagus, berries, tiny Alaskan shrimp, teal, and crabs fresh caught at Gearhart beach. He described home dinners as diamond shaped—light on soup as an appetizer and sorbet for dessert, but bulging in the middle.

At the age of 20, Beard abandoned Reed College to study opera in London, travel with a theater company in France, and reconnoiter bistros to absorb the cooking of fresh ingredients. He quickly discovered that an expensive dinner at Maxim's in Paris could not compare with the fare at country inns. Over a lifetime of wanderings, despite his fear of flying, he sampled exotica in Hawaii, most of the Western Hemisphere, Japan, and North Africa. At age 61, he credited palatal judgment and "taste memory" for recording the best flavors he encountered along the way.

While studying acting and opera in New York City in 1937, Beard supported himself by teaching English, French, and social studies at a private school in New Jersey. He joined Berlin-born cooks Bill and Irma Rhode in catering parties of Manhattan's "cocktail belt," the source of his first book, *Hors d'Oeuvre and Canapes* (1940). Beard's success in hustling cold cuts and vichyssoise cur-

Chef and food writer James Beard, the "Dean of American Cuisine," brought gourmet quality to the preparation of North American fare. His books, TV appearances, and cooking schools have inspired generations of professional and amateur chefs. *(Lee Lockwood/Time Life Pictures/ Getty Images)*

tailed his yearning to act in film and theater, for which he was too heavy. By the time rationing ended his catering concern, he recognized his true path as a food commentator and consultant, beginning with his employment by the Cognac Association, Cuisinart, and Sherry Wine and Spirits.

Over the next 15 years, Beard earned the titles of "Dean of American Cuisine" and "Father of American Gastronomy." To promote North American food heritage, he opened the James Beard Cooking School—first in New York City, then in Seaside, Oregon—and taught in short stints at civil clubs and women's societies. To support his travels, he endorsed Green Giant canned vegetables and Mouton Cadet wine. At the Four Seasons restaurant in New York City, he introduced New American Cuisine, a showcase of clams, hearts of palm, lobster, marinated lamb, and pigeon that predated the natural flavors and seasonal ingredients of nouvelle cuisine. His enthusiastic showmanship and loyalty to regional recipes influenced chefs Julia Child, Craig Claiborne, and Emeril Lagasse as well as members of Restaurant Associates, a top-ranked professional food consortium.

In syndicated newspaper columns and 31 books, five of them posthumous collections, Beard covered a range of styles—barbecuing and rotisserie cookery, beer busts, entertaining, casseroles, picnics—and kitchen interests, including Italian food, bread and sandwiches, low-budget meals, fish, fowl and game, and pasta. His text of *Cook It Outdoors* (1942) introduced camp cookery and grilling as serious cuisine and turned the chef into the first American food luminary. In a newspaper advisory, he explained how he met kitchen emergencies by stocking his pantry with broths, clams, corned beef, garlic, olives, pimientos, salmon, sardines, and truffles.

During World War II, Beard worked in cryptography for the U.S. Army Air Corps and as a farmhand in Pennsylvania Dutch country before establishing port canteens for the United Seamen's Service in Marseilles, France; Panama; Puerto Rico; and Rio de Janeiro, Brazil. By 1946, he braved television to produce America's first cooking show for NBC, *I Love to Eat,* an effort to boost American gastronomy from the postwar doldrums with French techniques. Among his culinary broadcasting innovations, he tricked the viewer's eye with ink enhancing the veins of Roquefort cheese and mashed potatoes posing as ice cream.

Diversification kept Beard afloat with freelance writing and cooking tours of France. His menus delighted guests at his Nantucket restaurant, Lucky Pierre on Steamboat Wharf; his food columns graced *Argosy, Gourmet, House & Garden,* and *Woman's Day.* His unpretentious approach to kitchen work also brought more males into menu planning and cooking. In the 1960s, he studied Mandarin fare under Sun Yung Chiang in San Francisco.

In 1976, the 73-year-old chef's wizardry enlivened service at Windows on the World, a tower restaurant in the World Trade Center. Catering to private members from as far away as New Zealand and Russia, the grill flourished at chicken hash, crab and lobster cakes, ham with pepper sauce, lamb chops, and striped bass. He considered his success an agency of civilization.

Beard took seriously the plight of the hungry. At age 78, he established Citymeals-on-Wheels, a service for the homebound throughout New York's five boroughs. At his death, from heart failure on January 23, 1985, he left a legacy of scholarships from the James Beard Foundation to ready a new generation for championing the American tradition and to administer the James Beard Foundation Awards, known as the "Oscars of the food world." His house in Greenwich Village became a culinary workshop for chefs and restaurateurs. His impact on American cuisine presaged the locavore movement.

See also: Child, Julia; Grilling.

Further Reading
Beard, James. *Beard on Food: The Best Recipes and Kitchen Wisdom from the Dean of American Cooking.* Ed. José Wilson. New York: Bloomsbury, 2007.
Clark, Robert. *James Beard: A Biography.* New York: HarperCollins, 1993.
Ferrone, John, ed. *The Armchair James Beard.* New York: Lyons, 1999.
Kafka, Barbara, ed. *A James Beard Memoir: The James Beard Celebration Cookbook.* New York: Wings, 1990.

Beef

The versatile, satisfying meat of bovines, beef supplies tables with savory protein food that cooks serve in individual slices of muscle and tongue, broth and stew, grilled kebabs and organ meats, dried jerky, and tripe soup. Wild beef consumption, as revealed in cave paintings at Lascaux, France, began with the aurochs, the ancestor of *Bos primigenius* (the first cattle), which thrived from sub-Saharan Africa into the Middle East and India. Middens revealed bones of cattle, the first tame herd animals, which revolutionized agriculture.

After cattle domestication in 8000 B.C.E., herders in the Indus Valley domesticated two scions, the gaur and the humped, long-horned zebu, ancestor of the Burundi, Rwanda, and Uganda Akole-Watusi species of cattle. In central Africa, one zebu produced enough meat to feed an entire clan of Tutsi. In contrast to these endangered ancestors, a present-day steer raised for two years on 8 acres (3.2 hectares) of pasture yields only 75 pounds (34 kilograms) of marketable meat.

Beef and Early Civilizations

Beef earned respect for its nutrition and instant energy. In the Chihuahua Desert of Mexico around 7500 B.C.E., Paleo-Indian herders became more sedentary and fed their families on the meat of steers and the cheese and milk of dairy cows. Much of the era's meat curing involved extracting fluids through air-drying and salting. Smoking dehydrated moist muscle meat while exterminating microbes and killing insects and parasites. Following the defatting of muscle meat, trimming of bone and gristle, and salting of rumps and shanks, the Inca of Peru sun- and wind-dried lean cuts to produce *charqui* (jerky), a dense, lightweight travel food.

The importance of beef to civilization recurs in records and temple art. To ensure rapid work on the three pyramids at Giza, between 2575 and 2465 B.C.E., the pharaoh Khufu and his successors instructed overseers to feed stonecutters beef. Around 500 B.C.E., Darius the Great of Persia indulged himself by having whole oxen cooked for his table. Roman food writer Columella exclaimed in 55 C.E. on the Umbrian Chianina, a beef cow praised for high yield of 65 percent quality lean. In the first century C.E., the Japanese imported Wagyu cattle from Korea to supply marbled beef admired for its juicy tenderness. *Trysts,* the Scots term for stockyards, appeared in the British Isles as trading centers for French Charolais and Limousin, English Herefords, Scots Aberdeen and Angus, and Alderney, Guernsey, and Jersey stock from the Channel Islands.

From the 200s to the 600s, wealthy diners ate boiled beef seasoned with oil and vinegar, while peasants contented themselves with beef heart, oxtails, tongue, and tripe. Sassanian cooks intensified flavors in ox haunches by steeping them in beef bouillon. Late in the seventh century, Muslims in Somalia celebrated Eid al-Fitr, the end of the Ramadan fast, with beef turnovers, an economical use of small cuts of meat. The Vikings predicated their cosmogeny on a primeval cow, Audumbla, the creator; Irish Druids sipped the broth made from a white bull and awaited dreams predicting selection of the next king.

Global Cuisine

Subsequent food history incorporates beef in significant cuisine developments. During a Mongol invasion of Moscow in the mid 1200s, Kublai Khan ate steak tartare, raw minced beef seasoned with capers that honored hardy Tartar horsemen. The formation of the 12 Yeomen Warders of the Tower of London in 1485 preceded their nickname "Beefeaters," after the kitchen of Henry VII rewarded his guards with beef, which roasters larded with bacon and cooked on iron spits. Under the influence of Catherine de' Médici on French cuisine after 1533, meat carvers invented filet mignon (tournedos of beef), an innovative slicing and arrangement on a platter of the heart of beef tenderloin. Her kitchen staff achieved fame for beef Stroganoff, a popular dish that wed savory meat bites with sour cream.

In Tudor England, while peasants ate salt cod and stockfish, menus for the privileged spotlighted beef and game served with soft, white wheat loaves. After Elizabeth I dispatched explorers to New World colonies, British naval provisioners and traders raised demand on corned beef as galley staples and supplies for the privateers at Tortuga, Haiti. In reference to British settlers in *The Generall Historie of Virginia* (1624), Captain John Smith became the first New World observer to refer to beef preservation in the West Indies as "meat jerking," the drying of a shelf-stable beef that remained edible at sea.

North and South American pastures extended open grasslands for the beef industry, which enriched itself on the commoner's reverence for meat as a symbol of the good life. By 1749, natural interbreeding between bison and domestic cattle produced the first beefalo. The Plains hybrid enabled ranchers to produce hardier grazing herds to withstand extremes of drought and blizzards. In fall 1766 in Rio de Janeiro, Brazil, British navigator Captain James Cook loaded fresh or jerked beef in the galleys of the *Endeavour* for an 11-year exploration of Pacific waters. In Hawaii in the 1800s, cooks abandoned whole fish entrées and showcased beef and dried beef jerky, which islanders called *pipikaula,* a traditional luau dish seasoned with ginger, honey, sesame, and soy sauce.

The broth from beef facilitated the planning of social reformers. In the late 1700s, British relief workers in London and Glasgow attempted to nourish the poor and homeless with daily servings of beef soup. Optician William Kitchiner's *Apicius Redivivus: The Cook's Oracle* (1817) compiled a soup recipe that flavored stewed beef strips and knucklebones with black pepper, celery, flour, leeks, salt, and split peas. Public distribution fed 600

families. London Reform Club chef Alexis Soyer summarized beef carvery that generated the leanest slices and tidbits for bouillon and stew.

In the Napoleonic era, the popularity of chateaubriand, a 2-inch (5-centimeter) cut of prime fillet served with béarnaise sauce, signaled a return of cachet to beef. Throughout the War of 1812, Caribbean planters profited from herd grazing and from contracting beef to the military. In 1843, the Puget Sound Agricultural Company, a subsidiary of the Hudson's Bay Company, distributed dairy products and beef to herd-poor locations in Alaska, Hawaii, and Tokyo. During the California gold rush of 1848, shippers sold miners beef, flour, and pork for $60 per barrel. From Southwestern chuck wagons, grillers stirred up beef brisket stew for cowboys; barbecuers soaked gristly cuts in vinegar as a tenderizer.

Commercial Beef

At the height of the Industrial Revolution, when farmhands deserted rural Europe for urban factories, Baron Justus von Liebig foresaw the need for body-strengthening beef extract for factory workers who could not afford roasts and steaks. In 1865, processors of Liebig Extract of Meat in Australia, Brazil, and Uruguay distributed beef stock cubes later called Oxo, an inexpensive meat substitute and health tonic. Within a half century, Oxo and Fray Bentos Corned Beef, Liebig's salted beef and glandular extracts, turned a substantial profit along with the recycling of bones, hides, manure, and tallow as beef byproducts. On his expedition inland from Zanzibar, African explorer Henry Morton Stanley popularized Liebig's beef extract.

Before the decline in the Australian salt beef trade in the 1860s, food processor Sizar Elliott anticipated a demand for tinned meat, particularly from the military. By 1869, shippers from Clarence, New South Wales, exported 14,331 cases of canned beef and processed gelatin, meat extract, and tallow. Simultaneously, Robert Mc-Cracken's Victoria Meat Preserving Company of Melbourne filled orders for canned beef in Japan as well as in England for Jewish kosher markets and the Royal Navy. As the British meat industry declined, Australia's laboring class relied on low-cost pickled and smoked beef.

On the American and Canadian plains, military demand for beef during the Indian Wars heightened profitability for homesteaders and stockmen. Beef Barons shipped their herds to Chicago in 1868, when A.A. Libby & Company first brined 200- to 250-pound (90- to 115-kilogram) quarters and packed them in barrels and casks. In urban areas, meat wagoneers distributed butchered beef to housewives, who made their selections in the street.

Established cattle ranches drove wild game farther from the Ute, leaving them dependent on government issues of dried beef. On the northern Texas border at Guthrie in 1870, Samuel Burk Burnett of the Four Sixes

Ranch hybridized tough desert longhorns by crossbreeding them with British Durham and Hereford cattle, sources of tenderer meat. Captain Richard King of Corpus Christi, owner of the 860,000-acre (350,000-hectare) King Ranch, collaborated with Burnett on drives to East Coast cities. Under protection of Texas Rangers, they exported American-bred Santa Gertrudis steers for the hotels and restaurants where diners demanded Texas beef entrées.

The first Midwestern threat to the New York meat market, Gustav Franklin Swift, Chicago's prime meat packer, conveyed freshly butchered beef to distant states. The transport of sides of beef rather than live cattle turned a seasonal business into a year-round bonanza for graziers and abattoirs. The immigration of Romanian Jews in 1872 added a new demand for thin-sliced pastrami, a delicatessen cut. In 1898, North American merchants on the Pacific Coast extended the output of fresh beef to Hawaii, Hong Kong, and the Philippines, where beef cuts appeared on inn and restaurant menus. A broader choice of meat cuts from polled (hornless) Scots Angus steers enabled chefs to refine their recipes to exact standards of flavor and texture. American beef kings controlled Pacific meat export until the 1876, when Argentine shippers sharpened competition by shipping chilled beef from Buenos Aires to France by refrigerated vessels.

By World War I, slaughterhouses distributed meat cuts to 25,000 communities by refrigerated railcar. Military demands, however, diminished supplies of cattle and meat products and caused U.S. government leaders to advocate replacing beef protein sources with whale meat. In Victoria, British Columbia, whale meat, called "sea beef," replaced beef cuts in meat rolls, shepherd's pie, steaks, and stew. New York restaurant menus featured fish as hors d'oeuvres, in *pot-au-feu* (stew), and salmon plank steaks until a postwar meat boom restored beef to the civilian market.

In 1926, long-distance refrigerated trucking linked consumers with fresh beef more rapidly and conveniently than trains. During the Great Depression, women on tight budgets ranked grocery stores primarily on the color and smell of their beef. In the 1940s, the interbreeding of large-muscled French Charolais cattle with plains herds raised standards for low fat, taste, and tenderness. In Nebraska in 1952, Omaha Steaks vacuum-packed filet mignon, porterhouse, and T-bones for wholesale. Tex-Mex restaurants of the 1960s adapted original menus with skirt steak for fajitas and string beef, a cooked-off-the-bone essential of chili con carne and taco salads. In 1973, extending the connection between macho diners and beef, Swanson's "Hungry-Man" dinners featured man-sized servings of charbroiled Angus beef sandwiches and beef enchiladas.

Asian beef cuisine made a global impact on menus. From the pervasive influence of Asian Indian cookery in the West Indies, curry dishes broadened beef entrées in Guyana, Jamaica, Tobago, and Trinidad. Tropical Indian turmeric tinged Sumatran *satay padang*, a skewered beef

topped with a deep yellow sauce. Szechuan cuisine balanced the fish and seafood focus of Shanghai with the hearty beef cookery of the Chinese interior. Szechuan style hot pot sizzled beef in hot pepper oil in preparation for seasoning with blood, brain, intestines, marrow, and tripe.

The launching of Internet food clubs has made gourmet burgers, filets, pot roast, ribs, and steaks readily available. Kenya, Malawi, Tanzania, Zambia, and Zimbabwe have ventured into agribusiness by developing commerce in beef. In a competitive environment, entrepreneurs import luxury cuts to satisfy travelers' demands for top-grade beef. The health conscious demand grass-fed meat, which contains fewer *Escherichia coli* (*E. coli*) microbes, herbicides, and pesticides than meat from cattle stall-fed on grain. In 1970, Mountain House, a division of Oregon Freeze Dry, first offered adventurers and campers zippered pouches of freeze-dried barbecue, beef stew, and chili for reconstituting in the wild.

British families began deserting the traditional beef roast in 1986, when bovine spongiform encephalopathy, or mad cow disease, first threatened meat eaters and spread to 14 European nations. Late in 2000 and into 2001, combined outbreaks of hoof-and-mouth and mad cow disease in Europe banished beef from home and public service and boosted sales of fish, kangaroo, ostrich, and vegetarian fare. Across Europe, beef consumption declined precipitously but temporarily.

See also: Animal Husbandry; Bouillon; Buffalo; Chili; Jerky; Szechuan Diet and Cuisine.

Further Reading

Denker, Joel. *The World on a Plate: A Tour Through the History of America's Ethnic Cuisine.* Lincoln: University of Nebraska Press, 2007.

Heine, Peter. *Food Culture in the Near East, Middle East, and North Africa.* Westport, CT: Greenwood, 2004.

Montgomery, M.R. *A Cow's Life.* New York: Walker, 2004.

Rimas, Andrew, and Evan Fraser. *Beef: The Untold Story of How Milk, Meat, and Muscle Shaped the World.* San Francisco: HarperCollins, 2009.

Beer

The world's oldest alcoholic drink, beer, sometimes called "liquid bread," shares with bread its beginnings in the grain-growing Fertile Crescent in the Neolithic age. At the beginning of culinary history, both barley and emmer wheat served home brewers as a basis for alcoholic beverages. Syrians first cultivated barley in 8500 B.C.E. at Abu Hureyra, where women superintended fermentation in tubs.

The production of ethanol foam from the feeding of yeast on carbohydrates plumped bread and fermented beer. After failure at raising loaves, experimenters may have turned dough into the basis of the first brewing operation. The commercial preparation of sourdough required a bacteria-rich inoculum, or starter, from previous batches or from beer or wine. To keep the starter viable, preparers fed the mass fresh leavening. Celebrants of early brews generated bar ditties to John Barleycorn as well as hymns, myths, and paeans to common culture.

Ancient Brews

During the Bronze Age, Sumerians thrived on baked yeast bread and sipped thick unfiltered beer through straws to avoid bitter dregs. The growth of cities increased demand for processed food, such as beer at Ur. Around 7500 B.C.E., Sumerians achieved a 40 percent surplus of grain for brewing eight varieties of emmer beers and eight of barley. Protofarmers across the east-west axis of Eurasia naturalized barley and wheat, two self-pollinating, early-maturing founder crops. Stonemasons shaped grinding stones and mortars and pestles for reducing grain heads into powdery grist. After the development of Babylonian beer in 7000 B.C.E., farmers enhanced revenues by diverting malted grain to vats in which they made 26 different brews. By 3000 B.C.E., the use of 40 percent of Babylonian cereal grains turned beer into a source of new social problems, inebriation and alcoholism.

Brewing flourished among Celts, Chinese, Germans, Iraqis, and Persians as well as North Africans. Nubian brewers in Sudan inadvertently produced antibiotic beer that included rudimentary tetracycline, a product of grain stored underground and contaminated with *Streptomyces* mold. In Egypt from 3150 B.C.E., predynastic citizens at El Omari, Faiyum, and Merimbole beni Salame learned to brew from Sumerian natural yeasting recipes. They valued emmer wheat for the era's staple cuisine, beer and sourdough bread.

Brewing gained economic and social significance at Heliopolis, Memphis, and Thebes, where vats maintained the microorganisms necessary to processing. Employers tended to pay workers in beer and groceries rather than cash. Around 1175 B.C.E., Ramses III endowed a large dole of beer and produce for artisans, priests, and tomb builders. On festival days around 1100 B.C.E., Egypt's royal pantry managers opened their storehouses to the public for unlimited distribution of beer to all petitioners, a political method of assuaging malcontents.

Funerary cults validated four types of beer as nourishment for the afterlife. A liquid power food called *bouza* (beer) resulted from steeping crushed loaves and water into mash in large resin-lined jars. Bouza so anchored the Egyptian cuisine that children carried skins of beer to school for lunch. Nutritional manuals named beer as a treatment for depression.

Beer flavored with herbs permeated the greater Mediterranean grain consumption of Greece, North Africa, Phoenicia, Rome, and Thrace. Herodotus's masterwork, *The Histories* (ca. 428 B.C.E.), credited the vigor of Egyptians to their addiction to barley beer. Around 100 B.C.E. in Mesoamerica, maguey (agave) beer entered Mexican gastronomy. Mexican cooks fermented agave heart into *pulque,* an indigenous beer that also served as a standard analgesic for adults and children. In Central American deserts, pulque rehydrated the body and heightened senses.

In the first century B.C.E., the posting of Roman legionaries throughout Africa, Asia Minor, and Europe introduced Italian men to regional beers, including the barley brew of Britannia's *tabernae* (pubs). After 100 C.E., the Roman Empire tapped Silk Road commodities in Alexandria, Egypt, and generated the first multicultural cuisine, which innkeepers offered at roadhouses. For expedience, the Emperor Trajan posted legionaries along the east-west highway to secure trade in Roman staples in exchange for Eastern beer, dairy products, and meat.

Medieval Innovations

Beginning in the Middle Ages, British and Scottish beech hedges produced fragrant mast for smoking beer and cheese. Both adults and children drank ale and beer, a culinary history reflected in the Finnish epic *Kalevala* (1835), a compilation of rural folk tradition of Scandinavian fen dwellers. Physicians fed beer sediment to anemic babies and lactating mothers. Hospitality from the eastern third of the Czech Republic featured artisanal beers and wines that influenced the cuisines of Austria, eastern Bohemia, Silesia, and western Slovakia. From the steppes west of the Ukraine, Russia's breadbasket, came cereal grains—barley, millet, rye, wheat—which reached markets as beer and grain products.

From the 800s C.E., growers protected their grain supply as a source of beer and bread. In *Capitulare de Villis* (*The Supervision of Manors,* ca. 800), an edict from Charlemagne, king of the Franks, ordered cleanliness in breweries, an industry that interested him personally. Moravian inns and pubs gained a reputation for hoisting a green bush to advertise a new run of dark beer, available at a reasonable price. Women embraced the tasks of the congregation kitchen with fervor, including soaking sour milk cheese in beer as a flavoring and preservative.

The Middle Ages introduced varied morning breaks with bitter hops beer, cheese, and oatcakes to feed laborers. In England, religious centers at Canterbury, Ely, Whitby, and Winchester gained fame for their brews, which bore alleged curative powers over leprosy and distension of the spleen. Priests substituted beer for holy water in baptismal fonts. At Burton-upon-Trent and along Italy's Po River in the 1000s, Benedictine and Cistercian monks, master brewers since the 600s, brushed cheese rinds with beer, brandy, brine, or saltwater to nourish mold, the type of crust and veining that distinguishes Brie and Limburger. The creation of a fuller morning meal elevated the worker's daily intake from two meals to three.

For good reason, medieval brewers fermented robust ales by building their vats next to bakeshops. By reusing starter from successful batches, they preserved zesty beer with flavorful yeast that initiated microorganisms in the next batch. Successful natural preservatives lengthened the time that ships could transport fresh kegs before they soured into vinegar. At a peak in the brewer's commerce in Holland and Belgium in the late thirteenth century, ships arrived up the Thames to London carrying as many as 200 casks of beer or wine each—in modern terms, 8,600 gallons (32,500 liters) per load.

Along the network of old Roman roads, organization of alehouses and coaching inns at the beginning of the Renaissance regulated brewed beverages. By the early 1500s, England's population of 2.7 million supported 17,000 pubs. In 1514, the Worshipful Company of Innholders unionized hostellers to better serve pilgrims and travelers. In 1516, William IV of Bavaria issued the first purity laws limiting additives to the basics—malt, water, and yeast.

New World Varieties

The New World entered the global beer business in the early sixteenth century. In the Bahamas and Cayman Islands, the Carib fermented manioc pulp into beer. Manioc also supplied South Americans with *chicha,* a coconut-flavored beer made from fiber chewed by brewers and fermented with salivary enzymes. Early in 1537 at Sorocotá, Juan de Castellanos's *Historia del Nuevo Reino de Granada (History of the New Kingdom of Spain,* 1886) reported on the Chibchan intake of bread made from roots and chicha. In the Peruvian Andes, Lima natives honored the sun god by pouring corn beer into a holy fountain. Poet and chronicler Garcilaso de la Vega's *Comentarios Reales de los Incas (The Royal Commentaries of the Incas,* 1609–1617) summarized the use of beer for nourishing the poor. Inca housewives organized a food collection feast of berry-flavored chicha and donated pantry goods.

To the north, because of the deft leadership of explorer John Smith, Londoners profited from investment in the first English settlement at Jamestown, Virginia. In February 1608, settlers, indentured to the company for seven years, immediately began brewing ale and beer from New World wheat. The drinks provided citizens with low-alcohol, bacteria-free beverages fermented according to northwestern European tradition.

The British maintained their dependence on brewing as an adjunct to cuisine. During the reign of James I, Scots in fishing communities poached eel and salmon in beer. Under the Puritan governance of Oliver Cromwell in 1650, however, religious prejudice against spirits forced beer drinkers to accept coffee as a breakfast beverage. The return of the monarchy in 1660 reestablished beer drinking as a national pleasure as well as a business in colonial Canada. In 1751, artist William Hogarth's sketch *Beer Street* satirized London's beer-sodden tipplers as pudgy and contented. By 1765, brewers industrialized the production process with the technological advances of hydrometers and thermometers.

At a time when shipboard provisions included alcoholic drinks, brewers in Alaska, Canada, New Zealand, and Norway flavored beer with spruce buds and greenery. Captain James Cook affirmed the belief that beer prevented scurvy. In 1766, during his four-year perusal of Newfoundland, his crew drank regular allotments of Canadian sugar-based spruce beer, an antiscorbutic known to Native Americans. The economical beverage was cheaper than lemon or lime antiscorbutics. Cooks on board the *Endeavour* brewed the drink from Sitka spruce (*Picea sitchensis*) using a recipe dating to the 1620s.

To feed Munich's 2,600 beggars, Count Rumford, an inventor and social strategist, established the Poor People's Institute in 1790. Calculating the maximum nutrition for the least expenditure, he concocted Rumford's Soup from barley, peas, and potatoes boiled in sour beer. To nourish the homeless, his feeding stations served beer-based soup three times a day. In a similar effort in Hawaii, after 1811, Andalusian horticulturist Francisco de Paula Marín became Hawaii's first commercial farmer and the first to recycle food by-products into beer. After 1832, German immigration boosted Cincinnati, Ohio, to a center of Teutonic beer. Honeymooners flocked to *Bierstuben* (beer halls) and inns. Tipplers from the University of Cincinnati gathered at the beer garden established by taverner Louis Mecklenburg.

The Ubiquitous Drink

Among North American immigrants, Hungarian, Jewish, and Scandinavian drinkers remained committed to mild birch beer or to lager beer, an alcoholic beverage brewed at low temperature. The cultural and religious mores of newcomer French, Germans, Irish, Italians, Jews, and Poles to North America validated a healthy respect for brandy, beer, and rum, often as additives to sauces and fruitcakes and a normal accompaniment to meals. In the federal period at Atlantic Coast oyster houses, travelers and workers washed down raw and fried bivalves with corn and pumpkin beer, maple sap, and persimmon beer, a brew of fruit with wheat bran. In this same period, the immigration of Eastern European and German brewers to the United States replaced cider with commercial beer.

An American tradition from colonial times, fermenting grain into beer brought distinction to commercial brew houses from Boston to Salt Lake City, Utah. Cities honored their brewmasters, coopers, and maltsters for distributing local beers, a mark of regional cuisine. In Poughkeepsie in New York's Hudson River valley, the Vassar Brewery dispensed 30,000 barrels per year. Some complexes, such as Bernhard Stroh's brewery in Detroit, Michigan; George Koenig Master Brewers in Cincinnati, Ohio; and Canandaigua in Victor, New York,

Modern American microbreweries, which produce high-quality craft beers and ales in relatively small quantities, follow in the long tradition of German, British, and Belgian artisanal brewing. *(Chuck Cook/Associated Press)*

recycled waste by making related products, including malt extract, near beer (alcohol content of 1 percent or less), and vinegar. To ensure quality, several breweries in St. Louis and San Francisco drew from spring water and stored kegs at a steady 55 degrees Fahrenheit (13 degrees Centigrade) above a system of sinkholes and natural limestone caverns or brick beer caves.

On the American frontier, saloons became the major distributors of brews. Beer halls drew lonely drovers, miners, and teamsters to sources of camaraderie, drinking, and entertainment from billiards, card playing, darts, music, and prostitution. The licensing of stand-alone bars and grog shops suited the demands of their clientele, mostly males who focused their social lives on alcohol and gambling. Drinks were cheap—a dime for a schooner of beer—and the ambience was limited to bare tables and chairs, brass spittoons, and floors covered in sawdust.

After the mid-1860s, an influx of ale, lager, malt liquor, pilsner, porter, steam beer, and stout drinkers from Czechoslovakia, Germany, Great Britain, and Poland created a beer culture that consumed 3.4 gallons (12.9 liters) per capita. The spirit of camaraderie and tippling increased tourism to festivals, such as American copies of Germany's Oktoberfest, the world's largest Volksfest, held in Munich, Bavaria, since 1810. To protect their interests during a period of temperance agitation, beer makers formed the U.S.

Brewers' Association to lobby legislators and the Bureau of Internal Revenue, which declared beer a luxury rather than a common beverage. By 1889, the U.S. Treasury levied $295,311,185 from brewers, a source of revenue to retire Civil War debts.

To satisfy local demand, German beer makers turned Brewerytown on the Schuylkill River in Philadelphia into the nation's prime brewing center. Farmers in Pennsylvania planted barley, hops, and soapwort, or bouncing bet (*Saponaria officinalis*), a common herb that stimulated froth. Malt houses stored bins of barley and malt, steeping tanks, and kilns. Wort masters left barrels of hops, malt, and water open in the brew house to encourage yeast to convert sugar into alcohol, the chemical change that determined flavor and alcohol content. By eliminating wild yeasts and spoilage bacteria, food processors applied pure spores to particular needs, such as pilsner beer, a pale Bohemian lager. After the Great Chicago Fire of October 8–10, 1871, Schlitz breweries in Milwaukee shipped barrels of beer and fresh water to survivors.

The first giant beer houses began operations in the late 1870s with Pabst in Milwaukee, Wisconsin, and Anheuser-Busch in St. Louis, Missouri. Industrialized brewing ensured jobs for bottle makers, brewmasters, grain vendors, keg builders, sugar refiners, yeast sellers, and van drivers, who delivered kegs directly to saloons and hotels. In St. Louis, Eberhard Anheuser, a prosperous German-born industrialist, established another U.S. beer dynasty and introduced pasteurization to protect Budweiser, a light Czech pilsner lager. For coast-to-coast transportation, his partner, Adolphus Busch of Kastel, Hesse, extended railroad icehouses and chilled freight cars. He introduced bottled beer, an innovative container that withstood humidity and climate change. By 1891, his vans had delivered more than 1 million barrels per year.

Prohibition

By 1890, the average American beer drinker put away 13.6 gallons (51.5 liters) per year. At Chicago, where alcohol generated one-quarter of city revenues, the Anti-Saloon League and the Woman's Christian Temperance Union crusaded for 70 years, making temperance a home and family issue. The backlash against a male social outlet did little to halt public consumption of beer, but it did sanction xenophobia against German, Italian, and Polish Catholics, for whom beer and wine defined cuisine and culture for men, women, and children.

In Britain, after Scots botanist Robert Fortune increased the profitability of the tea plantations of the British East India Company (BEIC), tea took precedence over beer, which the gentry castigated as a crude breakfast drink. Until competition from private companies forced dissolution of the BEIC in June 1874, the British monopoly commanded the planet's largest merchant navy and controlled half of world trade in such commodities as tea and beer. Anglo bureaucrats and soldiers in India popularized British pale ale, a highly hopped beverage from Allsopp brewery at Burton, England, which beer makers in Australia and North America imitated.

From passage on January 16, 1919, until repeal on December 5, 1933, the National Prohibition Act, or Volstead Act, impinged on the American wine and beer industries, which lagged until the revival of single-label brewpubs and craft beers in the 1980s. Since the early 1970s, the standard Tex-Mex entrée menu offers fajitas, a sizzling plate of marinated skirt steak with grilled peppers and onions, washed down with Corona beer or tequila. Patronage of local food markets supplies artisanal beers, cheese, and sausage to regional cafés and bistros. At Cinco de Mayo venues, hosts distribute barbecue, tacos, and pitchers of Mexican beer. Polish cooks simmer Lenten soup from beer thickened with crustless rye bread rubbed through a sieve. On St. Patrick's Day, bakeries shape cakes like shamrocks; barkeeps tint beer green, the traditional color of hope.

See also: Alcoholic Beverages; Manioc; Prohibition; Temperance; Yeast.

Further Reading

Hornsey, Ian Spencer. *A History of Beer and Brewing.* Cambridge, UK: Royal Society of Chemistry, 2003.
McFarland, Ben. *World's Best Beers: One Thousand Craft Brews from Cask to Glass.* New York: Sterling, 2009.
Mittelman, Amy. *Brewing Battles: A History of American Beer.* New York: Algora, 2008.
Nelson, Max. *The Barbarian's Beverage: A History of Beer in Ancient Europe.* New York: Routledge, 2005.
Sinclair, Thomas R., and Carol Janas Sinclair. *Bread, Beer and the Seeds of Change: Agriculture's Impact on World History.* Cambridge, MA: CABI, 2010.

Biopiracy

Biopiracy is the current term for the age-old theft and control of indigenous fungi, livestock, plants, and seeds for commercial exploitation. Plant and animal swapping and interbreeding is indigenous to agriculture, beginning with einkorn wheat from the Caucasus to China, Egypt, Europe, and India. Historically, such thievery dates to 1473 B.C.E., with Egyptian Pharaoh Hatshepsut's importation to Karnak from Somalia of myrrh and frankincense, natural resins for aromatic teas.

The purpose shifted to economic domination with the bioprospecting of Christopher Columbus in the Caribbean, the source of chilies, chocolate, corn, manioc, pawpaws, and tomatoes for Europe. Sanctioned on May 4, 1493, by Pope Alexander VI and his Bull of Donation, the series of voyages under the aegis of Spain's Ferdinand and Isabella extended the power of the Vatican as a Christian right granted to the "vicar of God," a forerunner of the concept of Manifest Destiny. As a result of colonial privilege, Portugal cornered the market on cloves, but it failed to monopolize nutmeg from the Banda Islands. The potato alone, one of about 180 food plants taken from the Quechua of Peru, nearly doubled the European head count between 1750 and 1850.

Trade Monopolies

After Scots trader and planter Charles Alexander Bruce introduced plants and seeds of *Camellia sinensis* tea from the Singhpo of Rangput, Assam, in 1834, the British East India Company (BEIC) launched a fleet of clipper ships to speed Indian beverages to Europe and the Americas. For the next 40 years, the British monopoly commanded the planet's largest merchant navy and controlled half of global trade in tea.

A similar transplantation occurred in Riverside, California, in 1870, when agronomist Eliza Tibbets grafted navel oranges (*Citrus sinensis*) from rootstock smuggled by missionaries from São Salvador de Bahia, Brazil. The successful orange, later called Sunkist, created an agricultural dynasty and fed the boom that advanced boxing, packing, and refrigerated rail transportation.

Monopolies grabbed unusual commodities for hoarding and profit—the Hawaiian taro, Thai jasmine rice, the breadfruit of Tonga, Colombian cassava, and the kakadu plum, bush tucker (bush food) among Australian Aborigines that the media billed as the world's richest source of vitamin C. In 1994, a Colorado firm hybridized and patented the Enola bean, a yellow legume that originated in Mexico; the lack of compensation robbed that nation of one of its biodiversified assets. A similar theft from Mexico occurred in 1999, when the Dutch corporation Quest International patented a substance found in *pozol,* a fermented corn drink invented by the Maya as early as 2000 B.C.E.

Looting began with the study of locations and climates for such marketable commodities. Late-twentieth-century prizes ranged from basmati rice and turmeric root from India and Pakistan to quinoa, a nutritious grain developed by the Inca of the Andes in Bolivia and Chile after 1200 C.E. In late April 2011, the illegal purchase of an Ongole bull from southeastern India represented an effort to increase milk yields at Brazilian dairies.

Ethics of Displacement

Only 10 percent of sustainable crops and livestock lie in the public domain. By patenting climate-ready crops capable of withstanding drought, flood, heat, and salt, such "gene giants" as Bayer, BASF, Ciba-Geigy, Dow, DuPont, Hoechst, Nestlé, Novartis, Syngenta, and Unilever claim rights to 77 percent of the foods of the future.

From the world's living treasures, scientists engineer and patent seeds, such as genetically altered soya and canola, an ingredient in confections, cooking oil, dairy products, ice cream, and margarine. The legal claim privatizes the plants as intellectual property and halts stock interbreeding and seed exchange, an essential among the wild rice growers of the Minnesota Chippewa and corn farmers in South Africa.

From these limitations have arisen international disputes between Japan and South Korean over *kimchi* and between the European Union and South Africa over grappa, a brandy first distilled from skins and pulp in Italy after 100 C.E. Compounding such ethical infractions, biopirates collect communal agricultural practice from shamans and villagers, an oral tradition of propagation and use. For example, the French company L'Oreal markets kava, a Fijian ceremonial beverage, to treat hair loss.

Hunting Grounds

Some 90 percent of native biota (flora and fauna) lies concentrated in the subtropics and tropics of preindustrial countries, most at the equator or in the Southern Hemisphere. Of the choice zones in Brazil, Congo, Costa Rica, Gabon, India, Indonesia, Mexico, the Philippines, and South Africa, Mexico contains 34 ecoclimates and an estimated 14.4 percent of the globe's living species. Historically, Mexicans domesticated 118 plants, notably corn. The countries most eager to control these living organisms include Australia, France, Great Britain, Germany, Holland, Japan, and the United States. Once companies develop these resources, the people in the original habitat lack funds to purchase the refined products.

Africa's wealth of edible plants and marine life dominates the cases of biopiracy currently under adjudication. Since 2000, eight varieties of groundnuts from Malawi, Mozambique, Nigeria, Senegal, and Sudan introduced wilt-resistant strains to farmers in Argentina and the United States, who paid nothing for appropriating the seed. In 2002, *hoodia,* an appetite-suppressing cactus valued by the Khoi and San bush people of South Africa, returned royalties from Pfizer, a British firm. Pfizer faced criticism for offering an unfair royalty in contrast to the plant's value for the control of obesity.

Because trademarking threatens the even distribution of nutrition worldwide, the United Nations continues to uphold food justice by thwarting the patent abuse that strips smallholders of food sovereignty. At a UN convention in Bonn, Germany, in 2008, the Coalition Against Biopiracy exposed theft by bestowing the Captain Hook Awards to shame capitalists for "pillaging the commons." Another effort in Norway, the Svalbard Global Seed Vault, completed on February 26, 2008, isolates seeds that existed before genetic modification and monopolies.

See also: Genetically Modified Food; Tea.

Further Reading

"Biopiracy: A New Threat to Indigenous Rights and Culture in Mexico." *New England Journal of International and Comparative Law* 7 (April 2001): 1–6.

Blakeney, Michael. *Intellectual Property Rights and Food Security.* Cambridge, MA: CABI, 2009.

Robinson, Daniel F. *Confronting Biopiracy: Challenges, Cases and International Debates.* Washington, DC: Earthscan, 2010.

Tansey, Geoff, and Tasmin Rajotte, eds. *The Future Control of Food: A Guide to International Negotiations and Rules on Intellectual Property, Biodiversity, and Food Security.* Sterling, VA: Earthscan, 2008.

Wynberg, Rachel, Doris Schroeder, and Roger Chennells. *Indigenous Peoples, Consent, and Benefit Sharing: Lessons from the San-Hoodia Case.* New York: Springer, 2009.

Biscuit

A ubiquitous travel bread for armies, navies, and expeditions, biscuit achieved its status as hardship rations for its stability on land and sea. Derived from Latin for "twice cooked," biscuit, called *biscotti* in Italian and *bizcocho* in Spanish, supplied pantries from ancient times with a clean, hard cracker. Egyptians baked the *dhourra* biscuit from millet and sorghum, a cheap sustenance for the underclass. Greeks used barley and chickpea flour, which they oven-dried and made chewable by soaking in oil or wine. The unleavened sea biscuit, or ship's biscuit, a dehydrated wafer of flour and water, earned the name *hardtack* for its toughness.

A recipe by culinary expert Apicius described the boiling of wheat flour for drying into hardened bars and serving with honey and pepper. In 77 B.C.E., Roman encyclopedist Pliny the Elder admired the bland biscuit for its impermeability by dampness and weevils. For military hardtack, legionary cooks double-baked *buccellatum* (biscuit) to issue to legionaries as *panis castrensis* (camp bread). As field pack food, the cracker traveled the Roman Empire, from Britannia and Germania to North Africa and Asia Minor.

Medieval Forms

Delivered in barrels, medieval biscuits anchored the hardy meals of the Irish and Scots; a lighter, more palatable variety fed Iberians. After 1189, Richard I, the Lionheart, departed on the Third Crusade with stores of "muslin biscuit" made from barley, bean, and rye flour. At the face-off with England by the Spanish Armada in 1588, Royal Navy recruits subsisted on a daily ration of a gallon (3.8 liters) of ale and a pound (450 grams) of biscuits, which consumers softened in brine, broth, coffee, milk, or wine. Subsequent fleet activity required stops at bakeries in Bombay and the Cape of Good Hope to replenish the ships' biscuit supply.

The French, who called their hard soldier's ration *pain biscuité* (twice-cooked bread), declared 3/4 pound (340 grams) of hardtack equal in nutrition to 1 pound of bread. They depended on it for a storable wartime food that remained edible for 30 days. Germans ate biscuits with stout to curb insomnia and biscuits soaked in wine to lessen gastric distress. Australian Aborigines and drovers cooked "damper," an unleavened bush bread heated on a baking stone in an earth oven. Another culinary method involved wrapping dough around sticks for cooking over a campfire and eating with smoked bacon.

Later History

British biscuit, baked in Carlisle, Deptford, Edinburgh, London, Norwich, Plymouth, and Reading, derived from a pressing machine invented in 1844 by T.T. Grant, storekeeper of the Royal Clarence Victualing Yard, Gosport. The device turned out wafers at the rate of 8,000 tons (7,300 metric tons) annually, each stamped with Queen Victoria's insignia. The single item formed a profitable export to Labrador, Newfoundland, and Nova Scotia as well as military supply to soldiers stationed in Cuba and Jamaica. Ships' surgeons treated dysentery with biscuit jelly, a boiled concoction of biscuits, cinnamon, sugar, and wine.

Captain's biscuit, a higher grade of wafer, earned more respect for its incorporation of butter, refined flour, and salt and for grilling into deviled biscuit, an hors d'oeuvre topped with anchovies and a cheese and mustard paste and peppered with cayenne. In 1771, Captain James Cook reported his biscuit supply remained edible for more than 36 months. Inmates in his brig survived for 30 days on nothing but hardtack. Sailors declared that the sound of teeth chewing sea biscuit resembled beans in a coffee mill.

In colonial North America, Theodore Pearson industrialized biscuit in 1792 at a bakery in Newburyport, Massachusetts. Along the New England coast, cooks made clam chowder by thickening cream-based clam soup with unsalted hardtack. On the frontier, families depended on bulk shipments of biscuits, dried beef, flour, grain, and salt. Shoppers snapped up fruit and sugary delicacies to enliven the daily cuisine of *pisco* (small birds) and tasteless wheat hardtack, made palatable by soaking in gravy, milk, or water. Alaskan camping and survival rations contained pilot bread, a high-energy biscuit served with applesauce and peanut butter.

By 1840, stamping machines increased biscuit making to use some six barrels of flour per day. Efficiency lowered the price for miners during the 1849 California gold rush and for workhouse inmates. Indians confined to desert reservations survived on canned beans and hardtack. At Fort Hays, Kansas, soldiers deserted because of cold, hunger, and illness from eating only bacon and hardtack, resulting in rampant scurvy. As commander of the Military Department of the Missouri, General Winfield Scott Hancock countered disease with antiscorbutics—servings of onions and potatoes to accompany military biscuit.

During the American Civil War, machine-rolled "Maryland biscuits" arrived from Baltimore to camp supply in 60-pound (27-kilogram) boxes. Soldiers complained that factories boxed biscuit too soon, causing it to mold and fill with larvae. By soaking a wafer in coffee or soup, a consumer could skim off the insects and find no change in the liquid flavor. While families in the North consumed apple pie with morning coffee, Union soldiers in the field soaked in water or coffee the biscuit left over from the Mexican War. General Ulysses S. Grant became so outraged by the quality of biscuit stacked among cargo at City Point, Virginia, that he refused the shipment.

Upon receipt of ten wafers per man per day, soldiers stored biscuit in their haversacks to keep it dry and used it as sandwich bread to hold raw "sow belly" (salt pork) or as a basis for stewed apples. They fried the squares in lard or leftover pork fat into "skillygalee," unimpressible by neglected teeth. Military cooks softened biscuit and stirred it into molasses and pork for a dish called "dandyfunck." While infantrymen toasted hardtack over the fire on a forked stick, they cherished memories of their mothers' cooking. Wealthier soldiers bought condensed milk or sugar to spread on biscuit.

Biscuit accompanied French social reformer François de la Rochefoucauld on his travels among the Canadian Iroquois in 1795, explorer John Lewis Burckhardt into

Nubia in 1819, the Turks into Arabia in 1829, and General Charles Gordon's men to the Siege of Khartoum, Sudan, in 1884. British beef burger, meat pasty, and sausage makers added biscuit to the meat mix to bind ingredients and hold moisture. During the Boer War, soldiers survived on rusk biscuits and coffee, which softened the crusts. In 1909, for the arduous trek to the Arctic Circle, Robert Peary carried only hardtack as bread to eat with condensed milk, pemmican, and tea.

In 1911, the U.S. military replaced hardtack with field bread. Industrialists augmented the basic recipe with the flavors of almonds, cinnamon, ginger, lemon, mace, nutmeg, orange, and vanilla. Biscuit survives in Dutch rusks eaten with lightly fermented grape juice and German zwieback, a common teething biscuit fed to infants. In Edinburgh, Scots bakers perpetuate the recipe for Abernethy biscuit, a digestive aid recommended by vegans and vegetarians. In 1888, Dr. John Abernethy devised the wafer to contain sugar for energy and caraway seeds for metabolism.

See also: Crackers; Seaman's Diet and Cuisine.

Further Reading

Dupree, Nathalie, and Cynthia Graubart. *Southern Biscuits.* Layton, UT: Gibbs Smith, 2011.

Haber, Barbara. *From Hardtack to Home Fries: An Uncommon History of American Cooks and Meals.* New York: Free Press, 2002.

Vilas, James. *Biscuit Bliss: 101 Foolproof Recipes for Fresh and Fluffy Biscuits in Just Minutes.* Boston: Harvard Common Press, 2003.

Volo, Dorothy Denneen, and James M. Volo. *Daily Life in Civil War America.* 2nd ed. Santa Barbara, CA: Greenwood, 2009.

Blenders and Food Processors

The technology of emulsification and pureeing of wet ingredients increased the cook's control of mouthfeel, taste, and texture, particularly in recipes involving hard grains, seeds, ice, or frozen ingredients. Bar, home, and restaurant models of blenders made possible batters and purees for infant and invalid diets, emulsification of hummus and mayonnaise, smooth dips and gravies, and specialty drinks—daiquiris, frosted mocha mixes, fruit slushies, and yogurt smoothies. Handheld immersion blenders simplified the preparation of cream soups, pesto, and spreads and enabled preparers to concentrate on small areas needing intense coalescing, such as beet vinaigrette, Caesar salad dressing, and hazelnut butter.

The blender design of Polish-born inventor Stephen John Poplawski in 1922 in Racine, Wisconsin, outper-

formed the meat grinder and stand mixer. The inventor encased a spinning blade in an aluminum or glass carafe securely capped at the top and sealed with rubber gaskets at both openings. Blending was less dangerous to the hands than crinkle-cutting and dicing with a wire mandoline or shredding lime zest or potatoes for latkes with a box grater or microplane.

Milk Shakes and Health Foods

In 1933, one-switch control made possible the popular frappe or milk shake at confectionaries, dime stores, ice cream parlors, and pharmacies. Operation became the specialty of the soda fountain clerk, called a "soda jerk." Decades of improvements to Hamilton Beach and Waring blenders enabled cooks to can and freeze foods prepared at variant speeds and to simplify the production of an ulcer diet.

Domestic equipment preceded the Dairy Queen soft-serve machine, an automatic large-batch blender that produced its first milk shake in 1940 in Joliet, Illinois. The company pioneered a faster emulsification of milk shake ingredients by using a creamier base for flavoring with chocolate, fruit, and vanilla syrups. The concept spawned Baskin-Robbins, Tastee Freez, and TCBY, which replaced ice cream with yogurt.

In Cleveland, Ohio, in 1949, W.G. Barnard introduced the Vitamix blender through the first televised infomercials aimed at caterers, coffee shops, cooking schools, hospitals, nightclubs, and restaurant chains. He demonstrated the use of a durable 3-horsepower motor to chop salsa and tapenade, grind coffee beans, juice root vegetables, and mix frozen desserts. Interchangeable agitators and pulse control extended the range of ingredients the Vitamix could flash blend, from delicate melon pulp for coulis and sorbet to tough cabbage leaves for chilled vegetable drinks and horseradish for hot dips.

The raw and health food movements of the late 1960s broadened interest in the swirling of peeled and unpeeled fruits and vegetables into broth, ice, milk, tea, and yogurt. At health food stores and milk bars, customers joined preparers in selection of nutritional supplements, including flax meal, gluten-free grains, herbs, nori, *spirulina,* sprouts, and whey powder.

Food Processing

Extending the closed-canister concept of blending in convenience cookery, in 1960, French caterer Pierre Verdun broadened the food maceration chores accomplished by a fixed blade in his Robot-Coupe. In 1976, New York engineer Carl G. Sontheimer patented the Cuisinart, an adaptable food mill that outpaced the blender.

The introduction of separate blades in a wide bowl for chopping cucumbers, grating cheese, grinding allspice, kneading pasta dough, pureeing strawberries, shredding cabbage, and slicing potatoes revolutionized food preparation. The use of feed tubes enabled the preparer to merge additional ingredients while blending, such as carrots into cabbage slaw and eggs into cookie dough.

See also: Fads; Oils.

Further Reading

Cole, David John, Eve Browning, and Fred E.H. Schroeder. *Encyclopedia of Modern Everyday Inventions.* Westport, CT: Greenwood, 2003.

Rodnitzky, Donna Pliner. *Low-Carb Smoothies: More Than 135 Recipes to Satisfy Your Sweet Tooth Without Guilt.* New York: Random House, 2005.

Smith, Andrew F., ed. *The Oxford Companion to American Food and Drink.* New York: Oxford University Press, 2007.

Sobey, Edwin J.C. *The Way Kitchens Work.* Chicago: Chicago Review, 2010.

Blueberries

From the exploration of North America by Europeans, newcomers from Alaska and Labrador to the Gulf Coast learned to value wild crops of blue-black berries indigenous to the continent. Berry bushes spread from deer, bear, and bird droppings and flourished on thornless shrubs in the forest understory amid the humus along streams and wet leas. From 11,000 B.C.E., Paleo-Indians ate berries raw, dried or smoked them, and used them to season venison, in stew and *sautauthig* (cornmeal pudding), and as a dye and medicines. Blueberry juice soothed coughs; its dried roots produced a tea to relax the muscles during childbirth. Amerindians prized the tiny pome fruit as a sweetener in cooking and an additive to deer fat and venison in the making of pemmican. By the mid-1800s, the availability of cane sugar increased interest in the tart berries, which canners in Cherryfield, Maine, sold to Union provisioners during the Civil War.

Hybrid blueberries were one of the few fruits introduced to the commercial market in the nineteenth century. Quaker fruit specialist and hybridizer Elizabeth Coleman "Lizzie" White earned the moniker "Mother of Cultivated Blueberries" and "The Blueberry Queen" for introducing the wild highbush blueberry to North American commercial farmers as a money crop. Near a 3,000-acre (1,200-hectare) cranberry bog, she grew up at Whitesbog farm in New Lisbon, New Jersey, a farm pioneered by her grandfather, Colonel James A. Fenwick. She taught herself cultivation of what locals called "huckleberries" and French Canadians called "bluets," a bush fruit indigenous to the acidic sand-peat loam of New England and north-central North America. After completing her schooling at the Friends Central School in Philadelphia, she studied at Drexel University.

On her own, White studied both swamp and upland berry bushes and handpicked the fruit in search of a money crop. She experimented with berry cultivation to produce no-waste fruit ready for picking in late June through mid-September and requiring no removal of seeds or hulls. Through self-education, she learned of the difficulty of domestic transplanting of wild root stock or growth from seed and of the importance of native blueberries to beekeeping and wild animal diets.

In addition to promoting bush cultivation by grafting and sucker propagation in low night temperatures, White sought cultivars producing fruit at least 3/4 inch (1.9 centimeters) in diameter for hand pollination to yield a berry 1 inch (2.5 centimeters) in diameter. She also researched means of protecting plants from katydid infestation. For the fruit industry, she issued a handbook on the culture of the cranberry (*Vaccinium oxycoccos*), a native fruit akin to the bilberry (*Vaccinium ericaceae*) and blueberry (*Vaccinium corymbosum* or *Vaccinium australe*).

Creative Hybridizing

In 1911, White collaborated with botanist Frederick Vernon Coville, author of "Experiments in Blueberry Culture" (1911). Over the next 20 years at the test plantation in Burlington County, New Jersey, the two devised ways of growing and selling the intraspecific hybrids of native blueberry, a flavorful light-blue fruit featuring small seeds. From interviews with woodsmen and hunter-gatherers in New Jersey's Pine Barrens, she identified qualities in variant strains in order to determine flavor, ripening time, and sustainability.

Research and cash bounties of up to $3 each for the largest berries in a 20-mile (32-kilometer) radius isolated the Rubel, a large, late-season cultivar suited to marketing that became White's keystone of blueberry breeding. By cross-fertilization, she developed Tru-Blu-Berries, the continent's first marketable blueberry. In 1916, she shipped the first 21 bushels of commercial fruit. For the propagation of the indigenous berry at Suningive, her 90-acre (36-hectare) bog nursery, and for promoting a complementary crop to cranberry growers, she became the first female farmer recognized by the New Jersey Department of Agriculture.

At her berry farm, White harvested 20,000 barrels of fruit annually from the Cabot, Katherine, and Pioneer strains, which sold well to hotels, restaurants, produce stores, and steamboat lines in Baltimore, Boston, and Philadelphia. She marketed rootstock in Connecticut, Michigan, New York, and North Carolina and introduced culture of the box or evergreen berry (*Vaccinium ovatum*) in northern California, Oregon, Washington State, and the Fraser Valley of British Columbia, the prime distributor of highbush berries. Her nursery pioneered the use of cellophane for packaging berries. In addition to being the first female member of the American Cranberry Association and, in 1927, the cofounder of the New Jersey Blueberry Cooperative Association, she published her findings in *Success* magazine and received honoraria from the horticultural societies of Massachusetts and Pennsylvania. By 1928, White had gathered 27,000 blueberry seedlings suitable for cross-pollinating.

Wonder Berry

White's fostering of the native berry helped to spread commercial farming on land unsuited to grain and vegetable culture. The dryland or lowbush *Vaccinium pallidum* and *Vaccinium Rubel* thrived from West Virginia to Minnesota and Wisconsin as far north as Quebec. The highbush rabbiteye (*Vaccinium ashei*) grows on stock as high as 15 feet (4.57 meters) in Mississippi, Texas, the Carolinas, Georgia, and Florida as far south as the Gulf of Mexico and to Argentina, Chile, China, South Africa, and Uruguay. Leading the United States in blueberry exportation, Maine flourished as the lowbush grower of the cold-hardy *Vaccinium augustifolium* and Michigan as the highbush center, producing plants from 3 to 10 feet (0.9 meter to 3 meters) tall. Additional sources of berries include the drought-tolerant mountain berry (*Vaccinium membranaceum*) from New Brunswick, Norway, Nova Scotia, and Prince Edward Island.

In the 1930s, Germany and Holland entered the competition for marketing hybrid blueberries, which spread in popularity to Austria, France, Hungary, Italy, Mexico, Poland, and Turkey. Merchants sold them under the names *bluets* (Canada), *bolleber* (Denmark), Pemberton *bilberry* (Finland), *airelle, myrtile, myrtillier* (France), *bosbes* (Holland), *mirtillo néro* (Italy), and *blea-berry* (Scotland). By the 1970s, the introduction of imported U.S. stock to Australia and New Zealand initiated a vigorous competitor from the Southern Hemisphere for production of frozen and dried berries, blueberry juice and purée, and jam and jelly, cobblers and pies, ice cream and dairy drinks, wine, salads and compotes, and additions to breakfast cereal, scones, muffins, cheesecake, and pastry fillings.

The blueberry won the regard of nutritionists as a superfood for its antioxidant value and for its protection of the brain. As of 2005, the U.S. blueberry crop approached $180 million in value. From the research of Amy Howell and Nicholi Vorsa at Rutgers University, publicity of the blueberry's value as an antioxidant and anti-inflammatory increased its value in Japan, Korea, and Taiwan in anticancer, anticholesterol, and antisenility diets. The fruit earned the nickname "brain berry," suggested by plant physiologist Mary Ann Lila Smith at the University of Illinois. Uncooked berries also enhance the regimens recommended for depression, hepatitis C, and high blood pressure and hinder blood clotting in strokes and the onset of Alzheimer's disease, bladder infections, and macular degeneration.

See also: Canning; New World Commodities; Pemmican; Refrigeration.

Further Reading

Draper, A. "Blueberry Breeding: Improving the Unwild Blueberry." *Journal of the American Pomological Society* 61:3 (2007): 140–143.

Harrison, Charles Hampton. *Tending the Garden State: Preserving New Jersey's Farming Legacy.* New Brunswick, NJ: Rivergate, 2007.

Minick, Jim. *The Blueberry Years: A Memoir of Farm and Family.* New York: Thomas Dunne, 2010.

Trehane, Jennifer. *Blueberries, Cranberries, and Other Vacciniums.* Portland, OR: Timber, 2004.

Boré, Jean Étienne de (1742–1820)

The founder of the Mississippi River delta sugar industry, Creole planter Jean Étienne de Boré de Mauléon revolutionized the dangerous job of boiling cane juice into crystallized sugar and broke the West Indian sugar monopoly.

Born to French nobility in Kaskaskia, Illinois, on December 27, 1742, he was the grandson of Robert de Boré, a postmaster and counselor to Louis XIV. From age four, Jean de Boré studied in Normandy and attended a military academy. At age 16, he entered the royal palace guard of Louis XV and advanced to captain of the Black Musketeers. Three years later in Paris, he married Marie Marguerite D'Estrehan des Tours, an heiress to land in the French colony of Louisiana.

In 1776, de Boré settled his family on a land grant in St. Charles Parish, a self-sustaining compound north of a loop of the Mississippi River. Risking his inheritance, he cultivated indigo and tobacco north of New Orleans, which was then an unimpressive colonial outpost. The loss of his slaves to malaria and his fields to wind damage and chenille worm infestation forced him to introduce a new crop.

With the aid of Antoine Morin, an industrialist from Santo Domingo's sugar plantations, de Boré introduced a hardy sugarcane in 1794 with seed he purchased from Brazil. On reclaimed swampland, he invested $4,000 in a drying shed and mill. He commanded his 40 male and female slaves with military precision. The following year, he introduced the *chaudron du sucre* (sugar kettle), a lidded reduction chamber that turned cane juice into granulated sugar and molasses. In 1796, his 100 hogsheads of cane sugar sold for 12.5 cents per pound (0.45

kilograms) and molasses for 12.5 cents per quart (0.95 liters), earning de Boré $12,000. Louisianans proclaimed him a savior.

Within one year, local planters shifted from indigo to top quality sugar and introduced the nation's first agro-industrial complex. Over 450,000 acres (182,000 acres) of 23 state parishes, the total income produced a multimillion-dollar industry. By 1801, Louisiana developed its prime location on a sea-lane and exported 500 tons (450 metric tons) of sugar per year. Applying science and technology, planters continued testing West Indian varieties of cane and methods of condensing its juice into sugar with bagasse (cane waste) as fuel. In 1802, de Boré achieved his largest crop, 40 tons (36 metric tons), which sold for 15 cents per pound.

In the final three weeks of French possession in 1803, Napoleon Bonaparte appointed de Boré as New Orleans's first mayor. A supporter of experimental crops and profit, de Boré cofounded the Bank of Louisiana. Under U.S. administration, he accepted appointment to the municipal legislative council and helped lead the movement for Louisiana statehood, achieved in 1812.

By tripling its slave population, New Orleans quadrupled its export trade and dominated the European sugar market. The success doubled the South's crops by adding sugar to "King Cotton." The demand for field labor derived from rapid depletion of workers to snake and alligator bites and machete accidents. The misery of cane fieldwork inspired the slave plaint of "sold down the river," a sure sentence of death.

At age 70, de Boré joined the press for Louisiana statehood. At that time, over a radius of 14 miles (23 kilometers), some 70 plantations on both banks of the Mississippi enriched the area with profits from 600 tons (540 metric tons) of sugar per year. Statehood brought a flood of slaves and American immigrants to work the cane fields and sugar refineries.

De Boré died on February 1, 1820, and was buried at Saint Louis Cemetery in New Orleans. His original sugar kettle remains on display at Louisiana State University in Baton Rouge.

See also: Creole Diet and Cuisine; Sugar and Sweeteners.

Further Reading

Alexander, Leslie M., and Walter C. Rucker, eds. *Encyclopedia of African American History.* Santa Barbara, CA: ABC-Clio, 2010.

Jones, Terry L. *The Louisiana Journey.* Salt Lake City, UT: Gibbs Smith, 2007.

Rodrigue, John C. *Reconstruction in the Cane Fields: From Slavery to Free Labor in Louisiana's Sugar Parishes, 1862–1880.* Baton Rouge: Louisiana State University Press, 2001.

Vernet, Julien. "More Than Symbolic: Pierre Clement de Laussat's Municipal Council and French Louisianian Protest Against American Territorial Government." *French Colonial History* 4 (2003): 133–144.

Borlaug, Norman
See Hybridization

Bouillon

A nourishing French broth or stock, bouillon captures in a single pot the aroma of herbs, the flavors of mirepoix, and the meaty zest of anchovies, beef, ham, mutton, ox, poultry, or shellfish. Stock makers begin with knuckle and marrow bones and boil the meat with fragrant allspice, bay leaf, garlic, onion, parsley, and thyme. According to Apicius, a Campanian food writer during the reign of the Emperor Tiberius, reducing broth, called *brodo* in Italian, required hours of slow simmering to marry flavors. A lighter recipe, called court bouillon (French for "short boil"), relies on minced herbs and vegetables in water or wine for a liquid in which to poach seafood.

Historically, bouillon referred to the herbed liquid in which cooks boiled or poached food. In Persia, the Sassanians of the third to the seventh century C.E. favored intense flavors, including ox meat simmered in beef bouillon. In the 800s, the Magyar horsemen of Hungary returned from swift winter gallops through the Ural Mountains to sip warming bouillon.

A staple basis of bisques, cereal grain or legume soup, creamy vichyssoise, French onion soup, glazes, gravy and sauce, and Russian borscht, bouillon became a regular restorative for religious fasts and an offering of street vendors, who heated stock in bulge pots (rounded kettles) over charcoal braziers. Bouillon softened the hard bread of prisoners and soldiers and strengthened the flavor of dumplings, pasta, or rice with the richness of bone marrow. A vegetarian version featured almonds and other nuts, eggs, mushrooms, tomatoes, and root vegetables. Cooks dried the stock on flannel until it formed a gel or strained the liquid through a broth napkin or sieve to yield a nourishing beverage for infants, invalids, and patients recovering from abdominal surgery. Hosts could choose to separate solids from bouillon just before serving to clarify a consommé.

Western European food writing recounted cookery in 1375, when Taillevent cited the intricacies of preparing beef bouillon. With a basic stock, cooks coated capons and stirred up black pudding, and grillers soaked brochettes before heating. In *Le Cuisinier François* (*The French Cook,* 1651), chef Pierre La Varenne systemized clear recipe ingredients and temperatures and codified methods of creating bouillon. His detailed instruction covered the bundling of herbs into a *bouquet garni* (garnished bouquet) for accentuating the aroma of reductions.

By the early eighteenth century, menus featured bouillon, either chilled or hot, accompanied by croutons as an introductory course to heavier entrées. In *The History of the Dividing Line Betwixt Virginia and North Carolina* (1728), William Byrd, the founder of Richmond, Virginia, recommended an on-the-trail snack of dried bouillon for quick energy. In 1765 in Paris, vintner A. Boulanger opened a bistro devoted to bouillon and *pot-au-feu* under the title *restaurant* (restoring), a dispenser of *restoratifs*. Refined buyers dipped soup from a tureen and ate their servings with long-handled soupspoons. The addition of chard to the stock tenderized leaves.

The industrial processing of dehydrated bouillon into a tiny cube, granules, or a lozenge offered convenience and transportability for the camper, home cook, and traveler. Filtration before drying ensured a product free of bacteria and mold. When rehydrated in sherry, vermouth, vinegar, water, or wine, the cube injected bouquet, heavy salt, and seasonings into beverages, casseroles, and chowders. Reduction of fluids resulted in a gel that dried rapidly in low humidity. Introduced in 1750s as defatted cake soup, meat extract, pocket soup, portable soup, quick soup, or veal blue, bouillon bolstered the pantries of ships' galleys and expeditionary tent kitchens with a shelf stable flavoring.

In 1756, English pharmacist William Cookworthy and his partner, a Mrs. Dubois of London, sold their thick soup-based cakes and paste to the Royal Navy as an alleged antidote to scurvy. Captain James Cook included bouillon in his supplies in 1768, when he commanded the HMS *Endeavour* on four expeditions to the Pacific. Subsequent stores of bouillon fed the crew of Meriwether Lewis and William Clark in 1804 on their exploration of the Missouri River and the Pacific Coast. In 1824, American idea man Peter Cooper developed the by-products of a New York abattoir into a domestic gelatin or portable soup for the convenience of housewives who had no time for the lengthy simmering of French-style bouillon.

Late-nineteenth-century culinary handbooks, such as Russian compiler Elena Burman Molokhovets's *A Gift to Young Housewives* (1861), detailed the lengthy processing of bouillon ingredients, beginning with the hand mincing of beef. In an 1863 recipe from French compiler Pierre Blot's *What to Eat and How to Cook It,* broth was the beginning of a pureed potage of mashed beans or peas. In Louisiana in 1880, a Bavarian immigrant, Madame Elizabeth Kettnring Dutrey Bégué, opened a coffeehouse in New Orleans's French Quarter and introduced brunch, a relaxed midmorning repast, with cups of court bouillon. By 1882, Swiss manufacturer Julius Maggi marketed inexpensive bouillon in cubes, the forerunner of instant soups and ramen packets.

See also: La Varenne, Pierre; Monosodium Glutamate; Russian Diet and Cuisine; Soups.

Further Reading

Dalby, Andrew. *Food in the Ancient World from A to Z.* London: Routledge, 2003.

Rumble, Victoria R. *Soup Through the Ages: A Culinary History with Period Recipes.* Jefferson, NC: McFarland, 2009.

Scully, D. Eleanor, and Terence Scully. *Early French Cookery: Sources, History, Original Recipes, and Modern Adaptations.* Ann Arbor: University of Michigan Press, 2002.

Toussaint-Samat, Maguelonne. *A History of Food.* Hoboken, NJ: Wiley-Blackwell, 2009.

Bread

The ingenuity of bread makers contributes a vital chapter to global food history. Emmer wheat, first domesticated around 17,000 B.C.E., served preparers as a source of a dense, high-fiber bread, which they grated into soup as a thickener. Hand grain milling, the world's oldest food industry, refined the flavor and palatability of bread flour and meal. After 9000 B.C.E., the domestication of wild einkorn wheat in southeastern Turkey prefaced the spread of dough recipes and bread artistry to Israel, Cyprus, India, Greece, and Crete. Wheat grain formed a weak mass that nomads shaped around a spit and bakers dropped onto hot surfaces for a quick wafer to accompany meat and vegetables.

The inflating action of yeast on dough intensified during processing and baking, creating the first risen bread. Yeast thrived on wheat gluten and augmented the versatility of high-protein dough. Leavening puffed air pockets in dough that gave the browned crust an elastic texture and nutty taste. In Gaul and Iberia, the kneading of dough from foamy beer produced batches of light, springy bread, the forerunner of sourdough.

Egyptian bakers pioneered leavened bread and produced light, chewy loaves, which the Greeks and Romans emulated. With the arrival of Alexander the Great to Alexandria in 332 B.C.E., emmer wheat gave place to durum wheat, a gluten-rich grain that baked into tight bread webbing. Greek cooks traditionally shaped dough into unleavened loaves that they baked in an oven and iced with honey. For elegant dinners, they fried wheat batter into drop biscuits or baked pancakes in crockery or under ash.

In Rome, the highest grade grain produced the whitest, tastiest rolls and loaves, the bread of the patrician class. After 27 B.C.E., bakers of the Roman Empire abandoned hard-hulled wheat for free-threshing bread wheat, the source of pie crusts and white loaves. With the spread of Christianity, bread for the Eucharist ritual took on a sacramental symbolism. Early medieval Italian bakers inscribed round loaves and buns with religious symbols. Around 1000 C.E., Scandinavian voyagers kneaded fibrous masses of barley, oats, and spelt into loaves for baking at the hearth or slathering

An illuminated page from the *Tacuinum Sanitatis,* a fourteenth-century handbook on health and well-being, depicts a baker putting loaves of dough into an oven. A simple, inexpensive, highly adaptable food, leavened wheat bread dates to around 3000 B.C.E. *(Alinari/Getty Images)*

on pottery shards for shardbread, the forerunner of shortbread.

Western Hemisphere

In the New World's agrarian culture, bakers valued the *duma,* a greased, convex soapstone or steatite slab, for cooking delicate, thin piki bread, a relative of the tortilla. The ash-blue corn batter rapidly conformed to the stone and baked into a crispy flatbread or corn chip. Piki anchored the diet with a carbohydrate finger food and utensil for scooping bites of salsa, mush, beans, and minced meat.

Until the introduction of metal cookware, Southwestern bakers made pones and tortillas on round stones, which they heated at a fire pit. At the Acoma Pueblo west of Albuquerque, New Mexico, cooks shaped their thin *mut-tze-nee* bread over hot loaf-sized stones; during long journeys, Choctaw cooks made flat corn cakes on portable baking slabs. The Zuñi crisped corn cakes by rubbing the bake stone with oil and resin to refine and lubricate the surface. Food workers so respected their stone griddles that they reduced their voices to a whisper to keep the dumas from cracking.

Unlike the Zuñi and other North American and Mesoamerican tribes that baked bread in concave slabs,

the Havasupai, who lived near the Grand Canyon, heated flat griddle stones in the fire, pulled them aside for cooking piki corn cakes, and then discarded the stones. Easy removal of the thin, curved bread required slicking the surface with pumpkin seed oil or suet. Handfuls of gruel sizzled on the surface and curled at the rim. The cook quickly pulled up edges and peeled the flexible corn wafer from the heat source before folding and rolling the bread into a convenient size and shape for holding juicy toppings.

Native American cooks also parboiled white corn grain in a covered vessel with slaked lime or wood ash as a preparation for bread making. The alkaline solution dissolved the grain's niacin bound in the endosperm by softening the outer shell and releasing a nutrient essential to well-being. Cherokee cooks made cornmeal into bean bread, a dough moistened with bean broth and augmented with sweet potato or squash pulp or nuts and seeds.

A pragmatic use of fire and rock, the hot stone method occurred in other cultures and under other names, for example, the Corsican *focolàre,* a baking stone heated over a hardwood fire for shaping *mullade,* a large crepe to eat with fresh goat curd cheese and fruit or jam. Among the Andaman Islanders in the Indian Ocean, cooks used hot rocks to make chapatis, a round, unleavened flatbread favored on the Indian subcontinent for wrapping fillings. On the plains outside Dayr az Zahrani, Lebanon, Bedouin cooks, seated barefoot in small work spaces, heated traditional unleavened bread in thin cakes spread over a convex cooking surface. The shape required little fuel for turning flattened dough balls into floury bowls to contain other elements of the meal.

Middle Ages

In the 1300s, English bakers recycled ale barm as a leavening for bread and for an egg batter fried into "cryspeys," a forerunner of the bagel, doughnut, fritter, funnel cake, and pretzel. During the late Middle Ages, the affluent bourgeois supped on manchet (soft wheat loaves), a slab that soaked up gravy and vegetable juices. At the end of a feast, hosts distributed the bread sops to the poor. For serfs, snacks of barley beer and oatcakes introduced the workers' breakfast, which initiated consumption of a third daily meal. The baking of batter bread enabled Scots troopers to enjoy hot, fresh oat bread on their march into Northumberland, while English soldiers had to make do on cold, unpalatable biscuit prepared in advance and stored in warehouses for military use. Because bread evolved into the essential comfort food, the loss of a baker to accident or epidemic devastated villagers until a replacement trained for the job.

The availability and cost of bread in the Middle Ages presented the peasant with a constant struggle. In 1266, the Assize of Bread and Ale ended the feast-or-famine cycle by stabilizing prices based on the cost of wheat. Such sumptuary laws limited profiteering and allowed the wealthy to consume 3 pounds (1.4 kilograms) daily of *paindemayne* (hand bread), a springy white loaf limited to wheat flour. By the beginning of the Renaissance, the dukes of Saxony regulated the supply of bread to artisans for breakfast and the evening meal. On pilgrimages to holy sites, European travelers packed cheese wedges and flatbread for travel food.

Nineteenth Century to the Present

On the North American frontier, hearth-style pones served native Canadian trappers, berry pickers, and lumberers. European settlers of the plains centered cookery on ashcake, johnnycake (or journeycake), and mock oysters (corn fritters), all convenient pocket or saddlebag meals. For native bread, camp cooks blended dough from wild rice flour to flatten on preheated rocks balanced over an open fire. Into the 1900s, flat bannocks, a moist bread with crisp crust, came in such varied forms as raisin bread, scones, and cheese biscuits.

During the Industrial Revolution, commercial bakers evolved softer wheat bread and pastries graced with a less fibrous, more elastic crumb. Immigrants to North America marveled at the contrast between Old World bread recipes and the refined slices of sandwich bread bought from a store. Housewives rummaged grocery stores in vain to find European types of flours for shaping of German-Jewish rye loaves and challah bread.

While the industrialized world flourished from better, cheaper, and more fuel-efficient bake ovens, rural Armenia doubled home heating as a form of bread making. One unusual dining arrangement involved the stoking of a *tonir* (pit oven), a ceramic cache similar to the tandoor oven of India, that held the coals at bottom with ashes spread on top. The stove chamber baked dough along the walls into *lavash* (bread) for eating with dried vegetables and raisins. While awaiting their meal, the family sat on top of the oven to keep warm.

After the processing of commercial yeast cakes in 1825, bakeries advanced the springy loaf with larger air cells. In Boston, the Parker House Hotel invented a yeast roll that commercial processors emulated. In 1912, Missouri inventor Otto Frederick Rohwedder standardized bread slices by inventing an automatic slicing machine. By the 1900s, grocery shelves displayed so wide a variety of dinner breads, sandwich buns, muffins, and holiday loaves that many homemakers abandoned the art of bread making. To American grain products, ethnic bakers added breakfast brioche and croissants, tortillas, naan, pitas, bagels, chapati, matzoh, and focaccia, an Italian yeast bread flavored with olive oil, tomatoes, and onions.

A mid-1970s health movement alerted diners to the absence of nutrition and fiber in carbohydrate-rich white bread made from over-milled, bleached flour. The Real Bread Campaign urged advocates of a wholesome diet to seek wholemeal grain bread. Commercial bakers supplied variety in selections of ciabatta, rice cakes, seven-grain loaves, African sorghum loaves, Mexican corn bread, and sourdough loaves. Twenty-first-century bakers also devise artisanal products from ancient grains that answer the need for gluten-free breads and pastries.

See also: Biscuit; Einkorn Wheat; Emmer Wheat; Linnaeus, Carolus; Manioc; Milling; Seaman's Diet and Cuisine; Sourdough; Tortillas; Tudor Diet and Cuisine; Yeast.

Further Reading
Cauvain, Stanley P. *Bread Making: Improving Quality.* Boca Raton, FL: CRC, 2003.
Preedy, Victor R., Ronald R. Watson, and Vinood B. Patel. *Flour and Breads and Their Fortification in Health and Disease Prevention.* Boston: Academic Press, 2011.
Rayner, Lisa. *Wild Bread: Hand-Baked Sourdough Artisan Breads in Your Own Kitchen.* Flagstaff, AZ: Lifeweaver, 2009.
Scully, Terence. *The Art of Cookery in the Middle Ages.* Rochester, NY: Woodbridge, 2005.

Breadfruit

A tender staple of Belize, the Caribbean, Oceania, and Southeast Asia, breadfruit (*Artocarpus altilis*) is an heirloom carbohydrate of the tropics. Trees fruit abundantly eight months of the year, usually in clumps of three. Whole breadfruit is highly perishable and requires storage in water. Unripe, it roasts within an hour in open fires and yields slices for pickling or eating raw.

Cultivated on the Moluccas and New Guinea around 2500 B.C.E., the heavy-fruiting plant once fed elephants in the wilds of Southeast Asia. It traveled as root cuttings over a 2,250-year span with Lapita voyagers to Melanesia, Fiji, Tonga, and Samoa. Grown up to 12 pounds (5.4 kilograms) on coral atolls and in well-drained soils, the pineapple-sized fruit was once the prize entrée of chiefs and royalty.

In prehistory, the tall shade tree provided leaves for food wrappers and bark, roots, and sap as treatments for dysentery and stomach upset. Cored and filled with codfish, crab, fruit, sugar, or taro, much like eggplant or rice, it absorbed the other flavors. During the off-season, the starchy pulp survived in leaf-lined caches as a fermented paste. The fibrous fruit, mixed with coconut and wrapped in banana leaves, baked into a loaf rich in vitamin C and potassium.

In 1595, Ferdinand de Quirós, a Portuguese fleet navigator on a voyage to Terra Australis, saw the breadfruit tree in the Solomon Islands and admired it for its efficiency and reliability. Islanders lengthened the shelf life of perishable harvests by fermenting them in pits and roasting or steaming them in *umus* (earth ovens). Balls of breadfruit paste saw natives through September and October, the stormy season.

Marquesan adventurers brought breadfruit tree stock to Hawaii. Preparers cooked breadfruit and sweet potatoes in a hot rock pit steamer. For ritual sea voyages by double-hulled canoe or outrigger back to Tahiti, mariners relied on "canoe foods," including fermented breadfruit and dried coconut pulp. Europeans likened the taste to artichokes, egg yolks, fresh bread, and potatoes.

Breadfruit showed promise to arboriculturists for feeding world colonists. In the estimation of English sea raider and cartographer William Dampier, who described the fruit in *A New Voyage Round the World* (1699), baked breadfruit served the natives of Guam and Mindanao as bread. In 1750, the French East India Company favored Mauritius and Réunion as well as the Seychelles as naval refueling stations and victuallers. To ensure provisions, island agronomists planted test nurseries with 3,000 specimens of pepper vines, mountain rice, and *le fruit à pain,* both seeded and unseeded.

On Captain James Cook's voyage to Tahiti aboard the *Endeavour* in 1769, he observed the offering of breadfruit as grave goods. Sir Joseph Banks, a naturalist on the voyage, and Swedish botanist Daniel Solander sampled bread-

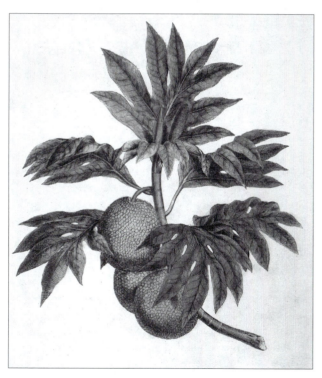

The breadfruit, depicted here in the account of James Cook's voyage around the world in 1768–1771, is a common source of carbohydrates in the Pacific islands and other tropical areas. European botanists viewed the high-yield plant as a symbol of paradise. *(The Granger Collection, New York)*

fruit and found it to be a cheap source of energy food. Because of its prolific yield, they identified the fruit as a symbol of a pastoral utopia. The *Endeavour* crew experimented with boiling and roasting breadfruit in the galley. When Cook published his journals and reported on his voyage to Tahiti to the Royal Society, lecturers pictured the breadfruit tree as a God-given blessing before the corruption of the Garden of Eden. French encyclopedist Denis Diderot extended the metaphor to a moral indictment. He charged European adventurers with introducing venereal disease among a virgin soil population.

After 1780, Banks, then president of the Royal Society, requested that George III import breadfruit trees to Jamaica to relieve cyclical famine. During consideration of the mission, in July 1787, André Thouin, head gardener of the Jardin des Plantes Médicinales in Paris, sought breadfruit saplings for transplant to French colonies. He distributed trees in Isle de France (present-day St. Bart's), Cayenne, Martinique, and St. Domingue as a vegetable ensuring human survival and providing fodder for livestock. Out of pride, Creoles rejected breadfruit as food intended for slaves. Greedy cane planters disdained the trees for taking up valuable space.

The British navy dispatched the HMS *Bounty* on December 23, 1787, to follow Captain Cook's route through the Society Islands to gather samples of the staple fruit for planting in the West Indies as slave food. The fateful mutiny on the *Bounty* delayed the venture but did not scuttle it. In February 1791, after an open-boat escape from mutineers 3,600 miles (5,800-kilometers) to Timor, Lieutenant William Bligh returned to the task as captain of the *Providence.* He succeeded in ferrying 2,126 Tahitian breadfruit plants in a specially designed shipboard greenhouse to the Caymans, Jamaica, St. Helena, and St. Vincent.

A parallel interpretation of prolific breadfruit as a Christian symbol influenced the spread of Methodism. In 1795, the Reverend Thomas Haweis, cofounder of the London Missionary Society, used the allure of breadfruit to attract recruits to the Pacific mission field. In articles for the *Evangelical Magazine,* he claimed that God provided breadfruit trees to nourish missionaries while they evangelized islanders. Politicians used the conversion effort as a justification for British imperialism.

The plant spread to Australia, Colombia, the Florida Keys, Honduras, India, Madagascar, the Maldives, Mesoamerica, the Philippines, Southeast Asia, Sri Lanka, St. Lucia, and Venezuela. Currently, on Samoa, breadfruit is an essential product of agroforestry and a source of fruit for canning in brine. Chefs enliven breadfruit and taro recipes with brown sugar or curry, a luxury spice from India. On Vanuatu, breadfruit pulp sprinkled with coconut milk makes a filling breakfast. Malayans peel and slice the fruit for frying in palm syrup. Hawaiians dice the pulp and cook it with bacon in milk as chowder.

Recipe: Breadfruit Seafood Chowder

In a soup kettle, fry two strips of bacon. In the fat, sauté 1/2 cup each of chopped carrots, celery, and shallots. Add 2 cups each of cream and shrimp and 1 cup of whole kernel corn. Cook the mixture on low heat for 10 minutes. Add 3 cups of chopped breadfruit and 1 cup of chopped parsley or taro leaves. Continue cooking for 10 minutes. Season with ground pepper and sea salt.

The tree yields more than pulp for fresh dishes. Puerto Ricans boil the flower spikes as a side dish or candy and sun-dry them. Costa Rican vendors sell the seeds to tourists. In Barbados, Fiji, Guam, Hawaii, and Trinidad, breadfruit comes to grocery stores as fresh fruit or chips. Canneries in Dominica and Trinidad ship breadfruit to London and New York.

See also: Cook, James; Lapérouse, Jean François Galaup; Polynesian Diet and Cuisine.

Further Reading

Casid, Jill H. *Sowing Empire: Landscape and Colonization.* Minneapolis: University of Minnesota Press, 2005.

Clarke, Austin. *Pig Tails 'n Breadfruit: A Culinary Memoir.* New York: New Press, 2004.

Newell, Jennifer. *Trading Nature: Tahitians, Europeans, and Ecological Exchange.* Honolulu: University of Hawaii Press, 2010.

Toensmeier, Eric. *Perennial Vegetables.* White River Junction, VT: Chelsea Green, 2007.

Breakfast

Historically, the type and extent of food service that began the day revealed the availability of foods for a quick, filling break to the night's fast and the leisure to enjoy it. Persians began the day with a power drink, molasses stirred into clabbered milk, but no formal meal. Arabs paired yogurt with dates or olives; Moroccans melded honey with grilled wheat to make *zemata,* a sweet porridge washed down with mint tea. For Republican Rome, as far north as the Italian Alps, daily meals began with a light *ientaculum* (breakfast) of bread, cheese, dried fruit, and olives. Soldiers on the march relied on *pulmentus,* a porridge roughly stirred together from ground grains. Country folk favored chicken, goose, or quail eggs, which cooks collected fresh each morning.

The Middle Ages introduced more variety in morning breaks with perfunctory barley beer and oatcakes, but still no formal table service. Ironically, in Asia and Europe, the medieval working and farming classes departed for manual labor in the mornings on empty stomachs. A Chinese plowman depended on a midmorning repast of a crust of bread wrapped around an onion bulb or garlic clove.

In contrast to peasants, the first meal of the day for aristocrats fortified them for a relaxed lifestyle. In the fourteenth century, Ibn Battuta, an Islamic Moroccan traveler, performed no manual labor while visiting foreign dignitaries and advising them on government and ethics. Nonetheless, he relished a breakfast of *mash* (peas) and enjoyed chapatis (thin slabs of bread) fried in ghee with meat kebabs, minced meat with nuts and onions, and damson plums.

Morning Meals in History

By the Renaissance, the study of diet and stamina introduced changes in attitude toward the necessity of a morning meal. Oxford-trained physician Andrew Boorde wrote in 1542 in his *Fyrst Boke of the Introduction of Knowledge* that day laborers required three full meals to accommodate the demands of toil. Boorde proposed a corollary, that the privileged class risked health and longevity by overeating. "Brevite and shortnes of lyfe doth folowe," he warned. Within the century, the morning menu in northwestern Europe began including boiled and poached eggs and bread with salt herring or curd cheese.

For African slaves in the Western Hemisphere, not much changed from medieval times to the seventeenth century. In the American colonies and the sugar islands of the West Indies, field hands cooked their own breakfast from leftover sweet potatoes or corn they grew in small kitchen gardens.

In contrast, a textured still life of a Spanish chocolate service painted by Antonio de Pereda y Salgado in 1652 establishes the atmosphere and mood of the pampered aristocrat. Closely arranged on a maroon cloth, a plate of pastries and cheeses alongside a lidded chocolate pot, a carved *molinillo* (swizzle stick), and pewter plate with cup, pitcher, and condiment jar connote a pleasant breakfast involving dipping pastries into the hot liquid.

The immigration patterns to North America throughout the eighteenth and nineteenth centuries exhibited the customs of varied motherlands transferred to the frontier in such breakfast fare as German *kuchen* and Jewish latkes (potato pancakes). In the early 1700s, reports of Swedish-American cuisine noted that breakfast consisted of pop robbin pudding, an egg batter boiled in milk. In Quebec, light crepes and heavier French toast vied for popularity. During winter 1777–1778, the Pennsylvania Dutch *schnitz* pie, made with dried apples, solaced the hungry Continental Army for breakfast at Valley Forge.

Peacetime brought together the media and the morning meal. In 1784, aphorist François de la Rochefoucauld commented on the connection between newspapers and breakfast. The perusal of an early-morning gazette accompanied the sipping of chocolate or coffee but impeded table talk. Unlike the dinners and banquets for which Georgian England and Regency France gained fame, breakfast was come-as-you-are casual. Diners could impale bread on toasting forks and hold them at the hearth to heat them enough to melt butter and absorb marmalade. At the Tuileries in Paris in 1799, even the Empress Joséphine enjoyed her morning meal as a social occasion by inviting female friends and their children for a pleasant meal devoid of imperial pomp.

The American Civil War era degraded the soldier's morning intake to fats and carbohydrates. For Johnny Reb, Confederate provisioners reduced breakfast to coush, a corn mush heated in a greased skillet. While families in the North consumed apple pie with morning coffee, Union soldiers in the field soaked hardtack in water or coffee and fried the squares in leftover meat grease. After wartime exigencies, in Trenton, New Jersey, John Taylor developed pork roll, a sausagelike pork product, in the late 1800s as a popular breakfast and sandwich meat throughout the Garden State.

On the western frontier, pragmatic housewives varied their corn-based meals with New England standards, johnnycake or corn pudding, a cooking style that emulated Amerindian cuisine. The term *hasty pudding* indicates the hurried stirring of molasses or maple syrup into corn mush for a quick morning repast, rounded out with cups of cider. Fireplace or campfire preparation for families on the move favored ashcakes wrapped in cabbage leaves and roasted in embers or hoecakes heated on a flat metal blade. Corn dodgers suited the horseman, including sheriffs' posses and salesmen, who stowed the compact edibles in sacks suspended from the saddle horn. For cowboys and wranglers, a delayed breakfast followed the initial ranch or stagecoach chores with a substantial spread, which featured hashed meat with fried eggs and potatoes sautéed with onion and chilies.

The English Way

Emulating Queen Victoria and Prince Albert, the English during the Victorian era expressed the middle-class preference for family togetherness with a breakfast sideboard spread of grilled mushrooms and tomatoes, kippers and sausage or chops, meat pasties, Brie or Roquefort cheese, and muffins and toast with jam and butter. Tea took precedence over beer, which the gentry considered too coarse for the morning table. Establishing a precedent at Buckingham Palace on February 10, 1840, French club chef Alexis Soyer catered a breakfast for 2,000 following Queen Victoria's coronation. Kitchen staff kept plover egg entrées and rashers of bacon warm in chafing dishes along with artichokes, asparagus, and sturgeon.

For the gentry and Americans emulating the British aristocracy, a breakfast around nine or ten in the morning preceded an amble on the grounds or in urban neighborhoods, where strollers worked up an appetite for a more substantial lunch of multiple dishes. Late risers made do with a hot drink, usually chocolate, coffee, or tea.

Following the flow of power, British morning menus permeated colonies around the world. The English morning food habits gave rise to elevenses, a midmorning snack, and to the bed-and-breakfast, a residential inn that provided travelers with a place to sleep and food before they set off for sightseeing or journeys. On Barbados, islanders customized colonial specialties with a native blend of broiled flying fish with a squeeze of lime juice. Bermudans clung to the British Isles with their imported Irish butter and scones. For the Welsh who could ill afford expensive breakfast foods, donkey tea, a stirring of burnt toast crumbs

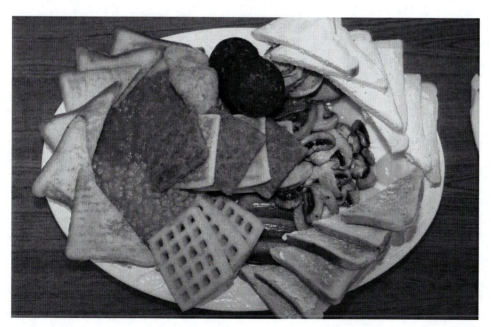

The full English breakfast—eggs, sausage or bacon, mushrooms, beans, tomatoes, toast, tea, and jam—dates to the Victorian era and spread throughout the empire. "To eat well in England," wrote Somerset Maugham, "you should have breakfast three times a day." *(Rex Features/Associated Press)*

in boiling water, produced a warming drink with little else to recommend it.

As a result of the colonial heritage of Antigua, islanders began the day with a substantial breakfast. According to the semiautobiographical writings of Jamaica Kincaid, schoolchildren ate arrowroot or corn porridge and eggs along with buttered bread, cheese, and grapefruit. On holidays and Sunday mornings, cocoa accompanied a breakfast of *antroba* (eggplant), boiled eggs, bread, salt fish, and souse, a pickled loaf made from the head and feet of pigs. Kincaid denounced the colonizer's insidious culture for insisting on English dishes rather than cheap, accessible island fruit, tree-ripened juices, and fresh seafood.

The Industrial Era

Factory-made breakfast foods ended the drudgery of early-morning preparation by replacing hot cereal with cold. In 1877, William Heston and Henry D. Seymour's Quaker Mill Company of Ravenna, Ohio, made cooked oats a staple of the American breakfast menu. Two Michigan brothers, John Harvey Kellogg and Will Keith Kellogg, introduced Americans to a wholesome, high-fiber breakfast food that required no cooking. In 1894, they manufactured ready-to-eat cereal flakes by baking thin layers of wheat paste. In 1906, the boom in breakfast cereals brought fame to the town of Battle Creek, from which the Kellogg brothers shipped 1,000 cases of bran, corn, and wheat flakes a day.

Charles William Post contributed Post Toasties, the beginning of a convenience food empire. In 1941, General Mills's introduction of Cheerios turned the staid oat cereal into a crisp doughnut, a shape that the Pennsylvania Dutch invented. Television ads of the early 1950s connected dry cereals with cartoon fun. Children identified breakfast cereals with Kellogg's Tony the Tiger or Trix Rabbit or Post's Sugar Bear. Worried mothers topped cereal confections with sliced bananas and berries, a concession to empty calories.

A&P, the Atlantic and Pacific Tea Company, prefaced an era of merchandise produced by company bakeries, factories, and meat packers, the beginnings of one-stop shopping. The company showcased its more successful product, Eight O'Clock Coffee, a light roast that became America's oldest name brand in 1859. The chain grocery added more house logos to its array, including Ann Page breakfast pastries.

Today, breakfast menus worldwide vary in detail but often focus on a single bread, fried cake, or cereal eaten with a hot drink of chocolate, tea, or coffee or with cold milk or yogurt. Grain gruel goes by many names, for example, Balinese porridge with coconut milk, Bangladeshi dal, Cambodian *babaw* (rice *congee*), Costa Rican rice with black beans and sour cream, English frumenty (spiced wheat in milk), Ghanian porridge, Italian polenta, Malaysian wheat noodles, Nigerian corn *ogi,* Rus-

sian *kasha* (oatmeal), and Vietnamese *pho* (rice noodles). In China, a thin rice congee and *baozi* (steamed buns) accompany fillings of chopped pork and green vegetable or sweetened bean paste. For commuters on bicycles, a quick out-of-hand breakfast of a boiled poultry egg or fried pastries from a sidewalk vendor suffice until there is time in midmorning for green tea.

Breakfast on Christian holidays bears ritual significance. On the fourth Sunday in Lent, English housewives around Bristol make mothering buns, an iced yeast bun topped with decorative candies and served with a hot beverage as a gesture of respect to mothers, the fount of renewal. In London on Good Friday, pastry cooks, such as the bakers of Old Chelsea Bun House in Jews' Row, advertise hot cross buns, a breakfast once endowed with curative powers. At Easter, the Polish baker aims for a delicate crumb in *baba,* a cake eaten after the sunrise Resurrection Service, when diners end the Lenten fast. Among Swedes, the kitchen work of children precedes a festal breakfast for adults served on December 13, St. Lucia Day, which preserves the virgin's martyrdom in 304 C.E. The oldest girl commands the kitchen and prepares a tray of coffee and Lussekatter, a furled sweet St. Lucia bun pocked with raisins, symbols of richness and innocence.

Americans select from wide choices of foods, from fried eggs and ham to pancakes and grits, a small-grained cereal the consistency of Tunisian couscous. Amish kitchen crews dole out ingredients in pinches and dabs rather than standard measures for such traditional foods as corn pie and sausage gravy, a breakfast staple thickened with spelt flour. The Creole influence in New Orleans infuses a sugary diet with more sweets at breakfast, including beignets sprinkled with powdered sugar and *calas,* fried rice cakes sold by black women on the streets. In South America, manioc becomes a common breakfast choice in the dough of *carimañolas* (filled fritters) served at breakfast buffets in Cartagena, Colombia.

By the 1970s, fast-food psychology among students, office workers, and drivers eroded the notion of the home breakfast table. The retailing of McDonald's Egg McMuffin and Burger King's Croisan'wich and French Toast Sticks with hot coffee created its own mystique enhanced by the electronic media. Schoolchildren made toaster meals from Pop-Tarts and frozen waffles. In 1975, the federal National School Lunch Program funded school breakfasts consisting of fresh fruit and toast or dry cereal with milk. The program subsidized free or reduced-priced morning meals to improve nutrition for the poor, especially parturient teens, and to establish a model of wise choices in breakfast menus for building strength and preventing tooth caries. Performance studies confirmed that a substantial amount of the day's nutrients eaten at breakfast improves pupil concentration and data retention.

In 1979, a U.S. Department of Agriculture study embarrassed cereal makers with a chart of popular brands and the proportion of sugar. Leading the sweets marketers, Kellogg laced Sugar Smacks with 56 percent sugar, as contrasted to Quaker puffed rice, which contained 0.1 percent sucrose. The appeal to children was obvious in merry product names—Alpha Bits, Froot Loops, Lucky Charms, and Sugar Crisp, all more than one-third sugar. Although cereals bore the brunt of criticism, fruit-flavored drinks came in second in misleading the public about nutritional content.

A health backlash popularized breakfast cereals enriched with niacin, riboflavin, and thiamine and orange juice enhanced with vitamins C and D. In 1971, the Food and Drug Administration recommended the addition of iron to breakfast cereals and baby foods. Invalids bolstered their intake with Carnation Instant Breakfast and Ensure and with power bars, a packable snack for eating with midmorning coffee. Heartier breakfasts anchored eating to nutrition with fruit smoothies served with granola or muesli, a European favorite composed of dried apricots and raisins, oats, and walnuts.

Families indulged in special-occasion brunches, a sideboard buffet served in late morning by the leisure class, who enjoyed broiled grapefruit halves with a cherry on top or challah toast, while clutching tumblers of Bloody Mary stirred with celery stalks. Northern menus featured lox with bagels and cream cheese; Southern fare tended toward cheese or shrimp grits and pitchers of mimosas. Western breakfast showcased Hispanic influence in burritos and huevos rancheros.

See also: Cereal; Holiday Dishes and Festival Foods; Medieval Diet and Cuisine; Roman Diet and Cuisine, Ancient.

Further Reading

Albala, Ken. *Food in Early Modern Europe.* Westport, CT: Greenwood, 2003.

Broomfield, Andrea. *Food and Cooking in Victorian England: A History.* Westport, CT: Greenwood, 2007.

Mason, Laura. *Food Culture in Great Britain.* Westport, CT: Greenwood, 2004.

Pilcher, Jeffrey M. *Food in World History.* New York: Taylor & Francis, 2006.

Brillat-Savarin, Jean Anthelme (1755–1826)

Author and protosociologist Jean Anthelme Brillat-Savarin, a provincial epicure during the Napoleonic era, developed the culinary essay as a literary genre.

Born Jean Anthelme Brillat on April 1, 1755, southwest of Geneva on the Alpine border of Savoy at Belley, he received tutoring at the family estate and introduction at the court of Louis XV. He completed obligatory studies at Dijon's Collège de Belley and, like his male forebears, practiced law. Accustomed to a refined table, he rejected the beans, boiled beef and mutton, and potatoes of the peasantry in favor of a Lucullan roast or a casserole, a popular dish of the era.

Conscious of the privileges of birth and wealth, he evinced a personal philosophy based on social rank. At Versailles at age 34, he practiced oratory in defense of martial law and the executions that followed the French Revolution of 1789. Upon the death of his aunt, Pierette Savarin, he inherited her estate on the condition that he add "Savarin" to his surname.

Brillat-Savarin's rise to a more refined class enabled him to enjoy opulent dining and the camaraderie of fellow gastronomes. The author's table company turned foodways into an intellectual synesthesia, a merger of sensual delights of the eye, nose, and mouth. Like the classical Greeks, he extolled friendship as the height of human relations and declared it the obligation of a friend to grace a shared meal with the best of dishes.

In his amiable views on haute cuisine, Brillat-Savarin displayed the ambiguities and inconsistencies of his times. Reflecting on early imperial Rome, he fantasized joining the poet Horace for conversation and simple fare—roast kid and poultry with a good Burgundy and a dessert of figs, grapes, and walnuts. Still rooted in his childhood tastes, he embraced the passionate love of food and invited to the table fellow gourmands who could not afford a pantry of exotic ingredients and a knowledgeable chef.

The democratizing of the post-Regency era hailed fellow rationalists of any class who preferred conviviality and table esthetics but abhorred gluttony and macho drinking bouts. As adjuncts to an appealing feast, Brillat-Savarin preferred elements of the ancien régime—a well-groomed staff and a sprinkling of fashionable female gourmands who contributed graceful manners and sparkle to conversation. At a time when the elite feared for their lives, he incurred republican approbation for past ties with the ruling class. From election to mayor of Belley, the author sank to outlaw and sought asylum in Switzerland from the Bonapartists. His wanderings took him to Holland and across New England and Philadelphia, where he earned a living teaching conversational French and playing violin in a theater orchestra.

In New York City, the author observed the delight of women eating ice cream from sidewalk vendors. Of Americans, he carped that they produced few national dishes but 32 religious sects. Among the U.S. foods he admired, Brillat-Savarin cited a recipe for oyster ketchup and praised the delicacy of American wild turkey. He rescinded his chauvinism in New Orleans, where Creole cuisine reminded him of the best of home. Of Louisiana's foods, he considered the blend of cocoa with sugar and

Recipe: Creole Bouillabaisse

Simmer 1 quart of fresh or canned tomatoes with the juice of one lemon, two chopped Vidalia onions, three fresh bay leaves, three chopped sprigs each of parsley and thyme, 1 teaspoon of ground allspice, 2 tablespoons of olive oil, and 1/2 cup of white wine After the sauce thickens, add 2 pounds of tilapia fillets. Simmer with 3/4 cup of Italian bread crumbs and salt and pepper for 15 minutes. When the fish shreds in the sauce, top with a dozen small shrimps or littleneck clams. As soon as the shrimps turn pink or the clams open, remove the bouillabaisse from the heat and serve with French bread.

vanilla the "ne plus ultra" of offerings and a forgivable obsession of the gourmand.

The exile returned home in September 1796 to an unstable political climate. In 1800, he advanced to the French Supreme Court and lived at peace on his estate at Vieu, northeast of Lyon, where he enjoyed shooting and wine making. Most pleasing to his indulgent lifestyle were the variety and subtleties of cosmopolitan cookery, such as crème brûlée, which he shared with dyspeptic friends as a restorative. He promoted the competition among restaurant chefs and the influence of a hearty menu on sociability and democratization.

In 1817, Brillat-Savarin, then known as the King of Clubs, began writing an epicurean classic. At age 69, he issued the gourmet's bible, *Physiologie du Goût (The Physiology of Taste,* 1825), which imitated obsolete Greek dialogues and ornate French aphorisms to capture the complex stimuli of the table. Much loved and quoted, his work avoided dull food chemistry yet elevated gastronomy to a science. Among his opinions, he noted the importance of *osmazome,* the scientific term for the flavor of roasted meat.

Brillat-Savarin's text advocated sensible dining and imbibing according to the philosophy of Epicurus, a fourth-century B.C.E. Greek lover of pleasure. The author favored a meaty diet low in sugar, carbohydrates, and refined flour, three sources of obesity. He also avoided "bad sleepers" as intolerable companions. For insomniacs, he banned from the menu asparagus, celery, duck, hare, pigeon, roast meat, spices, truffles, and vanilla. Of game, he noted that pheasants and partridges must hang in fresh air to age to optimal flavor.

Brillat-Savarin's table delights ranged from bouillabaisse (fish stew) and eggs cooked in lamb gravy to truffled turkey with pâté and champagne, which he sipped sparingly. He relished coffee as a sharpener of the senses but warned parents against serving it to children. He

recognized the physiological link between aroma and novel tastes and honored the French command of aromatic cookery as the height of civilization.

See also: French Diet and Cuisine; Restaurants.

Further Reading

Novero, Cecilia. *Antidiets of the Avant-Garde: From Futurist Cooking to Eat Art.* Minneapolis: University of Minnesota Press, 2010.

Schehr, Lawrence R., and Allen S. Weiss, eds. *French Food: On the Table, On the Page, and in French Culture.* New York: Routledge, 2001.

This, Hervé. *Kitchen Mysteries: Revealing the Science of Cooking.* New York: Columbia University Press, 2010.

———. *The Science of the Oven.* New York: Columbia University Press, 2009.

British East India Company

A joint-stock phenomenon for more than two and a half centuries (1600–1874), the British East India Company (BEIC) dominated international relations as well as world tastes in Asian foods and beverages. Established in London on December 31, 1600, the company issued £72,000 in stocks. The firm received a royal charter from Queen Elizabeth I to control English trade with central and eastern Asia.

Under the leadership of Admiral James (or John) Lancaster, skipper of the flagship *Red Dragon,* the BEIC launched its first voyage from Torbay in southwest England on February 13, 1601, with a companion fleet of the *Ascension, Guest, Hector,* and *Susan* and headed for the Malay Peninsula. At a Sumatran feast, Lancaster declared local rice wine to be as strong as aqua vitae, a distilled form of brandy. On his return trip from Java, Nicobar, and the Moluccas, scurvy killed 105 of his crew. Off the west coast of Africa, he harbored at St. Helena to purchase provisions of plantains and antiscorbutic lemons and oranges. Over the decade, reports of subsequent expeditions listed trade in local foodstuffs—alum for pickling and baking powder, areca nuts, black sugar (*jagra*), cardamom, China root (sarsaparilla), cinnamon, cloves, coconuts, ginger, pepper, rice, tamarinds, turmeric, and wax for sealing preserves.

The 3,000 investors in the BEIC dispatched up to 30 expeditions annually and reaped profits from £2 million in sales of coffee, cotton and silk, indigo, opium, sugar, and tea. Captains Lancaster and John Davis navigated treacherous waters to tap the pepper markets of the Malabar region of southern India and conducted private deals to supplement their salaries. To protect valuable cargoes from capture, on June 3, 1603, James I took financial and navigational risks to dominate the global pepper and spice trade. After the murder of Captain Davis by Japanese pirates off Sumatra in 1604, the king initiated a war on privateering by ordering the seizure of the marauders' lands and cargoes.

The sweeping of corsairs from sea-lanes encouraged capitalism in the global food market and set the tone of Captain William Hawkins's trade at Surat in the Gujarat region of India, in 1608, when he bargained for cloth and pepper. On his way east from Africa, Hawkins made landfall at the Seychelles and replenished his ship's stores with birds, coconuts, fish, and turtles. His ship, the *Hector,* was the first English trader to approach the Indian shores.

The exposure of British sailors and dealers to Indian cuisine made a permanent change in the English diet by popularizing meat and poultry curries. It also introduced the practice of the chewing of betel nut to curb indigestion. By 1773, the Norris Street Coffee House at London's Haymarket had added curry to its menu.

Indian Trade and Indian Cuisines

James I esteemed the work of the BEIC and, in 1609, extended its charter indefinitely on the condition that the company not incur losses for a period of 36 months. In the early years, the monopoly competed with the vigorous Dutch East India Company and, to a lesser extent, with the Portuguese East India Company. By bribing the luxury-loving Mughal Emperor Nuruddin Salim Jahangir with British goods, Captain Thomas Roe in mid-September 1615 affirmed the British monopoly at Surat. At Bombay (Mumbai) on the Indian west coast, the Mughal emperor issued a *firman* (royal decree) exempting the British from trade duties on exports of cotton, indigo, saltpeter, silk, and tea. On August 22, 1639, Francis Day, administrator of the BEIC, bought land from Venkatapathy, ruler of Vandavasi, and built a fort at Madras (now

Recipe: Curried Rice

Heat 4 tablespoons of ghee (clarified butter) in a heavy skillet and stir-fry four green cardamom pods, half a cinnamon stick, four cloves, and 1/2 tablespoon of cumin. Add 3 tablespoons of chopped green chilies, one minced garlic clove, and 1 tablespoon each of chopped ginger, coriander seeds, and rice vinegar, and 1 teaspoon each of tamarind paste and turmeric. Simmer for seven to ten minutes. Pour in 2 cups of basmati rice and stir for four minutes. Add 1 cup of cauliflower, green peas, sliced carrots, or bell pepper. Season with 2 tablespoons of sea salt and a sprinkle of ground pepper. Add 3 cups of water to the pilaf and steam for 20 minutes. Top with a scant handful of chopped basil, sliced almonds, or chickpeas.

known as Chennai), establishing a toehold, the seed of empire, on the Coromandel Coast of southeast India. By 1647, company factories (trading posts) extended from Surat, Madras, Bombay, and Calcutta (Kolkata) in the northeast to 23 locations on the Indian subcontinent.

Demands for exotic foods increased in the mid-1600s. Under the Puritan governance of Oliver Cromwell, in 1650, the English began drinking hot coffee at breakfast rather than beer. In 1657, Thomas Garraway touted tea to his coffeehouse customers as a health food effective against anemia, dropsy, and scurvy. Eight years later, the bubonic plague epidemic of 1665 boosted the value of nutmeg, which doctors declared a panacea against infection.

After years of poor management of the BEIC, Josiah Child, a naval chandler at Portsmouth, on the south coast of England, negotiated broader commercial rights with King Charles II, who renewed the company's charter. In 1668, the king granted the company a monopoly on activities in Bombay and allowed the BEIC to coin money, raise forces, negotiate truces, and hang violators of coffee and tea trade laws.

The Crown recognized the tea fad as a source of steady income. By 1684, tea drinkers were paying a tax rate of 5 shillings per pound on a shilling's worth of tea. To manage the hot drink, the English preferred handles on their Chinese porcelain teacups. At the shops of beverage vendors, called "penny universities" for the cover charge, aficionados drank tea while perusing newspapers and chatting with other customers. On August 24, 1690, chief BEIC agent Job Charnock purchased villages on the River Hooghly in West Bengal, India, and built a trading post at Calcutta. At Surat, John Ovington, the company chaplain, issued "An Essay upon the Nature and Qualities of Tea" (1699), a pamphlet advising tea fanciers on the purchase, storage, and enjoyment of the best varieties.

By 1711, the BEIC had opened a factory at Canton in southern China and bought tea with British silver. Shippers, banned from the city, occupied the island of Hainan from June to December while loading cargo. During the process, the Chinese demanded custody of English guns and ammunition. Under supervision of the Chinese imperial port master, dock employees conducted business in pidgin English and kept account of British silver that paid the bill for tea, porcelain, and lacquerware. The Chinese ban on the opium trade in 1729 made no inroads against British merchandisers, who continued until 1839 to smuggle 1.3 tons (1.2 metric tons) annually of the contraband narcotic through Calcutta to China to exchange for tea. In shady offshore transactions involving opium and slaves, Indians introduced triangular trade by making cash sales of Chinese tea to the BEIC.

Tea and War

Following the separation of Bengal, Gujarat, Oudh (Awadh) in central Uttar Pradesh, and Sind in northwest India (now part of Pakistan) from the Mughal Empire in a 1748 rebellion in the Punjab, the BEIC moved inland from coastal shipping posts to acquire Bengal. Governor-General Robert Clive captured the area from the Nawab Siraj ud-Daulah and pillaged its wealth. By 1785, the BEIC controlled 281,412 square miles (728,857 square kilometers), home to 27 million Indians. Because of Clive's appointment of Indian puppet monarchs in select districts, the takeover extended up the Ganges River to Delhi and over the southern portion of the subcontinent. During a drought in 1770, the company's forced reallocation of Bengali farmland from grain and rice cultivation to opium poppies initiated a famine that killed some 10 million people, reducing the population of Bengal by one-third.

Advancing company authority turned the BEIC into a colonial power. The British Parliament's Tea Act of May 10, 1773, allowed these favored traders to ship Chinese tea to the American colonies duty-free, thus underselling colonial food marketers and contributing to the American Revolution. Historians surmise that the British attempted to exploit more of Asia to compensate their markets for the loss of the American colonies. Under the leadership of Warren Hastings, India's first governor-general, extensive wars depleted BEIC profits. The India Act of 1784 established external control over the diplomatic and military elements of the BEIC, but the syndicate maintained control of the tea trade. Richard Wellesley, an Anglo-Irish colonial administrator, ousted the French from competition and turned the BEIC into an imperial power. The addition to company territory of Penang Island, west of the Malay peninsula, as a refueling stop on August 11, 1786, provided the region with protection from Siamese insurgents. In exchange, the BEIC acquired more stock for its food warehouses.

The colonial power of the BEIC reached unprecedented heights, providing the British economy with one-tenth of its annual revenues. A 1791 price list from merchants Morgan & Fenning of London divided tea, coffee, and chocolate beverages into four grades—good, fine, finest, and superfine. Green tea, which rose in popularity from 1610 to 1700, became the trade staple. Because 500 British coffeehouses served tea, it accounted for 60 percent of the nation's imported goods. The Ranelagh and Vauxhall Gardens in London began serving tea to late-night dancers around 1730. Domestic service of tea demanded a strong infusion taken with milk and sugar, along with plates of spiced cookies and cakes. From 1713 to 1813, total imports of tea rose from 213,554 pounds (96,866 kilograms) to 31.9 million pounds (14.5 million kilograms).

The Tea Capital

With the acquisition of Ceylon (Sri Lanka) and its coffee, tea, and rubber plantations in 1798, Crown colonies ruled world food commerce. Tea alone transformed London, where it replaced ale as the favored beverage. BEIC trade employed a majority of the city's populace at company warehouses on Leadenhall Street or on the Black-

wall Docks. On the north and south banks of the River Thames, company crews labored at building and repairing ships or blending, packing, and merchandising tea.

Anna Maria Stanhope, the duchess of Bedford, established afternoon tea at Belvoir Castle as a fashionable snack between lunch and dinner. To satisfy the tea-drinking public, Thomas Stamford Raffles bought the island of Singapore on behalf of the BEIC from the Sultan Hussein Shah of Johor on February 6, 1819, and created a major global shipping port. In 1823, Scots merchant Robert Bruce discovered *Camellia sinensis assamica,* a tea variety grown in the Assam high country of India. His brother, Charles Alexander Bruce, introduced the variety to European tea drinkers in the 1830s. After the BEIC began marketing the light-leafed Assam tea in 1838, the malty taste eclipsed Chinese tea in popularity at London's India House. Charles Bruce immediately ordered the clear-cutting of Assam jungles to accommodate more plantations.

The formal separation of spice-trading competitors in Indonesia in 1824 awarded Ceylon, India, Malacca, North Borneo, and Singapore to the British, leaving the rest of Malaysia to the Dutch. The BEIC acquired part of Burma in 1826 and seized the port city of Aden from Yemen on January 19, 1839. During a struggle with Chinese Emperor Dao Guang over the opium trade, the BEIC annexed the island of Hong Kong in retaliation for the Cantonese port authority's confiscation of 20,000 chests of opium. Victories at the Chinese Fujian city of Amoy (present-day Xiamen) on the Taiwan Strait in 1841 and Ninpo (present-day Ningbo) in eastern China and a threat to Nanking (Nanjing) on the Yangtze River delta in 1842 at the end of the first Opium War led to expanded British trading privileges following the Treaty of Nanking.

Interlopers, led by Jardine Matheson & Company (JM & Co.), jockeyed for independent tea patronage, sending the first private shipments of tea to England in 1834. JM & Co. promoted the occupation of Hong Kong, and the declaration on June 26, 1843, of Hong Kong as a colony under the Treaty of Nanking established the company as a major trading force.

In Burma, Rangoon (Yangon) offered another Asian port in 1852. The purchase of American clipper ships sped global food distribution in half the time deep-draft merchantmen required. Scots botanist Robert Fortune increased the profitability of British tea plantations by stealing plants and seeds from remote Chinese provinces. Entrepreneurs introduced Chinese tea varieties in Assam, Ceylon, and Java, where press gangs cultivated and picked tea under a tyranny known as the "planter raj."

Following Assam's ascendancy as a center of tea cultivation, a revolt swept India, beginning with unrest in the spring of 1857 that exploded on May 10, 1857, into mutiny among the sepoys, Indian soldiers employed by the BEIC. The conflict pitted BEIC troops against the British Raj. Because the company forced farmers to plant cash crops, families lacked subsistence crops to feed themselves and grew increasingly dependent on British colonists. At Bengal, Bombay, and Madras, some 257,000 sepoys (Indian mercenaries) remained loyal to the BEIC and rebelled against the Crown. The British put down the revolt and nationalized the BEIC; its Indian possessions, including its armed forces, were taken over by the Crown pursuant to the provisions of the Government of India Act 1858.

At its height, the BEIC commanded the planet's largest merchant navy and controlled half of world trade. After food entrepreneur John Dauglish, owner of the Aerated Bread Company chain of shops, introduced tea service at Islington in 1864, tea boutiques became a London fad. The light meal appealed to women, who visited with their friends over tea with scones and small sandwiches to socialize and enjoy the era's refined porcelain tableware. The BEIC disbanded in June 1874.

See also: Clipper Ships; Condiments; Curry; Dutch East India Company; French East India Company; Tea; Trading Vessels.

Further Reading

Bowen, H.V., Margarette Lincoln, and Nigel Rigby, eds. *The Worlds of the East India Company.* Woodbridge, UK: Boydell, 2002.

Carter, Mia, and Barbara Harlow, eds. *Archives of Empire: From the East India Company to the Suez Canal.* Durham, NC: Duke University Press, 2003.

Farrington, Anthony. *Trading Places: The East India Company and Asia, 1600–1834.* London: British Library, 2002.

Kiple, Kenneth F. *A Movable Feast: Ten Millennia of Food Globalization.* New York: Cambridge University Press, 2007.

Buffalo

A migratory wild ruminant that crossed the Beringia land bridge around 10,000 B.C.E., the American bison proliferated to 200 million, becoming the Earth's most populous megabeast. French trappers evolved the name *buffalo* for *Bos bison* from the French *boeuf* (cow or ox). Fed on savanna grass and prairie sedge, the bison reached heights of 6.5 feet (1.98 meters) and weights of 2,000 to 2,500 pounds (900 to 1150 kilograms). It traveled in herds as large as 10,000. Browsing at the rate of 10–20 acres (4–8 hectares) per animal per year, each lived up to 15 years along the largely treeless Great Bison Belt from central Mexico to the Arctic shore and as far east as the Appalachian foothills.

As early as 500 B.C.E. in Alberta, Montana, and Wyoming and south to Texas, buffalo herds ensured the survival on the Great Plains of 11 nomadic nations—the Sarsi in Canada; the Arapaho, Assiniboine, Blackfoot, Cheyenne, Crow, and Gros Ventre on the western plains;

and the Comanche, Kiowa, Kiowa-Apache, and Teton Sioux along the Great Lakes and Mississippi River valley. North American natives drove the animals over cliffs called *pishkuns* (buffalo jumps). At the bottom, for weeks at a time, tribes ate prime parts—brains, eyes, gut fat, snout gristle, teats, testicles, and the birth sac and hooves of unborn calves. A calf's head required pit roasting.

Around 4000 B.C.E., stone mallets reduced muscle to meat flour for stuffing intestines to make pemmican, a preservation style that prevailed from Texas to Manitoba and Saskatchewan. Despite predation, wise Indian husbandry enabled the buffalo population to reach 59 million by 1500. Around 1541, Spanish explorer Francisco Vásquez de Coronado observed the Kansa and Cheyenne eating raw buffalo fat as their staple food.

Meat

Each nation created indigenous recipes. The Blackfoot valued liver; the Cree, buffalo blood; and the Kootenai, the heart. The Crow relished blood pudding, made with minced meat mixed into the liquid. Most used bile from the gall bladder as a sauce and drank the blood as a ritual gift from the gods for an abundant life. The Hidatsa boiled gallons of lung blood with marrow fat and dried onions and turnips. Stirring with a splayed chokecherry sapling added flavor. Each adult consumed as much as 15 pounds (7 kilograms) of unmarbled meat a day.

Pursuers rack-dried enough jerky and softened enough hides with brain matter for provisions and trade. To disperse flies during meat processing, the women and children hung rawhide streamers to flap in the breeze. They prized the meat and milk of lactating cows and reserved buffalo bladders to hold marrow fat. When it was safe to light a fire, smoking reduced the weight of the tissue by some 83 percent and preserved it for up to 36 months. Cured fat, suspended from the smoke hole of a lodge, could be sliced and used like bread for jerky sandwiches.

Cooking required only elevating the paunch on a stick frame or tripod as a cauldron to stone boil the organs and viscera in a little liquid. After the roasting of leg bones in the fire, diners cracked them between stones to free the marrow. Children waited their turn for chunks of small intestines wrapped on skewers. With the ease of hunting buffalo came the luxury of fighting endless territorial skirmishes—Assiniboine with Sioux, Winnebago with Ojibwa. The arrival of the horse from the Spaniards around 1650 increased the range of tracking herds and the ease of returning meat by travois, a skin drag attached to a dog or horse by parallel poles.

Formation of the Hudson's Bay Company in 1670 earned profits for Native Americans as well as for its founders, interested chiefly in the fur trade. Great Lakes women taught white males the preservation of buffalo and moose by curing or smoking buffalo tongue and congealing pemmican, a native cache or pack supply and Canada's

A small herd of American buffalo (bison) grazes on a ranch in Colorado. Once numbering 60 million, the bison is now raised primarily for human consumption. Sweeter and tenderer than beef, bison is also lower in fat and cholesterol and higher in nutrients. *(Michael Smith/Newsmakers/Getty Images)*

first processed food. The women flavored mashed camassia (prairie turnips) with berries as accompaniments to meat dinners. The 1716 winter count (picture calendar) of the Brule Sioux record keeper Battiste Good at Rosebud, South Dakota, depicted the stalking of herds as a communal way of life.

On the Frontier

Introduction of Europeans to high-energy, low-fat meat enabled pioneers and soldiers to replace heavy stores of bread, porridge, and salt meat. Thus unencumbered, white expeditioners pushed farther north and west toward the Yukon goldfields and Russian Alaska. By 1749, natural interbreeding between bison and domestic cattle had produced the first beefalo.

Because of the spiritual nature of the buffalo, the Pawnee arranged skulls in geometric figures along the Platte River in Nebraska as a token of reverence for the source of their dietary staple. Simultaneous with the adoration of the huge beasts, plainsmen valued the herds as sources of chips and bones as fuel for cooking and heating. When settlers began grinding bones as fertilizer to enrich the soil, Indians unearthed skeletons around buffalo jumps to sell for sources of nitrates.

Indians and explorers followed herd trails in Indiana, Kentucky, Ohio, and Virginia, increasing losses among the 91 percent surviving drowning, falls, lightning, and

wildfire. For the white man, hunting brought easy money; for the Indian, it brought a sustaining cuisine. The introduction of 50 to 90 Sharps and Springfield buffalo rifles and bandoleers and the expertise of horse riders threatened the species as early as the 1830s. In an average year, the Hudson's Bay Company sold meat from 17,000 buffalo. The demand for buffalo tongue after 1826 rose from 1,923 every five years to a height of 25,657 in 1845.

Pioneers developed recipes for buffalo meat. Like the Indians, they began with hump meat, the most succulent cut. Cooks at Denver restaurants broiled and fried buffalo steaks, roasted ribs, and baked the nose. Stringier cuts suited stews and soups. Anticipating shifts in animal populations, Hudson's Bay Company officials at Fort Edmonton tried hybridizing more beefalo in 1844, a failed crossbreeding scheme involving penning up cattle with the more rambunctious buffalo.

Decimation

During an 18-year drought that ended in the 1860s, herds diminished, particularly in northern Mexico. On October 27, 1867, the Arapaho, Cheyenne, Comanche, and Kiowa signed the Treaty of Medicine Lodge, an idealistic accord with the U.S. government promising military protection of herds south of the Arkansas River. By 1868, tribes realized that they had to supplement their traditional meat-rich diet with small game and fish. The attrition coincided with the rise in demand for red meat to feed pioneers and railway crews. Hastening the animal's disappearance, fashion trends in the Atlantic states and in Europe favored hide rugs, robes, and belts and the display of horned skulls as trophies. New England restaurants featured buffalo tongue on their menus.

With the aid of federal marshals, crews of the Kansas Pacific and Santa Fe railroads laid lines along buffalo trails. By demanding that the great shaggy beasts be removed from tracks and telegraph lines to halt damage to engines and cars and delays to shipments, technological advancement disrupted migratory patterns thousands of years old. Around 1872, scouts and hunting teams north of the Arkansas River and around the Canadian, Cimarron, and Red rivers targeted herds and slew hundreds of animals per day. As the Santa Fe railroad tracks reached Dodge City, Kansas, wagons delivered heaps of meat from hunting parties. Provisioners paid 3¢ per pound for prime cuts. The rest rotted where the animal fell.

The eradication of wild herds by railroad provisioners and thrill seekers firing from train windows hastened an end to nomadic Indian life on the Great Plains. Outraged at the waste, Cheyenne, Comanche, and Kiowa on Oklahoma reservations violated the accord by plundering ranches and trading posts on the Texas Panhandle. Because Plains Indians relied on the buffalo for food and shelter, President Ulysses S. Grant refused to sign a congressional bill in 1874 to shield herds from stalkers.

On grazing grounds between the Arkansas and Cimarron rivers and around Fort Dodge, Iowa, the buffalo died at the rate of 1 million annually. Beginning in the eastern and southern plains, the slaughter of the buffalo paralleled overt attempts to annihilate Native Americans. In 1875, General Philip Sheridan violated terms of the Medicine Lodge accord by urging federal authorities to slaughter herds to starve out Plains tribes and make them amenable to reservation life. The Buffalo Hunters' War brought malnourished Comanche warriors into confrontation with Texas hunters. In December 1876, Chief Black Horse directed a war party of 170 from the Fort Sill Reservation in Oklahoma to Texas and halted rampant herd slaughter outside Lubbock. By 1878, the buffalo were too sparse to warrant tracking. Western tribes used Winchester rifles to decimate the remaining herds.

Back from Extinction

By 1884, except on federal parkland at Yellowstone, the buffalo, numbering 1,200 to 2,000, seemed fated for extermination. The novelty of eating the sweetish meat increased its worth at markets. With the arrival of trainloads of gentleman explorers, rising prices heightened the vulnerability of the buffalo.

In 1888 outside Garden City, Kansas, preservationist Charles Jesse Jones crossbred buffalo and longhorns to produce the first "cattalo," a blizzard-tolerant species that he

Recipe: Beefalo Meat Loaf

Blend in a food processor two eggs, 1 1/2 cups of Italian bread crumbs, 1 cup of prepared mustard, and sea salt and pepper. Chop 1 1/2 cups of celery ribs and leaves and 1 cup of bacon. Mix ingredients into 2 pounds of ground beefalo meat. Form into a ball and flatten into a casserole and bake for an hour at 350 degrees Fahrenheit.

sold in Liverpool, England. In 1902, Jones tended a herd at Yellowstone National Park, where he worked as the first game warden. He returned to cattalo ranching at Grand Canyon, Arizona, in 1906 by breeding buffalo cows with domestic bulls. A similar conservation effort began in 1899 in South Dakota from the herding of 50 buffalo by Scots rancher James Philip along the Missouri River. While most modern-day buffalo retain some cattle genes, genetically pure stock still exists in Yellowstone National Park and in some private herds.

By 1931, *Popular Mechanics* magazine reported the bison population at 10,000. In the 1950s, revival of the buffalo reached a population of 350,000. In the early twenty-first century, the number stabilized at about 500,000. Commercial bison ranching is on the rise, with many producers promoting grass-fed, all-natural meat that is leaner and 40 percent higher in protein than beef. Currently, consumers eat some 20,000 buffalo per year, compared with the butchering of 45.6 million cattle.

See also: Amerindian Diet; Caching; Dried Food; Hudson's Bay Company; Pemmican.

Further Reading

Brink, Jack. *Imagining Head-Smashed-In: Aboriginal Buffalo Hunting on the Northern Plains.* Edmonton, Canada: Athabasca University Press, 2008.

Lott, Dale F. *American Bison: A Natural History.* Berkeley: University of California Press, 2002.

Rinella, Steven. *American Buffalo: In Search of a Lost Icon.* New York: Random House, 2008.

Speth, John D. *The Paleoanthropology and Archaeology of Big-Game Hunting: Protein, Fat, or Politics?* New York: Springer, 2010.

Burbank, Luther (1849–1926)

To bolster the world's food choices and to make luxury produce available at a low price, botanist Luther Burbank, the "plant wizard," hybridized 800 varieties of fruits, nuts, and vegetables.

Born on a farm outside Lancaster, Massachusetts, on March 7, 1849, Burbank dreamed of becoming a physician. He studied for only two semesters at Lancaster Academy, where he focused on painting and sketching, the basis of his skill at observation. A self-directed reading program led him to the essays of glaciologist Louis Agassiz and philosopher Ralph Waldo Emerson and to a mystical faith in biology's life force.

At age 16, Burbank worked at patterning and machining for the Ames Plow Company. At his father's death in 1870, he and his mother, Olive Burpee Ross Burbank, bought a small truck farm near Lunenburg. In addition to selling vegetables and seeds, he marketed a seedless white table grape. After careful crossbreeding from one seed ball, he developed 23 seeds into the Early Rose potato, an oblong russet, forerunner of the Idaho russet, America's most popular staple food. In 1874, he sold rights to his improved potato for $150.

In 1875, before California became a horticultural paradise producing nearly one-third of the nation's food, Burbank moved to Petaluma to work for the W.H. Pepper nursery. He scouted chestnuts and wild yams and West Coast plums. At age 28, he bought 4 acres (1.6 hectares) north of San Francisco in Santa Rosa. Working as a carpenter, he supported his mother and his sister, Emma Louisa Burbank.

Using the work of Charles Darwin as a guide, Burbank became California's most innovative horticulturist. In his free time, he designed a greenhouse in 1889 and opened a nursery, which he sowed with imported seed from India, Iran, and Japan to raise 1,000 test plants. He grafted his "mother" trees with some 100 different varieties and raised experimental corn with 32 ears to a stalk. His practical trial-and-error system focused on consumer needs.

Burbank crossbred Patagonia squash and perfected Patagonia strawberries, a Chilean variety. He sold or burned all seedlings that failed to meet his standards for sturdy gene pools. With his empirical method of selection, he raised elephant garlic, low-acid tomatoes, and spineless prickly pear cacti, the latter valued as vegetable and fruit and as livestock feed for desert herders. Through persistent crossing of seven plum varieties, he produced the frost-resistant Alhambra plum. His fungus-resistant potato relieved the Irish of fear of future starvation.

Outside Sebastopol, Burbank expanded his botanic modification on the 18-acre (7-hectare) Gold Ridge Farm, where he managed 3,000 trials at a time. In June 1893, his catalog *New Creations in Fruits and Flowers* advertised the latest adaptations. His "Quality" wheat dominated plains fields into the mid-1900s. From 1905 to 1911, he obtained six $10,000 grants from the Carnegie Institution to develop the elephant heart plum, paper shell walnuts, pineapple quince, and thornless Himalayan blackberry. His winter crimson rhubarb became a best seller in Cape Town, South Africa.

Degreed agronomists ridiculed Burbank's plant mutations; ministers ranted from the pulpit that botanic experimentation was playing God. Yet the curious visited the test beds to assess his perceptive methods. European and South African farmers trusted his Elberta peach, Indian corn, quick-maturing chestnut, and dwarf sunflower.

For the American Breeders' Association, he wrote articles on heredity and species formation and announced his cactus improvements in *Popular Mechanics*. The Luther Burbank Press published the 12-volume *Luther Burbank: His Methods and Discoveries and Their Practical Application* (1915) and the eight-volume *How Plants Are Trained to Work for Man* (1921). Fellow food originators applied Burbank's theories of multigrafting and the crossing of species, such as the plumcot, a blend of the apricot and plum and ancestor of the pluot.

After weathering stomach and cardiac ailments, Burbank died on April 11, 1926. Four years later, Congress passed legislation to patent hybrids such as those propagated by Burbank. By 1945, California orchards fielded 2 million of Burbank's hybrid plum trees and distributed fresh fruit and prunes worldwide. His birth date, March 7, is marked each year in California as Arbor Day.

See also: Cacti; Ice Cream; Potatoes.

Further Reading

Kingsbury, Noel. *Hybrid: The History and Science of Plant Breeding.* Chicago: University of Chicago Press, 2009.

Sackman, Douglas Cazaux. *Orange Empire: California and the Fruits of Eden.* Berkeley: University of California Press, 2005.

Smith, Jane S. *The Garden of Invention: Luther Burbank and the Business of Breeding Plants.* New York: Penguin, 2009.

Stansfield, William D. "Luther Burbank: Honorary Member of the American Breeders' Association." *Journal of Heredity* 97:2 (2006): 95–99.

Bushmeat

A common source of protein where forest dwellers and logging communities kill animals in the wild for food, *viande de brousse* (bushmeat) supplements the human diet with sustainable game as well as endangered species. Following meat-eating patterns that date to the first settlers of Australia, Aboriginal hunters roast emus, kangaroos, and pythons directly over fire or in earth ovens as their traditional cuisine. On Guam, the fruit bat and flying fox are delicacies; orangutans carry the same distinction throughout Indonesia, where people generally lack the taste for domesticated meats.

Where meat markets fail to sell fresh beef, fish, goat, or poultry at an affordable price, such as rural Equatorial Guinea and Ghana and among the 800,000 refugees from Burundi and Rwanda camping in Tanzania, buffalo and antelope serve poor families as a free-for-the-taking alternative. In some Bantu dialects, "animal," "meat," and "food" are the same word. An ethical quandary arises from the battle between conservationists and humanitarians, who refuse to put the survival of animals over that of humans.

Like the American turkey on Thanksgiving, bushmeat carries cultural significance for health and libido, especially during harvest festivals. In southern Sudan, giraffe and zebra rank high as kill among illegal hunters. The only investment is ammunition or snares, the trap of choice in Kenya and Uganda. From the wild, the meat passes to chop bars for butchering and sale, such as the open-air counters in Nigeria, which lack refrigeration and running water.

For some 30 million rural poor in the Congo River basin, 80 percent of family meat supply comes from wild game, including bushpig, cane rat, duiker, guinea fowl, manatee, Nile crocodile, pangolin, porcupine, and snake. In the absence of affordable protein, hunters resort to poaching on game reserves and national parks. To conceal illegal meat from patrols, families cook it after dark. Large-bodied and slow-reproducing animals, particularly elephants and monitor lizards, suffer the greatest threat of extinction.

Because of the high cost of delivering domestic meats in refrigerated railcars or trucks, bushmeat has become a major source of income in Amazonia, central Africa, and Sumatra. In eastern Ecuador in the 1960s, the Huaorani advanced from subsistence hunting to selling smoked agouti and peccary as a full-time business. In the eastern Cameroon, smoked gorilla brings high profits. On the Ivory Coast, sides of antelope and hippopotamus dominate menus at barbecues and parties.

Reliance on terrestrial game generates crises among apes and tortoises, both dwindling species. Further reducing meat sources, clear-cutting of forests and road building in Africa and South America force stalkers deeper into the wild for bats and giant rodents. Scientists predict that the precipitate extinction of vulnerable species eventually will cause human malnutrition and starvation.

Hunters smoke or sun-dry their kill and peddle rare species for cash to chic urban restaurants as far away as Brussels, Guangzhou (Canton), London, Montreal, Paris, and Washington, D.C. Upscale immigrant populations willingly pay exorbitant rates for the wild taste of home. To meet the demand for luxury food, dealers pack meat in luggage for smuggling through major airports.

Unsanitary conditions encourage the spread of salmonella, which thrives in both cold- and warm-blooded animals. The dressing and consumption of apes, bonobos, and chimpanzees spreads such blood-borne pathogens as the fruit bat–borne Marburg hemorrhagic fever, identified in 1967 in Marburg, Germany, and the equine Hendra virus, first observed in 1994 in Brisbane, Australia. In 1976 in Zaire, the Ebola virus, a lethal zoonosis, passed from chimpanzees to humans, who died of hemorrhage and multiple organ failures. A more serious consideration of infected food is the evolution of the human immunodeficiency virus (HIV) from simian immunodeficiency virus (SIV), a related strain found in chimpanzees that reached pandemic proportions. Health officials fear that trafficking in illicit bushmeat may launch a new microbial threat to global populations.

The prophecy of epidemics spread by bushmeat continues to loom. In 1991, the bat- and pig-borne Nipah virus spread encephalitis in Malaysia and Singapore. Severe acute respiratory syndrome (SARS) emerged in Guangzhou, China, in 2003, apparently from the eating of civet cats. The list of connections to bushmeat extends to African squirrels, which carry monkey pox, and wild boars, which transmit trichinella, a parasite that survives in the raw meat of bears, foxes, raccoons, rats, and wolves.

See also: Australian Food Trade; Heritage Foods.

Further Reading

Davies, Glyn, and David Brown, eds. *Bushmeat and Livelihoods: Wildlife Management and Poverty Reduction.* Oxford, UK: Blackwell, 2007.

Greenfeld, Karl Taro. "Wild Flavor." *Paris Review* 175 (Fall/Winter 2005): 7–26.

Mills, Daniel S., and Jeremy N. Marchant-Forde, eds. *The Encyclopedia of Applied Animal Behaviour and Welfare.* Cambridge, MA: CABI, 2010.

Wolfe, Nathan D., Peter Daszak, A. Marm Kilpatrick, and Donald S. Burke. "Bushmeat Hunting, Deforestation, and Prediction of Zoonotic Disease." *Emerging Infectious Diseases* 11:12 (December 2005): 1822–1827.

Byzantine Diet and Cuisine

A merger of Greek and Roman foodways, the Byzantine diet and cuisine suited a class-structured society. From the founding of Byzantium in 667 B.C.E. to the reflective gastronomy text *On the Observance of Foods,* composed by the imperial physician Anthimus in 500 C.E., cookery reflected the catch of fishermen. At a peak in imperial fortunes in 324 C.E., the Roman Emperor Constantine proclaimed Constantinopolis the alternate capital of his realm. Officials regulated food commerce and set prices on fish from some 1,600 trawlers per day.

By avoiding shortfalls and famine, the cosmopolitan city remained central to global history until 1453 C.E. Authorities solidified grain contracts with merchants in Alexandria (Egypt), Mosul (Iraq), and Trebizond (Turkey) and went to war with Bulgaria over honey supplies. Citizens tolerated both Christian and Muslim feasts and street fairs and sampled holiday recipes from both cultures. A cross-cultural favorite, Christmas gingerbread, furthered the cult of St. Nicholas.

For the lowest-class Byzantine, barley, emmer wheat, and legumes dominated the communal pot. Side dishes ranged from ash-cooked loaves and olives to thistles, bulgur wheat balls with yogurt, and herbed broth. From small garden patches, householders harvested black-eyed peas and cabbage, eggplant, spinach, and zucchini, plus numerous root crops, including onions, radishes, and turnips. Bakers maintained privileged status for their contribution to urban meals of 80,000 loaves daily.

Travelers bought meat pasties and pies at taverns, baklava and soup from street vendors, and almonds, chickpeas, fresh fruit, pistachios, and walnuts at food stalls for pocket snacks. Inns featured fish stew on the menu. Innkeepers served citrus and pear preserves and frumenty, a grain porridge topped with carob seed, honey, and raisins. As sugar gained popularity, Byzantine chefs produced the first rose and violet sugar for sweetening aromatic beverages and candying citron and plums.

While soldiers made do on double-baked biscuits and cereal pottage washed down with *posca* (sour wine), creative cookery for the elite included cheese, doves, and partridges. Aristocrats chose among mackerel from the Black Sea, omelets, salad with oil and vinegar dressing, and shellfish as well as *garum* (fermented fish sauce). Around 20 C.E., the Roman geographer Strabo commented on tunny, a flavorful fish available off the Horn of Africa.

The windows of the imperial palace opened over the spice market to ensure air scented with artemisia, cubebs (Javanese pepper), and jasmine. For the table of Emperor Justinian in the early sixth century, the Empress Theodora hired chefs from Greece, India, Persia, and Syria. Specialists planned the three courses, an appetizer followed by grilled sea bass and sturgeon or roasted suckling pig served with yeast bread and lettuce. The meal concluded with honey cakes and rice pudding for dessert.

Byzantine preferences for colorful, fragrant, and savory foods survive in eyewitness accounts. Blends of meat and vegetables wrapped in grape leaves anticipated dolmades, a Cypriot Greek dish. One baked entrée, stuffed squid, got its flavor from pomegranates mixed with rice. A tenth-century recipe for roast kid called for a garlic, leek, and onion stuffing and garum sauce. More affordable than gazelles, hares, and lamb, swine produced salt meat and sausage as well as ember-broiled haunches and lard for seasoning and frying fritters and pancakes.

At the nexus between Asia and Europe, Constantinople's markets traded in exotic goods from Arabia, Italy, and Persia and Cretan and Macedonian wine. Christianity increased business with vintners to supply the Eucharist.

The flavoring of wine with absinthe, anise, chamomile, gentian, putchuk (thistle root), spignel (*Meum athamanticum*), spikenard rhizomes, storax (sweetgum resin), and valerian produced the forerunners of ouzo, retsina, and vermouth.

Spice markets stocked ambergris as well as anise, caraway, cinnamon, cumin, mastic, nutmeg, and pepper. Islamic merchants redirected rosemary and saffron from the druggist's shelf to the pantry. While the rest of Europe sank into the Dark Ages, the invention of marzipan, salted *bottarga* (mullet roe), the samovar (tea urn), and the table fork illustrates the innovations of the Byzantines.

Popular dietary handbooks introduced commoners to the balance of the four humors, an ancient scientific term for blood, phlegm, black bile, and yellow bile. To maintain nutritional harmony, authors paired *conditum* (wine concentrate) with spikenard and figs with salt.

In his treatise *On the Properties of Foods* (ca. 1075), Jewish nutritionist Symeon Seth, adviser to the Emperor Michael VII, illustrated period interest in eating. Seth encouraged meals of gazelle meat and asparagus and garlic and the choice of distilled water, juleps, and syrups for beverages. He suggested the serving of fresh fruit at the beginning of dinner but insisted that grapes be peeled and pitted. He was suspicious of cheese and millet and ruled out the eating of fish roe and very young pigs.

For religious ascetics, the *typika* (regulations) for monasteries placed severe limits on the consumption of cheese, eggs, fish, and meat. Rules grew more complex in the description of fasts, penance, and vigils. On Good Friday, monks and their guests ate equal portions of bread, raw greens, and water.

See also: Crusaders' Diet and Cuisine; Grilling; Maritime Trade Routes; Shellfish.

Further Reading

Dalby, Andrew. *Flavours of Byzantium*. London: Prospect, 2003.

———. *Food in the Ancient World from A to Z*. London: Routledge, 2003.

———. *Tastes of Byzantium: The Cuisine of a Legendary Empire*. London: I.B. Tauris, 2010.

Marks, Henry. "Dining with Angels: Cuisine and Dining in the Eastern Roman Empire." *Medieval History Magazine* 2:1 (September 2004): 16–23.

Thomas, John. *Byzantine Monastic Foundation Documents: A Complete Translation of the Surviving Founder's "Typika" and Testaments*. Washington, DC: Dumbarton Oaks Research Library, 2000.

Caching

From prehistory, caching—the hoarding of food, usually in a hidden place, for storage—has minimized the severity of food scarcities. A cache in a discrete site provided hunter-gatherers, nomads, mountain climbers, soldiers, and arctic explorers an underground storehouse or deep freeze for securing supplies. Copied from bear, coyote, magpie, rodent, squirrel, and wolf nest caching, this method of food, seed, and water preservation applies to holes in the ground, hollow logs, small caves, trees, and cavities in crags.

After the settlement of Mureybet and Abu Hureyra east of Aleppo in western Mesopotamia (Syria) circa 11,050 B.C.E., a millennium of drought forced the Natufians, the earliest settled people of Palestine, to adopt agrarianism by caching grain in storage pits as famine food. The ancient Chinese along the Yangtze River stored rice in pits, some of which survive to current times. North of the Aswan Dam in Egypt, the Wadi Kubbaniya inhabitants survived famine by caching smoked or sun-dried fish for up to five months.

Caching had its place in cultures beyond Eurasia. The Olmec and Tarahumara of north-central Mexico stockpiled dried corn on the cob, their staple food, in desert pits. In Queensland, Australia, Aborigines secured wild grain in hollow wooden bins or tied *bunya-bunya* (pine nuts) in skin bags coated in muddy straw. Grass-lined trenches served gatherers of cycad nuts, one of the world's most ancient foods, which they wrapped in tea tree bark. Tropical water lily roots and yams needed only drying and stacking at ground level. Africans of the southern deserts stored melon seeds and tamarind fruit for months at a time. As recently as 2002, during guerrilla warfare in Angola, women networked the transport and caching of edible supplies.

In the Americas, caching facilitated the spread of human subsistence to dry lands. From the first century C.E. in Arizona, the Hohokam laborers could gather and store as much as 175 pounds (80 kilograms) of dried mesquite pods a day, a substantial guarantee of winter rations. In south-central Mexico, as the Nahua of Cholula, Puebla, became urbanized around 500 C.E., caching helped to stabilize food distribution. During seasonal abandonment of dwellings, caches remained safe from digging animals and obscured from the eyes of human trespassers.

North of the Mexican border, Mono farmers made slatted, clay-coated bins to hold acorns, filberts, hickory nuts, mesquite beans, and piñon nuts. The Zuñi concealed snow mounds in the mountains to ensure a stock of fresh water and spare hunters from carrying the weight of water bags. The Hopi developed water trails over long journeys. Women followed men and buried water-filled gourds before returning home. On the men's return route, they retrieved the water to save time and relieve thirst.

The acorn caches of Eastern tribes survived in the cold mud surrounding springs and remained edible for as much as three decades. By digging a decoy storage hole, successful food preservers fooled raiders into seizing small stores of less palatable food rather than search out the main cellars.

The Eskimo of Nunivak Island, in the Bering Sea off the coast of Alaska, packed woven grass bags or walrus hides with meat, blubber, and seal or whale oil. They weighted their underground stores with stones to keep out foxes. Along the Mackenzie River in Canada, the Kutchin cached food on stilted platforms. On the Fraser River in British Columbia, the Kootenai people speared salmon, smoked the filleted flesh, then packed it in cedar boxes to store in cache trees above the reach of bears and dogs. Notched poles served as ladders. On Baffin Island in 1578, according to English voyager Martin Frobisher, the Canadian Eskimo hid fish and meat under stone cairns, as a method of supplying Arctic males on their return trek from hunting grounds.

Along the frontier, pioneer farmers, hunters, and trappers emulated the Native American caches, thus saving supplies from arson and thievery. Settlers referred to the burial spots as "wells" or "Indian barns." Late in the 1700s, Canadian Indians derived the term "cache" from the French *cacher,* to hide.

Methods of Food Cellaring

Caching evolved in different locales to suit the climate and address threats to provisions, especially along routes favored by foragers or where territorial boundaries met, such as the Great Lakes hunting grounds contested by the Dakota and Ojibwa. Along Lake Superior and Lake Michigan, the Ottawa, Potawatomi, and Winnebago buried wild rice or secured it in cedar bark bags. California and Colorado Indians braided ears of corn and dried them on adobe roofs for stocking rock-lined larder hoards. To keep out rodents, families overlapped rock slabs and chinked gaps with stones.

Farmers of the Atlantic Seaboard and New England buried sacks of corn ears or parched kernels as well as "corn smut" fungus, which they preserved along with strings of dried pumpkin and squash slices and bags of beans and sunflower seeds to supply them during winter. To parch corn for mush, they heated sand and spread handfuls of kernels over it. When the kernels popped open, preparers sifted out the sand and reserved the exploded grains for pounding into meal or boiling with beans.

The Iroquois of Canada and New York extended the use of surplus corn by charring it and burying it in bark-roofed cellars along with cured venison in rawhide rolls or envelopes called parfleches. After digging several holes about 1 yard wide (.91 meters) and 2 yards (1.83 meters) deep and drying them with fires, a family secured animal bladders filled with nutritious marrow fat, skins of dried berries and jerky, and prairie turnips in buffalo or deer hide or cedar bark bags. Women stacked the provisions atop a lining of bark, bunchgrass, charcoal, corncobs, leaves, or willow twigs and strung the sides with braided roots, such as those of the camas plant, a favorite of the Nisqually of western Washington.

In the Northwest, coastal Indians saved bear fat in liquid form in a gourd or animal bladder and hid dried fish in trees in storage containers of split cedar. The Thompson Indians of British Columbia placed berries and roots in baskets wrapped in birch bark in cellars, which they covered with poles topped with dirt and pine needles. Additional brush pantry containers held acorns, the source of flour. For seeds and liquid, women wove rushes into storage jars and waterproofed them with piñon gum and tar before burying them. Columbia River tribes pulverized fish between stone clappers, added berries and herbs for flavor, and stored the powder in grass and rush baskets lined with salmon skin. The Hidatsa of Montana retrieved beans, corn, squashes, and buffalo fat from cellars to make pounded mush, which they served in wood bowls to scoop out with horn or mussel shell spoons.

By choosing high ground or caching under shelving rock or inside a dwelling, Indians avoided water and rot in their granary pits and root cellars. In laying a fire pit over a cache, they concealed the true nature of the spot. A topping of ash, grass wall matting, gravel, leaves, sand, and a careful earth and sod cap sealed the cache from animals and thieves and waterproofed the storehouse.

In the Ohio Valley, the pits remained so secure that for years at a time families stored awls and flint knives, horn fishhooks and cooking implements, hammer stones, medicine bags, pottery, record sticks, ritual bones and adornments, and shell scrapers. In Ohio's Cahokia Mounds,

archaeologists have recovered limestone smoking pipes and leaf tobacco and seeds buried in bowls and jars. After the preservers emptied a storage cache, they turned it into a midden by backfilling it with ash, hearth debris, worn moccasins, other refuse, and kitchen waste. When tribes attacked enemies, they deliberately set fire to the caches.

Historical Caches

At Patuxet, Massachusetts, on November 16, 1620, shortly after the arrival of the *Mayflower* at Plymouth Colony, Governor William Bradford rejoiced in the discovery of a mound of sand adjacent to a harvest cornfield. Inside, he dug out a basket containing three or four bushels of Narragansett corn, a staple that the aborigines of southern New England had grown since 700 B.C.E. Reconnoitering two Indian houses, the English also commandeered beans and more corn. A year later, the Pilgrim settlers learned that the Wampanoag bore a grudge against food pilferage, which tribes ranked as a serious crime. Nonetheless, the Indians shared provisions with the English to assist them through a difficult winter. In spring 1621, Squanto joined Chief Massasoit in training the Pilgrims in growing and storing corn. To the south, in Jamestown, Virginia, however, the Powhatan War of March 22, 1622, resulted from the intent of indigenous people to punish English settlers for stealing pantry stores.

On the Great Plains, natives of the upper Missouri River valley scraped holes with an adze shaped from a buffalo scapula, then organized food in buffalo hide tarps. During the Lewis and Clark Expedition, in winter 1804–1805, explorers at Fort Mandan (present-day Washburn, North Dakota) found that Mandan women packed squash, the most perishable vegetable, in a store of shelled corn kernels. Corn ears pointed inward, leaving the dry stems, the least likely to rot from dampness, pointed outward. Both navigator Pierre Cruzatte and organizer Meriwether Lewis learned cache design for use later on their route over the Rocky Mountains.

In the 1830s, artist George Catlin observed food caching among tribes along the Missouri River. He described their drying of corn on the cob for caching with dried meat and pemmican, topped with bear grass. The jar-shaped deposits ranged from 2 yards (1.8 meters) at the bottom to a mouth less than 2 feet (0.6 meters) wide. After shoring up the sides with sticks and moss and blocking out seepage with skin linings, families concealed their caches from detection by sealing them with dirt and sod.

Farther south, Plains tribes' caches were deep enough to require a ladder to reach the bottom. After a buffalo kill, women filled and buried skin bags with leftover fat to be used in cooking.

See also: Arctic Diet and Cuisine; Beans and Legumes; Díaz, Bernal; Einkorn Wheat; Ice; Nuts and Seeds; Pemmican; Storage, Food.

Further Reading

Berzok, Linda Murray. *American Indian Food.* Westport, CT: Greenwood, 2005.

Dunn, Walter Scott. *People of the American Frontier: The Coming of the American Revolution.* Westport, CT: Greenwood, 2005.

Kantner, John. *Ancient Puebloan Southwest.* Cambridge and New York: Cambridge University Press, 2004.

Porter, Joy, ed. *Place and Native American Indian History and Culture.* Bern, Switzerland: Peter Lang, 2007.

Cacti

A ubiquitous species in hot, dry environments, the cactus provides desert and mountain dwellers with sources of candle material, food dye, fruit, flesh, and fluid. Cactus flourished in Central and South America and the Galapagos Islands, where it became a curiosity to European explorers. Spread across the Western Hemisphere around 100,000 B.C.E., the plant was a staple of the Nazca of Peru and among the Maya in Tlaxcala, Mexico, according to Spanish observers in 1519. The Zuñi made similar use of the tree cholla in ritual. The Huichol of west-central Mexico gathered the *tsuwiri* cactus to celebrate the harvest. The Acoma, Keres, and Laguna kept cactus as a fallback in starvation times.

In 1769, Franciscan missionaries introduced cacti from San Diego, California, south into Baja California. They harvested the "mission cactus" as a source of fruit and of mucilage for binding adobe brick. The Seri of northwestern Mexico used long poles for gathering the *Stenocereus gummosus* for fresh fruit and *cardón* seeds, which they ground into flour or pounded into mush. Peruvians made cactus into *cimora,* a psychotropic drink; the Tarahumara of central Mexico turned the sunami cactus into a sacred intoxicant. Farther north, the Blackfoot ate cactus fruit to treat enteritis and made the seeds into eye treatments.

After Christopher Columbus introduced the Caribbean *Melocactus,* or melon cactus, to Spain and described its use as a vegetable, the plant found its way east in ships and on land caravans. Travelers have relocated cacti to Corfu, Cyprus, Egypt, Eritrea, Ethiopia, Greece, India, Israel, Jordan, Libya, Malta, North and South Africa, and Southeast Asia and west to Hawaii and the South Pacific. In Sicily, slices from cactus stems served as plates. In Australia, the explosive growth of the prickly pear after its introduction in 1788 ruined 60 million acres (24 million hectares) of New South Wales and Queensland for other crops and forage.

Cooking methods varied by culture. Bolivian Indians harvested spherical cacti for boiling like potatoes for holy feast days. The Gosiute and Keres roasted cactus pads in damp sand and served with chili. In spring, the Papago sliced and boiled green buds and shoots like green beans or stewed them with onions and peppers. Dried cactus blossoms became pantry staples for the Cahuilla and Maricopa for dipping in syrup. The Indians of Zacatecas, Mexico, harvested cactus buds for frying and serving with chilies and eggs. In the Sonoran Desert, the Tohono O'odham baked cholla buds overnight in a fire pit to produce a storable food for boiling into gruel for the sick.

While traveling in the wild, desert Indians sliced the stem of the barrel cactus and crushed the tissue to allow liquid to collect. When cooked in honeyed water, the spongy pulp became a refreshing dessert. Travelers cut cores of the saguaro and chewed the cortex for moisture.

As a food, the cactus produces tasty berries and fruit, such as the red ovules with white pulp on the night-blooming cereus of Yucatán and the jelly congealed from the common saguaro fruit. Another species, the *garambullo* (*Myrtillocactus geometrizans*), rewarded the ancient Hohokam and the Apache, Papago, Pima, Sinagua, and Tewa with a currant-sized berry that they ate fresh or dried like raisins for mixing with *pinole*; the Diegueño of southern California dispatched their children to sell the dried fruit.

The Tequesta of southeastern Florida harvested the purplish-red fruit of the prickly pear (*Opuntia stricta*), also known as tuna or the Indian fig, and rolled it in sand to remove spines. The Havasupai and Navajo valued the tulip prickly pear for its pulp, which they made into a beverage. By crushing the fruit of columnar cacti, Indians extracted the juice, placing it in ollas (large earthenware jars) to ferment into vinegar or wine for drinking at rainmaking ceremonies. Harvesters found uses for leftover seeds in candy and porridge.

In 1912, California horticulturist Luther Burbank hybridized a spineless prickly pear as forage for cattle, hogs, and sheep. Currently, preparers hold the fruit in a gas flame to ready the pulp for preparing as candy, cheese, ice cream and sorbet, jam, lemonade, liqueur, margaritas, salad dressing, or syrup.

Mexico produces approximately 200,000 tons (180,000 metric tons) of cactus annually, two-thirds of the world's domestic crop. Mexican cuisine reprocesses the *Opuntia nopa* paddles pickled or deep fried with chili and cumin and as additions to egg casseroles, grilled vegetables, salads and salsa, and tortillas as well as the basis of an

Recipe: Desert Blush Lemonade

Score the peels of six lemons with a fork or zester. Slice and steep in 6 cups of boiling water. Add 1/2 cup of sugar and dissolve before stirring in 1/4 cup of prickly pear juice and four crushed lemon mint leaves. Serve over cracked ice.

alcoholic drink called *colonche*. Mixed with cow brains, *nopales* (cactus stems) produce a nutritious taco filling at roadside stands. As a healing plant, cactus aids in the dietary control of cholesterol and diabetes. Farmers also plant rows of cactus as a boundary fence to keep livestock out of food crops.

See also: Amerindian Diet; Peyote; Pit Cookery; Prohibition; Tex-Mex Diet and Cuisine; Vinegar.

Further Reading

Anderson, Edward F. *The Cactus Family.* Portland, OR: Timber, 2001.

Grigson, Jane. *Jane Grigson's Fruit Book.* Lincoln: University of Nebraska Press, 2007.

Jamison, Richard L., and Linda Jamison. *Primitive Skills and Crafts: An Outdoorsman's Guide to Shelters, Tools, Weapons, Tracking, Survival, and More.* New York: Skyhorse, 2007.

Van Atta, Marian. *Exotic Foods: A Kitchen and Garden Guide.* Sarasota, FL: Pineapple, 2002.

Cajun Diet and Cuisine

A southwestern Louisiana table tradition created by Acadians from New Brunswick and Nova Scotia, Cajun food combines seafood and wild game with local herbs and rice to yield a slow-cooked, zesty Southern fare. The corruption of the term "Acadian" into "Cajun" occurred from 1755 to 1788, when French colonists fled British rule. After the harrowing voyage down the Atlantic Coast to the Gulf of Mexico, they sustained themselves in the bayous west of the Mississippi River delta and lived free to speak French and practice Catholicism without restraint. A vigorous culture that once coexisted with the Micmac of Canada, Cajun lifestyle gravitated toward fellowship with other delta dwellers—African, Amerindian, coastal Mexicans, French, Iberian, and Italian.

The original Cajun hunter-gatherers and trappers lived in poverty and cooked whatever lay at hand. Unlike the high-toned Creoles, with their classic herbs, cream, beef and venison, and wheat bread, backcountry Cajuns depended on the beans, corn, greens, and peppers from their gardens and chicken and turkey eggs from the coop for custard pies. Extra eggs sold at the market bought shoes for churchgoing and *bals de maison* (house dances). From the Caddo and Choctaw, Cajun cuisine focused on alligator and turtle, birds and squirrels, pecans, and ground sassafras leaves for *filé* powder, as a thickening agent in soups and stews. From the wilds came blackberries, peaches, and plums for double-crusted pies and sorbet. Local waters teemed with blue crabs for stuffing, oysters for gratins, shrimp for spicy lemongrass soup, and soft-shell crabs for breading and frying.

Living on tracts from 4 to 12 acres (1.6 to 4.9 hectares) and hunting as far inland as the central Atchafalaya River basin, fiercely self-sufficient Cajuns sufficed on soul food. Using recipes from the mother country, they salted duck for duck confit and cooked sorghum into molasses, a standard table dip. Cooking style tended toward grilling, marinating, and smoking crawfish, shrimp, and tasso (pork shoulder). From Plaquemines Parish, where sailors discarded citrus fruit seeds, groves of blood oranges, grapefruits, kumquats, lemons, and satsumas yielded the juicy sections for ambrosia, a bright fruit extravaganza sweetened with coconut and sugarcane juice and decorated with fresh mint sprigs.

Communal events favored crab and crawfish boildowns and bouillabaisse as elements of a *bon temps* (good time). At a *Grande Boucherie des Cajuns* (Cajun pig slaughter) preceding Lent, cooks stuffed fresh *boudin* and the coarser *andouille* sausages. Women labored in teams to extract lard and tripe, cure pork belly in sea salt, and shape *platines* (pork patties) and souse, or head cheese, a cold cut congealed from pickled foot or head meat in meat jelly. Children anticipated *gratons,* the crackling pork skin that they crunched for the intense meat flavor.

Less refined than Creole chefs, Cajun cooks blackened chicken and bony "trash fish"—bream, croaker, drum, gar, and gaspergou—and slow-cooked them in broth in iron pots. Alongside cayenne, okra, onions, and mirlitons (chayotes), rice, the predominant meal stretcher and thickener, dominated *boudin noir* (black sausage) making and dirty rice, a mix of long grains with chopped organ meats. Like Creole recipes, Cajun entrées began with roux, a fried flour base for jambalaya and gumbo, a meaty puree served over rice or in broth seasoned with crawfish and shrimp heads. *Poutine,* a roux topping, consists of a thick savory gravy served with stewed beef over rice.

A standard flavoring in Cajun cooking, Tabasco pepper (*Capsicum frutescens*), a local specialty from Avery Island in Iberia Parish, came to market in 1869 from the factory of financier and confederate army paymaster Edmund McIlhenny. He cracked salt from the Avery salt dome with Central American red peppers for one month before adding white wine vinegar and aging the slurry for another month. Before bottling and corking the mix, he strained it to remove skins and seeds. Within a decade, his Tabasco sauce flavored dishes from Virginia City, Nevada, to England and Guam and accompanied the British army to the invasion of Khartoum in the Sudan. In the 1920s, the Cajun pepper sauce accentuated the Bloody Mary, a blend of tomato juice with vodka. Later purchases placed Tabasco in army MREs (Meals, Ready-to-Eat) and on space shuttle flights.

After Hurricane Katrina devastated the Mississippi River delta coastline and farms in August 2005, chefs John Besh and John Folse joined other food specialists in restoring Louisiana's economic basis. They provided 26,000 meals daily in St. Tammany Parish and distributed organic seed to farmers of herb and vegetable varieties necessary to Cajun recipes. Industrialists restored hand-

Recipe: Maque Choux

Chop and stir-fry one each of celery stalk, green bell pepper, onion, and tomato. Crumble and brown 1 pound of *andouille* sausage. Add together the stir-fried vegetables, the meat, and the milk and pulp sliced and scraped from a dozen ears of corn. Simmer at low heat for 30 minutes. Stir in 1/2 cup of light-brown roux, made of a blend of 4 tablespoons each of bacon fat and flour. Season with black pepper and cayenne and 1 teaspoon of sea salt. Serve with a sprinkling of chopped scallions.

crafted butters and sauces to the marketplace. A local program ensured that raisers of Berkshire hogs and white-faced cattle would find buyers close to home.

After hurricanes Gustav and Ike in late August–early September 2008, restaurateurs once more opened field kitchens and fed smallholders who were too poor to flee disaster. The familiar taste of spinach madeleine, green tomato pie, Canary Islands *caldo,* fig salad, crawfish corn bread dressing, and sweet potatoes in cane syrup restored the faith of Cajuns and others in the stewardship of the land and its food.

See also: Creole Diet and Cuisine; Grilling; North American Diet and Cuisine; Smoked Food.

Further Reading

Besh, John. *My New Orleans: The Cookbook.* Kansas City, MO: Andrews McMeel, 2009.

Bienvenu, Marcelle, Carl A. Brasseaux, and Ryan A. Brasseaux. *Stir the Pot: The History of Cajun Cuisine.* New York: Hippocrene, 2005.

Folse, John D. *The Encyclopedia of Cajun & Creole Cuisine.* Gonzales, LA: Chef John Folse, 2004.

———. *The Evolution of Cajun and Creole Cuisine.* Gonzales, LA: Chef John Folse, 1989.

Cannibalism

The ingestion of human flesh by humankind, anthropophagy, or cannibalism, is rare in the civilized world. In Paleolithic times, before ethical governments and priestly consortia outlawed the practice, however, consumers equated human bodies with other sources of nutrition. Eaters of human flesh applied the same practices they used on beasts—digging up and eating raw decomposing viscera and putrefying liquids, singeing and scraping, open-flame toasting, pit baking, wrapping in banana leaves for steaming whole, stuffing, skinning and disjointing, slicing and marinating, and boiling in ceramic pots.

Gnawing and flensing (de-fleshing) knife marks on human bones attest to the practice around 50,000 B.C.E. in Switzerland and after 13,000 B.C.E. at Gough's Cave in Somerset, England, perhaps as a means of discouraging raiders on hunter-gatherer clans. The practice warded off famine among Bohemians in 2000 B.C.E. and, after 1200 B.C.E., among the Anasazi of the Four Corners area of the Great Basin. Additional remnants of humans feasting on human meat marked Ethiopian foodways and Scythian funerals before 450 B.C.E., the Numantine War against the Roman Republic in north-central Spain in 134 B.C.E., the Muslim wars of 625 C.E., and the First Crusade (1096–1099). A unique form of bone eating in Egypt involved the grinding of mummies into medicine, a practice that continued until the late 1500s.

The New World astounded its conquerors with evidence of flesh eating. The Iroquois, for example, tortured and beheaded prisoners of war before spit-roasting them. The barbecuing of limbs and organs on a green wood grill marked the feasting of the West Indian Arawak and Carib, whom Christopher Columbus observed in December 1492. When the Spanish learned about a four-day Aztec cannibal festival that occurred in 1486, they recoiled from the assault on European aesthetics and coined the term *cannibal* to indicate a revolting blood crime. The Roman Catholic hierarchy formulated plans to end the practice by forcing the conversion of indigenous peoples and usurping their lands. The Aztec countered with an outsider's interpretation of transubstantiation, which claims that ritual bread and wine in Christian communion turns into the body and blood of Christ. Not only did Aztec altar murders continue, but the perpetrators of holy cannibalism also added captive Spaniards to their list of people to select for sacrifice and consumption at stone altars.

In the Marquesas Islands of the South Pacific, Norwegian expeditioner Thor Heyerdahl, author of *Fatu-Hiva: Back to Nature* (1974), found human remains dressed in tattered European garments. On Oipona terrace, he identified a temple god surrounded by heaps of human bones dating to 1887. Eyewitnesses still alive at the time of his visit attested to the propitiation of Polynesian gods with *kaikai enata* (eating people). The cannibalistic ritual required the pouring of human blood in shallow slots in a stone altar. Although on the wane, cannibalism also persisted into the 1900s in the Congo, Cook Islands, Fiji, Gold Coast, Liberia, New Zealand, Papua New Guinea, Sumatra, and Taiwan. The practice continued into the 2000s in Brazil, Colombia, Congo, Dominican Republic, Indonesia, Pakistan, Paraguay, Russia, Sierra Leone, and Uganda.

Anthropologists have divided victims of flesh eating into those resulting from extratribal and from intertribal relationships. Consumers of human flesh reasoned that exocannibalism, the eating of organs from adulterers, deserters, enemies, pedophiles, prisoners, spies, and traitors, especially the brain and heart, disempowered the victims and redirected their might to the cannibals, a belief of the Aztec, Cambodians, Sumatrans, and some Plains and Great Lakes Indians of the United States and Canada. In Cowboy Wash, Colorado, anthropologists examined skulls and bones cracked for their marrow in 1150 C.E. and cook pots containing human myoglobin (protein) from muscle tissue, which may have been an edible trophy.

To the Kwakiutl and Tlingit of the Pacific Northwest and a warrior cult in Basutoland, Africa, eating human flesh worked tribal magic. Farther north, the Inuit consumed the heart of a convicted witch as a means of exterminating evil. Melanesians ritualized sacred corpse meals by carving special forks out of wood. Among the Kaalurwonga of the Murray River basin in Australia, cannibals ate their enemies' extremities first to prevent ghosts from pursuing the consumers on foot or from hurling spears. In 1100, the Mohawk abandoned flesh eating with the conversion from cannibalism of Hiawatha, a mythic civilizer of the Longhouse society on Lake Ontario.

Endocannibalism, or mortuary flesh consumption, applied the same logic to the eating of wartime heroes as a ritual honor, a practice of the Dakota. Marco Polo, a visitor to the court of Kublai Khan in 1295, reported similar respectful feasting on warriors in the Andaman Islands, China, Sumatra, and Tibet. The dismembering and consumption of deceased friends and kin motivated Celtic and Peruvian tribes to console mourners with blood drinks. The ritual meal spared corpses the indignity of maggots and decay in the ground and retained beneficial spirits and strengths within the community of shamans.

Hunger extreme enough to overcome taboos has triggered one-of-a-kind episodes of cannibalism. Historians record consumption of human flesh during the Starving Time at the Jamestown colony in Virginia in the winter of 1609–1610 and among the Donner Party, pioneers snowbound in the Sierra Nevada mountains of California during the winter of 1846–1847. Subsequent cases of starvation and famine figure in the history of the Holodomor famine among Ukrainians in 1932–1933, the Siege of Leningrad from 1941 to 1944, the Mauthausen concentration camp in Austria shortly before liberation from the Nazis in 1945, the Great Chinese Famine of 1958–1961, and the North Korean Famine of 1995–1997. After the crash in the Andes of Uruguayan Air Force Flight 571 on October 13, 1972, 27 survivors stored the dead in snowbanks to preserve them for food. For two months, they struggled to feed their bodies to help them endure hunger, pain, and cold.

See also: Columbus, Christopher; Coprolites; Díaz, Bernal; Famine; Mexican Diet and Cuisine.

Further Reading

Avramescu, Catalin. *An Intellectual History of Cannibalism.* Princeton, NJ: Princeton University Press, 2009.
Constantine, Nathan. *A History of Cannibalism: From Ancient Cultures to Survival Stories and Modern Psychopaths.* Edison, NJ: Chartwell, 2006.
Feldman, George Franklin. *Cannibalism, Headhunting, and Human Sacrifice in North America: A History Forgotten.* Chambersburg, PA: Alan C. Hood, 2008.
Guest, Kristen, ed. *Eating Their Words: Cannibalism and the Boundaries of Cultural Identity.* Albany: State University of New York Press, 2001.
Raffaele, Paul. *Among the Cannibals: Adventures on the Trail of Man's Darkest Ritual.* New York: Smithsonian, 2008.

Canning

A technological advance over brining, drying, and fermenting, the canning of goods in glass or metal introduced a scientific process to the home food preserver. In 1809, to assist Napoleon's provisioners, French brewer Nicolas Appert perfected vacuum canning in glass, which he plugged with cork. The French navy applied the technology to fruit, meat, milk, and vegetables. Food processors extended the choices of perishables available to cooks, even those in remote areas, but slow production limited the value of canned food to the French.

The following year, British grocer Peter Durand improved on bottled foods by inventing the cylindrical metal can, a boon to the Royal Navy. Bryan Donkin and John Hall put the concept into production in 1811 by packing food in tinned wrought iron. In rural agrarian enclaves and along global shores, canneries employed women and the unskilled to preserve beef, pea soup, tomatoes, and tuna. By 1818, the British navy and Arctic expeditioners William Parry and James Ross had become regular customers of canned goods, which relieved the tedium of hardtack and salt pork while reducing incidence of scurvy.

Discoveries and improvements in canning methods marked the remainder of the 1800s. Sterile conditions suppressed the deadliest food-borne contagion, *Clostridium botulinum,* which paralyzed the face and respiratory system, especially in the elderly, infants, pregnant women, and sufferers from diabetes, and compromised immune systems. At Parramatta and Sydney, Australia, in 1819, the first 1,000 colonial farmers and herders opened canneries to preserve game birds and rabbits cured in brine.

In 1824, Ezra Draggett and Thomas Kensett increased canning possibilities in heat-tempered glass, which reduced the possibility of lead poisoning from metal soldering. In 1837, Jonas Yerkes, a Pennsylvania farmer, became the first U.S. commercializer of ketchup sold in pint and quart glass decanters. By the 1850s, pressure-canned cherries, corn, peas, soups, and tomatoes increased meal selection for frontier cavalry, hospital patients, and wranglers. In 1856, Gail Borden, an inventor from Norwich, New York, preserved stable, safe milk and dairy prod-

Shoppers stock up on canned goods at a food bank in San Francisco. In addition to preserving food for home convenience, the process of vacuum canning creates a cheap alternative to fresh produce and facilitates the distribution of food to the needy. *(Justin Sullivan/Getty Images)*

ucts, providing new possibilities for travel and trail food as well as infant feeding.

Sturdier jars improved processing in 1858, when Philadelphia tinsmith John Landis Mason patented thick glass strong enough to withstand the boiling that rid foods of bacteria. The use of pure pickling salt created a niche market for salt makers. In 1861, Gilbert Van Camp sold canned beans in tomato sauce. The availability of cane sugar increased interest in the tart blueberry, which canners in Cherryfield, Maine, sold to Union provisioners during the Civil War. In 1866, U.S. inventor J. Osterhoudt's removable tear strip and key wind simplified the opening of commercial tins of fish. The first cans of Campbell's soup appeared in grocery stores in 1869.

The narrow-neck canning jar served home canners in the late 1860s, as did John B. Bartlett's improved metal cap secured by elastic bands. In Baltimore in 1874, Isaac Solomon refined commercial pressure canning, experimenting with calcium chloride in the processing bath, thus reducing boiling time from 6 hours at 212 degrees Fahrenheit (100 degrees Celsius) to 40 minutes at 240 degrees Fahrenheit (116 degrees Celsius). His sterilization of fruits and vegetables during the canning process increased food safety and boosted the nation's dependence on inexpensive canned goods by 600 percent.

Far from extended families, frontier wives formed female sisterhoods that furnished camaraderie during canning season, a hot chore that dominated late summer. Home food preservation involved the young in coring pears for pear preserves and scalding tomatoes for canned soup mix. Preparers held lids in place with wire bails or galvanized metal screw-on caps until 1881, when Indiana inventor Alfred Louis Bernardin designed a canning jar

lid suited to high-acid foods. Families abandoned lean-tos and added root cellars, where stable temperatures kept glass jars from bursting during freezing weather. At the domestic tents at county and state fairs, the bright colors and shapes of green tomatoes, okra, and watermelon rind pickles generated interest in home food preservation.

Industrial Canneries

In 1893, at the height of North America's pickle mania, industrialist Henry John Heinz seized control of commercial canning at his factory in Sharpsburg, Pennsylvania. Heinz goods featured 57 pickle varieties plus bottled apple butter, baked beans, chutney, fish sauce, fruit preserves, horseradish, jelly, mustard, onions, sauerkraut, tomato and walnut ketchup, vinegar, and Worcestershire sauce. By promoting purity in his 200 products, the Heinz label earned the respect of consumers and home shoppers in every inhabited continent.

The William Underwood Company of Boston, Henry Heinz's competitor, added to canned meat selections by introducing deviled (seasoned) ground ham, chicken, turkey, tongue, and lobster. In Buffalo, New York, in 1872, suffragist Amanda Theodosia Jones patented a process of preserving fruit, meat, and vegetables by exhausting air from the container and replacing it with hot canning fluids. In 1890, she opened the Women's Canning and Preserving Company, a Chicago concern operated solely by females.

To the west, food preservation affected the course of history. In Sacramento, California, the Chinese labor force found jobs in a salmon cannery and, in 1876, at Joseph Routier's fruit cannery, where they hand made and soldered tin cans. The Hudson's Bay Company prospered from the sale of canned fish in North America. In the 1880s, the market for inexpensive canned meat increased the slaughter of baleen whales, a popular meat on the Atlantic Coast.

At the beginning of the twentieth century, Louise Andrea's *Home Canning, Drying and Preserving* (1918) featured photos of a preparer in an impeccable cook's uniform sterilizing jars. Her instructions covered the standard vegetables plus corn on the cob, Creole sauce, succotash, tomato paste, and tutti frutti. Guilt-producing ads in women's magazines hyped canned goods to improve children's diet, particularly evaporated milk. Sears supplied isolated farm wives with pantry needs, including canned fruit and sauces. The 1923 Sears catalog listed canned seafood, 25 varieties of canned vegetables, and ready-to-use fruit pie mix. For quick meals, Sears warehoused tinned clams, kippered herring, mock turtle soup made from calf offal, salmon, sardines in oil, shrimp, and smoked haddock.

In 1919, Freda Ehmann's olive cannery in Oakland, California, closed from the negative publicity of a botulism outbreak that killed 35 people. Temporarily, the news destroyed consumer confidence in safe canning techniques. Growers fought the toxin by sterilizing fruit containers with steam, rejecting windfalls and bruised fruit, removing picked fruit immediately from field contamination, and processing at 250 degrees Fahrenheit (121 degrees Celsius). A year later, Meyer Edward Jaffa, professor of nutrition at the University of California, reassured consumers that they could safely eat canned ripe olives.

Commodifying Perishables

The first quarter of the twentieth century brought the commodification of perishables to new heights. Industrialists profited on canned fruit concentrates, commercial chili powder and canned chili con carne from Texas, Heinz and Nestlé baby food, and sliced pineapple, a popular salad and dessert additive processed at Hawaiian plantations. Green beans and mushrooms, sliced and canned in factories, came to the table in uniform bites and consistent quality. Canned hearts of palm added texture to salads, soups, and stir-fries.

Infantry cooks during World War I dismayed frontline soldiers with a daily ration of British "bully beef" (corned beef), French canned chicken, and Italian spaghetti in meat sauce. Ensuring quality, the double seam protected tinned goods during lengthy convoys over rough terrain. During World War II, American farm agents opened neighborhood canneries as a hands-on teaching experience for homemakers in preserving the harvests of their Victory Gardens. In 1944, singer Kate Smith praised the women who preserved vegetables from some 20 million home plots. Overall, civilians raised 40 percent of their vegetables and canned 4.1 billion jars of food.

During the Korean War in 1950, Korean peasants survived starvation by acquiring from U.S. military sup-

ply canned ham and Spam, a chopped-meat product sold under an acronym for "shoulder of pork and ham." Native cooks nationalized recipes by flavoring tinned meat with chilis and *kimchi* (fermented vegetables). In 1966, food processors commercialized Korean ingenuity by canning kimchi for export.

The 1950s rid the canning industry of metal difficulties by applying flexible, lightweight aseptic packaging developed from laminated aluminum, nylon, polyester, and polypropylene. Cartons and retort pouches, a stackable type that holds U.S. military field rations, kept shelf stable for months a variety of perishables—chocolate drinks, coconut, custard, fruit juices, gravy, rice meals, soup mix, and tuna.

In 2007, U.S. food technologist Philip E. Nelson won the World Food Prize for his practical application of bulk aseptic processing and packaging to solving world hunger. The Tetra Pak, made in Lausanne, Switzerland, added a new wrinkle in canning—convenience and low cost as well as recyclable polyethylene.

See also: Disease, Food-Borne; North American Diet and Cuisine; Nutrition; Packaging; Poisonous Foods.

Further Reading

Astyk, Sharon. *Independence Days: A Guide to Sustainable Food Storage and Preservation.* Gabriola, British Columbia, Canada: New Society, 2009.
Shephard, Sue. *Pickled, Potted, and Canned: How the Art and Science of Food Preserving Changed the World.* New York: Simon & Schuster, 2000.
Tucker, Gary, and Susan Featherstone. *Essentials of Thermal Processing.* Ames, IA: Wiley-Blackwell, 2011.

Cantonese Diet and Cuisine

Imaginative Cantonese cuisine, the food of Guangdong Province, in southern China, acquired variety and innovation from local ingredients and the imports of the nation's first open port (Canton, or Guangzhou). The humid coast thrived on productive rice paddies, livestock, and agricultural abundance, including taro, tropical lychees and mangoes, and yams. New ideas—coconut milk and rice noodles from Thai cuisine, ginseng from Korea, mangoes from Vietnam, and peppers and tomatoes from Mesoamerica—expanded traditional pantry stock.

Because of the availability of just-caught seafood, Cantonese gastronomy developed recipes for abalone, jellyfish, octopus, sea cucumbers, shark fins, and squid. From 1600 B.C.E., Guangdong cooks served cat and dog meat and gained a reputation for turning any meat or plant into an edible. After 206 B.C.E., the kitchen stove and wok replaced hearth cookery with a more flexible heating method than the use of iron cauldrons. From the second century

B.C.E. along the Silk Road, cooks adopted coriander from Bactria, curries from India, and peaches from Samarkand. Persian traders, who introduced figs in Guangdong, welcomed relaxing morning and afternoon snacks of tea with dim sum (dumplings), tidy bites of meat and seafood wrapped in bamboo or lotus leaves.

A Heritage of Balance

From the publication of some of Guangdong's 2,000 recipes after 220 C.E., chefs earned a reputation for balancing the colors, flavors, and mouthfeel of dried and fresh ingredients. To highlight entrées, they limited the degree of spicing with chilies, mustard, oyster sauce, sesame, and vinegar. Their sensibility for subtle taste derived from Fujian cooks and Hakka nomads of the East River valley in central China traveling south in 317. The transients initiated the practice of cooking chicken in heated salt or hot soup. In the 600s, *koe-chiap,* a Cantonese fish brine flavored with herbs and spices, added the first "ketchup" to table condiments; stir-frying from Chaoshan to the northeast created a deft technique for rapid heating.

In the 1700s, Indonesian Muslims conducted a triangular trade with Australian Aborigines at Exmouth to supply edible invertebrates to Canton, particularly sea cucumbers for aphrodisiacs and dried and smoked gourmet dishes. A century later, vendors at Hong Kong's street stalls deep-fried *char siu* (barbecue pork) turnovers, ling balls, skewered meatballs, and vegetarian spring rolls. With sit-down snacks, waiters served bubble tea with tapioca pearls, noodles, oolong tea sweetened with evaporated milk, and rice *congee* (gruel).

Heritage dishes made the most of braised or poached beef brisket, chicken and duck eggs, cod bladder, frog's legs, pork ribs, scallops, shrimp, and squid. To meats, cooks wedded black beans, crab roe, fermented tofu, fried taro, pickled cabbage and daikon, and shiitake mushrooms. For light Cantonese desserts, menus featured sweet soups of red beans, sesame, and sweet potato as well as coconut candies, custards, ices, and mooncakes, a fall holiday pastry. A curative for skin ills, turtle jelly involved grinding together smilax root and the bottom shell from *Cuora trifasciata* (aquatic box turtle). The endangered reptile, which investors raised on farms and sold in Guangzhou's Qing Ping market, fueled a multibillion-dollar industry that spread to Hong Kong and Macau.

A Global Cuisine

The Cantonese diaspora from the Great Central Plains of the Yellow River carried regional recipes to Australia, California, Hawaii, India, Malaysia, the Philippines, and Singapore. During the importation of coolie labor to build the transcontinental railroad from California to Missouri

The location of Guangdong Province on the coast of the South China Sea makes seafood prominent in Cantonese cuisine; strong spices offset the fishy smell. Fish tanks are commonplace at restaurants and markets. *(Randy Olson/National Geographic/Getty Images)*

in the mid-1800s, Guangdong tastes and techniques became the first to influence North American restaurants along the track. The migration of Cantonese cooks to Taiwan in 1949 introduced *shacha* hot pot cookery, an ancestral form of shared one-pot meals.

In the 1980s, the Cantonese crock boiler became a national fad for simmering one-dish meals and restorative soups southern-style over a low flame. A family and take-out specialty, *lo foh tong* (slow-simmered soup) began as a clear consommé of fungi, crab, melon, or watercress, often enhanced with healing herbs. The closure of many urban street stalls in the 2000s forced the service of fried cuttlefish and wontons and skewered poultry gizzards indoors to cleaner, air-conditioned cafés. In April 2009, a letter to the *China Daily* protested the banning of roadside food service and ensuing joblessness.

Presently, Cantonese menus feature a range of meats, from bear, beef organs, chicken, duck, and monkey brains to lobster, prawns, salamanders, scallops, shrimp, snails, and snakes. A sapid restaurant fare compared to the bold savor of Szechuan, Thai, and Vietnamese cookery, lightly spiced Cantonese dim sum, either steamed or stir-fried, showcases the flavors of meat, rice, and vegetables. Favorite enhancements—cornstarch, jasmine syrup, longans, onion, oyster sauce, rice wine, salt, sesame, soy sauce, sugar, and vinegar—and sparse amounts of chili pepper and ginger allow the basic ingredients to dominate.

See also: Mandarin Diet and Cuisine; Pork; Szechuan Diet and Cuisine; Tea.

Further Reading

Chen, Teresa M. *A Tradition of Soup: Flavors from China's Pearl River Delta.* Foreword by Martin Yan. Berkeley, CA: North Atlantic, 2009.

Civitello, Linda. *Cuisine and Culture: A History of Food and People.* 3rd ed. Hoboken, NJ: John Wiley & Sons, 2011.

Wu, David Y.H., and Sidney C.H. Cheung, eds. *The Globalization of Chinese Food.* Honolulu: University of Hawaii Press, 2002.

Caravans

A means of transcontinental food trade from prehistory to the present, trains of domesticated pack animals have conveyed goods and passengers, bringing together consumers and exotic foodstuffs. Persians initiated the camel caravan, which linked North Africa and Arabia with the Middle East, China, and Outer Mongolia by convoys of asses, donkeys, double-humped and single-humped camels, horses, mules, oxen, and yaks. From bartering and swapping, traders and travelers engineered a global cuisine out of luxuries—alfalfa, asafetida, caraway, citrus fruit, coriander, cotton, eggplant, figs, millet, olive oil, quince, and sugar beets.

The taming of the camel in 1500 B.C.E. increased the efficiency, safety, and speed of caravanning. Each animal bore up to 400 pounds (180 kilograms) of goods during a journey that could last from a month to a year. After 500 B.C.E., the invention of the saddle and copper or leather shoes for the animals increased the flexibility of camel trains. The outreach ensured wheat for bread and bulgur in Ankara, Turkey, dried meat in Alexandria, Egypt, and ginger and tea in Kyakhta, a nexus separating northern Mongolia from Russia.

Caravanning involved Afghan and Berber route managers in balancing panniers or sacks on either side of each beast for daily journeys from 10 to 25 miles (16 to 40 kilometers). Nearly one-quarter of the cargo consisted of fodder for the dray animals. Cameleers connected camels with a hair nose-rope and led a file of 15–18 animals with a leash attached to the nostrils of the foremost animal. A full caravan consisted of 8–10 files. Each night, the caravan halted for animals to graze and receive first aid for foot lesions and pack sores. Upon arrival at an outpost, the supercargo (master trader) negotiated deals.

Caravan Cities

The trade routes promoted food markets in caravan cities, such as Aleppo, Syria; Benghazi and Tripoli, Libya; Fez and Marrakech, Morocco; Irkutsk and Orenburg, Russia; Lhasa, Tibet; Tabriz, Persia; and Trebizond, Armenia. One trade route city, Palmyra in south-central Syria, maintained a neutral junction that enabled Parthians and Romans to conduct peaceful business in spices and tea arriving from China and India. The Roman general Pompey Magnus ousted the Nabataeans from Petra, Jordan, in 63 B.C.E. and set legions over the trans-Jordanian caravan to end banditry. Under the Emperor Augustus, after 27 B.C.E., a frenzy for exotica developed culinary fads for chickpea fritters, dried eels and sturgeon, Persian lemons and saffron, pickled cucumbers, and Syrian marjoram.

From 300 to 1300 C.E., caravanning furthered international transport of foodstuffs and livestock, delivering Arabian and Indian dates, grains, horses, wheat, and wine to eager buyers in the Fertile Crescent and Egypt and among the isolated Berbers of North Africa. Trains moving east to markets around the Sahara Desert carried Arabian almonds and yogurt; Cantonese lotus seed and rice wine; Indian cardamom, curry spices, and dal; Syrian mutton; and Tientsin brick tea. The caravans returned with Abyssinian coffee, Algerian dates, Bedouin dried cheese, Garamantian olive oil and wine, Libyan sheep, and Malian kola nuts and salt from Timbuktu. With exchanges came details of clotting milk with rennet and clarifying grape wine with resins, food technology that expanded period cuisine.

Herodotus, the Greek historian, acknowledged the importance of long-distance caravanning to commerce and the importance of safety to trade along routes in Asia, North Africa, and southeastern Europe. He also commented on caravansaries, the inns that accommodated cof-

Moroccan traders lead a camel train from Ouarzazate to Algeria, following the ancient trade route from Spain across North Africa. The camel's ability to survive harsh conditions has been vital to desert trade and communication for thousands of years. *(Ton Koene/Gamma-Rapho/Getty Images)*

fee, pistachio, and spice merchants over 1,500 miles (2,400 kilometers) from Susa in Persia to Sardis, Turkey. The availability of food and water eased the burden of packing. While convoy leaders rested at a caravansary their servants tended animals and, in nearby stalls, guarded packs from robbers and sandstorms. In private, drivers shared cucumber and dill seeds for kitchen gardens as well as tips on clarifying butter into ghee and using natural yeasts to raise bread.

The Modern Era

In the 1400s C.E., Portuguese water transport competed with overland caravans for trade in crated and sacked goods, including coconuts and copra. In 1581 in Lower Galilee, Israel, Sinan Pasha, the Ottoman grand vizier, built a caravansary on Mount Tabor, where Syrian drovers herded cattle and horses to market. Caravanners traded with Palestinians from Nablus in apples, barley, cheese, eggs, figs, grapes, melons, poultry, raisins, rice, sesame, sugar, vegetables, and wheat.

In 1784, construction of the Khan al-Umdan caravansary at Acre in northern Galilee provided caravans with a grain and produce warehouse on the Mediterranean. When caravans reached Africa, eastern merchants encountered melegueta pepper, okra, and watermelons and secured seeds for Arabian gardeners. The creation of international borders and passport control initiated a de-

cline in caravanning. Still, 12 years after the November 17, 1869, completion of the Suez Canal, Baghdad merchants dispatched 2,000 camel loads to Damascus.

In 1866, the importation of 109 camels to New South Wales, Australia, from India and Palestine enabled Afghan traders to supply food to outlying stations. Harnessed like bullocks in colorful cording and announced by tinkling bells, a team of four could pull a wagon and 4-ton (3.6–metric ton) load 15 miles (24 kilometers) per day. During the 1881 drought, dromedary deliveries of food and iron tanks of water rescued miners in the Albert goldfields. Caravanning continues to deliver foodstuffs to areas remote from highways and airstrips.

See also: Ibn Battuta; Polo, Marco; Silk Road; Trade Routes; Trading Vessels.

Further Reading

Bernstein, Peter L. *The Power of Gold: The History of an Obsession.* New York: John Wiley & Sons, 2000.

Heiss, Mary Lou, and Robert J. Heiss. *The Story of Tea: A Cultural History and Drinking Guide.* New York: Random House, 2007.

Kelley, Laura. *The Silk Road Gourmet.* New York: iUniverse, 2009.

Kuz'mina, E.E. *The Prehistory of the Silk Road.* Philadelphia: University of Pennsylvania Press, 2008.

Carbonation and Carbonated Beverages

The invigoration of fluids with nontoxic carbon dioxide (CO_2) gas dissolved in water adds bounce and fizz to otherwise flat drinks. From prehistory, people favored natural effervescence in mineral waters as sources of health and the restoration of well-being. From a German spring site at Niederselters, near Wiesbaden, sparkling water acquired the name *seltzer*. In 1728, citizens jugged and corked the water and sold 600,000 stoneware jugs per year. The French dubbed the German water *"eau de seltz"*; Italians called it *"acqua di seltz."*

The first bottled pop to enter history lay in the sun around 1600. Puritan theologian Alexander Nowell, dean of St. Paul's Cathedral in London, noted that the uncorking of the warm ale produced a bang and foam. In 1767, English chemist Joseph Priestley, a Yorkshireman from outside Leeds, aerated the first glass of artificially carbonated water with CO_2. Swedish physicist Tobern Olof Bergmann of Katherinberg mechanized the process in 1770 by creating a machine that dropped sulfuric acid on chalk (calcium carbonate) to release CO_2 gas into liquids.

The manufacture of seltzer water in Stettin, Germany, in 1783, preceded similar businesses in France and England. King Frederick II funded the first operation to reduce alcohol imports. Medical applications of bubbly water became easier to swallow in 1807, when Philadelphia physician Philip Syng Physick first flavored carbonated curatives, which evolved into medicinal birch beer and sarsaparilla. In 1815, research chemist Frederick Struve of Dresden formulated the first artificial mineral water that bore the same carbonated qualities of natural springs. A decade later, he operated a pump room as a spa.

American inventor John Mathews enhanced the popularity of bottled drinks in 1832 in Charleston, South Carolina, with a carbonation machine. He sold his devices to drugstores as soda fountains. To these rough beginnings, pharmacists added alkaloid drugs; soda water marketers boosted appeal with aromatics and flavorings, forerunners of the first cola beverage, formulated in 1881 with the kola nut, an African stimulant and analgesic. Within the century, bottlers of ale and champagne exploited the gaseous discharge by fitting glass-bottled drinks with cork and a thread and adding caffeine to punch up the effects of effervescence.

By the late 1800s, soda pop makers extended the concept of bubbly water into exhilarating sweetened beverages, some marketed as patent curatives. In 1885, pharmacist Charles Alderton of Waco, Texas, concocted Dr. Pepper, a carbonated refresher high in cane sugar. The invention of the crimped or crown metal bottle cap in 1892 ensured that bottled drinks retained their fizz, an essential to Coca-Cola, which pharmacist John Pemberton formulated in 1886. Reducing prices on gaseous

drinks, the glass bottle machine, patented in the United States in 1899, blew blobs of molten glass into shapes more convenient for holding in one hand than previous stoneware jugs.

In the ensuing decades, carbonated beverages gained recognition as beneficial drinks for the sick. In the 1920s, the National Jewish Hospital for Consumption declared carbonation a means of slowing the advance of consumption with carbonic gas, which reputedly destroyed the tuberculosis bacillus. In Holland, dairiers discovered that carbonation prolonged the shelf life of butter.

Conveyor systems and mechanical filling apparatuses during the Great Depression expanded the use of carbonation to root beer and chocolate drinks. Bottlers proclaimed carbonated drinks safer than milk because no human hand touched the product during processing. To ensure sanitation, an amendment to the Federal Food and Drug Act in 1934 set standards for processing and gas delivery to liquids. Two years later, the reduction of spoilage in orange drinks allowed the marketing of carbonated beverages similar in appearance and flavor to orange juice.

Further applications of carbonation to food brought more enticing improvements. In 1952, consumers had access to the first diet soft drink; six years later, carbonated drinks appeared in aluminum cans. The invention of the pop-top in the 1960s and vending machines in the 1970s increased convenience. By 1991, containers shifted once more to polyethylene terephthalate (PET), which seized 25.6 percent of the carbonated bottling market. An inversion of food fads in the 1990s returned carbonated water to favor, making it the second most popular drink after colas.

In 1999, the International Society of Beverage Technologists set standards for the quality of CO_2 gas in beverages. The guidelines covered the mouthfeel of carbonation as well as the safety and purity of gas, which distributors typically filtered through carbon. In the twenty-first century, concern for osteoporosis produced a backlash against carbonation, which appeared to leach calcium from bones and teeth. In April 2010, environmental researchers linked PET with endocrine disruptors, a supposition about packaging of carbonated drinks that remained unsubstantiated. Today, in the United States alone, some 500 bottlers fill and seal 2,000 cans per minute of more than 450 different types of carbonated soft drinks.

See also: Packaging; Snack Food; Soft Drinks and Juices.

Further Reading

Allen, Gary, and Ken Albala. *The Business of Food: Encyclopedia of the Food and Drink Industries.* Westport, CT: Greenwood, 2007.

Hui, Yiu H., and J. Scott Smith, eds. *Food Processing: Principles and Applications.* Ames, IA: Blackwell, 2004.

McGee, Harold. *On Food and Cooking: The Science and Lore of the Kitchen.* New York: Simon & Schuster, 2004.

Shachman, Maurice. *The Soft Drinks Companion: A Technical Handbook for the Beverage Industry.* Boca Raton, FL: CRC, 2005.

Carême, Marie-Antoine (1784–1833)

The celebrated "King of Chefs and Chef of Kings," Marie-Antoine Carême elevated French cuisine to baroque style.

Born on June 8, 1874, Carême came of age during the French Revolution. At age 11, he lived abandoned on the streets of Paris and worked as a tavern potboy. At age 14, while educating himself at the Bibliothèque Nationale, he studied pastry under Sylvain Bailly and mastered displays of marzipan and spun sugar in the shape of classic arches and temples.

Carême's artistry included the creation of meringues and nougats, which he mounted on centerpieces at his boutique, La Pâtisserie de la Rue de la Paix. In March 1810, he baked a wedding cake for Napoleon's union with Marie Louis of Austria. From this era, at age 31, he published *Le Pâtissier Royal Parisien* (*The Royal Parisian Confectioner,* 1815).

By advancing his range to include all dining menus, Carême won a position at Château de Valençay, outside Paris, under the supervision of the diplomat Charles-Maurice de Talleyrand, a noted gourmand. To secure the post, Carême plotted a year's menu using seasonal herbs and vegetables. From Carême's inventive entrées, especially his signature soufflés tinged with gold, Europe's leaders acquired elevated tastes. Abandoning a holistic presentation known as *service à la Francaise,* diners anticipated courses offered via *service à la russe,* the separation of dishes for a unique presentation at each stage of the meal.

Carême spread what aficionados called the "first table in France" with such fare as Robin Redbreast pies and Bavarian creams. His service to royalty took him to London in 1816 to make pâté for the future king George IV at the Royal Pavilion at Brighton and, in 1819, to the Romanov kitchen as maître d'hôtel to Czar Alexander at St. Petersburg, Russia. His peripatetic cookery took him to diplomatic conferences at Minoritenplatz in Vienna and back to Paris in 1824 to superintend food service to financier Baron James de Rothschild, founder of a commercial dynasty.

Carême set out to rid refined tables of excessive spicing. He categorized the mother sauces as béchamel (white sauce), espagnole (brown sauce), hollandaise (butter sauce), and velouté (blond sauce). For the elite, he combed markets at Les Halles in Paris for calves' udders, cocks' teats, Isigny butter, and truffles, which he served with the best of Mocha coffee and champagne. In payment, the Rothschilds set his salary at 8,000 francs a year. For harmonizing flavors into a satisfying table experience, the chef crowned himself with the white toque, a hat that still marks the cook as a professional.

Carême worked as one of the last master chefs in private employ. During his residence in royal houses, he gleaned useful information from foreign diners to strengthen national security. To maintain his notoriety, he designed and named entrées for aristocrats—Pottage à Lady Morgan, Salmon à la Rothschild, Vol-au-vents à la Nesle. His set of decorative cooking swords skewered shrimp to whole fish. His subtly scented banquets pleased as many as 10,000 at a time.

Carême appears to have died of carbon monoxide poisoning from cooking over a charcoal fire without adequate ventilation. At his death at age 48, he towered over other chefs as the creator of French haute cuisine. He left unfinished his five-volume encyclopedia *L'Art de la Cuisine Française* (*The Art of French Cuisine,* 1833–1834), a compendium of his table settings, menus, and recipes. The completed three volumes covered the history of French gastronomy and plans for efficient kitchen layout. Central to his advice, education for cooks raised the level of discourse concerning fine fare and impressive table decor.

See also: Haute Cuisine; Pastry; Potatoes; Restaurants.

Further Reading
Civitello, Linda. *Cuisine and Culture: A History of Food and People.* 3rd ed. Hoboken, NJ: John Wiley & Sons, 2011.
Ferguson, Priscilla Parkhurst. *Accounting for Taste: The Triumph of French Cuisine.* Chicago: University of Chicago Press, 2004.
Kelly, Ian. *Cooking for Kings: The Life of Antonin Carême, the First Celebrity Chef.* New York: Walker, 2003.
Schehr, Lawrence R., and Allen S. Weiss, eds. *French Food: On the Table, on the Page, and in French Culture.* New York: Routledge, 2001.

Caribbean Diet and Cuisine

A crossroads table experience, Caribbean cuisine combines the ingredients and cooking techniques of Arawak, Taíno, Carib, Spanish, African, British, French, Dutch, Scandinavian, Chinese, and Indian inhabitants. The Arawak developed the barbeque, a unique enhancement of slow-cooked birds and ducks with savory green wood smoke. The Taíno introduced the one-pot meal simmered in clay urns, with bivalves, fish, land crabs, manatee, and turtles mixed into a chowder flavored by cassava, corn, guava, pawpaw, and yams.

On Dominica, Grenada, St. Vincent, and Tobago, the Carib shared with the Taíno the mounding of leaves into vegetable gardens called *conucos.* On each, cassavas, cubanelle peppers, lima beans, pumpkins, squashes, and starchy tubers grew together in a single clump such that something was in season year-round. From cassava, cooks made tapioca pudding, which doubled as a dentifrice. A subtle culinary addition from the Carib united tarpon and wild boar with lemon and lime juices and pepper sauce, one of the distinct recipes of the West Indies.

The least sophisticated West Indian meals come from Antigua, Barbuda, Dominica, Grenada, Montserrat, Nevis, and St. Kitts. Because these small islands relied heavily on imported seafood and vegetables, their standard table spread featured fresh meats, frog's legs, and produce for fish soup. To dockside offloads, after 1698, African slaves laboring on sugar plantations added from their yard gardens ackee, bananas, cornmeal, mango, okra, peanuts, and plantains.

Grenadans regularly feasted on callaloo with crab, oil down from salt cod cooked in coconut milk, and queen conch souse marinated in lime juice. Antiguans and Barbudans refined meat into pepper pot soup by adding *cassareep,* a fermented cassava juice cooked into a syrup and sweetened with brown sugar, cayenne, cinnamon, cloves, and salt. The antiseptic quality of cassareep kept foods safe for lengthy canoe journeys. A side dish of *fungi* combined two North American foods, cornmeal and okra, into a pudding. Dominicans developed a unique fried chicken recipe that began with the marinating of chicken in garlic and lime. Rolling in herbed flour preceded frying in oil.

Post-Columbian Cuisine

After the arrival of Spanish foodstuffs on Christopher Columbus's fleet in fall 1492, Cuban cookery, the earliest multicultural food in the West Indies, infused Andalucian recipes with Taíno and African methods and ingredients, including boniato and malanga tubers and *roucou,* an herb integral to picadillo sauce. From the island's history, cooks retained the omelet and the croquette, a mincing of conch and vegetables for binding with mashed tubers, milk, and egg and rolling in cassava flour for deep-frying.

Spanish grilling methods varied island menus. The empanada, a filled turnover, produced a similar marriage of textures and flavors, both savory and sweet. The Cuban sandwich served grilled Swiss cheese and ham on sweet *pan cubano* (Cuban yeast bread) with mustard and pickles, sometimes accompanied by a side dish of *Moros y Cristianos* (black beans and rice), wittily named for the Iberian face-off between black Moors and white Christians. When Cuban immigrants took their cuisine to Florida, culinary history dubbed it "Floribbean."

From similar roots, Puerto Ricans adapted Taíno, Mesoamerican, and Ethiopian tastes into a unique *cocina criolla* (Creole cookery), notably barbecued pig's ears, snouts, and tails flavored with an adobo spice rub blended from garlic, onion, oregano, pepper, and salt. Cooks stewed *arroz con gandules* from rice and pigeon peas, the island's national dish. To bland staples, they wrested flavor from annatto, bay leaves, capers, cumin, ham, olives, and *sofrito,* a combination of annatto seed, chili pepper, cilantro, gar-

lic, ham, onion, and oregano sautéed in lard. To wed spice to vegetable, they cooked the mix with a topping of banana leaf or plantain.

Jamaican cuisine, impacted by Danish and Portuguese sailors and British colonizers, developed *escabeche* (poached fish), "stamp and go" (cod patties), dunkanoo (corn dumplings), and ackee and salt cod, the national dish. From the British colonization of India, island cooks turned curried goat into a specialty along with moist, tender jerked chicken and pork cooked over pimiento wood and accompanied by kidney beans, pigeon peas, and rice. A flair for bright red pimiento and Scotch bonnet or habañero peppers and tomatoes and the fragrance of allspice, onions, and thyme heightened the sensual appeal of Jamaican jack fish and marlin dishes. A popular street food reflecting Rastafarian vegetarianism, aloo balls derived from mashed potatoes spiced with cumin and turmeric for deep frying and eating with Blue Mountain coffee, introduced on the island in 1728 from Martinique.

In the Lesser Antilles, Guadeloupe, Marie-Galante, Martinique, St. Bart's, and St. Martin adapted island ingredients to French cooking methods. To *machoui* (spit-roasted mutton), island cooks added egg dishes and elegant displays of carved pineapple and mango. A one-dish specialty, *pâté en pot* began with chopped lamb cooked into a stew flavored with basil, chili, and lemon and baked in a *tourtière* (pie pan). Simple luncheons involved the mincing of fresh vegetables into rice salad, a vegetarian dish soaked in a refreshing vinaigrette or yogurt.

Haiti, another French island, incorporated African cookery to produce *boulets* (bread-bound meatballs), blackberry or dewberry desserts, and *riz et pois colles* (rice and kidney beans). Saucing with béchamel from milk, *coquimol* from coconut, and *sauce ti-malice* from chili reserved local flavors in French-style creaming and whipping to top dishes featuring seafood and small, dark *djon djon* mushrooms. The Dominican Republic claimed as its national dish *sancocho,* a stew of *longaniza* (pork sausage) served with avocado over rice.

Immigrant Cooking

After the emancipation of slaves in the 1770s, the importation of Chinese laborers to sugarcane fields added bean curd, bok choy, mustard, and rice to the multinational cuisine. From Polynesia, English botanists brought breadfruit to the Grenadines, Jamaica, and St. Vincent. As beet sugar reduced the profits from cane sugar, growers began devoting more farm space to cinnamon, cloves, coconuts, corn, ginger, nutmeg, pineapples, soursops, and yams. The veritable rainbow of flavors spiced fish chowder, conch salad, and stewed shark.

Chinese-Caribbean style incorporated Asian cooking methods and textures for curried duck, fried chicken, and pork with egg noodles, a favorite in Jamaica. Stir-frying encouraged the quick heating of local greens with minced meats for a crisper mouthfeel and lighter meal.

Stuffing vegetables with ground fish contributed a common variant on seafood fried in oil.

A favorite dessert, konkee involved the wrapping of bananas or plantains in banana leaves for boiling in spiced coconut milk. Bush tea, ginger, guava, jujube, passion fruit, and tamarind contributed juices for refreshing non-alcoholic beverages that also restored health and vigor. More bracing drinks—daiquiri, malta, mauby, mojito, pina colada, rum punch, and sangria—were served to tourists and visitors.

North of the South American coast, Barbados created a regional Bajan Seasoning, a blend of green onions, marjoram, parsley, and thyme. Breakfast menus focused on fried flying fish, a tender, flavorful meat redolent with lime juice and served with steamed christophene (chayote). A peasant black pudding combined pig blood with rice for stuffing pig intestines. On Barbados Independence Day each November 30, hosts served platters of fish cakes and conkies, a fritter made from cornmeal, coconut, pumpkin, raisins, and sweet potatoes wrapped in banana leaf.

Likewise, Tobago and Trinidad imbued recipes with the taste and texture of coconut and sweet potatoes, which accompany coucou, a cornmeal mush, and pelau, a mix of rice with peas and pork. For *buljol* or cod bake, cooks shredded fish and blended it with coconut, olive oil, onion, pepper, and tomatoes. An accompaniment from India, roti, a griddle-baked wheat bread, wrapped around chutney, curries, and salsas to make them easier to eat. A patio favorite, Spanish pastelles consisted of corn pastries steamed in banana leaves.

Today, the popularity of the Caribbean diet derives from its emphasis on fresh produce and vibrant flavor. The combinations of fish, fruit, legumes, and vegetables bolster the diet with antioxidants, iron and potassium, omega-3 acids, vitamins A and C, and calcium. For the sake of wellness, roughage stabilizes blood glucose and regulates the colon. Dry rubs and liquid spice mixes invigorate digestion and suppress hunger.

See also: Barbecue; Breadfruit; Columbus, Christopher; Jerky; Manioc.

Further Reading

Blouet, Olwyn M. *The Contemporary Caribbean: History, Life, and Culture Since 1945.* London: Reaktion, 2007.

Harris, Dunstan A. *Island Cooking: Recipes from the Caribbean.* Berkeley, CA: Ten Speed, 2003.

Pilcher, Jeffrey M. *Food in World History.* New York: Taylor & Francis, 2006.

Rahamut, Wendy. *Modern Caribbean Cuisine.* Northampton, MA: Interlink, 2007.

Cassava
See Manioc

Demeter, the ancient Greek goddess of corn and the harvest (the counterpart to Ceres in ancient Rome), presents corn to the hero and demigod Triptolemus. In Greek mythology, Demeter taught Triptolemus the art of agriculture, which he disseminated to the rest of Greece. *(Dea/G. Dagli Orti/De Agostini/Getty Images)*

Cereal

The history of diet identifies cereals as the products of ubiquitous grains and grasses that nurture humankind. Emmer wheat sustained farmers in Israel from 17,000 B.C.E., some 5,000 years before humankind added einkorn wheat to Paleolithic cuisine. Around 11,050 B.C.E., after the settlement of Abu Hureyra in western Mesopotamia (Syria), a millennium of drought forced hunter-gatherers to sow and harvest the hardiest wild seeds, beginning with rye and advancing to barley, a nutritious cereal grain.

Parallel to these ancestral grasses of the Fertile Crescent, West Africans from Cape Verde to Lake Chad subsisted on *fonio,* a fast-maturing grain cultivated on dry, infertile savannas and made into couscous. Like Mediterranean myths, Malians considered fonio the grain from which the world evolved. Its unique taste made it popular with Malian and Nigerian chiefs and kings and as a remunerative bride price in Benin, Cameroon, Guinea, Senegal, Sierra Leone, and Togo.

Paleoethnobotanists have tracked the emergence of cereal crops in early civilizations. Developments in subsequent edible grains introduced dominant species region by region:

12,000 B.C.E.	rice	China
10,000 B.C.E.	wild rice	Great Lakes of North America
9600 B.C.E.	wheat	Iraq, Jordan
8500 B.C.E.	barley	Palestine
8300 B.C.E.	millet	China
6000 B.C.E.	amaranth	Mexico
5800 B.C.E.	quinoa	Peru
5000 B.C.E.	spelt	Caucasus
4000 B.C.E.	buckwheat	Japan
4000 B.C.E.	teff	Ethiopia
3200 B.C.E.	oats	Europe
1800 B.C.E.	rye	central Europe
1000 B.C.E.	sorghum	India, Pakistan

For harvest chores, growers created tools—the scythe, flail, basket fan, and winnowing fork. Threshing and wind winnowing enabled ancient communities to separate lightweight chaff from the nutritious grain. To accommodate preparers of cereal, potters molded earthenware into specific shapes for steaming cereal grains.

Cereals and Civilization

During the rise of agriculture, around 8000 B.C.E., and the addition of cereals to diet, humans declined in both body mass and well-being. Anthropologists noted a decrease in human height and the size of the bite as well as a spurt in dental decay from sticky carbohydrates clinging to teeth. As a result of community formation around productive fields, population density rose from one to 15 persons per square mile (from less than one to about six persons per square kilometer). The seasonal production of grain sustained the growth of communities into cities, where citizens pursued nonagrarian jobs and artisanal crafts.

Cereals introduced the young to adult foods. The shift from rough grains to porridge allowed women to wean infants sooner and to substitute pap and gruel for breast feeding. During the transition, the semiliquid cereal required no chopping or pureeing, offering mothers a shortcut to child feedings. The substitution of cooked cereals for breast milk shortened the period of nursing and thus the span between births.

Grains increased the range and complexity of barter systems. In sub-Saharan Africa after 1500 B.C.E., growers packed lightweight dried pearl millet, copra (coconut meat), and fish for trading in rural communities along major waterways. As far east as India and west to Spain, millet sold well as a parched grain, steamed couscous, and source of porridge, but it required immediate use rather than lengthy storage, for which it was unsuited.

Syrian author Ibn Sayyar al-Warraq summarized the Abbasid foodways of the Arabo-Islamic bourgeois in *Kitab al-Tabikh* (*Book of Dishes,* ca. 950 B.C.E.). The text enumerated recipes for cereal grains, including toasted wheat for travelers and *murri,* a fermented condiment revered as "the essence of food." Al-Warraq compiled innovative combinations of grain with beans and vegetables and seasoned wheat dishes and a stew of lentils, rice, and white beans with black pepper, cassia, galangal, and onion and a dollop of fat. His dietetic regimen for invalids centered on grain stews and rice porridge, which he also prescribed for indigestion and upset stomach. For barley broth, a reliever of respiratory congestion, he indicated slow cooking in a double boiler. He preferred his cereal dishes cooked fluffy and chewy in a *tannur* (clay oven) rather than creamy or mushy in a cauldron. For flavor, he suspended a roasting chicken, lamb, or beef ribs above the pot and allowed meat drippings to add complex flavors.

The Greeks valued cereal as a source of social change. Philosophically, diners acknowledged the civilizing aspect of cereal by which Demeter, the goddess of cereal grains, socialized bestial meat eaters and introduced mealtime courtesy and the sharing of communal dishes. In Bronze Age Greece, mythology about Demeter depicted her assigning Triptolemus, a chief of Eleusis, to sow cereal grains to feed the world. A standard rural meal among northern Greek pastoral people involved the boiling of einkorn flour with salt or wine must and either milk or water to produce a mildly sweetened porridge.

Cereals gained respect for providing more food energy than any other crop. Around 300 B.C.E., encyclopedist and educator Theophrastus of Lesbos evaluated cereals and pulses as grains useful as famine provisions for their ease of storage. Augustus Caesar's forces appear to have introduced hearty emmer wheat cereals to Italy after the Roman invasion of Egypt in 30 B.C.E. As the basis of farina, emmer wheat became the source of cooked porridge that dominated Roman *cena,* the main meal of the day. Cooks enhanced the blandness of barley with chopped garlic, leeks, and onion and sweetened oat gruel with honey.

Boosting Nutrition

In the early Middle Ages, watermill patrons could choose to retrieve the middlings for cereal or grits and to keep the bran in unbolted (unsieved) meal as a source of fats, minerals, protein, and vitamins. Both ingredients satisfied hunger while keeping food costs low. For the lowest-class Byzantine, barley and emmer wheat cereals and legumes stocked the communal pot. Armies subsisted on double-baked biscuit and cereal pottage washed down with wine.

After the Crusades, in the thirteenth century, the English began incorporating Levantine and Sicilian groat dishes in their diet. One example, the standard English porridge, became the oldest national dish. It acquired character as frumenty (or fermenty), cracked wheat cereal boiled in milk and flavored with fruit, spice, and sweeteners. Additives ranged from almonds, currants, and egg yolks to orange flower water, rum, saffron, and sugar.

In the early Renaissance, cereal cookery remained essential to stamina worldwide. During the Ming dynasty, which began in 1368, imperial Chinese food service required a cadre of 5,000 kitchen workers to plate the main meal of the day. Presented around 2 P.M., the courses featured entrées alongside cakes and cereals. After the Spanish conquest of the Americas, conquistadors discovered that the Inca kept their soldiers healthy on dried fish and quinoa, a common cereal grain. The Aztec ground corn for *atole,* a staple porridge flavored with chili and salt for eating from a spoon or sipping as a beverage. In Poland, *kasha* (buckwheat cereal) earned the title of "Jewish soul food" for sustaining families over a millennium.

American cooks associated cereal cookery with sustaining babies and the sick. In 1854, Bostonian writer Sarah Josepha Hale, author of *The New Household Receipt-Book,* advocated gruel as a food for toddlers. Her varied list of sickbed meals included cornmeal mush and oatmeal, both easily digested. For babies for whom cow's, goat's, or sheep's milk proved unpalatable, in 1867, German-born pharmacist Henri Nestlé of Vevey, Switzerland, formulated *Farine Lactée* (milk cereal), a powder of sweetened condensed cow's milk and malted wheat rusks. In the 1870s, he marketed it in the United States as an intermediate food under the logo "Best for Babies."

In 1877, the Quaker Mill Company of Ravenna, Ohio, popularized cooked oats as the mainstay of the breakfast menu, providing something "warm in the tummy" for schoolchildren. In 1894, Michigan brothers John Harvey Kellogg and Will Keith Kellogg introduced Americans to a wholesome, high-fiber breakfast food that required no measuring, stirring, and cooking. They manufactured ready-to-eat cereal by baking thin layers of wheat paste into flakes.

The heyday of cold cereals produced the corn flake, which vegetarian food faddist John Harvey Kellogg patented in Battle Creek, Michigan, in 1895. In 1906, the boom in breakfast cereals brought fame to the Kellogg factories, which shipped 1,000 cases of bran, corn, and wheat flakes a day. In 1908, Charles William Post contributed Post Toasties, the beginning of a convenience food empire. By 1911, consumers could select from 107 brands of corn flakes.

Industrialization reinvented cereal grains as fun foods. In 1941, General Mills's invention of Cheerios turned the amorphous oat cereal into a crisp, miniature doughnut, a shape invented in Pennsylvania Dutch kitchens. The burgeoning market in sugar after World War II turned shredded wheat and corn flakes into sweet snacks. Cereal companies also added small plastic toys and mascot figures to cereal box contents to entice child purchasers.

Television ads of the 1950s and 1960s connected dry cereals with friendly cartoon characters. Children identi-

fied breakfast cereals with the Trix rabbit, Cap'n Crunch, Tony the Tiger, Count Chocula, and Lucky the Leprechaun, spokesman for Lucky Charms. Endorsements from TV cowboy Hopalong Cassidy and puppet Howdy Doody increased cereal consumption of Post Raisin Bran and Kellogg's Rice Krispies. Health-conscious parents compromised on empty calories by topping General Mills's Cocoa Puffs and Kellogg's Sugar Smacks with bananas, raisins, and berries.

In 1970, after agronomist Norman Borlaug's genetic engineering of Asian grains, cereal crops increased yield by 10 percent, augmenting basic nutrition. Meanwhile, American cereal companies trivialized grain nutrition with harmful additives. The dyeing of grain cereal into Froot Loops, Franken Berries, and Boo-Berries intrigued children with Crayola colors. In the 1970s, pediatrician Ben Feingold of California identified artificial hues and flavors as causes of inattention and hyperactivity in young patients.

A health backlash popularized breakfast cereals enriched with niacin, riboflavin, and thiamine. In 1971, the U.S. Food and Drug Administration recommended the addition of iron to breakfast cereals and infant pablum. Invalids reinforced their intake with Carnation Instant Breakfast and power bars, a packable cereal snack for eating with midmorning coffee. Heartier breakfasts buttressed nutrition with fruit smoothies served with granola or muesli, a European cereal composed of walnuts, dried apricots and raisins, and oats.

Under the Child Nutrition Act, in 1972, the U.S. Department of Agriculture established the Women, Infants, and Children (WIC) Program, which distributed iron-fortified baby food and cereal to some 88,000 applicants. In 1975, the federal School Lunch Program promoted preschool breakfasts of dry cereal with milk. The program subsidized free or reduced-priced morning meals to improve nutrition for the poor, especially parturient teens, and to establish a model of wise breakfast selections.

In 1979, a U.S. Department of Agriculture initiative targeted food processors with a chart of popular cereals and the proportion of grain to sugar. Leading the sweets marketers, Kellogg overloaded Sugar Smacks with 56 percent sugar, as contrasted to Quaker puffed rice, which contained 0.1 percent sucrose. The appeal to children was obvious in merry product names—Sugar Crisp, Froot Loops, Alpha Bits, and Lucky Charms, all made up of more than one-third sugar. Although American cereals bore the brunt of criticism, British cooks traditionally sprinkled cereal with Barbados sugar, an additive that increased tooth loss.

Cereal and World Hunger

Cereal suits the human and situational needs of emergency food systems. The independence movement in sub-Saharan Africa in the early 1960s buoyed population so rapidly that the continent shifted from a cereal exporter to an importer in just four decades. The light cargo weight enabled rescuers to airlift sustenance to areas plagued by disease, flood, revolt, and starvation. Global food aid, much of it in the form of cereals, exceeded 10 million tons in some years during the early 2000s, though annual totals varied significantly.

Recent crises in Africa have required greater commitment to halting child mortality and relieving early childhood kwashiorkor and marasmus, which stunt physical growth and mental acuity. In 2010, the International Fund for Agricultural Development loaned Sudanese farmers cash for seeds and cereal for immediate famine relief. Growers repaid the loans with cereal from subsequent harvests. As the underclass raises itself out of calamity, positive indicators in Benin, Burkina Faso, Ghana, Mali, Mauritania, and Nigeria anticipate rapid increases in the cultivation of cereals. Similar programs relieve poverty in Guatemala and Haiti with cheaper cereals and sustainable grains.

See also: Baby Food and Infant Feeding; Breakfast; Corn and Maize; Einkorn Wheat; Emmer Wheat; Fertile Crescent Diet and Food Trade; Pan-European Diet and Cuisine; Rice.

Further Reading

Chakraverty, Amalendu, ed. *Handbook of Postharvest Technology: Cereals, Fruits, Vegetables, Tea, and Spices.* New York: Marcel Dekker, 2003.

Hui, Yiu H., ed. *Handbook of Food Products Manufacturing: Principles, Bakery, Beverages, Cereals, Cheese, Confectionary, Fats, Fruits, and Functional Foods.* Hoboken, NJ: Wiley-Interscience, 2007.

Kulp, Karel, and Joseph G. Ponte. *Handbook of Cereal Science and Technology.* New York: Marcel Dekker, 2000.

Charlemagne (ca. 742–814)

The king of the Franks and Lombards, Charlemagne, or Charles the Great, enlarged an empire over central and Western Europe and influenced the ample tables and jovial feasting of his era. His conquests incorporated numerous cultures, including those of Spain and Italy, where Pope Leo III crowned him first emperor of the Holy Roman Empire on Christmas Day 800. By shielding the papacy and crushing Saxon paganism, the king parlayed power far beyond his inheritance. Historians admire his reverence for monastic values and regard him as the father of Europe.

The king kept close watch on his assets and managed the food economy of his people. In addition to reforming currency, he superintended food pricing and, in 794, standardized weights and measures. For soldiers in the field, he organized supply trains to last for several weeks without restocking. His officers followed an orderly system of foraging and convoying. He admired a soldier who chewed meat from the bone and sucked out the marrow, evidence of vigor and avoidance of waste.

In 796, out of concern for pilgrims to Rome, Charlemagne funded food banks and the Schola Francorum, a hospice where travelers could seek meals and medicines. The schools he founded for youths stressed comportment as well as scholarship. He set an example of learning by listening to a lector at dinner read from the Bible and classic authors Augustine and Suetonius.

In his directive *Capitulare de Villis* (*The Supervision of Manors,* ca. 800), Charlemagne ordered cleanliness in the preparation of butter and cheese and in the milling of flour. He accorded honor to bakers as provisioners of the people. His standards affected the collection of honey and nuts and the malting of beer. The directive extended from vinegar and wine to the preparation of lard, mustard, and wax, of which he collected two-thirds for royal use. Out of parsimony, he instructed his poulterers to keep 100 chickens and 30 geese and to sell surplus eggs.

Charlemagne built the reputation of Carolingian kitchen largesse. For his entourage at Aachen, he maintained huge pantries of staples and wine and imported from peasant farms fresh beans and chickpeas. To ensure plenty, he ordered the keeping of the *Inventaire des Domaines* (*Domestic Inventory,* 810), an ongoing accounting of goods and livestock on royal estates. His penchant for observing the behavior of servants and lords enforced strict house rules of propriety and table manners.

Charlemagne dignified table customs as evidence of a civilized society. A handsome, stately ruler in gold diadem, he dressed in royal gems and embroidered cloaks for feasts, where he presided. According to Einhard, author of *Vita Karoli* (*The Life of Charlemagne,* ca. 817), the king preferred Frankish dishes—spit-roasted game accompanied by four side dishes. A follower of St. Benedict, the model of medieval hospitality, the king tended to concentrate on hearty food, especially roast boar and venison. He despised drunkenness and quelled medieval tendencies to eat and drink in excess. He also encouraged adventure stories from his table guests and enlivened the atmosphere with dancers, instrumentalists, and singers. Each of his four weddings coincided with lengthy festivals.

In his last month, chest pain forced Charlemagne to forgo eating. After his death from pleurisy in his early 70s in 814, monks illuminated manuscripts with images of the great host. Appropriately, after antipope Pascal III canonized him as Sanctus Karolus at Aix-la-Chapelle in 1165, Charlemagne acquired his own feast day, July 27, to honor his battles against Saracens and heathenism.

See also: Cider; Dairy Food; Mustard.

Further Reading

Barbero, Alessandro. *Charlemagne.* Berkeley: University of California Press, 2004.

Fletcher, Nichola. *Charlemagne's Tablecloth: A Piquant History of Feasting.* New York: St. Martin's, 2005.

McKitterick, Rosamond. *Charlemagne: The Formation of a European Identity.* New York: Cambridge University Press, 2008.

Story, Joanna. *Charlemagne: Empire and Society.* Manchester, UK: Manchester University Press, 2005.

Cheese

The details of cheese history remain lost in time, but the relevance of dairy food to the cuisine of Europe, the Middle East, and North America is invaluable. The coagulation of high-protein curds derives from a variety of milk—from the Arabian camel, African boar, Ceylonese zebu, Cretan sheep, Greek goats and cows, Italian water buffalo, North American white-tailed deer, Peruvian llama, Russian ass and mare, Scandinavian reindeer, Tibetan yak, and Tunisian camel. Archaeologists assume that storing fresh milk in a goat intestine or cow's stomach may have introduced enzymes that separated curds from the acidic whey.

As long ago as 9000 B.C.E., dried curds suited travelers as a portable dairy food less vulnerable to spoilage than milk or yogurt. Among the Bai of Yunnan Province, in southern China, pastoralists turned coagulated milk into a sheet or string cheese called *rushan*. Tibetans learned the process from the Bai and introduced a buttermilk cheese squeezed into leathery noodles for drying and tying in pretzel shapes or stringing on yak hair.

In the Chihuahua Desert on the Texas-Mexico border around 7500 B.C.E., Paleo-Indian farmers abandoned nomadism and consumed quantities of domesticated cheese and milk along with grain and meat. After 5200 B.C.E., Sumerian animal husbandry in the Tigris and Euphrates delta yielded secondary products from cattle, which added 5 quarts (4.7 liters) of butter and 7.5 quarts (7.1 liters) of cheese per cow to income. Families stored tart feta goat cheese in tall jars. In the Indus Valley, farmers enhanced their diet with butter and cheese from their herds, two sources of interregional trade.

In Asia in 4000 B.C.E., the Chinese tamed the water buffalo, a source of mozzarella cheese and curd. Cuisine relied on cheese, fish, and grain as staples. Chinese cheese makers removed oil from butter and processed the remaining buttermilk into a low-fat commodity that remained edible on the shelf. Worshippers carried altar gifts of butter oil and cheese blended with dates, grain, spice, and wine.

From goats and sheep in the south and cows in the north, the Greeks made cheese to extend the profitability of dairying. In the *Odyssey* (ca. 750 B.C.E.), Homer described the cyclops Polyphemus curdling goat's and sheep's milk with rennet and gathering the curds of *cynthos,* a forerunner of feta, in wicker baskets, which strained and shaped the solids. The grazing of flocks on *cytisus* (Scotch broom) gave the crumbly cheese its unique flavor and creamy texture. Pastoralists established a steady trade with the Romans, who found innovative ways of incorporating cynthos into cooking.

On Crete, shepherds kept busy daily curdling the output from sheep, which they milked twice a day. Farmers used tree roots, oak splits, and pear wood to make stirring sticks and whisks for whipping boiling milk into coagulation from the action of lamb's rennet. Lumps of solids hardened in a second boiling. Air-dried on wooden frames for 30 days, the wheels of sheep's milk cheese, called *mizithra,* ripened in mountain dugouts accessed by low tunnels. Traders loaded rounds into goatskin sacks

A cheese maker plunges his arm into a cauldron of curds while making blue cheese. As in the case of other hard cheeses, the curds must then be drained, cut into smaller pieces, scalded, and set in round moulds for ripening. *(Steven Senne/Associated Press)*

for shipping and for selling locally. Islanders ate mizithra in pies or with honey or olives. The physician Hippocrates validated it and other Mediterranean cheeses for their nourishment and ease of digestion.

From the Etruscans, the Romans learned to curdle milk with vegetable enzymes from artichokes, cardoons, figs, safflower seeds, and thistles. Around 70 B.C.E., the scholar Varro stated that Roman dairies advanced from kid and lamb enzymes to hare and goat rennet. Using complex methods of ripening solids, commercial dairies pressed and aged cheese for export. Fresh or soft ricotta cheese required air-drying and salting. After a soaking in cold water, workers shaped soft-paste mozzarella into rounds for immediate use.

Columella's agrarian encyclopedia *De Re Rustica* (*On Agriculture,* ca. 50 C.E.) detailed a longer dehydration or smoking of cheese over apple wood or straw followed by scalding with boiling water and hand shaping in wooden frames. The stored curd yielded hard cheese, which cooks flavored with pepper, pine nuts, and thyme. As described by encyclopedist Pliny the Elder's 37-book *Historia Naturae* (*Natural History,* ca. 77 C.E.), the cheese industry flourished at the beginning of the Roman Empire and contributed to cosmopolitan trade around the Mediterranean. The best Greek cheese came from Ceos and colonies in Sicily; the Romans ranked at the top Alpine, Apennine, and Vestinian cheeses from the Abruzzi hills and the worst from Gaul, where smoking overcame the natural sweetness.

Artisanal Cheese

Soft cheese achieved popularity for its fresh taste and low price. As a breakfast dish, ordinary Romans consumed it with bread and olives or vegetables. Wealthy consumers bought interesting dairy products from northwestern European sites, where bacteria and mold imparted unusual flavors. A favorite, semihard emmental, came from Helvetia; in Auvergne, France, mountain herders made cantal by pressing curds in a wooden cylinder called a formage, source of the French *fromage* (cheese). Gourmands reserved hard cheese, such as Bithynian varieties, as a dinner finger food or dessert nibble served with wine. Grated cheese topped gratins and contributed to the taste of bread, cakes, dips, and wine drinks.

Medieval cheese making, based on Roman methods adopted in river valleys, ensured supplies of Gorgonzola, Grana, Gruyère, provolone, and Roquefort as year-round pantry staples. Among Byzantine herders, halloumi, a Cypriot and Egyptian cheese, mixed goat's and sheep's milk flavors and remained fresh from a coating of mint leaves and storage in brine. Paneer, imported from India, derived from a curdling process that added lemon juice to milk. The coagulation satisfied the vegetarian needs of Hindus.

In the late 700s, Moorish herders brought goat cheese making to Poitou, France. Along Italy's Po River in the eleventh century, Benedictine and Cistercian monks preserved local cheeses as a gesture of hospitality to guests and patients at monastery clinics. The brushing of washed-rind cheese with beer, brandy, brine, or saltwater encouraged bacteria to produce mold, the type of crust and veining that distinguish Brie and Limburger. In northern Scotland, highland dairies employed stones in a metal frame to press whey from solids to make caboc cheese, which they sealed in oatmeal. A peasant favorite, crowdie, which coated the stomachs of whiskey drinkers, bore a coating of black pepper.

The end of the Dark Ages in 1000 derived from a livelier agricultural trade. From 1170, royal provisioners of Henry II bought tons of cheddar from Somerset, where dairies chopped and matured curds in humid caves for over a year. A century later, north-central Italians thrived on the sale of Parmigiano-Reggiano, a crumbly dairy food popular for grating into rice and soup and over pasta. At Lodi, farmers made short-aged mascarpone, a dessert cheese, from cream clotted with lemon juice. For Balkan, North African, and Turkish cuisine, feta and Kasar filled borek, a stuffed pastry encased in phyllo dough and deep-fried.

To the north, the Dutch made a similar success of Edam and Gouda. From the 1300s, sailing crews and home diners enjoyed Edam with melons and pome fruit. Gouda, coagulated with muriatic acid, had a pungent flavor that barkeeps served with ale. During the age of voyages, provisioners stored cheese in ships' galleys. After 1608, Samuel de Champlain introduced Canadienne cheese at Quebec, where dairies followed French techniques. The Pilgrims stocked the *Mayflower* with Holland cheese and, in 1620, brought northern European dairy skills to the Massachusetts Colony. In 1791, Marie Harel, a Norman farmer, sold the first Camembert, a creamy spread made from cow's milk in a style perfected by farmers from Brie.

Following the defaming of cheese in the late Renaissance as harmful to health, dairy foods revived in commercial importance during the 1800s. The Swiss introduced manufactured cheese in 1815; Norwegians followed industrial trends in the 1850s with the production of nutty, sweet Jarlsberg. Commercial production of uniform cheeses in the United States began in Rome, New York, in 1851, when grazier Jesse Williams built the nation's first factory distributing boxed cheeses. By 1859, John J. Smith, owner of Wisconsin's first cheese vat, opened a plant in Sheboygan County. From the late 1860s, cheese processors inoculated batches with scientific microbial culture rather than the lactobacilli, lactococci, and streptococci ambient in nature.

As former colonies developed indigenous styles of food production, cheese took on regional flavors. In Sydney, Australia, the production of creamy *buche noir* concluded with the dusting of wheels of goat's milk curds with the ashes of a vine. In 1881, Canadian dairier Édouard-André Barnard taught coagulation methods in Quebec at North America's first cheese-making school.

The initial commercial successes, Camembert and feta, preceded a lengthy history of experimentation and innovation in the use of herding products, which established Quebec as Canada's center of cheese excellence.

Production Today

Presently, world cheese consumption reaches 30 grams (1 ounce) per day among the British and 65 grams (2.3 ounces) for the Austrian, Danish, Dutch, French, German, Greek, Italian, Swedish, and Swiss diner. In twelfth place, American consumers eat cheese as often as diners in Finland, Iceland, and Norway. U.S. dairies allot one-third of their milk to the manufacture of 300 varieties of cheese.

To control the texture and melt, processors emulsify cheese with salt and add dyes, milk solids, and preservatives. Manufacturers market the results unsliced, sliced, shredded, or grated, or in aerosol cans, cheese mills, dips, and spreads. The popularity of pizza and string cheese boosts mozzarella to the top seller, followed closely by cheddar, the main ingredient in grilled cheese sandwiches and macaroni and cheese.

The local food and Slow Food movements augment demand for Asiago, Gorgonzola, and Havarti as well as chèvre and Muenster. The Ark of Taste, a catalog of heritage foods, honors sustainable cheeses for their contributions to regional cuisines, such as Abruzzi pecorino, American kunik, Austrian abgereifter, Brazilian sack cheese, British Dorset blue, Calabrian caprino, French rove brousse, Dutch leiden, Icelandic skyr, and Polish oscypek.

See also: Animal Husbandry; Charlemagne; Dairy Food; Fermented Foods; Travel Food.

Further Reading

Harbutt, Juliet. *The Complete Illustrated Guide to Cheeses of the World.* Leicester, UK: Hermes House, 1999.

Herbst, Sharon Tyler, and Ron Herbst. *The Cheese Lover's Companion: The Ultimate A-to-Z Cheese Guide with More Than 1,000 Listings for Cheeses and Cheese-Related Terms.* New York: William Morrow, 2007.

McCalman, Max, and David Gibbons. *Cheese: A Connoisseur's Guide to the World's Best.* New York: Clarkson Potter, 2005.

Thorpe, Liz. *The Cheese Chronicles: A Journey Through the Making and Selling of Cheese in America, From Field to Farm to Table.* New York: HarperCollins, 2009.

Chicle and Chewing Gum

A pungent natural latex grown from Brazil and Colombia north to Yucatán in Mexico and the Orinoco River valley of Venezuela and in the Philippines, chicle is the central ingredient of chewing gum. A familiar milky resin to the Maya from the sapodilla tree (*Manilkara chicle* or *zapota*) from 3000 B.C.E., chicle served as a thirst quencher as well as waterproofing, glue, mortar, and incense. From January to July, the inner bark of each tree dripped between 3 and 4 pounds (1.4 and 1.8 kilograms) of sap from v- or z-shaped slashes in the trunk. Trees remained productive for more than 15 years.

After Aztec collectors boiled away the 29 percent of liquid in vats, they produced a chewable mass and shaped it into bricks. For each mouthful of chewing gum, users mixed the chicle resin with wax and *Llaveia axin,* a greasy yellow insect larva. Along with improving digestion through the flow of saliva, the gum freshened breath and cleansed the mouth. Much as New England Indians shared spruce gum and pinesap with the Pilgrims, the Aztec offered chicle gum to Spanish conquerors arriving in Mexico City. Homemade recipes for the resin gained popularity as a confection with Europeans.

According to sixteenth-century Spanish ethnographer Bernardino de Sahagún, author of the *Florentine Codex,* the public chewing of gum by women and homosexuals bore a flirtatious connotation. For wives and widows, public chewing earned social disapproval. Still, a ban on gum chewing by the Catholic archdiocese failed to exterminate the habit.

Marketing

In the nineteenth century, General Antonio López de Santa Anna claimed to pay his Mexican army with the proceeds of chicle. After he introduced chicle chewing in New York City, foreign interests stole gum production from the Mexican *chicleros.* The commercialization of chicle replaced the chewing of spruce gum, America's first commodity gum.

An Ohio dentist, William F. Semple, patented a method of dissolving chicle in naphtha and alcohol in 1869. After drying the jellied mass for a week, he added chalk and flavored the gum with licorice root or oil of wintergreen and sugar. The process concluded with a coating of sweetened beeswax. He intended that his patients chew gum as a means of strengthening the jaws and scrubbing their teeth.

On Staten Island, glass merchant Thomas Adams, the first chewing gum millionaire, sold "Adams New York No. 1" in drugstores for a penny a stick for "snapping and stretching." He entered the flavored gum market in 1870 with Black Jack Gum, a licorice mouth and throat soother that sweetened smokers' breath. His company employed the first gum assembly line in the country and made gum one of America's first mass-produced processed foods.

Other manufacturers sweetened chicle with corn syrup and coated it in powdered sugar, which Canadian industrialist William John White of Ontario, the second chewing gum millionaire, added to his Yucatan brand in 1880. By 1888, gum chewers could buy Tutti-Frutti from vending machines in the New York City subway. Edwin E. Beeman, a physician from Cleveland, Ohio, added pepsin in 1891 to turn recreational gum into a digestive aid.

By 1897, the United States placed a tariff of $300 per ton on crude chicle.

In 1899, the American Chicle Company formed a binational monopoly from a merger of the trademarks of Adams, Beeman, and White plus companies in Baltimore; Chicago; Cleveland and Dayton, Ohio; Louisville, Kentucky; Newark, New Jersey; Philadelphia; Portland, Maine; Rochester, New York; St. Louis; and Toronto, Canada. New York City pharmacist Franklin V. Canning added a hygienic cavity preventer in 1899 with the creation of Dentyne.

William Wrigley of Chicago added fruit flavor and mint to rectangles of gum he called Chiclets. His voice for tariff relief urged Congress to reduce import duties on raw chicle. His products generated so much income that, in the early 1900s, sapodilla growing increased migration to Yucatán. In northern Belize, farmers planted some 23 sapodilla trees per acre (about 57 per hectare).

In 1906, Cadbury Adams marketed Chiclets, a candy-coated chewing gum available in peppermint and bright colors. The pellets sold well in fruit flavors throughout North America and Egypt as well as Belgium, Brazil, China, the Dominican Republic, Germany, Greece, Haiti, India, Iran, Italy, Japan, Peru, Portugal, Spain, and Turkey. Confectioner Frank Henry Fleer competed with fruit-flavored Dubble Bubble, which he sold with baseball trading cards.

Innovations

Before World War I, the U.S. military added chewing gum to boxed meals as a stress reliever and hygienic mouth cleaner for soldiers in the field. Although doctors warned that chomping permanently skewed the face, Americans in 1914 chewed 1.5 billion sticks of gum. Adams & Sons continued expanding that year with sour gums and the introduction of Clove, a spiced gum that became popular during the Prohibition era as a cover for alcohol on the breath. By 1924, Mexico earned $2 million from annual chicle exports to Britain, France, and the United States.

Gum reached market shelves as glazed sticks, ribbons, gumballs and jawbreakers, kosher gum, cubes, powder, extrusions, and pellets with liquid centers. Medicated gum delivered stamina-boosting caffeine and ginseng as well as green tea and *guarana,* an energy and memory aid valued by the Guaraní and Tupi of Paraguay.

U.S. GIs spread the fad to Western Europe in the 1940s—the golden age of chewing gum—when British kids yelled, "Hey, Joe! You got gum?" at passing Allied soldiers. Because of wartime sugar rationing, the Wrigley sugarless Orbit brand featured a natural sweetener devoid of sucrose in such exotic flavors as mango and watermelon. A decade later, Wrigley replaced natural resins with a petroleum-based synthetic rubber made from a butadiene polymer, which it distributed in the United States, Canada, and England under the logos Doublemint, Juicy Fruit, and Spearmint.

The U.S. Food and Drug Administration inveighed against the gum industry in 1970 with a ban on cyclamate sweetener. In 1975, Wrigley invented cinnamon-flavored Big Red and Freedent, a brand that doesn't adhere to dentures.

Mexican chicleros returned to the business of chicle gum making in 1995 and produced Chicza, an organic brand available in Great Britain. In 2010, Peppersmith brand reintroduced minted chicle gum in Great Britain and Holland. The makers based their formula on carnauba wax, rapeseed lecithin, gum arabic, and chicle from the Central American rain forest. Sweetening it with xylitol (wood sugar), they claimed, remineralized damaged tooth enamel.

See also: Cortés, Hernán de; New World Commodities.

Further Reading

Mathews, Jennifer P., and Gilliam P. Schultz. *Chicle: The Chewing Gum of the Americas, From the Ancient Maya to William Wrigley.* Tucson: University of Arizona Press, 2009.

Redclift, M.R. *Chewing Gum: The Fortunes of Taste.* New York: Routledge, 2004.

———. *Frontiers: Histories of Civil Society and Nature.* Cambridge, MA: MIT Press, 2006.

Schlesinger, Victoria. *Animals and Plants of the Ancient Maya: A Guide.* Austin: University of Texas Press, 2001.

Child, Julia (1912–2004)

A major influence on modern American cookery and cuisine, Julia Carolyn McWilliams Child infused uninitiated homemakers with vigor and daring through her television demonstrations and cookbooks.

Born the eldest of three on August 15, 1912, in Pasadena, California, to Julia Carolyn Weston and agronomist John McWilliams, Child attended a private boarding school and completed a degree in English at Smith College. After a stint in home furnishings advertising for W. & J. Sloane in New York City, she joined the Office of Strategic Services (OSS) in Washington, D.C., as a research assistant and traveled in Asia during World War II.

Intelligence work introduced Child to international haute cuisine in a variety of venues in China, Sri Lanka, and Europe. With her husband, cartographer and gourmand Paul Cushing Child, she sampled food in Marseilles, Paris, and Provence, a 1949 cultural odyssey summarized in her posthumous autobiography *My Life in France* (2006).

The couple settled in Paris, where she became a disciple of Georges Auguste Escoffier, the "Father of Modern French Cuisine." In 1949, she took classes at the Cordon

California-born chef, cookbook author, and television personality Julia Child introduced and adapted French cuisine to the American mainstream. Her enthusiasm and forgiving approach in the kitchen raised interest in fine cooking and dining. *(Bachrach/Getty Images)*

Bleu, the revered Parisian cooking school, studied privately under Belgian chef Max Bugnard, and joined a gastronomy club, the Cercle des Gourmettes. With Simone Beck and Louisette Bertholle, she opened a cooking school in her apartment on the Left Bank.

In her 30s at the family country house in Cambridge, Massachusetts, Child perfected her skills, from swinging a meat cleaver to melting cheese with a blowtorch. With her colleagues, Beck and Bertholle, she compiled a gastronomic classic, *Mastering the Art of French Cooking* (1961), and freelanced columns on artisanal kitchen skills for the *Boston Globe, House and Garden, House Beautiful, McCall's,* and *Parade.* Her maiden appearance on educational television for WGBH in Boston on February 11, 1963, launched an award-winning ten-year series, *The French Chef,* the first television program captioned for the deaf.

An upbeat, self-assured food master, Child gave credibility to the love of good food into the 1990s. She displayed the chef's knife and whisk, the buttered casserole, and the stockpot, all elements of the standard *batterie de cuisine* (kitchen equipment). She demystified boning chicken, chocolate sculpting, forming gnocchi, lobster boiling, creating phyllo pastry, and making a perfect meringue. Cus-

tomer demand for implements and ingredients increased the business of kitchen boutiques and fine-foods stores.

Child's lectures, televised program *Dinner at Julia's,* and books—*The French Chef Cookbook* (1968), *From Julia Child's Kitchen* (1975), *Julia Child & Company* (1978), and *The Way to Cook* (1989)—generated enthusiasm for fine dining at home, in restaurants, and in the White House of President Jimmy Carter. In 1981, with gastronomer James Beard and wine expert Robert Mondavi, she cofounded the American Institute of Wine and Food, a league of restaurants, to promote glamorous meals of fresh ingredients and table camaraderie. From the consortium came two publications, *American Wine and Food* and *The Journal of Gastronomy,* as well as the Julia Child Award.

In her 80s, Child broadcast three of her programs from her home kitchen, which Paul Child designed to accommodate cameras and set lighting. In a cover article, *Time* magazine dubbed her "Our Lady of the Ladle." She approved nouvelle cuisine and the local food movement but avoided the extremes of exotic food clubs, health obsessions, and veganism. She scoffed at dieting, temperance, organic foods, and free-range poultry and crusaded for the enjoyment of cooking and eating. In collaboration with Jacques Pepin on a subsequent television series, she retained her humor while educating viewers on international dishes.

In 2000, after years of conducting culinary tours of France, she was named chevalier of the Legion of Honor by the French government and elected as a fellow of the American Academy of Arts and Sciences. The following year, she appeared in Napa, California, at the unveiling of the American Center for Wine, Food, and the Arts, a 17-acre (7-hectare) culinary tutorial center. In 2003, she accepted the U.S. Presidential Medal of Freedom. The fervor of fans inspired a biopic, *Julie & Julia* (2009), a tribute to Child's culinary gusto.

See also: Beard, James; Film, Food in.

Further Reading

Child, Julia, and Alex Prud'homme. *My Life in France.* New York: Anchor, 2006.

Conant, Jennet. *A Covert Affair: Julia Child and Paul Child in the OSS.* New York: Simon & Schuster, 2011.

Shapiro, Laura. *Julia Child.* New York: Lipper/Viking, 2007.

Chili

A satisfying comfort dish and fast food, chili con carne combines beef with chili peppers, fat, and herbs to create a fiery one-pot meal. A product of the Great Basin of North America, chili dates to Papago, Pueblo, and Ute dishes made from fresh horse or venison, cornmeal, and peppers.

As revealed in army surgeon Stephen Compton Smith's *Chile con Carne; or the Camp and the Field* (1857), chili con carne nourished waves of westerers. American pioneers devised a convenient trail staple by pounding chili peppers, salt, and suet into beef jerky. The resulting blocks, called "chili bricks," traveled well and blossomed with flavor when rehydrated in boiling water and served with crackers and buttermilk.

In the mid-1800s, the devilishly hot stew fed travelers in depot cafés and on college campuses. Drovers and wranglers ate from the backs of chuck wagons, where camp "cookies" invigorated batches with onions, oregano, and smoky wild chilipiquíns (bird peppers). The washerwomen who served Texas militias braced goat stew with chili pepper and wild marjoram. For bulk, prison and ranch cooks added black beans, black-eyed peas, cracker meal, great northern beans, kitchen beans, *masa harina* (corn flour), and navy or pink beans. In 1890, food processor DeWitt Clinton Pendery simplified chili making by hawking his Chiltomaline chili powder, which he claimed aided digestion and fostered appetite and health.

Texas State Dish

The Texas frontier developed a reputation as a chili haven. Cooks delivered fresh batches daily by pushcart. By 1889, Oklahoma offered chili at lunch counters. Priests, fearing that the popular dish would inflame sexual appetites, preached chili abstinence. A San Antonio vendor introduced the stout stew to urbanites in Chicago at the 1893 Columbian Exposition, where programs referred to the dish as a "hash of meat and spices." British journalists, lacking a comparative to explain chili, called it "curry meat."

At Military Plaza Mercado between San Antonio's city hall and San Fernando Cathedral, from the 1880s, Latino women cooked pots of chili redolent with cayenne pepper and chili powder to sell to pedestrians. Known as "chili queens," the women turned their kitchen business into a unique fast food. They reheated pots of chili over charcoal and mesquite fires and, for a dime, served bowls of beans and chili and a tortilla to soldiers, tourists, and trail hands. The street earned the name La Plaza del Chile con Carne.

After the queens moved operations four blocks west to Haymarket Plaza, people of all classes ate together under colored lantern light to the music of mariachi bands. The egalitarian eateries flourished for a half century until September 12, 1937, when the city health department closed the open-air venue because of flies and unsanitary dish washing. San Antonio's chili market survived in author Stephen Crane's sketch "Stephen Crane in Texas" (1889) and O. Henry's "Seats of the Haughty" in *Heart of the West* (1904) and in the café business of Esperanza García, Juanita García, and Eufemia López.

Recipe: Texas-Style Chile con Carne

In a Dutch oven, brown 3 pounds of coarsely chopped lean beef shoulder, round steak, or ground buffalo meat in 2 tablespoons of lard or 2 ounces of beef kidney suet. Add two large chopped red onions and stir the mixture over medium-high heat. Complete the recipe with 1/2 cup of chopped ancho, red, or serrano peppers; 1/2 teaspoon of dried basil; 1 teaspoon each of paprika and Tabasco; 1 tablespoon each of cumin and oregano or marjoram; one can of tomato paste; two bay leaves; 2 cups of red wine vinegar; and 1 cup of water. Season with black pepper and coarse sea salt. Simmer on low for three hours. Chill overnight before skimming off the hardened fat. Reheat and serve with saltines or oyster crackers and a choice of chopped green onions, lime wedges, pickled jalapeños, shredded sharp cheddar cheese, and sour cream.

Industrialized Fare

Chili ingredients migrated from the Southwest throughout the globe. In 1896, Willie Gebhardt, a German immigrant and owner of the Phoenix Cafe in New Braunfels, Texas, imported ancho chilies from Mexico and ground them with black pepper, cumin, and oregano to bottle for sale as Eagle Brand Chili Powder. In 1908, he canned the first heat-and-eat chili.

Lyman T. Davis dispensed bowls of chili from the back of a wagon on the dirt streets of Corsicana, Texas. He distributed his stew in 1921 under the Wolf Brand Chili label. Promoters of Lyman's Pure Food Products drove a T-model Ford with a body shaped like a tin can. On the back, Davis's pet wolf, Kaiser Bill, rode in a round cage.

Texas families dispatched containers of Wolf Brand Chili to sons in service during World War II. In the field, soldiers reheated their gift food in helmets. To meet postwar demand, Lyman's factory added chili products—hot dog sauce, lean beef chili, and turkey with beans. In 1977, the popularity of Wolf Brand influenced the Texas legislature to drop barbecue and gumbo from the running and to name chili the state dish.

In the Great Depression, throughout the South and Southwest, chili parlors served up bowls of chili, both fresh and canned, with a side of corn bread or saltines. Innovators touted a variety of chili concoctions—chili burritos and omelets, chili cheese fries, chili-topped baked potatoes, corn bread casserole, Frito pie, layered chili salad, nachos, quesadillas, and taco pizza. Chefs originated menu items featuring allspice, beans, fried eggs, hamburgers, hot dogs, jalapeños, melted cheese, onions, sour cream, tomatoes, tortillas, and vinegar.

The Texas State Fair in Dallas enlivened competition in October 1952 by launching the World's Chili Championships. Stern rules limited experimentation with beans, corn or hominy, marinades, pasta, rice, and premixed spices. The contests ended at a specified time, when cooks presented the judges with a sample. Criteria ranged from aroma, consistency, and red color to taste and aftertaste, a common result of four-alarm recipes.

Chili dishes continue to emerge from rearrangements of standard ingredients. A green version, chili verde, begins with pork spiced with green chilies and tomatillos. The U.S. Army offers chili mac (with macaroni) as a Meal, Ready-to-Eat (MRE), a boxed field ration. Vegetarians favor chili made from beans, corn, potatoes, or tofu. Health promoters cook white chili from chicken or turkey breast and white beans. In Australia, Hawaii, and Great Britain, chili fans take their spicy meat over rice.

See also: Cook-Offs; Peppers; Street Food; Tex-Mex Diet and Cuisine.

Further Reading

Albala, Ken. *Beans: A History.* New York: Berg, 2007.

Denker, Joel. *The World on a Plate: A Tour Through the History of America's Ethnic Cuisine.* Lincoln: University of Nebraska Press, 2007.

Kimball, Yeffe, and Jean Anderson. *The Art of American Indian Cooking.* New York: Lyons, 2000.

Walsh, Robb. *The Tex-Mex Cookbook: A History in Photos and Recipes.* New York: Broadway, 2004.

Chinese Diet and Cuisine

See Cantonese Diet and Cuisine; Szechuan Diet and Cuisine

Chocolate

A food favorite for more than 3,000 years, chocolate derives from the cacao tree (*Theobroma cacao*), which originated in South America around 2000 B.C.E. By 1200 B.C.E., the Mexica of Chiapas and northern Hondurans were eating chocolate in both liquid and solid forms. Aborigines along the Amazon and Orinoco rivers cultivated the trees from 1100 B.C.E. and stored pods in ceramic vessels.

Among the Maya, the Nahuatl word *xocolatl* (bitter water) described the acrid taste that required fermentation to make it edible. The chemical conversion of carbohydrates into acids or alcohols transformed the tree pods into the first edible chocolate. Because Mesoamericans lacked cane sugar and milk, their chocolate tasted more like a vegetable than a sweet. After 1000 B.C.E., the Olmec cultivated cacao in Tabasco and Veracruz, Mexico. By 100 C.E., cacao beans received Mayan reverence as aphrodisiacs, currency, emblems of godhood, and a source of cooking sauces. Healers recommended bitter cocoa as a cure for cough, fever, and morning sickness. By 600, Mayans cultivated cacao trees at plantations throughout Yucatán. Trade to the north around 900 introduced the drink to Pueblo Indians of the Great Basin, the first major cacao importers.

In stone mortars, the Maya ground beans of the Criollo cacao tree into a fragrant paste to mix with chili, cornmeal, blossoms, and honey and make a thick chocolate drink sipped by royal courtiers. Worshippers dyed the drink red with achiote and presented the beverage as a ceremonial altar gift. In Guatemala, the Aztec filled bags with cacao beans to serve as coins. Rich Mesoamericans secured chocolate rounds in screw-top jars. Temple architecture featured carvings of cacao pods as the food of the agricultural god Quetzalcoatl.

Chocolate also figures in the *Codex Zouche-Nuttall* (1051) drawn on deer hide in the depiction of a bride offering chocolate to a pre-Columbian Mixtec ruler at Oaxaca. A scene in the late-sixteenth-century *Codex Tudela* demonstrates how Aztec servers generated foam on ritual pots of chocolate. Historians compared the precious drink to the Christian Eucharist and to agricultural tribute levied against conquered tribes. The accumulation of chocolate elevated the Aztec in power and authority.

From New World to Old

On November 7, 1504, Christopher Columbus completed a voyage to Nicaragua and returned to Spain with the first brown cacao beans seen in Europe. His discovery received little attention but eventually altered culinary tastes and cooking styles. On November 8, 1519, Hernán de Cortés's forces reached Mexico and observed chocolate consumption. Throughout the day, Aztec Emperor Montezuma II drank honeyed hot chocolate fragrant with vanilla. According to eyewitness Bernal Díaz, court servants stored the drink in thousands of jars and served it to businessmen, nobles, priests, and war heroes. The imperial court declared chocolate too intense an aphrodisiac for priests or women to taste.

In 1528, the conquistadors carried three chests of chocolate, chilies, and vanilla from Tenochtitlán back to King Charles V, along with the tools to stir the hot drink. The Spaniards accepted from Aztec servants cups of frothy hot chocolate spiced with chilies and the sultry aroma of vanilla. Cortés disliked the taste but realized the monetary value of the cacao bean, which he grew on a plantation in Cuernavaca after 1535.

The Spanish delegated secret chocolate making to Dominican monks, who revamped the Aztec recipe by adding allspice, cinnamon, cloves, nutmeg, sugar, and vanilla for a unique European taste. By 1585, the cacao bean became an international trade commodity, traveling by ship from Veracruz to Seville. As food and medicine, chocolate rose in value over the next two centuries in Austria, France, Germany, and Iberia as well as in the American colonies, Brazil, and the Philippines.

At Versailles, France's Louis XIV promoted the idea of chocolate as the food of seduction. Because of French, English, and Belgian fervor for the trendy drink, governments viewed cacao as a source of new luxury taxes. As seventeenth-century chocolate houses opened throughout major European cities, the Spanish lost control of the cacao monopoly.

In 1707, Irish physician and archivist Hans Sloane introduced milk drinkers to chocolate milk, which he promoted in England and Jamaica for nourishment and well-being. Physicians treated dysentery, inflammation, kidney stones, and tuberculosis with chocolate. Boston apothecaries sold chocolate imported from Europe. In 1741, to strengthen Swedish women, naturalist Carolus Linnaeus promoted the mix of ground cocoa, ambergris, cinnamon, sugar, and vanilla sold in drugstores. Viennese confectioners selected contrasting dark and white chocolate to mold candies called the nipples of Venus.

The Craze

By 1800, factories in Germany, Spain, and Switzerland had industrialized chocolate confections, thereby increasing the profitability of New World cacao plantations. The hydraulic cacao press, invented at Amsterdam in 1828 by Dutch chemist Conraad Johannes Van Houton, powered the "dutching" process, squeezing out acidity and bitterness in cocoa butter to smooth chocolate drinks into a pleasing consistency. The process fermented, cleaned, and dried cacao beans and roasted and winnowed the pods. Ground into cocoa cakes and cocoa liquor, the final product of cocoa butter and cocoa powder resulted from milling. The extrusion method reduced the cost and increased the popularity of chocolate at all socioeconomic levels. In 1851, U.S. fanciers admired chocolate bonbons and creams, manufactured by Quaker entrepreneur John Cadbury and featured at the London Exposition.

In the twentieth century, Quaker chocolatiers championed the beverage in the United States as a replacement for alcoholic drinks. In grocery stores, cooks found stocks of cocoa powder and baking chocolate mass-produced in Pennsylvania by the Milton Hershey Company, an international chocolatier on a par with Cadbury, Ghirardelli, Godiva, Lindt, Mars, and Nestlé. From the early 1900s, the homemaker could select baking chocolate and vanilla for delivery by mail from the Sears catalog. A flurry of candy bar manufacturing in the 1920s put some 40,000 brands on the market.

Distribution slowed during World War I and again in the late 1930s at the approach of World War II. In September 1939, the German bureaucracy denied civilians butter, chocolates, and whipped cream. In England, in lieu of rationed tea, older children received fruit and chocolate as nutrients. During U.S. airlifts along the Burma Road into China in April 1942, C rations arrived in tins containing a reassuring snack of chocolate, biscuits, instant coffee, and sugar cubes.

After World War II, veterans returned home with a yen for chocolate. Culinary schools and articles by essayist M.F.K. Fisher taught kitchen beginners how to hand-

Venezuelan plantation workers break open cacao pods to retrieve valuable Porcelana beans inside, used to make high-quality chocolate. The beans are then dried, roasted, milled, liquefied, and processed for final color, variety, and sweetness. *(Sipa/Associated Press)*

dip chocolates, which contained wax to firm up bonbons and cake decorations. In 1947, the Harry & David Company in Medford, Oregon, offered a gift-wrapped Tower of Treats containing chocolate truffles and shortbread. Corporations rewarded clients with Dean & DeLuca foil-wrapped chocolates and nuts in baskets.

Original Tex-Mex recipes incorporated Az-Mex spiced bitter chocolate *moles* (sauces) to complement meat entrées. In place of processed chocolate and sugary sweets, raw foodists flavored raw dark chocolate pie. In the 1950s, gourmet food co-ops experimented with innovative fondue by coating strawberries in chocolate. In the 1970s, food curiosity inspired such ventures as the Chocolate Connoisseur's Club and Popcorn of the Month, which featured white chocolate drizzles. In 1995, Godiva in Brussels, Belgium, added kosher varieties to its gourmet confections.

Before chocolate came to market as candy, drink mixes, icing, or powdered cocoa, New World food processors dyed it brown with caramel concentrate. A paraffin coating on chocolate bars prevented deterioration from bacteria, fungi, and light, even on army D rations and pantry supplies for space missions. For religious holidays, French and Italian confectioners formed chocolates in the shape of fish, a Christian symbol. In Australia, Lamington cube cakes combined cream or jam filling with a topping of chocolate and coconut, an icing also applied to German chocolate cake.

Today, shipments of cacao beans and cocoa powder from Ghana and the Ivory Coast feed the global demand for chocolate. A worldwide endeavor to root out child labor and stem slave trafficking lingers in the Ivory Coast, where exploiters may kidnap for sale some 12,000 underage beggars and orphans from Benin, Burkina Faso, Mali, and Togo. In 2001, the U.S. Congress charged enslavers with tricking and coercing boys and forcing them to carry heavy cacao sacks and machetes during a 100-hour week. The boys received no education. Some languished in farm prisons and died on the job. Manufacturers gave African overseers until 2005 to eradicate child slavery in the cacao market. By 2008, however, young press gangs still formed part of the labor force that generated 80 percent of the world's cocoa.

As of early 2012, the rest of the world supply of cocoa came primarily from Brazil, Colombia, Dominican Republic, Indonesia, Madagascar, and Venezuela. Many consumers preferred 60–70 percent cocoa for pure dark chocolate, a former luxury that health food advocates promoted as heart healthy and mood enhancing.

See also: Cortés, Hernán de; Currency, Food as; Dairy Food; Gourmet Cuisine; Pan-European Diet and Cuisine; Sloane, Hans.

Further Reading

Bradley, John. *Cadbury's Purple Reign: The Story Behind Chocolate's Best-Loved Brand.* West Sussex, UK: John Wiley & Sons, 2008.

Brown, Vincent. *The Reaper's Garden: Death and Power in the World of Atlantic Slavery.* Cambridge, MA: Harvard University Press, 2008.

Grivetti, Louis, and Howard-Yana Shapiro, eds. *Chocolate: History, Culture, and Heritage.* Hoboken, NJ: John Wiley & Sons, 2009.

Chowder

A broad term for a thickened seafood and vegetables stew, chowder is a filling one-dish meal suited to cold, blustery seasides. Named for the *chaudière,* a three-legged iron cauldron that seafarers heated by the shore for cooking fresh seafood, chowder flourished in fishing communities from ingredients at hand, including herbs and wine. Unlike the more refined pureed bisque soups, the improvisational chowder flourished in the 1500s in Brittany, France, and Cornwall, England, where the boil-up of a successful catch was reason for a community celebration.

Basque and French sailors carried the recipe for a creamy white fish soup to the Canadian Maritimes, where the native Micmac had their own tradition of fish stew. Acadian clam chowder followed traditional French recipes and came to the table with a sprinkle of dried dulse, a purple seaweed. Nova Scotian chowder employed haddock along with abundant scallops and lobster in fish stew. When explorer Joseph Banks visited Newfoundland in 1766, he described cod chowder as a food reserved for the poor.

Upon arrival among Algonquin Indians at Plymouth in Massachusetts Colony in 1620, the Pilgrims felt so amply supplied with clams that they had no reason to fish for stew meat. In Maine and at Nantucket Island, Channel Islanders reduced chowder to the basics of fish cooked in boiling water thickened with flour. Elsewhere along New England's 5,700-mile (9,200-kilometer) coast, cooks made clam chowder by thickening cream-based clam soup with unsalted hardtack, a rock-hard military biscuit carried on naval vessels. In 1751, the *Boston Evening Post* published a layered chowder recipe in verse form. At Georges Bank, Maine, clam diggers preferred the large, flavorful mahogany clam and the small, soft steamer clam. The larger ocean clams required seagoing dredges for retrieval.

In the 1750s, Italian-born New Yorkers augmented the New England recipe with allspice, clove, Rockaway clams, sage, and tomatoes. The resulting stew, later called Coney Island or Fulton Market clam chowder, paralleled the popularity of the creamier, New England original. Makers of the Long Island version compromised by blending the creamy white sauce with tomatoes and littleneck clams. The small, tender clam derived from Little Neck Bay, where diggers located them at low tide with their bare feet. Open-minded chowder fanciers tended to like both creamy and tomato sauces.

Rhode Islanders served both styles but excelled at a clear broth containing bacon, onions, potatoes, and quahogs, a hard-shelled clam that thrived at Narragansett Bay. Portuguese immigrants preferred the tomato-based stew, a recipe that traditional New England chowder aficionados declared anathema.

Regional ingredients localized U.S. chowders. The first American cookbook, Amelia Simmons's *American Cookery* (1796), issued at Hartford, Connecticut, substituted bass for clams. In 1802, Susannah Carter's *The Frugal Housewife* gave less definitive recipes, allowing the cook to choose a cup of beer, sliced lemon, or tomato ketchup as flavorings. According to *A Treatise of Domestic Medicine* (1824), physician Thomas Cooper, an English immigrant to Carlisle, Pennsylvania, spiked his chowder with anchovy sauce.

Miss Leslie's New Cookery Book (1857), compiled by Eliza Leslie of Philadelphia, departed from the cauldron method of making "Yankee chowder," instead recommending a lidded Dutch oven heaped with embers. At Boston, Elizabeth H. Putnam's 1858 recipe collection, *Mrs. Putnam's Receipt Book and Young Housekeeper's Assistant,* described a rich finish for chowder consisting of butter, cream, and flour. A Chicago cook reported in 1897 a new twist on thickening with the addition of rice as a binder. Delaware cooks centered their clam chowder on the flavor of fried salt pork. Virginians made the most of cod or cherrystone clams, a medium-sized specimen. Outer Banks restaurants in coastal North Carolina offered a similar blend of tastes, beginning with bacon. Farther inland, the absence of seafood precipitated a recipe for corn chowder, a compromise from Piedmont farmwives.

In St. Augustine, Florida, Minorcan clam chowder featured a hot chili pepper gathered by indentured laborers. Along the Florida Keys, an influx of Bahamians introduced a unique chowder made from conch meat. In San Francisco, cooks ladled New England–style white chowder into hollowed sourdough loaves. Farther north at Portland and Seattle, cooks replaced pork flavoring with smoked salmon or razor clams.

See also: Crackers; Fish and Fishing; North American Diet and Cuisine; Pennsylvania Dutch Diet and Cuisine; Restaurants; Soups.

Further Reading

Rumble, Victoria R. *Soup through the Ages: A Culinary History with Period Recipes.* Jefferson, NC: McFarland, 2009.

Walker, Jake, and Robert S. Cox. *A History of Chowder: Four Centuries of a New England Meal.* Charleston, SC: History Press, 2011.

White, Jasper. *50 Chowders: One-Pot Meals: Clam, Corn & Beyond.* New York: Simon & Schuster, 2000.

Chutney

A broad category of sweet-and-sour condiments from Southeast Asia, chutney derives from the mix of fresh or pickled fruits or vegetables with chilies, cilantro, mint, and spices. Whether cooked to the texture of jelly, preserves, or chunky salsa, chutney obtains its distinctive bite from fermentation in citrus juice, salt, and vinegar. A vegetarian meal accent and palate stimulant involves steamed dal, pulses, or taro served with green pepper and onion chutney. In northeastern India, coconut and soybeans form the basis of a spicy sauce.

In the 1600s, voyagers to India and the Spice Islands shipped native condiments to England, France, and Iberia for sale in upscale grocery shops. Hostesses served gooseberry chutney sauces and piccalilli (pickled vegetable relish) with breakfast toast, cheese and crackers at tiffin (snack time), and tea cakes. Portuguese fanciers topped beefsteak with mango chutney; Brazilians complemented goat, quail, and sausages with chutney. One complicated savory, devils on horseback, began with dates or pitted prunes stuffed with green mango chutney and wrapped in bacon for grilling and serving on toast points as a Yuletide appetizer in rural restaurants.

From Europe, colonial authorities carried chutney recipes to the American South, Australia, Brazil, British East and West Africa, Canada, Guiana, Indonesia, and South Africa, where cooks based a fruit relish on the grilled banana. Indonesian grilled lamb acquired complex tastes from a cashew and ginger marinade. In the West Indies, papaya chutney dominated table relishes with the tang of lime juice and rice wine vinegar and the color of fruit and red onion. Papain in raw papaya added tenderizer to marinades. Jamaican recipes favored the tart tamarind as a contrast to sweet mangos and pawpaws.

Recipe: New England Clam Chowder

In a heavy iron stew pot, melt 1 tablespoon of butter and sauté 1 cup each of diced celery and onion and 1/2 cup of diced bacon or pancetta. Add 3 1/2 cups of chopped clams, 2 quarts of clam juice, 2 bay leaves, and 1/2 teaspoon each of chopped summer savory and thyme. Bring to a boil. Melt 1 cup of butter in a skillet and stir in 1 cup of granulated flour to make a roux. Pour the roux into the clam mixture. Add 1 cup of peeled and finely sliced red potatoes and simmer for 20 minutes. Finish with 2 cups of half-and-half (half cream, half whole milk), pepper, and sea salt. Serve with oyster crackers.

In the Virginia Colony, green tomato chutney became a standard accompaniment to fish fillets and slices of chicken, ham, and pork. Another favorite blended bing cherries, nectarines, peaches, pineapple, or rhubarb with mint, onions, port wine, sugar, and red wine vinegar. Maryland barbecuers sauced slow-roasted pork with fruit chutney blended with bourbon whiskey and onions. In New Orleans, Louisiana, bottled chutney topped curried chicken sandwiches; cilantro chutney spiced crawfish balls. Galatoire's restaurant served foie gras with a fruity chutney made from black cherries, pears, and mangos flavored with champagne vinegar, garlic, scallions, and thyme.

New England cooks concocted an American original from indigenous blueberries or cranberries and tart apples, blended with allspice, candied citrus peel, clove, ginger, and mustard, and served the sauce with holiday turkey. Pennsylvania Dutch cooks made a homestead version of chutney by promoting "seven sweets sand seven sours," a contrast of flavors made by sweetening pickled chowchow (vegetable relish) with cane sugar and souring the mix with celery and mustard seeds, turmeric, and vinegar.

English and European manufacturers marketed imitations of Asian relish recipes under the brand names Bengal Club, Colonel Skinner's, and Major Grey's Mango Chutney, a fad condiment made with raisins and lime juice and sold in England and Singapore. After the formation of Crosse & Blackwell food brands in 1830, the company showcased Major Grey's label, which appeared in advertisements in the *Chinese Times*. By the mid-1800s, Anglo-Indians were serving chutney with curry at formal dinners and in restaurants as a stimulating dressing for meats and salads and accompanying plates of fruit and cheese. Unlike Asian cooks, who ground spices in a mortar, British factories boiled down apples, pears, or mangos and mixed them with onions, raisins, sugar, and vinegar.

To assist military wives living in India and Burma, British cookbooks, such as the anonymous soldier's *Anglo-Indian Recipe Book* (1840) and *Emma Tillotson's Recipe Book* (1842), enlightened them on the local produce suitable for homemade chutneys. Victorian hosts served the piquant sauces on dry beans and roast meats. From 1848 to 1849, the heavy application of cane sugar and molasses in bottled sauces resulted in Parliamentary debate of a chutney tax. In 1880, an international exhibition of foods in Melbourne, Australia, featured local bottled chutneys alongside imports from India.

By 1906, the port of New York collected a chutney tariff leveled on imported pickles, sauces, and "sweetmeats." Benjamin Smith Lyman's compendium *Vegetarian Diet and Dishes* (1917) and Louise Andrea's *Home Canning, Drying and Preserving* (1918) featured chutney dishes, which included a "grand salad" and apple, cranberry, green to-

Recipe: South Indian Tomato Chutney

Fry six red chilies in 1 tablespoon of sesame oil. Add one sprig of curry leaves, 1 tablespoon of whole coriander seeds, 1 teaspoon of sambar powder (pigeon peas and tamarind), 1/2 teaspoon of grated ginger, 1/4 cup chopped spring onion, and one pinch of asafetida and sauté. Add three chopped tomatoes and simmer until the pulp softens. Cool and grind the mix with 1 teaspoon of salt and 1/4 teaspoon of tamarind paste. In 1 tablespoon of sesame oil, heat a sprig of curry leaves with 1/2 teaspoon of black mustard seeds until the seeds pop. Pour this dressing over the tomato sauce mixture and stir. Serve with kebabs or vegetable pilaf.

mato, and mashed potato chutneys. Also in 1918, the *Bulletin of the U.S. Department of Agriculture* listed chutneys imported from Cambodia, China, and Samoa. Chutney making also provided employment for food processors in Jamaica and Puerto Rico.

See also: Arab Diet and Cuisine; Dal; Pickling; Restaurants.

Further Reading

Civitello, Linda. *Cuisine and Culture: A History of Food and People.* 3rd ed. Hoboken, NJ: John Wiley & Sons, 2011.

Davidson, Alan. *The Oxford Companion to Food.* Ed. Jane Davidson, Tom Jaine, and Helen Saberi. New York: Oxford University Press, 2006.

Laszlo, Pierre. *Citrus: A History.* Chicago: University of Chicago Press, 2008.

Toussaint-Samat, Maguelonne. *A History of Food.* Hoboken, NJ: Wiley-Blackwell, 2009.

Cider

A fermented apple juice, cider derives from the pressing of one variety of cider apple or from a blend of sweet, sharp, bittersharp, and bittersweet stock.

Ancient Origins

Apples appear in cave art from as early as 35,000 B.C.E. and in trade records from 6000 B.C.E. Although details are sketchy about the fermentation of cider, from 1300 B.C.E., apple juice or cider appears to have been popular with ancient Egyptians, Greeks, Israelites, and Phoenicians.

A specialty of East Anglia and southwest England, British cider dates to the first century B.C.E., when Iberian

Workers at an English orchard use a traditional hand press to squeeze and filter apple juice. Since the first century B.C.E., fruit pressers in England have converted juice to cider by fermenting it in wood casks. Cider remains extremely popular in the U.K. today. *(Fox Photos/ Getty Images)*

nomads introduced *shekar* (fermented cider). Whole fruit pressers extruded apple and pear juice and converted it in wood casks with the wild yeasts living in the air and on fruit skins. The conversion of sugar to alcohol by malolactic action preserved harvest time flavors year-round. Apple wine, made from dessert apples, contained the most sugar. Even windfalls found a place in cider commerce as scrumpy, a coarse, cloudy drink squeezed out of partially rotted, unmarketable fruit.

Apple cultivation spread across Roman conquests, including Iberia. After the Roman occupation of Kent in 55 B.C.E., the forces of Julius Caesar embraced Celtic cider and *posca* (cider vinegar) drinking for refreshment. Rather than apply local water to casualties in field hospitals, medics chose antiseptic apple beverages to cleanse and debride wounds. Veteran legionaries who received land allotments in Gaul, Iberia, and northern Italy grew apple orchards as an investment and turned fruit into *pomorum* (fruit drinks).

Middle Ages

After 800 C.E., the Frankish king and Holy Roman Emperor Charlemagne hired brewers to extract *pommé* (apple juice) and perry (pear juice) from his orchards. Following the Norman Conquest of England in 1066, monks specialized in the growing, grafting, and pruning of abbey *pomeria* (apple gardens) at Canterbury and Ely. They supervised fermentation and sale of cider, a

favorite thirst quencher of haymakers and corn harvesters, who accepted tuns of cider as some 20 percent of their wages.

The invention of the cider press in the 1200s increased late-medieval consumption of the fizzy juice and the use of cider and perry to pay rents and tithes. By the end of the Middle Ages, throughout England and Normandy, mulled cider flavored with allspice, cinnamon, clove, and nutmeg dominated table and recreational drinking. The English drank the health of their apple trees between December 24 and Twelfth Night by going

Recipe: Mulled Cider

Peel and core an apple and slice it into thin wedges. Place the wedges in a saucepan and add 1/2 gallon of cider, 1 tablespoon of honey or *muscovado* (dark brown) sugar, five whole cloves, two cardamom pods, one cinnamon stick, 1 inch of peeled, fresh gingerroot, and 1/2 teaspoon of allspice. Heat gently in an electric slow cooker. Add the juice and zest of one lemon and one orange and 6 tablespoons of cider brandy (Calvados). Ladle from a punch bowl into tall mugs and top each with a sprinkle of nutmeg.

wassailing, a ritual blessing of the coming year's cider apples to ensure wellness.

Advances

Renaissance tree grafting and cultivation of orchards improved in France, where orchardists preferred the Costard, Pearmain, and Pomme d'Espice varieties for draft cider. The latter cultivar was the favorite of Francis I, who kept a private stock of cider barrels. The reputation of French apples intrigued Henry VIII, who had his fruiterer, Richard Harris, import pippin saplings to Teynham, Kent, in 1533. Apple specialist Guillaume D'Ursus recorded his success on the Cherbourg Peninsula in March 1553, where he practiced Basque cider-making skills. The blending of sour-sweet fruit for delicate flavor with acid fruit for clarity resulted in a distinguished cider renowned for its aroma and flavor.

In 1588, Norman cider maker and physician Julien Le Paulmier issued *De Vino et Pomaceo* (*On Wine and Cider*), a treatise that named 82 apple varieties and extolled apple juice as a healthful drink. During the reign of Louis XIII (1610–1643), Norman farmers avoided heavy taxes on vineyards by replacing them with apple orchards. In the mid-1700s, heirloom apples and prize runs of cider won agricultural awards. Because canker destroyed English orchards in the 1810s, growers returned to France to buy Medaille d'Or and Michelin cultivars to graft onto British varieties, the Albemarle Pippin, Foxwhelp, Kingston Black, Morgan's Sweet, Redstreak, Sweet Alford, and Woodbine.

New World

North American aborigines made crab apple cider in prehistory. The colonial era differentiated between eating and cooking apples and cider apples, which included small wild crab apples and the Shawmut, planted at Boston in 1623. By 1635, America's first apple cultivar, the Yellow Sweeting, was growing at Rhode Island homesteads. Along the Chesapeake Sound, women superintended the cidering process.

In 1647 at New Amsterdam (later, New York), Dutch immigrants grafted orchard stock with the Summer Bonchretien, a juicy, sweet pear. Huguenots brought the Pomme Royale (or Spice Apple) in 1600; the Newtown Pippin flourished as a "tankard apple" from 1730. As settlers pushed west, they spread apple and pear residue and seeds over their fields, encouraging the sprouting of new trees from Atlantic Coast stock.

In 1792, John Chapman, the legendary Johnny Appleseed, opened a Pennsylvania nursery in the Susquehanna Valley and spread fruit tree seedlings throughout Ohio and Indiana as a means of improving government land grants. To spread apple harvesting over the seasons, orchardists grafted a single trunk with different varieties of apples that ripened from early spring to autumn. The extended season supplied farm cider mills with fruit for beverages to replace questionable water sources.

America's National Drink

The lack of grain alcohol at tap houses produced a demand for beverages, which growers supplied with corn and pumpkin beer, fermented maple sap, and persimmon beer. To turn sugar into alcohol, they fermented apple drinks into sweet (or fresh) cider and hard (or fermented) cider, the country's national drink. Because the complex flavors paired well with entrées and desserts and as travelers' refreshment, barrels of cider served country folk as bartering elements.

Philadelphians preferred applejack, America's indigenous distilled beverage. A strong cider brandy, it results from "jacking," or freezing, hard cider through the winter to concentrate flavors and raise the alcohol content. In New Jersey, road builders accepted jugged applejack in lieu of wages. From Laird & Company in Scobeyville, New Jersey, the oldest applejack distillery, the manufacture of strong apple drink spread to Virginia, Tennessee, the Carolinas, and Georgia. Applejack suited the soaking of pound cake and the basting of roast meats, such as a pig shoulder coated in pepper and onions.

From abundant Liberty, Macintosh, and Northern Spy apples, colonial cider makers produced pleasing drinks at the rate of 300,000 gallons (1.14 million liters) a year. The drink suited the tastes of the Continental Army as well as the first presidents, George Washington, John Adams, and Thomas Jefferson. Promoters linked cider drinking three times a day with longevity.

By 1800, Massachusetts residents were drinking 35 gallons (132 liters) of cider per person annually. Parents soaked pomace (apple pulp) in water for ciderkin, a children's drink mixed with ginger and molasses. (Perkin, a similar drink made from pear pulp, never gained the popularity of ciderkin.) Soldiers during the Civil War bought cider, ciderkin, and applejack from commissaries. By 1872, American orchardists raised nearly 1,100 apple cultivars. Trees produced varied stock for blended ciders and cider vinegars, which merchants exported to the British Isles, Europe, and the West Indies.

Decline and Resurgence

During this same period, the immigration of Eastern European and German brewers to the United States raised the popularity of beer over cider. As urban populations grew, the shrinking number of smallholders continued the traditional cider making as an annual chore. To increase the appeal of cider, fermenters added honey, raisins, rum, and sugar to boost alcoholic content from 2 percent to 7.5 percent. At restaurants and saloons, barkeeps fermented apple juice with glucose, pepper, vinegar, and whiskey, thus destroying the reputation of a favorite country beverage.

In England, the Industrial Revolution lured farmworkers to the city and decreased interest in cider making. In the late 1800s, disease altered the fruit harvests on both sides of the Atlantic. In the United States, apple scab and codling moths precipitated the burning of apple orchards and cider mills. At the same time, because of fungus in grapevines, French apple orchards increased in three decades from 4 million hectares (10 million acres) to 14 million hectares (35 million acres).

As World War I began in Europe in 1914, French ciderists agreed to government seizure of cider tuns to provide alcohol for defense needs. The temperance movement and Prohibition in 1919 ended the commercial success of U.S. cider, lowering production to 13 million gallons (49 million liters)—from 55 million gallons (208 million liters) at the height of popularity in 1899. After Prohibition, brewing ale became more profitable than making cider.

World War II unleashed devastation on British and Continental orchards. Postwar commodities development subsequently abandoned traditional apple pressing and cider making until gourmet drinkers rediscovered the drink in the 1990s.

In the 2000s, a resurgence of interest in artisanal or heritage and Slow Foods in the United States and Europe invigorated demand for the Baldwin and Roxbury Russet apples and restored cider to popularity. In Germany, the making of *apfelwein* (apple wine) from Bramley and Granny Smith cultivars required the addition of *Sorbus domestica,* or astringent serviceberries for flavoring. Newcomers to cider drinking boosted the sale of beverages from small cider houses to farmer's markets and to buyers in China. Health authorities list applesauce and cider as reducers of bad cholesterol in the arteries and preventers of cancer and coronary disease.

See also: Adulterated Food; Alcoholic Beverages; Fermented Foods; Honey; Medieval Diet and Cuisine; Prohibition.

Further Reading

Maclaran, Pauline, and Lorna Stevens. "Magners Man: Irish Cider, Representations of Masculinity, and the 'Burning Celtic Soul.'" *Irish Marketing Review* 20:2 (2009): 77–88.

Meacham, Sarah Hand. *Every Home a Distillery: Alcohol, Gender, and Technology in the Colonial Chesapeake.* Baltimore: Johns Hopkins University Press, 2009.

Watson, Ben. *Cider, Hard and Sweet: History, Traditions, and Making Your Own.* 2nd ed. Woodstock, VT: Countryman, 2009.

Clipper Ships

From the late 1770s to 1869, hydrodynamically efficient clipper ships sped global food distribution at the rate of 400 miles (640 kilometers) per day. Clippers traveled at four times the speed of deep-draft merchantmen, thereby delivering fresher produce to markets in London, Baltimore, Boston, New York, and Salem. Built in England, Scotland, and the United States, with some competition from Canada, France, and Holland, the canvas-heavy topsail schooner featured a U-shaped hull and an uplifted concave bow that sliced through ocean waters.

Captains set their courses to follow ocean currents and trade winds. Ranging above sleek, yacht-like hulls some 20 stories, an elaborate web of canvas and rope required precision teamwork by skilled seamen. On return trips to Canton (Guangzhou) in China, some carried apples as well as ice slabs cut from ponds and packed in straw for use in hospitals and restaurants in the tropics. During the War of 1812, the American clipper forerunners *Harvey* and *Pride of Baltimore II* captured British traders and redirected to American warehouses the provisions intended for the British army. For their beauty and craftsmanship, the multiuse clippers earned the name "queens of the sea."

By 1819, square-riggers, called "tall ships," acquired a rakish reputation for their use in speeding opium from China to India. For the delivery of coffee, indigo, rice, spices, and tea, the British East India Company (BEIC) favored trading vessels that hastened over trade routes around the globe and crewed them with British seamen, some veterans of the Royal Navy. On the journey from Java or Malabar to England, coffee beans mellowed to a rich, low-acid flavor, a boon to profits. With the introduction of *Camellia sinensis assamica* tea from Assam, India, in the late 1830s, the BEIC purchased American clipper ships to sate world demand for Asian beverages.

American redesign of the clipper in 1841 thrust the U.S. merchant marine into direct competition for Asian goods. New demand for foodstuffs and equipment for miners following the California Gold Rush of 1848 offered clipper owners the handsome exchange of overpriced goods to pioneers wielding the unprecedented purchasing power of gold dust. Shippers sold beef, flour, and pork for $60 per barrel and coffee, sugar, and tea for $4 per pound. Whiskey brought $40 per quart and laudanum $1 per drop.

Commerce and Nationalism

During the Age of Transportation, clippers boosted the American ego in a race to surpass British dominance in food transport and marketing. In the late 1840s, the profits from fast sails around Cape Horn, Chile, inspired Robert Henry "Bully Bob" Waterman, the New York–born captain of the *Sea Witch,* to padlock ropes to prevent crew from reducing sail over the dangerous route around Tierra del Fuego. His records for speed still stand, as does his reputation for harsh discipline of slackers.

In 1851, Boston shipwright Donald McKay, an immigrant from Nova Scotia, launched the *Flying Cloud,* the first of a series of bigger, faster "extreme clippers," which carried high-profit perishables from Australia, China, the

East Indies, and Hawaii. His pride in accomplishment appeared in the naming of subsequent clippers, the *Sovereign of the Seas, Chariot of Fame,* and *Great Republic,* at 400 feet (122 meters) the largest clipper ever built.

Captains anchored their vessels off Chinese harbors in mid-June to await processing of the April pekoe harvest, a high-priced commodity known as "first flush" tea. After Foochow (Fuzhou), the port of choice following the 1842 Treaty of Nanking (Nanjing), opened five ports to trade with Great Britain, agents negotiated commodity prices. Junks, lighters, and sampans delivered rattan-wrapped tea chests around the clock. Clipper crews measured the chests with calipers and hammered them into place in the hold. A tight pack above planking covering ballast of beach pebbles or scrap metal stopped the lightweight tea from shifting on the passage. Topped with a tarpaulin, the chests held firm in hatches sealed tight against leakage or swamping by heavy seas. The clippers' iron-over-wood hulls featured gutta-percha caulk, which kept holds dry and tea safe from unforeseen soaks in seawater.

Clipper Engineering

To escape food tariffs and port dues, Alexander Hall and Sons of Aberdeen, Scotland, designed the *Scottish Maid* to reduce hull tonnage. From 1844 to 1846, American naval designer John Willis Griffiths's promotion of the *Rainbow, Houqua,* and *Sea Witch* advanced rapid global voyages, covering the New York–to–Canton route in as little as 78 days. American ships began making headlines in 1850, when the *Oriental,* the first U.S. clipper to trade in London, carried 1,600 tons (1,450 metric tons) of tea from Canton and earned $48,000, a cargo fee nearly equal to the cost of the ship's construction.

In 1866, the Great Tea Race pitted the top contenders—the Scots-built *Ariel* and *Taeping*—in a dash from China to London with the year's first tea picking. On September 12, the clippers arrived on the same tide. The *Taeping* won by ten minutes after a 16,000-mile (26,000-kilometer) sail that encompassed the South China Sea, Indian Ocean, Atlantic Ocean, and English Channel. Tea companies rewarded the winner for delivering the season's first batch, which tea snobs began purchasing the next morning.

For its dash and trim looks, the clipper earned the name "greyhound of the sea." At Manhattan dockyards, leather merchant George Francis Gilman and dry goods clerk George Huntington Hartford, the original partners of the Great American Tea Company, sold cut-rate Chinese and Japanese tea straight from the cargo holds by negotiating price directly with the crew and edging out the middleman. In this manner, consumers could buy tea as well as allspice, cinnamon, clove, ginger, mustard, and pepper on credit at bulk rates of one-third retail cost. A full-page ad in the 1865 *Horticulturist* exploited the glamour of the clipper ship by announcing the importation of 22,000 half chests of tea aboard the *Golden State,* owned by Jacob Aaron Westervelt, mayor of New York City.

The spread of coffee rust, a plant fungus, in Ceylon, China, and Malaysia raised coffee prices and fueled demand for tea. Ad copy targeted tea drinkers with the choice of Assam, Bey-Jop, Celinrus, Congo, Foochow, Formosa, green gunpowder, young Hyson, imperial, moyune, oolong, orange pekoe, silver leaf, souchong, and sun-dried varieties grown on the Great American Tea Company's private tea plantations. In 1869, Hartford renamed his company the Great Atlantic & Pacific Tea Company, which developed into the modern grocery chain known as A&P.

See also: British East India Company; Maritime Trade Routes; Spices; Tea; Trading Vessels.

Further Reading

Crothers, William L. *The American-Built Clipper Ship, 1850–1856: Characteristics, Construction, and Details.* Camden, ME: International Marine, 1997.

Cutler, Carl C. *Greyhounds of the Sea: The Story of the American Clipper Ship.* 3rd ed. Annapolis, MD: Naval Institute Press, 1984.

Martin, Laura C. *Tea: The Drink That Changed the World.* Rutland, VT: Tuttle, 2007.

Paine, Lincoln P. *Ships of Discovery and Exploration.* New York: Houghton Mifflin, 2002.

Coconut

A wholesome, versatile native of the tropics, the coconut palm bolsters the world's wild foods with the water and flesh of the fruit, which also yields coconut jelly, milk, and oil. A high-protein energy food rich in iron, phosphorus, and zinc, the coconut originated in Melanesia and flourished between the Tropic of Cancer and the Tropic of Capricorn as a trade item. For a half million years, it provided nourishment from its natural dish. The willowy *Cocos nucifera* palm spread about the world by ocean currents, and after 2000 B.C.E., with the aid of Polynesian colonizers, the tree journeyed by outrigger from New Guinea to Tahiti. Arab traders extended the fame of the coconut, which they transported from the Maldives and Zanzibar to England.

The nutrition from coconuts balanced the island diet, providing benefits for dental health, weight control, and medicines from palm roots for dysentery and cholera. Mariners bore the coconut west over the Indian Ocean to Madagascar, the Cape Verde Islands, and Angola by 60 C.E. and completed the encircling of the globe in 86 countries by planting the palm in Central and South America, Egypt, and Queensland, Australia. On the Nicobar Islands, palm fruit became so valuable that it doubled as currency.

The coconut appears in Sanskrit and Tamil writings and in the Hindu epic *Ramayana* (ca. 400 B.C.E.) and in food ritual emerging from the Puranas (200–400 C.E.), the creation lore of the Gupta Empire. In 1501, the reports of Portuguese mariner Vasco da Gama to King Manuel I lauded the coconut as a source of arrack (liquor), sugar, vinegar, and wine and as a handy travel food.

Ferdinand Magellan, the first circumnavigator of the world, replenished failing ship's stores on Guam in March 1521 by loading the galley with coconuts. In the mid-1500s, Portuguese and Spanish seafarers made a joke about the three eyes on the blossom end, which they named "coco" for "grinning face." In *A New Voyage Round the World* (1699), English sea raider and cartographer William Dampier found ample coconut palms in New Guinea. In 1686, he discoursed at length on the young fruit in India as a source of "pap," a soft, jellied flesh scooped out like pudding, and of water for boiling poultry or rice.

Upon receipt of coconuts from sailors, the British turned the grated meat into a flavoring for cakes and cookies and used whole coconuts for toss games called the Coconut Shy. In the early 1800s, imported coconut oil replaced whale oil and tallow in hand soaps. Cigarettes featured charcoal filters made from husks; solids provided high-energy food for racehorses. Investors met demand by establishing plantations in Australia, the Caribbean, the Dutch East Indies, Fiji, Malaya, and Sri Lanka.

In 1888, brothers Josiah and Henry Vavasseur, British engineers, proposed a more cost-effective method of importing coconuts to Europe. By drying the meat into copra, they made packing easier and lighter without lowering quality. In 1900, annual shipments rose tenfold to 60,000 tons (54,400 metric tons). In 1895, Philadelphia food miller Franklin Baker further simplified shipping from the Philippines by selling coconut flesh shredded and dehydrated.

The availability from Philippine plantations of coconut removed from the shell and ready for cooking initiated a U.S. food fad in the early 1900s for coconut cake, cream pie, custard, frosting, and macaroons. For Southern ambrosia, a Yuletide treat, cooks layered shredded coconut with orange slices, sprinkled on confectioner's sugar, and topped the mix with Southern Comfort, a sweet whiskey liqueur. Canned hearts of palm added texture to salads, soups, and stir-fries.

Coconut profits remained high until the Great Depression. During World War II, medical units short of intravenous glucose substituted coconut water, which arrived sterile in the shell. The Pacific War of the 1940s curtailed coconut exports, producing a global dearth of vegetable oil.

Coconut remains a pantropical arboricultural foodstuff. In the southern Malay Peninsula and Thailand, grove managers train Sunda macaques to harvest the nuts. Hainan Islanders express coconut juice to sell in China and Southeast Asia. In Vietnam, pushcarts display whole fruit

sold for nut water. A coconut knife or screwdriver inserted into the open end extracts a spiral of meat for eating fresh. Freezing softens the meat and reduces its natural crunch.

Copra, the dehydrated flesh of the coconut, requires fire- or sun-drying, smoking, or layering in ovens, often fueled by burning palm husks. Pressure during milling or centrifuging releases oil from the thick fiber, a by-product that farmers feed to livestock. The oil is a common additive to confections and nondairy creamers.

In southern Asia, cooks make coconut milk by shredding the flesh into a cloth, pouring on hot water, and rolling and squeezing the cloth to express a cooking cream. Melanesians heat the cream to evaporate the water. The sweet milk enhances the bland taste of cassava, fish, rice, sweet potato, tapioca, taro, and yams. Fermented sap yields a powerful alcoholic drink and, when evaporated, produces sugar. Because coconut oil is stable at high heat, it is valuable for deep-frying and popping corn.

After some 70 years of blame for clogging arteries, the coconut returned to respectability in the 2000s. Consumers sip coconut water through a straw and scoop the jelly with a spoon. Recipes specify the oil for flavoring chutney, curry, ice cream, jam, muesli, oatmeal, pastry, raw food and vegan meals, stir-fries, and diets for diabetics. Because of the oil's similarity to human breast milk, it bolsters baby formula and children's toddy.

Despite thousands of years of anecdotal evidence to the contrary, muddled understanding of saturated fats in the 1950s defamed the coconut as a dangerous food. Although hydrogenated coconut oil contains trans fat, virgin coconut oil appears to be harmless to the cardiovascular system. Recent studies reclaim the coconut as a thyroid stimulant, cholesterol and hypoglycemia control, boost to the immune system, fungus and yeast deterrent, and suppressor of human immunodeficienty virus (HIV).

See also: Heritage Foods; Ibn Battuta; Maritime Trade Routes; Polo, Marco; Storage, Food.

Further Reading

Clark, Melissa. "Once a Villain, Coconut Oil Charms the Health Food World." *The New York Times*, March 1, 2011.

Fife, Bruce. *Coconut Lover's Cookbook*. Colorado Springs, CO: Piccadilly, 2004.

———. *Virgin Coconut Oil: Nature's Miracle Medicine*. Colorado Springs, CO: Piccadilly, 2006.

Ohler, J.G. *Coconut: Tree of Life*. Rome, Italy: Food and Agriculture Organization of the United Nations, 1984.

Cod

A popular food fish in Great Britain, Iberia, North America, and Scandinavia, cod has amplified the economies of nations in the Northern Hemisphere since the 1500s. From prehistory, preserving fresh catches involved whole families, who gathered on seashores and cliff sides to gut and filet the easily boned body and to smoke two delicacies, the roe and liver. The air-dried fish had a shelf life of several years, thus supplying daily needs as well as ensuring famine food during crises and disasters.

A cod-based cuisine developed north of the equator in maritime cultures. From 5400 B.C.E., the Mesolithic Erte-bolle, hunter-gatherers of Denmark, relied on cod for subsistence, as did the Alaskan Tlingit in 3000 B.C.E. From 50 C.E., the Abenaki of Damariscotta River, Maine, varied their cod intake with alewife, clam, eider duck, oysters, shad, sturgeon, and venison. The Inuit ate cod livers with bilberries, cranberries, and crowberries. On Chinese junks, the crews' 1,900-calorie daily meal consisted of 1,000 grams (35 ounces), or 53 percent, of cod or herring and the remaining 47 percent of cabbage, rice, and tea.

Salt Cod Industry

For transport, salting extended the shelf life of cod or stockfish, which absorbed the brine readily because of its low fat content. In the 700s, Italian *baccalà* (salt cod) provided the peasant cook with a cheap, convenient main dish seasoned with garlic and mustard. A transportable food at a low price, heavily salted filets required soaking in several changes of water before grilling or frying. Elements of the Mediterranean diet—anchovies, cheese, eggs, garlic, olives and olive oil, onions, and wine vinegar—contributed to satisfying Portuguese fish dishes, including *baccalao* (cod stew).

Around 800, the availability of salt enabled the Vikings to establish salting stations in Iceland and Greenland and to market Baltic cod, which achieved a demand far from marine centers. In the 900s, Viking trade networks developed long boat holds to accommodate bulk stowage of dried Norwegian cod from Ribe in Jutland to sell in Asia, Greenland, and Western Europe, where the French pickled the fish in brine. By 1000, Nordic fishermen expanded their seafood processing to Newfoundland. Varangian and Viking trading vessels bore dried cod and mead as far south as Byzantium.

By desiccating and salting fish, dealers drew out excess water, reducing the weight of their unscaled catch by up to 80 percent and simplifying packing and transport. Along the North Sea, Norwegians dehydrated cod as the basis of their food industry and as currency. New England and the Grand Banks east of Newfoundland profited from salt cod, which they marketed in eastern South America, West Africa, and the West Indies. Additional fisheries flourished in Brittany and Holland.

Dried fish remained abundant in imports from the Faeroe Islands, Iceland, and Norway and supplied the cuisines of Brazil, the Caribbean, the Mediterranean, and Northern Europe. *Le Viandier* (*The Provisioner,* ca. 1375), a sourcebook of medieval cuisine by Taillevent, the head chef of King Charles V of France, advised readers on how to leach salt from cod to freshen a sweet, densely flaked fish and top it with mustard sauce. By the 1390s, the Hanseatic League, a trade alliance in Lübeck, Germany, superintended cod and grain commerce from Novgorod, Russia, southeast over the Baltic Sea through Riga and Danzig to Lübeck and Hamburg and over the North Sea to Bergen and Bruges.

In the 1400s, Basques abandoned whale drying and began processing cod, a popular food throughout the Mediterranean and North Africa for its lean, white meat. Approval by the Catholic Church increased demand for fish on holy days. Portuguese fish processors drew on saltworks in Aveiro and Setúbal for supplies. From Basque and Portuguese settlers of the Canadian Maritime provinces, the Beothuk of Newfoundland and the Micmac of Nova Scotia and the Gaspé Peninsula of Quebec learned to layer cod, oysters, and venison in barrels with generous sprinklings of rock salt. The shore industry was still in operation in 1497, when English explorer John Cabot made his observations of teeming schools of cod.

As red meat consumption decreased, the consumption of cod spread far beyond cold northern waters as a Renaissance fad. Catalans baked cod to flavor with *allioli* (garlic mayonnaise). Andalusians made a salad of cod with orange slices, simmered it into chowder, or cooked the fish with beans. Basque chefs folded fish chunks in tortillas. In 1442 in Naples, Catalan cooks introduced the fish as *baccalà*, flavored with honey, pine nuts, and prunes, fried into fritters, or turned into soup with wild mushrooms.

Throughout the Renaissance, cod maintained a reputation as the food of peasants, sailors, and slaves. During the Spanish colonization of Mesoamerica after 1519, Dominican priest and chronicler of Spanish history Bartolomé de Las Casas surveyed and defended the lifestyle of Indians from Cuba to Peru. He resented the enslavement of Lucayan pearl divers, who lived on cod and corn bread while diving repeatedly in search of oysters. Because of fatigue and malnutrition, few divers lived longer than a year in service to the Spanish.

In Tudor England, stockfish fed the commoner. Table fare of aristocrats favored beef and game served with soft white wheat loaves and relegated boiled vegetable potage, oat or rye bread, and salt cod to paupers. As expeditions departed the naval marinas of Elizabeth I, the British navy heightened demand for imported corned beef and salt cod as galley provisions. Fishermen met the demand, catching as many as 400 cod daily per man and stowing up to 25,000 per trawler in salt holds.

During the 1600s, when salt was cheap, families awaited fresh catches of cod for drying. French West Indians subsisted on salt cod and cassava root, the main source of bread for workers and slaves. Portuguese mariners received measured amounts of biscuit and stockfish as their daily rations. On long voyages to Brazil, Guinea, and India, a high death rate from scurvy sapped Portuguese naval crews, who had relied on cod for galley supplies.

At the close of the Renaissance, 60 percent of European fish purchases were cod, which sold for 4 cents in Spain per 100 grams (3.5 ounces), as opposed to 4.5 cents for tuna, 5.7 cents for mutton, and 8 cents for hake. From the Popham experiment, the Pilgrims learned how to prepare for difficult winters by setting up fishing stations to provide enough cod and shellfish to sustain a colony until spring.

In 1614, Captain John Smith led an expedition from the English settlement at Jamestown, Virginia, to study the New England coastline from Penobscot Bay, Maine, to Cape Cod, Massachusetts. He realized that salt cod promised wealth to American shippers and enriched himself selling dried fish to the English and Spanish. Smith's prediction proved true in the colonies, which supported 1,000 fishermen in 440 trawlers by 1675. Fisheries profited by producing 6,900 tons (6,250 metric tons) of fish annually and by shipping salt cod to slaving camps in West Africa.

Into the late 1600s, the salt cod industry increased its business by 300 percent. One upsurge came from traders who supplied dried beef and salt cod to the privateers at Tortuga, Haiti. During the cod-fishing and whaling heyday, the cracker industry became one of North America's first processed food industries. A period recipe for party chowder combined cod with crackers and salt pork to feed "a large fishing party." English cook Robert May, author of *The Accomplisht Cook* (1685), recommended cod pie, an elaborate mincemeat concoction of apple, caraway seed, cinnamon, currants, dates, ginger, lemon, pepper, raisins, rosewater, sugar, verjuice (green grape juice), and wine.

Commerce

Ironically, while Atlantic hostilities escalated over fishing rights for the next century, few fleets targeted the Pacific cod off the Fox Islands of Alaska, which remained virtually unfished. The nomadic Canadian Eskimo flourished at commercial open-water fishing for cod and halibut, two Scandinavian staples. At the conclusion of the Seven Years' War in 1763, France ceded North American territory to the British but kept the cod fisheries off Newfoundland, Miquelon, and Saint Pierre.

British statesman William Pitt regretted that England gave up a profitable food industry. His lament proved prophetic of the growth of the cod trade in Massachusetts and Newfoundland and the reciprocal trade between New England fishermen and Caribbean molasses vendors. The "codfish aristocracy" of Massachusetts flaunted the source of their prosperity by decorating their mansions and the Boston Town Hall with carved fish.

Beginning in 1774, the Royal Greenland Trade Department (Den Kongelige Grønlandske Handel, or KGH) monopolized commerce between the Inuit and Denmark for the next two centuries. The Hudson's Bay Company commodities trade succeeded at a global interchange of cod and wheat. By the early 1800s, the salt cod industry undergirded the economy of Labrador and Newfoundland.

The poor welcomed methods of cooking stockfish to full advantage. *Mrs. Hale's Receipts for the Million* (1852), by cookbook compiler Sarah Josepha Hale, suggested uses for cod heads as a means of trimming kitchen waste. In Jamaica and Puerto Rico, a popular island recipe called for the boiling of rice and salt pork with cod tails and scraps for a make-do peasant dish. An upscale recipe from Neapolitan food writer Ippolito Cavalcanti's *Cucina Casereccia in Dialetto Napolitano* (*Home Cooking in Neapolitan Dialect*, 1847) introduced the tomato to fish sauce as a complement to the delicate flavor of stockfish.

The addition of cod liver oil to orange juice decreased the incidence of rickets and scurvy by supplying the body with vitamins A, D, and E and omega-3 fatty acids. Adults consumed the oil to boost the nutrition of breast milk and as a treatment for arthritis. In 1865, German Baron von Liebig, the founder of physiological chemistry, began manufacturing Extract of Malt, a nutritious food more palatable to children than cod liver oil, which left a fishy aftertaste.

In a period when fishermen processed Pacific catches of cod at San Francisco and Sausalito, California, and at Pirate Cove and Unga, Alaska, the West Coast never attained the success of New England and Newfoundland. In 1893, when the Sears catalog was advertising pantry stocks of crackers and salt cod, the future of cheap salt fish seemed

A period engraving depicts cod fishing, curing, and drying in Newfoundland during the 1730s. As a key item in the triangle trade network, salted Atlantic cod, the first major commodity of the New World, found buyers in Europe, Africa, and the Caribbean. *(The Granger Collection, New York)*

unfavorable. Denmark charged the British with endangering fishing grounds off the Faeroe Islands. Confiscation of British trawlers resulted in fines and the impounding of vessels and their catch. In April 1899, Danes arrested the captain and fired on the British trawler *Caspian,* which escaped back to England. Hostility between Denmark and England over fishing grounds continued until the beginning of World War I.

In the 1900s, cod fishing gained strength in the Bering Sea and the Aleutian Islands as far south as Puget Sound, Washington, in part because of the investment of Edward Pond. His profits dwindled from hostile engagements with Russian gunboats. The financial picture shifted in 1920, when nutritionists began debating the health benefits of cod liver oil, which evidence in the *Journal of the American Medical Association* championed as a treatment for consumption and rickets. In 1940, grocery store advertisements lauded healthful, high-energy foods, especially oatmeal and cod liver oil.

Threatened Species
Because of the suppression of the fishing industry during World War II, enormous schools of cod thrived in the Barents Sea, English Channel, Irish Sea, and North Sea. The exploitation, or overfishing, of cod in the 1950s threatened the range of diet available to shore folk. The resulting Cod Wars between Iceland and the United Kingdom exacerbated quandaries over the future of cod in the North Atlantic. When the Icelandic Coast Guard tried to enforce quotas within a 13-mile (21-kilometer) limit, the British Royal Navy shielded English fleets and engaged in net cutting and ramming of competing fishing vessels. The squabble ended in 1976 after the North Atlantic Treaty Organization (NATO) brokered a concession from the British that they would cease infringing on Iceland's territorial waters. Nonetheless, the protection of fish habitats failed to halt the 1980 crash of cod stock.

Currently, cod remains much in demand. Ice fishing among the Siberian Nenets and the Alaskan Aleut yields char and polar cod. The cuisine of some 50,000 Northern Sami of Norway and Sweden as well as Canadian menus feature lutefisk, a gelatinous entrée of cod or pollock softened and cured with lye that leached from birch ash. Dating to the Renaissance, the aromatic dish requires spices or butter to enhance the mild flavor.

Cod remains on the endangered species advisories of Greenpeace, Seafood Watch, and the World Wildlife Fund, with catches down by 70 percent. Scientists predict that a 15-year moratorium on fishing may enable the former schools to regain strength and numbers. Canada continues to prohibit cod fishing in the Gulf of St. Lawrence and northeastern Newfoundland, but dishonest fishermen conceal illegal cod as "bycatch" or unintended targets. The short supply of cod forced British fish-and-chips shops to change their menus to include dogfish, haddock, hake, plaice, and skate.

In Australia and Canada, urban farming with aquaponics reduces the mileage that such crops as barramundi and cod travel to market, making local produce both cheaper and fresher. While Icelandic buffets continue displaying cod liver sausage and smoked milt and roe as well as wind-dried *saltfiskur* (cod), a traditional favorite, the British have retreated from the threatened species and embraced pollock as an inexpensive, sustainable substitute. Birds Eye, an international brand of frozen foods, followed a similar trend by replacing cod with pollock in fish sticks.

See also: Allergies, Food; Hudson's Bay Company; Maritime Trade Routes; Pan-European Diet and Cuisine; Salt; Smoked Food; Virginia Company of Plymouth.

Further Reading
Harris, Michael. *Lament for an Ocean: The Collapse of the Atlantic Cod Fishery.* Toronto: McClelland & Stewart, 1999.

Innis, Harold Adams. *The Cod Fisheries: The History of an International Economy.* Rev. ed. Toronto: University of Toronto Press, 1978.

Kurlansky, Mark. *Cod: A Biography of the Fish That Changed the World.* New York: Walker, 1997.

Coffee
A staple brewed beverage identifiable on menus worldwide, coffee is the planet's largest cash crop and most popular social lubricant. Release of enticing coffee aromas and savory oils requires roasting for 20 minutes at 500 degrees Fahrenheit (260 degrees Celsius), which doubles the size of the bean. As addictive as chocolate, cola, *guarana, ilex guayusa,* tea, and yerba maté, coffee floods the nervous system with caffeine, a vegetable alkaloid that stimulates adrenaline flow and flushes the urinary system. Coffee fans favor the stimulus and sense of well-being, especially in the early morning.

The Oromo, a Cushite people of Ethiopia, Kenya, and Somalia, promoted the brewing of *Coffea arabica* in the ninth century C.E. Discoverers, according to Roman monk and educator Antonio Fausto Naironi's *De Saluberrima Potione Cahue (On Coffee, a Most Healthful Drink,* 1671), admired the scent of roasting beans and the stimulation of *qahwa,* ground coffee boiled in water. The Persian physician Rhazes's nine-volume medical text *Al-Haiwi (The Virtuous Life,* ca. 930) recommended hot coffee for the stomach. A century later, Persian author Avicenna's *Al-Ganum fit-Tebb (The Canon of Medicine,* 1025) recognized the energizing effects of coffee on the limbs.

The cult of coffee breaks offered Muslims a bracing drink to replace the alcoholic beverages forbidden by Islam. Coffee service became a social equalizer and favorite creature comfort. At the same time, Arabian medical compendia also warned that too much coffee could cause confusion, depression, headache, heart palpitations, insomnia, and tremors. From the 1100s until the 1850s, officials of the Ethiopian Orthodox Church allowed religious prejudice to overrule taste by stigmatizing coffee as a Muslim drink.

In the 1400s, Sufist monks in Yemen drank coffee as a devotional revitalizer for midnight prayers. Galla nomads traversing North Africa cooked coffee porridge and formed coffee berries and fat into fist-sized balls to sustain them during raids on Abyssinia. Throughout the fifteenth century, Muslim pilgrims carried their favorite drink across the Levant and North Africa. Both Mecca and Cairo boasted *kaveh kanes* (coffeehouses) in 1500. In 1511, an Arabic poem praised the pleasant energizer as "the beverage of the friends of God." At mid-decade, after Turkish middlemen eased into bean exports from their holdings in Yemen, Constantinople saw the establishment of a coffee culture.

Controversy arose over the allegation that coffee fostered gambling and illicit sex. In 1570, imams (prayer leaders) complained that the devout preferred a visit to the coffee bar rather than worship in the mosques. Conservative males in Yemen denounced coffee as a source of frivolity, sensual music, hashish consumption, and harmful gossip. Suppression of the drink in Cairo and Mecca resulted in closure of secular espresso bars until Ottoman Turkish authorities overruled the ban in 1580. Although dealers forbade the removal of viable beans from Yemen, an Arab traveler, Baba Budan, smuggled ripe berries from the port of Mocha to Karnataka, India, thus spreading cultivation to Bali, Celebes, Java, Malabar, Sumatra, Sunda, and Timor.

From East to West

By the 1610s, Europeans discovered that Turks spent easeful hours in cafés conversing, partaking of opium and tobacco in hookahs (water pipes), playing backgammon, and sipping hot coffee. When Turks fell ill, they fasted and subsisted on coffee alone. Travelers noted the refreshment available in shaded marketplaces and cool cafés in Damascus, where Syrian males played checkers and chess and listened to storytellers. Trade with Middle Easterners brought arabica beans to St. Mark's Square in Venice, the first European coffee venue. In 1600, Pope Clement VIII alleviated guilt in Christians that they preferred a Muslim drink to tea.

Speculators for the British East India Company and Dutch East India Company imported Europe's first Turkish coffee. In 1637, Greek student Nathaniel Conopios, the future bishop of Smyrna, was England's first known coffee drinker. The nation's initial coffee service began in 1650 at Oxford's Grand Café and two years later in London at the establishment of Armenian restaurateur Pasqua Rosée in Cornhill. Cafés specializing in the hot brew developed into intellectual gathering spots for men seeking respite from taverns.

English patrons of any persuasion paid a penny entrance and tuppence (two pennies) a cup. In high-back seating, they received their mail, smoked and wrote letters, treated friends, and discussed the economy and politics. Partisans could choose Jesuit, Jewish, Papist, or Puritan cafés. Will's Coffeehouse appealed to intellectuals and the clergy; Man's, the fop's café, drew the fashionable as well as French spies. Seamen, middle-class merchants, cattlemen, and attorneys preferred Jonathan's. Those overcome by caffeinism (too much coffee) took a glass of cinnamon water or sarsaparilla as an antidote.

Health Effects

In addition to egalitarian café society and travel accommodation at caravansaries and inns, coffee drinking influenced the medical world. British physician William Harvey stimulated blood flow and treated drunkenness with coffee. A coffee ad from 1657 specified the use of coffee to cure consumption, dropsy (edema), eye sores, gout, headache, respiratory ills, scrofula, and scurvy. Medical writer Gideon Harvey's *Advice Against Plague* (1665) proclaimed coffee a deterrent to contagion. "The Women's Petition Against Coffee" (1674), intended to empty coffeehouses of recalcitrant husbands, declared the drink a "base, black, thick, nasty bitter stinking, nauseous Puddle water." Nonetheless, Englishmen continued to throng cafés as relaxing men's clubs promoting a civil drink. From consortia of coffee drinkers grew the Banker's Clearing-House, Lloyd's of London, the Royal Society, Stock Exchange, and the first newspapers, *The Tatler* and *The Spectator*.

By 1700, coffeehouses drew devotees in Amsterdam, Hamburg, Marseilles, Paris, Boston, New York, and Philadelphia. In Vienna, brewmasters dispensed polite servings in demitasse cups, which came to the table with diminutive spoons for sugaring and stirring. Spanish barkeeps poured *carajillo*, a cup of coffee with a shot of brandy. Outside the British Isles, men and women flirted over steaming cups and overcame old approbation against mixed genders conversing in public. In Germany, women took a respite from housewifery with *Kaffeeklatsch*, a feminine version of the coffeehouse.

Because of coffee's immediate physical effects, Europeans forbade consumption by women of childbearing age to prevent infertility, miscarriages, and stillbirths. Females maintained that coffee was the cause of male impotence. In 1706, Daniel Duncan, a medical teacher at Montpellier, France, issued an advisory against abuse of hot chocolate, coffee, and tea. The French philosopher Voltaire countered that coffee had a "cerebral" effect. The source of the controversy, caffeine, remained unidentified until the collaboration of physician Friedlieb Ferdinand

Runge with Johann Wolfgang von Goethe in 1819, when the two extracted the stimulant from Arabian mocha beans.

Crops and Culture

In the Western Hemisphere, the first coffee plantation on Martinique in 1720 precipitated culture of the bean in Argentina, Brazil, Costa Rica, French Guiana, Guadeloupe, Haiti, Martinique, and Mexico. From there, planters carried the plant to Ceylon, Kenya, Réunion, Sumatra, and Tanzania. Conditions for laborers turned bean production into a cause of uprisings and the eventual emancipation of slaves. In French colonies, maroons (runaway slaves) raided the plantations that produced 60 percent of the world's coffee. Insurgents set fire to hundreds of coffee plantations to impress whites with black outrage at profiteering at the expense of African slaves. The outbreak of the Haitian Revolution in 1791 precipitated a 13-year clash that ended in freedom for black islanders.

During the American Civil War, the absence of authentic coffee permeated journals and media articles with the need for a favorite drink. Southern cooks tested numerous substitute plants for the absent coffee bean. The most successful were acorns, beets, chicory, corn, dandelions, holly berries, melon seeds, okra seeds, peanuts, sweet potatoes, wheat, and yams. On July 8, 1861, when coffee was still available, the Sumter, South Carolina, *Tri-Weekly Watchman* advised cooks to cut ground coffee evenly with cornmeal to make supplies last. The Charleston, South Carolina, *Mercury* of February 8, 1862, offered a recipe for boiling and parching rye for coffee. As the war entered its last months, the demand for a coffee substitute reached epidemic proportions. The Yorkville, Georgia, *Enquirer* of January 21, 1863, offered a method of parching and grinding cane seed for coffee. The November 18 issue of the *Confederate Baptist* of Columbia, South Carolina, suggested blending dried potatoes with persimmon seed for coffee. Perhaps the worst substitute, English pea coffee, turned up in the June 30, 1864, edition of the Albany, Georgia, *Patriot*.

Coffee culture established itself in the social behaviors of industrialized nations. In the late 1800s, temperance activists advocated coffee as a substitute for beer, whiskey, and wine. A factory in Buffalo, New York, offered the first designated midmorning and midafternoon work stoppage in 1902. A half century later, the creation of the term *coffee break* from a Pan-American Coffee Bureau advertisement validated a minimeal dating to fifteenth-century Constantinople. Factories and offices complied with the trend by providing coffee vending machines and coffeemakers in canteens and cafeterias. The relaxation from labor figured in union negotiations of worker benefits, in combat, and even in the daily food intake of astronauts aboard the space shuttle. Computer operators identify improved eye-hand coordination, rea-

soning power, and visual acuity from a single cup of coffee.

Currently, coffee plantations thrive on the bean belt, the growing area between the Tropic of Cancer and the Tropic of Capricorn. The most common bean, arabica coffee, suits the taste of 70 percent of aficionados, more than twice the number of those who prefer bitter robusta (*Coffea canephora*). The latter is a high-caffeine, high-yield species discovered in central Africa in 1895 and grown in Brazil, India, Indonesia, and Vietnam. The major roasters of coffee, Philip Morris, Procter & Gamble, Nestlé, and Sara Lee, thrive on the profits from pure arabica and blends.

Coffee Time, Starbucks, Torrefazione Italia, and other chain coffee shops flourish at serving gourmet flavors, which vary the diluted American version with additions of chocolate syrup, condensed or fresh milk, cream, dry foam, half-and-half, ice, or whipped cream. Europeans favor espresso, a concentrated brew that forces pressurized hot water through a fine grind of dark roast beans. Additional flavorings—almond extract, brandy, brown sugar, cocoa, grappa, Irish whiskey, kirsch, lime or orange peel, mint syrup, and vanilla—add sweetness, alcohol, and fragrance.

See also: Adulterated Food; Freeze-Drying; Plant Disease and Prevention; Restaurants; South American Diet and Cuisine; Tea.

Further Reading

Antol, Marie Nadine. *Confessions of a Coffee Bean: The Complete Guide to Coffee Cuisine.* Garden City Park, NY: Square One, 2002.

Cowan, Brian William. *The Social Life of Coffee: The Emergence of the British Coffeehouse.* New Haven, CT: Yale University Press, 2005.

Pendergrast, Mark. *Uncommon Grounds: The History of Coffee and How It Transformed Our World.* New York: Basic Books, 2010.

Weinberg, Bennett Alan, and Bonnie K. Bealer. *The World of Caffeine: The Science and Culture of the World's Most Popular Drug.* New York: Routledge, 2001.

Wild, Antony. *Coffee: A Dark History.* New York: W.W. Norton, 2005.

Columbus, Christopher (ca. 1451–1506)

The landing of Christopher Columbus, a Genoan navigator representing the Spanish Crown, on the Bahamian island of San Salvador in the West Indies on October 12, 1492, produced the high-water mark of global food exchange and dietary diversification.

Born to a wool weaver, Columbus went to sea in 1461. He worked on trading vessels across the Mediterranean and as far north as the British Isles and Iceland and south along the Guinea Coast of Africa. In 1479, he settled at Lisbon, Portugal. Columbus formulated an investment venture to propose to John II of Portugal and Henry VII of England. Rejected in both courts and in Genoa and Venice, he returned to Iberia to seek funding. At the court of Ferdinand II and Isabella I of Castile in May 1486, Columbus exploited the national fever for colonization. After initially spurning his idea, the queen kept her options open and changed her mind about investing in potential trade missions to the west.

On August 2, 1492, Columbus set out on the merchant ship *Santa María* on the first of four voyages to the Western Hemisphere. Influencing his expectations, his readings of Aristotle's philosophies prepared him to look for similar food plants in the same global latitudes. A study of *The Travels of Marco Polo* (ca. 1300) raised anticipation of commerce in the Spice Islands, one of the wealthiest food trading sites on the planet. His fleet included the *Niña* and the *Pinta,* which carried crews of 18 each, plus a stock of almonds, anchovies and sardines, beans and lentils, biscuit, chickpeas, flour, honey, molasses, oil, raisins, rice, salt cod and red meat, vinegar, water, and wine. Cooks prepared meals on deck at a single open firebox fueled by logs. On October 2, nearing land, the men caught tuna, a welcome change in the ship's mess.

Landing in the Bahamas on October 12, 1492, Columbus anticipated meeting the Great Khan of China. He viewed flora, such as the papaya and sea grape, that might be useful to Ferdinand and Isabella but regretted that he could not identify additional plants that supplied curatives, dyes, food, or spices.

Exploring the Bahamas and Cuba

In daybooks, Columbus praised the New World for its fertility and promise of a rewarding enterprise. He lamented that he had no time to ascertain the medicinal powers and nutritional worth of herbs and trees. From foot travel among the Arawak, Carib, Lucayan, and Taíno, he summarized a panoply of taste sensations and reciprocated with gifts of European edibles, usually bread with honey and cups of wine. The Arawak brought popcorn to trade. The Carib made extensive use of the palmetto or cabbage palm as a source of hut materials and of nuts and hearts of palm, a fibrous vegetable. In exchange for tender palm cores, Columbus offered the Spanish onion, a much larger allium bulb than native wild onions.

On October 16 at the island he named Fernandina (present-day Long Island), Columbus observed native corn and kidney beans in the fields. After two crewmen brought him corn flour, the first eaten by a European, he found it tasty. Three days later at Guanahani (San Salvador in the Lucayan Archipelago), he ate iguana, which he compared to the taste of chicken. At Cape Isleo, he collected a half

ton (454 kilograms) of aloe, which he honored in his journal with grapes, olives, and wheat as the four vegetables indispensable to human wellness.

Farther west, Columbus misidentified the island of Cuba as mainland China. On October 28, 1492, he encountered the potato, which reminded him of the taste of chestnuts. He identified amaranth and purslane as edible but, on November 16, disdained a meal of huge "snails," which may have been conches that the Bahamian Taíno valued. For the first time in European history, he observed the recreational smoking of tobacco, the same leaf that the Taíno offered as a gift. He examined specimens of mastic, an aromatic tree resin he believed cured cholera, but he rejected a spice his men collected from the canella tree and misidentified as cinnamon. His food sampling included corn, green beans, kidney beans, manioc bread, and sweet potatoes. Rather than examine them objectively, he contrasted the new flavors and textures to what he had known in Europe.

Hospitality on Hispaniola

In December 1492, the Castilians reached the island of Hispaniola (Haiti and the Dominican Republic), which earned the title "Cradle of the Americas." On December 16, Columbus declared the environment as desirable a source of provisions as anyone could want. He entertained Guacanagarí, an Arawak cacique, with European food and offered a flask of orange flower water, a substance and fragrance unknown in the West Indies. At Guacanagarí's royal compound (at present-day En Bas Saline), east of Cap Haitian, Columbus learned how the Taíno made bread by grating manioc root and kneading the pulp into flatbread. The natives fed his crew well on bread, fish, shrimp, yams, and spiced drinks. The day after Christmas, the Taíno of the area where Columbus established La Nueva Isabela (Santo Domingo) in 1496 offered Columbus *ají,* their favorite red chili pepper or cayenne. He called it pimiento and planned to deliver peppers to Spain by the shipload.

Columbus had mixed luck at farming experiments. Near Cap Haitien on December 24, he stationed 39 sailors at Villa de la Navidad, the first European colony in the Americas, to plant European crops. Rather than adapt to the island flora, his men tried to produce crops new to the hemisphere, such as citron, lemon, lime, and orange trees. Meanwhile, their imported supplies rotted in the tropical humidity, which also encouraged the mosquitoes that spread malaria and yellow fever. The attempt to coerce nature wearied the settlers with constant shortages and famine while endangering the island's ecosystem. On January 1, 1493, sailors took a shore boat to the island of Amiga and collected rhubarb to introduce to Castilian farmers. The root proved to have no commercial value.

On March 4, 1493, Columbus returned aboard the *Niña* to the Seville court of Ferdinand and Isabella. In lieu of gold, the voyager presented to the court new foods, parakeets, and six members of an unidentified New World tribe, whom he called "Indians." His discoveries broadened European cuisine almost immediately by introducing chili peppers and sweet potatoes to a bland Continental cuisine dominated by beans and peas, bread, cabbage, cheese, mutton, and salted herring and pork. He began planning his next voyage to the land of wonders.

The Columbian Exchange
Setting sail from Cadiz on September 24, 1493, aboard the *María Galante* with a 17-ship fleet, Columbus added four pairs of live pigs to his ship's stores, as well as cattle, chickens, dogs, goats, horses, sheep, and sugarcane for introduction to foreign shores. He crossed the Atlantic to more food discoveries at numerous landfalls in Hispaniola.

One crew member, Michele da Cuneo, wrote of the expansive oyster beds and of the sailors' collection of six boatloads of oysters, none of which produced a pearl. Other sources of West Indian meals, such as fish, pigeons, snakes, and turtles, delighted Cuneo. From European livestock, islanders acquired not only riding horses and new sources of meat, but also butter, cheese, cream, and milk.

On November 3 at the island of Marie-Galante in the Antilles, which Columbus named Santa Maria la Galante after his flagship, Castilian sailors burned their tongues on the poisonous manchineel fruit (*Hippomane mancinella*). At Barbuda, Columbus tasted a sweet fruit, probably a guava or papaya. At Guadeloupe, he enjoyed pineapple, which islanders made into wine and used as an abortifacient and vermifuge. On November 22 on Hispaniola the crew ate monkey meat and observed Indians feasting on lizards and snakes. When Antonio de Torres arrived from Spain with relief supplies in winter 1494, the explorers rallied to supplies of food, medicines, and wine.

Permanent Change
As European agrarianism took hold in the Caribbean, clear-cutting, heavy plowing, monoculture, and soil compacting replaced the land-friendly Taíno system of the digging stick and hoe for growing a variety of vegetables in small plots. The Indians applied an energy efficient system of planting beans to grow up mounded corn stalks and squash as a ground cover underneath. For animal protein, they respected seasonal limits by fishing with wooden weirs and used game surrounds to drive big mammals toward hunters.

By respecting finite nature, the Taíno had avoided overkill of a single species. But the abrupt alteration of the island ecosystem now caused unforeseen damage. Herd animals introduced by the Spaniards rapidly depleted native Haitian grasses and denuded pastures, causing island soil to thin from rain and wind erosion. Extraneous wild plants—the daisy, dandelion, and nettle—displaced indigenous herbs. The introduction of sources for red

Recipe: Original Jamaican Jerk Snapper

Halve a 2-pound snapper. Rub with a slurry of two chopped hot peppers (*habañero* or Scotch bonnet), two sprigs of thyme, 2 tablespoons of allspice, 1/4 cup of vinegar, and cayenne pepper and sea salt to taste. Place snapper halves on a grill and cook for 15 minutes on each side while continuing to coat the fish with the slurry.

meat, the staple of the Castilian elite, generated a social stratification that made the Taíno dependent on their conquerors.

Like his crew member Cuneo, Columbus showed ongoing concern for matters of hunger and food. He attempted an exchange on Hispaniola, where he introduced seeds of cucumber, melon, squash, and radish. His experimental agriculture failed to grow barley, beans, chickpeas, lettuce, onions, and scallions. He pioneered the planting of wheat, the first grown in the Western Hemisphere, which his colony needed for malting and livestock forage. In Jamaica, he discovered allspice, a source of oil and an essential of the Arawaks' jerked (spiced) meat for its mingling of aroma and flavor reminiscent of cinnamon, clove, and nutmeg. On April 2, 1494, at Santo Tomás (St. Thomas), he introduced European food technology by building a gristmill.

The second voyage continued to surprise and inform Columbus. In Cuba, he ate fish and *hutias,* rodents served in a peppered stew. Diego Álvarez Chanca, his physician and fellow enthusiast for discovery, identified red pepper as a member of the capsicum family. Chanca claimed that produce on Hispaniola grew 2.5 times faster than its Spanish counterpart.

The homeward journey began from Hispaniola on August 20, 1494. Columbus's survey of the Azores, Canaries, and Cape Verde Islands implanted an insight into the ecological disaster to come from the stripping of forest canopies and introducing European agricultural theory to virgin tropical soil. More dire for the Taíno, their numbers fell rapidly from European diseases and enforced labor in sugarcane fields and mines.

Further Exploration
On the third expedition, embarking on May 30, 1498, Columbus led six ships from Spain to Trinidad in two months. He explored Venezuela, the Orinoco River, Tobago, and Grenada. On August 6, he offered gifts of beads, brass bells, and sugar to Carib traders who approached his fleet in a canoe. The natives presented Columbus with bread, corn, fruit drinks, and beer made from corn. South of Trinidad, the mainland, which the Caribs called Paria,

flourished with wild grapes and orchards. The chief welcomed Columbus and his men with feasting and gifts of parrots and pearls. The voyage taxed the navigator with fever and gout as well as an eye inflammation that rendered him nearly blind.

For the fourth and final voyage, Columbus covered the sea route between Cadiz and the Antilles in 35 days, arriving at Martinique on June 15, 1502. He visited Jamaica before exploring the coast of Honduras, Nicaragua, Costa Rica, the Cayman Islands, and the Darién peninsula of Panama, the home of more advanced peoples than the Arawak and Carib of Haiti. At Guanaja Island off Honduras on July 30, his brother, Bartolomew Columbus, encountered 25 Maya in a trading dugout. The Indians carried cacao beans, which they used as currency, but the Castilians, bent on finding gold, were unimpressed. On August 18 at an area in Honduras he named Costa de la Oreja, Columbus feasted on chicken, bread, red and white beans, and roast fish. Into early fall, he explored the coast of Nicaragua. On the Mosquito Coast, he sampled bananas, coconuts, and a luscious fruit he misidentified as *myrobalan*.

At Jamaica on July 7, 1503, Columbus made another culinary discovery, a wild turkey with feathers he described as woolly. During a year stranded among the Taíno, he cajoled them into supplying his men with food by predicting the lunar eclipse of February 29, 1504. On November 7, 1504, he arrived back in Spain with details of barbecuing, the first chocolate seen in Europe, and samples of chili pepper and Jamaican allspice, substitutes for cinnamon, clove, and peppercorns.

Ironically, although Columbus introduced the roots of the world's future commercial wealth, he parried complaints from investors that his expeditions had returned little profit, especially lacking pearls and precious ores. Men of little vision overlooked the Columbian exchange, which brought tobacco and the wild turkey to Europe. A treasury of foodstuffs and cuisine additives eventually flowed from the New World—avocados, blueberries, butter beans, cashews, chicle, cranberries, gooseberries, green beans, Jerusalem artichokes, kidney and lima beans, maple syrup, muscadines, passion fruit, peanuts, pecans, sarsaparilla, and vanilla.

By the mid-1500s, Spanish agronomists had planted European produce in Columbia, Mexico, Peru, the Philippines, Puerto Rico, Venezuela, and the West Indies. The Antilles acquired cauliflower, citrus groves, figs, lettuce, and pomegranates, new food crops that increased food choices and nutrition in the Caribbean. From the Spanish toehold in the Philippines, trade took chocolate to China and added to sophisticated European tables more types of Chinese fruit, rice, and spice than gourmands had ever seen.

Boosting the cost of exotic goods, the water–land–water transport from the Philippines to Acapulco and from Veracruz to Spain endangered costly stores from seawater, salt air, and attrition. Nonetheless, the arrival of green beans, potatoes, and tomatoes generated a boom in truck gardening and farmer's markets. The olive flourished in Peru. The French embraced haricots verts (green beans); Italian innovators, wearied of the pulse-based cuisine of the ancient Romans, turned tomatoes into sauce for pasta and pizza and found use for the New World zucchini. Corn generated new plantings and food traditions in Lombardy and Romania. In England and Ireland, the American potato became the basis of mashed potatoes and shepherd's pie.

See also: Agriculture; Amerindian Diet; Barbecue; Jerky; Manioc; Maritime Trade Routes; New World Commodities; Peppers; Pickling; Potatoes; Sauces and Saucing.

Further Reading

Columbus, Christopher. *The Diario of Christopher Columbus's First Voyage to America, 1492–1493, Abstracted by Fray Bartolomé de las Casas.* Ed. Oliver Dunn and James E. Kelley, Jr. Norman: University of Oklahoma Press, 1989.

Gerbi, Antonello. *Nature in the New World: From Christopher Columbus to Gonzalo Fernandez de Oviedo.* Trans. Jeremy Moyle. Pittsburgh, PA: University of Pittsburgh Press, 1985.

Rubin, Lawrence C., ed. *Food for Thought: Essays on Eating and Culture.* Jefferson, NC: McFarland, 2008.

Sale, Kirkpatrick. *Christopher Columbus and the Conquest of Paradise.* 2nd ed. New York: Tauris Parke, 2006.

Commodity Regulation

Because most nations import and export edibles, the guarantee of wholesome, clearly labeled edibles relies on laws that require global oversight of quality, correct measures, and sanitation. Commodity regulation deals in the specifics of dairy foods, fruits, grains, meats, seafood, vegetables, and water. Prescripts are as old as the Mosaic code and as current as directives from the European Union, United Nations, and World Health Organization on genetic modification.

After 3000 B.C.E., Egyptian priests restricted the sale of meat to healthy, unblemished animals slaughtered in plain sight according to market ordinance. In the 1600s B.C.E., Sumerian King Hammurabi II regulated dairy commerce as stringently as he did butchering. From as early as 850 B.C.E. through the Talmudic period ending in 500 C.E., Hebrew market agents in Palestine attached clay inspection labels to oil and wine amphorae stating date of filling and the identity of the bonded warehouse. Among Athenians, wine inspectors handed out fines and penalties for food hoaxers. Strict temple ordinances controlled the age and condition of a sacrificial beast or bird and its slaughter and cooking and distribution of altar portions.

From 439 B.C.E., Roman civil law abandoned the arbitrary legal principle of caveat emptor (let the buyer beware) by necessitating accurate labels and weights and measures. After 388 B.C.E., aediles elected to the office of public works supervised fresh and smoked meats and grain and provision markets as well as the water supply from aqueducts and fountains. Agents oversaw meat curing with statutes that protected the consumer from fraud, such as the substitution of goat meat for more appealing ingredients. Nevertheless, smugglers avoided the price jumps and tariffs inflicted by regulators and maintained thieves' markets, unmonitored exchanges where peasants bought and sold under an illicit economy.

The Lex Fannia, legislation sponsored by Consul Caius Fannius Strabo in 161 B.C.E., regulated the amount citizens could spend on fish and meat and on the weight of silverware at table. Under Augustus, the first emperor, sumptuary laws restricted *luxuria* (extravagances), particularly commerce in Asian imports. Austerity imposed a return to early Roman values instituted by a pastoral culture, a means of upholding the virtues of simple country beans, pork, and spelt that the mythographer Ovid urged in *Fasti (Holidays,* 8 C.E.).

Surveillance increased suspicion of the edibility and safety of imported goods and foreign sauces that marketers hawked in a cosmopolitan city. At a peak in imperial fortunes in 324 C.E., the Roman Emperor Constantine proclaimed Constantinopolis the alternate capital of his realm. Officials regulated grain and meat commerce and set standards on fish from some 1,600 trawlers per day.

Early Modern Regulation

Health regulations got their start in the Middle Ages with consumer edicts governing the safety of beer, bread, cheese, eggs, sausage, and wine. Along the network of old Roman roads, collaboration among alehouses and coaching inns regulated the dispensing of brewed and fermented beverages. Kosher housewives patronized a network of abattoirs, bakeries, delis, fish markets, picklers, and wineries that observed rabbinic strictures. They chose merchants governed by respect for scriptural food and sanitation edicts. Similarly, under Islamic law, the governance of commodity exchange fell to clerics rather than state bureaucrats.

In 732 C.E., in response to Germanic paganism, Pope Gregory III issued a ban to St. Boniface, a missionary to Germany, on the eating of horses, which the church valued as companions and as mounts for cavalry under assault by an Islamic army. Under Pope Zachary I after 741, Boniface extended commodity regulation to the eating of uncooked bacon and pork and the consumption of meat from animals killed by accident, disease, or starvation. These codes illustrated the centrality of the meat diet and the economic value of the meat industry to the Holy Roman Empire, which eventually came under control of the Mecklenburg city bailiff and the thirteenth-century butchers' guild at Augsburg and Basel.

In 1215, King John's signing of the Magna Carta returned to Roman concern for getting one's money's worth by codifying England's statutes governing weights and measures. Common law and guild principles protected the consumer from rancid meat, rotted cheese, and deliberate commodity adulteration of aromatics and condiments. The Pepperers Guild outlined deceptive practices in the packaging and sale of spices, especially the most expensive—alum, cloves, ginger, pepper, and saffron. Agents combated false claims of freshness and quality in fish and milk. In 1266, the Assize of Bread set loaf ingredients and proportions of flour per pound of bread, as overseen by justices of the peace. In 1291, French statutes forbade the concealment of original wine casks, the mixing of two wines, and the marketing of vintages by false names or ages.

German commodity law tended to punish falsifiers with brutal executions. In Augsburg, bakers and their employees using unwholesome flour or short-weighting loaves underwent a lethal ducking in a muddy pond. Nuremberg regulators terrified food adulterers by public immolation. In 1444, the state incinerated a food cheat by burning him with his adulterated saffron. At Biebrich, Hesse, in 1482, a wine falsifier had to swallow 1.5 gallons (5.7 liters) of adulterated wine in a few minutes, a sure death sentence.

In 1540, English law empowered physicians to search and analyze the quality and cleanliness of foodstuffs and spices dispensed by apothecaries and to destroy offensive stock. After 1558, Elizabeth I fought such faulty commodities by proclaiming a purity act in 1580 that required bona fide labeling of honey with a hot iron inscribed with the seller's initials. Those selling counterfeit produce risked a penalty of 6 shillings 8 pence. The following year, similar stringent regulations forbade the contamination of wax with resin, tallow, or turpentine. James I standardized medicinal dosages in April 1618 by issuing the *Pharmacopoeia Londinensis,* which prescribed the dispensing of spices and chemicals. The decree represented a larger program of regulating foreign and home commerce in corn, pepper, and other edible commodities in standard measures and weights. The British Adulteration of Tea and Coffee Act of 1724 further standardized luxury purchases.

New World Regulations

North American food inspection lagged behind that of its European counterparts. During the Civil War, President Abraham Lincoln signed the False Claims Act of 1863 prohibiting profiteering from the U.S. government by making deceptive or false claims, such as the ingredients of pharmaceuticals and processed foods, particularly biscuit, coffee, and portable soup, three major purchases of the Army of the Potomac. In the 1870s, Grange members, led by Oliver Hudson Kelley, a staff member of the U.S. Department of Agriculture, protected grain and forage farmers by promoting Granger laws in Illinois, Iowa, Minnesota, and Wisconsin. The legislation fought corrupt middlemen by superintending the sanitation of cooperative silos, grain elevators, rail transportation facilities, stockyards, and warehousing.

Meanwhile, meat marketing allowed unscrupulous license. Consumers in Austria, England, France, Germany, and Italy campaigned against unfit salt pork. In 1879, prohibitions against the sale of one U.S. commodity—bacon—reduced the export of trichina in swine products. The U.S. Congress passed inspection regulations in 1890 that guaranteed the quality of bacon and salt pork. Within months, Chicago opened a food laboratory conducting microscopic inspection of pork for trichina. In 1895, federal law empowered regulators to destroy condemned meat. Canadian law followed the U.S. example.

Twentieth Century and Beyond

The U.S. Pure Food and Drug Act of June 10, 1906, called for the creation of the Food and Drug Administration (FDA), the nation's oldest consumer protection agency and main commodities regulator. After Upton Sinclair's muckraking novel *The Jungle* (1906) disclosed corruption in the meatpacking industry, President Theodore Roosevelt championed the Meat Inspection Act of June 30, 1906. The first law prohibiting adulterating and misbranding meat from cattle, goats, horses, sheep, and swine, the legislation began a crusade for sanitary abattoirs and processing plants. Technology upgraded U.S. merchant marine fleets under the Shipping Act of 1916, which applied stringent rules to food shipments by Great Lakes and oceangoing barges and merchant vessels.

The onset of World War I required new edicts establishing fairness to buyer and trader and ensuring minimum waste of foodstuffs during global combat. In England, fixed ingredients and prices for flour, grain, milk, sugar, and tea restricted profiteering and discouraged food swindles. Scofflaws risked a fine of £100 and six months at hard labor.

The highway system, port inspections, and supermarkets improved food quality for suburban shopping. The 1938 Federal Food, Drug, and Cosmetic Act (or Wiley Act) fought medical quackery, pesticide residue, food adulterants and dyes, and deliberate misbranding by replacing widely varying state regulations with a firm national standard of purity. Scrutiny of food handling and distribution increased with the addition of standards and frequent spot inspections, especially of imported prepackaged fish, meats, and tea from Argentina, China, Japan, and New Zealand. In 1949, Arnold J. Lehman, the "Father of American Toxicology," equipped the FDA with a guidebook, "Procedures for the Appraisal of the Toxicity of Chemicals in Food," a manual that initiated government oversight of processed food.

The past decades have produced consistency in global commodities standards. On January 1, 1958, the Food Additives Amendment identified 700 safe food substances. The Delaney Clause banned such carcinogens as cyclamate and lead and halogenated compounds. Throughout Europe since the 1970s, criteria for ingredients in commercial foods insisted on uniform, identifiable plant varieties rather than wild insect- and wind-pollinated plants. In defiance of agrarian regulation of traditional foodstuffs, botanists have established heirloom arboretums and seed banks.

U.S. consumer agencies increased health warnings, resulting in 1983 with the Federal Anti-Tampering Act and in 1986 with a ban on Alar, a growth regulation spray for apples. Further surveillance of food colorants and flavorings scrutinized additives to baby food. In 1990, the Nutritional Labeling and Education Act required full disclosure of food ingredients by proportion.

In January 2001, Dole Food Company, the world's largest fruit and vegetable seller, entered organic marketing by distributing bananas grown without bioengineering or chemical enhancements. The firm's advance into a limited specialties market coincided with issuance of the first national organic food standards by the U.S. Department of Agriculture, which regulates produce nationwide, beginning in August 2002. U.S. border rejections of African foods tended toward the ridding of cereals, dried fruit, nuts, and vegetables of foreign matter and microbes. In 2011, health and purity ordinances passed by the European Union increased overhead, notably the cost of analyzing and inspecting seafood, maintaining quality control, removing pesticide residues, and tracing aflatoxins.

See also: Endangered Species; Genetically Modified Food; Heirloom Plants; Organic Foods; Rationing; Taboos, Food; Trading Vessels.

Further Reading

Berggren, Lars, Nils Hybel, and Annette Landen, eds. *Cogs, Cargoes, and Commerce: Maritime Bulk Trade in Northern Europe, 1150–1400.* Toronto: Pontifical Institute of Mediaeval Studies, 2002.

Fortin, Neal D. *Food Regulation: Law, Science, Policy, and Practice.* Hoboken, NJ: John Wiley & Sons, 2009.

Jansen, Kees, and Sietze Vellema, eds. *Agribusiness and Society: Corporate Responses to Environmentalism, Market Opportunities, and Public Regulation.* New York: Zed, 2004.

Commodity Riots

A dynamic of the struggle for property and power, rioting against food profiteers and commodity hoarders tends to follow harvest failures, inflation, and wartime price-fixing and rationing. Examples during the American Revolution of 1776, the French Revolution of July 1789, and the fall of the Romanov dynasty in Russia in 1917 illustrate the power of starvation and inflated prices to arouse nationalism and bring down governments. With food as a symbol of social imparity, the underclass uses child malnutrition as justification for coercing and disempowering the privileged class.

During subsistence emergencies throughout the Roman Empire for two centuries following the mid-300s C.E., the plebeian class of Alexandria, Antioch, Constantinople, and Thessalonica as well as Rome faced periods of famine while aristocrats flourished. Urban security decreased while mendicants and petty criminals overran marketplaces and plotters plundered granaries and burned property. Mobs demanded a bread dole from grain shipped to the warehouses at Ostia from Egypt and Sicily. At the imperial capital, the senatorial class had little choice but to distribute flour, oil, pork, and wine in the Suburra, southwestern Rome's ghetto. In 100 C.E., satirist Juvenal predicted the class impasse with the term *panem et circenses* (bread and circuses), a snide comment on shallow politicians who chose short-term appeasement of recurrent crises.

Opposing Commercialization

The decline of European feudalism created additional agitation among the needy. The rise of a market economy angered peasants, who had previously enjoyed prices adjusted to their means by aristocratic paternalism. In Tudor England, fury emerged in the artisanal class between 1585 and 1603, when the war against the Spanish Armada and the Nine Years' War fixed prices and diverted provisions to the military. On November 17, 1596, a failed harvest and mounting poverty triggered revolt in Oxfordshire against commercialization of the food supply. To set an example, Elizabeth I had two ringleaders hanged, drawn, and quartered but, in 1597, she relented in her anger toward the destitute by passing the Act for the Relief of the Poor.

A parallel revolt against food commercialization in China during the Ming dynasty resulted from the growth of cities and the demand for bread. Peasants raged against the transport of harvests to urban areas and for trade with the Dutch, Portuguese, and Spanish. During the reign of Emperor Wanli, the riots began with roadblocks, which occurred in Shanxi in 1583 and Jiangxi in 1588. Thousands of the rural poor confronted grain factors to prevent hoarding by speculators. To draw attention to the rebellion, leaders banged gongs and floated banners before seizing the grain for free distribution or for sale by local dealers at a reasonable rate.

In 1594, food insecurity in Fuzhou compelled infantryman Deng San to fight back against profiteers who defied caps on the price of rice. He led a throng to the home of Li San, the obdurate rice factor, for looting and intimidation. After three days of lawlessness, militia ended the riot. A more serious insurrection on April 12, 1620, aroused 10,000 Suzhou rioters against wealthy gain merchants. For ten days, rebels sacked and burned the houses of the rich and closed the market.

In England, bread insurrections took unpredictable turns, such as the lifting of a symbolic loaf with a pitchfork and the tying of expensive loaves in black ribbon, the acts of canny instigators. Passage of the Riot Act on August 1, 1714, had little effect on food protests, whether premeditated or spontaneous. In September 1766, lace makers in Honiton removed corn from rural barns to alleviate shortages. The throng marketed the grain and returned cash and corn sacks to the growers. At Nottingham on October 2, 1766, a rally at the Goose Fair protested the removal of 6,000 cheeses by Lincolnshire traders. A three-day disturbance had cheese wheels rolling through Peck Lane and Wheeler Gate, knocking the mayor into the mud.

Foot rioting originated legends about the motivation of local unrest. At Halifax on August 16, 1783, the hanging of rabble-rouser Thomas Spencer, a leader of revolt against grain prices, resulted in his martyrdom by fellow rioters for his seizing corn and wheat from wagons and warehouses. A meat protest at Market Place in Nottingham on May 12, 1788, intimidated the village butcher. The confrontation resulted in a bonfire being made from the butcher's records, doors, and shutters, a gesture of contempt for his low-quality goods. On the anniversary of the riot in 1792, when meat prices rose again, townspeople restaged the rampage.

Riot Tactics

Near the end of the eighteenth century, dissent strategy called for the interception of food in transit and at piers and loading docks. Preceding demonstrations, runners distributed handbills denouncing exploitation of the poor. In England in 1795, female shoppers engineered a nonviolent food riot by advancing on bakeshops, proffering a reasonable amount of money for their purchases, and departing with the overpriced goods. The food demands and grocer coercion continued into the early 1800s, when Napoleon's blockades kept supply vessels from reaching England.

Food scarcity, currency deflation, and unprecedented inflation and taxation during the American Civil War forced Southerners to demand food relief. In the first half of the four-year conflict, baking needs rose 200 percent in cost; dairy goods quadrupled in price. The redirection of salt to military use deprived civilians, prohibiting them from preserving precious meat. Rebellion arose in Atlanta, Augusta, Columbus, Macon, Milledgeville, and Savannah, Georgia. Clashes with price gougers and speculators resulted in pilfering of flour, meal, and salt barrels and sacks of bacon, dried beans, and peas. Housewives snatched what they could carry from warehouses and load into wagons.

To enforce government cost controls, women in Salisbury, North Carolina, on March 18, 1863, wielded axes and hatchets and forced dealers to open stores. A month later, Governor Zebulon B. Vance urged mobs to leave law enforcement to appointed agents. An autumn flour rebellion in Mobile, Alabama, on September 4 of that year, sent women raging into dry goods emporiums on Dauphin Street. According to an October issue of the *Country Gentleman,* agitators waved placards reading "Bread or Peace" and "Food or Death." Militia brandished bayonets against females armed only with fists. A year later, the situation worsened with the rising price of stove wood and the rationing of sugar and molasses.

In another episode in 1864, women from the Belvidere Hill Baptist Church in Richmond, Virginia, followed mob leader Mary Jackson on a rampage at Capital Square. Wielding cleavers, hatchets, and pistols against shopkeepers, raiders raged for two hours until Governor John Letcher intervened. At the order of Confederate President Jefferson Davis, public authorities dispersed the crowd with threats of firing on mobs. The food rioters faced 16 counts of misdemeanor larceny and a felony charge against Jackson for fomenting a riot. To prevent future food riots, the state police placed cannon in range of supply depots and calmed outraged women with rations of rice.

Public frenzy continued to dot periods of food insecurity in the United States. In 1902, riots in New York City's Lower East Side revealed the exasperation of mothers, who led militant males in politicizing everyday dealings with the kosher butcher. High prices so incensed Jewish homemakers that they trampled meat in the streets and collared bystanders who refused to take part.

During World War I, American shoppers waited in mile-long lines for bread. Consumers charged bakeshop owners for adulterating wheat flour with barley, oats, and rye to stretch supplies and augment profits. On February 20, 1917, women rallied against the inflationary cost of chicken, fish, onions, and potatoes by confronting the pushcart vendors of New York City. Their march to City Hall to press for food relief spread to consumers in Boston, Chicago, Philadelphia, and Toronto.

Contemporary World Uprisings

Capricious changes in food availability and pricing continued to spark antigovernment forays across the globe. On January 17, 1977, spontaneous revolt from Alexandria to Aswan, Egypt, followed President Anwar Sadat's cancellation of $250 million in state food subsidies on flour, oil, and rice. A clash between millions of the destitute and the middle class raged for 48 hours. Despite the dispatch of military squads to rout the mob, 79 citizens died and 800 required medical treatment. The virulence of the hungry forced Sadat to restore previous food policies.

Between 2004 and 2011, as investment lapsed and food stockpiles dwindled worldwide, food prices doubled. In late 2007, with 33 nations at risk of social mutiny against food crises, clashes erupted in Bangladesh, Bolivia, Mauritania, Mexico, Morocco, Pakistan, South Africa, Sri Lanka, Uzbekistan, and Yemen. On February 22, 2008, urbanites in Burkina Faso rebelled against price

increases of 65 percent. To calm citizens, the government removed tariffs and taxes on dairy goods, infant food, oil, rice, salt, and wheat and distributed free meals at hospitals and schools.

Riot forces in Ivory Coast on March 31, 2008, fired tear gas at market protesters, who protested the rise in beef costs of nearly 25 percent. A similar emergency response in Cameroon denounced import duties on fish, flour, and rice. Bread shortages in Egypt the following April 8 provoked demonstrations in which police shot a child in the head. In the same week, the 50 percent boost in costs of beans, condensed milk, fruit, and rice in Haiti sent dissenters into the street to revile Prime Minister Jacques-Édouard Alexis.

Spring 2008 exposed to the world media a growing outcry against hunger. Southern Yemenites resorted to arson and roadblocks against army tanks. In Dakar, Senegal, food rioters claimed that police tortured protesters of inflation. Egyptian families stood in queues from dawn to buy *baladi,* the nation's staple flatbread. In protest of uneven commodity distribution, arsonists in Mahalla burned tires on railroad tracks and set fire to two schools. Black marketers increased tensions by charging $377 for 220 pounds (100 kilograms) of flour worth $3.14.

Turmoil in North Africa worsened in summer 2011, when global food prices reached a record high. Jordanians opposed the cost of staples; Libyan impatience with grocery pricing reached a boiling point. Additional uprisings threatened commercial districts in Chile, Morocco, and Mozambique. Mobs in Algeria and Tunisia challenged police in street battles. The scramble for food resulted in the death of 100 citizens and the destabilization of both governments.

See also: Proust, Joseph-Louis; Rationing; Salt.

Further Reading

Allen, Gary, and Ken Albala. *The Business of Food: Encyclopedia of the Food and Drink Industries.* Westport, CT: Greenwood, 2007.

Bohstedt, John. *The Politics of Provisions: Food Riots, Moral Economy, and Market Transition in England, c. 1550–1850.* Burlington, VT: Ashgate, 2010.

"The World Food Crisis." *The New York Times,* April 10, 2008.

Condiments

The complementary taste and smell of liquid and semiliquid condiments, pickles, and flavoring sauces can make or break an entrée. National and regional favorites depend on small quantities of savor or sweetness, as with French onion dip on chips, horseradish on beef, ketchup or mayonnaise on fries, molasses on biscuits, red currant jelly on lamb, and whipped cream on pecan pie. Some additives, including duck sauce atop spring rolls, miso and *shoyu* (soy sauce) with Japanese rice dishes, *sofrito* on Haitian cod, and vinegar in Caribbean callaloo, ensure authenticity in ethnic cuisine. Menus retain the traditional pairings of Irish lamb with mint sauce, pork loin with applesauce, tartar sauce on fried flounder, toast with anchovy paste, and wasabi on sushi.

Fish roe, honey, pepper, rue, salt, seaweed, and vinegar figure in the earliest recorded recipes as seasonings and digestive aids. In 5000 B.C.E., Egyptians and Hebrews valued cinnamon oil as a cordial, coriander and cumin as aromatics, dill and honey as dressings for altar gifts, and the hot bite of horseradish and capers grated over meat as an appetite stimulant. Mustard intensified the first curry powder, which occupants of Mohenjo Daro in the Indus Valley in 4000 B.C.E. husked and winnowed before pounding the seed in mortars. Chinese cooks introduced fermented soy sauce around 2800 B.C.E. as a food accessory. The Romans turned honey and vinegar into complementary pantry staples and factory-made *garum* and *liquamen* (both fish sauces) into major exports for embellishing porridge.

Medieval Advances

After a decline in condiment demand, early medieval chefs experimented with creamy bread sauce, tartar sauce, and verjuice squeezed from unripe grapes to intensify dishes for the wealthy. Condiments traveled well, as exemplified by the mustard paste ferried north to the Celts by Roman legionaries. Horseradish enlivened the cold meats and spreads of Britons, Germans, and Scandinavians. Central European Jews favored horseradish to serve with gefilte fish and to treat sinus and urinary infections.

Monastery cooks made *cameline* from cinnamon in vinegar, caudell from ale and egg yolk, galantyne from jellied meat drippings, and *poivre jaunet et noir* from green and black pepper. In the 800s, French monks turned mustard into a moneymaking flavoring, which hawkers sold on Paris streets. Coulis, a puree of orchard fruit or vegetables, sometimes incorporated roast meat drippings or the flesh of crustaceans and fish.

To medieval Islamic platters, cooks applied dabs of *murri* (fermented barley) and olive oil, a foodstuff too expensive as a general ingredient. A cheesy condiment, *khamakh rijal* involved the placement of milk in a gourd to ripen for three months before the addition of garlic, mint, nigella, and rose leaves. With a distinctive taste, *amba,* a pickle common to Iraqi cooking, flavored mango with fenugreek, mustard, and turmeric to spread on pita sandwiches.

Post-Columbian Flavor Boom

The introduction of Christopher Columbus's crew to barbecue in Hispaniola in 1492 informed Europeans of the savory sauce accompanying wood-smoked pork and poultry. The blend of spice and sweetener with tomato and vinegar soaked into the dish and heightened aroma while tenderizing the meat. A similar union of *chimichurri* with *asado,* the barbecue of Argentina, Brazil, Chile, Colombia, Nicaragua, Paraguay, and Uruguay, created a titillating main dish. An oily combination of garlic, lemon, onion, parsley, pepper, and salt, chimichurri served as both condiment and marinade in the same way that the Chinese used hoisin sauce as a specialty dip and glaze for beef and poultry.

In the early Renaissance, chefs turned condiment making into a profession, beginning with the purchase of almond powder and sugar from pharmacists. Processing of condiments grew so contentious that, around 1550, governments cracked down on adulteration and contamination, particularly the addition of coal-tar dye and pumpkin to ketchup. The Genoans updated Roman *moretum* (cheese spread) into pesto sauce, a creaming of basil, garlic, and pine nuts with olive oil and grated cheese; Scots creamed peas into mushy peas as a dressing for cod and salmon and condiment with steak pie. In *Le Grand Cuisinier* (*The Elegant Cook,* 1583), an anonymous recipe for Barbe Robert sauce suggests the combination of fried onions, mustard, verjuice, and vinegar for topping duck, eggs, fried fish, and roast hare. Consumers in Tudor England equated such quality saucing with the best in dining.

In the 1600s, the French brought Continental cooking to a historic height. Chefs produced *chasseur,* Lyonnaise, Mornay, and port, all variations of white sauce. Credited to Philippe de Mornay, these four contributed zest to seventeenth-century meats and vegetables. Chasseur, a brown sauce made from mushrooms and shallots in wine, topped game and pheasants. A fifth period favorite, béchamel, invented by Louis de Béchamel, head steward to Louis XIV, or by the king's chief chef, Pierre La Varenne, flavored dried cod.

English mustard makers had a monopoly on manufacture by 1658 and formed a professional guild. During this same period, British colonial cooks adopted chutney, saffron, and turmeric from Indian table garnishes. When voyagers returned from the Far East, they described the appeal of soy sauce. Lacking soybeans, food processors imitated the taste with kidney beans and mushrooms and added their wares to hash, ragout, and soup. Royalist food writer Robert May's *The Accomplisht Cook; or, The Art and Mystery of Cookery* (1660), a survey of 1,300 entrées served to the court of Charles II, summarized the influence of French gastronomy during the king's retreat from the Puritan Commonwealth. To celebrate regal alimentary standards during the Restoration, May compiled 13 categories of condiments to accompany meat entrées, including dressings for fricasseed frog's legs and snails and ambergris on nightingale.

In the 1690s, the Chinese bottled the first commercial soy sauce and *ke-tsiap* (ketchup) from spiced fish

Worcestershire sauce, ketchup, and HP brown sauce—along with mustard, mayonnaise, barbecue sauce, and salsa—are among the most popular condiments in modern Western cuisine. Liquid flavor enhancers are as old and diverse as world cooking itself. *(Business Wire/Getty Images)*

Mayonnaise became a global condiment, featuring regional alterations in the original recipe. Aioli, a garlicky mayonnaise, originated in Provence as a sauce for fried hake; a variant, rémoulade, added anchovy paste, capers, curry, and pickles to mayonnaise for saucing cold crab, plaice, salmon, and sole. Belgians and Dutch added creamy mayonnaise to dishes of cold chicken and hard-boiled eggs. Russians made mayonnaise the binder in a salad of meat, potatoes, and vegetables.

Pre-Modern Innovations

The era of experimentation generated more complicated condiments from simple beginnings. An emulsification of clarified butter and egg yolk, Hollandaise garnished steamed asparagus from the 1650s. Hollandaise preceded béarnaise, a condiment invented in 1836 by Jules Colette, the chef at Le Pavillon Henri IV in Paris. The bright yellow cream sauce got its unique flavor from the addition of herbs, nutmeg, peppercorns, shallots, tarragon, and vinegar for topping pike.

The nineteenth century inspired industrialists to manufacture condiments, including creamy horseradish, HP sauce (brown sauce), malt cake, and tomato ketchup. Grist miller Jeremiah Colman of Norwich blended brown and white seeds in 1804 to produce Colman's mustard, a brand name popular with Queen Victoria's household. Worcestershire sauce, an anchovy dressing bottled by chemists John Wheeley Lea and William Henry Perrins in 1835 and marketed in 1837, added zip to Caesar salad, oysters, and Welsh rarebit as well as mixed drinks. Cooks in Australia, Canada, China, Indonesia, and Thailand found additional uses for the famed "English sauce." Food inventor Jean Naigeon of Burgundy refined brown mustard in 1856 by replacing vinegar with verjuice. The smooth, pleasant taste appeared in markets as Dijon mustard.

In the United States, moral reformer Sylvester Graham joined temperance activists in denouncing sexual promiscuity and American dietary standards for debauching youth. In 1831, he led a crusade against gastronomic stimulants. Among his targets—coffee, liquor, meat, opium, tea, tobacco—he railed against curry powder, pepper, salt, and spices as anatomical mischief makers. In his *Lectures on the Science of Human Life* (1839), Graham called for a ban on cinnamon, ketchup, and mustard as enervators of the body and precipitators of dyspepsia and exhaustion. A fellow zealot, educator William Andrus Alcott, extended the list to include cucumber, garlic, ginger, gravy, lettuce, pickles, and sauces, which he condemned as licentious drugs and temptations to carnality. By 1840, the ranting over condiments ceased.

Commercial condiments provided convenience and lower prices in the early 1900s but limited diversity and imagination. U.S. industrialist Henry John Heinz profited by shipping 46-gallon (174-liter) tuns of ketchup, Ameri-

pickle or brined shellfish. Within a decade, British explorers introduced both ketchup and soy sauce to Europe. Innovative ketchup recipes included anchovies, cucumbers, gooseberries, herring, kidney beans, liver, mushrooms, oysters, pome fruit, and walnuts as basic ingredients before the early 1800s. Afterward, tomatoes anchored batches, producing a bright flavor and color. From the Regency period into the mid-Victorian age, the rage for ketchup appeared in the writings of Lord Byron, Jane Austen, Charles Dickens, and Rudyard Kipling.

Mayonnaise dates to an exact time, June 29, 1756, the era in which velouté, a cream and egg yolk white sauce, reached perfection. To celebrate a victory over the British, the chef of the duke of Richelieu substituted olive oil for the cream in velouté to emulsify a condiment named "mahonnaise" for Mahon, Minorca. Subsequent concoctions deepened the delicate flavor with lemon juice, pepper, and sea salt.

ca's national sauce, to Australia, Canada, China, Great Britain, Japan, New Zealand, South Africa, and South America. In New York City after 1910, delicatessen worker Nina Hellman marketed Hellman's mayonnaise in glass jars, the forerunner of a ubiquitous product that currently holds 45 percent of U.S. sales in jarred mayonnaise.

Presently, American menus feature condiments by name with entrées, especially balsamic vinegar on baby greens, barbecue with mustard sauce, red pepper on pizza, and turkey with cranberry relish, either jellied or chopped with oranges and walnuts. Shakers of cinnamon sugar complement apple desserts and cocoa; special salts complement popcorn and seafood with bacon, celery, chili, citrus, garlic, and smoke flavors. Hot sauce remains a table standard in Cajun and Tex-Mex cafés and the fish camps of the American South. For dishes such as cheddar fries, nachos, and taco salads, melted cheese, *pico de gallo,* and salsa are more recipe essentials than condiments.

See also: Carême, Marie-Antoine; Chutney; Curry; Grilling; Ketchup; Mustard; Pickling; Roman Diet and Cuisine, Ancient; Salt; Scandinavian Diet and Cuisine; Spices; Sugar and Sweeteners.

Further Reading

Costenbader, Carol W. *Mustards, Ketchups and Vinegars.* Pownal, VT: Storey, 1996.

Freedman, Paul H. *Food: The History of Taste.* Berkeley: University of California Press, 2007.

Gunst, Kathy. *Condiments!* New York: Putnam, 1984.

Smith, Andrew F. *Encyclopedia of Junk Food and Fast Food.* Westport, CT: Greenwood, 2006.

Consumer Protection Laws

To prevent fraud and unscrupulous practices in the marketplace, consumer protection laws promote competition and honest representation of goods. In the United States, the Food and Drug Administration (FDA), empowered by the Pure Food and Drug Act of 1906, stamps imported bottled water, eggs, meat, and poultry as edible. Consumers trust goods certified free of antimicrobial resistance, cloning, drugs, genetic engineering, irradiation, and pesticides. Examples of infractions include excessive caffeine in bottled cola, mislabeling of genetically modified corn in snack chips, dioxin in fish, expired baked goods, mutton from cloned sheep, irradiated exotic fruits, and dichlorodiphenyltrichloroethane (DDT) on peppers and tomatoes imported from Mexico.

A series of follow-up laws and modifications of standards increased the safety of food and water. The Federal Meat Inspection Act of 1907 shields the public from unsanitary conditions in Chicago abattoirs, tainted egg farms

in Iowa, and adulterated cold cuts, ham, potted meat, and sausage in supermarkets. In 1923, strict scrutiny advanced to dairy products to prevent addition of fats and oils as fillers in skim milk. Criminal investigations involved a network of agents from Customs and Border Protection, the Department of Justice, the Federal Bureau of Investigation, and Interpol as well as local and state agencies and the U.S. Coast Guard.

In the European Union (EU), a league of 27 member states, a similar integrated approach to food quality and animal health depends on a farm-to-table supervision by the European Food Safety Authority, impaneled in January 2002. Inspectors select at random from cartons and flats of produce to search for fungicides and herbicides on brussels sprouts, cucumbers, hops, olives, soybeans, and sunflower seeds. Among concerns are residues in honey, aflatoxin in peanuts from Argentina, and carcinogens in Pai You Guo capsules and tea, a fad Chinese weight-loss supplement that causes addiction, fainting, heart palpitations, and insomnia.

Under the Consumer Product Safety Act of 1972, the U.S. Consumer Product Safety Commission sets mandatory standards. Regulation aids industry in developing voluntary quality control and evaluation of transportation by railcar and tanker truck and temperature controls for frozen and refrigerated commodities. The commission can recall or ban from retail marketing and secondhand sale dangerous foods and drugs or equipment, such as suspect naturopathic elixirs, bodybuilding enhancers, barbecue grills, coffeemakers, and infant feeding devices.

Also in the United States, in 1974, passage of the Safe Drinking Water Act established purity standards for public water systems by curtailing the injection of wastes underground and eliminating lead soldering of plumbing pipes. Inspections of water tanks on commercial aircraft found contents contaminated with *Escherichia coli* (*E. coli*) in 15 percent of planes examined for microbes. In 1996, passage of the Food Quality Protection Act targeted another covert threat, insecticide residues and veterinary medicines in comestibles, particularly those consumed by children.

International regulatory safeguards protect consumers from questionable standards in imported goods. In 2007, a recall of Chinese seafood and toothpaste and subsequent import bans on rice protein adulterated with melamine involved consumer watchdogs in the United States as well as Australia, Canada, the European Union, and New Zealand. On July 10, 2007, the Chinese government executed its food and drug administration chairman, Zheng Xiaoyu, for compromising quality goods by taking bribes. Xiaoyu's corruption of standards resulted in the deaths of 13 infants in 2004 from feedings of adulterated powdered milk. To maintain the reputation of Chinese foods among Western buyers, a tracking system imposed by the Chinese Agriculture Ministry in 2011 encouraged grocers to determine sources of adulterated food.

Currently, the U.S. Federal Trade Commission (FTC) monitors the media and investigates such deceptive practices as the injection of brine or broth in turkeys, the padding of TV dinners with gravy and sauce rather than whole foods, and the coloring of peanut butter with cocoa butter and malt. Another market problem involves false or misleading advertising, a common complaint against food labels claiming that contents are "green" (eco-friendly), "light," or "organic." To halt ambiguous and misleading claims, such as the United Egg Producers' "animal care certified" eggs, the FTC requires corrective advertisements to disclose a true representation of the product, particularly claims of vitamin C in soft drinks, vegetarian pork and beans, and 100 percent beef in hot dogs.

Passage of the 2011 U.S. Food Safety Modernization Act improved consumer protection by setting guidelines for preventing food-borne illness. Statutes address defilement during harvesting, processing, packaging, and transport. Among changes in handling regulations, the law requires importer accountability of foods from foreign suppliers and certification of high-risk foods, including berries, fresh fruits and herbs, and juices. The law focuses on seafood, 75 percent of which comes from offshore sources, some from rogue traders. Expanding on the 2002 Bioterrorism Act, the new Food Safety Modernization law requires mandatory seizure and recall of suspicious foods that fail to meet U.S. standards.

Worldwide, the transfer of food from port to port demands stepped-up scrutiny. In 2010, the Canadian Food Inspection Agency intercepted meat pies containing undeclared milk. In Australia, the Competition and Consumer Commission recalled weight-loss products made from poisonous oleander seeds and Lindt milk chocolate containing peanuts, an unlisted allergen that can cause death. The Australian commission intervened in the marketing of substandard almonds, calamari, chorizo, dried kelp, pine nuts, salmon, and smoked trout. Following an earthquake that caused leakage from the Fukushima nuclear power plant in Japan on March 11, 2011, the EU took action against radioactivity by limiting imports of beef, fish, fruit, mollusks, mushrooms, and vegetables from the region.

See also: Additives, Food; Adulterated Food; Sanitation.

Further Reading

Cartwright, Peter. *Consumer Protection and the Criminal Law: Law, Theory, and Policy in the UK.* New York: Cambridge University Press, 2001.

Griggs, Lynden, Eileen Webb, and A.Y.M. Freilich. *Consumer Protection Law.* New York: Oxford University Press, 2008.

Jin, Chaowu, and Wei Luo. *Competition Law in China.* Buffalo, NY: W.S. Hein, 2002.

O'Rourke, Raymond. *European Food Law.* London: Sweet & Maxwell, 2005.

Williams, Elizabeth M., and Stephanie J. Carter. *The A–Z Encyclopedia of Food Controversies and the Law.* Santa Barbara, CA: ABC-Clio, 2011.

Cook, James (1728–1779)

Explorer, cartographer, and a primary source of observations on the Pacific diet and culture, Captain James Cook chose to study people living on the opposite side of the globe from Europe.

A Yorkshireman, he was born at Marton, near Middlesbrough in England, on November 7, 1728, to Grace Pace and James Cook, a Scots farmer. After study at the Postgate School and apprenticing to a grocer, he went to sea at age 17 on a coal coaster. After educating himself in astronomy, mathematics, and navigation, he sailed aboard traders to the Baltic Sea. During the Seven Years' War, he rose in the ranks of the Royal Navy and earned commendation in Quebec.

In 1766, during his four-year exploration of Newfoundland, his crew warded off scurvy by drinking Canadian spruce beer, which was cheaper than lemon or lime antiscorbutics. Cooks on board brewed the drink from Sitka spruce using a recipe dating to the 1620s. Upon reaching Nootka Sound, Captain Cook sent shore parties in search of spruce to replenish hogsheads of beer.

Also in 1766, the admiralty assigned Cook command of the HMS *Endeavour*, a 369-ton (335-metric-ton) research bark. With funding from King George III, Cook made four expeditions to the Pacific.

On his first voyage from Plymouth on August 26, 1768, he and 94 others sailed for the Royal Society around Cape Horn, Chile, to Tahiti and eastern Australia. Among the provisions for 18 months, Cook stocked a goat, hens, and pigs along with beer, brandy, cheese, oatmeal, oil, peas, rum, salt, and sugar. On September 12 at Madeira, he added fresh beef, fruit, greens, onions, sweets, and wine for the next leg to Rio de Janeiro, Brazil. In mid-November, he restocked fresh and jerked beef, greens, and pumpkins for the risky rounding of Cape Horn. He noted that Brazilian traders made the most of their location by charging exorbitant prices for cassava, grain, pork, poultry, and yams.

Beginning with landfall at the Bay of Good Success in Tierra del Fuego, Chile, on January 15, 1769, Cook's botanists, Joseph Banks and Daniel Solander, collected the first of a total of 3,000 plant specimens, many of them unknown in Europe. Observations of the diet of southern South America reported native dependence on the meat of the guanaco, a member of the llama family, as well as cranberries, limpets, mussels, and wild celery.

The *Endeavour* reached Tahiti on April 10 and remained there until July 13 before searching for Terra Australis Incognita (Unknown Southern Land), which geographers wrongly surmised lay separate from Australia. Cook and his surgeon, William Monkhouse, took precautions against scurvy by dispensing malt wort (malt extract), portable (dehydrated) soup, and sauerkraut. The crew cultivated friendships with native traders in canoes, who bartered coconuts and fruit for cloth and iron. The Tahitian chief, dubbed Lycurgus by the crew, feted Cook and his officers with broiled fish and coconuts and offered plantain trees to take back to England. Other gifts of breadfruit and pigs symbolized trust.

At Poverty Bay, New Zealand, Cook admired the wellness and sturdy frames of elderly Maori, who remained energetic into advanced age. In his observations of Gweagal hunter-gatherers at Botany Bay, Australia, he found their simple lifestyle far more satisfactory than European lives. They lived serenely and stockpiled no food, but relied on nature to provide necessities. The voyage concluded with a long layover near the Great Barrier Reef, off the coast of Queensland in northeast Australia, and a return route past Possession Island in the Torres Strait Islands off the coast of northern Queensland, and Batavia (Jakarta), Indonesia, then around the Cape of Good Hope at the southern tip of Africa.

Cook and his crew reached Dover on July 12, 1771, without a single loss to scurvy. Physicians acknowledged his wisdom in stocking the ship's pantries with fresh food. Both he and naturalist Joseph Banks published journals, which Cook recorded in triplicate for posting to the Royal Admiralty.

In 1772, Cook accepted a second commission from the Royal Society to locate the reputedly massive continent of Terra Australis. On the HMS *Resolution*, Commander Cook paralleled the route of a sister ship, the HMS *Adventure*, and, on January 31, 1774, reached Antarctic waters. His Pacific route via Easter Island, the Friendly Islands, New Caledonia, Norfolk Island, and Vanuatu quashed the myth of a Terra Australis that connected to Antarctica. A premature retirement preceded a third expedition to locate the fabled Northwest Passage, a sea route from the Atlantic to the Pacific through Arctic waters.

In 1776, Captain Cook sailed the HMS *Resolution* and led the HMS *Discovery* to Tahiti and north in 1778 to the Hawaiian cluster, which he named the Sandwich Islands. He surveyed Nootka Sound at Vancouver Island and spent a month trading metal objects for sea otter pelts in Yuquot Indian villages. During his forays north to the Bering Strait, his crew sampled walrus meat but found it inedible.

After his journey south to Kealakekua Bay, Hawaii, he observed Makahiki, the harvest festival for the god Lono. Hawaiian natives murdered Cook and four mariners on February 14, 1779. Upon the return of his ships in October 1780, Captain James King completed Cook's journal. Historians lauded Cook's circumnavigation of the globe without crew losses to scurvy and his observations on Pacific peoples.

See also: Breadfruit; Jerky; Lapérouse, Jean François Galaup; Seaman's Diet and Cuisine; Soups.

Further Reading

Horwitz, Tony. *Blue Latitudes: Boldly Going Where Captain Cook Has Gone Before.* New York: Macmillan, 2003.

Thomas, Nicholas. *Cook: The Extraordinary Voyages of Captain James Cook.* New York: Walker, 2003.

Williams, Glyndwr, ed. *Captain Cook: Explorations and Reassessments.* Rochester, NY: Boydell, 2004.

Cookbooks

A culinary reference source from early times to the present, cookbooks compile distinctive collections of recipes that reflect regional ingredients and individual tastes in cuisine. Published food chronicles fall into two broad categories—a compendium of dishes on a particular subject, such as barbecuing, Indian curry, or frozen desserts, and a tutorial for professional caterers, chefs, and institutional cooks.

Ritual cookbooks from Mesopotamia exemplified local enthusiasm for refined cookery of birds, shellfish, and turtles. In 1900 B.C.E., Sumerian-Akkadian cooks cataloged 800 sophisticated dishes and beverages. Recipes from the state dinners of Assyria and Elam consist of clay pot and metal cauldron cookery of gazelle, kid, partridge, and pigeon and turnip stew.

Two centuries later, Mesopotamians summarized banquets in cuneiform on three clay tablets, one of the earliest recipe books committed to writing. Among the details, the food writers described the stuffing of meat into sausage casings, fermenting fish and grasshoppers into a condiment, and solidifying cream cheese. More than taste, they lauded the aroma of fat-fried meat and onions as essential to good eating.

Early in the first century C.E., the Roman merchant and author Marcus Gavius Apicius described in *De Re Coquinaria* (*On Cookery*, ca. 35 C.E.) the pickling of anchovies in *garum* (fish sauce), a savory touch during the reign of the Emperor Tiberius. In 77, Roman encyclopedist Pliny the Elder identified 1,000 species of fish for the table and complementary flavors but cited no cooking instructions. Written in Egypt, Greek gourmand Athenaeus's 15-volume miscellany *Deipnosophistae* (*The Banquet Philosophers,* ca. 190) recorded the Greek love of men-only table fare and jolly conversation near brazier fires. Among his recipes, *kandaulos* illustrates the stewing of meat with anise, breadcrumbs, and grated cheese to create an aphrodisiac. Simpler recipes tend toward Attic figs, honey and sesame cakes, roasted boar, fried cakes, spitted apples, and fragrant berries fermented into vinegar.

Medieval Kitchen Guides

Medieval food writing focused on the culinary advances of the period. Syrian author Ibn Sayyar al-Warraq summarized the Abbasid foodways and etiquette of the Arabo-Islamic bourgeois in *Kitab al-Tabikh* (*Book of Dishes,* ca. 950 B.C.E.). A thorough examination of medieval tastes in 132 chapters, it enumerated 600 hot and cold dishes, featuring bird pies, dips, cereal grains, fried meats, roasted game and kid, pudding, saucing, spicing, and stuffing. Al-Warraq's comprehensive food knowledge and experience enabled him to describe Mediterranean specialties, including Egyptian raisin wine and Persian antelope cooked in onion juice. He advocated the use of apricots, honey, prunes, and vinegar to orchestrate sweet and sour dishes. Several of his recipes for *harissa,* a savory paste, required labor-intensive shredding, grinding, beating, and straining of chicken, fat, milk, rice, and sugar for cooking on a three-legged brazier.

A subsequent cookbook of the same name, written in 1235 by Hassan al-Baghdadi, listed only the 160 recipes he liked. The text revealed a profusion of herbs and spices—celery, cinnamon, coriander, cumin, dill, ginger, gum mastic, mint, peppercorns, saffron, sesame, sumac, and thyme—the flavors of pastries, pickles, salads, and vinegars that had aroused the appetites of Crusaders. Not listed by dry measure, the apricot and lamb *tagines* (slow-cooked stew) thickened with ground almonds and perfumed with rosewater and orange blossoms required the cook's instinctive skill at balancing aroma, flavor, and texture.

After the publication of two anonymous classics, the Latinate *Liber de Coquina* (*Book of Cooking,* ca. 1300), compiled anonymously in Naples, and the first German cookbook, *Daz Buch von Guter Spise* (*The Book of Good Food,* ca. 1350), the Norman French contributed a unique survey of medieval kitchen techniques and cuisine in Taillevent's *Le Viandier* (*The Provisioner,* ca. 1375). Two of his suggestions, a description of entremets (palate cleansers) and herbed chicken broth, presaged the refined food service that the French developed into haute cuisine. None of the three forerunners matched the influence of the anonymous *Le Ménagier de Paris* (*The Goodman of Paris,* 1393), a didactic handbook for brides. The text advanced from meat cook-

A home chef uses a recipe from the original *Joy of Cooking* (1931) to make a German potato salad. Self-published by St. Louis homemaker Irma S. Rombauer, *The Joy of Cooking* has sold more than 18 million copies in multiple editions. (*MCT/Getty Images*)

ery to a variety of instructions for incorporating eggs, frogs and snails, pastry, and vegetable soups in the diet.

The first Chinese cookbook concentrated on food for the privileged. From service to the mid-thirteenth-century Celestial Throne, Huou recorded pantry tastes and feasts honoring the Emperor Kublai Khan. Huou's three-volume survey, *Yin-shan Zheng-yao* (*Proper and Essential Things for the Emperor's Food and Drink,* 1330), listed court details, particularly for making and serving soups. Late in the Middle Ages, Eurasian communication increased along the Silk Road, China's main link with the West.

Renaissance Advances

The printing press turned cookbooks into an affordable resource for wealthy domestic and professional cooks, who read aloud to illiterate servants. The shift from mundane potages and roast meats reached a height of professional cookery in *Forme of Cury* (*Forms of Cookery,* ca. 1390) from the household of Richard II and Bartolomeo Platina's *De Honesta Voluptate et Valetudine* (*On Honorable Pleasure and Health,* ca. 1465). The first work introduced the French terms *blancmange,* a costly food paste, and *pain fondue,* bread for dipping into sauce. In 1570, chef Bartolemeo Scappi issued recipes in Italian for marzipan in his 1,000-recipe collection, *Opera dell'Arte del Cucinare* (*Culinary Works of Art*). He stressed dishes incorporating goose liver and Parmesan cheese and listed egg, fruit, nut, and rice recipes for meatless meals.

In England, Sir Kenelm Digby, a polymath and privateer, wrote *The Closet of the Eminently Learned Sir Kenelme Digbie Knight Opened* (1669). A private journal published

Recipe: Lamb and Apricot Tagine

Sauté two chopped red onions in 2 tablespoons of vegetable oil. Add 2 1/2 cups of water, 2 pounds of cubed lamb shoulder, 1 1/2 teaspoons of cinnamon, 1 1/2 inches of ginger sliced, 1/2 teaspoon of cumin, and 1/4 teaspoon of chili powder. Simmer the mixture on low heat for 90 minutes, remoistening as necessary. Season with ground pepper and sea salt to taste. Add 1 pound dried apricots and 1/4 cup of raisins and simmer another 30 minutes.

posthumously by Digby's son John and Hartman, the household steward, the free-form text explains the food preferences of the late Renaissance. Courses range from meat pasties and vegetable potage to jelly, pies, and *syllabub,* a milk punch. Digby elaborated on the fermentation of cider, metheglin, and wine. With less pomposity, Hannah Wooley, the first female cookbook compiler, produced *The Queen-like Closet; or Rich Cabinet* (1670). The text reported the womanly arts of the Restoration era, including the candying and preserving supervised by the queen, Catherine of Braganza.

At the end of the Renaissance, French food writer François Massialot, the chef to Philippe I, duke of Orléans, saluted the aristocratic table with *Nouveau Cuisinier Royal et Bourgeois (New Cookery for Royalty and the Middle Class,* 1692). He expressed his intent to please princes and "people of the first rank" with elaborate crème brûlée and meringue. His text introduced alphabetized recipes, a forerunner of the gastronomic encyclopedia, and remained a kitchen resource for the next five decades.

The Age of Wisdom

Eighteenth-century cookbooks deserted royal kitchens and focused on the everyday eating and curative foods of Americans and Europeans as viewed by females. In Williamsburg, Virginia, Eliza Smith's best seller, *The Compleat Housewife; Or, Accomplished Gentlewomen's Companion* (1727), summarized kitchen duties, from breakfast, lunch, and dinner to trays for invalids and home simples for contagious diseases. Published in the American colonies in 1742, Smith's directives instructed women on housewifely issues of dressing eels and pickling mushrooms and mapped out the kitchen as a female domain. She encouraged women to distribute tasty foods to their neighbors and to share recipes for beverages, jellies, pickles, and preserves along with cordials, ointments, syrups, and tonics. Lacking from her era of food writing were dish size, precise measurements and portions, and exact temperatures. In their place appeared "a pinch," "a penny's worth," "a piece of butter," "a glassful," "warming temperature," and "a slow oven."

A colonial kitchen landmark, Martha Custis Washington's *Book of Cookery* (1749), a handwritten heirloom, served the cooks at Mount Vernon for a half century. A bride gift from Frances Parke Custis to her 18-year-old daughter-in-law, the compilation derived from British cookery. Recipes maintained ties with the mother country in its Elizabethan and Jacobean menus and table style. Into the federalist period, cooks imported key ingredients—almonds, oranges, wines. The 500 recipes retained homey touches in instructions for chicken pie, fritters, and raspberry marmalade.

A shift toward indigenous ingredients took the redirection of English food author Hannah Glasse's *The Art of Cookery Made Plain and Easy* (1747). Susannah Carter's *The Frugal Housewife* (1772) featured North America's food legacy in corn and cornmeal, cranberry sauce, Jerusalem artichokes, molasses, pumpkin, and squash and introduced American cooks to pearl ash, an early form of baking powder. Connecticut writer Amelia Simmons's self-published *American Cookery* (1796), the nation's first original guide to fireplace techniques. Although Simmons plagiarized recipes from a previous collection, her work banished frippery and excess and revealed to the inexperienced kitchen worker pragmatic methods of reducing waste and producing meals suited to a limited budget. Later editions of Simmons's collection promoted patriotic cookery of Election Cake, Federal Cake, and Independence Cake.

Cookbooks as History

The emerging no-nonsense style of food writing influenced Mary Randolph, author of *The Virginia House-Wife* (1824), who documented the foodways of the new nation. Among the Southern dishes popularized in her book, she outlined recipes for barbecued pork, beaten biscuits, catfish, gumbo, and okra. Philadelphia cook Eliza Leslie followed Randolph's practical advice with a book on desserts, *Seventy-Five Receipts for Pastry, Cakes, and Sweetmeats* (1828), a testimonial to her kitchen business. Among the Americanized treats, she introduced Indian Pound Cake, a four-ingredient dessert that replaced cake flour with cornmeal.

By the Industrial Revolution, cookbook publication burgeoned in response to a concern for a healthful diet and temperance. Eliza Acton, author of *Modern Cookery for Private Families* (1845), originated a uniform code of exact timing and quantities of ingredients. Educator and domestic expert Catharine Esther Beecher's *Miss Beecher's Domestic Receipt-Book: Designed as a Supplement to Her Treatise on Domestic Economy* (1846) took a scientific approach to home management. She incorporated her views on mothering and wellness into recipes for weanlings and invalids. Reformer Alexis Soyer summarized simple meal planning in *A Shilling Cookery for the People* (1854), in which he informed the poor that vegetables offer more nutrition than ale, bread, and cheese.

Throughout the 1800s, self-conscious decorative cooking gave way to the national diets that arose from common staples. In place of imported haute cuisine, Poles reclaimed sausage; Jamaicans celebrated the pepper pot. In the American colonies, clam chowder and Christmas ambrosia denoted high points in comfort food, the featured dishes that marked family tradition and clan solidarity. Editors Lydia Maria Child and Sarah Josepha Hale created a stir with Child's *The American Frugal Housewife* (1829) and Hale's *The Good Housekeeper* (1839) and *Mrs. Hale's Receipts for the Million* (1852), all favorites with working-class housewives. Child offered hands-on advice, such as the boiling of a calf's head with the esophagus hanging out of the pot as an escape route for scum. Hale suggested uses for calf's knuckles, cod heads, and haunches of venison, which she valued fresh-killed as sources of soup.

In the era of the coal cookstove, Isabella Mary Beeton, the touchstone of Victorian cuisine, reached culinary stardom with *Mrs. Beeton's Book of Household Management* (1861). The first recipe book to list ingredients before preparation instructions, the text also estimated preparation cost and time—for example, the one-hour chilling of almond cream or simmering a large ham for six hours. Her collection of 900 recipes remained in print for a century and, as demonstrated in the BBC-TV drama *The Secret Life of Mrs. Beeton* (2007), the collection earned respect as a monument to cultural and social history.

During the American Civil War, women's groups introduced a regional branch of food authorship by issuing the first fund-raising cookbooks. Their pamphlets aided the Sanitary Commission in opening and equipping rehabilitation centers for the wounded. The first charity collection, *Camp Cookery and Hospital Diet, for the Use of U.S. Volunteers, Now in Service* (1861), proved a valuable outlet for women who wanted to aid the war effort. Their decision to turn home-style recipes into salable commodities prefaced the subsequent suffrage movement and women's use of publication as self-expression and consciousness-raising, the purpose of *The Woman Suffrage Cook Book* (1886) and *The Settlement Cookbook: The Way to a Man's Heart* (1901). The latter, in circulation for a half century, introduced beginning cooks to level measures, fireless cookers, and pasteurizing milk to protect children from contagious disease.

European food writers produced valuable overviews of period gastronomy. Cookbook compiler Elena Burman Molokhovets preserved classic menus in her household text *A Gift to Young Housewives* (1861), which reached a print run of 295,000 copies. In the last 56 years of the Romanov dynasty, she taught the Russian bourgeois housekeeper how to ferment fruit liqueurs and how to plate and garnish pâté and mousse for a feast. Another regional best seller, Italian author Pellegrino Artusi's *La Scienza in Cucina e l'Arte di Mangiar Bene* (*Kitchen Science and the Art of Eating Well*, 1891), achieved fame in translations into Dutch, English, German, Portuguese, and Spanish.

The Gilded Age returned ornate dishes to prominence. Charles Ranhofer's grand *The Epicurean* (1894) surveyed the culinary feats of Delmonico's chefs in New York City. His contemporary, French chef Georges Auguste Escoffier, published the first comprehensive cookbook for chefs, *Le Guide Culinaire* (*The Culinary Guide*, 1903), a meticulous compilation of over 5,000 recipes. Whereas Ranhofer named his dishes for prominent people—a salad for novelist Alexandre Dumas and a potato dish for actor Sarah Bernhardt—Escoffier retreated from grandeur to focus on teaching the next generation of chefs.

Home Economics Movement

Professional kitchen work showcased the artistry of home economists Juliet Corson, Mary Johnson Lincoln, Maria Parloa, and Sarah Tyson Rorer, all cookbook authors, who debuted cooking school techniques and scientific food analysis to the home kitchen. Following the introduction of all-electric cookery at the 1893 Chicago World Fair, food writing voiced precise cooking instructions for predictable results. Women's magazines—*Better Homes and Gardens, Godey's Lady's Book, Good Housekeeping, McCall's, Woman's World*—published recipes and culinary lessons, which editors issued in book form. A favorite, *The Good Housekeeping Woman's Home Cook Book* (1909), replaced the work of well-known food writers with the gleanings of recipes sent to the magazine for testing in the in-house kitchen. *The Better Homes and Gardens New Cook Book* (1930) sold 20 million copies by emphasizing good-tasting meat loaf, scalloped potatoes, and fruit pies.

To accommodate a sedentary lifestyle, home economist Fannie Merritt Farmer, America's top culinary writer, composed in longhand the bible of the American kitchen, *The Boston Cooking-School Cook Book* (1896). The text introduced the first scientific formulation of measurements and methods for the home kitchen. Her 12-course holiday feasts captured the spirit of families seeking social attainment through food service of such exquisite dishes as calf's-food jelly and mock turtle soup. Farmer's perspective and tone influenced a subsequent classic, Irma Starkloff Rombauer's *The Joy of Cooking* (1931), which, in turn, set standards for food maven Julia Child, the great celebrity food writer of the twentieth century. General Mills exploited women's demand for recipes with *Betty Crocker's $25,000 Recipe Set* (1933), the beginning of a series of household favorites. With *Betty Crocker's Picture Cookbook* (1950), the company introduced branding, prepackaged ingredients, and inexpensive one-dish meals.

In 1938, French editor Prosper Montagné issued *Larousse Gastronomique: The Encyclopedia of Food, Wine, and Cookery*, a culinary gem containing 3,800 recipes. A vast sourcebook on the provenance of foods and their preparation for cooking, the work entered its third edition in 2001 under the subtitle *The World's Greatest Culinary Encyclopedia*. Among the traditional French strategies the chef demystified were braising, forcemeats, and wine selection.

World War II advanced concepts of kitchen technology by specifying mixer speed and freezing temperatures for ices. Food processors involved homemakers in the compilation of cookbooks, notably, the Pillsbury Bake-Off texts first published in 1949. Women's clubs marketed their expertise. The oldest, *Charleston Receipts* (1950), derived from South Carolinians in the Junior League. American experiences in distant settings increased interest in Asian food, which Lin Tsuifeng encouraged with *Cooking with the Chinese Flavor* (1956), an introduction to implements and ingredients unfamiliar to most American cooks. The book preceded the era's monolith, Julia Child's *Mastering the Art of French Cooking* (1961), a training course in culinary expertise.

The eco-friendly approach to cooking reached the public in Frances Moore Lappé's *Diet for a Small Planet*

(1971), a humanitarian's guide to foods less wasteful of Earth's resources. Lappé used the book's success as a springboard to informing readers about climate crisis and world hunger. Her concept of complementary animal and plant proteins angered vegetarians, who riposted with facts about human nutritional needs.

The past half century has favored multicultural kitchen instruction on everything from Kosher and soul food to Cajun, Tex-Mex, and Thai. Television spawned illustrated recipe collections the quality of bridal suppers in Martha Stewart's *Entertaining* (1982) and homey entrees in Rachael Ray's *30-Minute Meals* (1999), a boon to the workingwoman. In the health-conscious 2000s, food writing has targeted specific ills, for example, Robyn Webb's *The American Diabetes Association Diabetes Comfort Food Cookbook* (2011), Carol Fenster's *1,000 Gluten-Free Recipes* to help sufferers from celiac disease, and *Giving Hearts Cookbook* (2011), a police department collection from Aurora, Colorado, dedicated to cancer survivors.

See also: Apicius; Athenaeus; Beard, James; Câreme, Marie-Antoine; Child, Julia; Food Network; Huou; Ice Cream; *Larousse Gastronomique*; La Varenne, Pierre; Medieval Diet and Cuisine; Pan-European Diet and Cuisine; Pasta; Pennsylvania Dutch Diet and Cuisine; Soul Food; Soyer, Alexis; Taillevent; Tofu; Tudor Diet and Cuisine.

Further Reading

al-Warraq, ibn Sayyar. *Annals of the Caliphs' Kitchens: Ibn Sayyar al-Warraq's Tenth-Century Baghdadi Cookbook.* Boston: Brill, 2007.
Civitello, Linda. *Cuisine and Culture: A History of Food and People.* 3rd ed. Hoboken, NJ: John Wiley & Sons, 2011.
Fisher, Carol. *The American Cookbook: A History.* Jefferson, NC: McFarland, 2006.
Snodgrass, Mary Ellen. *Encyclopedia of Kitchen History.* New York: Fitzroy Dearborn, 2004.
Theophano, Janet. *Eat My Words.* New York: Palgrave Macmillan, 2002.

Cooking Schools

Culinary schools prepare students for operating an efficient, hygienic kitchen that produces attractive, nutritious dishes and drinks for varied occasions.

Le Cordon Bleu

In the 1600s, *cordon-bleu* (blue ribbon) became a superlative applied to anyone who succeeded in any profession, particularly cookery. The term derived from an exclusive sixteenth-century order of knights, *L'Ordre du Saint Esprit* (Order of the Holy Spirit). Founded by Henry III of France in 1578, the order honored royalty and nobles and awarded them gold crosses on broad blue ribbons, the school's emblem of excellence. In memory of distinguished aristocrats, acclaimed chefs prepared the period's most elegant menus. The blue ribbon epitomized the high standards of the In-

stitut de Saint-Louis, a private laboratory school opened in 1686 at Saint-Cyr, France.

Françoise d'Aubigne, the royal consort of Louis XIV, founded the institute to prepare young women for food service in strict classical style. She limited the student body to 250 daughters of impoverished aristocrats and army officers. D'Aubigne supervised curriculum, stocked the pantry, demonstrated recipes, and observed institutional thrift, down to napkins and aprons. Backers for the project included playwright Jean Racine, poet Nicolas Boileau, minister François Fénelon, composer Jean-Baptiste Lulli, and speech teacher Madame de Brinon. On graduation, each chef received a dowry of 3,000 crowns and the blue ribbon, a symbol eventually worn by the school's 1,121 diplomates.

No name resonates so impressively among cooking institutes as Le Cordon Bleu of Paris, the source of a rigorous culinary education and the world's model of kitchen professionalism. The school derived from a weekly newsletter, *La Cuisinière Cordon Bleu* (*The Blue Cord Cook*), published by French journalist Marthe Distel in 1895. The text offered illustrative and tutorial articles by famous chefs as well as food prep advice, discussions of gourmet dining, and a world-class recipe collection.

At the Palais Royal, Distel organized free classes in *cuisine pratique* (practical cooking) and *haute cuisine classique* (elegant classical cookery), the revered cuisine of Georges Auguste Escoffier and Marie-Antoine Carême. Distel initiated the first hands-on training where students sampled their teachers' dishes. The school evolved into a network of 27 divisions in 17 countries.

For chefs in training, celebrity pastry chef Charles Barthélémy, food writer Auguste Colombe, curriculum director Charles Driessens, and caterer Charles Poulain demonstrated their arts and, without charge, taught kitchen skills to subscribers. One distinguished faculty member, Henri-Paul Pellaprat, taught at the school for 40 years. While on staff, he compiled *Les Secrets Culinaires: Une Belle Table de Bonnes Recettes* (*Culinary Secrets: The Handsome Table of Good Recipes*, 1930), *L'Art Culinaire Moderne: La Bonne Table Française et Etrangère* (*Modern Culinary Art: The Good Table, French and Foreign*, 1949), and *La Cuisine Familiale et Pratique* (*Practical Home Cooking*, 1955).

The Cordon Bleu grew into the leading gastronomic institution by attracting promising pupils worldwide. In 1933, chefs Dione Lucas and Rosemary Hume, two of Pellaprat's protégés, opened London's L'Ecole d'Petit Cordon Bleu, the institute's first branch, and added British dishes to the standard French menu. In the late 1930s, Elizabeth Brassart superintended the Paris institute and modernized the traditional *cours de cuisine* (curriculum) to suit future needs.

Cooking as a Profession

The culinary arts drew students to the thriving home economics movement, which got its start in 1879 from educator Fannie Merritt Farmer's classes for immigrant women at the Boston Cooking School. Two reformers, Juliet Corson and Maria Parloa, extended the training of chefs through public lectures and coursework at the New York Cooking School, which advanced from cookstoves to chafing dishes, urns, and other tableside appliances.

At food laboratories in large cities, class method involved students in work sessions that educated them in food chemistry and dietetics for cafeterias, hospitals, missions, rehabilitation centers, and retirement homes. The schools also offered meaningful training to women who chose home economics as a profession. Among the burgeoning educators for black women, Mary McLeod Bethune opened Bethune-Cookman College in Daytona Beach, Florida, in 1904 as an introduction to domestic science and the operation of a commercial kitchen.

After the attack on Pearl Harbor, Hawaii, on December 7, 1941, the U.S. Army prepared men for institutional food service. At the Army Cooking School at Fort Meade, Maryland, trainees for the Quartermaster Corps learned to stretch 42¢ per day to feed soldiers hearty meals of chicken and beef. To assess the appeal of military chow, budding chefs analyzed plate scrapings to determine which entrées and side dishes were less appealing.

At the end of World War II, the Pentagon accredited the Cordon Bleu in Paris and the Culinary Institute of America (CIA) in Hyde Park, New York, the nation's first academic cooking school, for training U.S. military veterans. According to the memoir *My Life in France* (2006), author Julia Child of the class of 1950 and chef Simone Beck spread the Cordon Bleu spirit of excellence to North America. In 1953, graduates Rosemary Hume and Constance Spry served cold chicken in mango chutney to foreign dignitaries at the coronation luncheon for England's Elizabeth II.

In 1960, the CIA initiated continuing education to keep students current with changing ingredients and methods. In the next decade, the CIA staff launched a culinary library and learning resource center. For its attainments in curriculum development, *Life* magazine dubbed the school the "Harvard of Haute Cuisine."

International Education

To maintain impartiality in the styles and tastes of the next generation of master chefs, cooking schools recruited American, Canadian, French, English, Spanish, and Japanese pupils. Students learned international cuisine, beginning with classic French and branching out to Asian, German, Mediterranean, Pan-Pacific, and South American cookery. Typically, professors distributed boxes of ingredients to prepare by prescribed recipes. In addition to displaying international buffets and formal dinners, students dined with chefs at world-class restaurants and hosted regional and ethnic dinners. Success netted each a diploma, a ticket to high-paying jobs as prestigious food specialists.

Because the Cordon Bleu and its famed blue ribbon gained a reputation for tradition, expertise, refinement, and innovation, it established locations in Ottawa, Sydney, and Tokyo. In 1988, it opened the Ottawa Culinary Arts Institute, Canada's first branch, and published a reference guide, *Le Cordon Bleu Complete Cooking Techniques* (1998). In 15 chapters, the institute's master chefs instructed home cooks on a variety of dishes in clear, concise language. In 2000, Le Cordon Bleu joined with Career Education Corporation to establish a Parisian cooking school in the United States in Mendota Heights, Minnesota; Pasadena, California; Pittsburgh, Pennsylvania; Portland, Oregon; and Scottsdale, Arizona.

Simultaneously, the CIA operated a variety of campus restaurants. To demonstrate Continental menus, students managed the Escoffier and the Ristorante Caterina de' Medici, venues for classic European dishes. American fare dominated the St. Andrew's Café, the Apple Pie Bakery, and the CIA Bakery Café in San Antonio.

Contemporary Training

Currently, culinary school certification in a broad range of skills prepares graduates for jobs with airlines and resorts, on cruise ships and trains, and in dormitories, hospitals, and restaurants. Vocational training in hospitality and resort management at the Box Hill Institute in Melbourne, Australia; the Cilantro Culinary Academy in Subang Jaya, Malaysia; Paul Smith's College at Adirondack State Park, New York; and the University of Santo Tomas in Manila, Philippines, retrieves academic kitchen management from an artisanal craft to a money-making profession.

Specialty schools—DCT University Center in Lucerne, Switzerland; Johnson and Wales in Providence, Rhode Island; and Stratford University in Falls Church, Virginia—add a strong business basis to the study of baking, dietetics, food service, and hotel and tourism management. Escuela de Gastronomía Mexicana limits ingredients and techniques to Central American cuisine. At Lokichoggio, Kenya, students at the Culinary Institute of Africa learn solar cooking, a method that employs an aluminum-lined heat retention box as a heat source. For Asian industrial cookery, pupils apply to the Bhakti Industrial School of Cooking in Chennai, India. A one-on-one tutorial at the Nimmy Paul Cooking School in Kochi, India, focuses on the flavors of the subcontinent, including coconut milk, cumin, masala, and turmeric. In New Mexico, the Santa Fe School of Cooking introduces beginners to elements of Native American cuisine, such as annatto seed, chard, *epazote,* frybread, juniper berries, nuts, piki corn, posole, and prickly pear syrup, and to walking tours of restaurants over four routes.

Gastronomy preparation incorporates peripheral knowledge. Grégoire-Ferrandi in Paris focuses on catering and artisanal foods as well as restaurant design and kitchen layout. To ensure mastery of entrepreneurial cookery, Chicago's Kendall College in Evanston, Illinois, partners with the National Restaurant Association to stress health and business standards in food storage and preparation. Sullivan University in Louisville, Kentucky, expands its outreach through e-learning via online programs in hospitality.

Less comprehensive programs by the Alain & Marie Culinary Institute LeNôtre in Houston, Texas; Cambridge School of Culinary Arts in Cambridge, Massachusetts; Dumaguete Academy for Culinary Arts in Negros Oriental, Philippines; and Japanese Culinary Institute in Surry Hills, Australia, offer individualized coursework. Students may specialize in beverages, cake decoration, chocolate, ethnic cuisine, finger food, knife skills, meat and poultry, pastry, special diets, Sichuan cuisine, and sushi. The Culinary School of the Rockies in Boulder, Colorado, extends food internships with a farm-to-table study of biodynamics, including distilling, game butchery, recreational cuisine, root cellaring, and vine espaliering.

See also: Beard, James; Child, Julia.

Further Reading

Culinary Institute of America. www.ciachef.edu.

Le Cordon Bleu. *Le Cordon Bleu Cuisine Foundations.* Clifton Park, NY: Delmar, 2011.

———. www.cordonbleu.edu.

Smith, Andrew F. *Eating History: 30 Turning Points in the Making of American Cuisine.* New York: Columbia University Press, 2009.

Snodgrass, Mary Ellen. *Encyclopedia of Kitchen History.* New York: Fitzroy Dearborn, 2004.

Cook-Offs

A culinary competition featuring one ingredient or style, a cook-off or bake-off channels recreational cooking into a charity, fair, or media event. The concept of cooking for prizes or blue ribbons began at agricultural fairs early in the nineteenth century. Some events required entries to contain a regional ingredient, such as cheese, chili peppers, pecans, or shrimp. The concept gained enthusiasm for state and international championships.

Most cook-offs have space and time limits. Judges dock cooks for unfair application of aluminum foil and for messy countertops or unclean cookware. Rules sometimes limit contestants to children and youths and reward them with cash and appliances. Recipes may appear in published collections, such as *California State Fair Demonstration Recipes, 1949–1959* (2010) and *The Harrow Fair Cookbook* (2010), compiled in Harrow, Ontario.

Participants in biscuit, butter bean, chocolate, corn bread, eggs, garlic, horseradish, olive oil, onion, pie, pine-

The Georgia Cowboy Poetry Gathering hosts the annual Southeastern Chuck Wagon Cook-Off in the town of Cartersville. Teams use period ingredients to prepare a beef roast, beans, potatoes, biscuits, and dessert on an open wood fire. *(Dayton P. Strickland/Daily Tribune News/Associated Press)*

apple, potato, ramp (wild onion), spinach, and vegetarian/vegan cooking contests sometimes compete against specialists, such as chefs at Commander's Palace and Galatoire's in New Orleans. Some competitions involve name brands, including Golden Band, Kikkoman, Kona, Spam, and Martha White. The most popular cook-offs feature meats—barbecue, beef, catfish, chicken, chili, étouffée, gumbo, hamburgers, hot dogs, jambalaya, menudo (beef stomach), ribs, seafood, and Tex-Mex.

Many cook-offs are organized to aid community campaigns of one kind or another. Canada's Largest Ribfest, an annual cook-off in Burlington, Ontario, boosts tourism and raises funds for Habitat for Humanity, the Salvation Army, and Scout troops. A similar rib festival in London, Ontario, features food stalls, kitchen demonstrations, and music. In a departure from meat-centered cuisine, in summer 2010, People for the Ethical Treatment of Animals involved contestants from England and North America in a vegan cook-off, which awarded first prize to an oat and onion roast.

A contest unique to the North American frontier, Dutch oven events—called DOGs for "Dutch Oven

Gatherings"—ban gas or electric stoves and require log fires and tripods. DOG competitions, such as the Llano River Chuck Wagon Cook-Off in Llano, Texas, and the Chandler Museum Chuck Wagon Cook-off in Chandler, Arizona, imitate the outdoor cookery of pioneers. Using authentic equipment and unprocessed foods, participants vie in the bean, dessert, meat, potato, pie, stew, and sourdough or yeast bread divisions. All "cookies" prepare dishes from scratch in iron cookware.

As a more individualized contest, the bake-off encourages originality and innovation with a broader range of recipes. In 1949, Pillsbury initiated its annual contest, a salute to Americana and name brands. The event took place in 100 minikitchens in a ballroom of the Waldorf-Astoria Hotel in New York City. The results helped set trends in regional recipes for scratch cakes, cookies, pies, quick and yeast breads, and sweet rolls, such as the Orange Kiss-Me Cake in 1950 and Mardi Gras Party Cake in 1959. The challenge paralleled a resurgence in American baking and the influence of such television paradigms as Norwegian housewife Marta Hansen on *Mama* (1949–1957) and Margaret Anderson, the suburban mother on *Father Knows Best* (1949–1960).

Bake-off focus shifted in the 1960s as more women went to work. Pillsbury encouraged contestants to use cake mix, canned meat, frozen vegetables, potato flakes, processed cheese, and refrigerated dough and piecrust for Dilly Casserole Bread in 1960 and Magic Marshmallow Crescent Puffs in 1969. Ethnic ingredients and techniques broadened the bake-off spectrum in the 1970s, when cooks grew confident adding herbs and spices and using food processors and microwave ovens to simplify preparation of a streusel cake, Danish rolls, and chicken and broccoli pot pie. In 1978, the bake-off altered from an annual contest to a semiannual event.

Speed and shortcuts marked the next three decades of Pillsbury bake-offs. The 1980s featured international dishes and healthful meals as well as eye-catching garnishes on Almond-Filled Cookie Cake in 1982 and Chocolate Praline Layer Cake in 1984. More imaginative recipes in the 1990s called for blueberries, couscous, custard, and salsa. In 1996, Kurt Wait became the first male contestant to win the $1 million grand prize by preparing a macadamia fudge torte. The 2000s stressed variants of the tried and true in a granola pie and Florentine panini.

See also: Barbecue; Chili.

Further Reading

Fraioli, James O. *The Best Recipes from America's Food Festivals.* New York: Alpha Books, 2007.

Henderson, Mindy B. *The Great Southern Food Festival Cookbook.* Nashville, TN: T. Nelson, 2008.

Mercuri, Becky. *Food Festival, U.S.A.* San Diego, CA: Laurel Glen, 2002.

Sutherland, Amy. *Cookoff: Recipe Fever in America.* New York: Penguin, 2003.

Cookware

The creation of containers and implements to facilitate heating food permeates the history of human manipulation of natural and manufactured goods. From the earliest kitchen work, forked sticks held raw ingredients in place for roasting over embers or flame, the earliest form of cookery. The second most common culinary method, hypocendric baking, required heaping roots, truffles, and tubers with coals. Cooks handled baked pieces with tongs made from antlers, shells, or wood.

To distribute heat more evenly and delay charring, cooks coated fish, haunches of meat, and tubers with clay or wrapped them in banana and ti leaves. As early as 10,000 B.C.E. in Faiyum, Egypt, and elsewhere, preparers secured ingredients in bamboo tubes or baskets woven from birchbark, grass, palm, reeds, roots, rushes, vines, willow withes, or yucca. These advances made food more healthful and savory and shortened eating time.

Boiling eggs, seafood, and vegetables required waterproof containers, including animal craniums, clay pits, coconut husks, large mollusk shells, or turtle carapaces. In a container elevated on a stick frame or tripod, such as Havasupai and Zuñi baskets in the U.S. Great Basin and stone bowls in Tehuacán, Mexico, from 8000 B.C.E., ears of corn, muscle meat, and viscera cooked in a little liquid. A fireside staple from 7000 B.C.E., the first soups emerged from pit cookery or stone boiling, the dropping of heated stones into pouch hides, the bladders

Recipe: Cherry-Apple Dutch Oven Pie

Sift together 2 cups of flour and 1 teaspoon of salt. Blend in 2 cups of shortening. Gradually add 5 tablespoons of ice water to form a dough. Divide the dough into two balls. Roll out the first ball and spread over bottom and sides of a Dutch oven. In a bowl, stir 2 cups of dried cherries, 1 cup of sugar, 3 tablespoons of cornstarch, 1 tablespoon of vanilla, and 3/4 teaspoons each of cinnamon, ground clove, and nutmeg into 4 cups of peeled, cored, and sliced Granny Smith apples. Pour this mixture into the crust. Roll out the second dough ball and spread over the top of the pie. Seal in steam by crimping the edges together with a fork. Dress the top crust with one egg beaten with 1 tablespoon each of sugar and water. Bake for 40 to 50 minutes.

or stomachs of large animals, stone bowls, turtle shells, or wooden troughs.

Clayware

When clay separated from the outsides of baskets or gourds, cooks recycled the earthenware into the first clay cook pots. The concave shapes preceded the molding of pottery for such specific purposes as holding water for poaching birds and fish and steaming cereal grains and seaweed. Cooks soaked Chinese sand pots, *tagines,* and tandoor pots in water to create a moist enclosure for tenderizing meats. Flared edges facilitated pouring and transferring liquids. Lids directed condensation back into ingredients, producing complex flavors and moistening meats to tenderize them. Users tied lids in place to seal in steam and natural juices, the forerunner of gravy.

Fireproof earthenware and dense stoneware increased hearthside flexibility. Potters modeled useful shapes by coiling, paddling, and press molding. Before the building of kilns, cookware makers in Pakistan, Mesopotamia, and Nigeria sun-dried orange-brown terra-cotta. The rounded profile, such as the ware made at Catal Huyuk, Turkey, in 6500 B.C.E., aided stirring and spread heat evenly from the fire to all sides of ingredients.

Iberian terra-cotta produced the *cazuela,* a workhorse vessel that worked directly over heat for sautéing onions with saffron, simmering a Portuguese bean or cardoon and potato soup, or stirring up an aromatic *sofrito* from peppers and tomatoes. The smooth surfaces prevented evaporation of juices and easily soaked clean. A liability of earthenware, grit loosened by stirring tended to abrade tooth surfaces.

Experimenters used a variety of waterproofing—asphaltum, gums, piñon pitch, resins, soap root, and tar—to seal earthenware *ollas,* splint baskets, and woven rice steamers. A tight seal facilitated the cooking of a one-pot meal. In the classic *olla podrida,* Iberian cooks evolved main courses of pork slow-cooked with beans or chickpeas.

In the 1600s B.C.E., Babylonian householders dipped cooking baskets in molten bitumen. In Asia, ash, salt, and vitreous glazes sealed pores in carved teapots and clay tagines, some of which makers tempered by slow heating at the hearth or in a kiln. In Australia, Aborigines mixed cement from ash and gum to make conical baskets watertight.

From prehistory, the Zapotec of Oaxaca, Mexico, produced a cured *barro negro* (black clay) cookware that resisted shattering. After 1600 B.C.E., Chinese potters of the Shang dynasty shaped sturdy stoneware vessels and ritual cooking items for ancestor worship. The British pipkin, a lightweight saucepan on three legs, nestled in hot embers. Users inserted a wooden handle in the hollow nib at the side for ease of movement without endangering hands.

Metal Cookware

Metal pots advanced civilization by applying improved technology to the heating of delicate ingredients, particularly fish, porridge, and vegetables. After 1500 B.C.E., when the Hittites of Anatolia discovered iron ore smelting, they poured liquid metal into packed sand molds. Metal containers advanced cooking technology by conducting heat from flame into ingredients to render raw food more flavorful and easier to chew. Dark matte finishes absorbed heat and shortened the time needed for braising and simmering.

From the Roman era, iron kitchen *batterie de cuisine* (equipment) included elevated braziers and pots and pans on legs for setting on tripods and trivets or directly in the fire. For large cooking chores, overhead cranes suspended cauldrons. Cooks rotated the crane with angle irons to swing dishes outward for tasting, seasoning, and serving or for thickening with bread crumbs from an iron grater.

During the Middle Ages, a bottle jack or wind-up clock jack rotated meats in front of hearths and reflecting screens to ensure even roasting. A stiletto (iron pin) wrapped in dough and held over a pot enabled the cook to drop noodles directly into broth, a culinary technique invented by the Chinese after 25 C.E. Basket skimmers enabled the cook to fry directly in oil and to remove fish and pork slabs at the height of doneness.

As metallurgy developed, cookware conducted heat directly to ingredients, such as meringues and whipped toppings whisked in copper bulge pots and double boilers, tortillas on *comals,* and chapatis and waffles on griddles or gridirons. Eggs and meat slabs cooked directly on metal in fry pans, skillets, and spiders, three-legged skillets that nestled directly over hot embers. One dish, the Italian and Spanish *cassola* (casserole), cooked over flame or coals atop the vitreous glaze on the ceramic material.

The salamander, an iron plate on legs, provided a sturdy source of reflected heat for holding over dishes for broiling, browning, or toasting. Use of the salamander increased the success of endoring, the early Renaissance method of gilding or glazing the crust of a presentation piece—caul-wrapped kidneys, pigeon pie, roast kid, sturgeon, or veal's head—with savory egg yolk and saffron mixtures. Chefs to royalty extended endoring with real gold leaf and other metallic finishes hardened in lidded tureens or before metal screens.

Advanced Cookware

While the poor continued to cook in earthen pots and urns, housewares makers in the 1500s offered the wealthy expensive bronze, copper, and ceramic kitchen containers made to order. In 1679, French physicist Denis Papin added a new dimension to cuisine with his "marmite digester," the prototype of the pressure cooker. His application of steam under pressure cooked meats and vegetables faster than did ordinary pots, but it subjected cooks to scalds from explosions and spewing steam and cooking liquids. The concept remained unworkable until the presentation of the first commercial pressure cooker at the 1939 New York World's Fair.

A heavy material, cast iron yielded heavy-lidded pans and grills for suspending over campfires and hearths. Wrought iron, a cheap alternative, offered a high melting point but tended to scorch heavy fruit and vegetable mixtures and stews. The metal proved more practical as a source of tough griddles and turning forks. From the 1700s, cast iron suited the slow, even cooking of soups and stews. It required seasoning with oil or fat to prevent rust and sticking, a difficulty encountered by pioneers and chuck wagon chefs simmering pork and beans and baking corn bread and fruit cobblers in Dutch ovens.

Some metals left a metallic taste, as from the chemical reactions of copper or cast iron to acid from simmering tomatoes and vinegar or wine at high heat. The best in Renaissance cooking sets—copper cookware tinned on the inside—offset problems with off-flavors. In 1789, American patriot Thomas Jefferson, upon his return from a two-year embassy to France, equipped his kitchen at Monticello, Virginia, with 60 articles of iron and copper suited to French cuisine. Europe's latest designs included the *poissonnière* (fish cooker), *réchaud en cuivre* (chafing dish), and footed *tourtière,* a tart pan topped with a copper lid. His daughter, Martha Jefferson Randolph, used the trendy kitchen devices over charcoal fires to make omelets, pickles, and tomato gumbo. Because tin rapidly wore thin, itinerant tinkers traveled the country restoring linings, plugging holes in teakettles, and mending handles and lids.

Upon retirement from the military to Mount Vernon in 1785, George Washington provided his wife, Martha Custis Washington, with a model brick and slate kitchen. A grand fireplace held copper ewers and pudding molds, an iron spit rack, and kettles, pans, and pots clustered at the hearth. Slaves Hercules, Lucy, and Nathan cooked in embers or baked apples and custard pies in the brick bake oven. Implements on hooks swung cauldrons onto the flame with a crane for boiling cured ham and game. For himself, Washington operated five copper stills to extract barley, corn, and rye whiskey each year, a kitchen business that provided most of his income.

Iron cauldrons, roasting jacks (spits), and rotisseries and tinned bains-marie (double boilers), kettles, reflector ovens, sauce pots, and springform tart pans increased variety in cooking techniques. A metal hot closet kept dishes from cooling and warmed serving platters. One specialty cake pan, the tube pan, popularized in the 1880s, conducted heat to a cake's center and negated problems with damp spots and "sad streaks" (gummy batter).

Iron was cheaper and easier to find than copper and tin, but iron cookware proved more brittle and more easily corroded than bronze or tin. Maintenance of kitchen containers required daily polishing with ash or stove pol-

ish and constant repairs, especially of long-handled basting and saucing spoons and the spouts of teapots and coffee urns. To protect kitchen staff from burns, spills, and cuts, blacksmiths welded loose handles and finished raw edges with files, grinders, and wire brushes.

Scientific Cookware

Innovations designed for cooks continued to fill kitchens with new ideas, such as Margaret A. Wilcox's addition of a hot water tank to a stove flue in 1893. The receptacle recycled heat while keeping water at a usable temperature for blanching vegetables and scalding poultry. Clay roasters, popular in Germany and Scandinavia, accommodated whole poultry for braising without liquid.

Enameling with porcelain increased the usability of cast iron with a nonreactive, nonstick surface in black, blue, brown, and gray but increased the weight, endangering young cooks and people with arthritis. Industrial chemist Ellen Swallow Richards, author of *Food Materials and Their Adulterations* (1886), increased stovetop safety by adding a pouring lip on each side of saucepans. Her simple adjustment directed the flow of hot liquids while accommodating both right- and left-handed users.

The 1895 Montgomery Ward catalog promotes rustproof aluminum as the "coming metal," soon to replace tin. Scientific advances have made cookware more specialized and efficient. Lighter than tin and iron, aluminum conducts heat more evenly. (*The Granger Collection, New York*)

The era of scientific household inventions profited in January 1900 from the formation of the Good Housekeeping Institute, which opened in Springfield, Massachusetts. Critiques in the institute's magazine introduced homemakers to thrifty investments in kitchen utensils and small appliances—electric skillets, percolators, sandwich grills, toasters, and wafer irons for making ice cream cones. Practical advice explained how to butter iron gem pans for making muffins and spiders for cooking omelets, to grease iron racks for baking halibut, and to oil griddles for pancakes.

Aluminum offered a lighter frame for cookware and even conductivity of heat. WearEver introduced the innovative, rustproof metal in 1903. Six years later, Admiral Robert Peary took a set of WearEver cookware on his expedition to the North Pole. In 1910, *Good Housekeeping* magazine touted the Caloric Fireless Cook Stove from Janesville, Wisconsin. Among its assets, commentary named aluminum kettles and steatite (soapstone) roasting radiators. In 1911, Harvey W. Wiley, the Good Housekeeping Institute's director, ranked aluminum saucepans above copper, iron, nickel, and silver. Within decades, aluminum accounted for 40 percent of U.S. cookware sales.

Whether anodized (thickened) or cast (molded) aluminum, the metal alloyed well with copper, bronze, and magnesium to produce biscuit and cookie sheets, canners, loaf pans, roasters, and stockpots. Cast aluminum suited the slow cooking styles of cake pans and Dutch ovens. In 1919, the Kewaskum Aluminum Company of Kewaskum, Wisconsin, patented Regal Ware as *waterless cookware.* The term drew homemakers to the brand for its promise of nonstick, nonscorching containers. In 1925, Le Creuset, a cookware manufacturer in Fresnoy-le-Grand, France, distributed the first enameled Dutch oven, which the company offered in bright blue, brown, and cream.

Stainless steel, distributed by the Stainless Metals Company, introduced more beauty and durability to the cookware market in the 1930s. The wonder metal of the era offered an alternative to heavy pieces but heated as slowly as cast iron. Carbon steel heated faster, an advantage for sautéing and searing in a crepe or paella pan or low-oil stir-frying in a wok. Enameled steel, popular with campers, produced a workable, easily cleaned stockpot for water-based cuisine. Cladding solved individual drawbacks by layering aluminum, copper, and steel over baking pans, coffee urns, and samovars.

U.S. designers increased the convenience of cookware with ceramics, glass, porcelain, and silicone. Porcelain teapots in England tended to have spouts situated low to access the strongest brew at the base; ceramic and glass coffee pots offer spouts higher up to avoid the grounds that settle to the bottom during brewing. In 1915, Pyrex, a borosilicate glassware name brand made by Corning in Charleroi, Pennsylvania, manufactured the first kitchen casserole to tolerate freezing and baking and to stack with overturned lids in place.

In 1938, polytetrafluoroethylene further simplified kitchen chores by lining inner surfaces with a nonstick coating of powdered ceramic or titanium. Silicone ladles and spoons increased flexibility, a quality that also suited nonwoven oven mitts and hot pads. Colette and Marc Gregoire created a boom in French cookware with T-Fal, a combination of Teflon and aluminum. Teflon, invented by Roy Plunkett for Du Pont in 1938, proved ingenious for cookware because it ended the need for high-calorie fats to keep foods from sticking. The Gregoires sold 36,500 T-Fal pans a year. Tupperware, a plastic phenomenon of the 1940s, survived to the present as a modern marketing legend with innovative series for freezing and microwaving.

The latter part of the twentieth century produced dramatic new conveniences for the cook. In 1951, engineer David Dalquist designed the Bundt pan, a cast-aluminum cake pan with a center tube and scalloped sides, for Nordic Ware of Minneapolis, Minnesota. One of the container's distributors, Williams-Sonoma in Northern California, founded by kitchen specialist Chuck Williams in 1956, added the Bundt pan to a line of cookware gleaned from England, France, Germany, and Italy. The cake pan gained publicity from the 1966 Pillsbury Bake-Off, which Ella Helfrich won with the Tunnel of Fudge Cake.

By the mid-1950s west of Elmira, New York, Corning distributed glass ceramics that tolerated oven and stovetop heating for casseroles that went from stovetop to table. In 1965, Tappan debuted the microwave cooking center with a conventional range topped by a microwave oven. In the mid-1970s, as Corning, Tupperware, and other designers created containers for use in microwave ovens, more changes in cookware lessened the weight of casseroles and pans and increased their versatility. Food processors invested in food packaging that contained ingredients during heating, notably, the film microwave popcorn bag.

Small appliances restored to home cooking the convenience and slow-simmered flavor of past ages. The electric slow cooker, devised by Rival in Kansas City, Missouri, in 1971 and sold as the Crock-Pot, turned a brand name into a culinary style involving roasting and stewing in an unattended container. In the 1980s, the introduction of the bread machine created a trend toward home-risen loaf baking in a small appliance. Governed by a timer, the countertop baker also mixed and kneaded dough for panettone, pasta, pizza, and rice cakes.

See also: Bamboo; Blenders and Food Processors; Pit Cookery; Soups; Rumford, Count.

Further Reading

Civitello, Linda. *Cuisine and Culture: A History of Food and People.* 3rd ed. Hoboken, NJ: John Wiley & Sons, 2011.

Ruth, Jamee. *The Cookware Cookbook: Great Recipes for Broiling, Steaming, Boiling, Poaching, Braising, Deglazing, Frying, Simmering, and Sautéing.* San Francisco: Chronicle, 2005.

Snodgrass, Mary Ellen. *Encyclopedia of Kitchen History.* New York: Fitzroy Dearborn, 2004.

Wrangham, Richard. *Catching Fire: How Cooking Made Us Human.* New York: Basic Books, 2009.

Cooperatives, Food

A grocery store or chain operated by a private consortium, a food cooperative, or co-op, reflects the tastes and needs of a limited membership. To their mutual benefit, individuals seek joint ownership of the enterprise and manage it democratically by majority vote. In exchange for investment in the buying agency, families cut out the middleman and deal directly with growers.

Cooperatives save consumers on food costs through bulk buying, the initial purpose of the Berkeley Buyers' Club, which formed in California in 1936, and England's Northern Milk Partnership, founded in 1993. Nonprofit food clubs led the initiative toward ingredient identification, nutritional labeling, and unit pricing. Members received politically correct, eco-friendly products along with high-quality discount wines, organic produce and meats, and vegan specialties, including coconut cream and nondairy butter.

History

The procurement co-op concept started in 1832 in Nuneaton, England, with the Lockhurst Lane Industrial Co-operative Society, later renamed Heart of England Co-operative Society Limited (HECS). At Warwickshire, factory laborers enjoyed wholesale food prices at club supermarkets, which expanded to 33 locations. In addition to general foodstuffs, members purchased lunches and sandwiches. Subsequent dietary initiatives directed shoppers to quality foods and healthful cuisine. Some families have maintained membership in HECS for four generations.

The Rochdale Society of Equitable Pioneers formed a model consumer consortium in 1844, a time of socialist experimentation in England influenced by the utopian philosophy of Robert Owen, owner of the New Lanmark mills. The 28 flannel weavers who formed the buying club strove to overcome the fiscal losses and food adulteration incurred during the Industrial Revolution. By opening their own cash-and-carry grocery store, the society pooled money to purchase the club's first commodities—butter, candles, flour, oatmeal, and sugar. The co-op accepted any volunteer, regardless of gender, race, or religion, and adopted altruism and duty as goals promising a boost in quality of life. Members agreed to share surplus funds prorated by individual amounts of trade.

Shoppers examine the produce at a food co-op in Burlington, Vermont. With growing concerns about food safety, a preference for healthy eating, and a desire to support local farms, more Americans rely on groceries owned and operated by members. *(Toby Talbot/Associated Press)*

Owenism, the spark that fueled the food co-op, engendered additional attempts at group savings on groceries. In 1863, the Co-operative Wholesale Society began in Lancashire and Yorkshire, England. Later food-purchasing consortia founded the Puget Consumers Co-op in Seattle, Washington, in 1953 and the Mondragón Corporation in Mondragón, Spain, in 1956. In 1999, the National Cooperative Grocers Association began selling natural foods in Iowa City, Iowa. Expanded to 160 stores in 34 states, the food co-op joined some 300 food-buying consortia nationwide. In 2002, Coop Norden formed in Scandinavia, serving Denmark, Norway, and Sweden with grocers, supermarkets, and hypermarkets. Finland joined the trend toward wholesale food cooperatives in 2005.

Concept and Operations

Shoppers patronize food co-ops like other stores, where clerks and managers facilitate purchases. Some clubs schedule members to work shifts on the premises, where child care is often available. The target clientele sets standards for purity and quality of out-of-the-ordinary farm commodities—courgettes, daikon radishes, galangal, goat's milk, kumquats, organic goji berries and granola, mung beans, nutritional yeast, and pine nuts—at the lowest price. Meat choices extend from free-range chicken, grass-fed beef, and kosher chicken livers and cold cuts to wild boar and other game. Annually, the club collects dues and distributes profits proportionally.

Membership enables individuals to control aspects of the family diet, primarily a diversification of natural foods, the object of Uhuru Foods, opened by the African People's Solidarity Committee in Oakland, California, in 1979, and Keimblatt, a green market organized in 1995 in Vorpommern, Germany. The Ypsilanti Food Co-op in Ypsilanti, Michigan, stocks honey from its own beehives and powers its bake ovens with solar panels. In Madison, Wisconsin, the Willy Street Co-op sells fresh soups and juices and teaches cooking and health classes. The George Street Co-op in New Brunswick, New Jersey, offers bulk herbs and vitamins, gluten-free bakery items, and meatless bologna and hot dogs, featuring minimal additives, allergens, and processing. The New Pioneer Food Co-op in Iowa City, Iowa, specializes in antibiotic- and steroid-free chicken, local lamb, French-style hearth bread, microbrewery beers, lactose-free products, seven-grain flour, and sustainable, hormone-free seafood.

Larger stores advertise cruelty-free beauty and health aids and household goods, fair trade items, and the elimination of corn syrup, genetic modification, and trans fats from edibles. The People's Food Co-op in Portland, Oregon, models energy and water conservation with a geothermal exchange heating system and rainwater harvesting. Alfalfa House in Sydney, Australia, advertises farmer-direct produce and minimal packaging. Clubs also receive unique benefits, for example, education in vintages by the Australian Wine Consumers' Co-operative, founded in 1946, and the Organic Field School, and certified organic shopping and farm tours, introduced in 2008 at the Wedge Community Co-op in Minneapolis, Minnesota.

Social Activism

As conduits of social action, food cooperatives sometimes express member protest, especially the exploitation of migrant workers who harvest grapes and lettuce. The Park Slope Food Coop in Brooklyn, New York, which formed in 1973, opted to boycott Coca-Cola, Minute Maid, and Odwalla products for their exploitation of world farmers. Additional activism banned from shelves Chilean grapes, Nestlé products, and goods from South Africa during apartheid.

More recent resolutions discontinued the sale of bottled water and use of non-biodegradable plastic shopping bags as well as ended dealings with Flaum kosher products for labor law violations. In 2009, the sanctioning of Israeli products to oppose the occupation of Palestine involved Park Slope Food Coop members as well as the Rainbow Grocery Cooperative in San Francisco in addressing the ethical ramifications of imported foods. The

success and moral example of Park Slope influenced other buyer's clubs, including the Cooperative Grocery of Emeryville, California.

Currently, Japan sets the example for rural and urban cooperatives, which began competing aggressively against retail food markets in the 1890s. A locavore group purchasing club, the Han Group, suits the needs of small neighborhood buying clubs that submit weekly electronic orders and receive fresh produce and staples by truck. Payment entails automatic bank transfers. The convenience to the 1.2 million members is particularly beneficial to the disabled, elderly, homebound, working women, and young parents.

One of world's largest food cooperatives, Co-op Kobe, opened in Japan in 2003 and set an example of ethical and human practices and recycling based on the Christian pacifist principles of labor reformer Toyohiko Kagawa. The Kobe company used waste from bean curd and cooking oil to feed livestock and to generate electricity from its Rokko Island plant. In April 2011, the club's 1.3 million members began offering home delivery of packaged meals in Nishinomiya City.

See also: Agriculture; Local Food Movement; Sanitation.

Further Reading
Cox, Craig A. *Storefront Revolution: Food Co-ops and the Counterculture.* New Brunswick, NJ: Rutgers University Press, 1994.

Duram, Leslie A., ed. *Encyclopedia of Organic, Sustainable, and Local Food.* Santa Barbara, CA: ABC-Clio, 2010.

Wickstrom, Lois. *The Food Conspiracy Cookbook: How to Start a Neighborhood Buying Club and Eat Cheaply.* San Francisco: 101 Productions, 1974.

Coprolites

Fossil traces of digestion and diet, human coprolites (also called bezoar stones or paleofeces) retain mineral and organic evidence of nutrition, health, and cooking and eating styles. Archaeologists obtain specimens from ancient latrines, middens, caves, and human interment, including the colons of mummies.

By assessing the contents of coprolites—algae, undigested animal hair and soft tissue, bark, charcoal, feathers, fish bones and scales, fruit pits, insect shells, pollen, seeds, shells, spores, and stems—archaeologists gain insights into the availability of foodstuffs in a particular time and place and into the health and longevity of a single person. For example, at Wadi Kubbaniya in Egypt, analysis of infant coprolites from 17,000 B.C.E. indicates that women alternated breast feeding with a high-carbohydrate diet of root vegetables.

By extension, researchers can use traces of magnesium, sulfides, and other mineral components from drinking water to assess the overall health of clans, social classes, and tribes as well as their annual or seasonal location. Endoparasite eggs, such as hookworm found at Antelope House in Canyon de Chelly, Arizona, indicate the level of sanitation, which degrades as population density increases.

From studies of the physical condition of maize kernels and cactus and millet seeds in coprolites, analysts have identified various methods of food preparation—grinding or pounding seeds to break the husks or roasting before grinding. Abrasion and mastication offer clues to dental disease and tooth attrition. The recovery of Mexican buckeye seeds along with coprolites containing minnow bones attests to prehistoric knowledge of the use of buckeye as a fish poison in West Texas.

William Buckland, a geologist at the University of Oxford in England, initiated interest in excrement analysis. Basing his study of fecal science on the work of English fossil expert Mary Anning, a paleontologist at Lyme Regis, Dorset, in 1829 Buckland called the desiccated objects coprolites (from the Greek *kopros lithikos*, "stone dung"). In 1896, John William Harshberger, a botanist at the University of Pennsylvania, established the significance of fossilized feces to the study of ancient ecosystems, carnivores, cannibalism, disease, food diversity, and the discovery and use of fire.

In 1960, Eric Ottleban Callen, a professor of plant pathology at McGill University in Montreal, became the first coprolite specialist. He standardized analytic techniques for studying fungi, macrofossils, mollusks, parasites, and pollen as elements of diet patterns. He also overviewed prehistoric Peruvian diet at Huaca Prieta and the Pikimachay (Flea Cave) in the Ayacucho Valley and found maguey (agave) beer common to Mexican diet of 100 B.C.E. A decade later, scientists at Texas A&M University added pathogens to the regimen of fecal analysis.

The study of digested food enhanced ethnobotany. From studies of wheat seeds, scientists deduced that farmers in the southern Balkans grew einkorn wheat, perhaps the world's first cultivated grain. Trace amounts of creosote bush, ephedra, goosefoot, and willow attested to early pharmacopoeia for treating diarrhea, fever, intestinal parasites, and urinary disorders. Archaeologists began contributing data for perusal at archaeoparasitology laboratories in Brazil, Canada, Chile, England, Peru, and the United States. To recover human excrement from underwater sites, retrievers sample sunken storage jars, ships' bilges, and river or sea floors under sunken vessels. Until samples reach the lab, freezing protects pollen and tissue from fungus and microbes and preserves myosins and myoglobin (both types of proteins found in muscle tissue), evidence of the consumption of human flesh.

Coprolitic analysis requires protecting samples from contamination with masks, gloves, sterile forceps, and specimen bags or cups. Separation of particles begins with reconstituting the mass to its former pliability using a solution of trisodium phosphate. Analysts can deter-

mine food harvesting methods, consumption of raw foods, and the sophistication of cooking methods, whether on a drying rack, among rocks, on a spit, in a rock pit, on a parching tray, or in a clay or copper container.

Agave, one of the complex food staples of North American desert people, requires much preparation to soften tough fibers, including steaming or roasting in a rock-pit oven. In contrast, meals of cactus pads and sotol plants need less kitchen time and technology. In the Ozark Mountains of Arkansas, acorns demand leaching techniques to rid valuable nutmeats of bitter tannins; in contrast, a sweeter acorn that grows in the Lower Pecos area of Texas is edible raw or parched. Missing from the overall examination of diet, salad materials and leafy greens leave little recoverable residue after mastication and digestion.

Recovery of fish tapeworms shows that prehistoric humans in Chile and Peru ate raw fish. Identification of bark and eggs in samples from Hogup Cave in northwestern Utah adds dogwood and body lice to cacti, pickleweed seed, and rabbit, the list of colon contents from hunter-gatherers of 6800 B.C.E.

The study of human excrement, whether charred, dried, or frozen, by specialists Vaughn M. Bryant, Karl J. Reinhard, and Kristin D. Sobolik has illuminated the climate and eating habits of humans in a variety of world archaeological sites, even identifying the subjects' ages. Paleobiologists identify levels of estrogen and testosterone to identify gender. Cataloguing of seasonal plants and pollens establishes the arrival of hunter-gatherers at particular sites.

Because of the dry climate of southwestern North America and Mexico, coprolites have survived intact in the Chihuahuan Desert, Colorado Plateau, Great Basin, Great Gypsum Plain, Mojave Desert, and Tehuacán Valley. Coprolite findings at other sites in Chile, England, France, Holland, Israel, Peru, Sudan, and Tanzania have advanced comparative studies of world diet and nutrition.

In 2005, Eske Willerslev studied the DNA of 14 coprolites from Paisley Caves in the Summer Lake basin near Eugene, Oregon, at his lab at the University of Copenhagen. He established for the first time that Paleo-Indians of North America arrived as early as 12,300 B.C.E. He also surmised that food from the paleo-environment included biscuit root (wild parsley), bird, bison, dog, fish, grass, squirrel, sunflower, and possibly meat from a coyote, red fox, or wolf.

See also: Cannibalism; Fertile Crescent Diet and Food Trade; Middens; Nutrition; Paleolithic Diet.

Further Reading

Curry, Andrew. "Ancient Excrement." *Archaeology* 61:4 (July/August 2008): 42–45.

Ellis, Linda. *Archaeological Method and Theory: An Encyclopedia.* New York: Taylor & Francis, 2000.

Kelly, Robert L., and David Hurst Thomas. *Archaeology.* Belmont, CA: Wadsworth, 2010.

Stanford, Craig B., and Henry T. Bunn, eds. *Meat-Eating & Human Evolution.* New York: Oxford University Press, 2001.

Whittle, A.W.R. *The Archaeology of People: Dimensions of Neolithic Life.* New York: Routledge, 2003.

Corn and Maize

In a triad with rice and wheat, for 12 millennia, corn has nourished civilizations from cave and hut to cities and empires. A uniquely vulnerable grain, it requires human planting rather than dispersal by birds or wind. Its prehistoric name, *maize,* derives from the West Indian Taíno word *mahiz,* meaning "sustenance." The words *maize* and *corn* survive simultaneously in the Americas and the United Kingdom. South Africans prefer the Portuguese word *mealie.*

In the milk stage, early young ears, known as "sweet corn," are tender enough for eating raw or for grating into creamed corn, an accompaniment to green beans. Later harvests, called "field corn," yield dry kernels for pressing for corn oil, hydrolizing into corn syrup, distilling into grain alcohol and bourbon whiskey, mixing with gasoline for ethanol biofuel, or grinding into cornstarch, meal, or pet food. Farmers make the most of their investment by grinding stalks into silage for winter livestock feed.

Paleocorn

According to geneticist and Nobelist George Wells Beadle (in Physiology or Medicine, 1958), Mesoamericans domesticated corn from small-seeded teosinte (*Zea mays*) between Jalisco and Oaxaca, Mexico, around 10,000 B.C.E. Because of its rough exterior, teosinte declined in importance, but its offspring developed from a grass into a dietary keystone. The Olmec and Maya unlocked corn's nutritional wealth through *nixtamalization,* a process of soaking kernels in slaked lime water or wood ash. They balanced their diet with amaranth, beans, chia, fish, and meat, sources of complete proteins.

Around 3600 B.C.E., Amerindians discovered popcorn, a food the Iroquois served at the first Thanksgiving in 1621 and Americans continued to eat as an inexpensive snack through the Great Depression and as a substitute for sweets during the rationing of sugar in World War II. In 1700 B.C.E., corn determined Mesoamerican foodways, religion, and identity. In the first millennium C.E., cultivation spread north through Arizona, New Mexico, and Texas.

The Hopi domesticated piki, a blue corn readily processed into meal for thin tortillas, a daily demonstration of female culinary skills. In the Mississippi River valley, the Mesquakie and Sauk developed kernels into flour, *masa* (dough), and posole or hominy, a soaked kernel eaten like a vegetable. The Narragansett of New England, who relied on corn for winter sustenance, stored dried grains in caches lined with grass.

History and Myth

Indians revered the symbiotic "three sisters" of gardening: beans, corn, and squash. The Cherokee turned kernels into hominy, a puffed vegetable, and *sofkee,* a hot beverage. Adaptation to a colder climate and shorter growing season evolved in the Great Plains and, by 1200 C.E., in Ontario, Canada. Around 1250 C.E., the Pawnee grew flint corn, a hard-kerneled variety, in the cold, wet climate of the Great Plains as a source of hominy. Cornfields eventually flourished from Argentina to California and the Dakotas and into the lower St. Lawrence River valley of Canada.

In the era of global voyages, Christopher Columbus first saw corn on November 5, 1492, when two sailors brought ears from Cuba. The explorer introduced corn seed in Iberia, France, and Italy by 1494. The Portuguese carried the grain to China in 1516. In 1535, French expeditioner Jacques Cartier found extensive corn cultivation in Montreal. In 1643, Roger Williams observed how Indians

Harvested feed corn shoots out of an augur wagon and into a truck for delivery to a storage elevator or processing plant. With an astonishing range of uses, American corn dominates global farm crops. *(Bloomberg/Getty Images)*

Recipe: Corn Pudding

Make a slurry of three eggs, 1 cup of shredded Monterey Jack cheese, 1/4 cup of shredded pecorino cheese, and sea salt and pepper. Mix with 1 1/2 cups of fresh sweet corn. An optional ingredient, 1 cup of tomato pulp, adds an interesting acidic flavor. Pour the mixture into a buttered casserole dish and bake for 20 minutes at 350 degrees Fahrenheit.

carried corn in burden baskets as travel food and secured cornmeal in leather belts. The Mahican and Muscogee revered corn in planting ceremonies and the Green Corn ritual, a harvest celebration that renewed the soil for the next year's planting.

Corn's versatility made it a welcome crop in North Africa, the Balkans, India, the Philippines, and the East Indies. The omission of the nixtamalization process spread pellagra and kwashiorkor among growers, who knew nothing about the enhancement of calcium, protein, and vitamin B3 (niacin). European settlers of the Americas centered cookery on kernels for corn pudding and succotash. They reserved canisters of cornmeal for ashcake, corn dodgers or hush puppies, johnnycake, mock oysters (corn fritters), and pone, all convenient travel food.

Wasting nothing, pioneers recycled cobs into smoking pipes and husks into dolls, mattress stuffing, and wrappings for tamales. A Southern breakfast tradition, ground hominy produced grits, a soft side dish flavored with butter or redeye gravy, a deglazing of country ham drippings with coffee. Tidewater Virginia contributed eggs and milk to corn bread recipes to produce spoon bread, a delectable side dish and showpiece soufflé.

In 1860, in preparation for the Civil War, Confederates boosted corn production from 30 million to 55 million bushels but faced increasing starvation as armies robbed farms of laborers and emancipation set slaves free. Rebel army cooks turned cornmeal or leftover pone into coush-coush, a breakfast stir-up of African origin. At Castle Sorghum on the Saluda River, South Carolina, a Union prisoner, Captain Willard Worcester Glazier of Albany, New York, reported meals of little more than corn cakes and molasses, the cause of chronic enteritis. By 1866, Southern cornfields lay scorched and weedy.

Reviving a Staple

Corn continued to serve new uses in the late 1800s, notably in amusement park and theater concessions, beginning in 1893 with a popcorn booth at the Columbia Exposition in Chicago. The heyday of cold cereals produced the cornflake, which vegetarian food faddist John Harvey Kellogg patented in Battle Creek, Michigan, in 1895. By 1911, shoppers faced 107 brands of cornflakes from which to choose.

In the 1920s, battered hot dogs on a stick rose to popularity as corn dogs, which vendors sold at the Texas State Fair in 1938. The corn-wrapped wiener also gained fame as street food in Argentina, Australia, Canada, New Zealand, and Vietnam, where diners popularized baby ears and waxy corn, a gelatinous variety. In South Korea, roasted kernels soaked in boiling water produced *oksusu cha*, a naturally sweet corn tea touted as a treatment for diabetes and kidney disease. The Taiwanese favor grilled corn on a skewer topped with cayenne, garlic, onions, and soy sauce.

In the 1930s, corn became equated with poverty meals. Works Progress Administration artist Lowell Houser captured the beginnings of corn culture in 1938 on a mural for the Ames, Iowa, post office. The three panels pictured a Mayan grower and corn gods and an American picker centered with an emblematic corn kernel, stalk, and ear. Social novelist John Steinbeck's *The Grapes of Wrath*, filmed in 1940, depicted nomadic Okies fleeing the Dust Bowl and frying corn mush balls in grease as subsistence meals.

In the South, the Great Depression placed hardships on mountaineers, who made higher profits on distilled "corn squeezin's" (moonshine) than on corn sold as grain. To avoid federal revenue agents, "'shine" runners stripped cars to accommodate fast deliveries to city centers. Lionized in the 1958 movie *Thunder Road,* moonshiners' cars became the ancestors of NASCAR racers.

Hybridization of corn extended shelf life and, in the 1950s, increased sweetness, a discovery of Jerald K. Pataky, a plant pathologist at the University of Illinois. A decade later, Arthur Lee Hooker, a corn specialist at the same university, boosted resistance to rust fungus. In 1966, Frito-Lay of Atlanta, Georgia, and Memphis, Tennessee, the distributor of Fritos, invented Doritos corn chips, a snack fad adapted from tostados (toasted tortillas). In 1969, amylomaize, a unique cornstarch, coated food for the *Apollo I* spaceflight to prevent crumbs from permeating the atmosphere in the space capsule.

At 366 million tons (332 million metric tons) per year, corn dominates American farm crops. Of the three major grains worldwide—corn, rice, and wheat—corn accounted for 817 million, or 37.5 percent of crops, in 2009. During harvest, combines strip cobs from the stalk and husk and shell the corn, which provides 21 percent of the world's human food. The development of full popping and hull-less kernels satisfies the public's demand for an aromatic, easily activated snack, often cooked in a microwave oven. As a sweetener, corn syrup flavors more than 2,000 processed foods.

Indeed, according to Michael Pollan, author of *The Omnivore's Dilemma* (2006) and other acclaimed works on the modern food system, corn is a keystone of the American food industry. More than a quarter of the 45,000 items available in U.S. supermarkets, he maintains, contain corn—most of it cheap. Corn's overuse, he argues, is a direct cause of the growing problem of obesity in America.

See also: African Diet and Cuisine, Sub-Saharan; Agriculture; Aztec Diet and Cuisine; Plant Disease and Prevention; Prohibition; Snack Food; Standish, Miles; Swedish West India Company; Tortillas; Verrazzano, Giovanni da.

Further Reading

Betrán, Javier, Edward C.A. Runge, and C. Wayne Smith, eds. *Corn: Origin, History, Technology, and Production.* Hoboken, NJ: Wiley, 2004.

Pollan, Michael. *The Omnivore's Dilemma: A Natural History of Four Meals.* New York: Penguin, 2006.

Smith, Andrew F. *Eating History: 30 Turning Points in the Making of American Cuisine.* New York: Columbia University Press, 2009.

Warman, Arturo. *Corn & Capitalism: How a Botanical Bastard Grew to Global Dominance.* Chapel Hill: University of North Carolina Press, 2003.

Cortés, Hernán de (1485–1547)

With the Spanish conquest of Aztec Mexico in 1519–1521, Hernán de Cortés witnessed a unique culture capable of pitiless blood sacrifice and responsible for introducing chicle, chocolate, corn, pepper, and turkeys to the world.

A native of Medellín, Spain, Cortés studied classical languages and law at the University of Salamanca. During his work as a notary, he learned of Christopher Columbus's voyages to the New World and his return with potatoes and other culinary wealth. In 1504, Cortés departed for Hispaniola. At a village outside Santo Domingo, he received a colonial allotment of land and Taíno laborers. After establishing his reputation as a conqueror of Cuba and treasury officer for the Crown, he advanced to colonial magistrate. While serving as mayor of Havana, he raised cattle and horses and dabbled at mining.

Much of Cortés's Central American experience appears in the history of New Spain and Mexico City compiled by infantryman Bernal Díaz del Castillo. Without permission from Holy Roman Emperor Charles V, Cortés set out for the Yucatán on February 19, 1519, with 600 soldiers and 20 horses. Upon encountering Maya, he hosted them with food and wine, a new experience for the Indians. Through trade, he acquired 20 Indian females from Tabasco to soak, hull, and grind corn for tortillas.

On March 4, the Spaniards burned their boats and marched inland from Vera Cruz with the aid of Cortés's mistress, translator Doña Marina, called Malinali Tenépal or La Malinche, who spoke Mayan and Nahuatl. His 150-pound (68-kilogram) mastiffs alarmed the Mexica, who raised only small Chihuahuas for meat. On Easter Sunday, the slave Cuitlalpitoc anticipated that the Spaniards would sacrifice and eat him. To his surprise, Cortés invited him to Sunday Mass and dinner.

Aztec Abundance

In mid-August 1519, the convoy moved west 200 miles (320 miles) toward Tenochtitlán, raising terror in natives by slaying citizens and burning property. After receiving gifts and foods from the Mexica allies, Cortés offered trinkets—beads, mirrors, needles, pins, and scissors. He angered the Indians by proselytizing them with Catholic dogma and by demanding an audience with Aztec Emperor Montezuma II. The Mexica deserted the Spaniards, leaving them to survive on shellfish and the remains of moldy ship's stores of cassava bread from Havana.

Cortés got a glimpse of New World foodstuffs from the next envoys. Some 50 Tlaxcalans brought him food gifts—beans, cherries and figs, corn cakes, fish, and roast turkey, an unfamiliar poultry breed to Castilians. As a grisly token of blessing, the Indians sprinkled the food with the blood of freshly slain Totonac boys. La Malinche warned that the carriers actually spied for the emperor to reconnoiter the camp and the military strength of men and horses. To refute legends that the insurgents represented the plumed serpent god Quetzalcoatl, the envoys returned to Montezuma with news that the Spaniards acted like normal humans.

On November 8, 1519, Montezuma received the conquistadors with gold treasures and enough rations for several days. Cortés realized that Tenochtitlán was as populous as Córdoba or Seville, with perhaps as many as 200,000 people. He discovered the food wealth of the capital city in a huge farmer's market at Tlatelolco that was twice the size of the square in Salamanca. To feed so dense a populace, vendors offered 300 varieties of produce. To lure business, prostitutes smacked chicle (chewing gum), another unfamiliar New World product.

From Lake Xochimilco, farmers who grew peppers, corn, and tomatoes on *chinampas* (floating gardens) poled their goods through public canals. The agrarian islets yielded fruit and 50,000 tons (45,000 metric tons) of corn per year. For bartering and trade, merchants used cocoa beans as currency. For crises as deadly as the famines of 1450–1454 and 1505, magistrates stored corn in warehouses. In better times, citizens paid their taxes in beans, corn, and sage.

In a second dispatch to Charles V dated October 30, 1520, Cortés reported on the availability of birds and ducks, deer, dogs, and rabbits as well as *ollas,* pottery cooking jars. Apothecaries prescribed herbs and medicinal roots. Greengrocers stocked artichokes, borage, garlic, leeks and onions, nasturtiums, thistles, and watercress. Cortés cataloged honey, cherries, plums, sugar, and wine. Vendors displayed corn on the cob, cornmeal, and corn bread. While restaurants sold food and drink, diners on street fare ate bird and fish paté and eggs as well as cashews and peanuts. Cortés marveled at wells and a double water conduit into the city but found less appealing the idols shaped from ground legumes and seeds mixed with blood from the hearts of Aztec victims.

From Grandeur to Ruin

Montezuma received daily food service in grand courtyards, including his regular service of honeyed cocoa, which he drank as an aphrodisiac as often as 50 times a day. Cleanliness required the washing of hands before and after each meal and immediate replacement of used tableware. Some 400 young servants brought dishes to the emperor and heated cooling platters over charcoal braziers. He ate along with courtiers and shared with five or six elderly caciques (native chiefs) the entrées and peppery sauces from his own dishes. Choices ranged from poultry such as parrot, partridge, pheasant, quail, and turkey to the meat of boar, dog, iguana, and venison. Emulating Montezuma's table luxuries, Cortés's soldiers accustomed themselves to a leisurely breakfast at 10:00 A.M., when they ate two types of tamales, either honeyed or flavored with pimiento.

Following a rout of Spaniards from their headquarters at Tenochtitlán on June 24, 1521, and a loss of 600 conquistadors, angry Aztec rebels stoned their emperor for his complicity with the insurgents. Bringing reinforcements, Cortés attacked by boat over Lake Texcoco and began squeezing Tenochtitlán's supply lines. During an 80-day siege, the Aztecs rapidly depleted their stores of corn. After hunger, wounds, and rampant dysentery and smallpox sapped the city's citizenry of 100,000, the survivors capitulated on August 13, 1521, and fled the capital.

On October 12, 1524, Cortés led a two-year expedition to Honduras to colonize it for Spain. He provisioned the journey up the Tabasco River by 20 canoes relaying goods from caravels. At Cupilco Province, he found ample fisheries and cacao; at Chilapan, he arrived just as sweet corn was ripening. Along the long, swampy trail, his provisioners found either fresh or dried corn to feed the troops and their mounts until they reached the rain-soaked trail beyond Ixtapan. For the rest of the mission, despair and hunger alternated with hope and plenty.

Upon Cortés's safe return, the Mexica greeted him with cacao, fruits, and turkeys and swept the road before him while showering him with blossoms. In his fifth letter to Charles V, dated October 23, 1525, he described the hardships of overland marches and the meager rations at Teucix of cooked herbs, dates, and palm buds. At Taniha, he killed the pigs he brought along and ate unsalted pork with boiled palmetto and hearts of palm. Worsening relations with the Crown sent the expeditioner home in 1528, when Charles V demoted him to viceroy.

In 1530, Cortés retired to Cuernavaca to the palace he built upon returning from his expedition. While building ships, he cultivated sugarcane in new territory and erected a sugar mill operated by African slaves. Three years later, in the vessel *Concepción,* he explored the Pacific coast of Mexico and Baja, where he encountered Guaycura divers harvesting pearls from 30 oyster beds in La Paz Bay in May 1535. One of his introductions, Spanish grapevines, presaged the Central American wine industry. Cortés died of pleurisy in Seville on December 2, 1547.

See also: Biscuit; Díaz, Bernal; Mexican Diet and Cuisine; Pork; Religion and Food; Seaman's Diet and Cuisine; Tortillas.

Further Reading

Aguilar-Moreno, Manuel. *Handbook to Life in the Aztec World.* New York: Oxford University Press, 2007.

Kirkwood, Burton. *The History of Mexico.* Santa Barbara, CA: ABC-Clio, 2010.

Koestler-Grack, Rachel A. *Hernando Cortes and the Fall of the Aztecs.* Philadelphia: Chelsea House, 2006.

Wagner, Heather Lehr. *Hernán Cortés.* New York: Chelsea House, 2009.

Wolfe, David. *Naked Chocolate: The Astonishing Truth About the World's Greatest Food.* San Diego, CA: Maul Brothers, 2005.

Crackers

A convenience and finger food baked from flour dough pressed flat, crackers provide grain nourishment in an easily stored and transported form. Whether salted or unsalted, leavened with bicarbonate of soda to reduce acidity or unleavened, thin layers of dough rest for up to four hours to slacken gluten. In a hot oven, the flattened wafers bake quickly and uniformly. Perforations simplify the variance of size to suit dipping, eating in soup, or topping with a complementary food, such as cheese.

Over time, crackers have accompanied meals in the form of flatbread, pita chips, Passover matzoh, Eucharist host, teething biscuits, dehydrated sea biscuits, naan, and rusks. Small, hard biscuits derived from Mesopotamia as

Recipe: Hot Cocoa, Aztec Style

Bring 2 cups of water to a boil, add one seeded chili, and cook for a half hour. Remove the pepper. Warm 2 1/2 pints of cream, flavored with a cinnamon stick and 1 teaspoon of vanilla extract. On low heat, add 1/2 pound unsweetened dark chocolate and 2 tablespoons of honey. When the chocolate melts, remove the cinnamon stick and pour in the boiled pepper water. Top the cocoa with chocolate shavings.

travel food made from oil, a small quantity of water, and ground acorns, bones, or grains. For military hardtack, Roman cooks double-baked *buccellum* (biscuit) to harden it for issuance to legionaries. As field pack food, the crackers traveled the Roman Empire, from Britannia to North Africa and Asia Minor.

Crackers in History

In the Middle Ages, crusaders carried crisp flatbread over long journeys from Europe to the Holy Lands. After 1189, Richard I departed on the Third Crusade with a "muslin biscuit" made from barley, bean, and rye flour. Soldiers returned home with recipes for plain or seeded Middle Eastern varieties, including Arabic *khubz* and Egyptian *dhourra*.

At the face-off with England by the Spanish Armada in 1588, Royal Navy recruits subsisted on a daily allotment of 1 gallon (3.8 liters) of ale and 1 pound (0.45 kilograms) of biscuit. This dreary diet continued until 1667, when navy provisioner Samuel Pepys added variety to ships' pantries. Under Queen Victoria, the English soldier identified biscuit from the Royal Clarence Victualing Yard at Gosport by the Crown's seal. Military bakers in Japan and Korea provided the same hard cracker as a long-lived ships' staple.

Under less stringent circumstances, hardtack entered the diet of Hawaiians and Alaskans as common stores. Germans cut crackers into imaginative shapes to decorate Christmas trees. Yule wafers became the forerunners of alphabet- and animal-shaped crackers, designed to delight toddlers while they learned to chew solid food. Native American cooks enhanced the flavor of acorn and nut crackers with bear grease and duck or goose fat.

The Industrialized Cracker

During the cod-fishing and whaling era, the cracker industry became one of North America's first food industries. In 1792 at Newburyport, Massachusetts, John Pearson of Pearson & Son Bakery shaped flour and water into pilot bread, a flat, dry, tasteless ship's biscuit intended to remain edible at sea in galley pantries in all climates and temperatures. Before meals, the ship's cook soaked the wafers in milk, coffee, brine, or broth. Ships' doctors recommended sea biscuit as a digestive aid but joined the officers' mess for captain's biscuit, a more refined version of the sea dog's daily issue.

The concoction earned the name *cracker* in 1801 from Josiah Bent, a Boston baker who identified the crackle of cooling biscuits emerging from the oven, a sound reminiscent of firecrackers. His establishment distributed Crown Pilot Crackers, a lightly flavored wafer, as an accompaniment to New England clam chowder and to the fish houses of Canada's Maritime Provinces. Barrels of crackers followed pioneers west and satisfied the need for bar food in the frontier saloons of Denver and Pasadena. In 1822, a British brand, Huntley & Palmers of London, came to grocers' shelves in metal tins to prevent crumbling during coach travel. Cooks recommended lining tureens with crackers before ladling in broth and serving the mix to the sick and feeble.

Under factory conditions, the piercing of crackers with a docking stamp produced holes. The ventilation released pockets of steam formed in the dough by heat and facilitated an even shape, even for the hexagonal oysterette. Bite-size oyster crackers or water crackers originated in 1847 in the Trenton, New Jersey, factory of English immigrants Adam and John Exton as a crunchy accompaniment to soup and chowder.

A year later, competitor Ezekiel Pullen packed his Original Trenton Cracker or "OTC" in a wagon for sale door-to-door. In 1861, he supplied the Army of the Potomac with crackers sold in rounded lumps similar in shape to pretzel nuggets and served for breakfast and supper with salt pork and coffee. Soldiers, who called the wafers "McClellan pies" and "Monitors," bought private stashes from sutlers. Homemakers relied on saltines as a makeshift ingredient in appleless apple pie and other dishes created out of the few staples still available during wartime shortages. On April 7, 1862, Mary Ann Bickerdyke, chief nurse and dietician under General Ulysses S. Grant, assuaged survivors of the Battle of Shiloh with dwindling stores of crackers, tea, and whiskey.

Advances in baking technology increased productivity by rolling and stamping the dough. Although homemakers could shape their own wafers, by the 1870s, barrels of standardized crackers drew loafers and shoppers in general stores. In 1874, the Premium Saltine Company, with an automated factory in St. Joseph, Missouri, answered a demand for boardinghouse and restaurant accompaniments to salads and stews. In 1898, the Crown Pilot Company grew into the National Biscuit Company, maker of Nabisco snack crackers and cookies.

A Boston competitor of Crown Pilot Crackers, Educator Brand Crackers, came on the market in 1885. A dentist, William L. Johnson, formulated baking times for the whole-wheat dough to exercise teeth and gums. He contracted with Butler's Bakery in Newburyport, Massachusetts, to produce the Johnson Educator Cracker, which developed a fan base. By the twentieth century, the company distributed Beer Chasers, Butter Thins, Corn Meal Crackers, Diabetic Crackers, Kremex, Luncheon Biscuits, Scotch Chasers, Sea Pilots, Sesame Crax, Toasterettes, Vee-Gee Crax, and Wheatless Crackers among its 140 variants of the original dental stimulant.

Sold at the rate of a dime per pound, Educator Crackers were a godsend to the poor. Manuals on family nourishment mentioned Johnson's cracker by name as a chewable food for small children and a digestible accompaniment to cocoa. In 1894, the *Medical and Surgical*

Reporter recommended a meal of cream and Johnson's crackers for rehabilitating patients.

The Modern Cracker

Crackers left factory conveyor lines in a variety of shapes and flavors, including beef broth, cheese, pepper, sesame, shortening, and coarse sea salt. Sealed in moisture-proof waxed paper, they remained dry and crisp. Caterers anchored hors d'oeuvres trays with crackers to hold egg salad, mousse, pâté, and seafood spreads. Saltier varieties accompanied bowls of soup and oyster stew.

In 1917, Russian Mennonites imported to Canada an unfamiliar child food, the teething biscuit zwieback, named for the German "twice baked." A brittle cracker, zwieback acquired sweetness from the double oven time, which turned starch into sugar.

In 1923, Nabisco designer Sydney S. Stern created Ritz Crackers, a buttery scalloped disc that paired well with cheese and cold cuts. The inexpensive but filling food gained popularity during the Great Depression as a filler for meatloaf and beef stew or as a meal in itself spread with peanut butter, cocktail sauce, or evaporated milk, a common hobo food. In the late 1940s, crackers and other snack foods suited the eating style of prospering Americans. A healthful snack cracker in 1962 derived from Pepperidge Farm's distribution of Goldfish. In 2012, Nabisco, Pepperidge Farm, and Special K merged the qualities of the cracker with the chip.

See also: Finger Food; Hearth Cookery; Salad and Salad Bars; Snack Food.

Further Reading

Haber, Barbara. *From Hardtack to Home Fries: An Uncommon History of American Cooks and Meals.* New York: Free Press, 2002.

Kulp, Karel, and Joseph G. Ponte. *Handbook of Cereal Science and Technology.* New York: Marcel Dekker, 2000.

McDaniel, Rick. *An Irresistible History of Southern Food: Four Centuries of Black-eyed Peas, Collard Greens & Whole Hog Barbecue.* Charleston, SC: History Press, 2011.

Smith, Andrew F., ed. *The Oxford Companion to American Food and Drink.* New York: Oxford University Press, 2007.

Creole Diet and Cuisine

From the settlement of Mobile in 1704 and of New Orleans in 1722, the Creole cuisine of Louisiana Territory evolved from the blending of African okra and Choctaw sassafras leaves (*filé*) with classic French and Italian gastronomy. In 1704, Governor Jean-Baptiste Bienville, father of both capital cities, imported 500 French orphan girls and undesirables, *filles à la cassette* (casket girls), as potential mates for French soldiers. To introduce the females to cooking wild game and produce with Amerindian recipes,

Bienville employed his Choctaw French cousin, Madame Langlois, to hold cooking classes. From the union of immigrant women with the first slaves, imported in 1719, came the first Creoles, the French-speaking free people of color who settled the Gulf of Mexico.

More elegant than rural, game-based Cajun food, haute Creole or native cookery began with roux, a sauce blended from flour fried in butter with broth or tomato pulp. The substantial essence, flavored by the chemical changes of the Maillard reaction (a kind of browning), turned fresh market staples—catfish, crawfish, grits, mirlitons (squash), oysters, peppers, pork, rice, shrimp, tomatoes—into multicultural entrées that emulated European originals.

Aristocratic without overwhelming the diner with tedious refinements, Creole dishes featured the savor of Greek, Portuguese, Spanish, and West African cookery, the tastes typically found in port cities such as Mobile and New Orleans. One model, jambalaya with ham, pepper sauce, and *andouille* sausage, yielded a riot of flavors and textures in one of North America's most spirited recipes. Another, chicory coffee, emerged from rationing after a blockade in 1808 halted shipments of coffee and cane sugar.

Creole style profited from the professional discipline, ingenuity, and intuition requisite to luxury. In the French Quarter of New Orleans, Antoine's, a restaurant founded on Rue Saint Louis in 1840, introduced *pompano en papillote,* fish steamed in a parchment paper bag. Before sealing the container, the chef soaked a fillet with velouté, a shrimp and white wine sauce laced with crab meat and flavored with a *bouquet garni* of bay leaf, parsley, and thyme. Patrons varied from prominent families to riverboat captains and their mistresses, a New Orleans–style juxtaposition of the sedate with the tawdry. To perpetuate Creole flair after the Civil War, Commander's Palace, a restaurant on Washington Avenue in the Garden District, trained a number of successful Creole chefs, among them current celebrity Emeril Lagasse and Paul Prudhomme, inventor of nouvelle Creole.

Creole tastes acknowledged the strand of slave cooking derived from the cultural memory of Africa and the bondsmen who passed through the Dominican Republic and coastal South America on the way to North America. Dishes featuring black-eyed peas, caramelized onion, sweet potatoes, pineapple, and bananas, a Honduran treat introduced in 1866, flourished at the nineteenth-century hearths of convents, plantations, inns, and restaurants, particularly Arnaud's, Broussard's, and Galatoire's, a classic triad of New Orleans fare.

In 1880, a Bavarian immigrant, Madame Elizabeth Kettenring Dutrey Bégué, opened a coffeehouse at the corner of Decatur and Madison streets in the French Quarter. There she introduced brunch, a relaxed midmorning repast that included court bouillon (poaching liquid) and cream-topped trifle, or bread pudding with whiskey

Creole jambalaya—a slow-cooked rice dish of sausage, chicken, tomatoes, celery, onions, peppers, and spices—originated in the French Quarter of New Orleans, melding French and Spanish influences in a unique local style. *(MCT/Getty Images)*

sauce, suited to the unhurried lifestyle of New Orleans. Travelers found Creole menus in other cities—at Galt House in Louisville, Maison Dorée in New York, Maxwell House in Nashville, the Peabody Hotel in Memphis, and the colonial pavilion at the Paris Exposition of 1889.

In 1885, travel writer Lafcadio Hearn collected Creole flavors in his first compilation, *La Cuisine Creole: A Collection of Culinary Recipes, from Leading Chefs and Noted Creole Housewives, Who Have Made New Orleans Famous for Its Cuisine.* That same year, the Christian Woman's Exchange issued *The Creole Cookery Book,* a generous list of soups, fish and shellfish dishes, sauces, poultry and meats, vegetables, breads and cakes, custards and puddings, and pickles. The two anthologies testified to the centrality of cosmopolitan classics—Sicilian biscuits, trout à la Venitienne, turkey à la Perigord, *riz au laid,* ladyfingers, coffee custard—to family fellowship and to hospitality, the mark of well-bred gentry. In Natchitoches, fried meat pies sold door-to-door during the Great Depression enabled women to profit from the kitchen skills of original Spanish pioneers.

Creole specialties permeate modern American pop culture, beginning with Hank Williams's country classic "Jambalaya" (1952). Local dishes color fiction and film, from Tennessee Williams's play *A Streetcar Named Desire* (film, 1951) and Robert Penn Warren's *Band of Angels* (1957) to *The Big Easy* (1987), a noir crime movie rich in music, dance, and crawfish étouffée, and *Grand Isle* (1991), a screen version of Kate Chopin's feminist novella *The Awakening* (1899). Distinct from the southeastern gastronomy of the Gullah recipes of Charleston, South Carolina, and the Tidewater fare of Richmond, Virginia, original Louisiana Creole featured crowd-pleasing combinations—

bloody bull cocktails preceding the gumbos and shrimp bisque served from steaming tureens along with side dishes of dirty rice, red beans, and sauce picante (a spicy tomato-based sauce). The serious diner topped off the meal with slices of pecan pie, bananas Foster, pralines, and beignets.

In the 1960s, Leah Chase, a purveyor of African Creole gastronomy, drew civil rights leaders to her Orleans Avenue restaurant, Dooky Chase. There, she created a meatless special for Lent, gumbo z'herbes, a puree of mustard greens, spinach, and turnips based on West African pot greens and the French *potage aux herbes.* Her establishment survived flooding from Hurricane Katrina in August 2005. After the deluge and a fire following Hurricane Ike in 2008, Brennan's on Royal Street, one of the famous Creole venues, resurged to popularity at Mardi Gras 2010. Nonetheless, the combined devastation wrought by hurricanes and the BP oil spill from April 20 to July 15, 2010, threatened the integrity of Creole ingredients, particularly coastal crab, crawfish, shrimp, and oysters. Gulf pollutants left aficionados fearful for the future of an American food phenomenon.

See also: Boré, Jean Étienne de; Cajun Diet and Cuisine; Grilling; Moravian Diet and Cuisine.

Further Reading

Goody, Cynthia, and Lorena Drago, eds. *Cultural Food Practices.* Chicago: American Dietetic Association, 2010.

Kein, Sybil. *Creole: The History and Legacy of Louisiana's Free People of Color.* Baton Rouge: Louisiana State University Press, 2000.

Rumble, Victoria R. *Soup Through the Ages: A Culinary History with Period Recipes.* Jefferson, NC: McFarland, 2009.

Tucker, Susan. *New Orleans Cuisine: Fourteen Signature Dishes and Their Histories.* Foreword by S. Frederick Starr. Jackson: University Press of Mississippi, 2009.

Crusaders' Diet and Cuisine

A series of Christian military expeditions from the eleventh to the fourteenth centuries to recapture the Holy Land from Muslims, the Crusades introduced European armies to the biota and foods of Asia Minor and Africa and to the spiced dishes common to the Near East. The culinary shift occurred at a time when both the upper classes and peasants invested more than half of their income on food and beverage and when farmers paid their bills and taxes in foodstuffs. After the launch of the First Crusade in 1096, tens of thousands of foot soldiers experienced a broadening of tastes and cuisines.

First Crusade

Organized by Pope Urban II at Clermont in southern France in August 1095, the crusaders left Europe on August 15, 1096. The huge endeavor produced unforeseen changes in the wine industry. Some nobles abandoned their vineyards to monasteries in exchange for ongoing prayers from monks for victory over the Saracens who ruled Jerusalem. Other landowners left vineyards in their wills to churchmen who prayed for their salvation in the afterlife. Within three centuries, Cistercian brothers managed Europe's largest grape-growing territory.

On the First Crusade, the Christian forces departed in the midst of famine without adequate food, a problem that perpetually threatened a badly organized siege on Islamic territory. While supply trains imported dried fruit and starchy staples—barley, beans, chickpeas, lentils, and wheat—some 3,000 miles (4,800 kilometers) to the Middle East, Christian soldiers passing through Champagne and Rouen outraged French Jews by their demands for donated supplies. German provisioners, led by Walter Sans-Avoir, and Franks commanded by Godfrey de Bouillon bought food from Byzantine sellers in Hungary and Bulgaria to feed troops on the way to Constantinople.

A year later, produce and meat sellers along the route to Jerusalem either offered goods at inflated prices or refused to sell to an army of strangers in exchange for foreign currency. Peter the Hermit, leading 40,000 crusaders, bargained for lower food prices and negotiated with the Byzantine Emperor Alexios I for imperial "hospitality" and donations.

More fearful of starving than of the attacking Turks, the men of the First Crusade spread into the Balkans and raided markets for their immediate needs. According to William of Tyre, in October 1097, newcomers to the eastern Mediterranean area foraged around Antioch in northern Syria for 30 weeks for edible plunder—Sidonian wine, Palestinian olive oil, Syrian grain, Galilean dried fish, Sicilian bacon and tuna, Jerusalem honey, Tyrian sugar, cheese, and yogurt. Anselm of Laon added pepper to the list of troop necessaries of bread and candles.

After crusaders captured Antioch, eyewitness Raymond d'Aguilers described in his chronicle how troops from Provençal continued to live off local supplements throughout the cold months of 1097 and 1098, when Saracens cached their pantries and retreated to caves. In a gloomy winter of famine and epidemic typhoid fever, the Calabrian Prince Bohemond, Robert of Flanders, and Tancred of Normandy led 20,000 raiders, who excelled at foraging for cattle, corn, fodder, and wine along the Orontes River through Lebanon, Syria, and Turkey. Others sailed for Cyprus in search of provisions. Supply ships from Europe arrived at the ports of Joppa (Jaffa in present-day Israel) and Nicaea (Íznik in present-day Turkey) with only enough sustenance to maintain crusaders for short periods.

Troops, inured to cookery far from Europe, adapted their tastes to local rations and styles of preparation and seasoning. In 1099, Fulcher of Chartres recalled how Frankish troops marching through the Holy Lands staved off hunger by chewing sugarcane, which the Arabs had cultivated since 700 C.E. As a result of hybrid cookery, international trade spread Arab cuisine to the West, notably honey cakes and *lebkuchen* (sweet cake), the forerunners of gingerbread, a staple of German Easter pastry.

On his deathbed in spring 1118 from eating spoiled fish from the Nile River, the Frankish general Baldwin, who became King Baldwin I of Jerusalem, so trusted Egyptian spice that he ordered his cook, Oddo, to embalm and return his remains to Jerusalem for interment. Oddo gutted Baldwin's corpse and seasoned it with spices, salt, and balm of Gilead (also balsam) for the return journey. The corpse remained incorrupt until its burial.

Second and Third Crusades

In 1147, at the beginning of the Second Crusade, English fishermen and yeomen from Bristol, East Anglia, Hastings, Kent, London, and Southampton set out from Dartmouth in 164 ships. At Adalia, Turkey, in January 1148, crusaders paid outrageous prices for Byzantine foodstuffs. According to historian Odo of Deuil, because of malnutrition and exhaustion, soldiers died at a rapid rate from an unidentified epidemic, possibly bubonic plague or typhoid. Those fleeing the pestilence met their end from Turkish attacks. The few who survived, as well as some 10,000 turncoats who accepted posts as Muslim mercenaries, began to adopt Moorish dress, domestic life, medical practice, and cuisine, settling in Sicily and as far west as Spain.

Upon their return to England, veterans incorporated eastern Mediterranean fare into British cookery. Eleanor of Aquitaine, the queen of Henry II and a veteran crusader, enhanced the royal pantry at Winchester with almonds, cinnamon, cumin, and pepper. Later in the century, London merchants stocked Babylonian palm oil, pepper, spices, and Mediterranean wines. From northwestern Sicilian markets at Palermo came melons, lemons, and oranges as well as figs, pine and pistachio nuts, pomegranates in syrup, and tahina paste made from roasted and ground sesame seeds.

Hildegard of Bingen, a Rhineland Benedictine abbess, incorporated aromatic plants, spices, and wines in her *Physica* (*Medicines*), an herbal handbook. The text advised correct dosages of simples (herbs) for disease:

Herbs & Spices	Ailments Treated
cinnamon	malaria and soreness
cloves	head cold, hiccups, septic wounds, and edema
cumin	lung congestion and heart pain
fennel	nausea and sore eyes
galangal	palsy, back pain, and reflux
ginger	weak eyes and constipation
horehound	deafness and sore throat
lavender	liver pain and chest congestion
licorice	intestinal complaints and hepatitis
nigella	ulcers and flatulence
nutmeg	halitosis and depression
pepper	pleurisy and a diseased spleen
sage	excess phlegm, fungus, and senility
thyme	scabies and leprosy
zedoary	tremors and snakebite

By the Third Crusade, assistance from the Armenians and Turks raised spirits for the Christians' march through Asia Minor. By relieving crusaders of foraging duties, the volunteers restored the European ranks to full strength. During the siege of Acre, Israel, initiated against the Arab Saladin, a Kurdish general from Lebanon, by the French knight Guy of Lusignan on August 28, 1189, food arrived by sea to Haifa on an erratic schedule.

By late February 1191, scurvy-ridden crusaders were feeding on grass, bones, and meat from their depleted mounts. King Richard I of England, known as Richard the Lionheart, arrived in early June with ample food and weapons to supply his army until July 12, when it starved out the Muslim garrison at Acre. During Richard's initial dealings with Muslims the previous month, Saladin treated him to sherbet (granita), a flavored ice made from fruit puree and snow.

War in the Thirteenth Century

For the 1203 conquest of Constantinople during the Fourth Crusade, initiated by Pope Innocent III in 1201 and begun on June 24, 1202, Italian Christians chose food marketing over piety. Crusaders found Genoan, Pisan, and Venetian moneylenders eager for commerce via trading vessels. Two historians, Robert of Clari and Geof-

frey de Villehardouin, exonerated the Venetian Doge Enrico Dandolo of greed for trying to balance a contract market economy thrown awry by 12,000 soldiers marching through the Republic of Venice. The livelihood of fleet commanders and provisioners hung in the balance as West fought East for possession of the Holy Lands.

Fortunately for investors, control of the African and Asian spice trade passed from Constantinople to Venice. Trade in old spices—pepper and saffron—and new spices—aloes, cinnamon, cloves, cumin, nutmeg, and powdered rhubarb—as well as sugar and suckets (candied citrus fruits) made Venetian merchants on the city docks phenomenally wealthy.

The push into Alexandria, Egypt, in 1204 revived the question of where and how provisioners would buy necessities. Frankish soldiers robbed and raided markets unmercifully to make up for past hunger and sickness. In 1205, King John of England extended Queen Eleanor's shopping list with imported cloves, ginger, nutmeg, rice, saffron, and sugar, an expensive commodity used to make medicines and syrup for preserving fruit.

During Louis IX's bivouac along the Nile in February 1250, in the third year of the Seventh Crusade, Muslims at Al Mansurah (Mansoura), Egypt, cut off 80 Christian supply ships. Louis's troops relied for food on burbot, a scavenger fish that fed on corpses. As the French army retreated to Damietta at the Nile River delta, the supply convoy carried away some 25,000 knights sickened by their makeshift rations and by scurvy and dysentery. For treatment of casualties returning to France, encyclopedist Vincent of Beauvais, Louis's chaplain, prescribed cinnamon and pepper as cure-alls.

Living Among Arabs

Throughout the 174-year crusader residency in the eastern Mediterranean, the sanitary lifestyle and lavish diet of the Arab elite astonished English, Frankish, and German soldiers, some of whom languished from scurvy and malnutrition, intestinal parasites, dysentery, malarial fevers, trachoma, and food poisoning.

Servants in Arab households arranged a variety of meats—boar, deer, hare, partridge, and quail as well as beef, goat, and mutton—on painted lusterware platters. Fresh herbs grew wild—fennel, fern, mint, parsley, rue, sage, and thyme. Arab banquets featured ample vegetables—artichokes, asparagus, cabbage, lettuce, pickled turnips, spinach, and truffles. Cooks stuffed onions with fruit and lentils, flavored lamb with peaches and turmeric, baked eggplant with allspice and currants, fried cheese fritters, simmered lamb in mint and pomegranate juice for soup, filled dates with cardamom and coconut, and spiced other dishes with cinnamon, coriander, cumin, ginger, mastic, and pepper.

Residents refreshed themselves with snow-chilled sorbet, semolina pudding, and shredded pineapple frozen with rose petals and sugar. From Mamluk glass beakers and footed Persian beverage cups, diners sipped herbed mare's milk and drinks made from pureed apricots, bananas, citron, dates, figs, grapes, lemons, oranges, pomelos, and quince, the fruit of Damascene orchards. After-dinner trays offered apples, cherries, pears, pomegranates, and walnuts.

In Egypt, the nexus between Far Asian trade into the Red Sea and Middle Eastern kitchens, the reign of Saladin unified Arabic cookery with disparate elements from Egypt, Iraq, Lebanon, and Syria. Iraqi cuisine tended toward simple foodstuffs heavily flavored with sweet and savory additives—spices, sugar, and oil and vinegar. From Lebanese merchants trained in India, European crusaders learned how to cultivate sugarcane and extracted dry crystals from its juice for food and medicine. By the twelfth century, most of Europe imported sugar from the Middle East.

The maritime force that patrolled trade routes from the Red Sea through the Mediterranean derived from the Fatimid dynasty in Egypt, which dominated trade and demanded custom duties from the Catalanese, English, French, and Germans. The revenues proved so lucrative and steady that the Christian Church, although leery of commerce with Muslim infidels, began to view food traders as respectable for their contributions to the compounding of cough syrups, painkillers, and cordials, used as tonics for the heart.

Arab Cuisine in Europe

The English began incorporating Levantine and Sicilian dishes into their diet between 1100 and 1135. New spending on luxuries gave rise to a merchant class, whose profits on foodstuffs produced envy in aristocrats. In the mansions of the rich, imported anise, caraway, cardamom, cinnamon, clove, coriander, cumin, garlic, ginger, mace, mustard, nutmeg, pepper, saffron, and turmeric brightened the flavors of familiar recipes. One example, the standard English porridge, acquired glamour as frumenty, wheat cereal boiled in milk and flavored with spice, fruit, and sugar or honey as a sweetener.

New plants and taste treats bombarded European palates. The Duke of Anjou returned from Syria with the damson, a fruit originally called "Damascene." Italian vendors and Muslim traders in Sicily and Spain, the conduits for Eastern foodstuffs, enriched themselves on the flow of Mediterranean goods from the ports of Jerusalem and Alexandria. John Adrian made a fortune from imported cinnamon, dates, and gingerbread. Along with a wider choice of harmoniously seasoned foods and distilled beverages, according to the inventories in the Testament of Count Eudes de Nevers in Acre (1266), crusaders imported to their homelands elegant table settings, sophisticated utensils, flamboyant carving and serving styles, and dining manners suited to conspicuous consumption.

Religious leaders acquired balm, a gum resin burned as incense for Christian services and valued in hospices for

Recipe: Medieval Frumenty

Remove the hulls of 1 cup of wheat kernels by crushing in a mortar. Add the cracked grain to 4 cups of water, 1/2 cup of milk, and 1/2 cup of cream. Simmer for 15 minutes. Cover and let the mixture rest. When the grain softens, stir in 4 teaspoons of honey, two egg yolks, and a pinch of nutmeg. Add 1 cup of raisins, currants, stewed apricots, or stewed prunes and a pinch of saffron for color. Serve with fish or venison.

treatment of pain, coughs, and abrasions. English distributors, known as pepperers and *speciarii* (spicers), compounded aromatics at herb shops and *spicerias*. With the adoption of Arab distilling equipment, the trade evolved into the establishment of pharmacies in Boston, Lincoln, London, Lynn, and Southampton. Robert de Montpellier, royal apothecary-spicer to Henry III, opened London's first pharmacy at Cheapside in 1245, where he stocked pyonada (ground pine nuts) and colored sugar flavored with attar of roses and violets for making hippocras (spiced wine). City spicer John Adrian made a fortune from the sale of imported cinnamon, dates, and gingerbread.

By 1299, the English demand for exotic dyes and flavorings resulted in an offering of 53 kinds of spice as well as pine nuts and Morocco and rock sugar at the Boston Fair in Lincolnshire. The recipe for *viande Cyprus* (Cyprus meat) called for stewed chicken prepared with dates, Cyprus sugar, cinnamon, pine nuts, rice flour, and sweet wine.

The Countess of Leicester kept estate spices locked in the wardrobe. Henry III, her brother, sent guards from Winchester to purchase dates, figs, and raisins. In 1264, Henry's queen, Eleanor of Provence, ordered a saucery built in the upper story of Windsor Castle. The income from an almond, spice, and Cyprus sugar monopoly at the St. Giles Fair at Winchester supported the Benedictine priory of St. Swithun. At St. Ives in Cornwall, 20 spice boutiques flourished throughout the 1280s. Mediterranean food additives became so costly that recipes numbered them, such as ten white peppercorns, a dozen cloves, or eight saffron curls.

See also: Byzantine Diet and Cuisine; Crackers; Famine; Pan-European Diet and Cuisine; Spices; Sugar and Sweeteners; Travel Food.

Further Reading

Civitello, Linda. *Cuisine and Culture: A History of Food and People.* 3rd ed. Hoboken, NJ: John Wiley & Sons, 2011.

Harpur, James. *The Crusades: An Illustrated History.* New York: Thunder's Mouth, 2005.

Harris, Jonathan. *Byzantium and the Crusades.* London: Hambledon Continuum, 2003.

Mitchell, Piers D. *Medicine in the Crusades: Warfare, Wounds, and the Medieval Surgeon.* Cambridge, UK: Cambridge University Press, 2004.

Riley-Smith, Jonathan. *The Crusades: A History.* New York: Continuum, 2005.

Culpeper, Nicholas (1616–1654)

The English naturopath and populist author Nicholas Culpeper enhanced seventeenth-century understanding of holistic nutrition and curative foods as elements of alternative medicine.

Born in Sussex on October 18, 1616, and trained in Greek and Latin and in herbology by his maternal grandfather, Culpeper completed his education at Cambridge. His family disowned him for rejecting a degree in theology in favor of medicine. After apprenticing with a druggist at Bishopsgate, he opened a pharmacy in Spitalfields outside London's East End. Culpeper developed a hatred for supercilious physicians, who kept secret pharmaceutical knowledge to extort fees from the ignorant. He maligned pompous doctors as "bloodsuckers, true vampires." His enemies lambasted him with charges of drunkenness, fraud, and lechery.

With botanic specimens gathered in the countryside, Culpeper treated the indigent at a rate of 40 patients per day. He chose the freshest plants for food and medication and stored preserves in clay pots. His simples, or vegetable treatments, included the cooking of beans and peas with savory (*Satureja hortensis*) to ease flatulence and the sipping of barley water to reduce fever and pain. Culpeper advocated ample vegetables in the diet, especially asparagus, carrots, and parsnips, which sucked minerals from the soil into their roots. His respect for dandelion greens and duck

meat derived from their cleansing of the urinary passages. He also believed that cooking with bay leaves diminished cyclical headaches and that cherries and mint sparked appetite. Moderating his success, the Society of Apothecaries inveighed against clinical herbalism as "white witchcraft," a benevolent form of sorcery.

In 1643, during the second year of the English Civil War, Culpeper practiced combat surgery and translated medical texts from Latin to English. His intent was to supply ordinary people with handbooks, notably *The English Physitian* (1652), a best seller in Britain and its colonies. He followed that with *The Complete Herbal* (1653), a guide to home cookery to treat common ailments, such as bittersweet for vertigo, beets for stuffy nose, vinegar for whitening teeth, and mustard to combat lethargy.

On January 10, 1654, while recuperating from a shrapnel wound to his left shoulder incurred at the siege of Reading, Culpeper died of the combined effects of tuberculosis, smoking, and overwork at age 37. His concern for women's travails in *A Directory for Midwives* (1651) earned him the title "Father of Midwifery." The Culpeper chain of herb shops still flourishes today in India and the United Kingdom as well as on the Internet.

See also: London Virginia Company; Mustard; Peppers.

Further Reading

Debus, Allen G. *The Chemical Philosophy: Paracelsian Science and Medicine in the Sixteenth and Seventeenth Centuries.* Mineola, NY: Dover, 2002.

Furdell, Elizabeth Lane. *Publishing and Medicine in Early Modern England.* Rochester, NY: University of Rochester Press, 2002.

Potterton, David. *Culpeper's Color Herbal.* Foreword by E.J. Shellard. New York: Sterling, 2007.

Taavitsainen, Irma, and Päivi Pahta. *Medical Writing in Early Modern English.* Cambridge, UK: Cambridge University Press, 2011.

Woolley, Benjamin. *Heal Thyself: Nicholas Culpeper and the Seventeenth-Century Struggle to Bring Medicine to the People.* New York: HarperCollins, 2004.

Curative Foods

In oral tradition and medical writing, folk cures are a mainstay of preliterate and uneducated peoples. From prehistory, culinary advice advocated flavorful foods that prevented and treated disease.

Honey, the original health food, gained respect because it required no digestion, preparation, or additives. Theoreticians from Zenon to Dioscorides advised the mixing of honey in foods and beverages to prevent scurvy and treat surface wounds. In Egypt papyri as early as

Recipe: Easter Cake

For postholiday cleansing of the body, Nicholas Culpeper advised the baking of tansy cake: "Add seven beaten eggs to a pint of cream, the juice of spinach and of a small quantity of tansy pounded in a mortar, a quarter of a pound of Naples biscuits [sponge cakes made from ground pine nuts], sugar to taste, a glass of white wine, and nutmeg." After thickening the mix over low heat, the cook placed it in a cake tin and baked it in an oven.

3500 B.C.E., lists of healing compounds extolled honey and characterized it as a respiratory aid, perhaps because it soothed raw mouths and throats and quieted coughs. Around 2000 B.C.E., Mesopotamian patients chose between the surgeon and the *asu* (herbalist), both of whom valued honey as a foundation of medicines. The Vedas, Sanskrit scriptures begun in 1500 B.C.E., contained prayers to the mother herb and relied on ghee (clarified butter) mixed with honey as an alimentary soother. Around 60 B.C.E., the Roman poet Lucretius found honey helpful in the treatment of infants.

Ayurvedic Diet

In prehistoric India, healers recognized cooks as allies. From 3000 B.C.E., India developed Ayurveda, a unified dietary system featuring wellness as its goal. Essential to Ayurvedic recipes, yogurt and ghee balanced energy with nutrition. The Upanishads, the mystic Vedas, bolstered wellness through fresh vegetables, the basis of health. To maintain stamina, Hindu housewives found ways of combining fruit, grain, legumes, and vegetables with herbs and roots, notably *ashwagandha*, a stress reliever, and *ramacham*, a purifier.

Ayurvedic texts promoted paired foods. Recipes featured palatable choices and advised plating hot servings in reasonable proportions to prevent gluttony. Families sought harmony in table atmosphere and chewed slowly to direct nutrients to needy parts of the body. In 1000 B.C.E., Ayurvedic texts compiled recipes for fragrant oils and restorative menus. At Varanasi around 800 B.C.E., Sushruta, a surgeon and clinician of Ayurvedic healing, compounded a butter-honey skin dressing that cleansed wounds. For purifying the body, cooks focused on greens and stews that combined dal, herbs, and rice, with vegetables.

Chinese Therapeutic Diets

Simultaneous with the rise of Indian Ayurvedic healing, Chinese herbologists focused on herbs and healthful staples. Around 2695 B.C.E., the Emperor Shennong (Shen Nung), the "Father of Chinese Medicine and Pharmacology," systematized consumer shopping and summarized the benefits of produce and condiments. A vegetarian, he combed the countryside for palatable healing ginseng and tested on himself the effects of ma huang tea and medicinal mushrooms. In a treatise, *Pen Tsao Kang Mu* (Chinese pharmacopoeia), he warned cooks of such plant poisons as aconite and mandrake. In 1122 B.C.E., aides of the Emperor Cheng Wang interviewed dietitians to superintend the imperial diet.

A collection of health lore and superstitions from the Zhou dynasty, the *Tao Te Ching* (*The Classic Way*, ca. 300 B.C.E.) named the nutraceuticals (nutritional pharmaceuticals) of the Chinese savant Laozi (Lao Tse). His philosophy of eating for longevity stressed the addition of herbs, mushrooms, nuts and seeds, and seaweed to greens and steamed root crops.

In medieval Asia, practicality outweighed arcane methodology. "Diet doctors" confirmed the consensus that spring rainwater and a hearty folk diet served the body better than the overdressed fare of court feasts. In 1368, Chia Ming, an aged politician from Zhejiang (Chekiang) Province, published *Essential Knowledge for Eating and Drinking*, a directive to the Ming dynasty on long life and health through preventive diet. Chinese culinary historian Li Shih Chen listed 1,800 hot and cold herbs and offered homemakers 18,000 recipes in *Compendium of Materia Medica* (1578), the outgrowth of a lifetime of research. From these beginnings, Chinese kitchen cures of the early twenty-first century maintain a dependence on such natural foods and beverages as *tang kuei* for female reproductive health and *ho shou wu*, an organ energizer.

Mediterranean Cures

Along the Mediterranean shores, domestic and monastic publications featured *gestivos* (digestive compounds). In 1550 B.C.E. at Luxor, Egypt, the Ebers papyri named chants and herbal dosages that improved blood flow to the heart. Recipes featured pantry staples—dates, grain, honey, milk, and oil—as well as cardamom, garlic, sesame seed, and tamarind, all beneficial to metabolism. The thorough study of restorative foods mentioned fenugreek and onions to relieve swelling, dill and beer to ease depression, and licorice to combat bloating and dyspepsia. The compilers showed special interest in causes of blindness, for which they prescribed roasted ox liver and pigs' eyes.

The first Greek clinical advisories advanced from food choices to meal preparation. Around 550 B.C.E., the Samian mathematician Pythagoras of Croton, the "Father of Vegetarianism," set the example of health foods for his community of disciples. He developed a strict code of exercise and meatless fare. His faith in healthful meals echoed that of a contemporary, Siddhartha Gautama (later, the Buddha), who promoted peaceful well-being with a ritual meal of milk and rice.

Greek dietitians educated Romans on fragrant unguents to stem disquiet and the preparation of liver to cure night blindness arising from a vitamin A deficiency. Imperial chefs prevented senility by serving watercress sprinkled with vinegar. After 54 C.E., the Emperor Nero trusted healing foods to preserve his talents. For singing and speaking, he commanded a daily serving of stewed leeks to shield his larynx and broaden his vocal range.

Roman encyclopedist Pliny the Elder, the compiler of *Natural History* (ca. 77 C.E.), amassed a range of data on a healing diet. He cited a recipe for frogs that healed diseased eyes and named lettuce and onions as deterrents to insomnia. He quoted Cato on the choice of curly cabbage over smooth for maximum energy. Pliny valued physic garden staples, particularly holly berries and ivy, and respected mead, but he reserved his strongest praise for grapes as "creating more for our benefit even than for our pleasure."

Medieval Herbology

In the early Christian era, monks and nuns cultivated plants as sources of food and treatment for the sick. They grew meadowsweet and dandelion alongside rhubarb, a dependable body purifier. For *De Cultura Hortarum* (*On Gardening,* ca. 840), Walafrid Strabo, a Frankish monk, researched fresh and dried plants at Reichenau Abbey on Lake Constance. His poetic descriptions pictured both fennel and pennyroyal as jolting energy to the intestines. Of the melon, he described the gush of juice and seeds as a delightful refreshment. For the treatment of ills, he prioritized cures for the stomach, the "king of the body."

Around 1140, St. Bernard of Clairvaux echoed Pliny and Strabo in relying on common herbs as inexpensive, easily tolerated cures for ailments. During a malaria outbreak, Bernard warned Italian Cistercians that pharmaceuticals threatened health and violated vows of poverty because of their high cost. His pointed comments hinted at disrespect for Benedictine monk-physicians, who violated the stoic philosophy of forbearance with their fraudulent medicines.

In homes, the treatment of invalids and the enfeebled fell on housewives. Into the Renaissance, women prepared meals and nostrums in the kitchen, the female nerve center of the house. Physic beds grew the leaves and fruits for broths, cordials, infusions, and tonics. A common gift to guests and travelers, evening possets of valerian promised untroubled sleep. The thrifty offered a glut of fresh and dried plants and roots for barter and sale or for distribution to the poor during epidemics.

American Frontier Curatives

When immigrants reached the New World, Amerindian shamans demonstrated oral traditions of 200 plant curatives, including willow bark and mayapple. In the Carolinas and Georgia, native doctors compounded bitters in oil to pour into the ear canal to ease stiff joints. The Cheyenne healed fevers with decoctions of black cherry and purple coneflower. For soothing digestion, medicine men prescribed a dish of wild yam or pokeweed greens; wild blueberries and sassafras tea heightened stamina and alertness. Native cooks taught pioneers to respect New World biota and their powers of nutrition and cure, including juniper tea for scurvy and blue cohosh for women's reproductive ills.

South of the Rio Grande, Indian cooks fermented agave hearts into *pulque,* an Indian beer that served as a standard analgesic for adults and children. In Mexican deserts, pulque rehydrated the body and sharpened senses. Throughout the Southwest, pioneers relied on whiskey to

quiet suffering and ease labor pains. Food cures were as close as a blackberry or elderberry bush or a pot of collard greens or dish of sauerkraut. Oatmeal water alleviated rash and sunburn. A single clove bud anesthetized an abscessed tooth.

Into the twenty-first century, folk dieting holds out hope against catastrophic ills as virulent as pancreatic cancer and as insidious as brain tumors. Regimens tend to extremes—such as protein but no carbohydrates or raw fruits and vegetables to the exclusion of gluten and white sugar. Physician-made menus ban hydrogenated fats and alcohol as well as red meat and prohibit smoking. Ironically, the health conscious often return to the curative dishes of the ancient world—raw vegetables and fruit juices and pure water from springs.

See also: Culpeper, Nicholas; Jacobean Diet and Cuisine; Lapérouse, Jean François Galaup; Liebig, Justus von; Lind, James; Physic Gardening; Pliny the Elder; Polo, Marco; Seacole, Mary Jane; Seaman's Diet and Cuisine; Seaweed; Shellfish; Taro; Theophrastus; Tofu; Virginia Company of Plymouth.

Further Reading

Kitchen Cures: Homemade Remedies for Your Health. New York: Reader's Digest, 2011.

Mitchem, Stephanie Y. *African American Folk Healing.* New York: New York University Press, 2007.

Parrish, Christopher C., Nancy J. Turner, and Shirley M. Solberg, eds. *Resetting the Kitchen Table: Food Security, Culture, Health and Resilience in Coastal Communities.* New York: Nova Science, 2008.

Wilkins, John M., and Shaun Hill. *Food in the Ancient World.* Malden, MA: Wiley-Blackwell, 2006.

Curing

Since ancient times, the processing of fish, fish roe, and meat by smoking, marinating, or dry rubbing with rock salt and sugar plus nitrates or nitrites has preserved fats and proteins and prolonged their use over long winters and hard times. In Babylonia, Greece, and Samaria, rock salt gained prominence in trade as a meat preservative. Around 590 B.C.E., Chinese sausage makers approached curing with a more complex recipe. They added bean sauce, ginger, green onions, and pepper to salted minced goat and lamb to produce a long-lived fermented sausage. For slaves, the curing of a onetime kill or fish seining extended wild game usage over months instead of days. The process suited the saving of a variety of game, from duck, hare, gazelle, and reindeer to smelt and whale blubber.

The Romans followed the curing principles of author Cato the Elder's *De Agricultura* (*On Agriculture,* ca. 160 B.C.E.) and regulated pork curing with guidelines to

A curemaster examines one of hundreds of raw hams coated in salt and brown sugar for aging in a cold curing facility in North Carolina. After curing for up to six months, the hams absorb flavor from a wood-fired smoker and then age for several months longer. *(MCT/Getty Images)*

protect the consumer. In the next century, the poet Varro reported that the Roman taste for cured meats fueled a thriving import business in Gallic ham. Julius Caesar's legionnaires, who dined on Gallic dry sausage, spread the popularity of cured meat throughout conquest lands. A recipe from the early empire listed honey, mustard, rock salt or saltpeter (potassium nitrate), vinegar, and water as a brine to preserve cooked meat.

The French continued to lead world production of preserved meats. Cooks evolved charcuterie, or pork preservation, for convenience. Curing increased the shelf life and storage stability of fresh pork as bacon, confit (coated meat), forcemeat, *galantine* (deboned stuffed meat), ham, pâté (meat spread), or terrine (meat loaf). Variety suited the French flair for adaptable foodstuffs that made appealing table presentations.

Drying and Smoking

Much of meat curing involves extracting fluids. Smoking combines dehydration of moist external tissue with the fumigation of insects and extermination of microbes in beef and pork, cheeses, haddock and salmon, malt whiskey, nuts, prunes, salt, and tea. The Romans mixed pork

sausage with garlic, onions, and pepper before stuffing into casings for smoking to shrink the finished product. Salt containing streaks of nitrate produced the most appealing pink tint.

Along the North Sea, medieval fishing crews turned smoked herring and stockfish into an industry. Despite the need for soaking, herring became the most popular pickled species for Scandinavian smorgasbords. Canada's Grand Banks and New England made a similar bonanza from rack-dried flounder and hake and from salt cod, which they marketed in eastern South America, West Africa, and the West Indies. By drying and salting fish, dealers drew out excess water, reducing the weight of their unscaled catch by up to 80 percent and simplifying packing and transport. The processing also softened pickerel and shad and made them easier to fillet. Restaurants served cured fish with potatoes as a means of balancing the salty taste.

Variance of heat sources permeated tissue with such identifiable flavors as applewood and mesquite in the United States and alder and oak, the choice for curing European lamb. Other substances—animal dung, aromatic spruce boughs, corncobs, peat, sawdust, whiskey-soaked hardwood chips—imparted unique flavors, whether applied at low or high temperatures in the closed quarters of a metal chamber smoker or walk-in smokehouse.

Cured Foods

A number of regional dishes evolved from cured specialties, notably Alaskan eulachon (candlefish), Chinese Jinhua ham, Egyptian *batarekh* (mullet roe), Romanian pastrami, Ecuadoran ceviches, Italian prosciutto and Toscano ham, Virginia ham, Faeroe cured mutton, Icelandic gravlax, Mexican shark and shrimp, and tender Montreal brisket. Brazilian cured poultry, a rarity among national preserved meats, defeated problems with salmonella, the main threat of chicken and duck sausage. Spanish Serrano and Iberian ham, made from rustic pigs, gained such a reputation for dry curing that the country currently produces some 40 million hams annually.

In the southeastern United States, the evolution of native barbecue in Texas and the Carolinas enabled the underclass to elevate cheap cuts of meats and their unique sweet-and-sour sauces to signature dishes. In the Appalachian hill country of the Carolinas and Georgia, families salted pork chines (backbones) in wood barrels and boxes in the proportion of 8 pounds (3.6 kilograms) of salt to 100 pounds (45 kilograms) of meat. The addition of 2 ounces (57 grams) each of black and red pepper and 1 quart (0.95 liter) of molasses plus borax to kill blowflies resulted in a mountain staple, salt-and-pepper ham. Some hung the cured meat in cloth bags; others buried it in cornmeal, hickory ashes, or shelled corn, all of which absorbed briny runoff.

Meat Processing

Nineteenth-century butchers increased the penetration of brine or stabilizing nitrite pickle by injecting solutions into animal muscles or arteries with a perforated needle. To prevent gray areas and soured meat near the bone, industrial food processors enhanced circulation of curative liquids by piercing a haunch with a rank of needles. By hand massaging or tumbling the meat, the processor broke down membranes and increased distribution of the pickle or marinade throughout tissues. In 1917, George F. Doran patented the first U.S. nitrite curing process, a system that enhanced meat savor.

Sausage, a Hungarian and Polish delicacy, derived its texture and taste from salt and vinegar, which slowed oxidation and the growth of bacteria. German sausage makers boosted the flavor with juniper berries and branches on the cook fire. French guilds developed techniques of preserving coarsely chopped salt pork as forcemeat pressed into intestinal casings. To ensure quality, makers inserted pieces of former batches into the mix to inoculate bacteria.

Butchers sold sausage in two forms, uncooked and cooked or ready-to-eat. More refined chopped meat required baking in a mold as pâté or terrine, which chefs served cold on antipasto platters along with boiled eggs, pickles, and raw vegetables. Similar delicacies, the galantine and roulade involved pounding poultry and rolling it in skin for poaching in liquid.

Sugaring with dextrose, honey, lactose, or corn or maple syrup altered the flavor of streaked pork belly to produce bacon. Cooks buoyed the bacon industry by serving the meat boiled or fried, by sprinkling bacon bits on salads and baked Idaho potatoes, and by using it to lard pheasant, roasts, and venison or to wrap around blander meats, including meat loaf and scallops. A leaner cut, Canadian bacon, or back bacon, comes from the boneless pork loin.

More invasive of the taste and appearance of meat than flavorings, nitrates and nitrites suppress *Clostridium botulinum* spores (which cause botulism) and oxidation and enhance the color of red tissue. U.S. Food and Drug Administration studies of the formation of nitrosamines in 1972 established that bologna, corned beef, hot dogs, pepperoni, and salami contain carcinogens that can cause leukemia in children and colorectal cancer and emphysema in adults. Nonetheless, smoked meat still accounts for 30 percent of the U.S. meat market. In October 2011, the World Cancer Research Fund continued to warn that consumption of 50 grams of processed meat per day upped bowel cancer risk by 20 percent.

See also: Amerindian Diet; Barbecue; Jerky; Pemmican; Pork; Salt; Sausage; Smoked Food.

Further Reading

Aberle, Elton David, John C. Forrest, David E. Gerrard, and Edward W. Mills. *Principles of Meat Science.* Dubuque, IA: Kendall/Hunt, 2001.

Gisslen, Wayne. *Professional Cooking.* Hoboken, NJ: John Wiley & Sons, 2007.

Marianski, Stanley, Adam Marianski, and Robert Marianski. *Meat Smoking and Smokehouse Design.* Seminole, FL: Bookmagic, 2009.

Pegg, Ronald B., and Fereidoon Shahidi. *Nitrite Curing of Meat: The N-Nitrosamine Problem and Nitrite Alternatives.* Trumbull, CT: Food & Nutrition, 2000.

Toldrá, Fidel, ed. *Handbook of Fermented Meat and Poultry.* Ames, IA: Blackwell, 2007.

Currency, Food as

By association, food currencies have, from ancient times, allied the exact worth of edibles with other commodities, from land to armor and weapons, boats, slaves, and wives. For the Babylonians, barley equaled cash; for Mongolians, tea bricks liquidated easily into currency. Far to the north, Norwegians entered the Middle Ages with an economy based on butter and dried cod.

The cannibals of Borneo, Ecuador, and Peru retained human skulls as money and shrank the craniums to make them easier to carry. New Guinean women arrived at markets with bundles of banana leaves, the indispensable cooking sheaths that flavored pit-roasted meals. In Japan and the Philippines, into the seventh century C.E., shoppers carried purses of rice until copper coins replaced grains as money. After the establishment of the West Indian cane fields in the eighteenth century, barterers in Barbados, Jamaica, and the Leeward Islands bought goods with leaf tobacco, twists of chewing tobacco, and loaf sugar.

The variety of foods used as money derives from local tastes and available commodities, such as pemmican among Amerindians, corn as "country money" in colonial New England, and tulip bulbs, the edible commodity that saved the Dutch from starvation during World War II. In ancient Russia and Scandinavia, Sami and Siberians paid blood money, bride prices, court fines, and taxes with cheese and reindeer. Farther west, Caucasians used cattle or oxen as cash, a system paralleling the trade in livestock among the Anakalang, Lamboya, and Lauli of Sumba, Indonesia. At Darwaz, cakes of dried mulberry, leaf tobacco, sugar, tea bricks, and vodka equated as Afghan currency. As late as 1917 and the end of the Romanov czarist dynasty, isolated Russian peasants exchanged pots of jam for goods and services.

African Commodities

African vendors bartered with cowrie shells and feathers as well as kola nuts and salt cakes or cylinders. In the 600s B.C.E., Egyptians determined bridewealth in household goods as well as livestock. Negotiated between the bride's father and the groom, the *shep en sehemet* (marriage contract) determined the types and amounts of gifts that would cement a social and political union of families that suited male ambitions.

After 500 C.E., the coconut contributed another form of food currency, which spread across the Mediterranean and Polynesia as far north as Kaho'olawe, Hawaii's smallest island, and south to the Nicobar Islands. Food assets stabilized familial relations and ensured that the bride could count on a long marriage untroubled by desertion or nonsupport.

Before coinage in sub-Saharan Africa, Kenyan, Madagascan, Tanzanian, and Ugandan traders set their monetary standards on the worth of cattle and goats as well as grain and beer. Other folk currencies included spotted peas, salt, and tobacco in the Cameroon; gin and yams in Nigeria; brick or slab salt in Abyssinia, Ethiopia, Mali, and Zambia; and camels and millet among the Somali. Guinea established a unique economy based on black pepper and rice; Liberia relied on palm kernels and oil. The Sudanese bartered with millet, onions, tobacco, livestock and poultry, and salt bars. Libyans became the only African traders to value corn as money.

Edible fish and mammals supported currencies readily converted into meals. Mozambique traded in a wide variety of goods, including dogs, ducks, and chickens. In the 1930s, Lord William Malcolm Hailey, a supervisor of British colonies, foresaw the depletion of pastures from too many animals penned up in readiness for trade. In his treatise *African Survey: A Study of Problems Arising in Africa South of the Sahara* (1938), Hailey proposed to rescue arable land by replacing livestock money with coins incised with individual likenesses of cows and goats to indicate worth; however, the imposition of a symbolic coinage failed to eradicate the centuries-old system. Even in the 1980s, Angolans lost faith in the *kwanza* currency and regressed to trade in Beck's, Heineken, or Stella Artois beer.

Salt Money

Because of the necessity of salt to humans and domesticated animals, traders from China and India to the Black Sea, Burma, and New Guinea traveled salt routes across deserts and seas and used salt in barter to even out swaps. Mine slaves on the Dnieper River delta who set ocean water to evaporate in shallow depressions lived a miserable existence as caustic substances inflamed their eyes, lungs, and skin. Into the Iron Age at Cheshire, East Anglia, Salinae, Teeside, Tyneside, and Worcestershire, British salt making provided granular currency through grueling labor.

History provides scenarios in which slaves turned salt into cash. In 1275, Marco Polo observed salt boiling along the Yalu and Yangtze rivers and, in Tibet, the stamping of salt cakes with the khan's imperial logo, which set the value at 2¢ each. Mid-fourteenth-century travel writer Ibn Battuta of Tangiers compiled eyewitness accounts of Malian salt makers evaporating brackish water and loading salt slabs on camels for trade at Walata, in southeastern Mauritania.

After the Romans abandoned the *pecus* (cow) for other forms of *pecunia* (money), their carters wore a trail known as the Via Salaria (Salarian Way) to the artificial port of Ostia for trade throughout the Mediterranean. Their goods served soldiers as *salarium argentum* (salt money), a salt allowance that doubled as cash in remote parts of the empire. Additional evidence of salt money in Abyssinia, India, and Tibet suggests a widespread buying power of the food additive. From sharp-eyed dealers came the equal-armed *libra*, or balance-beam scale, a device that weighed salt and other food money via gravity in a *bilanx* (paired pans), source of the word *balance*.

From Salt to Spice and Cocoa

By the fall of Rome, the world shifted away from grain and salt to the more lucrative spice trade, the economic fulcrum of the Middle Ages. In 410 C.E., Alaric I ransomed Rome in exchange for 1.5 tons (1.4 metric tons) of pepper, the prime ingredient in Gothic sausage. By 412, his Visigoths set up an annual pepper tithe of 300 pounds

(140 kilograms). Exchange in the lightweight grains made transport easy to places where the exchange rate advanced to higher profits than Alaric could expect from ordinary plunder.

New World money systems similarly relied on easily borne edible currency. After 1000 B.C.E., the Olmec cultivated cacao, which originated along the Amazon and Orinoco rivers. By 100 C.E., the Aztec and Maya revered cocoa beans as aphrodisiacs, food, money, and symbols of deity. The Aztecs of Guatemala carried purses of cocoa beans to farmer's markets to buy beans, bread, and meat. Wealthy Mesoamericans guarded screw-top jars filled with chocolate patties, their money in the bank.

In 1519, Spanish conquistador Hérnan Cortés recognized government control of cacao planting as a means of halting inflation. At Aguadulce, Panama, customs agents guarded the local treasury, which was stacked with bags of cocoa beans. In 1712, Brazil's economy maintained the food currency system by paying military salaries in cocoa beans as well as cloves, sugar, and tobacco. Guatemalans continued carrying the beans as pocket change, along with eggs, another transportable exchange medium.

In Ireland, trade in females as currency suited a primitive Druidic society. The arrival of St. Patrick in the 400s B.C.E. introduced a Christian humanity that forbade enslavement. To replace bondage as money, before 465 C.E., the Irish accepted the *Senchus Mor,* the law code of St. Benignus, who compiled tables of equivalents. According to his calculations, the former price of one woman equaled 5,184 wheat kernels, 72 sheep, 18 heifers, or three cows. The agrarian monetary system dominated barter until the advent of metal coins in the 700s.

See also: Animal Husbandry; Chocolate; Manioc; Pemmican; Salt.

Further Reading

Biggs, Barton M. *Wealth, War & Wisdom.* Hoboken, NJ: John Wiley & Sons, 2009.

Burnham, Terry, and Jay Phelan. *Mean Genes: From Sex to Money to Food, Taming Our Primal Instincts.* Cambridge, MA: Perseus, 2000.

Gintis, Herbert. *Moral Sentiments and Material Interests: The Foundations of Cooperation in Economic Life.* Cambridge, MA: MIT Press, 2005.

Kurlansky, Mark. *Salt: A World History.* New York: Penguin, 2003.

Snodgrass, Mary Ellen. *Coins and Currency: An Historical Encyclopedia.* Jefferson, NC: McFarland, 2007.

Curry

A cooking tradition based on coriander, cumin, and turmeric, curry encompasses a complex food culture from Pakistan to Southeast Asia. Curry derives from the mortars and pestles of Mohenjo Daro, a settlement in the Indus Valley dating to about 2600 B.C.E., where tamarind pods, cumin, fennel, and mustard were ground into a cooking powder. A bit farther north, their contemporaries, the Harappans, harvested cardamom, pepper, and turmeric, which they added to the region's gastronomy. By 1700 B.C.E., the beginnings of curry cuisine reached Sumer, where temple cooks offered spiced meat to the god Marduk.

The term curry, which originally meant "sauce," entered English in *Forme of Cury (Forms of Cookery,* ca. 1390), compiled by the chef of Richard II. Etymologists surmise that the word crossed the spice route from India, first as the Tamil word *kari,* translated into English as "cury." To Indians, curry identified a pungent or astringent gravy made in the pot juices of fish, fruit, herbs, legumes, meats, spices, and vegetables. To the English, curry was an additive to a finished dish.

Curry actualizes the Ayurvedic concept of balancing hot with cold and wet with dry, a dietary method once used to boost intelligence and to treat diabetes. Recipes incorporate the vibrant taste and aroma of roasted whole spices into vegetable, fish, and meat dishes served with flatbread.

Across Asia, curries vary in flavor and degree of heat. The Telugu cookery of southeastern India generates fragrance and intensity with combinations of anise, bay leaf, black pepper, chilies, cinnamon, clove, nutmeg, and leaves of the Indian curry tree (*Murraya koenigii*). A more distinctive taste derives in Bangladesh and Bengal from additions of mustard and poppy seeds. In southwestern India at Karnataka, cooks temper spice with coconut and jaggery, an unrefined cane sugar. The dairy-based fare of Kashmir calls for more piquant ghee (clarified butter) and a yogurt and rice base.

Other variants typify regional curries, such as the garlic and tomato dishes of Pakistan, the ginger and onion flavors of Punjabi cuisine, and the simpler, unenhanced foodways of the Pashtun around Kabul, Afghanistan. The Tamil of Sri Lanka broaden their cookery with the tastes of central India plus fenugreek, rosewater, and tamarind, a sour fruit pulp. Indian recipes influence Chinese entrées, which temper peppers and onions with hot sauce and soy sauce. Burmese curries tend toward fresh onion and chili paste. Japanese curry favors the taste of pickled vegetables and spices purchased in brick form. The subtle essences of Kaffir lime and lemongrass combine with shrimp paste and tamarind in Indonesian meals. The Vietnamese render curry as a soup flavored with cilantro and green onions. In Samoa, curry is a luxury spice enlivening bland breadfruit or taro.

From centuries of exploiting Asian conquests, the British established their own version of curry, a mongrelization that continues to raise issues of political correctness. The taste first tingled their mouths in the seventeenth century with the exploits of the British East India

Company. In a historic cookbook, Hannah Glasse's *The Art of Cookery Made Plain and Easy* (1747), Asian recipes listed only coriander and pepper as elements of curry. Later editions included ginger and the traditional yellow of turmeric, but not hot chilies.

In the early 1800s, indentured Indian nationals worked colonial plantations in Africa, the Caribbean, and Southeast Asia. For a taste of home, they carried with them stashes of curry powder. At each site, locals adapted Indian flavorings to local foodstuffs, such as the rum that West Indians added to curry sauce.

By 1837, Lea & Perrins, a British-made liquid condiment fermented by apothecaries, offered a curry additive and appetite stimulant in simple drop form known as Worcestershire Sauce. Not until Isabella Mary Beeton published *Mrs. Beeton's Book of Household Management* (1861) did British curry achieve its savory bonanza from the addition of allspice, cayenne, cinnamon, fenugreek, and mustard. The collection recommended that cooks obtain seasonings in powder form from a spice shop.

Through colonial fusion cookery, curry influenced the beef and seafood restaurants of Guyana, Jamaica, Tobago, and Trinidad. A German invention, currywurst dates to the cookery of housewife Herta Heuwer in postwar Germany in September 1949, when city workers removing the bombing rubble bought street food for lunch. The recipe involved the spicing of slices of grilled pork sausage with curry ketchup and curry powder, a cult snack featured by wayside food trucks and stand-up snack shops in Berlin.

By the 1950s, British curry sauces also incorporated fennel, paprika, raisins, and vinegar. In the following decades, cookbooks, magazines, travel guides, and gourmet clubs encouraged experimentation with regional Indian gastronomy. Snack trays displayed hearty curried finger foods—shrimp satay, spicy cheddar bites, curried corn fritters and deviled eggs, and lamb wontons. In May 1991, English gourmand Pat Chapman, a noted food writer, issued the first Curry Awards to England's top curry restaurants. One venue, Madhu's Southall in Hilton Park Lane, London, won the award in 2001, 2004, 2006, and 2007.

Nutritional studies of the twenty-first century have examined the bioactivity of curcuminoids found in turmeric. Research links curry with the control of arthritis and the prevention of the protein plaque that causes Alzheimer's disease and the carcinogens that generate colorectal cancer. Unlike pharmaceuticals, which overtax the liver and kidneys, curry produces no known side effects.

Practitioners of Ayurvedic medicine value the curry leaf for stimulating the digestive and immune systems and alleviating inflammation and the disfigurement of psoriasis. Additional claims of muscle regeneration, protection from pesticides, treatment of cystic fibrosis and sexually transmitted disease, and antimetastatic action against breast tumors and skin cancer currently boost

dietary use of Indian cooking styles dating back 5,000 years.

See also: Fast Food; Heritage Foods; Lunch; Mustard.

Further Reading

Collingham, Lizzie. *Curry: A Tale of Cooks and Conquerors.* New York: Oxford University Press, 2006.

Iyer, Raghavan. *660 Curries.* New York: Workman, 2008.

Kessler, Roman. "The Craze over Currywurst." *Wall Street Journal,* August 27, 2009.

Madavan, Vijay. *Cooking the Indian Way.* Minneapolis, MN: Lerner, 2002.

Monroe, Jo. *Star of India: The Spicy Adventures of Curry.* Chichester, UK: John Wiley & Sons, 2005.

Cussy, Louis, Marquis de (1766–1837)

Culinary writer and food historian Louis, Marquis de Cussy, respected cuisine as a microcosm of human experience. Born to wealth, he ran an exacting Paris kitchen. Fine cooks gravitated to him for his command of roasting and sauces, which he dubbed "enlightened chemistry."

The chef vilified the stultifying menus of classical Greece and Rome and disdained the decorative fare of the court of Louis XIV. Instead, he touted the expertise of middle-class Parisian caterers, especially in preparing spring and summer vegetables. His political observations credited the Reformation as a backlash of Christians against too many Catholic fast days. Among his regrets, he named the fragmentation of the French wine country during the revolution of 1789.

Cussy squandered a fortune on a gracious table decked with fine food. His weekly dinners accommodated no more than 11 guests. He based quality cooking on mushrooms in dry wine and regarded truffles as the "diamonds of the kitchen." His table behavior began with abstemious portions and sips of liqueurs and halted before he reached satiation. He declared that he could cure gout easily through such controlled diet.

Cussy's first coup as a celebrity chef came from the patronage of Marie Antoinette. From attendance on her table, he presented French royalty specialty chicken dishes, which he basted solely with butter. He honored the *jésuite* (turkey) and regaled tablemates with the history of a Paraguayan turkey imported by Jesuits for the wedding feast of Charles IX and Elisabeth of Austria in 1570. Cussy's praise of rivals established his interest in food done right rather than building his own reputation. In 1804, at age 38, he entered the household of diplomat Charles Maurice de Talleyrand, a noted gourmand, as pastry chef under head chef Boucher.

During his rise to prominence, Cussy served Napoleon I as palace prefect. The emperor was indifferent to food and expected unscheduled meals of cutlets and roast fowl, with hot coffee served at the table rather than in the salon after dinner. He especially appreciated the chef's innovative kidney bean salad in oil. Cussy honored Lent with a favorite onion soup, which required the frying of tiny bulbs in butter to a hint of gold. He finished the dish with a bit of sugar, broth, cognac, and buttered bread for thickener. The soup preceded his favorite combination, salmon with asparagus.

Cussy served the emperor as escort for the Empress Marie Louise to Vienna. Upon returning to the Tuileries, he discovered his patronage at an end following Napoleon's political demise at Waterloo in 1815. Cussy won a pardon as a Bonapartist from Louis XVIII by soaking the king's strawberries in champagne and cream.

On his deathbed, Cussy chose his favorite poultry, red partridges, as a last meal. He surveyed food history in "L'Art Culinaire," issued in an 1843 compendium, *Les Classiques de la Table* (*Table Classics*). He showcased his dishes in sparkling prose, the hallmark of a new era of table conversationalists and food writers. Among the chef's beliefs towered a faith in gastronomy and hospitality as emblems of a nation's greatness.

Further Reading

Kelly, Ian. *Cooking for Kings: The Life of Antonin Carême, the First Celebrity Chef.* New York: Walker, 2003.

Young, Carolin C. *Apples of Gold in Settings of Silver: Stories of Dinner as a Work of Art.* New York: Simon & Schuster, 2002.

Customs, Food

Food preparation lies at the core of many of the world's folk and religious customs—for example, the sharing of *syllabub,* a sweet brandy punch with whipped cream on top that Charlestonian cooks ladle into cups at Christmas; the mischievous pouring of tea down the backs of diners at a Laotian New Year's banquet; and the festive cinnamon cup that Nazareth's Arab women steep and serve visitors to a birthing chamber. Newfoundlanders cook a jiggs dinner of salt beef and peas pudding to serve at a scoff, a gathering for eating, dancing, singing, and storytelling.

The Eid al-Fitr, a three- or four-day celebration of the end of Ramadan, begins at dawn with dates or another sweet fruit before Muslim prayers for forgiveness and mercy. Devout Bangladeshis, Burmese, and Fijians take their sweet fruit with milk and spaghetti. A gathering of friends and relatives in Tunisia begins with special biscuits and baklava. Saudi Arabians distribute gift candy to children and deposit rice and staples at the doors of the poor.

Kitchen preparations commonly accompany and enhance life passages. In India, women cater to pregnant women by preparing tempting dishes equal to the number of months of pregnancy. The extra kitchen work readies the mother for bearing a well-rounded baby or for

a peaceful passage to the afterlife if she should die in childbirth. In Indonesia, cooks steam rice and spread a *rijstaffel* (rice table) to celebrate a first birthday. At funerals, the Laguna of New Mexico expect food sharing. Clan members spread a table to feed grave diggers.

Food from the Gods

For religious rituals, food preparation and service typically follow age-old formalities, a culturally stabilizing influence. In India, Hindus sing hymns that characterize the importance of sacral meals and the soma plant to healing and wellness. In the Vajasaneya Samhita (Black Vedas, ca. 600 B.C.E.), a prayer for food supplies a pantry list of common staples:

> May for me prosper, through the sacrifice, milk, sap, ghee, honey, eating and drinking at the common table, plowing, rains, conquest, victory, wealth, riches. May for me prosper, through the sacrifice, low-grade food, freedom from hunger, rice, barley, sesame, kidney beans, vetches, wheat, lentils, millet, panicum grain, and wild rice.

Prose liturgy advises the worshipper on rites to win the heart of the god Brahman to ensure a pantry supplied with a variety of edibles.

Tradition links special dishes with the propitiation of gods as though they were banquet guests. In Sanur, Bali, barefoot women prepare festal bowls of fruit, duck, and rice cakes. In procession, they move toward one of the island's Buddhist temples bearing heavy loads on their heads. At Tulikup, Bali, a similar religious parade ends a 3-mile (4.8-kilometer) walk to the Indian Ocean, where participants join in the yearly purification of the sea. At the completion of their honorarium, they share the bowls of delicacies.

In China, Confucius, a sixth-century sage, recognized an earthly need for preparing and sharing dishes. He respected good cooking and elevated cuisine to prime importance as a social unifier and harmonizer. He believed that group rituals teach virtue. Like the Hebrew Passover and the Christian *agape* (love feast), Chinese temple ritual required communal sampling of food platters. In his *Analects,* Confucius insisted that the meals be fresh, flavorful, and properly blended. He spurned fussy manners and showy banquets in favor of well-cooked peasant entrées of polished white rice, finely chopped meat, and sauce.

Chinese Customs

A festive time for the Chinese occurred over an extensive celebration of the Lunar New Year, a tradition eventually shared by Japanese, Koreans, Malaysians, and Vietnamese. For a month, the Chinese rested and displayed affection and forgiveness in the form of conversation. Because servants went home during the holiday, families stocked pantries with easily prepared goods for themselves and callers. With their tea, they served their favorite spring roll or egg roll, which got its name from the season of the year it marked.

During the Ming dynasty, which began in 1368, cooks shaped dumplings like gold coins to guarantee prosperity. Other foods acquired significance for puns on their names: *lin ngau* (lotus root), which sounds like "every year there will be abundance"; *hoe see fat choy* (dried oysters in seaweed), a homophone for "good business" and "prosperity"; *saang choy* (scallops stir-fried with lettuce), a soundalike for "growing fortune"; and *yu* (fish), a play on the word *desire*.

New Year cookery requires planning for the wide array of sweet cakes, lychees and candies, and main dishes chosen for their color and shape, such as green spinach and snowpea shoots to symbolize money and round buns to resemble coins. Chinese homemakers shape bite-size dumplings and pot stickers and mold moon cakes with a bean paste filling, scalloped edges, and an embossed symbol of the moon goddess. They harmonize table presentations with shades of red and gold, symbolic of luck and wealth. Eating an entire fowl traditionally promotes wholeness; fish advances prospects of marriage.

Asian Holiday Preparations

New Year's cuisine has influenced other parts of Asia as well. Because the Tet holiday means a time of rest, Vietnamese cooks prepare ahead *banh tet,* a boxy rice cake encasing mung beans and pork and wrapped in banana leaves. In Malaysia, families pickle vegetables, a chore prefaced by the grinding of spices and slicing and blanching of root crops, which Chinese immigrants eat at the New Year and island Muslims serve at Ramadan.

In Japan, New Year's calls for drying shiitake mushrooms and pounding rice for *mochi* (glutinous rice) desserts in advance of the holiday display of three large round cakes. On New Year's morning, housewives serve red rice and special taro soup, also cooked the night before to prevent having to light the stove on a holiday. In the afternoon, relatives visit to feast. In place of an old-style house-to-house procession, celebrants gather at one table. On the last day of the seven-day holiday, cooks make seven-herb soup for supper. The next morning, they reduce the menu to tea and beans. On the fourteenth day after New Year's, the cook shapes mochi into squares and rectangles and puts coins into round cakes that hang on branches in the kitchen and stable and on the front door. For distant kin and friends, housewives send gifts of mushrooms, rice, and mochi.

Mediterranean Food Ritual

In ancient Greece, celebrants of the grape offered food at altars dedicated to wine making. For the late February feast of Anthesteria, a first flowering and coming-of-age ritual, Athenian worshippers honored Dionysus, the god

Recipe: Panspermia

Soak a handful each of common beans, lentils, peas, corn, and bulgur wheat in water overnight. Parboil in fresh water for ten minutes. Drain, add fresh water, and cook for an hour. Sweat two cloves of garlic and one large chopped onion in olive oil. Mix the ingredients, adding 1 cup of red wine and enough water to cover, and stew for 45 minutes. Add the juice of one lemon, pepper, and sea salt and bring to a boil. Serve with toppings of snipped dill or parsley and more lemon juice, bread, and cheese.

of wine, and his son Pan, a goat-footed sprite. The holiday immortalized Ikarios, the introducer of wine in Attica whom Dionysus transformed into a star. The period gave its name to the month of Anthesterion, the time of flowering and of unsealing and tasting the new wine.

Activities began the first day with the opening of the *pithoi* (wine jars). On the second day, libations poured from the 3-quart (2.8-liter) *khous* (pitcher) preceded heavy imbibing. On the third day, the devout stewed fruit in a large earthenware casserole and carried the dish to the altar to pour into a pit. The fruit pleased Hermes, the messenger linking the living with the dead. Another dish, *panspermia,* a honeyed gruel of vegetables and grains, treated deceased ancestors and honored the Earth Mother.

In the style of its Greek neighbors, Italy produced its own cookery customs based on family and community values. In Abruzzo during the Renaissance, the celebration of family milestones and such patriotic and religious occasions as the feast of Saint Antonio of Abate on January 17 and the distribution of *panis benedictus* (holy bread) on the first Sunday in May coincided with an all-night festival known as a *panarda.* The spread of 30 to 60 courses—traditional antipasti, herbed omelets, pasta, fried fish and game, sausages, cheese and bread, and desserts—along with complementary wines demanded that women work rapidly to preserve freshness in ingredients. Served to men only, the food bash included singing and celebrating.

New World Feasting

In the seventeenth century, culinary history acquired the written observations of Europeans newly arrived in the Americas. In the Peruvian Andes, poet and chronicler Garcilaso de la Vega's *Comentarios Reales de los Incas (The Royal Commentaries of the Incas,* 1609–1617) summarized native behaviors from an aboriginal perspective. His people's rivals, the Huanca of the Xauxa River valley of Peru, worshipped dogs, which native cooks raised, fattened, and sacrificed at ritual feasts.

Quechua-speaking natives shared their foodstuffs with the less fortunate. To aid the hungry, housewives organized a food collection feast. Before pouring mugs of *chicha,* a ritual corn beer flavored with berries, the hostess brought baskets and draped a serape or poncho on the veranda to receive donated staples. At the end of the drinking fest, the needy homemaker joined in a thanksgiving prayer and gathered items to store in her kitchen. The principle of gift giving respected fate and reciprocity: "Today, this is for you; tomorrow, it may be for me."

In the southeastern United States, the Cherokee liquefied a caffeinated black drink from parched holly (*yaupon* or *dahoon*) leaves, the main beverage at an annual Green Corn Dance. Because the bitter tea purged the stomach, bladder, and liver, the black drink centered purification rites, which concluded with steaming the body in a sweat lodge. Similar cleansing rituals employed emetic beverages prepared by Alabama, Creek, and Huron practitioners. European colonists attempted to add the black drink to their diet but abandoned it in favor of tea and coffee.

In the Massachusetts Bay Colony, the Puritans of Boston arranged to feed the family without violating the Sabbath. To ready dishes on Saturday evenings, they filled the bean pot, a lidded ceramic casserole settled near the dying fire at sundown. Its bulbous shape enhanced the mingling of bean flavor with layers of salt pork and molasses. The building of brick ovens added to the one-dish meal other slow-cooked regional specialties, including berry cobbler; pandowdy, a deep-dish sweetened apple dessert; and slump, savory stewed fruit with biscuit topping.

See also: Holiday Dishes and Festival Foods; Idiocuisine; Polo, Marco; Tea; Tea Ceremony.

Further Reading

Broomfield, Andrea. *Food and Cooking in Victorian England: A History.* Westport, CT: Greenwood, 2007.

Freedman, Paul H. *Food: The History of Taste.* Berkeley: University of California Press, 2007.

Houston, Lynn Marie. *Food Culture in the Caribbean.* Westport, CT: Greenwood, 2005.

Zanger, Mark. *The American Ethnic Cookbook for Students.* Santa Barbara, CA: ABC-Clio, 2001.

Ziegelman, Jane. *97 Orchard: An Edible History of Five Immigrant Families in One New York Tenement.* New York: Smithsonian/HarperCollins, 2010.

Dairy Food

Dairy products derive from processing the milk from buffalo, camels, cows, goats, horses, llamas, reindeer, sheep, yaks, and zebras. Because of the refreshing taste and high nutrient content of milk products, cultures such as the Khoikhoi of southern Africa, the Masai of East Africa, and Tunisians of North Africa value dairy foods, either raw or cooked, as integral parts of national diet and cuisine. The dairier's efficient use of the environment sustains the pastoral life, even on unpromising soil, such as that of northern Greece, the Australian interior, and the Navajo herding lands of the Four Corners (Arizona, Colorado, New Mexico, and Utah).

After neolithic hunter-gatherers in Germany, Iraq, and southeastern Turkey shifted from nomadism and a heavy wild game meat diet to raising domestic animals around 9000 B.C.E., they discovered the value of herding and dairying as a steady, reliable source of food. The symbiotic relationship between humankind and herd advanced in 8000 B.C.E., when herders in India raised zebu for meat and evolved dairy foods from cows. Transport, which began with knotted skins, improved with the use of bladder and stomach bags introduced by the Tuareg of the Sahara and the nomads of Anatolia and the Caucasus. In Iran, innovations to the New Stone Age diet advanced the taming of goats as herd animals, as pictured in colored frescos of milking and churning cream into butter, a luxury food. Balearic Islanders and Corsicans advanced coagulation with fig tree sap and thistle buds; the British used bedstraw. Farther west, Berber *smen* (fermented butter) in North Africa became the basis for frying other foods.

Originally a Sumerian product of buffalo, camel, cow, ewe, goat, reindeer, or yak milk, yogurt coagulated naturally in the pouches that nomads shaped from sheep stomachs as early as 6000 B.C.E. By the 1600s B.C.E., Hammurabi II regulated dairy sales as stringently as he did butchering. Blended with wild herbs for Balkan sour soups and in bulgur (cracked wheat) and millet balls, the combination of yogurt with other flavors appealed to the Fulani of Nigeria.

Historic Innovations

Where goats, horses, and sheep adapted to rough terrain, female dairy maids developed other milk variants that diversified Middle Eastern cuisine. Russians sipped liquid yogurt like buttermilk. Scythians, according to the Greek historian Herodotus, invented koumiss, the world's first fast food, from curdled mare's milk. They maintained a stable of lactating mares to produce milk for a fermented drink valued as an aphrodisiac and cure-all.

Buddhist, Hindu, and Jainist scripture set the tone and style of the peasant diet with ghee (clarified butter), an emollient integral to anointing and burial rituals. Ghee appeared in the Akkadian-Sumerian *Epic of Gilgamesh* (ca. 1800 B.C.E.) and in India and Pakistan in the Rig-Veda (1200 B.C.E.) as a skillet lubricant and fuel for holy lamps. The milk solids, smeared on bread, produced a simple daily meal. Heritage foods from the early Israelite culture in 1200 B.C.E. centered on barley bread and dairy items from goats and sheep. In Homeric Ionia, the invention of the woven rush cheese strainer facilitated the removal of whey from soft goat curds. In the *Iliad* (eighth century B.C.E.), a healer grated cheese into restorative Pramnian wine during the Greek siege of Troy.

Around 800 B.C.E., the Baudhayana Sutra, a collection of manuals on behavior, warned the Hindu devout to keep silent, sit with crossed legs each evening, and eat sparingly of grains and dairy products, both easily digested. For sacramental gifts, the devout purchased milk products rather than meat, which Hindus denounced for causing death to animals that would otherwise continue producing nourishing dairy food.

Pastoral Cuisine

People in temperate zones relished dairy products unavailable in tropical climes, primarily because there were no meadows for pasturing herds. In India, cooks turned to milk and chickpeas to make halvah, a dense confection suited to hospitality and dinner parties. In China from 200 B.C.E., cooks mixed rice with frozen milk for an early sherbet. Romans mocked Iberian cooking with butter and based Italian meals on smoked Ligurian and Tuscan cheese wheels with *punicum* (flatcake) paired with olives, a Mediterranean staple. Gala dinners ended with gelato, a honey- and snow-based dessert and forerunner of Renaissance ice cream in Arabia, Egypt, France, Iraq, and Syria.

Early medieval dairiers in Benedictine and Cistercian monasteries in the Alps and throughout northwestern

A Tibetan nomad milks a yak at a pasture in Qinghai Province, China. Tibetan nomads make their living from livestock and their products, which also form an integral part of the herders' diet. *(China Photos/Getty Images)*

Europe preserved artisanal cheese making, including Port du Salut, named for an abbey. Monk-made milk products surprised Charlemagne with the sharp taste of molded sheep cheese. The monks' recipes favored compressed curd products as a substitute for forbidden meats and extended their shelf life by brining, cellaring, drying, or smoking. According to the Avesta (ca. 530 C.E.), the Zoroastrian scripture composed during the Sassanid dynasty, the prophet Zarathustra lived on cheese for two decades to prepare for his ministry. In Ireland, the devout honored Saint Brigid with spreads of dairy foods and gorged on milk products, eggs, and meat before Lent. The eleventh-century medical school dietary guide *Regimen Sanitatis Salernitanum (Code of Health of the School of Salernum)* treated depression with dairy products. In Poland, icehouses extended the shelf life of fresh butter, milk, and yogurt as well as of cheese rounds, which peasants used in lieu of cash to pay church tithes.

In the late thirteenth century, Marco Polo cited popular recipes of nomadic Mongolian hunter-gatherers. Lacking settled farmland, they relied heavily on the milk of ewes and mares. He described fermented milk as a pleasant drink that satisfied his hunger. In 1215, Genghis Khan credited koumiss, yogurt made from mare's milk, with boosting the efficiency of his soldiers, who conquered Mongolia. Polo's dictated writings described sun-dried milk as an on-the-march paste consumed by the Tatar forces of Kublai Khan from 10-pound (4.5-kilogram) packs. In the 1500s, Spanish colonists added milk products to the largely vegetarian Aztec regimen. Contrary to tastes in Catalonia and Provence, chefs in central France enamored of butter added it in one-third of their recipes.

Haute Cuisine, Desserts, and Processed Foods

Following the popularity of simple clabber among highland Scots and whey drinks in coffeehouses in the mid-1700s, sweet French dessert cheeses and festive custard and berry ice cream in London cookbooks migrated to the colonial tables of Benjamin Franklin, Martha and Thomas Jefferson, Dolley and James Madison, and George and Martha Washington. Haute cuisine, a product of the early 1800s, introduced the European bourgeois to new versions of dairy products—crème fraîche on lobster bisque and asparagus soup, powdered milk in caramels, and *smetana* (sour cream) on Russian borscht. Dessert tables featured English clotted cream topping lemon tarts and varied cheeses and ripe pears at the end of the meal.

Winter dairying and industrialization boosted the application of milk to processed goods year-round. In 1832, Russian chemist M. Dirchoff streamlined the drying of milk for commerce. After French inventor Nicolas Appert condensed milk in 1820, Gail Borden's production of canned milk in vacuum pans in 1856 and the invention of pasteurization in France in 1862 enlarged the pantry even more with stable, safe milk and dairy products. The Civil War popularized sweetened condensed milk as a standard field ration, which remained fresh because sugar prevented spoilage. By 1872, dairier William Lawrence sold America's first cream cheese under the Philadelphia brand. Three years later, the world's first industrial dairy opened in Normandy, augmenting the reputation of the French as global cheese masters. Long-distance refrigerated trucking linked an increasing number of consumers with perishable dairy goods.

Concern for purity drove the infant food industry, which got its start before World War I. Parents demanded the testing of dairy herds for staphylococcal and tuberculin pathogens. Consumers petitioned governments to curtail the watering of raw milk and the preservation of dairy products with borax and formaldehyde.

For the Dairy Division of the U.S. Department of Agriculture, microbiologist Alice Catherine Evans researched microbes in milk and cheese. In 1917, Evans tested milk directly from the udder to prove that the *Bacillus abortus* in fresh milk spread brucellosis, or undulant fever, in cows, goats, and humans. For more than a decade, she campaigned to upgrade the dairy industry by informing doctors, public health authorities, veterinarians, and dairy farmers of sepsis in milk. Universal pasteurization became an industry standard in the 1930s.

In 1919 at a shop in Barcelona, a Spanish physician, Isaac Carasso, commercialized pure cultured yogurt to prevent milk intolerance and gastrointestinal distress. He obtained the antidote from Ukrainian microbiologist Ilya Ilyich Mechnikov, winner of the 1908 Nobel Prize in Medicine.

During World War II food rationing in Europe, British Minister of Food Frederick James Woolton forced dairiers to slaughter herds to free pastures for growing grain and vegetables. The abrupt shift in agriculture produced an immediate milk scarcity. The war also advanced concepts of naval readiness by adding milk products to the seagoing diet. After the war, the concept of bolstering bones and teeth with milk applied to schoolchildren in Australia, Ireland, New Zealand, and the United States. More recent concerns target modern-day additives to milk products, particularly antibiotics and growth hormones in cattle and guar gum in cottage cheese, both of which impact children's health.

Today, reefer ships speed dairy products directly to grocers in small coastal towns. Food processors manipulate raw milk by reducing fat and water content, condensing and homogenizing it to spread cream throughout, flavoring it with strawberries and chocolate, and enriching with vitamins for infant formula. Factory dairy manipulation involves evaporation of milk for Malaysian coffee, churning of white butter for couscous in Arabia, coagulating liquid into ricotta for Italian mascarpone, and fermenting into Yakult in Brazil.

The addition of yeast in India produces a fermented curd preferred by Hindu vegetarians. Indians also turn cream into *cham cham,* a block candy topped with coconut. The dairy-based fare of Kashmir calls for more piquant ghee and yogurt added to rice dishes. Tibetans drink butter tea with churned yak's milk; Czechs and Latvians use *quark* (unaged cheese) as a sandwich filler and basis for cheesecake. In the Punjab, celebrants drink sugared or herbed buttermilk from street vendors. Russians bake and caramelize milk for use in desserts.

See also: Animal Husbandry; Cheese; Guar; Hormones in Food; Marshall, Agnes; Polo, Marco; Scandinavian Diet and Cuisine; Trading Vessels; Yogurt.

Further Reading

Clark, Stephanie, Michael Costello, Mary Anne Drake, and Floyd Bodyfelt, eds. *The Sensory Evaluation of Dairy Products.* New York: Springer, 2009.

Duram, Leslie A., ed. *Encyclopedia of Organic, Sustainable, and Local Food.* Santa Barbara, CA: ABC-Clio, 2010.

Toussaint-Samat, Maguelonne. *A History of Food.* Hoboken, NJ: Wiley-Blackwell, 2009.

Yildez, Fatih, ed. *Development and Manufacture of Yogurt and Other Functional Dairy Products.* New York: Taylor & Francis, 2010.

Dal

A husked chickpea, kidney or mung bean, red or yellow lentil, pigeon pea, or vetch, dal (also daal, dahl, or dhal) is any of 50 varieties of split pulse that add fiber and protein to a vegetarian diet. In India, dal occupies the place that cheese and meat fill in other cuisines. Connoisseurs rank the variant dishes from gourmet class to crude peasant porridge and food fit only for livestock.

To increase palatability, cooks since early times have decorticated lentils by soaking and loosening skins between wet towels, either by hand or with a rolling pin. The preparation readies yellow split peas for a popular dish among Southern Asians and the Indian settlers of Canada, Guyana, Trinidad, and the United States. The addition of lime juice, turmeric, and a garnish precedes serving with brown or white basmati rice, a fragrant long grain grown in the Punjab.

A dietary stable from Nepal south to Sri Lanka from 3000 B.C.E., dal grew in plots cultivated by Aryans in the Indus Valley of northern Pakistan and the Punjab in northwestern India. The Punjab developed more dal recipes than any other Indian state. Practitioners of Ayurvedic medicine prescribed monodiets on dal as a body purifier and stabilizer after childbirth or surgery and as an aid to memory. Dal anchored a popular stew in Bangladesh and Pakistan, complementing roti (toasted flatbread) and rice pilau.

Consumers bought ingredients in bazaars or ready-to-eat dal or *khichri* (dal with wheat) in cookhouses. The poor resorted to grinding dal with barley, India's cheapest food crop, for baking into chapatis. In Sind, Pakistan, the destitute ate kesari dal (*Lathyrus sativus*), a toxic grain that caused chronic joint pain, hives, and eventual leg paralysis. Diagnosticians claimed that kesari dal produced white spots that degenerated into leprosy. Famines in Afghanistan, Eritrea, Ethiopia, and India caused extended reliance on kesari dal and greater evidence of emaciation of the gluteus and leg muscles.

A digestible food after removal of the seed aril, dal cooks slowly over charcoal heat. It absorbs the flavors of fresh tomatoes or of asafetida, bamboo shoots, coconut, coriander, cumin, fenugreek, garam masala, jaggery (unrefined palm sugar), mustard, red chilies, or turmeric sautéed in ghee (clarified butter). Another use involves serving dal as a fluffy grained side dish or grinding it into flour for thickening sauces and stirring into pancake batter.

Dal recipes appeared in Sanskrit compendia as native comfort foods made from the world's earliest domesticated plants. In 6 C.E., Tamil holiday literature referred to the service of mung dal with sugar and milk for a mid-January festival and named *idli,* a spongy dal breakfast food or snack.

Indians fermented black gram (lentils) into the savory idli cake and served it with condiments. Around 900, Jain writer Shivakotiacharya, author of the devotional poem *Vaddaradhane* (*Worship of the Venerable*), described the fermentation process. Subsequent recipes characterize chutney, curds, and ghee as common accompaniments to idli. A more detailed recipe appeared in the seventh chapter of the *Lokopakara* (*For the People's Benefit,* ca. 1025), a Sanskrit encyclopedia, detailing the use of buttermilk to soak urad dal (black beans) and listing dosages of mung dal for arthritis.

Indian cuisine particularizes dal dishes by region, such as vetch in Patna and *mag* dal (yellow lentils) in Gujarat, where parents feed the soft legumes and rice to weanlings. In Rajasthani cuisine from northwestern India, *pachrangi* dal features five types of dried legumes in proportion—1 part *channa* (sweet yellow split peas), 2 parts *mung* (green beans), 3 parts *masoor* (red lentils), 4 parts *toor* (yellow pigeon peas), and 1 part *urad* (black beans)—soaked overnight and cooked Mogul or Persian style in hot ghee. A dal cracker called *papadum* accompa-

Recipe: Sweet Potato Dal

Soak 1 cup *channa* dal (a sweet yellow split pea) in water for two hours and drain. Brown one chopped onion in 1 teaspoon of crushed cumin and 3 tablespoons of vegetable oil. Add three chopped chilies, two diced tomatoes, 1/2 teaspoon of turmeric, and 1 teaspoon each of chopped garlic, coriander powder, and crushed ginger. Simmer the mixture until the tomatoes soften. Add the dal, 4 cups of water, and 2 cups of diced sweet potatoes. Cook covered on low heat until creamy. Serve with basmati rice and garnish with chopped cilantro.

nies meals and snacks either plain or topped with chopped onion. Other regional cooks produce West Indian dal curry and fermented dal, *rasam* (mung bean soup) cooked in tamarind or tomato juice, and sambar, or pigeon peas spiced with asafetida and tamarind in South India. Eastern Indian dishes pair dal with pickles and rice.

From the 1500s, the Portuguese influence turned the bland puree fiery hot with the addition of chilies and sweet from blends with sweet potatoes. Cooks prepare the dish ahead of time, but the seasonings require sautéing immediately before serving. In Britain and the United States, cooks season dal with butter and cream. A popular fast food, *dosas* consist of ground dal and rice fermented in a dough and cooked into crepes.

See also: Curry; Dried Food; Heritage Foods; Indian Diet and Cuisine; Lunch; Mustard.

Further Reading

Banerji, Chitrita. *Eating India: An Odyssey into the Food and Culture of the Land of Spices.* New York: Bloomsbury, 2007.

Dalal, Tarla. *Dals.* Mumbai, India: Sanjay, 2007.

Erskine, William, et al. *The Lentil: Botany, Production and Uses.* Cambridge, MA: CABI, 2009.

Hughes, Martin, Sheema Mookherjee, and Richard Delacy. *World Food: India.* Oakland, CA: Lonely Planet, 2001.

Danish East India Company

From 1616 to 1772, the Danish East India Company (Dansk Østindisk Kompagni or OK) joined the world marketing frenzy to dominate a lucrative trade in cloves, nutmeg, pepper, and tea.

Founded in 1615 by Herman Rosenkranz and Jan de Willum, immigrants to Denmark from the Netherlands, the company received a charter from King Christian IV of

Denmark and Norway on Mary 17, 1616, to import tea from China, India, Ceylon, and Japan. In a period of decline in Scandinavian prominence in world affairs, the king oversaw the establishment of the Danish stock market. He intended economic ventures to boost Danish influence in both food imports and the spread of Lutheranism.

From 1620, the OK headquartered in southeastern India at the Tamil town of Tranquebar, which the Danes bought from the rajah of Tanjore for an annual tribute of 4,000 rupees. Under colonial governor Ove Gjedde, traders modeled their administration on that of Dutch mercantilism and built OK revenue from shipments of Malabar pepper.

Lacking economic clout, the Danes struggled to compete against the larger ships and crew of the dominant food exporter, the British East India Company. Each year, the OK equipped two outward-bound merchantmen and two returning vessels. The Danish ship *København* imported Malayan pepper from Siam (present-day Thailand) to Tranquebar (present-day Tharangambadi) for global distribution. In 1624, shipper Roland Crappé plotted a route to Makassar on Celebes Island (Sulawesi) to add Indonesian cloves to the company's inventory. He opened warehouses at Balasore (Baleswar), Masulipatnam (Machilipatnam), and Pipeley in India and installations in Japan, Java, and Sumatra.

In addition to trade in cloves, which the Danes monopolized, the OK bought cotton, porcelain, sandalwood, silks, sugar, tea, and turtle shell. The firm profited from smuggling tea into Britain, where food dealers eagerly bought the Danish wares to avoid British import taxes. A year later, the OK leased its seagoing trade ships to carry Portuguese wares from Makassar over the Bay of Bengal. Financial mismanagement forced the Danes to accept Dutch help in 1628 in manning Fort Danesborg at Tranquebar.

The OK chose violence as its modus operandi in subduing its Indian colony and bartered military naval support with its prospective clients in exchange for goods. Beginning in 1642, captains profited from naval attacks on some 30 Mughal ships from Bengal and from the looting of spice and tea shipments. The death of King Christian IV and the lackluster financial acumen of his successor, Frederick III, weakened Danish support for global trade until 1671, when King Christian V, Frederick's successor, offered the OK a new royal charter. In 1672, the company made greater inroads into the Asian food trade by expanding voyages to China, Japan, and Tonkin (Vietnam). To smooth the way with China, the Danish king corresponded with the Emperor Kangxi of China and dispatched the *Fortuna* from Copenhagen to Fuzhou in 1674 with Scandinavian and Indian goods.

While the Dutch and English engaged in religious wars, the Danes turned neutrality to their advantage. By 1675, the Danes rivaled both Dutch and English in trading from India. Danish merchants added Oddeway Torre,

a pepper clearinghouse on the Malabar coast, in 1696 and, two years later, added Gondalpara, southeast of Chandernagore (Chandannagar). Beginning in 1699, the Danes extended operations to the Nicobar Islands and Frederiksnagore (present-day Serampore) in Bengal, named for King Frederick V. The Crown colonies became a haven for Lutheran missionaries, who proselytized the Indians.

Trade declined during Denmark's war with Sweden, an 11-year conflict that stripped the OK of its operating capital. At war's end in 1720, the situation was unsalvageable. During the governorship of Rasmus Hansen Attrup at Tranquebar, the company foundered in 1729. It reorganized in 1732 under Governor Diderich Mühlenport as the Asiatic Company (Asiatisk Kompagni), which monopolized the Indian tea trade until the company's bankruptcy in 1772. In 1845, the Danes sold Tranquebar to the British East India Company.

See also: Seaman's Diet and Cuisine.

Further Reading

Bredsdorff, Asta. *The Trials and Travels of Willem Leyel: An Account of the Danish East India Company in Tranquebar, 1639–48.* Copenhagen, Denmark: University of Copenhagen, 2009.

Brødsgaard, Kjeld Erik, and Mads Kirkebaek. *China and Denmark: Relations Since 1674.* Copenhagen, Denmark: NIAS, 2000.

Dijk, Wil O. *Seventeenth-Century Burma and the Dutch East India Company, 1634–1680.* Singapore: Singapore University Press, 2006.

Gepken-Jager, Ella, Gerard van Solinge, and Levinus Timmerman. *VOC 1602–2002: 400 Years of Company Law.* Deventer, Netherlands: Kluwer Legal, 2005.

Danish West India Company

From 1671 to 1776, the Danish West India Company (Dansk Vestindisk Kompagni) maintained Caribbean colonies that reaped the profits of cotton and tobacco cultivation. Within decades, the Danes dominated sugar production in the Lesser Antilles.

From 1654, Danish commerce in West Africa built investment capital from trade in gold, ivory, palm oil, and sugar. In 1659, to profit from the Caribbean sugar and tobacco trade in St. Croix, St. John, and St. Thomas (now the U.S. Virgin Islands), Dutch traders Isaac Coymans and Nicolaes Pancras sold shares in a limited Danish charter firm called the Danish Africa Company (Dansk Afrikanske Kompagni). In competition with the Dutch, Danish colonists settled Africa's Gold Coast (present-day Ghana) and the Danish Virgin Islands. Pioneers organized a triangular trade in molasses, rum, and slaves and to a lesser degree in ginger and indigo.

In 1662, Admiral Erick Nielsen Smit (or Schmidt) superintended commerce from St. Thomas under the aegis of King Frederick III and turned the island harbor into a major entrepôt. The colony incorporated not only Danes, but also Dutch, English, Flemish, French, German, and Sephardic Jewish immigrants. The dominant languages were Dutch and English.

Food plants broadened the tastes of Europeans by adding cashews, coconuts, custard apples, mameys, mangoes, pawpaws, soursop, and tamarind to pantry staples of arrowroot, cassava, and sweet potatoes. Farmers planted beans, corn, okra, pepper, plantain, sorrel, and squash and harvested cacao to make chocolate. Local healers treated malaria and yellow fever with eucalyptus and yellow love vine leaves and with healing regimens involving eggs and raw lizards. Fruits and vegetables joined imported cattle and swine and native conch, crab, herring, lobster, mackerel, oysters, sardines, shrimp, snapper, tarpon, and turtles on plantation tables to create a fusion cuisine.

Epidemics and the death of Governor Smit sapped the infant colony of purpose and direction. British pirates drove the settlers from St. Thomas in 1667.

A New Start

Under the financial direction of King Christian V, the Danes once more invested in sugar plantations and global commerce in cotton, dyes, spices, and tobacco. In 1672, the king chartered the Danish West India Company under company governor Jørgen Iversen Dyppel, who imported indentured servants and convicts to found the port of Charlotte Amalie on the island. Of some 200 pioneers, only 29 remained in the St. Thomas colony by the time of its desertion in 1673. A renewed effort imported slaves from Guinea, veterans of farms in hot, wet climates.

By 1680, plantations powered by windmills flourished on St. Thomas under the direction of 156 whites and the labor of 175 black slaves. The northeast trade winds turned the mill sails, powering iron-plated rollers that extracted juice from sugarcane. In 1691, St. Thomas boasted 101 plantations. Its importers profited from the neutrality of Denmark during European wars. At the capital, Charlotte Amalie, wharves stacked with building materials, hogsheads of sugar, and puncheons of rum carried the stamps of global entrepreneurs. In the main street, marketers set up butcher stalls and displays of fish, bananas, herbs, melons, mangoes, and vegetables.

On March 23, 1718, Governor Erick Bredal attempted a similar settlement on St. John, where he imported five soldiers, 16 slaves, and 20 planters. Pioneering required forest clearing, terracing of hillsides, and the plowing and seeding of open land. Within a decade, a population of 123 Europeans and 677 slaves operated 87 plantations.

The 518-acre (210-hectare) Annaberg sugar factory, built in 1718, set the example of profitability for the island's 20 sugarworks, which averaged 80–90 acres (32–36 hectares) in size. For 20 hours each day, slaves watered sugarcane plants by hand. They completed the sugaring process by cutting and bundling cane and, using a windmill, crushed the canes to extrude up to 500 gallons (1,900 liters) of juice per hour. After boiling down in copper kettles into crystals, the brown sugar filled wood barrels holding 1,600 pounds (725 kilograms) each. The remaining concentrate formed molasses, the basis of rum.

Despite a disruptive Akwamu (Ghanian) slave revolt at the Coral Bay fort, the St. John economy grew to 109 plantations by 1739.

The Third Island

In 1733, when the Danish West India Company negotiated with the French for St. Croix, Denmark's third foothold in the Caribbean, colonizers benefited from the mistakes made by the settlers of St. Thomas and St. John. From the company plantation at La Grange, Dutch-style stone windmills extruded cane juice. Managers recycled fiber waste, called bagasse, into fuel to heat copper boilers. The raw sugar advanced by ship to refineries in Denmark, where law required the purchase of materials from the Virgin Islands at a fixed price.

The clearing of St. Croix timberlands for more sugar plantations upped the demand for slaves. During transport over the Middle Passage from Guinea, ship captains increased survival rates by supplementing the typical slave diet of barley gruel, beans, millet, and salt pork with rum and tobacco. Humanitarians, concerned for the high death rate among both African abductees and European sailors, ended the slave trade in 1803, but did not abolish slavery on St. Croix.

Recipe: Virgin Islands Pepper Pot

Soak four eddo or tannia leaves and 1 pound of spinach in salted water. In fresh water, soak 8 ounces of chopped pumpkin, three small squash, and 1 pound each of chopped eggplant, okra, and green pawpaw with 2 pounds of chopped beef. Stir-fry meat and two chopped onions in vegetable oil for five minutes. Add vegetables, meat or seafood, and onion to 2 quarts of water. Cook until tender. Add 1/2 cup each of minced chive, parsley, and thyme. Season with four whole cloves, one minced garlic clove, two hot peppers cut into pieces, a 1 inch–long cinnamon stick, and salt and pepper. Simmer until thickened. Instead of beef, this dish also can be made with conch or fish; alter the cooking times accordingly.

In addition to commercial agriculture, Arawak and Carib farmers wrested from the land two annual crops of cassava, corn, and vegetables. Slaves swelled their monthly provision allotments with loot from plantation pantries of beer, cod, flour, ham, rum, and wine. Daily meat and produce markets supplied islanders with chickens and pigeons, oranges, potatoes, and wild berries and plums. By candlelight, shoppers flocked late in the evenings to Christiansted's produce stalls to buy cabbage, eggs, pumpkins, tomatoes, and yams. To the European cuisine, slaves added black-eyed peas, cornmeal cakes, roasted sweet potatoes, and African versions of the Carib specialty, callaloo pepper pot—fresh greens flavored with red pepper, a high source of fiber.

Demand during the American Revolution raised St. Croix sugar exports to nearly 8,400 tons (7,600 metric tons). During the War of 1812, production burgeoned to 23,000 tons (20,900 metric tons). Island plantations also profited from pasturing herds and from the sale of beef, mutton, and pork. Competition from sugar beet growers in Europe and from sugarcane-growing in Brazil Cuba, India, and Mauritius caused economic decline of the Danish Virgin Islands and forced planters out of business. Huge land blocks required division into farms for the cultivation of diverse crops by rural homesteaders. In 1917, the United States bought the three islands, known as the U.S. Virgin Islands, and promoted tourism.

See also: Manioc.

Further Reading

Bastian, Jeannette Allis. *Owning Memory: How a Caribbean Community Lost Its Archives and Found Its History.* Westport, CT: Libraries Unlimited, 2003.

Donoghue, Eddie. *Black Breeding Machines: The Breeding of Negro Slaves in the Diaspora.* Bloomington, IN: Authorhouse, 2008.

Dookhan, Isaac. *A History of the Virgin Islands of the United States.* Kingston, Jamaica: Canoe, 2002.

Darwin, Charles (1809–1882)

Naturalist Charles Robert Darwin observed and tasted unusual foods on his voyage around the world, filling his writings with culinary details.

A native of Shrewsbury, Shropshire, he was born on February 12, 1809, to physician Robert Waring Darwin and Susannah Wedgwood Darwin, who died when he was eight years old. Reared in the Unitarian faith, he studied medicine at the University of Edinburgh and biology at Cambridge University. As president of the Glutton Club at Cambridge, he led members in samplings of bittern, hawk, and owl.

On an around-the-world study voyage beginning December 27, 1831, he traveled five years aboard the HMS *Beagle* to the Cape Verde Islands, Brazil, Argentina, Chile, and the Galápagos Islands west of Ecuador. After crossing the Pacific to Tahiti, where ferns anchored the island diet, he continued his survey of edible plants and animals in Australia and at St. Helena in the South Atlantic Ocean.

In *A Naturalist's Voyage Round the World* (1860), Darwin expounded on world diet, such as the provisioning of Brazilian cavalry with mare's meat. He gathered ostrich eggs, which provided 11 times the amount of sustenance as chicken eggs, and ate manioc bread, which natives made from pounded manioc root. Befitting a banquet guest, at a plantation in Socego, Brazil, on April 13, 1832, he ate of each dish—beans, beef, rice, venison— but regretted the appearance of roast pork and turkey, which threatened to overstuff him. Because of the low vegetable variety at Tierra del Fuego, off the southernmost tip of the South American mainland, he theorized that it was the only place in the world that considered fungus (*Cyttaria darwinii*) a kitchen staple. In contrast, Chile offered an abundance of beans, corn, and wheat as well as an appealing fruit menu of figs, grapes, and peaches.

On Darwin Island (initially called Culpepper Island and renamed in honor of Darwin) in the Galápagos Islands group west of Peru, the naturalist reported his observations of species mutation and natural selection. At Asilo de Paz on Floreana Island, also in the Galápagos group, he encountered rare species of animals and plants, including a croton tree whose leaves made an aromatic tea. His journal recorded details of native thatched huts and Peruvian plantations growing bananas, corn, sugarcane, and sweet potatoes. He characterized the native "Robinson Crusoe" protein sources as feral goats and pigs, turtle eggs, and tortoises. A feast with an island governor included manioc bread, melons, plantain, pumpkin, and tea poured from tortoiseshell pitchers. He hunted for the *Beagle* crew's food supply of deer, tuna, and turtles and also ate armadillos, a rare rhea, guinea pigs, land iguanas, and a 20-pound (9-kilogram) rodent that he declared the best meat he had ever eaten.

For convenience, Robert FitzRoy, the commander and surveyor of the *Beagle,* brought on board saddleback land tortoises, which survived for months without either food or water. FitzRoy's crew loaded 30 "elephant tortoises" from Chatham Island (Rekohu), the largest island of the Chatham Islands group in the south Pacific Ocean off the eastern coast of New Zealand. Each tortoise required six men to transport, but the ungainly beast was worth the effort for its "excellent and extremely wholesome food." Each tortoise supplied 8 gallons (30 liters) of oil for the Pacific crossing and some 200 pounds (90 kilograms) of meat. The beast was so convenient a catch for passing ships that by the 1830s, visitors to Charles, Hood, and James islands had nearly destroyed the species.

The world tour gave Darwin much material to ponder concerning human sustenance. Readings in Thomas Malthus's *Essay on the Principle of Population* (1797) impressed Darwin with the concept that the global population would grow exponentially until it outpaced the food supply. In Darwin's landmark book *On the Origin of Species* (1859), he predicted that, by the next millennium, competition for food would plunge humankind into turmoil and create a vicious struggle between species.

Darwin's theories of struggle and survival within living organisms revolutionized science. Among the failsafes for the human table, he added to the list of foods that people considered edible. In *The Expression of the Emotions in Man and Animals* (1872), he observed the universal response to contemptible, disgusting, or socially unacceptable food through gagging, retching, spitting, and vomiting. In Tierra del Fuego, a native had disgusted the scientist by touching his serving of cold preserved meat, which the Fuegan found too soft for palatability. He also discusses the converse reaction, salivation, which prepares a diner for tempting servings that appeal by sight, aroma, texture, or the memory of a previous satisfying experience.

See also: Manioc.

Further Reading

Berra, Tim M. *Charles Darwin: The Concise Story of an Extraordinary Man.* Baltimore, MD: Johns Hopkins University Press, 2009.

Browne, E. Janet. *Charles Darwin: The Power of Place.* Princeton, NJ: Princeton University Press, 2002.

Grant, K. Thalia, and Gregory B. Estes. *Darwin in Galapagos: Footsteps to a New World.* Princeton, NJ: Princeton University Press, 2009.

Krull, Kathleen. *Charles Darwin.* New York: Penguin, 2010.

Daubenton, Louis Jean-Marie (1716–1799)

French vegetable physiologist and comparative anatomist Louis Jean-Marie Daubenton, one of the four founders of French biology, applied the intellectualism of the Enlightenment to matters of food and digestion.

A native Burgundian from Montbard, Daubenton began his education under Jesuits. He studied medicine at Reims and dedicated himself to biological fieldwork, writings, and illustration. At the Jardin du Roi in Paris in 1742, he collaborated with encyclopedist Georges-Louis Leclerc de Buffon in compiling and illustrating the first 15 segments of the 36-volume *Histoire Naturelle, Générale et Particulière* (*Natural History, General and Specific,* 1749–1789). The quality of Daubenton's work earned him a royal cabinet appointment in Paris at age 29.

While chairing general zoology at the Collège de France, lecturing on rural economy, and directing the Museum of Natural History in Paris, Daubenton influenced the farming, beekeeping, and herding preferences of his time. He corresponded with American polymath Benjamin Franklin and introduced Europeans to the cultivation of the date palm.

Daubenton's evaluation of the Spanish Merino sheep in *Instructions of Shepherds and the Proprietors of Flocks* (1784) spurred vast shifts in the mutton and wool market. His commentary on fattening four-year-old sheep for slaughter insisted on stall-feeding with clover and fescue plus bread, oats, hemp or rape seed, and hazelnuts. He recommended a vegetable diet for herds of cabbages, carrots, corn, potatoes, and turnips, a regimen that Louis XVI employed at his sheepcotes at Rambouillet.

In his studies of practical medicine, Daubenton noted the slowing of digestion in the middle-aged and elderly human and recommended vegetarianism to prevent dyspepsia and flatulence. With *Memoire sur les Indigestions* (*Treatise on Dyspepsia,* 1785), he pioneered the use of ipecac in small amounts as a treatment for indigestion. Like the action of after-dinner cayenne pepper, ginger, and rhubarb, by stimulating peristalsis, the natural rhythmic contractions of the stomach, the dosage energized gastric glands to produce mucus. Taken in jelly, lozenge, water, or wine, the ipecac treatment expedited the movement of food through the stomach without causing nausea or pain.

Daubenton survived the Reign of Terror, the mass deaths of aristocrats and royal appointees during the French Revolution of 1789–1799, by maintaining his role as agronomist and herder. Before his death on December 31, 1799, from stroke, he directed the Luxembourg Gardens in Paris and introduced fruits from around the world as well as cultivation of the potato.

Further Reading

Crossley, Ceri. *Consumable Metaphors: Attitudes Towards Animals and Vegetarianism in Nineteenth-Century France.* Bern, Switzerland: Peter Lang, 2005.

Spary, Emma C. *Utopia's Garden: French Natural History from Old Regime to Revolution.* Chicago: University of Chicago Press, 2000.

David, Elizabeth (1913–1992)

In the mid-1900s, English culinary historian and kitchen master Elizabeth Gwynne David revived enthusiasm for home cooking of heritage foods and traditional recipes.

She was born into an upper-crust family in Sussex on December 26, 1913, and educated at High Wycombe and Tunbridge Wells, where she came to despise cheerless boarding school meals of limp fried fish and canned apricots served over custard. She trained in art and theater in Paris at the Sorbonne and savored her first taste of mussels. In 1931, she took lessons in German in Munich, where sage-flavored fried eel nauseated her. During World War II, on a voyage from England to Greece, she wrestled with galley cookery aboard the sloop *Evelyn Hope.* On the island of Syros, she shopped at an open-air market and cooked over a brazier outdoors at her cottage, where she embraced the simplicity of daily meals from fresh supplies.

Fleeing German invaders, Gwynne settled in Alexandria, Egypt, where she enjoyed the cosmopolitan influence of Arabs, Armenians, Copts, Syrians, and Turks. She took posts in Cairo as a cryptographer for the British navy and librarian for the Ministry of Information. Under the tutelage of her cooks, Kyriacou and Suleiman, she learned to enjoy herbed vegetables, octopus in thyme branches, quail kebabs, and charcoal-grilled pigeon, a Nile-side specialty. During bohemian experiences cooking on Primus stoves and a tin box oven, she displayed touches of identity and uniqueness.

Revitalizing English Cuisine

Upon her return to England at war's end, the author combated high food prices and frumpy kitchens with their stores of dehydrated egg packets and tasteless powdered soup. She chose as a weapon elegant articles about the regional Mediterranean diet for *Harper's Bazaar, Nova, Vogue,* and the *Sunday Times.* Still rationed, English supplies of butter, olives, tea, and tomatoes remained scarce and Parmigiano-Reggiano cheese and eggplant unknown. For a decade, readers learned details of the imaginative French and Italian use of basil and marjoram, langoustine and octopus, mountain herbs, Parma ham, peppers, saffron, and salami. She aimed to retrieve French table style from "a snob's preserve" to cookery within the grasp of the English middle class. At her urging, grocers tempted English shoppers with courgettes, croissants, fava beans, olive oil, pimientos, sheep's milk cheese, and zucchini.

At the age of 47, David and husband, Tony David, settled in Chelsea. To re-create the ambience of Syros, she decorated the kitchen in the Mediterranean style, with terra-cotta pots and baskets of eggs and lemons and without the "clanking ironmongery" of overdone English kitchens. In 1950, she issued an illustrated manual titled *A Book of Mediterranean Food,* a compendium of sensual pleasures laced with food commentary by authors Lawrence Durrell, Henry James, D.H. Lawrence, and Gertrude Stein.

Flavors of France, Italy, and Beyond

David followed with *French Country Cooking* (1951), in which she identified the flavors and textures of Alsace, Brittany, Burgundy, Île de France, Normandy, Provence, and Savoy. The text introduced English cooks to the

mandoline, mezzaluna, and moulinette, all essential European equipment for slicing, chopping, and pureeing. After a tour of Venice, she summarized the style and flair of regional cookery in *Italian Food* (1954). The text admired the verve of Neapolitan and Sicilian caponata and ice cream eaters and listed essential ingredients—capers, chickpeas, Gaeta olives, garlic, pasta, pine nuts, porcini mushrooms, prosciutto, tuna—that the English pantry lacked.

David's global interests came together in *Summer Cooking* (1955), a collection of dishes from England, the Mediterranean, India, Mauritius, and Russia to grace "la bonne table." She mocked the pretensions of Michelin Guides and their awarding of stars to self-important restaurants. A more thorough study of fundamentals, *French Provincial Cooking* (1960) deconstructed the elements in classic dishes, particularly *pot-au-feu* (beef stew) and everyday pâtés and terrines. She carried specificity to great lengths, even describing a favorite charcuterie in Ardèche.

Recovering from a cerebral hemorrhage at the National Hospital for Nervous Diseases in London, David suffered a loss of vigor and agility as well as part of her speech and some of her sense of taste. In November 1963, she set up in the kitchen trade in Pimlico and sold cookbooks, imported Tuscan oil, and imported equipment to dedicated cooks. Her love of vivid color inspired Le Creuset to distribute cast-iron cookware enameled in blue. Her standards for cuisine demanded authentic photos of ingredients and a minimum of out-of-season imports and "food in fancy dress."

Tutoring the English Homemaker

After two decades of focusing on Mediterranean cuisine, David shifted her emphasis to British fare. Her articles scolded the English for investing in bouillon cubes, gravy mix, ketchup, and other commercial flavorings and for limiting herbs to rosemary and sage. In place of too many processed flavorings, she proposed reliance on good wines. She researched recipes for smoked fish, stewed steak, Indian curry, mince pie, and fruit pickles for *Spices, Salt and Aromatics in the English Kitchen* (1970) and recommended Tuscan salt, the key ingredient of Gorgona anchovies. After closing her kitchen shop, she wrote an award-winning cuisine retrospective, *English Bread and Yeast Cookery* (1977), from a hospital bed following a car accident. Her zeal for wholemeal (whole wheat) loaves generated an English rebellion against mass-produced baked goods.

David's autocratic critiques of table arts earned her membership in the Royal Society of Literature and a Commander of the Most Excellent Order of the British Empire. In declining health, David compiled an omnibus edition of her essays, *An Omelette and a Glass of Wine* (1984), which lauded French markets, whiskey in the kitchen, and the eateries of Iberia and Morocco. Her papers and

Recipe: Ratatouille

2 onions	4 ripe tomatoes
olive oil	2 cloves garlic
2 eggplants	a dozen coriander seeds
2 large red bell peppers	parsley or basil

Chop the onions fairly small and put them to stew in a sauté pan or deep frying pan in half a tumbler of olive oil. Meanwhile, cut the eggplants, leaving on their skins, into 1/2-inch squares and put them, sprinkled with coarse salt, into a colander so that some of the water drains away from them. When the onions have cooked about ten minutes and are beginning to get soft (but not fried), add the eggplants and then the peppers, also cut into small pieces. Cover the pan and let them simmer for 30 to 40 minutes. Now, add the chopped tomatoes, the garlic, and the coriander seeds. Continue cooking until the tomatoes have melted. Should the oil dry up, add a little more, remembering that the liquid from the tomatoes will also make the ratatouille more liquid, and the final result must not be too mushy. When cold, garnish with chopped parsley or basil. Drain off any excess oil before serving.

collected cookbooks survive at Harvard's Schlesinger Library, the Warburg Institute in London, and the London Guildhall Library. In 2006, the British Broadcasting Corporation (BBC) recapped her accomplishments in a film, *Elizabeth David: A Life in Recipes*.

See also: Grilling; Ice Cream; Nouvelle Cuisine.

Further Reading

Cooper, Artemis. *Writing at the Kitchen Table: The Authorized Biography of Elizabeth David.* New York: Ecco, 2000.

David, Elizabeth. *An Omelette and a Glass of Wine.* 1984. Guilford, CT: Lyons, 2010.

Reichl, Ruth, ed. *Endless Feasts: Sixty Years of Writing from Gourmet.* New York: Random House, 2003.

De Soto, Hernando (ca. 1496–1542)

Spanish explorer Hernando de Soto paid a heavy price for mounting a four-year expedition to the Americas without adequate provisions. A native of southwestern Spain reared in a middle-class household, he led the first European expedition (1539–1542) to the Mississippi River.

At age 18, De Soto sailed to Mesoamerica with fantasies of subduing tribes and conquering territory for Spain. From Nicaragua, he pressed along Yucatán in search of a sea route to Asia and looted Cajamarca, Peru, the capital of Inca Emperor Atahualpa. Under the leadership of Francisco Pizarro, De Soto joined the rifling of Cuzco, Peru, to add gold and silver to that stolen from Atahualpa. By the time De Soto departed Peru in 1536, his wealth rivaled most of the world's richest individuals.

On a second expedition to the Caribbean in May 1539, De Soto assumed the governorship of Cuba, a post granted by Holy Roman Emperor Charles V. De Soto's entourage brought to Cuba weapons and ammunition as well as horses and mules, plows, and seeds for establishing gardens at potential colonies.

On May 18, 1539, De Soto, leading a fleet of eight ships and 620 men, set out from Havana to North America on the flagship *San Christoval* to claim land for the king. He took with him Vasco Porcallo de Figueroa, a rich Cuban who organized equipment, horses and pigs, and 3,000 loads of cassava bread, bacon, and corn, a storable, transportable form of nutrition. Other goods filled barrels, casks, and pottery containers. For the next four years, corn served the Spaniards as survival food. Before De Soto's disembarkation at west-central Florida, his vanguard collected berries and forage for their horses. North of the landing, De Soto found good hunting—birds, deer, and turkeys—enough to feed the expedition for six weeks.

De Soto herded domestic swine as famine food and possible trade items as well as for the main courses of feasts. He released into the wild long-nosed, tusked pigs from Extremadura, Spain, the ancestors of the American razorback. Because feral pigs were omnivores that stored 35 percent of the food energy from the offal, acorns, chestnuts, mushrooms, lizards, moles, snakes, and worms that they ate, they promised a source of fat and meat for future Spanish colonization.

At Ocale (present-day Ocala, Florida) De Soto and his men traded glass beads and iron tools with village chiefs for beans, corn, and dog meat. Food availability was so limited that the Spaniards raided the nearby home of the Acuera people on the Ocklawaha River for more corn. Theft and abduction set a pattern for the Spanish advance. De Soto also countenanced kidnapping of Indian women to perform the labor-intensive job of pounding dried corn into grits, baking corn cakes, and cooking beans and squash and of youths as porters for supplies and utensils.

Feeding the Troops

Beginning in August 1539, a meandering four-year march routed the expedition from Port Charlotte, Florida, east into Indian societies less urbanized than the Aztec or Inca, who warehoused food for large cities. The absence of provisions forced De Soto to dispatch Captain Baltasar de Gallegos and 180 men in foraging teams to find birds, fish, small game, and herbs and roots. At present-day Tampa to Urriparacoxi (Sumter County) and north to Napituca (Live Oak, Florida), in mid-September, the Spanish harvested a three-months' supply of green corn from lush fields. Their journals report grapes, muscadines, mulberries, and plums, chestnuts, hazelnuts, and walnuts, and butter made from acorns. Obscure descriptions of fruits similar in flavor to pears and strawberries leave in question the exact species.

Rumors of corrals of deer and turkeys in Uqueten (Dade City), Ocale Province, north of Tampa Bay, lured the Spanish onward. Over a swampy trail, hunger compelled them to stew wild greens and herbs. Risking sickness and possible poisoning, the men roasted and gobbled unknown roots. Soldiers stacked firewood, crushed corn in mortars and pestles, and sifted meal for bread through their chain mail. They spread cornmeal dough on earthenware griddles above coals in the fire. Men in a hurry parched corn directly on metal armor and stewed it whole. At the Withlacoochee River, they ate the fibrous cores of cabbage palmetto known as hearts of palm.

In Indian villages, De Soto remarked on the ready stores of honey and the melted fat of bear and oil from black walnuts, which they poured into gourds for use in cooking and healing. In July 1539, he encountered a vast phosphate ridge that supplied enough pasturage and grain fields to sustain the conquistadors; however, the constant fording of black-water rivers depleted men weary of foraging and hungry for salt meat. Building bridges and wading through swamps left no time for fishing, gathering shellfish, or shooting the ample herons, ibis, storks, or wild turkeys.

At the Santa Fe River in north-central Florida, the Spaniards found the Alachua living on raised platforms and caching provisions in pits. In addition to collecting hickory nuts and palm berries, the Alachua used clay pots to cook blue gill, bream, catfish, muskrat, opossum, rabbit, raccoon, and squirrel. On August 15, 1539, at Cholupaha (near Citrus Spring), soldiers gathered water

Recipe: Pickled Hearts of Palm

Remove hearts from emergent palm fronds of scrub palmetto. Lop off the tops and bottoms to expose the tender inner tissue. Soak in a brine of 3 cups of water, 1 cup of white vinegar, 1 teaspoon of alum, and 1/4 cup of sea salt. Cover and soak for a week before draining. Store hearts of palm in glass refrigerator containers and keep moistened with diluted vinegar. Eat raw in salads or add to trays of olives and cucumber pickles.

chinquapins, a dwarf chestnut that provided edible seeds and tubers. Northwest through Apalachee territory on the Florida panhandle, vegetable gardening spread so far across the land that the Spanish spent five months in comfort and plenty.

De Soto passed through Apalachen (Tallahassee), where Indians harvested tasty snacks of black cherries and wild yellow plums. Native gardeners grew beans, corn, gourds, and squash. The troops carried only enough provisions for 12 days of marching, primarily roasted corn kernels. Each trooper bore his personal share in his backpack. They varied their vegetable diet with birds and fish. The Spanish discovery of fragrant sassafras root offered a possibility of trade in a New World commodity valuable as a spice and as a drug to treat venereal disease.

The herd had grown to some 300 pigs, contributing protein to the Spanish diet. Foraging parties packed biscuits and cheese from the dwindling travel larder. In Georgia, the forces encountered the Muscogee (Creek) Indians near the Ocmulgee River at present-day Macon, where the fall line between the piedmont and coastal plain supported a diet of fish and forage plants. The ravenous Spaniards devoured green corn, cob and all. If tribes hesitated to supply rations, the Spaniards threatened to release Bruto, the chief war dog of their meat-hungry bloodhounds, which were trained for manhunts.

At Cofitachequi (Camden, South Carolina), on May 1, 1540, near-starvation forced the remaining 550 men of the De Soto campaign from one tribe to the next. When news of the approaching force passed up the Indian grapevine, one tribe donated 700 turkeys to the troops. In July, after covering 1,300 miles (2,100 kilometers), the expedition reached present-day Knoxville, Tennessee. Ground corn supplied both the Spaniards and their 230 mounts for the journey into the Carolinas, southwest along the Tennessee River to Alabama, and north to the alluvial plains of Mississippi and back to the Appalachian Mountains of Tennessee. At Quizquiz (Clarksdale) on the Mississippi, Indians rewarded the newcomers with edible bricks made from compressed red plums. On the way through Mississippi, the conquistador succeeded in supplying his expedition by holding native chiefs hostage.

Violent Foraging

De Soto's brutal methods of extorting provisions for hundreds of men and animals antagonized Native Americans. Simultaneously, the interlopers unintentionally disrupted villages by spreading chicken pox, influenza, measles, and smallpox throughout the Southeast.

Along the Gulf of Mexico on October 18, 1540, the theft of food and women from the Choctaw provoked combat at Mabila (Mobile, Alabama). After a nine-hour pitched battle, some 2,500 Indians succumbed to cavalry forays, superior armor and weaponry, and the burning of the palisades. Arson killed Chief Tascalusa and obliterated the Atahachi nation and culture. While only 22 of De Soto's forces died in the conflict, he lost so much equipment and harness that his men ate seven dead horses to spare any waste.

During winter on the Tombigbee River, the Spaniards ate well on corn, pecans, and rabbits. The crossing of the Mississippi River in June 1541 required the building of rafts to carry 400 Spaniards to dry land. After the expedition advanced northwest to Hot Springs, Arkansas, in March 1542, the troops located a wealth of beans, corn, and dried plums at the confluence of the Arkansas River with the Mississippi. De Soto, emotionally devastated and thwarted in his hopes of riches, contracted fever and died on the Arkansas side of the Mississippi on May 21, 1542, possibly near Ferriday, Louisiana.

Europe's longest foray into native America, De Soto's expedition exhibited to future conquistadors the value of dried fruit, ground corn, and nuts in sustaining an oversized phalanx of men on the move. Even a one-day delay meant skimpy rations and possible death of men and mounts.

New dining experiences awaited Castillians unaccustomed to barbecued hens, the corn-based Timucuan diet grown along the St. Johns River, or the buffalo eaten by well-fed Arkansas plains tribes. The Spaniards consumed so many indigenous barkless dogs that the breed neared extinction. Among the Mococo and Uzita hunter-gatherers of south-central Florida, the Spanish recorded a unique food culture based on fishing and hunting and the foraging for goosefoot, marsh elder, and smartweed, shellfish, and wild birds and animals. At Toa (Dawson, Georgia), the Europeans admired plastered and stilted summer huts featuring kitchen facilities for storing corn and sunflower seeds and baking bread. In the Ouachita Valley in south-central Arkansas, patient Indians taught De Soto's men how to snare rabbits, a method of provisioning making each man responsible for his own nourishment.

Under the leadership of Peruvian commander Luís de Moscoso, the scarcity of food forced the expedition's 311 survivors to build four flat-bottomed boats, pilot them down the Mississippi River delta, and end the march at the Panuco River below Tampico, Mexico. Although De Soto found no precious metals, he provided Spain with information on aboriginal cultures that had survived in the Southeast for 14,000 years.

See also: Barbecue; Manioc; Pork; Salt.

Further Reading

Clayton, Lawrence A., Vernon James Knight, Jr., and Edward C. Moore, eds. *The De Soto Chronicles: The Expedition of Hernando de Soto to North America in 1539–1543.* Tuscaloosa: University of Alabama Press, 1993.

Koch, Peter O. *Imaginary Cities of Gold: The Spanish Quest for Treasure in North America.* Jefferson, NC: McFarland, 2009.

Milanich, Jerald T., and Charles Hudson. *Hernando de Soto and the Indians of Florida.* Gainesville: University Press of Florida, 1994.

Delessert, Benjamin (1773–1847)

In a food war between the Old World and the New, industrialist, philanthropist, and herb collector Jules Paul Benjamin Delessert introduced beet-sugar refining to the Napoleonic Empire.

The son of a Swiss financier, Delessert, a native of Lyon, France, and his sister and brother received home training in botany through lectures and live specimens mailed from philosopher Jean-Jacques Rousseau. While studying science at the University of Edinburgh, Delessert traveled to Birmingham, England, to view James Watt's steam engine, the beginning of the Frenchman's interest in the factory system.

At age 20 during the French Revolution, Captain Delessert led an artillery company for the French National Guard in combat in Belgium and Holland. After accepting the presidency of the Savings Bank of Paris, he mechanized a model cotton factory at Passy, the first in France. He collected 250,000 specimens of 86,000 plant species at the Musée Botanique in Geneva that benefited world agriculture.

In 1802, Delessert opened a sugar-refining business. He stripped yellow beet juice of its color through purification, a success that earned him the title of baron of the empire. He applied his wealth to establishing 30 soup kitchens in Paris, a forerunner of the Société Philantropique.

A decade later, during serious food shortages in France, he pioneered a new food art: he bypassed the typical ingredients of chestnut, grape, honey, potato, and wheat to manufacture sugar loaves from beets, the vegetable with the highest sugar content. To improve the aroma and flavor during the extraction of crystalline sweetener, Delessert filtered the juice through charcoal, a clarifying agent. His process improved the technology created in 1747 by Prussian chemist Andreas Sigismund Marggraf, who had boiled beets in alcohol before crystallizing the juice. The French method produced grains as fine as those from West Indian cane sucrose. For expert staff, he employed Spanish prisoners of war who had operated cane mills in the Caribbean. Delessert presented his first granular product at the royal palace and shared the technology with his rivals, who distributed sugar at medicine shops for the making of sugar syrups and sugar water, viewed as a healthful drink and tonic.

With money from the Emperor Napoleon I, Delessert filled a gap in military provisioning after the British blockade halted imports of West Indian cane sugar and raised the price to $1.20 per pound. On August 22, 1810, the emperor was so desperate for supplies that he invested $40,000 in 12 test laboratories to promote the crystallization of sugar from grapes to undermine England's world sucrose monopoly. In the next year, on March 25, Napoleon turned his attention to beets and ordered the Société d'Encouragement pour l'Industrie Nationale to fund beet planting on 80,000 acres (32,400 hectares). Education began at six agrarian schools, where 100 students earned scholarships to train for managing the beet sugar industry. A valuable by-product, beet solids suited the meat industry as cattle feed.

Delessert, the French sugar king, opened the first sucrose mill near Brussels at an abandoned abbey to crystallize pearl sugar. Made from beets, this coarse grain sweetener had the advantage of a high resistance to dissolution.

On January 2, 1812, Napoleon arrived at Passy to award Delessert the Cross of the Legion of Honor for his efforts on behalf of French trade. The emperor ordered the industrialist immediately to build a network of ten sugar refineries in temperate climates that could sustain beet fields. Despite complaints from the fastidious that beet sugar was inferior to imported goods, chemists attested that the grains of beet sucrose exhibited the same color, flavor, and weight as cane sugar. The mills produced tons of sugar annually and experimented with useful improvements and methods. Cooks turned sugar into a pantry staple for gelling sorbet, blending wine cordial restoratives and liqueurs, candying fruit, sweetening café au lait, and making delicate pastries, custards, and jam.

By 1813, French efforts, superintended by Delessert, had manufactured more than 2,200 tons (2,000 metric tons) of beet sugar. The next year, his concept spread to 40 sugar refineries across Europe—to Austria, Belgium, France, and Germany. By 1838, there were 581 factories refining beets into sugar in France alone and an emerging sugar beet industry in the United States. Shifts in tariffs and treaties and the abolition of slavery in the Indies transformed the industry. In the 1890s, beet sugar supplanted cane sugar in the sweetener market and lowered the price of sweeteners for home use. From the inventor's name, restaurateurs added a "Dessert" course to menus.

Further Reading

Abramson, Julia Luisa. *Food Culture in France.* Westport, CT: Greenwood, 2007.

Smith, Michael Stephen. *The Emergence of Modern Business Enterprise in France, 1800–1930.* Cambridge, MA: Harvard University Press, 2005.

Desalination

Processes removing salt from water make available more potable water for home use and crop irrigation. The quest for purification methods in North Africa dates to Egyp-

tian water sedimentation and decanting, which servants operated as early as 1450 B.C.E. Along the Fertile Crescent of western Asia after 850 B.C.E., the Persians devised primitive filtration systems by pouring heated water through gravel or sand, over porous stone, or into the seed pods of the *Strychnos potatorum,* a nut tree recommended for healing in Ayurvedic medicine.

According to the Sanskrit medical writings in the *Sushruta Samhita (Sushruta's Precepts,* ca. 600 B.C.E.), potable water resulted from boiling, solar heating, or plunging heated iron rods into brackish water. Around 360 B.C.E., Hippocrates, the Greek father of medicine, proposed straining boiled water through a cloth bag. Subsequent Roman methods replaced the filtration sack with clay filters, wick siphons, crushed laurel stems, coral, barley, sand, and fibrous cord.

Drinking water at sea and on arid shores prompted research into desalination. The United States began ridding water of salt on ships in 1791 at the instigation of Thomas Jefferson, then secretary of state under President George Washington. During World War II, mobile units desalinated water on large naval vessels traveling to North Africa and the Pacific. By the mid-1900s, desalination had become a global issue. The formation of Israel in 1948 raised questions of sustainability, which the nation's first prime minister, David Ben Gurion, interpreted as a need for desalinated seawater for municipal and farm and orchard use.

Under the U.S. Saline Water Conversion Act of 1952, hydrologists and engineers experimented with methods of cutting costs of desalination plants. The first demonstration facility, built in 1961 at Freeport, Texas, used vertical tube distillation to convert 1 million gallons (3.8 million liters) per day. For military purposes, hydrological techniques of ridding seawater of minerals enabled ships and submarines to remain at sea without calling at ports to fill their tanks. By the 1980s, desalination had become a commercial enterprise. In 2007, a U.S. facility at Tampa Bay, Florida, began providing 171 million gallons (647 million liters) of water per day for use over a 2,000-square-mile (5,200-square-kilometer) area.

The demand for such facilities grows annually as the world's population requires more fresh water for agrarian, domestic, and industrial use. The cost of building new water plants falls heavily on needy areas in China, the Colorado River basin, Gaza, the Jordan River basin, Spain, Tobago, and Trinidad. A thrifty method of desalting water, cogeneration involves directing excess heat from nuclear power plants to distillation mechanisms, a common cost reducer in Australia, India, Japan, Russia, and Saudi Arabia.

To ensure equity in global water use, the United Nations General Assembly in July 2010 declared water justice a human right. Proposals for alleviating human suffering from catastrophes and droughts and resultant epidemics and famine include building desalination

The Hadera seawater reverse-osmosis (SWRO) desalination plant, on the Mediterranean coast of Israel, is the largest of its kind in the world. Desalination in Israel, one of the most arid countries on the planet, accounts for a majority of the nation's drinking water. *(Ariel Schalit/Associated Press)*

plants. Currently, the United Arab Emirates operates the world's largest electrodialysis processing plant, at Jebel Ali southwest of Dubai. By changing water to steam, the mechanism rapidly distills potable water. The flash distillation technique produces 64 percent of the world's desalinated water.

Osmosis competes with distillation by yielding more water at a lower cost. In Hadera, Israel, the world's largest reverse osmosis facility cost $500 million, an outlay that supplies 16 percent of Israelis, or more than 1.2 million people. Brackish water passes through a water-permeable ceramic or polymer membrane at high pressure to separate minerals. The proficiency of the reverse osmosis process keeps costs at 50¢ per cubic meter (38¢ per cubic yard).

Use of desalination systems protects the environment by limiting the overdraining of groundwater, lakes, and streams. Negative elements—air pollution, fossil fuel use, greenhouse gas emission, mortality of fish and plankton—raise questions of how and where to establish intakes and methods of debrining outflow into calm waters, including the Persian Gulf, Red Sea, and tropical lagoons. One possibility is through solar desalination of open ponds and the reclamation of salt for sale.

See also: Irrigation; Salt; Water.

Further Reading

Cotruvo, Joseph, et al., eds. *Desalination Technology: Health and Environmental Impacts.* Boca Raton, FL: CRC, 2010.

Rizzuti, Lucio, Hisham Mohamed Ettouney, and Andrea Cipollina. *Solar Desalination for the 21st Century.* New York: Springer, 2007.

Shiva, Vandana. *Water Wars: Privatization, Pollution and Profit.* Cambridge, MA: South End, 2002.

Solomon, Steven. *Water: The Epic Struggle for Wealth, Power, and Civilization.* New York: Harper Perennial, 2011.

Díaz, Bernal (1492–1585)

A chronicler of Hernán de Cortés's conquest of Mexico, Bernal Díaz del Castillo, an ordinary infantryman in 119 battles, preserved details of Mexica (or Aztec) culture and religion in a stirring New World history.

Reared in genteel poverty in Medina del Campo, Spain, Díaz went to sea in his mid-teens but abandoned hopes of wealth from his adventures in Tierra Firme (Panama). Disappointment in Cuba and Yucatán ended his illusions of New World promise. A subsequent role in the Spanish invasion of Aztec Mexico on February 10, 1519, placed him under the command of Cortés, the commander of a fleet of 11 ships. For the voyage, the *nao* (or carrack, a three- or four-masted sailing ship) stocked the standard seaman's diet—anchovies and sardines, bacon, biscuits, cassava flour, cheese, chickpeas, onions, salt pork, and wine. Additional stores fed war steeds, which the Spanish introduced to battle for the first time in Mesoamerica in April 1519 at Potochan (present-day Tabasco).

Upon disembarkation in Mexico, Díaz adapted to the Mesoamerican diet. His daily ration consisted of *aji* (peppers), cactus fruit, cassava, chayote, corn smut and tortillas, jicama, mushrooms, and the leaves of amaranth and goosefoot. Both Aztec and Spaniard found cause to complain of the dietary changes they encountered as the two cultures clashed: the Aztec at the tastelessness of wheat biscuit and the revolting texture of pork fat, the Spanish insurgents at the consumption of small dogs and *animalitos* (reptiles and vermin). Díaz also quailed at the flaying of sacrificed humans, whose remains priests served at festivals with a pepper and tomato sauce.

On August 31, 1519, the Spanish cortege accepted gifts of 20 baskets of tortillas and 300 turkeys from King Xicotenga in south-central Mexico at Tlaxcala. The 40,000 native Otomi deliberately overfed their enemy before attacking them. That night, after Cortés's men overwhelmed the Otomi, military physicians dressed the Spaniards' wounds with fat rendered from the corpses of Indians.

When the Spanish advanced northwest toward Mexico City on November 1, they took new allies, 6,000 Otomi warriors. The Texcoco, another nation resentful of the Aztec, provisioned the grand army. The Emperor Montezuma II capitulated to the Europeans but begged them not to return to collect the annual tribute. He cited a pragmatic reason: The Aztec lacked the provisions for feeding so large an annual influx of Spanish.

The Aztec Way

Upon their arrival at Tenochtitlán (Mexico City) on November 8, 1519, the big-city life of Mexican Indians amazed Díaz. Opposite the great pyramid of the war god Huitzilopochtli, the Spaniards encountered an urban center housing 200,000–300,000 Aztec. Díaz commented on the need for controlled water distribution and on the orderly conveyance of food from outlying farms. At the arcaded central plaza, he gawked at the variety of vegetables and fruits, organ meats, and ready-to-eat stews and tamales offered to some 25,000 shoppers. Farmers delivered fresh goods by canoe from *chinampas* (floating gardens) on Lake Xochimilco. The huge market featured separate sections for specific foods, utensils, and slaves. In addition to tobacco, vendors stocked indigenous medicinal herbs, sweet-smelling salves, and seeds, but nothing from the outside world, not even cotton or salt. Royal inspectors collected taxes, settled commercial disputes, and examined the quality of salt, fish, flint kitchen knives, and loaves of bread baked from dried alga gathered from the lake, a spongy product the author com-

pared to cheese. In response to Cortés's insulting remarks about pagan idols, Montezuma retorted that Aztec gods were responsible for providing food and water and for nourishing the cornfields, the source of *atole,* a corn beverage, and tortillas, the Indian staff of life.

Díaz observed the extravagant habits of daily feasting at the emperor's palace, which required some 400 waitstaff bearing fragrant poultry, corn specialties, and hen and egg entrées along with side dishes of salad and vegetables in broth. Another 1,000 portions served the royal security guard. Pages spread the table with silvered and gilded fowl and the heads of calves, deer, and swine and kept each platter warm over fires kindled in clay braziers. Proper presentation demanded the adornment of tamales with beans and seeds and the shaping of corn cakes into animals and butterflies, a symbol of deceased warriors' spirits winging back to Earth. Meal service continued throughout the day for Montezuma, who sat behind a screen on a cushioned stool. He ate in silence and shared tidbits with four distinguished elders. Servants disposed of hand-washing implements for before- and after-meal cleansing and tossed out the emperor's dishes, which received only one use. Leftover food went to favored dancers, musicians, and hunchback jesters. Throughout the day, the emperor and his advisers walked the court, munching on snacks and sandwiches.

In 1520 during a celebratory feast, Díaz wrote of the shaping of corn tortillas into tacos filled with pork. Aztec table manners required the holding of a rolled tortilla in the left hand for dipping into a clay dish of *mole* (sauce) held in the right hand. The elite ended their meals with smoking and cups of hot cocoa.

In 1521, a 75-day siege from May 26 to mid-August ground down Aztec defiance of their conquerors. In his observations of this confrontation, Díaz mentioned cherries and figs as a relief from a steady diet of corn and as refreshment for combat casualties. For the beleaguered Aztec at Tenochtitlán, famine forced them to turn to lizards, rats, and snakes for sustenance. When those resources failed, Indians ate bark, grass, insects, leaves, moss, and roots and drank brackish lake water. Nonetheless, even perishing mothers and their toddlers glared at their conquerors and refused to plead for mercy.

After the Spanish victory over Montezuma on August 13, 1521, the death count from dehydration, disease, and hunger reached 240,000 Aztec and 30,000 of Cortés's Tlaxcalan allies. In celebration of the conquest, Díaz joined the feasting and revelry at Cuyoacan, the city center. Cortés rewarded the Aztec with haunches of enemy bodies salted to preserve them for cooking and eating. Spanish soldiers celebrated so excessively that Father Bartolomé de Olmedo, chaplain of the expedition, had to discipline them.

A Soldier's Fare

On the march south toward Espíritu Santo Bay in Yucatán on the Gulf of Mexico on October 12, 1524, Díaz earned his commander's regard for foraging, a survival skill that kept the army healthy and strong. Upon arrival southeast of Veracruz at Chilapan province, the soldiers found the deserted city of Tamaztepec north of Tuxtla burned to the ground, but with granaries still intact and corn and fruit still in the fields. While resources allowed, the troops shed their gloom and ate well.

In these hard times, hungry marchers built a bridge over a three-day period, during which they survived on meals of grass and a root—*quecuenque*—that burned their mouths. The Mexican chiefs of Tezcuco and Tlacuba staved off hunger by baking native victims between stones until Cortés commanded an end to cannibalism. At a swamp, the expedition seemed doomed until Díaz returned from a foraging expedition with eight chickens, honey, beans, and 130 loads of corn. Soldiers pounced on the booty before the officers could intervene and mete out the provisions fairly.

During Lent in 1525, the paucity of provisions aroused suspicion and infighting. Díaz blamed the commander for failing to send an escort to guard the supply train. Fortunately, Díaz had the foresight to cache corn, hens, and honey to feed Cortés and his staff. To the commander's concern for the feeding of company priests, Díaz assured him that soldiers respected their confessors enough to save them from starvation.

On a second foray into the countryside, Díaz superintended 100 native porters carrying provisions. The Mexican chiefs detected that famine caused a breakdown in discipline and proposed a camp mutiny. When Cortés learned of the plot, he hanged the kings of Mexico and Tlacuba to set an example of order and recompense for the exploitation of hard times.

Local chiefs, viewing the greed with which an army could strip natives of their stores, urged the Spaniards to proceed to the Mayan town of Nito, Honduras, an eight-day march crossing Guatemala. For provisions, the high command dispatched 80 men by canoe to outlying pueblos. Feasting and merrymaking resumed at the stockaded pueblo of Izancanac (Palenque, Mexico) in Acalan province and at a subsequent hunt with the Mazatec of Oaxaca, which yielded 20 deer. As weary men toiled up steep slopes, their horses died from cuts and falls. The scanty trail food consisted of unsalted cabbage palm seasoned with pork.

Upon reunion with the Spanish community of Nito, Díaz reported an unappealing diet of fish, vegetables, and *sapotes*, a creamy fruit similar in flavor to peaches. The arrival of a supply ship jeopardized the malnourished men, some of whom died from gorging on pork and other provisions. Foraging by raft deep into Guatemala along the Polochic River provided Mesoamerican staples—beans, corn, and cocoa—which Cortés rafted downstream to his camp. To sustain the colony at the port of Trujillo, Honduras, Cortés sent loot by two ships to Cuba and Jamaica to pay for livestock and plants to trade and to upgrade the diet of pioneers.

European Excess

Upon Cortés's triumphant return to Mexico, Díaz added to his descriptions of baroque court overindulgence with his recorded memories of a banquet held in Tenochtitlán's central plaza in June 1538. The sumptuous display set an example of Spanish snobbery and distaste for enchiladas, tamales, and other peasant cuisine. From sunset until after midnight, to the music of flute, harp, and trumpet, courses of dove, kid, oxen, pork, and marinated quail issued from the palace kitchen, accompanied by servings of beef and mutton, cabbage and turnips, and garbanzo beans. Ingenious presentations of platters took the form of classical tableaux. The opening of empanadas (turnovers) released live rabbits and birds. Servants poured chocolate from thousands of jars and served carob, mead, and spiced wine as prefaces to servings of blancmange and dessert trays of cardoons, cheeses, fruit, and olives. Montezuma himself sipped a vanilla-flavored chocolate beverage.

After Díaz's appointment in 1541 as governor of Santiago, Guatemala, he abandoned the military. At age 76, he began compiling his combat experiences to correct misinformation issued by Francisco López de Gómara, a former chaplain of the Cortés family and author of *Crónica de la Conquista de Nueva España* (*Chronicle of the Conquest of New Spain*, 1522). Díaz's collected episodes form *Historia Verdadera de la Conquista de la Nueva España* (*The True History of the Conquest of New Spain*, 1632), a working-class view of Cortés's expeditions. Critics question Díaz's skewed European perspective but credit him with detailing Aztec food marketing, table manners, and cuisine.

See also: Aztec Diet and Cuisine; Manioc; Seaman's Diet and Cuisine.

Further Reading

Cantú, Norma Elia, ed. *Moctezuma's Table: Rolando Briseño's Mexican and Chicano Tablescapes.* College Station: Texas A&M University Press, 2010.

Long-Solis, Janet, and Luis Alberto Vargas. *Food Culture in Mexico.* Westport, CT: Greenwood, 2005.

Dinner

A focus of sit-down communal eating, dinner is the main meal of the day as well as of festivals and religious banquets honoring holidays and special occasions. For the sake of hospitality, the assembled diners may groom their hands and hair, dress formally, and observe unusual protocol to honor the host. Diners may sit at appointed places, offer chants or prayers, and use more dishes, glasses, cups, and utensils than usual. Courtesy limits table conversation to prevent insults and squabbles.

Evolution of a Meal

The heavy meal in classical Rome, *cena* (dinner) followed the style of the Greek *deipnon* and latened from noon to early evening. Preceding service, hosts offered pinches of food at the home altar to the *lares* (guardian spirits) and *penates* (ancestral spirits). On divans in the *triclinium* (dining room), during the Roman Empire, male and female patricians reclined to consume three courses of finger foods: *gustatio* (appetizers), *mensa prima* (main course), and *mensa secunda* (dessert).

To make the most of sunlight, medieval diners broke the workday with *prandium,* a prenoon meal, the first food of the day. Workers, who began work at daybreak, followed a set pattern of eating a smaller meal at nightfall shortly before going to bed. In abbeys ruled by canonical hours, the timing of food intake at None (mid-afternoon) and Vespers (evening) reflected set times for worship and prayers.

For feudal nobles, the noon dinner offered a dramatic setting for a display of power and ostentation, showcasing the presentation of heavily garnished whole beasts and main dishes carried by a procession of servants. Meat received the greatest obeisance. Carving and proper plating set a tone of dignity and civility.

In later centuries, the British trader and shopkeeper halted business around 3 P.M. for dinner. The tradition, still honored by the Italian and Spanish siesta, set the pattern for two midday rush hours before and after dinner. The principal meal hour for the leisured classes advanced from 3 P.M. in the 1700s to an evening spread after 6 P.M. in the next century. Enhancing elaborate settings and table service, overhead candlelight and wall sconces softened lighting and created an intimate mood. The lateness of dinner generated a need for breakfast, which became ampler and more standardized in the late 1800s to satisfy the appetite during a long day.

In Japan in the 1830s, a gendered approach to dinner demanded that housewives stay home with the children while businessmen dined together in restaurants. Groups reserved banquet rooms and awaited a *table d'hôte,* or set menu, paid for in advance. To relieve the male-only tedium, geishas, professional hostesses, provided hospitality and sparkling conversation.

In colonial North America, fieldworkers and schoolchildren gathered at home around noon for the largest meal of the day. The factory and mine whistles that announced work stoppage signaled homemakers of the regimented hours or half hours. Women introduced teatime as a polite, relaxing snack and social hour in late afternoon to stave off the hunger preceding dinner. By the 1840s, tea service fueled a demand for tearooms, a

Swanson introduced TV dinners in 1954 with a Thanksgiving-style meal of turkey with gravy, mashed potatoes, and peas. At 98 cents each, the original TV dinner sold 10 million units in the first year—to the detriment of dinner table conversation. *(The Granger Collection, New York)*

feminine business that expanded opportunities for women in baking, jam making, and food service.

After urban gas service and electrification altered the life rhythms of rural people, it became less necessary to eat the principal meal at midday. Children and laborers deferred to sack lunches and saved the major eating event for early evening, when housewives dished up a meat and two vegetables along with hot bread and dessert. For the gentry as well, an evening meal replaced the noon lunch in importance. Evening entertainments and theater performances kept the moneyed class up later and generated a need for supper, a small dinner served as late as midnight.

In the early 1900s, dinner service in the United States took place by 4 P.M. for factory workers and miners and around 6 P.M. or later for white-collar workers. Jewish families gathered at sundown on Friday for a Sabbath meal enriched by symbolic blessings of children and food, candles, and *kiddush* (prayer). Braided challah (egg bread), carrot stew, and fragrant fish or meat soups accentuated the ritual, which dated to ancient Babylonia.

Modern Adaptations

The evening dinner hour defined household timeliness and togetherness in the Western world until the late 1940s, when families began abandoning seven-day-a-week rituals for five-day-a-week home meals and fast food on weekends. Simultaneously, snacks randomized hunger and fulfillment and diminished the camaraderie of the nuclear family.

In Peoria, Illinois, in 1954, C.A. Swanson & Sons designer Gerry Thomas responded to a surfeit of Thanksgiving turkeys by inventing the TV dinner, a covered, three-compartment serving for one. Heated in the oven, it resembled an airline dinner. Young and old took their individual servings to metal trays in the living room or den to eat while watching television. In 1955, at the height of *I Love Lucy*, *The Lawrence Welk Show*, and *What's My Line?*, the company sold 10 million TV meals.

At a cost of 98¢ each, the Swanson frozen time-saver allowed families a choice of fried chicken, haddock filet, meatloaf, Salisbury steak, or turkey. Banquet, a competitor in Omaha, Nebraska, augmented selections by packaging meat pies, chicken breast tenders and wings, and fruit pies. In 1958, Freezer Queen of Buffalo, New York, entered the frozen dinner market and pioneered onion gravy and broccoli in cheese sauce. Amid dinnertime innovations, home economists warned that convenience meals were replacing home cooking with conveyor belt gastronomy.

With the advent of microwaving in the late 1960s, plastic trays replaced aluminum. In 1973, Swanson's "Hungry-Man" dinners offered larger portions and selections ranging from charbroiled Angus beef sandwiches and chicken strips to beef enchiladas, fried chicken, lasa-gna, pork ribs, spiced ham, steak, and veal parmigiana. A twenty-first-century communication revolution interrupts meals by cell phones and iPods, which draw the attention of youth from dinner to social networking.

See also: Beans and Legumes; Cereal; Feasting; Luau; Salad and Salad Bars.

Further Reading

Clarkson, Janet. *Menus from History: Historic Meals and Recipes for Every Day of the Year.* Santa Barbara, CA: Greenwood, 2009.

Inch, Arthur, and Arlene Hirst. *Dinner Is Served: An English Butler's Guide to the Art of the Table.* Philadelphia: Running Press, 2003.

McMillan, Sherrie. "What Time Is Dinner?" *History Magazine* 3:1 (October/November 2001): 21–24.

Visser, Margaret. *Much Depends on Dinner: The Extraordinary History and Mythology, Allure and Obsessions, Perils and Taboos of an Ordinary Meal.* New York: Grove, 2010.

Disease, Food-Borne

In addition to hydrating and nourishing the body, edibles also harbor fungi, parasites, and pathogens, some of which cause critical illness, long-term impairment, or death. Historically, sickness from food and water has weakened populations from early times. A common cause of epidemic results from polluted food and water sources, such as the contaminated drinking water in Babylon that spread typhoid to Alexander the Great and his forces and cholera in India during seasonal floods between 1900 and 1920, which killed 8 million people. Additional epidemics dot history: *Serratia marcescens* in medieval Eucharists that inflamed eyes and urinary tracts, giardia in Christian crusaders in Palestine during the eleventh and twelfth centuries, ergotism among victims of seventeenth-century witch trials, and dysentery that killed prisoners of war during the American Civil War.

Global food distribution, combined with spotty inspection of edibles, increases the flow of tainted goods to consumers. The sources of contamination appear at all stages of the handling of produce and meats—picking, washing, transporting, processing, warehousing, distribution, cooking, and consumption. One example, scombrotoxin, from bacterial decay of tuna, can inflict diarrhea and vomiting, headache, muscle cramp, and even blindness. Symptoms of brucellosis, a milk-borne disease carried by dogs, camels, cattle, goats, and pigs, may include flulike chills and fatigue, joint pain, swollen glands, and weakness. Unlike most food-borne disease, which passes within days, brucellosis may cause relapses over several years.

A daunting list of bacteria, fungi, parasites, and viruses—Creutzfeldt-Jakob disease, *Cryptosporidium parvum, Giardia lamblia,* hepatitis A, *Listeria monocytogenes,* norovirus, *Rotovirus gastroenteritis,* shigellosis, *Staphylococcus aureus,* and trichinosis—can corrupt food and pass through the mouth and stomach to habitats in intestinal walls and the bladder, heart, kidneys, liver, and lungs. Infectious hepatitis, which can originate in polluted shellfish, causes jaundice, a yellowing of the eyes and skin that may last for months. Some 25 percent of victims of listeria incur the disorder from deli meat and hot dogs and die from meningitis. The deadliest food-borne contagion, *Clostridium botulinum,* generates a paralytic toxin in canned foods that are heated at temperatures too low to kill bacteria. Most at risk are infants, the elderly, pregnant women, and patients suffering from diabetes, human immunodeficiency virus (HIV), lupus, radiation depletion, or other immune suppressants.

The most common food-borne threats come from *Campylobacter jejuni, Escherichia coli* (*E. coli*), and *Salmonella typhimurium.* Campylobacter bacteria thrive in raw poultry and inflict serious gastrointestinal suffering from Guillain-Barre syndrome. *E. coli,* a bacteria that lives in ruminants, enters human food or water through fecal contamination. Gut impairment can result from hemolytic uremic poisoning, a preface to anemia, bloody dysentery, and kidney failure. Salmonella, a third food-borne bacteria, lives in birds, mammals, and reptiles and enters the body through polluted water, infected meltwater from frozen poultry, and unclean kitchens. In healthy people, the discomfort is chiefly short-term fever, abdominal cramps, and diarrhea; in compromised immune systems, the disease infects the bloodstream with lethal sepsis.

The norovirus, a more difficult diagnosis, initiates vomiting and inflammation of the alimentary canal. Because the pathogen passes between humans, investigators tend to locate the origin in food handlers and waiters who cut and arrange salad bars and sandwiches. The outbreak reaches endemic proportions at gatherings, such as catered receptions and family reunions, or from service of infected food at delis, grocery stores, hospitals, prisons, restaurants, and schools. Another source of contamination comes from the hands of seafood harvesters and sorters who unknowingly infect clams, mussels, oysters, and other filtering shellfish.

Annually, food-borne illness afflicts 30 percent of the world's people. Over 48 million Americans incur disease from eating and drinking, most commonly from salmonella. Of these, 3,000 die and 128,000 enter hospitals. Tracking by the Centers for Disease Control and health departments begins with a culture of stool samples. Before the specimens produce verifiable pathogens, individuals remedy dehydration from loss of body sera and electrolytes with extra fluids. More serious treatment combats fever and intestinal bleeding. Physicians cau-

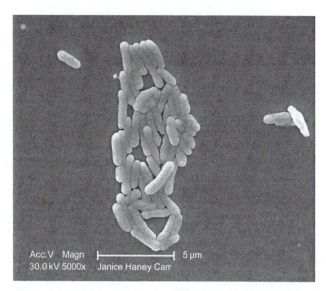

A colorized photomicrograph, at a magnification of 5000x, reveals a cluster of salmonella bacteria linked to an outbreak of food poisoning in spring 2008. More than 1,300 cases of salmonellosis were reported in 43 states. *(CDC/ Associated Press)*

tiously prescribe antibiotics because of the emergence of such resistant strains of bacteria as methicillin-resistant *Staphyloccus aureus* (MRSA).

Clustered illnesses require graphing of victims, their meals, and the places where they may have encountered or purchased contaminated food or water. For example, *Giardia lamblia,* a zoonotic transmitted from beaver, cows, deer, and sheep, may infect consumers of well water or swimmers in ponds and wilderness streams. Statistical evaluation of toxic ingredients leads to original sources, such as salmonella from a single poultry farm or alfalfa sprout grower, or *E. coli* from hamburger ground on unwashed abattoir equipment and marketed by a chain grocer. Inspectors look for contaminated cutting boards and field and orchard collection baskets as well as points of recontamination from animal blood, raw shellfish, and unpasteurized eggs, juice, or milk.

In 2010, the U.S. Food and Drug Administration introduced standards intended to reduce bacterial infection of foodstuffs and water by 60 percent. In July 2010, egg producers installed new precautions against *Salmonella enteritidis* involving bird sanitation and egg storage and initiated additional safeguards intended for completion over the next two years. Veterinarians contributed safety policies regarding slaughtering and processing of poultry, beginning with preventive medicines for flocks. The Partnership for Food Protection mandated similar upgrades in sanitation involving restaurant inspection and domestic and imported baby formula, pet foods, and fruits, such as the Mexican papayas that caused a salmonella outbreak in 23 states in July 2011.

See also: Alcoholic Beverages; Allergies, Food; Inspection and Safety, Food; Pork; Veganism; Vegetarianism.

Further Reading
Bjorklund, Ruth. *Food Borne Illnesses.* New York: Marshall Cavendish Benchmark, 2006.
Derby, Mary Patricia. *Poison Control Center Foodborne Illness Surveillance.* Ann Arbor, MI: UMI, 2008.
Hui, Yiu H., et al., eds. *Foodborne Disease Handbook.* Vol. 2, *Viruses, Parasites, Pathogens, and HACCP.* New York: Marcel Dekker, 2001.
Snodgrass, Mary Ellen. *World Epidemics: A Cultural Chronology of Disease from Prehistory to the Era of SARS.* Jefferson, NC: McFarland, 2003.

Dried Food

Whether by natural sunlight, oven, or open fire, the drying of food, the world's first preservation method, extends table use by slowing enzymatic action and removing sources of infestation and spoilage. In prehistory, hunter-gathers in Asia and the Middle East relied on solar energy to preserve berries, fish, game, nuts, seaweed, seeds, vegetables, and vine fruit. In Armenia, fruit purees dried in the sun into *bastegh* (fruit leather), a thin, malleable layer that preparers cut into slices for storage in jars. Perishables also dried on a smoking rack, among rocks, on a spit, in a rock pit, on a parching tray, or in a shell or clay container. In heat and smoke, fish, meat, plantains, and yams shrank from extraction of up to 80 percent of liquids. The resulting food remained high in energy and fiber and low in fat.

Ancient Fare

From 11,000 B.C.E., Paleo-Indians dried and smoked berries to season fish, turtle, and venison stews. Shrinkage of jerky and fruit leather on birch bark trays or wooden slabs increased the value of both as barter items and pack food. Similarly, Libyans and Ethiopians bartered with lake salt, which they dehydrated in brackish pools. Yogurt, first coagulated naturally in Sumer in 6000 B.C.E., dehydrated into a traveler's snack. Armenians and Egyptians spiced and wind-dried camel and goat meat for *pastirma,* a ready-to-eat meal requiring intense chewing. From 2100 B.C.E., south-central China evolved a cuisine noted for the robust flavor of dried vegetables. By 1500 B.C.E., the Babylonians and Chinese air-dried sausage, a meat preservation technique that involved blending ground meat with salt, spices, and sugar.

Dehydrated produce lasted longer than salt-dried or smoked food and weighed up to one-third less than fresh. In sub-Saharan Africa, traders packed palm oil and lightweight dried cereal, copra (coconut meat), and fish for transport by major waterways. The yield of the floodplain and amicable relations in river ports enabled vendors to supply dense populations, which developed into the continent's first city-states—Gao in the Songhai Empire, Jenne-Jeno in Sudan, Timbuktu in Mali, and Zanzibar.

Between Iceland and Scotland in 1000 B.C.E., Faeroe Islanders made dolphins, porpoises, and long-finned pilot whales a staple of their cuisine by salting and air-drying the meat and flavoring it with dried fish as a condiment. On the island of Tonga in the same era, Polynesian cooks used pottery jars for parboiling fish in herbed water to ready the meat for drying. For ritual sea voyages by double-hulled canoe or outrigger back to Tahiti, mariners packed desiccated coconut pulp and fish as "canoe food." Along the Mediterranean, Hesiod's *Works and Days* (700 B.C.E.) described the air-drying of grapes to temper the flavor before packing them in terra-cotta jars.

The concept of air-, fire-, and sun-drying cuts of meat suited the needs of desert nomads, pueblo dwellers, and Phoenician seafarers, who carried compact, lightweight meals on journeys around the Mediterranean. On Crete, the sun-drying of wheat stirred into sour goat or sheep milk yielded *xinochondros,* a stabilized breakfast food dehydrated into nuggets in large trays. From the first century C.E. in Arizona, Hohokam laborers ensured winter rations by gathering 175 pounds (80 kilograms) of dried mesquite pods a day for storage. The *garambullo* cactus (*Myrtillocactus geometrizans*) provided the Hohokam and the Apache, Papago, Pima, Sinagua, Tewa, and Ute with a grape-sized berry that they dried like raisins for sweetening *pinole* (corn porridge).

For indigenous people in temperate to tropical climes, dried foods held up to changes in humidity and temperature. Indians in Santiago, Chile, valued the daylily, the root of which they dried in an oven and ground into meal for making pastries. In the Great Basin, the Cahuilla and Maricopa sorted and dried cactus blossoms for dipping in syrup. The Pomo of northern California dried seaweed on the beach to serve in tortillas or to fry in oil. California and Colorado Indians braided ears of corn and spread them on adobe roofs in the sun before stacking them in rock-lined pantries. Mission Indian women commandeered the caching and drying of acorns, the chief carbohydrate.

To the east, Middle Atlantic and New England growers buried sacks of corn ears, parched kernels, and corn smut, along with strings of dehydrated pumpkin and squash slices, to supply them during winter. The Iroquois of Canada and New York extended the use of surplus corn by charring it and burying it in bark-roofed caches. Among the Timucua of northern Florida, the drying of squash strips into curls and the roast-drying of oysters guaranteed plentiful stores during hurricane season.

North of the Aswan Dam in Egypt, the Kubbaniya survived famine by caching smoke- or sun-dried fish for up to five months. Honeyed and salt-dried jerky supplied the tombs of Amenhotep II and Thutmose III with grave goods. In Hokkaido, Japan, processors boiled seaweed in iron kettles filled with fresh water before drying fronds on bamboo racks. The Inca of Peru trimmed bone, fat, and gristle from cattle, deer, elk, horse, and llama muscle and heat-dried it to produce dense, lightweight meals. After salting the rumps and shanks, Inca processors sun- and wind-dried them into *charqui* (jerky). In Kamchatka, Russia, hunter-gatherers added cloudberries, cranberries, crowberries, raspberries, whortleberries, and wild garlic to sweeten a diet of dried salmon and trout. Cooks softened dried fish by dipping it into salmon oil.

During the Iron Age, after the Chinese and Japanese fished or "jigged" for cuttlefish and squid at night by lantern light, they dried the meat for barter or sale. Celtic hunter-gatherers from the British Isles to Eastern Europe depended year-round on dehydrated currants, heather, rowan berries, and seaweed. For winter, they stored beechnuts and hazelnuts, flax, and dried bilberries, dewberries, and hawthorn and juniper fruits in sealed containers. Herbs suspended in warm, airy environments remained flavorful and easily shredded for adding to crab apple vinegar and sloe and wild plum wine.

From 400 C.E., the Chinese extended papermaking technology to drying seaweed in strips. After pulverizing it, they made stock to thicken meat dishes or simmered seaweed in vegetables or rice to produce a taste like anchovies or caviar. In Iceland during the tenth century, Norse chieftains favored dried dulse as a fiber food. The Irish cached dehydrated seaweed to cook in fish dishes, oatcakes, and potatoes. Healers recommended dried or powdered dulse in the diet for the fluoride content, which prevented dental cavities. In Scotland and the Hebrides, fishermen and crofters relished dried and stewed seaweed as a vegetable or condiment and as forage for sheep. In storage sheds, they draped dulse and carrageen for air-drying.

Middle Ages and Renaissance

During the Middle Ages, preservation of food by desiccation in a still house became a cornerstone of the economy and general well-being. Afghans dried mulberry cakes to spend like coins. Similarly, Norwegians dried cod as the basis of their food industry and as currency. Stores from Ribe, in Jutland, packed easily on ships and sold well in Asia, Greenland, and Western Europe. According to *De Cultura Hortarum* (*On Gardening*, ca. 840), author Walafrid Strabo, a Frankish monk, dried plants at Reichenau Abbey to maintain wellness through regulated digestion. Early medieval dairiers in Benedictine and Cistercian monasteries in the Alps and throughout northwestern Europe stored curd products as a substitute for forbidden meats and extended their shelf life by brining, drying, or smoking. Before cooking, preparers soaked curds in milk, dehydrated fish in water, and dried fruit in brandy or wine.

Dehydrated goods provisioned armies and fleets. During the First Crusade, after 1096, Christian supply trains imported dried fruit to the Middle East as a source of energy and nourishment for badly malnourished troops. *The Travels of Marco Polo* (ca. 1300) described sun-dried milk as an on-the-march paste consumed by the Tatar forces of Kublai Khan. Chinese sailing crews ate dried ginger rhizomes to prevent seasickness and consumed oysters desiccated in seaweed. On long trading missions, both foods remained free from fungus and decay.

After 1492, the age of voyages introduced the Spanish to Native American pantry stock. The dehydrated vanilla bean entered world cuisine in the Totonac diet of Veracruz. Curing began with blanching the beans in hot water and sun-drying them to one-quarter the former weight. On a larger scale, the Olmec and Tarahumara of north-central Mexico stockpiled their staple, dried corn on the cob, in desert pits. Taíno bread makers dehydrated cassava to shape into loaves on clay griddles. For Aztec women, grinding dried corn involved kneeling at a stone mano and metate and pressing the roller until it crushed hard kernels into meal. In another labor-intensive preservation task, the Inca of Peru sliced llama meat for drying and tenderized the strips by pounding them between stones. Desiccation promoted a long shelf life in stone silos and warehouses and portability in pouches for journeys.

The Carib of the West Indies considered food drying a daily chore. They built sheltered food storage near their homes and vented air-drying and smoking through the unthatched sides. To perform the daily job of drying and pulverizing corn into grits, Spanish explorer Hernando de Soto approved the kidnap of Indian women as slave labor in 1539. Three years later, after his expedition advanced northwest to Hot Springs, Arkansas, the troops located a wealth of dried beans, corn, and plums and added the goods to military stores for the captive women to cook.

During the Renaissance, food dehydration extended to more than fish, fruit, grain, and meat. The poorest of England's 4 million subjects turned ground dried peas into maslin (brown bread) or horse bread, the lowest grade of baked loaves.

Among Japanese fishermen in Kuzaki on Enshu Bay east of Osaka, sacred offerings of seafood required a special preparation of the abalone catch. They excised the circular abalone muscle in an unbroken strip and sun-dried the length for home use. They also secured dried sardines in lidded baskets and air-dried shiitake mushrooms to ready the household for a New Year dinner. Dried tofu accompanied the tea service in the late 1500s as a complement to the beverage. Hosts mixed tofu blocks with chili sauce, dried shrimp, onion, or soy sauce for breakfast. In the Philippines, dried tofu topped with palm syrup produced a sweet dessert.

In 1607, the 45 English adventurers from the Virginia Company of Plymouth returned home with a store of dried greenbrier (*Smilex regelii*), the source of sarsaparilla. The drink proved popular in England because of rumors that it cured venereal disease. In 1620, the Pilgrims of Plymouth, Massachusetts, learned from returnees at Popham colony at Sagadahoc, Maine, how to survive hunger during dire winters. In imitation of coastal Algonquins, the English garnered clams and oysters and bartered quahogs (hard clams) with inland tribes.

During the 1600s, when salt was inexpensive and families awaited fresh catches of cod for drying and sale to fleets, a high rate of death from scurvy sapped Portuguese naval strength. On voyages to Brazil, Guinea, and India, mariners received measured amounts of baked biscuit and dried cod, the standard sailor's fare, which lacked ascorbic acid. In addition, the ship's cook laid in stores of almonds, lentils, prunes and raisins, and sardines. For sickbay meals, they reserved the dried fruit, which had limited effect on bleeding gums and flaccid muscles.

For long voyages, Spanish sailors converted Pacific island goats into *carne seca* (dried meat) to stock their galleys with an adaptable jerky. In reference to the drying method, in *The Generall Historie of Virginia* (1624), Captain John Smith named the technique "meat jerking." Hunters of the North American plains rack-dried enough buffalo meat for clan provisions and barter. Packing the jerked flanks with mint discouraged vermin during caching. Preparers sliced cured fat, suspended from the smoke hole of a lodge, and used dehydrated slabs like bread for jerky sandwiches.

Food for Colonies

The colonial era revealed to Europeans the preservation methods of indigenous people. In the Caribbean during the seventeenth century, food writer Gonzalo Fernández de Oviedo observed the Arawak, Carib, and Taíno air-drying alligator and fish on racks of bearded fig wood raised on saplings. The Pee-Posh of the lower Colorado River, the Yukon of northwestern Canada, and the Hare of Alberta and Alaska added pantries to the hogan, igloo, or lodge as storage space for baskets of dried berries and grain or as a shelter for dried plums and herbs and smoked meats and fish. Rising heat from hearths protected the foodstuffs by preventing moisture from invading them.

Cooking styles passed from Indians to white settlers, who had limited experience with survival food. According to the writings of philosopher and provincial founder William Penn, Pennsylvania Indians taught settlers how to dry and beat corn kernels and boil them in water to produce hominy. Native women demonstrated how to crush corn with a pestle in a hollow log mortar. By placing a flat stone on top of the corn and pounding with a stone hammer, workers reduced labor and waste and produced an evenly crushed meal. Native cooks mixed the meal with water and shaped the dough into corn cakes for wrapping in corn shucks and baking in ashes.

Among most North American Indians, trade in surplus corn and dried fish augmented supplies for winter, when red meat was scarce. The Canadian Huron gathered and air-dried berries, corn, and sweet prairie turnips

(*Psoralea esculenta*). At Patuxet, Massachusetts, on November 16, 1620, Miles Standish and his hungry followers pounced on a basket of dried cranberries and bushels of husked Narragansett corn, a staple that the aborigines of southern New England had grown since 700 B.C.E. The discovery impressed on naive English settlers the importance of dehydrating food for hard times.

Heat-drying shortened the desiccation process while protecting foodstuffs from inclement weather and infestation. Quebec masons built semi-indoor ovens and flues, in which rising heat dried bean pods and grain sheaves to ward off mildew and yeast and dehydrated strings of beans and peppers, bags of chestnuts and peanuts, braided onions, loops of pemmican, tubers and herbs, and rounds of pumpkin and winter squash. In imitation of native industry, settlers of Canada's Grand Banks and New England initiated global trade in rack-dried flounder and hake, which acquired a smoky savor from the drying process.

The tea trade encouraged complementary food business in dried leaves, milk, and sugar. After 1706, Eastern Europeans developed a tea culture from Lapsang souchong, a tea smoke-dried in bamboo baskets over pinewood fires. The strong, savory leaves traveled by camel caravan on a 6,000-mile (9,600-kilometer) route through Russia, thus raising prices for supplies of chai (tea blended with sweetening, spices, and milk). Complementing hot tea, plantations in Barbados and the Virgin Islands chopped sugarcane for dehydration. After sun-drying and curing in tins, the hardened crystals passed to wind-powered pounders, which smashed hard sugar into coarse, crunchy chunks. The hang-drying of calf stomachs preserved rennet for the curdling of milk into sour cream, an English additive to tea service.

Establishment of a penal colony in New South Wales on January 26, 1788, necessitated the preservation of foodstuffs until English prisoners and soldiers could acclimate to their island habitat. In Queensland, the newcomers observed Australian Aborigines air-drying tropical waterlily roots and yams. In a world apart from Aborigines, the English fed themselves temporarily on a two-year stock of cheese and dried beef. In Tasmania, settlers dehydrated goat meat, mushrooms, underground fungus, and brined fish. They also air-dried apple slices, the beginning of a world export business in dehydrated pome fruit.

Dried foods quickly increased the economic stability of New World settlements. In his treatise *A Description of Greenland* (1818), travel writer Hans Egede observed the Inuit cuisine and reported the consumption of boiled, dried, and raw meat from hares, partridges, and reindeer and of air-dried halibut and salmon roe. The convenience of desiccated food generated a demand for commercial stocks. In British Columbia in 1827, the Hudson's Bay Company added dried salmon to trade offerings of jerky and pemmican.

Brisk Atlantic trade between Great Britain, the West Indies, and the American ports of Charles Town,

Boston, New York, Newport, and Philadelphia required constant surveillance to protect stores of dried fish. Emulating the ramadas of Southwestern Indians, frontier families constructed brush arbors and slatted sheds facing south to maintain the texture of dried meat. Daily inspection and excising of spoiled tissue prevented rot from destroying the entire batch. Turning ensured even dehydration of thicker portions.

Technical Advances

To primitive guesswork, science contributed new methods of drying and processing foods. German organic chemist Justus von Liebig made artificial human breast milk with proportional blends of carbohydrates, fats, and protein in a farinaceous food called Liebig's Soluble Food for Babies. In 1867, his Registered Concentrated Milk Company in London shipped the simulated mother's milk to American and European markets. Liebig followed the liquid version with a powder of dried cow's milk, malt and wheat flour, and potassium bicarbonate for reconstitution with milk and water. A letter to the *Medical Times and Gazette* in 1877 proclaimed the formulation a boon to children for its ease of use and nutritional value.

In Chicago in 1887, advertisements for pharmacist James Horlick's malted milk, another form of dried milk combined with dried sprouted barley, promised health benefits in a nonperishable dairy food. The powdered product, the forerunner of Ovaltine, proved more popular with polar explorers than with babies. In the 1890s, Nestlé's Milk Food debuted dried milk especially for hot weather infant feeding. Magazines introduced the product to mothers by mailing samples to readers and hyping a product reputedly more beneficial than the milk of wet nurses.

World War I and the Great Depression produced the first global demand for dried foods. During the rationing of World War II, 160 dehydration plants went into operation in the United States. Factories produced food more calorically dense than fresh produce but lower in vitamins A and C, which air and heat destroyed. Batchelors, a leader in food desiccation in Sheffield, England, excelled at the production of noodles, peas, and soups, the forerunner of Lipton's Cup a Soup. Dehydration of food stocks brought to the homemaker's table powdered egg yolk, fruit, milk, and soup. In lieu of tea, older children thrived on high-energy fruit juice, dried fruit, and chocolate. Pregnant and nursing women drank a pint of reconstituted dried milk a day.

The end of wartime rationing did not halt the sale of dehydrated food. By the 1970s, imported goods from Australia and New Zealand initiated a vigorous competition from the Southern Hemisphere in frozen and dried berries. Warehousing of dried foods kept stocks at hand for emergencies and weather disasters. In the 1990s in India, where 62 percent of children suffered malnutrition, impoverished families received infant formula and dried milk dispatched by charitable outreaches, including CARE and UNICEF.

Today, desiccation methods continue to extend the life of foodstuffs, such as the roof-drying of tomatoes in Italy and breadfruit in Sri Lanka. In Rajasthani cuisine from northwestern India, *pachrangi* dal features five types of dried legumes in proportion. For the Inuit of North America, the world's purest hunting society, a protein- and fat-focused regimen ranges from rack-dried capelin and ptarmigan and kittiwake eggs to smoke-dried bowhead whale and reindeer tongue. For the Pribilof Islanders on the Bering Sea, dehydrated salmon and eider ducks provide winter subsistence. An Icelandic delicacy, *hákarl,* requires the curing in sand and the hang-drying of basking shark for up to 20 weeks. An Icelandic buffet features liver sausage as well as wind-dried cod and haddock.

In Polynesia, the hazard of cyclones and freak winds necessitates emergency food reserves. The cooks of Oceania sun-dry or smoke-dry snapper and tuna, which also supply voyagers on canoe expeditions. The light pack weight of dried bread mix, milk, cereal, rice, and instant tea enables rescuers to ferry sustenance to areas plagued by famine, flood, epidemic, and siege.

See also: Caching; Curing; Fish and Fishing; Freeze-Drying; Jerky; Liebig, Justus von; Sausage; Standish, Miles; Tea.

Further Reading

DeLong, Deanna. *How to Dry Foods.* New York: Penguin, 2006.

Hui, Yiu H., et al., eds. *Food Drying Science and Technology: Microbiology, Chemistry, Applications.* Lancaster, PA: DEStech, 2008.

Ratti, Cristina. *Advances in Food Dehydration.* Boca Raton, FL: CRC, 2009.

Symons, Michael. *A History of Cooks and Cooking.* Urbana: University of Illinois Press, 2000.

Dubois, Félix Urbain (1818–1901)

In 1869, French chef Félix Urbain Dubois popularized *service à la russe,* the presentation of dinner in separate courses on individual plates rather than in grand displays. He based his early style on the example of master chef Marie-Antoine Carême. Dubois gained renown for architectural creations adorned with inedible ferns and animal statuary to entertain and amuse diners. For home-style reference, he compiled *Le Livre de la Ménagère; ou, Petite Encyclopedie de la Famille (The Book of the Housekeeper, or Small Encyclopedia for the Family,* 1870), a practical handbook on the coating and saucing of meat for 180 family menus.

With his two-volume *La Cuisine Classique (Classic Cookery,* 1856), coauthored by Émile Bernard, the cook of

Napoleon III, Dubois contributed to gastronomy a respect for food at the height of readiness. At St. Petersburg, he developed the concept while serving from 1850 to 1869 as head chef of Prince Nikolai Alexeevich Orlov, the worldly Russian ambassador to Belgium, Britain, France, and the Austro-Hungarian Empire. Dubois remained on the prince's staff during the Congress of Paris of 1856 at the end of the Crimean War, a peak of prominence that involved the chef in constant social and political activity.

The revolutionary shift in table decor affected all aspects of cookery. The former French style of plating presented hot dishes and cold dishes in separate batches. The grouping of entrées, a leftover of the Middle Ages, allowed the heated platters to cool and the cold specialties to wilt under warm candlelight. Dubois chose to serve individual entrees one by one at the height of edibility.

A model of Dubois's Russian-style entrées, veal Prince Orlov consisted of a braised loin sliced into thin leaves and interlarded with a puree of mushrooms and onions. For the finished dish, Dubois topped the meat with béchamel (white sauce) and broiled the surface into a brown crust.

In retirement in the 1880s, Dubois continued traveling between Nice and Monte Carlo to dine at the Grand Hotel and propose recipes for his collection, *La Cuisine d'Aujourd'hui: Ecole des Jeunes Cuisiniers* (*Today's Cuisine: School of Young Cooks*, 1897), a standard culinary text. Commentary explained the etymology of culinary terms, including the union of firm and soft dough to make *pain bâtard*, or torpedo loaf. His mentoring of Auguste Escoffier influenced the wealth of European restaurants that opened in the early 1900s.

See also: Escoffier, Georges Auguste.

Further Reading

Donovan, Mary, ed. *Remarkable Service.* Hoboken, NJ: John Wiley & Sons, 2009.

Fischer, John. "Table Service." *Gastronomica* 1:3 (Summer 2001): 90–91.

James, Kenneth. *Escoffier: The King of Chefs.* London: Continuum, 2006.

Mennell, Stephen. *All Manners of Food: Eating and Taste in England and France from the Middle Ages to the Present.* Urbana: University of Illinois Press, 1995.

Durante, Castor (1529–1590)

Italian court physician and botanist Castor Durante da Gualdo compiled an influential guide to diet and wellness in the sixteenth century.

Born at Gualdo, near Spoleto, Durante came of age at the height of Renaissance interest in global foodstuffs

and cuisine. A man of his time, he completed medical studies at Perugia and called himself a *"cittadino Romano"* (Roman citizen). In 1567, he became Gualdo's town doctor.

Under Vatican patronage of Pope Gregory XIII, Durante wrote works on diet, hygiene, and rest. For invigoration of the senses, he urged the pope to exercise outdoors. Durante's texts advocated meals of hedgehogs and rats and extolled frog meat as a cure for snakebite. His culinary advisories featured easily swallowed foods as well as the use of tobacco, a leafy North American plant, as a cure-all for pulmonary distress. At issue among his contemporaries lay questions of meal organization and service, particularly the placement of salads and sweets among courses. Because of Durante's felicitous writing style and succinct advice on therapeutic food concerns, his books went through numerous editions and translations. His popularity as an adviser on herbalism earned him a papal appointment and a university chair at Salerno.

In 1565, Durante published in Latin hexameters *De Bonitate et Vitio Alimentorum Centauria* (*On the Goodness and Medicinal Faults of Foods*), a handy guidebook subtitled *How to Preserve Health and Prolong Life; Treating Nature, Food, and Remedies for Illness*. Translators rendered the text in Italian under the more familiar title *Il Tesoro della Sanita* (*The Treasury of Health*, 1586), a common reference manual for medical doctors.

Durante opened his discourse with comments on air quality and suggested leaving bread in the open to gauge humidity and the presence of air pollutants. The scholarly dietary organizes tidy entries on wheat, pasta, and bread and covers beans, chickpeas, lentils, greens and spinach, asparagus, herbs, lettuce, radishes and carrots, and mushrooms. Each entry makes claims about the aspect of wellness that individual foods bolster, such as the pharmacological wonders of salads and vegetable medleys. Durante valued borage for relief of depression and for enhancement of memory, a belief anchored in the classical Greek writings of Dioscorides and Hippocrates.

Durante fostered a proactive diet. He recommended eating salad at the beginning of each meal. Of songbirds as entrées, he preferred the thrush, especially the ones fed on aromatic juniper and myrtle berries. He favored boiling rather than roasting meat and recommended using beans only as accompaniments to other ingredients. Of fava beans, he warned that they encouraged a limp sponginess in muscle tissue. His recipe for dried broad beans required skinning them to rid them of indigestible cortex and pounding them before simmering in leeks, onions, oil, and spices. The addition of oregano and fennel discouraged dyspepsia and flatulence.

Concerning the *pomi d'oro* (tomato), a recent import from New World gardens, he advised preparing it, like eggplant, with oil, pepper, and salt. Like most Europeans, he doubted the nutritional value of the tomato and blamed *tartufi* (potatoes) for head and nervous disorders, but he repeated the common belief that potatoes fostered sperm production.

Durante's orderly listing of fruits, nuts, oils, and condiments preceded a gradual lead-up to fish, poultry, and red meat. The herbalist recommended the meat of birds over mutton and veal from quadrupeds. He valued game above domestic meat because wild animals exercised in fresh air and ate from nature. He believed that wild meat enlivened the human vascular system. Like the ancient Greek physician Galen, Durante advocated pork for its food value.

More significant to health was his lengthy discussion of water and wine. To prevent an imbalance of the body's humors, he disallowed cooling wine and water with ice or snow. In a society where popes and eminent prelates flaunted gluttony, Durante's work advocated prudence and body wisdom about the combinations and quantities of foods needed for health and satisfaction. As the physician to Pope Sextus V, Durante espoused frugality and temperance.

Durante's first publication flourished for a century. He followed this with the illustrated *Herbario Nuovo* (*New Herbarium,* 1585), an A-to-Z study of more than 900 plants and their value to nutrition and healing based on classical and medieval dietary theory. Published in Venice, the herbarium went through four revivals. The woodcuts, drawn by teen wonder Leonardo Parasole Norsini and engraved by Parasole's wife Isabella, provided elegant detail of species, flower, and fruit. Interest in Durante's comments on spices illustrated the involvement of Venetians in the spice trade and advances in the spicing of food.

Further Reading

Albala, Ken. *Eating Right in the Renaissance.* Berkeley: University of California Press, 2002.

Appelbaum, Robert. *Aguecheek's Beef, Belch's Hiccup, and Other Gastronomic Interjections: Literature, Culture, and Food among the Early Moderns.* Chicago: University of Chicago Press, 2006.

Riley, Gillian. *The Oxford Companion to Italian Food.* New York: Oxford University Press, 2008.

Dutch East India Company

The world's first stock company and first multinational corporation, the Dutch East India Company monopolized the Indonesian pepper and spice trade from 1602 to 1769. Known in Dutch as the Vereenigde Oost-Indische Compagnie (VOC), the conglomerate originally traded with Asian colonies. At its height, the company operated 4,785 vessels and employed 1 million laborers to trade millions of tons of merchandise from Asia. Central to the company's success, the dispersal of pepper to the West

altered the aroma and flavor of cooking, giving it a new pungency, particularly in Chinese cuisine of the Wanli dynasty. Beverages acquired a sharp tang and lasting aftertaste from a sprinkle of pepper grains. For two centuries, VOC investors earned dividends of 18 percent until the firm's bankruptcy and dissolution on December 31, 1800.

To best its Portuguese competitors, stockholder Jan Huyghen van Linschoten and explorer Cornelis de Houtman began seizing trade routes along the Javanese north shore in 1580. De Houtman reached Bantam (now Banten), West Java's main source of the extra-hot long pepper, a staple of Indonesian cooking and of Indian vegetable pickling for its supposed effects on human longevity. The most profitable regional commodity, pepper passed from European warehouses to condiment shops in Poland, Russia, and the Ottoman Empire.

For centuries, the Egyptians had prized pepper as an ingredient in embalming fluid; in India and China, healers had valued pepper as a restorative of appetite, energy, and sexual potency. As a pharmaceutical, pepper soothed the digestive tract, heart, liver, and throat and relieved cholera, colic, diabetes, dysentery, epilepsy, fever, malaria, pruritus, toothache, typhoid, and vertigo. Largely from pepper sales, the VOC gained the power to print currency, construct forts and colonize lands, negotiate treaties, raise armies, and declare war in its territories, the Dutch East Indies.

A Profitable Monopoly

In March 1599, Captain Jacob Cornelius van Neck's eight-ship fleet reached the Malukan Spice Islands in eastern Indonesia. He quadrupled investors' funds from profits on 500 tons (450 metric tons) of cloves and pepper, plus stores of cinnamon bark, a fumigant and cure for chapped lips, halitosis, inflamed gums, and low sperm count, and of mace and nutmeg, a meat preserver and an aphrodisiac extracted from the same nut. At the time, cloves cost three times the price of pepper; mace and nutmeg cost even more.

The Dutch created a cuisine that added grated nutmeg rind to beans, brussels sprouts, cauliflower, cider, eggnog, pudding, sausage, and wine. Continental Europeans prized the spicy aroma and flavor in baked goods, potato dishes, sauces, and soups and for seasoning meats. Mace, the outer aril (covering) of the nutmeg, yielded a more delicate taste and smell as well as oils for use in preservatives, sweets, syrup, and treatments for diarrhea, enlarged heart, halitosis, seasickness, and skin rash

In 1600, Dutch traders negotiated a monopoly on pepper and cloves from Hitu at Ambon in the Molucca chain, where fleet commander Steven van der Hagen seized control. Following the formation of the British East India Company in 1600, the Dutch organized their own cartel in 1602, which headquartered at Bantam, a prime nexus of international commerce. Two years later,

65 more Dutch traders strengthened the Netherlands' presence in the Asian trade and introduced barter with the Chinese for tea in exchange for dried sage, which the Dutch promoted as a cure-all. By 1611, the VOC boosted business by opening a second outpost at Batavia. The governor-general, posted at Ambon, superintended trade wars against the Chinese and the English, who headquartered in Java and Sumatra.

Fighting Competition

The food trade wars required military backing. After overpowering a Portuguese fort at Ambon in 1613, the Dutch faced a defiant competitor, which made a stand at West Timor. On May 30, 1619, Governor-General Jan Pieterszoon Coen led 19 ships on the Java Sea against Batavia, routed the Portuguese, and opened a new beachhead overlooking trade routes. After murdering or expelling natives, Dutch planters exported cloves, mace, and nutmeg from the Banda Islands and expanded commerce with Asia, which profited from European technology. The Dutch penetrated Japanese commerce with trade at Dejima, in southern Japan. In 1640, the VOC added to its exports cinnamon from the fortified port of Galle, Ceylon (now Sri Lanka), also a source of areca nuts, cardamom, ginger, pepper, and exotic wood.

In 1652, colonial administrator Jan van Riebeeck, manager of the VOC post in Tonkin, Vietnam, opened a supply post at the Cape of Good Hope for vessels rounding South Africa on their way east. The Dutch firm hosted a treatment center for scurvy-weakened sailors. In 1658, soldier Gerard Pieterszen Hulft seized Colombo, in west-central Sri Lanka, and drove the Portuguese from southwestern India's Malabar Coast, where pepper plants grew wild. Commercial centers in Persia, Bengal, Macassar, Thailand, Canton, Taiwan, and Coromandel, India, extended Dutch income from its colonies in cocoa, coffee, macassar oil, mother of pearl, rattan, rice, and rubber. At its height in 1669, the VOC, the world's richest corporation, boasted 150 merchant ships, 40 warships, 50,000 clerks, 10,000 soldiers, and a 40 percent annual dividend.

The Dutch trading empire stumbled in 1670 during dynastic changes in China from Ming to Qing and because of an economic decline in Japan. The English took advantage of regional upheaval to seize European pepper markets. After the publication of VOC Governor Hendrik van Rheede's 12-volume botanical encyclopedia *Hortus Indicus Malabaricus* (*A Malabar Indian Garden*, 1678–1703), Danish and French traders entered European competition for the pepper and spice trade. In 1715, Indian potentates, seeking independence, renounced alliances with the Dutch. By 1721, the English had gained the upper hand with Indian traders and undermined Dutch control. To restore high profits, the VOC expanded its fleet and manpower by 125 percent and diversified products to include coffee, cotton, dyes, opium, seashells, sugar, tea, and textiles.

Poor management and dishonest employees, however, contributed to declines in income and profitability. Simultaneous with a drop in the sugar market in 1720, the Dutch lost control of trade in Bengal, Malabar, Persia, and Surat in northwestern India. After 1730, the unwieldy VOC distributed more dividends than it earned, filling the gap with disastrous short-term loans. Still attempting to support 25,000 dealers in ten Asian countries for a half century after 1750, the company foundered in 1799, when the Dutch crown took control and the English commandeered the pepper trade.

See also: British East India Company; Maritime Trade Routes; Peppers.

Further Reading

Boxer, Charls Ralph. *The Dutch Seaborne Empire, 1600–1800.* New York: Penguin, 1990.

Chaudhuri, K.N. *Trade and Civilization in the Indian Ocean: An Economic History from the Rise of Islam to 1750.* New York: Cambridge University Press, 1985.

Farrington, Anthony. *Trading Places: The East India Company and Asia, 1600–1834.* London: British Library, 2002.

Jacobs, E.M. *Merchant in Asia: The Trade of the Dutch East India Company During the Eighteenth Century.* Leiden, Netherlands: CNWS, 2006.

Ravindran, P.N, ed. *Black Pepper: Piper Nigrum.* Amsterdam, Netherlands: Overseas, 2000.

Recipe: Dutch Spice Cookies

Stir 5 ounces of soft butter until smooth. Mix in four eggs. Add 34 ounces of brown sugar and a pinch of salt. Mix thoroughly with 1/2 teaspoon of cardamom, 1/2 teaspoon of ginger powder, 1/2 teaspoon of ground anise, 1/2 teaspoon of ground clove, 1/2 teaspoon of ground nutmeg, and two 2 teaspoons of ground cinnamon. Sift in 38 ounces of flour and 1 tablespoon of baking powder. Knead the dough and refrigerate for two hours. Roll out dough until it is 1/4 inch thick. Cut out cookies. Brush with 5 tablespoons of beer and sprinkle with 6 ounces of coarse sugar. Bake at 400 degrees Fahrenheit for 20 minutes. Cool on a baker's rack.

Dye, Food

Dye heightens the visual appeal of food by intensifying natural colors. As civilization developed, food dyes achieved value in world trade.

From 2000 B.C.E., the extraction of the crocus stigma in Assyria yielded a brilliant yellow dye valued as an aphrodisiac, a mood elevator, and a tea and wine colorant. Alexander the Great ate saffron rice, drank saffron tea, and bathed in saffron water to heal combat wounds. At the outbreak of the Black Death in the fourteenth century, the fearful laced their food with costly saffron, which rose in price between the ports of Genoa, Rhodes, and Venice and destinations in the western Mediterranean. Saffron maintained a prominent place in food dye history. Spanish restaurants produced a lustrous yellow in paella. The French added saffron to bouillabaise; the Italians, to Milanese risotto. Pennsylvania Dutch cooks tinted their noodles and cake flour with saffron. In 2010, researchers found saffron beneficial in the treatment of Alzheimer's disease, macular degeneration, and retinitis pigmentosa.

A rival of saffron, Indian turmeric, grown in the tropics, colors curry and Sumatran *satay padang,* a skewered beef topped with a deep yellow sauce. The Japanese of Okinawa prize turmeric tea. In the United States, turmeric heightens the tone of biscuits, chicken broth, dairy products, orange juice, pickles, popcorn, and yogurt. Current evaluation of medicinal value of the curcumin in turmeric suggests applications to Alzheimer's disease, arthritis, cancer, and pancreatitis.

The Aztec and Maya profited from cochineal, a dye extracted from a scaly parasite living on opuntia cacti. Trading vessels carried the colorant to England, India, and Spain, where alchemists, clothiers, cooks, and painters paid top price for red pigments. In the mid-1800s, cochineal production expanded to the Canary Islands, Guatemala, North Africa, and Spain, where collection of 70,000 insects produced 1 pound (0.45 kilogram) of carmine dye. Cochineal lost value in the next century after the invention of alizarin crimson, an artificial dye. In 2005, the Canary Islands, Chile, Mexico, and Peru continued to ship carmine to top distributors of gelatin, marinades, and surimi in France, Italy, and Japan, but not to Islamic or Jewish consumers, who forbid the addition of insect-based dye to edibles.

A common dye in Filipino, Latin American, and West Indian cuisine, annatto derived from the seeds of the achiote, a tropical tree native to South America. Aztec priests employed it in ritual and body painting and as ink for manuscripts. Recipes for achiote paste and *arroz con pollo* (chicken with rice) take their yellow hue from annatto. In London in 1860, the colorant brightened cheddar cheese and butter.

Modern Diversity

Employing the hues of alfalfa, algae, annatto, beets, blueberries, butterfly peas, caramelized sugar, carmine, carrots, cochineal, elderberries, grapes, mushrooms, pandanus, paprika, saffron, and turmeric, colorants boost the blander tints of bubble gum and candies, cheese, citrus fruit, jelly, pickles, sausage, vitamins, and wine. Pandanus tints and flavors rice pudding in Bangladesh, Burma, Indonesia, and Thailand; in Hungary and Spain, paprika, an antioxidant, gives a rust-red hue to rice-and-meat soups and stews. The carmine coloring of maraschino cherries from Scarlet GN (an artificial azo dye) satisfies consumers' expectations of a deep red, which they associate with intense aroma and flavor. Similarly, elderberry darkens St.-Germain liqueur in France and purple syrups and tisanes in Germany and Italy.

Caramel concentrate, one of the most traditional and least suspect food dyes, provides a familiar brown hue in

Natural and artificial food coloring has little or no effect on food taste but is essential to modern consumer marketing. The manufacturer of Jell-O uses combinations of seven federally approved artificial dyes to color its gelatin fruit flavors. *(MCT/Getty Images)*

beer, bread, chocolate, fish, ice cream, potato chips, and soft drinks. Synthetic tinting with betanin from beet juice conceals variants in bacon and soups and restores lost intensity to oranges, salmon, and tomato pulp. Bakers choose vegetable dye as a means of coloring icing for drawing shapes, numbers, and letters on cakes and cookies.

For children, Gatorade, Hawaiian Punch, Kraft Mac and Cheese, Minute Maid Lemonade, Pop-Tarts, Skittles, and Velveeta display the Crayola colors that grab attention. The dyeing of grain cereal into colorful children's breakfast cereals adds fun to scooping up floating bits from milk. In the 1970s, however, pediatrician Ben Feingold of California treated inattention and hyperactivity in young patients by ridding the diet of artificial colors and flavors. His findings set the scientific community in search of harmful additives.

Imitators

Suspect among food dyes, azo dyes trigger asthma, edema, and hives as well as bladder cancer and cardiac arrhythmias. In 1976, the U.S. Food and Drug Administration (FDA) banned an artificial dye known as Amaranth—the infamous Red Dye No. 2—a reddish purple coloring linked to malignancies. The deep hue had previously tinted chocolate pudding, hot dogs, grape soda, and gravy mix. General Foods, the last to halt Amaranth usage, reformulated Gaines dog food, Jell-O, and Kool-Aid. Food processors protested that rats grew cancers only after being force-fed large amounts of the dye.

As new colorants burst on the scene after 2005, making food more kid-friendly, a replacement hue, Allura Red AC, the colorant of red cotton candy, Gummy Bears, medications, and strawberry beverages, appeared to target children's diet. Along with Azorubine, Ponceau 4R, and Red 2G, additional red dyes, the Allura shade came under scrutiny in England with a 2007 University of Southampton study of lowering IQs in children and increasing hyperactivity and anomalies in bladder, bone marrow, colon, and stomach. British food producers began a two-year phase-out of the dye. Allura maintained its presence in U.S. foods, but the United States, Canada, Japan, Norway, and Sweden banned Azorubine.

The illicit use of synthetic dyes, such as the carcinogen Sudan 1 in chili and paprika in England in 2003, require constant monitoring in international markets. A broad ruling in Norway governing such artificial dyes as Brilliant Black BN, Brown HT, Fast Yellow AB, Lithol Rubine BK, Orange B, Para Red, Sunset Yellow, and Yellow 2G raises issues of allergies and attention deficit disorder in consumers. Among the most suspect, tartrazine, a yellow shade also used in green tints, may negatively affect hepatic and renal function, inflame gastric linings, lower sperm count, and alter behavior in children from the effects of sodium benzoate.

On June 30, 2010, Michael Jacobson, director of the Center for Science in the Public Interest in Washington, D.C., recommended banning tartrazine for its disruption of children's behavior and for possibly causing cancer. He backed his statement by insisting that such dyes serve no health purpose and may contain neurotoxins. Manufacturers showed interest in returning to natural dyes—beet juice, carrots, pumpkin, strawberries, and turmeric—but recognized that they might spend more money and achieve a less stable product.

After decades of assurance to the public that food dye is safe, the FDA in March 2011 signaled its willingness to re-examine evidence of behavior and health problems. A new panel began considering warning labels indicating that the nine artificial dyes approved for food processing cause cancer and exacerbate hyperactivity. Taking the opposite stance, the Grocery Manufacturers Association sided with artificial food dye makers in demanding clinical proof of harm. Kraft Foods took a cautious approach by introducing color-free Capri Sun juices, Kool-Aid Invisible, and Macaroni and Cheese Organic White Cheddar. A stronger approach from Trader Joe's and Whole Foods Markets involves the refusal to stock foods that are artificially colored.

See also: Additives, Food; Australian Food Trade; Blueberries; Sanitation.

Further Reading

Potera, Carol. "The Artificial Food Dye Blues." *Environmental Health Perspectives* 118:10 (October 2010): A428.

Sharma, Vinita, Harold T. McKone, and Peter G. Markow. "A Global Perspective on the History, Use, and Identification of Synthetic Food Dyes." *Journal of Chemical Education* 88:1 (2011): 24–28.

Ecofeminism

A woman-centered ecological crusade for the common good, ecofeminism nurtures fragile life-forms and promotes stewardship of Earth's flora and fauna. In the name of the metaphoric Earth Mother, conservationists celebrate feminine instincts for reverence and protection of resources, especially food and water. Since the Industrial Revolution unleashed social havoc and accelerated the destruction of nature, the reciprocity of feminine sensibility has benefited families inundated by commercial profiteering.

One utopian fantasy, Charlotte Perkins Gilman's *Herland* (1915), set female vegetarians in a self-sustaining organic haven. Of the equality of their mission, she stated, "Neither did they start off on predatory excursions to get more land from somebody else, or to get more food from somebody else." Instead, 3 million farmers established and tended fruit and nut orchards and replenished the land with recycled green waste. The novel established common ground for ecofeminists by saluting female Earth keepers from prehistory.

Ecocritical idealists Marjorie Kinnan Rawlings, Sarah Orne Jewett, Barbara Kingsolver, and Willa Cather issued social and political truths that charged squanderers and polluters with befouling Earth's fecundity and bounty. Reclaiming ancient food wisdom, sci-fi author Ursula K. Le Guin's Earthsea sextet dramatized eating styles close to the source and the drying, smoking, and salting that preserved surpluses before the industrialization of food. In a glimpse of twentieth-century predations, Laguna Pueblo novelist Leslie Marmon Silko's diatribe *Almanac of the Dead* (1991) charged patriarchal governments with funding weapons and death while ignoring the homeless and hungry. Her clan witnessed skewed U.S. values on July 16, 1945, when an atomic blast outside the Los Alamos, New Mexico, laboratory obliterated apricot orchards and melon gardens and permeated groundwater with toxic radioactive rubble. She labeled the profanation of Earth an extreme example of white man's folly.

In *Yellow Woman and a Beauty of the Spirit* (1996), Silko acknowledged the planetary life network by asserting that "None can survive unless all survive." Through the character Wilson Weasel Tail, she projected a rebirth of the buffalo, the Lakota equivalent of heavenly manna. In her edenic novel *Gardens in the Dunes* (1999), she pic-

tured the altruism of the Sand Lizard tribe, a female clan of hunter-gatherers who modeled stewardship and frugality as well as the sharing with the needy of piñon nut flour, cattail roots, palm dates, sprouted seeds, and wild gourd vines.

At the core of ecofeminism lie issues of globalism and whole Earth conservation. In 1998, essayist Marilynne Robinson alerted readers to the shrinking habitats of whales and to the eventual despoliation of the sea as a source of food, a disaster of unfathomable proportions. In New Delhi, India, philosopher Vandana Shiva began a national movement in the 1990s to reverse destruction by empowering women in the green movements in Africa, Asia, Europe, and Latin America. Her projects emphasize native seed and organic food growing as bases of human well-being.

See also: Genetically Modified Food; Local Food Movement.

Further Reading

Nhanenge, Jytte. *Ecofeminism: Towards Integrating the Concerns of Women, Poor People, and Nature into Development.* Lanham, MD: University Press of America, 2011.

Sandilands, Catriona. *The Good-Natured Feminist: Ecofeminism and the Quest for Democracy.* Minneapolis: University of Minnesota Press, 1999.

Warren, Karen J., and Nisvan Erkal, eds. *Ecofeminism: Women, Culture, Nature.* Bloomington: Indiana University Press, 1997.

Egyptian Diet and Cuisine, Ancient

Diet and meal service in pharaonic Egypt demanded planning and order that set patterns of social class. Egyptian royalty believed that food made the nation content: By filling the people's bellies, the pharaoh kept anarchy and revolt under control. From around 3100 to 30 B.C.E., peasants, who made up 95 percent of the population of some 3 million Egyptians, maintained one of the highest standards of living in the region. At the banks of the Nile River, they obtained fish and the water to irrigate barley, emmer wheat, and flax fields—the source of beer, bread, oil, and seed. If farmers and their families acquired a surplus, they sold it for cash to buy other goods. They also produced a liquid power food called *bouza* (beer) by crushing bread in water and fermenting the mash in large resin-lined jars. Bouza so anchored the cuisine that children carried skins of beer to school for lunch.

Bureaucratic records from around 2400 B.C.E. revealed the importance of the food distribution system in considerable detail. After the annual June flood of melted snow from the Ethiopian highlands, planting in alluvial mud involved broadcasting by hand and treading seed into the soil by goats and sheep and channeling water through canals from the river by *shaduf,* a counterweighted dip bucket on a long pole. During unending toil, which included pulling plows in lieu of draft animals, men drank from leather water flasks and hung them in the shade to cool. Constant vigilance against crocodiles and hippopotamuses protected plants from trampling and workers from attack. After 2100 B.C.E., Egyptians chanted a praise anthem to the Nile for maintaining nature's balance and for making farmers self-sufficient.

On the threshing floor at harvest time in April and May, winnowers drove cattle, donkeys, oxen, and sheep over grain shafts to separate kernels from husks. Tax collectors recorded the yield and apportioned the amount the farmer owed the pharaoh. During a poor season, a diet of lily loaves, papyrus pith, and roasted lotus bulb bread contributed to malnutrition in peasants. A high yield supported nobles and the artisanal class, who developed high standards of accounting, canal engineering, charioteering, medicine and midwifery, pottery, toolmaking, and weaving. During the imperial age, from 1539 to 1075 B.C.E., the demand for crushed grain for porridge or flat cakes rose so high in Nubia and the Fertile Crescent in western Asia that Egyptian farmers had no spare forage for raising domesticated cattle and geese. In the tenth century B.C.E., however, the book of Exodus characterized Egypt as the best place for starving nations to seek relief. Rome, the major grain purchaser, depended on Egyptian harvests to stave off mass famine.

The Average Egyptian

Archaeologists have deduced from digs at Amarna, Deir el-Medina, and Kahun that most Egyptian families possessed simple clay oil jugs, limestone mortars, rush baskets, and saddle querns for kitchen chores and salt bins for preserving carp, catfish, eel, mullet, and perch. The poor grew *ben* nut (moringa) trees along the riverbanks to crush for cooking oil and also rendered castor oil from *kiki,* a medicinal herb.

Daily meal preparation required intense grinding of sun-toasted grain on hand mills and the removal of chaff as well as insects and rocks with rush sieves. Stems and hulls went into animal feed or the molding of fibrous mud brick. Bread making concluded with kneading flour with water, salt, and leaven or sourdough starter in dough vats, a process invented at Memphis. Cooks baked dough in hot sand, on hearth slabs, or on shelves in earthen ovens heated at bottom with charcoal, dung, or wood.

Enlivening a grain-based diet over time, Egyptians revered garlic, leeks, and onions, all varieties of the sacred *Allium* family. Additional flavor and nutrition derived from broad beans and cowpeas, cabbage, chicory, cucumber, lentils, melon, *Raphanus* (wild radish), romaine, spinach, and turnips. Laborers also grew herbs in home gardens as both food and medicine, which the Egyptians honored as the "necessary art." Couples used a kitchen recipe of honey, milk and cream, and "red salt" (natron or sodium) on fiber as a contraceptive and blended beer, dates, frankincense, and oil to encourage childbearing. The concept of treating *similia similibus* (like with like) caused doctors to prescribe ostrich egg to a patient suffering a cranial fracture, a worm-shaped carob fruit as a vermifuge, and the milky juice of lettuce to promote fertility.

Dining areas featured occasional tables, where people knelt to eat without utensils from flat baskets and to drink from cups. Air filtration through woven mats suspended over doors and windows kept flying insects out of food. Light came from twists of burning plant fiber permeated with sesame oil. The serving of wheat cakes with honey and the pulp of dates, figs, and grapes rounded out a meal.

Respect for the dead dictated many practices. Mourners abstained from food until the post-funeral banquet. Loaves accompanied the deceased to their tombs, such as the barley loaves left at Sakkarah, the necropolis at Memphis, around 3475 B.C.E. to honor a noblewoman. Funerary cults listed a wide range of appropriate nourishment—16 types of bread and pastry, 11 fruit varieties, ten meat entrées, six types of wine, five species of poultry, and four types of beer. They avoided fish because of its odor.

A hieroglyphic list from after 2600 B.C.E. at Dahshur, south of Cairo, pictured uniformed handmaidens delivering appropriate grave foods to the dead on trays. A menu inscribed on the tomb wall reminded servants in the afterlife of the favorite foods of the deceased. Exactly 40 days after the funeral, survivors brought provisions to the cemetery and distributed them to the poor, a gesture accruing goodwill from judges in the underworld. Food left at the site drew jackals and wolves, giving rise to the myth that the animals guarded burial sites.

Marketing, Barter, and Theft

Farmers reserved lentils, lotus seed, and *Raphanus* oil for market, which they reached by camel or donkey. In good years, commerce moved briskly along the Nile River delta. In bad years, low flooding silted in branches leading from the capital at Memphis to the Mediterranean Sea, impeding transport of produce to buyers. During famines, laborers and quarriers became the first to suffer malnutrition or starvation. To limit the loss to the labor pool, the state operated grain silos and reservoirs that stored surpluses for times of dearth and allotted handouts in standard amounts. At public kitchens, the needy and homeless used tall mortars and poles for pounding and communal mills for cleaning hulled grain.

Wages tended to take the form of beer, bread loaves, grain, oil, or vegetables rather than coins. To ensure rapid work on the three pyramids at Giza, one of the Seven Wonders of the Ancient World, between 2575 and 2465 B.C.E., overseers employed by the pharaoh Khufu and his successors appear to have fed laborers beef. Soldiers received plaster ration tokens in the shape of a cylindrical, oval, or round loaf for presentation at the supply depot, which also distributed salt fish. Sailors earned a similar bread dole that equaled half the amount apportioned to the captain, first mate, and ship's watch.

Exotic trade goods, especially coconuts, mandrake, and olives, set the wealthy apart from peasants and drones. Professional hunters killed cranes, herons, and pelicans with throwing sticks or arrows and netted small birds and pintail ducks for sale. The rich adorned their tables with glass chalices for wine and with servings of red meat, which included pork in the delta region and, at Memphis, gazelles, oryxes, and ostriches, big game stalked by pharaohs and courtiers. The tomb art honoring the grain accountant Nebamun around 1500 B.C.E. pictured him wielding a serpentine throwing stick at marshland birds and waterfowl and dining in luxury. Privileged artisans and temple priests received meat portions on holidays and game birds from successful hunts.

Refined Dining

Crouched at floor level over bronze, copper, and terra-cotta cookware, chefs prepared food in the open air of a courtyard or flat roof, flavoring recipes for mullet roe cake and spit-roasted geese and pigeon with coriander, cumin, dill, lettuce and mustard seed, marjoram, mint, and vinegar. The palace of Thutmose IV (r. ca. 1512–ca. 1504 B.C.E.) produced an innovation: a separate kitchen streamlined with three ovens and an in-floor cistern, plus storage amphorae accessed from openings in the bottoms dispensing condiments, grain, legumes, and spices.

Skilled chefs added mallow to soup, tigernuts to cake, fish roe to pickles, and carob, grape and plum must, honey, jujube, knotgrass, lotus, *seneb* berries, and wine to marinades. They omitted fish from the menu as an unclean creature suited to consumption by the lower class. In a hot climate, milk required immediate use or processing into butter or sour cream. Ceremonial bread, a high-gluten specialty, rose in conical or cylindrical molds. Because the baker broke the mold to extract the loaves, the bread making generated exorbitant costs.

Seating on carved chairs and food service on bronze, gold, or silver dishes contrasted with the lowly huts and clay tableware of the poor. To enhance the palatial atmosphere, stewards employed *kyphi,* an air freshener and lung-purifying drink blended from cassia, cedar, cinnamon, honey, juniper berries, raisins, resins, sedge, spikenard, and wine. A more complex recipe from Edfu Temple mentions cardamom, mint, pine kernels, and saffron. Before the distribution of entrées, maidservants rinsed the hands of guests. Butlers strained wine through metal strainers into goblets and passed them to wine tasters to sample the vintage. Flatbread with hollows in the center served as bowls for beans and vegetables.

Diners lifted bites of raw songbirds or quail or roasted waterfowl with the thumb and first two fingers, an affectation of the elegant. They dipped lettuce in salted oil or goose fat and dabbled their soiled fingertips in bowls of scented water. Dessert might consist of fried sweet pancakes or sweet rolls, made by stuffing dried fruit into dough. As a digestive, diners sipped diluted cumin crushed in water.

Mustard water combated more debilitating illnesses, such as fainting or seizures. The bitter cucumber (also known as wild gourd) purged the bowels and aborted pregnancies. Autopsies of mummies recognized the value of curative foods, but questioned the Egyptian diet for encouraging heart disease, obesity, and tooth decay.

The Developing Cuisine

Egyptian cuisine acquired new flavors and textures from imports, particularly apples, juniper berries, olives, and pomegranates. Because attempts at establishing olive groves in Alexandria and the Faiyum had mixed success, Egypt proved a steady customer for Greek olive oil. The Nuer, a pastoral tribe of southern Sudan, introduced cattle. Thutmose III (r. ca. 1504–1450 B.C.E.) brought chickens from Syria, the culture that also refined beer and wine fermentation. From Persia, the Egyptians acquired mulberries and pomegranates. From the Romans, the pharaoh's gardeners acquired almonds, cherries, citrus fruit, peaches, and pears and, as early as 1400 B.C.E., learned the art of espaliering branches along garden walls. To the south, Nubians bartered with millet and sorghum; Libya and Ethiopia provided dried lake salt. Fenugreek, used as a pickling spice and brewed to make tea, and pepper apparently reached Egypt from India or the Fertile Crescent. For oil, the Egyptians pressed almonds, *ben* nuts, cole seed, linseed, *Raphanus,* safflower, and sesame. The upper class enjoyed a highly intoxicating fig wine as well as date and pomegranate vintages, but like the Greeks and Romans, repudiated public drunkenness as boorish.

Special prayers and ritual sprinklings accompanied the temple slaughter of calves and oxen. Priests reverenced the liver and spleen and preserved bloody runoff for blood sausage. They either cast the animal head into the river or sold it to impious Greeks. In 1350 B.C.E., Egypt's first monotheist, Akhenaten (also called Amenhotep IV), the husband of Nefertiti and father of Tutankhamen, began closing temples and seizing sacred property as a means of enforcing Atenism, his radical religious reform. The loss of sacred plantations and the swine herds of Abydos threatened the nation with economic collapse.

Around 1175 B.C.E., Ramses III endowed a large dole of beer, bread, cattle, dried dates, garlic, geese, raisins, waterfowl, and wheat for artisans, priests, and tomb builders at Heliopolis, Memphis, and Thebes. Five years later, during attacks by the Sea Peoples (a confederacy of seafaring raiders), the loss of the pharaoh's food allotment resulted in a labor strike at the necropolis at Deir el-Medina, the first employee walkout in history. Ramses's viziers restored the barley and wheat supply and cajoled palace artisans to resume work on royal tombs.

Under Ramses IV (r. 1151–1145 B.C.E.), the provisioning of Deir el-Medina grew more erratic, provoking a backlash of tomb robberies and six decades of governmental instability. The cost of palace cuisine reached a pinnacle under Ramses IV, who led a royal quarry expedition of 9,368 people. His household required the specialties of confectioners and pastry chefs, bakers and brewers, butchers, meat managers, and sommeliers.

See also: Bread; Emmer Wheat; Espaliering; Irrigation; Maritime Trade Routes; Poultry; Shellfish; Trade Routes; Trading Vessels; Yeast.

Further Reading

Berriedale-Johnson, Michelle. *Food Fit for Pharaohs: An Ancient Egyptian Cookbook.* London: British Museum, 2008.

Kemp, Barry J. *Ancient Egypt: Anatomy of a Civilization.* New York: Routledge, 2006.

Robins, Gay. *The Art of Ancient Egypt.* Cambridge, MA: Harvard University Press, 2008.

Silverman, David P. *Ancient Egypt.* New York: Oxford University Press, 2003.

Einkorn Wheat

From the Mediterranean shores to the northern coniferous forests, einkorn (*Triticum monococcum*), or single-grain, wheat flourished as one of the first domesticated crops cultivated in the Middle East. The seed of einkorn wheat—the name "einkorn" comes from the German for "one seed"—is a pale red kernel naturally carapaced against disease and insect infestation.

The sturdy-hulled wheat, which is the domestic version of wild wheat (*Triticum boeoticum*), contributed to the domestication of hunter-gatherers in the western end of the Fertile Crescent in western Asia. During the Neolithic revolution around 12,000 B.C.E., einkorn's large seeds found a place at campfires as sources of digestible roasted grains. Pouches of charred or roasted einkorn bore an aromatic, flavorful, and stable travel food easily carried and eaten without further cooking.

After the settlement of Mureybit and Abu Hureyra east of Aleppo in western Mesopotamia (in present-day Syria) in 11,050 B.C.E., a millennium of drought forced the Natufians, the earliest settled people of Palestine, to

Einkorn wheat, a protein-rich wild species native to the Middle East, was one of the first grain crops domesticated by humans. Paleobotanists have found evidence of cultivation in the Fertile Crescent some 12,000 years ago. (*David Q. Cabagnaro/Getty Images*)

adopt agrarianism by caching grain in storage pits to stave off famine. To cultivate wild seeds, Natufian settlers fenced in fields and broadcast seeds in open spots near fruit trees and berry patches. Because of the ease of harvesting wild stands growing 3 feet (1 meter) tall, a family could amass a year's supply of grain from three weeks' work. As a result of clan clustering around the wettest, most productive fields, population density rose from 1 to 15 people per square mile (3 to 39 people per square kilometer).

To feed all, protofarmers across the east-west axis of Eurasia domesticated eight self-pollinating, early-maturing founder crops, which featured einkorn wheat. The choice favored a variety resistant to fungus and frost. The use of hulled wheat as food required the tools of grain preparation—sickles for harvesting, grinding stones for removal of chaff from tightly wrapped kernels, and mortars hammered out of bedrock for refining grain into a fine yellow flour.

Low-yielding but protein-rich, einkorn wheat provided low-fiber gruel suitable for nurturing invalids and weaning babies. The variety failed at loaf making because of its poor rising capability; however, it may have been the basis of the first beer.

Wheat in Early Civilization

Paleobotanists studying food sources in Mycenae (present-day mainland Greece), Sumer, in Mesopotamia (present-day Iraq), and Troy (northwestern Turkey) have concluded that domesticated wheat varieties flourished in a single latitude from about 10,500 B.C.E. and contributed to the baking styles that undergirded urbanization. Baking flatbread consisted of hand-crushing grains, adding water, and spreading the mix on a heated stone. A covering of hot ashes finished the cooking process. The Sumerians became the first ancient peoples to mix naturally yeasting sourdough with an unleavened mass to form risen loaves.

Cultivation in Jordan and Turkey spread across the Balkans to Serbia, the Danube delta, and the mouth of the Rhine; as far west as northern Italy and Valencia, Spain; and north to Denmark and Britain. Einkorn grew in North Africa, but not in the hotter climates to the south in Ethiopia and southern Egypt or in the irrigated fields of Mesopotamia.

In about 9000 B.C.E., the planting and harvesting of wild einkorn, a more productive cereal grain than its cousin, emmer wheat, introduced wheat cultivation in southeastern Turkey. Harvested in Jericho in 8000 B.C.E., in Cyprus, the Indus Valley where the Harappan culture thrived, and Kurdistan in 7000 B.C.E., and in Argissa, Greece, and Crete in 6000 B.C.E., einkorn shared growing space with emmer wheat and barley, forming a triad of founder crops that flourished in clay and marl soils.

With the addition of salt, einkorn formed an inelastic dough that required no kneading and a short baking time. The survival of massive grindstones indicates the production of bulk wheat flour. The growing of einkorn reached the northern Greek peninsula—to Macedonia, Thessaly, and Thrace—after 5200 B.C.E. and the Bug and Dniester valleys of Russia about 4500 B.C.E. The 1991 recovery in the Italian Alps of Ötzi the Iceman, Europe's most ancient mummy, established the use of einkorn bread in 3300 B.C.E. on the mountainous ridge separating present-day Austria and Switzerland.

Classical and Modern Grains

In Bronze Age Greece, mythology about Demeter, the goddess of cereal grains, depicted her charging Triptolemus, a chief of Eleusis, with sowing seeds to feed humankind. Homer's *Odyssey* (ca. 800 B.C.E.) referred to einkorn wheat as *zeia*, a term indicating one-seeded wheat. A standard rural meal among northern pastoral people involved the boiling of einkorn flour at the hearth with salt or *siraion* (wine must) and either milk or water to produce sweetened porridge. Meals concluded with cups of plain or honeyed wine.

According to Hippocrates's *Regimen II* (ca. 400 B.C.E.), Greek cooks traditionally formed ground wheat into unleavened cakes that they baked in an oven and drizzled with honey. More elaborate recipes for *diepnon* (the main or evening meal) called for frying wheat batter into drop biscuits or pancakes, baking dough in crockery or under ash, or stirring wheat in an urn to make sweetened *maza* (porridge), the main Greek dish. Diners rounded out meals simply with dates, figs, grapes, nuts, and wine.

During the Roman monarchy from 753 to 508 B.C.E., the pastoral community made a simple porridge from einkorn flour, water, and salt. By the time of the republic, Romans formed 75 percent of their daily diet around einkorn, either ground or pounded on a saddle quern for simmering into gruel. Although preparers sieved the flour through cloth or wickerwork, the remaining stone grit in wheat recipes compromised the enamel of teeth. Nonetheless, the devout revered the grain for funeral meals and grave gifts.

More sophisticated cuisine replaced traditional cookery after 300 B.C.E., when Greek kitchen styles influenced Roman cooks. To punish disobedient soldiers in the early third century B.C.E., according to historians Livy and Plutarch, officers replaced wheat rations with barley, a crude grain associated with pack animals, poor peasants, and slaves. Professional milling and baking, an urban necessity for patrician Romans, began around 174 B.C.E. Around 150 B.C.E., Cato the Censor advised cooks on the art of gruel making—wash and husk the wheat and rinse thoroughly. After the initial cooking, Cato explained the gradual liquefying of the mush by adding milk.

As legionary power encroached around the Mediterranean, central Italian food styles influenced less cosmopolitan areas. For grain meals in the second century C.E., Galen, a Turco-Roman physician, valued einkorn more than oats, which he considered famine food for its low nutrition. In Anatolia in western Turkey, conquered peoples paid their tax assessment to Rome in einkorn grain and sold surpluses to feed Roman soldiers and their mounts. At Pergamum in western Anatolia, einkorn served communities as a source of low-grade flour.

After 27 B.C.E., the first years of the Roman empire saw a shift from hard-hulled wheat to free-threshing varieties of bread wheat to grace Roman tables with pastry and white bread. After the Roman occupation of Britain in 43 C.E., provisioners may have parched wheat in grain-drying kilns to simplify threshing and chaff removal. In the 700s C.E., einkorn became the main Anglo-Saxon cereal crop. Slowly, Britain's agrarian traditions shifted toward bread wheat, in part because of culinary habit and resistance to agricultural innovation.

As new varieties of wheat evolved, farmers abandoned einkorn in favor of easier milled hull-less grain. During the Industrial Revolution (starting in Britain in the late eighteenth century), cooks favored softer wheat varieties that gave bread and pastries more elasticity and a less fibrous crumb.

The health-conscious twenty-first-century baker rediscovered artisanal breads from ancient grains and returned highly digestible einkorn wheat to popularity. Cake, pita bread, and pasta made from einkorn wheat appears to suit the gluten-free diet of victims of celiac sprue, an autoimmune ailment of the small intestine. Nutritionists laud einkorn wheat for its low toxicity and for containing antioxidants, beta-carotene, lutein, phosphorus, potassium, riboflavin, and vitamin A.

Still grown in the Kurdish uplands from Anatolia through the Zagros Mountains in Iran, einkorn is used for animal feed, bedding and thatching, and materials for basketry. In the kitchen, bulgur (parboiled and husked wheat) appears in recipes for baked goods, *kibbeh* (meat-stuffed croquettes), pilau (pilaf), soup, stuffing, and tabbouleh, a salad of cooked grain mixed with mint, onion, parsley, and tomato and seasoned with vinaigrette.

See also: Agriculture; Emmer Wheat; Hybridization; Paleolithic Diet; Theophrastus.

Further Reading

Barker, Graeme. *Prehistoric Farming in Europe.* New York: Cambridge University Press, 1985.

Hornsey, Ian Spencer. *A History of Beer and Brewing.* Cambridge, UK: Royal Society of Chemistry, 2003.

Prance, Ghillean T., and Mark Nesbitt. *The Cultural History of Plants.* New York: Taylor & Francis, 2005.

Eliot, Jared (1685–1763)

Agronomist Jared Eliot, the first clerical physician in the colony of Connecticut, compiled the first North American guide to intensive horticulture, which defined farm wealth as a means of strengthening the colonies.

The third in a lineage of public-spirited New England farmers, Eliot grew up in Guilford. He studied books on farming that he inherited from his grandfather and, in 1706, completed his studies at Yale College. With a master's degree from Harvard College in 1709, he entered the ministry at the Congregational church in Killingworth, Connecticut.

Networking with agrarians in Boston, London, New Haven, and Philadelphia, he encouraged pragmatic enlightenment that bolstered a market economy. In 1747, he published "Essay upon Field Husbandry" in the *New York Gazette,* which published three subsequent essays by Eliot in 1753 and a fifth essay in 1754. A Boston printer issued a compendium of Eliot's essays in 1761 that aroused enthusiasm for generating greater wheat yields.

With the exegetical style and tone of a pulpit preacher, Eliot introduced uses for the American black cherry and

devised a way to turn a hilltop well into a hillside spring. He described the soaking of corn kernels in water to improve digestion and a similar soaking of corn with oats to fatten horses. At age 62, he shifted his focus from physical maladies to experimental agriculture and the breeding of a sturdier strain of sheep. Because of widespread soil depletion in New England, he recommended the drainage of swamps to flood farmland with nutrient-rich sludge. The introduction of calcareous sand from a Guilford beach provided much-needed lime; dry ash boosted the production of corn. He recommended the planting of red clover and timothy for the sake of the soil and the health of herd animals and advocated the cultivation of cabbage, corn, flax, hemp, kale, and turnips. He imported Russian watermelon seed from Archangel and reported a first harvest of melons weighing more than 15 pounds (6.8 kilograms).

The looming conflict with Georgian England turned Eliot's attention to pragmatic agrarian problems that kept colonists dependent on transatlantic trade and imports from the West Indies. After the English prohibited the importation of molasses and sugar from the West Indies, he proposed turning apple cider into molasses. During a wheat shortage in 1747, he suggested grinding a half peck (4.4 liters) of white beans with a bushel (17.6 liters) of rye to make imitation wheat flour for bread.

His planting instructions valued intercropping oats with summer rye, barley with wheat, and oats with peas, which vined up the grain shaft, making double use of a single furrow. He foresaw the improvement of varied species of grain to spread wheat growing into the frontier and the planting of potatoes as ways to increase food crops. All such innovations aimed at alleviating a colonial "diet mean and coarse."

After publishing the first essay, Eliot continued exchanging farming advice with John Adams and Benjamin Franklin in Philadelphia and farmers in Europe. According to his second essay, a shortage of corn, which farmers shipped from Connecticut, resulted in weak dray animals. Eliot deduced that greater use of alfalfa, clover, and sainfoin in meadows would alleviate the dearth of forage for oxen. By turning sheep and swine into harvested fields, the animals would fatten while scavenging cornstalks and, simultaneously, trample their dung into the soil to fertilize the next year's crops. In a region short on manure, he listed ways of recycling ash, creek mud, fertilizer, hair, horn shavings, kelp, and rags, all of which avoided the "filth and nastiness" of dung as well as its load of weed seeds. His third essay proposed crop diversification to increase food variety, a means of limiting colonial dependence on imports from the mother country.

The fourth essay, issued in 1751, introduced the Norfolk system, which replaced fallowing with a four-crop rotation that included clover and turnips. He also enriched his fields with mulched leaves, nitrous sea salt, seaweed, and swamp dredgings. In the fifth essay, Eliot

Americanized British inventor Jethro Tull's theories of tillage and contour plowing and promoted his own device to drill turnip and wheat seed directly into furrows. Benjamin Franklin wrote a letter to Eliot in 1753 praising his commentary on Barbary barley, a significant beer and bread grain in world diets.

Eliot's sixth essay, composed in 1759 during the onset of war in Quebec, turned to problems of farm labor drafted into the Continental Army. Eliot proposed that the remaining farmers halt experiments in food cultivation and put their energies toward the establishment of fruit and nut trees and the growth of mulberry trees to foster the silk industry.

Eliot extolled the colonies for their contributions to food exports, particularly rice from the Carolinas, apples from New England, and fish from coastal sources. He described trade relations with the "British Sugar Islands" as circular, a reciprocal arrangement that enhanced the colonial table while enriching settlers from sale of cash crops. He enumerated ways of putting food plants into full use, such as harvesting berries for wine, fodder for poultry and swine, and ships' timbers from mulberry stands. His expansive views honored New England husbandry as a means of avoiding slavery and uniting farmers in a soil-based patriotism. By 1850, Eliot's methods were common practice throughout New England.

See also: Tull, Jethro.

Further Reading

Breen, Timothy H. *The Marketplace of Revolution: How Consumer Politics Shaped American Independence.* New York: Oxford University Press, 2004.

Donahue, Brian. *The Great Meadow: Farmers and the Land in Colonial Concord.* New Haven, CT: Yale University Press, 2004.

Fitzgerald, Deborah Kay. *Every Farm a Factory: The Industrial Ideal in American Agriculture.* New Haven, CT: Yale University Press, 2003.

Grasso, Christopher. "The Experimental Philosophy of Farming: Jared Eliot and the Cultivation of Connecticut." *The William and Mary Quarterly* 50:3 (July 1993): 502–528.

Emmer Wheat

One of the first domesticated crops planted in the Middle East, emmer wheat (*Triticum dicoccum*) derived from a wild cereal grain native to the western end of the Fertile Crescent in western Asia. A hardy but low-yielding grain resistant to fungus and salty soil, it flourished at uniform height in damp and rocky soils in both spring and winter, producing the first viable agrarian economy.

The emerging staff of life in northern Iran, emmer wheat appears to be a cross between wild einkorn wheat (*Triticum monococcum*) and wild goat grass (*Aegilops taus-*

chii), an ancestor of bread wheat. Endowed with large, abundant grains, emmer wheat was the most nutritious and palatable grain and the easiest to harvest in prehistory. According to ethnobotanical studies, the species fed the Assyrians, Babylonians, and Egyptians at 80 percent of excavated sites.

Now called farro, emmer wheat serves brewers as a basis for beer and cooks as a source of high-fiber bread and a thickener for soup. Its chewy texture and nutty flavor satisfy hunger and introduce dietary fiber while supplying calcium, iron, magnesium, protein, and vitamins A and C.

Earliest Evidence

The earliest proof of emmer consumption was found at an archaeological dig in the Rift Valley of Israel, where seeds of the self-sowing hulled wheat surrounded a grinding stone in the late Paleolithic Age around 17,000 B.C.E. The grain required hulling and milling to prepare it for kitchen uses. In the Neolithic era, after the settlement of Abu Hureyra in western Mesopotamia (Syria) in 11,050 B.C.E., a millennium of drought forced inhabitants to cultivate wild seeds. As a result of clan clustering around the wettest, most productive fields, population density rose from 1 to 15 people per square mile (3 to 39 people per square kilometer). To feed all, protofarmers domesticated eight self-pollinating, early-maturing founder crops, which featured emmer wheat.

Dating to 9800 B.C.E., emmer grew wild in Israel and on the West Bank of the Jordan River valley. In the Euphrates-Tigris basin, emmer wheat planting in Sanliurfa, Turkey, appears to have begun around 9000 B.C.E. Using only digging sticks and flint sickles, which cut stalks with a single stroke, from 8000 B.C.E., a head of household could feed could feed a family on the proceeds of less than 5 acres (2 hectares) of land. Cropped stalks remained standing for grazing. Additional cropland provided seed for the next season's planting and for use as animal feed.

From 7700 B.C.E., when emmer flourished at Damascus, Syria, agrarianism rapidly replaced the more rigorous and risky hunter-gathering lifestyle. Sumerians achieved a 40 percent surplus of grain for brewing eight varieties of emmer beers. In Babylonia and at Mehargarh, India, farmers planted emmer wheat as early as 7000 B.C.E.; grain crops appeared in Greece in 6800 B.C.E. and in Crete and Germany in 6000 B.C.E. Beginning in 3400 B.C.E., northeastern Europeans managed a tripartite grain cultivation of barley and einkorn and emmer wheat. From 3150 B.C.E., predynastic Egyptians at Faiyum, El Omari, and Merimbole beni Salame valued emmer wheat for the era's staple fare of beer and sourdough bread, which they learned to make from Sumerian natural yeasting recipes.

Egypt, Rome, and Beyond

Throughout the classical period, the grain remained a primary crop. Long after the decline of emmer wheat cultivation in the Near East, Egyptian dealers traded surplus grain to Canaan, Mesopotamia, Nubia, and Syria. Their bakers experimented with yeast bread and produced lighter, fluffier wheat loaves, which the Greeks and Romans emulated. Emmer grain earned the name the "Pharaoh's wheat" for its storage in pyramids in bulk form and for funerary loaves shaped like animals.

In the book of Exodus, set around 1250 B.C.E., Pharaoh Rameses II placed the Hebrew Joseph, the vizier of Egypt, in charge of granaries of emmer wheat. On the walls of the tomb of Ramses III, artists depicted the rigors of bread making, which included pounding grain heads with sticks and milling on a saddle quern before baking loaves in portable clay bake ovens and in open-topped brick ovens. Emmer wheat dominated Egyptian cuisine until the arrival of durum wheat with the troops of Alexander the Great in 332 B.C.E.

Subsequent cultivation of a wider variety of grains around the Mediterranean Sea did not exclude emmer wheat, which the Phoenicians raised at Volubilis, Morocco, as did the Jews in Israel. In Mesopotamia, the spe-

cies remained dominant until 3000 B.C.E., when barley advanced to the prime cereal crop. Around 800 B.C.E., Homer described fertile grain fields as "emmer-bearing."

Julius Caesar's forces appear to have introduced the hearty cereal to Italy after the Roman invasion of Egypt in 30 B.C.E. As the basis for *farina* flour, emmer wheat became the source of the gruel that dominated Roman cuisine. Because Rome's metropolis depended on grain imports from Egypt, Roman agronomists experimented at growing wheat varieties along the Nile.

Numa, Rome's second king, introduced an annual harvest thanksgiving called the Feast of the Ovens, during which worshippers roasted emmer groats as a sacred gift. For three centuries, the Romans ate only emmer cereal. As a token of the hearth and nourishment of the family, nuptial couples ate farro as part of a *confarreatio* (wedding) and the *confarati,* shared marriage vows.

In *Historia Naturae* (*Natural History,* ca. 79 C.E.), Roman encyclopedist Pliny the Elder referred to the emmer species generally as *far adoreum* (glorious grain) and specifically as *semen adoreum* (glorious seed), an elevation linked to its role in altar offerings and in state gifts to victorious generals. Pliny described rigorous bread making in Ancona, Italy, on the Adriatic coast. Bakers steeped *alica* (emmer groats) for nine days in raisin wine before kneading. After forming a long roll, bread makers baked the dough in a clay pan and soaked the finished *panis depsticius* (shaped loaf) in milk or dessert wine before serving. Until the Middle Ages, emmer wheat dominated grain production north of the Black Sea in Moldovia and the Ukraine until the arrival of bread-wheat seed to central Asia.

In current times, soft, hull-less bread wheat prevails, especially in industrialized countries, but farmers still grow wild emmer in Ethiopia, India, Iran, Iraq, Israel, Jordan, Syria, and Turkey. Because of twenty-first century demand, cultivation of emmer wheat is advancing in Albania, Italy, Morocco, Spain, and Switzerland. In Sagalassos, Turkey, boiled bulgur wheat is a popular winter food in rural areas. Italian farro, the modern descendent of emmer wheat and a relative of durum wheat, anchors a number of foods including biscuits, boiled cereals, cookies, macaroni, and spaghetti. Its high-protein makeup and structure suit the needs of people with gluten allergies as well as famine food banks, local foods restaurants, and gourmet and vegetarian markets.

See also: Agriculture; Cereal; Einkorn Wheat; Fertile Crescent Diet and Food Trade; Hybridization.

Further Reading

Bakels, C.C. *The Western European Loess Belt: Agrarian History, 5300 B.C.E.–C.E. 1000.* New York: Springer, 2009.

Nevo, Eviatarl, Abraham B. Korol, Avigdor Beiles, and Tzion Fahima. *Evolution of Wild Emmer and Wheat Improvement.* New York: Springer, 2002.

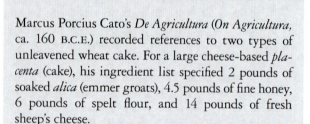

Recipe: Roman Wheat Cakes

Marcus Porcius Cato's *De Agricultura* (*On Agricultura,* ca. 160 B.C.E.) recorded references to two types of unleavened wheat cake. For a large cheese-based *placenta* (cake), his ingredient list specified 2 pounds of soaked *alica* (emmer groats), 4.5 pounds of fine honey, 6 pounds of spelt flour, and 14 pounds of fresh sheep's cheese.

The baker kneaded groats and flour in a mortar and shaped the mass into pastry strips. The dough dried in a wicker basket before a brushing with oil. The cheese required washing and draining three times and breaking in a mortar, before the cook passed the curds through a sieve. Shaping of the placenta began with wrapping flour strips and layers of cheese and honey. The cook shaped the cake on oiled bay leaves and covered it with the remaining flour strips. The cake baked slowly on a hot hearth under a clay pot covered with hot embers. Presentation followed spreading the top with honey.

A simpler *libum* (hard flat cake) required 1 pound of emmer flour, 1 egg, and 2 pounds of cheese. The baker kneaded the ingredients and placed the mass on bay leaves to bake slowly on a hot hearth under a clay pot. After presentation at Jupiter's altar for sacred offerings, the cakes became the property of priests.

Zohary, Daniel, and Maria Hopf. *Domestication of Plants in the Old World: The Origin and Spread of Cultivated Plants in West Asia, Europe, and the Nile Valley.* Oxford, UK: Oxford University Press, 2000.

Endangered Species

A plant or animal that sinks too low in numbers to survive, an endangered species heightens depletion of the world's nutritional and medicinal security and dietary diversity. For example, the extinct aurochs and pupfish left no free-ranging populations to replenish their kind; no spores remain to pollinate stands of giant fern, a common famine food and thirst quencher.

Currently, the International Union for Conservation of Nature oversees the status of 1,556 organisms threatened by disease, overharvesting, pollution, and climate change. Among them, 700 are food items. The most threatened habitats exist in the Americas, followed by Russia and Africa. In Sweden, forestry techniques infringe on habitats of berries and mushrooms that constitute heirloom plants and heritage foods. In China, the exploitation of exotic flora and fauna—bear, crocodile, ginseng, pangolin anteater, pine nuts, rhinoceros, tortoise—for medicines and tonics perpetuates folk demand for spurious health foods as sources of well-being and longevity.

Some wild food types—the Bactrian camel, baobab, Chinese alligator, hazelnut, leatherback sea turtle, monk seal, ohelo berry, pawpaw—exist in critically limited supply. Of concern are such species as American bison, baobab and butternut trees, conch, flying squirrel, milkvetch, narwhal, New Zealand mollusk, polar bear, round-leaf shadbush, sea lion, sturgeon, and wild water buffalo. In 1973, the Endangered Species Act protected imperiled amphibians, fish, mammals, and poultry as well as crustaceans and mollusks by shielding their habitats from biocides, human encroachment, and poaching. Resultant conservation has effectively increased populations of some vulnerable edibles, including aloe, gentian, ginseng, gray whale, grizzly bear, Hawaiian goose, key deer, pineapple cactus, sea algae, and wild buckwheat.

The loss, exploitation, or lessening of coastal staples—such as abalone, Aleutian geese, auk, cod, kelp, lobster, wild salmon—as well as the impacts of ecological deterioration, industrial contamination, and invasive species threaten the range of diet available to shoreline populations. Regulation of exploited areas interferes with corporate profits, sources of jobs, and multinational competition for a stressed ecosystem. As a result, habitats such as the fisheries off Newfoundland, Hong Kong, Japan, and the oil-damaged Gulf of Mexico have less opportunity to repair and recover sustainability. When shore harvesters and trophy fishermen vie for the remaining supply—such as green turtles, North Sea herring, right whales, sea otters, sharks, and sockeye salmon—commodities develop a cachet as exotic cuisine and luxury dishes, notably bluegreen algae, fugu, shark fin soup, and turtle eggs.

Because wild foods gathered and consumed by nomads and isolated hunter-gatherers have no commercial value, species salvagers underestimate their worth, as with black walnuts prized by Southwestern Indians. Since the World Food Summit of 1996 in Rome, 187 nations have promoted the United Nations demands for food that is environmentally sound and socially just. The goal is global food access and nutritional security, such as the preservation of large rodents and wild pigs eaten in Latin

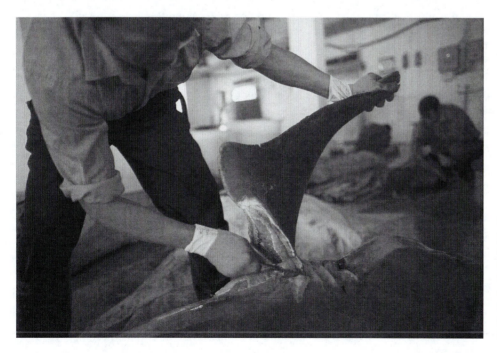

Workers at a Chinese fish-processing facility remove a shark's fin, a delicacy in high demand for traditional shark fin soup. A billion-dollar industry, finning constitutes a serious threat to the global shark population. *(China-FotoPress/Getty Images)*

America and the abalone, eulachon smelt, and suckers that feed indigenous peoples of the Upper Klamath Lake in the Pacific Northwest.

One answer to the decrease of wild species, botanic gardens and greenhouses preserve specimen plants for future development, such as the Swedish mycorrhizal mushroom. Another rescue method, farm-raised stock augments the supply of bluefin tuna, salmon, tilapia, and turtles. Starter pieces of coral permeated with endangered seaweed protect the dwindling supply, as raised in land-locked ponds in Molokai, Hawaii, until it is ready for transplanting. An oblique philosophy supported by vege-tarians and vegans proposes that the abandonment of meat in the diet offers a quicker and fairer means of restoring animal species to wild habitats.

See also: Buffalo; Cod; Fish and Fishing; Seed Trade; Taboos, Food; Whaling.

Further Reading

Evans, Kimberly Masters. *Endangered Species: Protecting Biodiver-sity.* Detroit, MI: Thomson Gale, 2007.

Kittler, Pamela Goyan, and Kathryn Sucher. *Food and Culture.* Belmont, CA: Wadsworth/Thomson Learning, 2004.

Sheehan, Sean. *Endangered Species.* Pleasantville, NY: Gareth Stevens, 2009.

Stonich, Susan C., ed. *Endangered Peoples of Latin America: Struggles to Survive and Thrive.* Westport, CT: Greenwood, 2001.

Escoffier, Georges Auguste (1846–1935)

From the Napoleonic era to the belle epoque, Georges Auguste Escoffier, the "Father of Modern French Cuisine," enhanced French cooking by designing color-matched meals and striking ice sculptures.

Born in Villeneuve Loubet on Oct. 28, 1846, Es-coffier apprenticed at age 12 with his uncle as a saucier at the Restaurant Français in Nice, where he became the first great chef to learn his art in a public venue. His em-ployment at the Petit Moulin Rouge in Paris ended in 1870 for kitchen service to the Army of the Rhine during the Franco-Prussian War. In peacetime, he made celebrity appearances at the Grand Hotel in Monte Carlo and the Hotel National in Lucerne, Switzerland, and opened at Cannes his own restaurant, Le Faisan d'Or (The Golden Pheasant).

In 1890, Escoffier brought Gallic flair to London's Savoy Hotel, where he shared supervision with hotelier César Jean Ritz. Escoffier's coordination of the *brigade de cuisine* (kitchen staff) demanded cleanliness. He gener-ated order in the first à la carte menu and Russian-style service, presenting one course at a time. His squad of culi-nary officers specialized in particulars—the *garde manger* presiding over cold food, the *entremetier* over soup and veg-

Dubbed "the King of Chefs and the Chef of Kings," Au-guste Escoffier simplified, modernized, and popularized classical French cooking in the early twentieth century. His *Guide Culinaire* (1903) remains a classic of French haute cuisine. *(Hulton Archive/Getty Images)*

etables, the *rôtisseur* over grills and roasts, the *saucier* over sauces and *fumets* (fragrant additives), and the *pâtissier* over pastry. His style in the preparation and plating of hearty dishes earned the praise of the Prince of Wales, Austrian singer Nellie Melba, French actress Sarah Bernhardt, and Italian composer Gioachino Rossini.

With Ritz's aid, Escoffier quickly turned foreign princes and British gourmands into proponents of haute cuisine. Innovators in the late 1890s, the duo established the kitchens of the Paris Ritz, the Grand Hotel in Rome, and London's Carlton Hotel and staffed them with cooks trained in the splendor and operatic drama of French table art. Mentored by chef Félix Urbain Dubois, Escoffier influ-enced the wealth of European restaurants that opened in the early 1900s and served some 500 guests daily. He in-sisted on the best in equipment and urged his workers toward speedier food presentation at appropriate tempera-tures. The Michelin Guides promoted luxury hotels in 1900 by listing nonpareil food that suited diners' habits and tastes.

Escoffier captured the fundamentals of *haute cuisine classique* (classical elegant cookery) in a monumental text, *Le Guide Culinaire* (1903), a meticulous compilation of more than 5,000 recipes. He sold house label sauces, which offered in bottles the savory mixes he invented. For Hamburg-Amerika Lines, he installed the first à la carte dining aboard ocean liners with such specialties as young venison, asparagus with mousseline sauce, pureed chestnuts, peach Melba, and flaming plum pudding. He finished fish, meats, and vegetables with the best of butter, caviar, champagne, cherries, grated parmesan, hearts of romaine, olive oil, truffles, and velouté sauce.

On June 18, 1906, table service aboard the SS *Amerika* began with Swedish hors d'oeuvres, Greek lettuce, and iced consommé and included sole in Rhine wine, quail with raisins, and Soufflé Surprise d'Orange. The meal so impressed Kaiser Wilhelm II that he dubbed Escoffier the "Emperor of Chefs."

Escoffier set the standard of wartime cookery and earned a French Legion of Honor award for sending food packages to troops and their families. He trained professionals at the Carlton and influenced Chinese pastry chef Ho Chi Minh and English food professional Agnes Marshall, who introduced the English to the ornate glories of assemblies and receptions. After retirement in 1919, he expended his energies at professional expositions and in writing *Ma Cuisine* (*My Cooking*, 1934). His disciples, including American chef Julia Child, formed culinary associations in America, Europe, and Japan.

See also: Dubois, Félix Urbain; French Diet and Cuisine; Grilling; Haute Cuisine; Sauces and Saucing.

Further Reading
Escoffier, August. *Auguste Escoffier: Memories of My Life.* New York: Van Nostrand Reinhold, 1997.

Ferguson, Priscilla Parkhurst. *Accounting for Taste: The Triumph of French Cuisine.* Chicago: University of Chicago Press, 2004.

James, Kenneth. *Escoffier: The King of Chefs.* London: Continuum, 2006.

Trubek, Amy B. *Haute Cuisine: How the French Invented the Culinary Profession.* Philadelphia: University of Pennsylvania Press, 2000.

Espaliering

A practical use of gardening space, espaliering spreads the branches of shrubs and trees horizontally over a flat plane. Tidy pruning inhibits shoots branching obliquely or vertically, a horticultural style that George Washington applied to crab apples at Mount Vernon, Virginia.

An ancient, high-maintenance method of training vines and fruit trees against a stationary object, espaliering developed into living sculpture, such as the heavily pruned vines at Yufeng Temple, built outside Lijiang, Yunnan, in 1756. The method derived its name from the French for "shouldering," a Prussian military term for the shouldering-in of infantrymen in a tight row. The concept enhanced beauty and privacy while making use of limited space and sunlight in walled cities, screening out wilderness and surrounding culinary rows made unsightly by

gradual harvesting of cole plants and the digging of root crops. In Japan, espaliering gave outlets to dwarfing specialists who engineered miniature fruit orchards.

Throughout Belgium, France, Germany, and Holland, trellised fruiting patterns provided visual interest to otherwise dull architecture. Cast-iron nails prevented rust and the dislodging of mortar, but some specialists preferred sheepshanks and wood pegs. Branch ties varied from cloth and chamois leather to more naturalistic bast, bulrushes, osier, and withy. Italian gardeners sometimes placed glass wine flasks over budding fruit and harvested the full piece for bottling in syrup.

In open spaces, free-standing trellised plants formed *contre-espaliers*, natural dividers usually low enough to avoid shading herbs, knot gardens, and low-growing vegetables. Low walls were more suited to currants, dwarf stone fruit, gooseberries, and raspberries. For walkways or pergolas, U-shaped frames and interconnecting wires trained limbs into a shady tunnel, such as one at Foxglove Spires in Tilba Tilba, New South Wales. Another creative form of trellising used a latticed hedge of apples to make fruit reachable for netting and harvesting.

Architectural Gardening
In the Middle Ages, pruned fruit and nut trees adhered to a trellis chimney, or rampart-decked walled castles, manses, and monasteries. During the Renaissance, Europeans rediscovered ancient Chinese espaliering techniques for growing the jujube and loquat in Y shapes. In Italy in the early 1500s, a belvedere on Isola Madre on Lake Maggiore supported espaliered vines and Ligurian citron and lemon trees that shaded the interior while supplying fragrant blooms and fruit. A common espaliered plant of the period, the tomato advanced from hotbeds to sunny walls to grow as ornamentals and sources of aphrodisiacs.

The flight of Huguenots from persecution in Flanders and France after the St. Bartholomew's Day Massacre of 1572 sent market gardeners to a refuge in England. Their trademarks throughout East Anglia, Kent, and London involved hedges of dwarf apple and plum trees grown on a lath trellis into fruit partitions. After 1610, Jacques Boyceau, the gardener for Louis XIII and author of *Traité du Jardinage* (Treatise on Gardening, 1638), advised on pruning and training plants to mimic nature. Because of the Dutch landscaping introduced to England with the crowning of King William in 1689, the English turned dwarfing trees and trellising into a gardening craze.

Eighteenth-century landscapers used trellising as a means of imposing geometric order and symmetry on wild nature, such as the netting grove at Villa La Quiete in Florence, home of Anna Maria Luisa de' Medici, and the recessed fruit arcades at Plympton House in England, planted in the early 1700s. At Versailles, the Potager du Roi (king's kitchen garden) of Louis XIV displayed 44 complex mazes of procumbent plant limbs groomed and harvested daily within a hand-reach. His master gardener,

Jean-Baptiste de la Quintinye, increased fruit diversity by grafting fruit to foreign stock and by anchoring multiple cultivars in a small space, thus enabling cross-pollination. His use of sun-heated walls engineered a microclimate, a basis of present-day solar cultivation of fruits and vegetables.

Advanced Orchardry

During the early Victorian era, the trellising of orchards fell into disfavor. Landscapers grubbed out stock that had been in place for 150 years. In the second half of the nineteenth century, intellectual curiosity prompted gardeners to return to grooming and forcing techniques. Scientific interests influenced such experiments as the grafting of pear limbs on hawthorn. In 1868, Irish gardener William Robinson advanced neater trellising with eyed nails and wire that he ratcheted tight. The final effect kept the understory warm in spring and placed fruited limbs at child height, encouraging early interest in botany and food production and harvesting. The cultivation of espaliered fruit spread to the British colonies, producing fragrant pomegranate walls in India for fruit used in beverages, sherbet, and sweets.

Currently, espaliering enhances the view while encouraging early growth against the solar-heated stone confines of gardens and courtyards. By choosing a south wall, the gardener shields fragile growth and unripe fruit from wind and nudges fruit to early ripeness in plants normally limited to a warmer clime. The shaping of euonymus, holly, pyracantha, rosemary, and yew creates a windscreen and limits dense growth that reduces air circulation and harbors pests. The method intertwines apples and pears and the shaping of trees, such as almond, apricot, cherry, citrus, crab apple, fig, olive, peach and nectarine, plum and quince, and pomegranate, and grapevines, melons, and sea grapes. Espaliering also stimulates the growth of plants and trees that provide valued aromas, medicinal properties, and flavorings, particularly anise, juniper, myrtle, and witch hazel.

By restraining new growth and shaping it in artistic candelabras, cordons (rope ladders), diamonds, fans, hedges, lattices, loops, palmettes, pyramids, T's, and umbrellas, the gardener channels plant energy into a higher yield and oversized fruit, such as a pear produced in Guernsey, one of the Channel Islands, weighing 28 ounces (794 grams). In the twenty-first century, espaliering remains in vogue as a form of permaculture, a creation of permanent landscaping with berry bushes and fruit and nut trees.

See also: Japanese Diet and Cuisine; Medieval Diet and Cuisine; Silk Road; Theophrastus.

Further Reading

Campbell, Susan. *A History of Kitchen Gardening.* London: Frances Lincoln, 2005.

Forsyth, Holly Kerr. *The Constant Gardener: A Botanical Bible.* Carlton, Victoria, Australia: Melbourne University Publishing, 2007.

Liebreich, Karen, Jutta Wagner, and Annette Wendland. *The Family Kitchen Garden.* London: Frances Lincoln, 2009.

Reich, Lee. *Landscaping with Fruit: A Homeowner's Guide.* North Adams, MA: Storey, 2009.

Exotic Food Clubs

The exotic food fancier has thrived from ancient times on meals of atypical or taboo ingredients, some imported over great distances. Just as Romans valued dormice as prestige foods, Spanish conquistadors carried chocolate and chilies from the New World back to aristocratic European tables. In the 1870s, eastern U.S. restaurants turned buffalo tongue into a must-have entrée for the elite. The fad hastened the demise of migrating buffalo herds.

In England, the absence of variety during World War II spurred decades of group gourmet initiatives. In 1949, the privations of rationing and shortages inspired historian Raymond Postgate to found the Good Food Club. Members sampled and critiqued the most venturesome of London restaurants in the *Good Food Guide,* founded in 1951. From the stimulus, British gourmands began tasting Chilean pinot noir, duck heart risotto, herbed vinegar, and Thai fish cakes. In the United Kingdom, as a service of the Fine Food Club, Bernice Hurst, a cultural consultant in Reading, Berkshire, accommodated tastes by offering mail-order rarities.

Food maven Julia Child got her start in cooking in a Paris food club, the Cercle des Gourmettes. In the United States in the mid-1960s, followers of her television show from WGBH in Boston spawned their own cuisine clubs. Neophyte French chefs imitated Child's methods in lacing up a holiday goose, reaming Israeli blood oranges, and whisking a smooth sabayon (a sauce of egg yolks, wine, and seasonings). Fervid Julia fans purchased German cleavers and French raclette pans as well as unusual spices and flour from foreign dealers. The group adoration inspired a feature biopic, *Julie & Julia* (2009), a re-creation of a blog in which author Julie Powell chronicles her mastering of Child's recipes.

In the 1970s, food curiosity inspired such ventures as the Cheese and Wine Club, Chocolate Connoisseur's Club, International Food Club in the Florida Keys, and Popcorn of the Month, which featured Cajun, peanut butter, pecan, and white chocolate drizzles. In mockery of conspicuous consumption, counterculture groups turned hippie food samplings into perusals of power by serving working-class menus—Mediterranean bouillabaisse and paella, Moroccan mutton tagine, and Mississippi River delta alligator gumbo with red beans and rice. Craig Claiborne, food critic for *The New York Times,* supported ventures into proletarian fare by introducing readers to ethnic menus.

Distance determined the exoticism of foods, which could be ordinary in remote places but rarefied by inaccessibility. After the Vietnam War, returning soldiers sought the unique foods of Southeast Asia—ant eggs, bull penis, cobra heart, pigeon heads, silkworm larva, snails with noodles, and snake bones. At the head of the list of memorable meals, Westerners popularized *nuoc mam* (fermented fish sauce), a common salty soup flavoring or topping for raw entrées and salads. A parallel upsurge in sushi in the 1970s claimed a Japanese specialty as a healthful combination of raw fish and rice. The pursuit of Asian delicacies turned some food club members into purchasers of imported fugu, a poisonous fish. Club members also became regulars at immigrant mom-and-pop restaurants in major cities and popularizers of chai tea, pad thai, and sashimi.

Foodies, the slang term for culinary hobbyists, cherished memories of foreign table exotica, such as the square Malaysian watermelon grown in a glass box or roasted baby goat's head. Museums established foreign food clubs for youths, a boost to children's table sophistication. In the Philippines, Western diners sought alien fare in Angono, Rizal, where they chose between monitor lizard and tree snake.

In July 1989, the eighty-fifth annual dinner of the Explorer's Club at the Waldorf-Astoria in New York City showcased an exotic food banquet. The menu featured dishes from Asia and the Pacific Rim: Australian hare with kiwi and yams, China Sea grouper, Malaysian dove with bamboo shoots, Seychelle Islands reef fish, Southeast Asian reptile stew in paprika sauce, and Tibetan roast yak and ram curry. The spread kept pace with other club dinners, for which chefs stir-fried worms and presented maggot-ridden strawberries, duck tongues on endive, kangaroo meatballs, and scorpions on toast.

Adventuresome travelers choose China as a reliable source of varied exotica, such as black rice, a popular item with the Beijing Exotic Foods Club. In Canton, entrées of butterfly cocoons, cat and dog stew, fertilized duck or quail eggs, live octopus, roast rat, scorpion canapés, and sea cucumber satisfy curiosity about food oddities. The use of metaphoric names—Dragon and Tiger Fighting—elevates the spectacle of such place marvels as snake with tripe. Dishes of live shrimp and squirming fish for sushi surprise Western gourmands, who are not used to killing their own selections.

Immigrant populations further the formation of exotic food clubs. Denmark foodies promote the tastes and traditions of enclaves of Africans, Chinese, Pakistanis, Thais, and Turks. Other locales offer authentic street food,

a strollers' choice of Filipino eel and frog's legs, Korean *eo-muk* (pureed whitefish on a stick), or fried Chinese beetle larva or crickets on a skewer. In July 2011, a New York City gastronomy club gathered around a Korean food truck to sample a menu of century eggs, grilled chicken gizzards, pig's blood and chive salad, and sea snails.

The launching of Internet food clubs has made available such flavorful game as alligator and rattlesnake, free of antibiotics and growth hormones. Cuts of bison from Ultimate Food Club in Washington, New Jersey, and other U.S. suppliers parallel beef butchery with burgers, filets, pot roast, prairie-raised chops, ribs, and steaks. Choices of buffalo or rabbit sausage, elk medallions, and wild boar loin tempt red meat eaters. Other entrées—breast of pheasant, ground ostrich, and whole Muscovy duck with foie gras—vary the standard poultry recipes. The Rare Olive Oil Club identifies samples by name—Frantoio from Chile, Pasolivo from northern California, Peranzana from Molise, Italy, Roi from Liguria, and Yellingbo from Australia. Investors in unique oils order stock online from Zingerman's in Ann Arbor, Michigan.

The availability of rare edibles introduces American and European members of gourmet food-of-the-month clubs to unusual aromas, color, flavors, and textures. Samplers taste subtropical betel leaf, durian, Jerusalem artichoke, loquat, mangosteen, nogal, rosemyrtle berries, Surinam cherry, and satsuma. Carambola, or starfruit, and kiwi have gained favor more as garnishes than as featured ingredients. Successful matches between tastes and food explorers have increased world demand for carob, chayote, jujube, lychee, and sapodilla and a following for produce from the California Rare Fruit Growers. Processed foods offer artisanal cheeses and wines, caviar spreads, lemon curd, panko crumbs, and fruit salsas made from guava and mango. The discerning have turned key lime, pita chips, pomegranate, sun-dried tomatoes, and water chestnuts into kitchen and restaurant staples.

See also: Child, Julia; Haute Cuisine; Lapérouse, Jean François Galaup; Maritime Trade Routes; Taboos, Food.

Further Reading

Burnett, John. *England Eats Out: A Social History of Eating Out in England from 1830 to the Present.* Harlow, UK: Pearson/Longman, 2004.

Johnston, Josée, and Shyon Baumann. *Foodies: Democracy and Distinction in the Gourmet Foodscape.* New York: Routledge, 2010.

Van Atta, Marian. *Exotic Foods: A Kitchen and Garden Guide.* Sarasota, FL: Pineapple, 2002.

Fads

Eating patterns based on fads may ignore long-term health needs while satisfying the individual's urge to follow the crowd. Historically, food crazes have circumvented heritage cuisines by focusing on fashionable ingredients, such as chai tea, quinoa, roasted peppers, soy sprouts, sun-dried tomatoes, tofu, wraps, and yogurt. Popular dishes—cupcakes, curry, hummus, pineapple upside-down cake, pita sandwiches, and Swedish meatballs—have accorded temporary chic to unusual food combinations and elevated to a food frenzy such oddities as deep-fried dill pickles and Twinkies. More detrimental to nutrition, fad cures make unsubstantiated claims that wheat germ and trail mix boost stamina and the grapefruit diet burns fat. In addition to exaggerated commentary on diet, trendy cures tend to demonize a particular regimen or food type, such as all carbohydrates or fats.

Over time, cooking techniques and equipment spawned a royal demand for Arabian sherbet and live songbirds baked in a pie in the early Middle Ages, gingerbread imported in the 1000s during the Crusades, the beginning of the Japanese tea cult in 1190, Mongolian koumiss in China in 1280, macaroni and frankfurters in the 1500s, and a rush to buy ice cream freezers and dessert molds in the 1880s. Decade by decade, food faddists created a demand for technological marvels—blenders and juicers for fruit smoothies and diet drinks in the 1930s, barbecue grills and Bundt pans in the 1960s, Sterno-fired fondue sets for coating bread in melted cheese or strawberries in chocolate in the late 1960s, Crock-pots for slow-simmered stews and chili in 1971, and fry pots for deep-frying turkeys in the early 2000s. In May 2011, the famous Chelsea Flower Show in London presented edible flowers, ranging from old favorites—chives, lavender, nasturtiums, rose hips, and violas—to Asian salad herbs and squash flowers for stuffing.

Food processors launch new ideas by hyping ingredient manipulation, such as Spam, Cheetos, and Krispy Kreme doughnuts. In the 1950s, television spurred enthusiasm for Jell-O, TV dinners, and frozen fish sticks and vegetables. Waves of zeal for brand names—Graham crackers, Grape Nuts, Häagen-Dazs, Kool-Aid, and Tang—often derived from successful advertising visuals and popular jingles. The food snobbery of the 1980s elevated pink peppercorns, pineapple chutney, and sushi as the exotica of the moment. The media exploited nutritional ignorance by broadcasting unsubstantiated medical claims and glittering generalities about kefir for soothing the stomach, pomegranates and acai and goji berries for their high vitamin C content, and salmon for its omega-3 fatty acids, which protect the heart.

The thrust of fast-food psychology on students, office workers, and drivers eroded the notion of breakfast, lunch, and dinner. The retailing of boxed takeout, microwave popcorn, and carbonated fountain drinks created a period allure enhanced by the electronic media. Driven by instant gratification rather than the satisfaction of preparing nutritious foodstuffs into well-rounded servings, food trendiness catered to convenience and eye appeal rather than adherence to food wisdom. Individuals filled their stomachs with fad foods—yogurt in a tube, nachos, power drinks—in the same way that they replenished their gas tanks, with gulp-and-go fuel that immediately energized.

Sociologists list a number of interlinking attitudes and perceptions that keep the American diet and restaurant business in flux. Because of a history of waves of immigration, the national diet has shifted periodically, as with the importation of Jewish dill pickles, German lager beer and sausages, Italian pasta, and Mexican tacos and salsa. Wherever it occurs, capitalism seizes on new tastes, aromas, and textures—black rice bran, egg rolls, energy bars, fajitas, gyros, pad thai, even designer water—and commercializes their mystique.

See also: Exotic Food Clubs; Fusion Cuisine; Gourmet Cuisine; Nouvelle Cuisine; Slow Food.

Further Reading

Allen, Gary, and Ken Albala. *The Business of Food: Encyclopedia of the Food and Drink Industries.* Westport, CT: Greenwood, 2007.

Belasco, Warren James, and Philip Scranton. *Food Nations: Selling Taste to Consumer Societies.* New York: Routledge, 2002.

Liberman, Sherri, ed. *American Food by the Decades.* Santa Barbara, CA: ABC-Clio, 2011.

Lovegren, Sylvia. *Fashionable Food: Seven Decades of Food Fads.* Chicago: University of Chicago Press, 2005.

Famine

Prolonged hunger and lethal malnutrition attest to the centrality of food distribution and stockpiling in human survival. Historically, the lack of sustenance repeatedly threatened China, Egypt, England, Ethiopia, India, Japan, Russia, and Somalia. In 1051, starvation destroyed the Toltec of central Mexico. Natural causes—cold, crop failure, drought, flood, insects and vermin, and typhoons—share blame with human factors such as inadequate food distribution and rationing, profiteering, tyranny, and violence, and the impacts of inflation, migration, and epidemic diseases.

War produced its own forms of torment, such as the Assyrian spread of mineral salts and weed seeds over destroyed cities. The concept of killing future agriculture recurred in Pope Boniface VIII's plowing and sowing of the town of Palestrina in salt in 146 B.C.E., the decimation of Mesoamerica by sixteenth-century conquistadors, and the starvation during the German occupation of Holland in winter 1944–1945 that forced the Dutch to unearth and consume flower bulbs.

During the famines of prehistory, subject tribes migrated to richer strongholds to barter for subsistence foods or applied the strategies of hunter-gatherers. After the settlement of Mureybet and Abu Hureyra east of Aleppo in western Mesopotamia (Syria) in 11,050 B.C.E., a millennium of drought forced the Natufians, the earliest settled people of Palestine, to adopt agrarianism by caching grain in storage pits as famine food. The experience presaged future civic planning that protected clans from starvation and the need for food raiding. Preparation for drought and crop failure prevented lengthy migrations to sources of water and sustenance.

Africa and Asia set a global example of coping with food shortages. A drought in 2150 B.C.E. struck Upper Egypt from Thebes southward, causing the demise of the Old Kingdom. Field workers and quarriers became the first to die from want and malnutrition. Official documents stated that starving adults cannibalized their children. To minimize losses in the labor pool, the state operated grain silos and reservoirs that stored surpluses for times of meager harvests. To address uneven grain distribution, bureaucrats allotted standard portions to citizens. Royal agencies paid workers in beer, bread loaves, grain, oil, or vegetables rather than cash.

Because of wise administration, Egypt became a source of relief to surrounding nations in famine times. In the tenth century B.C.E., the book of Exodus described the plight of the Canaanites of Palestine. The Hebrew patriarch Jacob, the sire of a dozen sons, sought to buy grain in Egypt, where Joseph, the lost eleventh son, had spent seven years storing food surfeits against a prophesied famine. On the family's second journey to purchase grain, Jacob offered cash as well as almonds, balm, honey, myrrh, pistachio nuts, and spices in trade. As a hedge against future suffering, Joseph resettled his aged father in Egypt, North Africa's model civilization for protecting citizens from catastrophe.

The Middle East and Rome

In western Asia, empires in the Fertile Crescent initially fed more people with less effort than neighbors in China and India. Beginning with the Medes in 1000 B.C.E. and advancing to the Achaemenid Empire in 550 B.C.E., Persia grew into the ancient world's largest empire and the most noted for abundance and generosity to the needy. Under the Achaemenid kings, government control and stockpiling prevented famine.

In northern India, Kautilya, a Brahmin adviser to the emerging Maurya Empire, composed the *Arthashastra* (*Statecraft,* ca. 300 B.C.E.), which advised the Emperor Chandragupta on citizen entitlement to sustenance. Kautilya asserted the emperor's responsibility to open the imperial storehouse of grain and seeds and to use food as pay for public workers completing irrigation lines and military installations. Kautilya also stressed that farmers deserved tax exemptions as well as free irrigation systems and seeds. Because of India's security, a 140-year period of peace and prosperity furthered agriculture, education, law, and trade with Malaysia for spices and exotic food. An innovative use of border tribes turned food gatherers and dealers into trappers of wild animals and lookouts for marauders.

To the west, Rome emerged as an urban metropolis that grew no crops. Citizens depended on Egypt, the ancient world's major grain seller, to stave off food shortages. Because of its burgeoning population and reliance on wheat imports, the Roman Republic dispatched Consul Gnaeus Fulvius in 230 B.C.E. to stop Illyrian pirates from waylaying grain convoys from Egypt, North Africa, and Sicily. Within two years, Fulvius ensured a steady grain supply by suppressing piracy around the Black Sea and along the Red Sea. Safer sea-lanes restored the Roman military to full provisions and rid Rome of its fear of famine.

To feed the plebeian class, Augustus, Rome's first emperor (r. 27 B.C.E.–14 C.E.), instituted the *annona* (poverty relief), for which he imported 14 million bushels of wheat per year. Decades later, encyclopedist Pliny the Elder lauded the Italian Piedmont for producing *secale* (rye), a local famine food that was easily transported over Roman roads.

In 284 C.E., the Emperor Diocletian feared a migratory trend to the city and the desertion of farms, which threatened food markets. In Rome's declining days in the late 300s C.E., after the failure of taxation and the economy, food transportation ceased. Authorities banished aliens and travelers, which the city could no longer support. The siege of the Visigoths in September 408 C.E. forced the city into a food panic, and the reduction of the daily wheat ration from one-half to one-third precipitated the fall of the Roman Empire. Over the next four centuries, Rome's population declined by 90 percent from hunger and disease.

Asia

The defeated Roman Empire resettled at Byzantium and faced more waves of drought and famine to the east and south in Arabia, India, and the Levant. In 638, perishing Bedouins, trapped by hunger and epidemic, sought a last chance at urban food rationing stations in western Arabia at Medina. To rescue them, Caliph Umar ibn al-Khattab coordinated an ingathering of supplies from Iraq, Palestine, and Syria. The caravan of Abu Ubaidah, governor of Syria, stretched from his warehouses to Medina's refugee camps. He traveled with the provisions to the famine center to manage disaster relief. With the supplies, Umar fed evening meals to some 100,000 beggars. When the rains returned in 639, he quartered displaced persons until they could reestablish themselves.

Some two centuries later, profligacy with the food supply threatened to depopulate eastern China. Under the Tang Emperor Yizong, the nation incurred drought and flooding beginning in 860 that destroyed cropland. While the imperial court pursued extravagance and military conquest, peasants struggled to continue buying seed and to locate disaster and tax relief. A rebellion in 875 threatened Henan Province with a military coup. Because of seven years of grassroots revolt, destruction of farmland and the coercion of men into uniform left the region in worse condition. When provisions failed, soldiers turned to cannibalism.

On the First Crusade in 1096, grain scarcity proved more lethal than arrows. The Christian vanguard foolishly traversed lands that lacked the provisions to sustain armies. While supply trains imported barley, beans, chickpeas, dried fruit, lentils, and wheat more than 3,000 miles (4,800 kilometers) from Europe to the Middle East, Christian soldiers violated Jewish farms in Champagne and Rouen by demanding food donations. In 1097, France suffered both epidemic and starvation and the loss of 100,000 lives. Farther southeast along the route to Jerusalem, Palestine lost 500,000 people to famine.

Provençal forces continued to live off local supplements throughout winter 1097–1098, when Saracens cached their pantries and retreated to caves. In cold months made gloomy by starvation and epidemic typhoid fever, the Calabrian Captain Bohemond, Robert of Flanders, and Tancred of Normandy led 20,000 soldiers to purloin cattle, corn, fodder, and wine along the Orontes River through Lebanon, Syria, and Turkey. Others sailed for Cyprus in search of famine relief, which enabled crusaders to capture Antioch on June 28, 1098.

Western Hemisphere

In the New World, preparation for calamity involved stockpiling of fish and meat along with herbs and berries.

Proactive plans protected native peoples from shortfalls. During periods of high productivity, they worked to prevent future starvation through numerous food preservation methods—brining, caching, dehydrating, drying, fermenting, freezing, and smoking.

When famine assailed the Inuit of Greenland, they consumed catfish and red seaweed as well as discarded pelts and partridge and reindeer intestines along with the animals' dung. At Barbuda, agropastoralists staked out animals to manure plots of dasheen, a nourishing South American famine food. Cooks adapted hillside greens to varied recipes. Amaranth and manioc leaves, collards, mustard greens, and sorrel provided salads, steamed vegetables, and thickeners for fish stew and meat soup. Islanders boiled callaloo and plantain with eddo and yam and flavored the mix with cayenne pepper and sea salt.

Catastrophe struck aborigines to the southwest from 800 to 1000 C.E., destabilizing the Maya of Mesoamerica and their empire. In Peru, to protect the Inca from grain and meat scarcity, rulers controlled the hunting of wild game to allow nature to replenish itself. Imperial agents stockpiled as much as a seven-year supply of food in silos and warehouses. Over extensive territory, the state guaranteed peasant survival by networking food distribution to even out crop failures with abundant harvests from other regions.

In February 1502, Queen Isabella appointed Friar Nicolás de Ovando, a Spanish colonial governor, to direct a fleet of 30 Spanish ships to Hispaniola. Cave paintings illustrate the attempts of the Taíno to welcome their conquerors with native bread delivered by boat at the landing.

The settlement of 2,500 colonists threatened the survival of 500,000 Arawak, Carib, and Taíno aborigines of the West Indies. From a combination of atrocities, despair, enslavement in cane fields, epidemic smallpox, infanticide, and starvation, the Indian population fell by 88 percent, to 60,000. After the colonists imported African slaves to replace Indian press gangs, the Taíno led African runaways into the hill country to escape the mounting genocide, surviving on meals of lizards, spiders, and tree roots.

Historic Struggles

In horrendous case studies, historians have analyzed the elements of starvation for interrelated causes. In British-controlled Bengal and Bihar during a drought in 1769, the British East India Company forced reallocation of Bengali farmland from grain and rice cultivation to indigo and opium poppies, sources of tax revenue. Hungry farm laborers, lime workers, and weavers retreated to the jungle to forage for bark, grass, leaves, and nuts.

In Patna in January 1770, some 8,000 beggars clogged the streets, dying at the rate of 50 per day. In Calcutta in April, corpses lay in the highways, attracting jackals and vultures. Street sweepers collected remains and hurled them into the Ganges. Rumors of cannibalism, consumption of taboo cows, and the spread of smallpox coincided with depopulation. From summer to fall, the loss of food crops to rural people in the lower Ganges plain initiated a famine that killed 10 million, reducing the population of Bengal by one-third. In 1771, British mismanagement of rice distribution allowed profiteers to elevate prices to ten times the normal cost, excerbating the malnutrition that ravaged the Bengali. From hunger grew crime, as gangs of thugs seized food shipments for sale to the highest bidder.

Irish Potato Famine

One of the most publicized famines of history, the Irish Potato Famine of 1845–1848, a severe period of starvation for the island's poor, resulted during English domination of smallholders. Forced to earn cash by selling their dairy products and grain, peasants kept none for their own use. During the Great Hunger, their typical daily per person consumption of up to 12 pounds (5.4 kilograms) of fish, meat, and cabbages, potatoes, and turnips from home gardens fell to little and then none.

News of the onset of famine on the Isle of Wight reached Tory Prime Minister Robert Peel in August 1845, but he, Whig leader John Russell, and Queen Victoria took virtually no action to feed the needy. Landlords, backed by the Crown, refused to exempt farmers from rents for the duration, thus forcing the poor into beggary.

Unlike previous crop failures and market dearths, Ireland's tragedy stemmed from dependence on "lumper" potatoes, a single homegrown staple, and the lack of cash to buy other foodstuffs. Planted in small kitchen plots extending from front door to front gate, the potato returned twice the yield of oats and wheat in Irish fields from Connaught to Munster. During a spurt in Ireland's population to 8 million in 1841, tubers nourished and enriched rural agrarians and supplied herds with forage. The population increase made the island nation the world's densest area and the most susceptible to a food deficit. In west Ireland, farmers, who delighted in the potato's easy cultivation, rotated no crops and sought no new strains or clean seed to supply their kitchens with potatoes for the national dish, "tattie" cakes, which they consumed with buttermilk.

Because lumper tubers were offshoots of the parent crop, the *Phytophthora infestans* fungus, perhaps imported from Peru in 1844 in a shipment of guano, devastated potato fields. During a moist growing season, the one variety of potato succumbed universally to an air- and waterborne blight of leaf, stem, and tuber rot. The decay proved so foul that families had to leave their doors and windows open. The tubers that survived spread rot in storage. Those who ate putrefying crops died, and those who fed them to livestock caused death in cattle and swine herds as well.

The Irish had no safety net beyond fishing. Agrarian families fell behind in rents, sold their belongings, and incurred eviction. The dispossessed fled to the bogs and turned to holes in the ground roofed with turf to house themselves. Lacking provisions, children degenerated to skeletal limbs and succumbed to cholera, influenza, marasmus, and tuberculosis.

While the British dominated food import and distribution worldwide, the destitute died on land and sea en route to opportunity in industrialized America and Canada. Because English landlords and tax collectors continued to bear down on the peasantry, the global media began viewing the situation as genocide. On September 9, 1845, the British press declared a state of emergency, which British Prime Minister Robert Peel attempted to alleviate with stores of corn and meal from India and the United States. Peel's relief commission employed 140,000 peasants to upgrade the Irish infrastructure with bridge, canal, dock, drainage, and road projects. Emaciated laborers often died in ditches with shovels in hand. To ease poverty, on May 15, 1846, the government repealed the Corn Laws, a tariff on imported grain, and set aside £365,000 in loans. It was too little too late, however, as the increase in jobs and aid failed to feed the hungry and compounded the problem by creating a welfare-dependent subclass of bitter, landless Irish paupers.

Analysis by the Horticultural Society of London on February 16, 1846, predicted the subsequent annual shortfall of potatoes due to the disease. The year's crop failure plus the government's closure of relief programs forced families to eat boiled cabbage leaves, nettles, roots, and seaweed. Beggars roamed Cork and Dublin. In ditches and sod huts, typhus killed off the weak.

To stem a protest march in Roscommon, the government called out mounted dragoons. Meanwhile, charity took the form of grain shipments from the Ottoman Turks and funds amassed from the Choctaw in Oklahoma, Pope Pius IX, Queen Victoria, and soldiers and employees of the East India Company in Calcutta. Protestant relief workers destroyed their credibility by doling out meals along with condemnations of Catholicism.

Homeless widows and orphans camped in the woods, living like foraging animals and cannibalizing the remains of the dead. Some had themselves arrested to take refuge in jail, where they at least had a bed and guaranteed prison food. Others hoped to be transported to British penal colonies in Australia. Of the many children boarded at Skibbereen workhouses, more than half died. To save themselves, the surviving Irish, some of the best of the nation's farmers, launched a vast diaspora approaching 1 million emigrants by the beginning of 1846.

Those left behind lived through the spring and summer to suffer "Black '47," the late-winter depth of Ireland's misery, when another 100,000 set out for North America. Through the worst of want, satirists writing for *Punch* perpetuated stereotypes of the Irish as coarse, potato-eating ne'er-do-wells. An editorial in the London *Times* declared that such louts deserved to starve. To the most cynical

English, famine rid Ireland of criminals and overpopulation, a subtextual swipe at Catholicism for encouraging large families.

Realizing that their original measures were inadequate, English officials feared that resentment could fuel an Irish revolution. The government introduced a novel answer to mass hunger—nationwide famine relief. Agents directed relief stations on Ireland's streets, set up soup kitchens, and distributed staples to 3 million poor. Unfamiliar grains introduced corn bread to the Irish diet, just as the Filipino sweet potato had saved the Chinese from famine in 1594.

The era's most famous cook, Alexis Benoist Soyer, London's Reform Club chef, led volunteers to Ireland to set up innovative feeding programs. His model kitchen called for a mobile wood shed 200 feet (60 meters) long. With a steam boiler in its center, the shed held a 300-gallon (1,140-liter) cauldron and an oven at the far end. In addition, the makeshift refectory required cutting tables, chopping blocks, and condiment boxes attached to the roof supports. Soyer's kitchen closed in winter 1847 from lack of funds, then reopened in January 1848.

Meanwhile, world charities, spearheaded by a Quaker outreach, battled malnutrition along with deaths from exposure and epidemics of consumption, dysentery, pneumonia, and typhus. As of 1849, some 932,000 Irish smallholders still were unable to grow enough grain or vegetables for themselves. With mass emigration and the deaths of 1.1 million from hunger and disease, the island population fell to 6.5 million. Those who resettled in Canada and the eastern United States shifted their lifestyles from homeowners and farmers to that of a burgeoning class of servants and wage laborers.

China in the Twentieth Century

During the Great Leap Forward campaign of Chairman Mao Zedong, from 1958 to 1961, China endured a devastating famine that killed 45 million from deprivation, exposure, overwork, and violence. Bureaucratic meddling in farming forced deep plowing below topsoil and the planting of seedlings at six times the normal density. During a series of droughts and flooding of the Yellow River, the government failed to prepare for advancing malnutrition in eastern China. By summer 1958, despite communal kitchens and boarding kindergartens, peasants began to show nutritional strain. Yunnan farmers dropped dead from slaving over furnaces that reduced equipment to steel ingots. Beggars lined the highways.

While land productivity dropped by 15 percent, farmers adulterated grain by adding sand. Exporters slaughtered herds, leaving the Chinese virtually meatless. The unscrupulous resorted to stealing, smuggling, and torture. As China continued to export corn and sorghum to Africa and Cuba, Communist bureaucrats lost their positions for posting the true dearth of food. While corrupt managers allowed stock to rot and grain to lie unhar-

vested, homeowners tore their homes apart and traded bricks for staples. Women sold themselves for a meal. In Nanjing, half of violent crimes stemmed from disputes over food. The poor scrounged for roots, poisoned ponds to extract fish, swallowed mud, or committed suicide in despair.

Relief efforts and importation from the West in winter 1960–1961 fell short of need. Collective canteens doled out sustenance by the spoonful. At water conservation projects, laborers died of overwork and malnutrition as scheduled hours increased and food rationing reduced caloric intake. The storehouses of Hebei and Henan remained closed to the poor. Szechuan Province reported a death rate of 14.3 percent; Guangshan County lost one-third of its population. World estimates of 20 to 43 million deaths swamped the official Communist Party count of 15 million. Charges against the regime claimed that Communists used selective genocide to rid the country of the disabled, elderly, and sick.

Africa in the Twenty-First Century

Into the twenty-first century, as predicted in 1984 by the Famine Early Warning System, food scarcity remained virulent in parts of postcolonial Africa. The Sahel, a 3,400-mile (5,500-kilometer) ecological band from Senegal and southern Mauritania east to Eritrea, Ethiopia, Kenya, Somalia, and Sudan, provided too little sustenance from grasslands and savannas for a burgeoning population. Mounting desertification stripped pastures of grass and robbed forests of combustibles for cooking fires.

On January 1, 2010, the International Food Policy Research Institute predicted that environmental degradation and water mismanagement could reduce sustainability of fragile lands in Burkina Faso, Chad, and Niger. Farmers diverted fields from cassava and wheat to export-for-cash commodities such as peanuts, sesame, and shea nuts. Medair, a Swiss-based relief agency, examined the lack of produce in Sudan and found 46 percent of its children starving. Hunger forced families to migrate from country to country, such as the male villagers of Gueza, Niger, working in Nigeria. Diasporas increased mob violence north and south of the Sahel. In response, the Emergency Food Security and Rural Development Programme identified and aided the most vulnerable farm families, strengthening irrigation and crop transportation for rice and wheat.

As heat waves and dust storms compromised farming and tropical rains shifted to the south, the drought of June 2010 destroyed Nigerian crops and pastures, putting 1.2 million at risk of starvation. Hydrologists studied ancient aquifers for sources of water for wells to return the Sahel to agriculture and pasturage. Appeals to global charities directed concerns toward child mortality in Chad and Niger, but abduction and banditry throughout the Sahel threatened the aid workers who investigated. To reduce chancy overland deliveries, the United Nations employed C-130 transport planes to deliver sacks of rice to Rumbak, Sudan.

Despite various dangers, relief work continued. The International Fund for Agricultural Development loaned farmers cash for seeds and cereal for immediate famine relief; farm families repaid the loans with cereal from subsequent harvests. Doctors Without Borders measured children's arms to test for muscle atrophy and set up therapeutic feeding programs offering supplemental rations. Desperate cases required hospitalization at Magaria, which saw 6,200 starving children within the first six weeks of 2011. UNICEF delivered a free spread called Plumpy'Nut at 204 feeding stations in Niger to improve nutrition for children.

In February 2011, the London media warned that the Sahel suffered from "virtual kleptocracies," the theft of food by despots and warlords, but lauded the rising revenue from Kenya's Green Belt movement and foreign investment by such conglomerates as Coca-Cola, Kentucky Fried Chicken, and Walmart. The locus of 60 percent of the world's uncultivated arable land, Africa, according to pundits, could surprise the world by controlling cyclical disasters through bioengineering that boosts profits from coffee, corn, millet, peanuts, and sesame.

See also: Agriculture; Caching; Famine Relief; Jacobean Diet and Cuisine; Linnaeus, Carolus; Malnutrition; Manioc; Plant Disease and Prevention; Potatoes; Standish, Miles.

Further Reading

Boesche, Roger. *The First Great Political Realist: Kautilya and His Arthashastra.* Lanham, MD: Lexington, 2002.

Dikötter, Frank. *Mao's Great Famine: The History of China's Most Devastating Catastrophe, 1958–1962.* New York: Walker, 2010.

Fraser, Evan D.G., and Andrew Rimas. *Empires of Food: Feast, Famine, and the Rise and Fall of Civilizations.* New York: Simon & Schuster, 2010.

Walter, John, and Roger Schofield, eds. *Famine, Disease, and the Social Order in Early Modern Society.* New York: Cambridge University Press, 1989.

Famine Relief

A group effort to rescue victims of starvation, famine relief recurs in history during upheavals that threaten regions with malnourishment and death, especially for vulnerable children and the elderly. Famine presents a moral dilemma by victimizing people who live in chronic poverty. Without access to transportation from war, harvest failure, and natural disasters, the poor struggle with inadequate food supplies under worsening conditions, such as lack of shelter and sanitation and advancing epidemics.

Global famine raises questions about the nature of charity and responsibility to the unfortunate. According to Australian bioethicist Peter Singer's essay "Famine, Affluence, and Morality" (1971), privileged nations have an obligation to relieve suffering, even at a high cost to donors. In 1996, New York philosopher Peter K. Unger defended Singer's premise in the ethical treatise *Living High and Letting Die: Our Illusion of Innocence.*

Essential to relief efforts, early warning systems avert or ameliorate disaster, such as that suffered in colonial Vietnam after 1862 and during the Russian famine of 1919–1922, the Sahelian famine of 1973, and hunger in drought-stricken Darfur, Sudan, in 1984–1985. Long-range assistance aims to sustain starving people temporarily until they can regroup, reap a sufficient harvest, and plot autonomous subsistence for the future. The emergency aid to Cambodia in 1975 and 1979 rescued refugees displaced by tyranny and mass killings under Pol Pot and the Khmer Rouge. In the largest food, seed, fertilizer, and tool distribution effort to date, the combined efforts of CARE and UNICEF on the Cambodia-Thailand border fed 25,000 people a day, handing out supplies of 22 to 66 pounds (10 to 30 kilograms) of rice. Out of the original population of 8 million Cambodians, over the next two decades, the 66 percent who survived reinvigorated the agrarian strengths of Southeast Asia's rice bowl.

Aid to the suffering is an essential of urban planning. As a proactive measure, Chinese engineers protect low-lying rice beds and wheat fields by maintaining a watch on flood conditions. If famine threatens from harvest failure in sodden fields, food warders distribute food free to the needy. During the Ming dynasty (1368–1644), philanthropists protected the lower Yangtze River valley and the food security of central and southern China. In 1644, the Manchus ensured agrarian abundance by improving efficiency of flood control and grain storage. The proficiency of these measures raised China's standard of living to unprecedented peace and prosperity for 300 million people.

Because of a political ideology that set state intervention policy, the Chinese led world theoreticians in studying protracted food scarcities. State leaders applied Confucian beliefs in tao (the way) to prevent mortality: Official granaries stockpiled grain when prices were low and sold it during inflationary periods to stabilize food costs. In the 1700s, the Qing emperors entered the golden age of famine relief, the result of years of preventing food scarcity via realistic methods of predicting weather catastrophes and gauging the human ability to endure urgent shortfalls.

In addition to plotting supply and demand, distributive justice requires control of opposing dynamics. The thwarting of clan wars, genocide, population displacement, food speculators, tyrants, and hoarders ensures that nourishment arrives at the right place with minimal waste. Another problem with aid delivery, the marginalizing of female farmers, who grow up to 80 percent of food in

A Turkana native carries food aid from a relief distribution center in northwest Kenya in 2011, when a drought across East Africa threatened famine for more than 13 million people. Humanitarian agencies raised over $1 billion in aid—still not enough. *(Stringer/AFP/Getty Images)*

developing countries, removes from the relief equation people who can provide supplies directly to resolve crisis situations.

Widespread combat raises complex obstacles based on national loyalties. Bengali philosopher Amartya Sen issued warnings about food insecurity in *Poverty and Famines: An Essay on Entitlement and Deprivation* (1981), a study of the 1943 Bengal famine, which occurred in the midst of World War II. He blamed price gouging, panic buying, warehousing, wartime inflation, and military provisioning for driving prices beyond the reach of rural laborers. Even though food production remained high, victims had no means to buy it.

Benevolence to famine victims requires logistics, as in the case of food shipments to northern India in the 1960s, which slowed because of inadequate port facilities. In 1969, Frederick C. Cuny, an engineer and urban planner from New Haven, Connecticut, initiated a career in such humanitarian relief efforts as food distribution and water purification projects, beginning with hands-on work with migrant farm laborers in Kingsville, Texas. As a United Nations agent and the founder of Intertect Institute, a private relief agency headquartered in Dallas, Texas, Cuny instituted technical assistance with minimum delay to the needy in Biafra, Bosnia, Cambodia, Ethiopia, Guatemala, India, Iraq, Kurdistan, Mexico, Somalia, and Thailand.

Cuny's pilots—veterans of the Korean and Vietnam wars, mercenaries, Israelis, and Air America pilots—delivered food packets dispatched by CARE, Inter-Church Aid, and the Red Cross. Crews paved roads to speed aid trucks, repaired gas lines to fuel stoves, distributed vegetable seeds for windowbox gardens, restocked herds, and set up sanitation facilities to prevent disease. While negotiating a cease-fire in Chechnya in April 1995, Cuny disappeared, possibly executed by Chechen rebels in Bamut. His legacy survives in the Cuny Center of Arlington, Virginia, founded in 2002 to expedite disaster relief with practical solutions.

See also: Airlifts, Food; Charlemagne; Famine; International Food Aid; Jiménez de Quesada, Gonzalo; Malnutrition; Maritime Trade Routes; Potatoes; Soyer, Alexis; Taro.

Further Reading

Amstutz, Mark R. *International Ethics: Concepts, Theories, and Cases in Global Politics.* Lanham, MD: Rowman & Littlefield, 2008.

Conklin, Alfred R., and Thomas C. Stilwell. *World Food: Production and Use.* Hoboken, NJ: Wiley-Interscience, 2007.

De Waal, Alexander. *Famine That Kills: Darfur, Sudan.* New York: Oxford University Press, 2005.

Li, Lillian M. *Fighting Famine in North China: State, Market, and Environmental Decline, 1690s-1990s.* Stanford, CA: Stanford University Press, 2007.

Nguyen, Marshall, Van. *In Search of Moral Authority: The Discourse on Poverty, Poor Relief, and Charity in French Colonial Vietnam.* New York: Peter Lang, 2008.

Farm Subsidies and Government Agricultural Programs

Governmental assistance to farmers supplements agrarian income while regulating the supply of commodities to prevent surpluses and drops in food prices. In the United States before the Great Depression, the 1922 Grain Futures Act shielded the heartland from price instability, primarily in corn, cotton, dairy, peanuts, rice, soybeans, sugar, vegetable oil, and wheat. In 1929, the Agricultural Marketing Act, followed in 1933 by the Agricultural Adjustment Act, set the tone and style of New Deal protectionism, which guaranteed price floors by warehousing surplus food. As a result, the protectionism from supplemental payments rid farming of market competition.

The effort failed to halt falling prices and did little to aid some 8.5 million tenant farmers and sharecroppers in Alabama, Arkansas, Mississippi, Missouri, and Tennessee. Representing the bottom of the agrarian realm, these serflike farmers lived at the mercy of landlords. The loss of income from cotton, hay, and rice and the violence instigated by landowners left some farm families homeless and jobless. Payments to landowners enabled them to purchase farm machinery that further displaced poor laborers.

Money for Not Planting

A novel approach in May 1933, the Agricultural Adjustment Act, the first modern U.S. farm bill, paid farmers for not planting and for slaughtering excess livestock to avoid food surpluses. In the midst of World War II, President Franklin D. Roosevelt warned that lowering price supports could boost living costs and inflation. Wrangling in the postwar years forced President Harry S. Truman to maintain subsidies and President Dwight D. Eisenhower to pledge administrative support for flexible price aid based on land productivity.

American farmers profited from demand in 1972, when crop failures in the Soviet Union spiked the market for wheat. As a result, subsidies fell to their lowest point at 2 percent of total farm income. The picture shifted in 1985, when farm financial crises spawned Farm Aid concerts to protect rural families from bankruptcy. A peak in agricultural research in 1994 generated ideas for genetic modification and livestock breeding. Scientific support increased yield to solve the developing world's population growth and demand for more food, notably in China.

Twenty-First Century

By 2000, U.S. farm protectionism averaged 47 percent of total agrarian income. Five years later, the World Trade Organization warned the United States that North American subsidies competed unfairly with world food production and pricing. Disparities forced developing nations further into poverty and food dependency. A similar aid system in Canada shielded farmers with tariffs on cheese, chicken, eggs, and milk at the rate of $8 billion a year.

From 2002 to 2007, U.S. crop subsidies altered from fixed remuneration for market losses to the flexible payments originally proposed by President Eisenhower. After the May 2002 Farm Security and Rural Investment Act boosted payments to $16.5 billion per year, loan deficiency payments, irrigation and export credits, and marketing loan guarantees supported production of cotton, dairy, feed grain, honey, oilseed, peanuts, rice, soybeans, sugar, tobacco, vegetable oil, and wheat. The bill raised the guaranteed wheat price to $3.92 per bushel, plus a Food and Drug Administration payout of $.52. Opponents of the Farm Act complained that payments of $180 billion to farmers enlarged the subsidy program by 70 percent and generated feedlot situations requiring antibiotics to combat *Escherichia coli (E. coli).* The World Trade Organization proclaimed the subsidies an obstacle to fair trade.

Unsold corn following Hurricane Katrina and the scramble for fossil fuel alternatives in 2005 elevated payments for corn to $7.3 billion per year for the production of ethanol. By 2009, 62 percent of U.S. farm earnings—$180.9 billion—came from the government. The majority of receivers resided in Texas, Iowa, and Illinois on commercial farms. Only 9 percent remunerated rural residence operations.

Alternatives

Global opinions of farm protectionism fluctuated according to circumstances. In 1984, New Zealand farmers stopped receiving financial aid, as economic authorities sought to control overproduction and inflated land costs by alleviating market controls on food exports. Surprisingly, as New Zealanders reduced production of surplus fatty sheep and turned to viticulture (the cultivation of grapes) and pasturage for feeding cattle that produce milk higher in protein and lower in butterfat, farm prices rose 40 percent and bankruptcies failed to materialize for all but 1 percent of New Zealand farmers.

As contrasted with U.S. subsidies, which compose 22 percent of the value of agrarian produce, New Zealand provided only 1 percent in farm aid, which applied only to agricultural research. The loss of regular payments in New Zealand and reduced subsidies in Australia forced suppliers of fertilizer, implements, and seed to reduce their profiteering. To meet market demand, dairy farmers explored future markets for kosher and antibody-rich milk and chocolate cheese.

Restructured Protectionism

Beginning in 2006, Malawi distributed vouchers to corn, rice, and tobacco growers to reduce the financial burden of seed and fertilizer by some 33 percent. Although the country became self-sufficient, opponents termed the Malawi model a short-term gain promising eventual disaster. The United States clung to its 90-year subsidy program, which enabled multinational corporations to dump surpluses on the world market. Surpluses forced rising deficits on poor farmers in sub-Saharan Benin, Burkina Faso, and Mali and suppressed conservation methods—biodiversity, sustainable cropping, wildlife protection, and regeneration of ecosystems. Tariffs and the incentives systems in Japan and the United States ensured high food prices, such as those for Brazilian cane sugar, as well as poverty among vulnerable smallholders in such nations as Angola, India, and Nigeria.

Because world cotton, dairy, and sugar prices tumbled in 2009, the United Kingdom and the United States restored subsidies and erected barriers to free trade with Australia and New Zealand. Health providers blamed the low cost of sweet drinks and fattening snack foods, as opposed to the higher cost of healthy staples, for contributing to an obesity epidemic. In 2010, while the European Union subsidized agribusiness and fisheries, U.S. authorities pondered setting a cap on direct payments to farmers earning less than $750,000. The proposal acknowledged that farm households earned $77,654, or 17 percent more than the average family, from a form of government welfare.

In August 2011, economic instability, increasing exports of pork and soybeans to China, and a boom in milk and grain prices forced U.S. politicians to consider scrapping the Depression-era subsidy initiative. European farm programs faced cuts in Belgium, where the European Union set a cap on aid to limit profits to large agro-industrial corporations. Protectors of farm aid feared a complete loss of the safety net. Britain's National Farmer's Union predicted that caps would endanger some 800 farms. Some warned that dependence on foreign food imports subjects buyers to lower crop quality and sanitation standards as well as potential unmonitored genetic modification of livestock and seed.

See also: Agriculture; Cereal; Lunch.

Further Reading

Arnold, Wayne. "Surviving Without Subsidies." *The New York Times,* August 2, 2007.

Kilman, Scott. "Crop Prices Erode Farm Subsidy Program." *Wall Street Journal,* July 25, 2011.

Marlow, Michael L. *The Myth of Fair and Efficient Government: Why the Government You Want Is Not the One You Get.* Santa Barbara, CA: Praeger, 2011.

Peterson, E. Wesley F. *A Billion Dollars a Day: The Economics and Politics of Agricultural Subsidies.* Hoboken, NJ: Wiley-Blackwell, 2009.

Farmer's Markets
See Local Food Movement

Fast Food

Quick-serve meals have appealed to consumers, shoppers, soldiers, and travelers from ancient times. Street fare historically caters to the hurried diner. In 1700 B.C.E., the brick counter at Ur stocked bread and spitted meats grilled on charcoal braziers, an early model of convenience food. According to the Greek historian Herodotus and travel writer Marco Polo, the world's first fast food began with curdled koumiss (or *kumish*), a mare's milk refresher originally fermented by the Scythians. In Ostia, Pompeii, and Rome, citizens of the Roman Republic and subsequent Empire had their own version of handy takeout at open-air cafes, where hawkers recommended stew with side dishes of chickpea fritters and olives served with wine.

In the Middle Ages, sailors and strollers took advantage of crepes, curry, flatbread, pancakes, and pasties cooked in the commercial districts of London, Paris, and Venice. Near ports, outdoor cooks steamed rice cakes and grilled kebabs and oysters. The pilgrim march through Santiago de Compostela in northern Spain demanded wine restoratives, which barkeeps sold with fried cakes dipped in honey retrieved from rock crevices. In the Yangtze River delta of China, street cooks in the market town of Shanghai offered bowls of noodles and fried dumplings with tofu. Complaints about culinary chicanery and shoddy preparation resulted in laws protecting buyers from such trickery as carp roe sold as sturgeon caviar and the heavy peppering of goat meat to conceal spoilage.

Urban Fare

The Renaissance strengthened the urban demand for street eats, from calzone in Italy to honey nut pastries in Morocco. Vendors cooked at plazas to the specifications of purchasers, such as roasting meat tidbits with vinegar sauce and marking *gaufres* (waffles) with the Chi-Rho or cross on Christian holidays. In India in the 1500s, *dosas* consisted of fermented dal-and-rice crepes, a popular quick hot snack served with coriander or tamarind chutney. Street cooks in the Middle East offered grilled eggplant and sardines and almond and sesame sweets. After 1519, Spanish conquerors of Mesoamerica found the food court of Montezuma II offering seafood empanadas. The 1600s introduced military dinner wagons and sutlers' barrows, which served hot fare to forces maintaining sieges around city walls.

A Greek street vendor slices meat from a rotisserie to serve in a gyro—a pita pocket with roasted meat, onion, tomato, and *tzatziki* (yogurt sauce). A centuries-old fast food, the gyro is a close relative of the Arab shawarma and the Turkish doner kebab. *(Michael Gottschalk/AFP/Getty Images)*

In the 1800s, Thailand produced its canal-side fast food in Bangkok with *khao pad* (fried rice) and pad thai (noodles with eggs and vegetables). In 1867, Charles Feltman, a German American entrepreneur, introduced the hot dog on a bun, served from his charcoal-heated cart at the amusement park at Coney Island, New York. The concept translated into rapid sales at the 1893 World's Columbian Exposition in Chicago and the 1904 Louisiana Purchase Exposition in St. Louis. From fair venues, individual vendors equipped self-contained hot dog carts and wienie vans, modeled on the Western chuck wagon.

A satisfying comfort dish and fast food on the American frontier, chili con carne thrived at Military Plaza Mercado between San Antonio's city hall and San Fernando Cathedral from the 1880s. Latina women let the aroma of cayenne and chili powder lure late-evening traffic to pots of chili heated over charcoal and mesquite flame. At La Plaza del Chile con Carne, a dime bowl and a tortilla served shoppers, soldiers, and wranglers. Public health concerns regarding the washing and reusing of bowls resulted in the closure of the impromptu chili business.

Early-twentieth-century Reform Judaism abandoned kosher rules, which tended to isolate Jews from fast-food restaurants, a common element of mainstream society. Jews felt exonerated for purchasing cheese pizza in Naples, doner kebabs in Halifax, gyros in Athens, and *poulet-crudités* (chicken and vegetables) in baguettes on the French Riviera. For fast food in Israel, snackers chose falafel, fried chickpea croquettes in pita, a national craze. In 1912 in Leeds, England, Harry Ramsden opened a fast-food business in fish and chips, a British favorite since 1860. As the result of a dearth of cod, British fish-and-chips shops

later began dispensing dogfish, haddock, hake, plaice, and skate in the standard quick-serve dish.

The Age of Hurry Up

In the United States, impatient drivers began patronizing gas-station convenience stores that stocked sandwiches and nachos. Teens with cars promoted fast-food franchising, which began with A&W Root Beer in 1919, a roller-skating curb service in Lodi, California, and White Castle burgers two years later in Wichita, Kansas. By 1925, Howard Deering Johnson raised the cachet of hurried meals by opening Howard Johnson's, or "HoJos," the first standardized ready-serve dinners and ice creams in Quincy, Massachusetts. In 1932, the opening of Krystal in Chattanooga, Tennessee, marketed the slider, a low-price burger, sold with coffee for 35 cents. In British Columbia, Carl Karcher initiated Canadian fast food in 1941 with Carl's Jr., a drive-in barbecue. Mobile army canteens during World War II brought Allied infantrymen face to face with female servers in hard hats distributing doughnuts, sandwiches, and tea.

For the Western world, the evening dinner hour defined household timeliness and togetherness until the late 1940s. Families began abandoning seven-day-a-week rituals for five-day-a-week home meals and weekend runs for burgers and fries and fried chicken and fish. Food on demand demolished dining timetables. Snacks randomized hunger and fulfillment. Meals on demand diminished the camaraderie of the nuclear family while dulling the expectations of consumers for a wide array of flavors and food combinations and the pleasure of conversation and table courtesy.

In the 1950s, the growth of fast food standardized eating out of hand buns and rolls with meaty fillings and of chicken legs, fish sticks, fried pies, and kebabs, as well as egg rolls from Jack in the Box in San Diego in 1951 and "value combos" at Burger Chef in Indianapolis in 1954. In 1956, a year after Ray Kroc opened his first McDonald's franchise in Des Plaines, Illinois, and three years after the opening of Burger King in Jacksonville, Florida, Charles Woodrow Pappe and Troy Nuel Smith revamped the skating carhops at the Sonic Drive-in, a burger stand that opened in Woodward, Oklahoma. In midcentury, fast food grew faster than formal restaurants. Drive-throughs degraded the waiter-diner relationship with industrialized food service. Fast-paced kitchens depended on automation to time the frying of potatoes in wire baskets and the squirting of soft-serve ice cream into cups and lowered the quality of ingredients and commercial cooking skills to monotonous minimum-wage jobs.

The mushrooming of franchises began with Hardee's in St. Louis in 1960 and extended to Subway in 1965 in New York City, Roy Rogers in Frederick, Maryland, in 1968, and Wendy's in Columbus, Ohio, a year later. Papa John's Pizza joined the competition in 1983 in Jeffersonville, Indiana. Minority communities sprouted chicken take-out sites labeled Bojangles, Church's, and Popeyes, venues of unhealthful fried food that encouraged obesity and declining health among the poor.

The industry continued to spread in the early twenty-first century. In 2000 in Brazil and Mexico, Alberto Saraíva, owner of Habib's, introduced open-faced Lebanese meat pies as fast food. The fast-food model influenced hospital and school cafeterias to replace a broad meal plan with french fries, hamburgers, and pizza. In addition to assaults on child nutrition, the fallout from paper, plastic, and Styrofoam wrappings and utensils forced civic authorities to combat roadside litter.

In 2000, the Vegetarian Legal Action Network petitioned the Food and Drug Administration to mandate that all fast-food giants label flavorings and preservatives. Activists from People for the Ethical Treatment of Animals focused on unnecessary animal suffering in abattoirs. Reformers denounced the food mill approach to animal husbandry and targeted Burger King and McDonald's fast-food restaurants in Miami to protest large-scale slaughter of cattle to feed a voracious public.

Public demand for lower trans fats forced the reformulation of quick snacks and finger food processed in oil at high temperatures. Companies reducing trans fats included Arby's, Burger King, Chick-fil-A, Kentucky Fried Chicken, McDonald's, Taco Bell, Walt Disney Company, and Wendy's. Erich Schlosser's 2001 best-selling book *Fast Food Nation: The Dark Side of the All-American Meal* (2001), Scott Ingram's *Want Fries with That? Obesity and the Supersizing of America* (2005), and Morgan Spurlock's documentary film *Super Size Me* (2004) attacked the

American quickie diet for children. In the wake of public pressure, as of July 2008, New York City banned trans fats from all restaurants.

Currently in Africa and Asia, up to 50 percent of urban food purchasing occurs at fast-food venues. Hurry-up meals offer outlets for female entrepreneurs, who assemble Third World kitchen businesses from home experience and such local ingredients as peanuts and yams. Street food remains a bargain for homeless and low-income patrons, who rely on mobile dim sum and dumpling bars and falafel and taco stands rather than equip and stock a home kitchen. Liabilities to depending on fast food range from undependable service and traffic congestion to contaminated water, high-calorie choices, and unrefrigerated perishables breeding *Escherichia coli* (*E. coli*) and salmonella microbes. Despite the negative impact on diet, American convenience food fans in October 2011 concurred with Yum! Brands—Kentucky Fried Chicken, Long John Silver, Pizza Hut, and Taco Bell—in demanding that federal food stamps apply to take-out meals.

See also: Carbonation and Carbonated Beverages; Chili; Kebabs; McDonald's; Soft Drinks and Juices; Street Food; Trans Fat.

Further Reading
Ingram, Scott. *Want Fries with That? Obesity and the Supersizing of America.* New York: Franklin Watts, 2005.

Schlosser Eric. *Fast Food Nation: The Dark Side of the All-American Meal.* Boston: Houghton Mifflin, 2001.

Smith, Andrew F. *Encyclopedia of Junk Food and Fast Food.* Westport, CT: Greenwood, 2006.

Wilk, Richard R., ed. *Fast Food/Slow Food: The Cultural Economy of the Global Food System.* Lanham, MD: Altamira, 2006.

Feasting

In folklore everywhere throughout history, the banquet table represents a gustatory and social welcome as well as honor for important people and special days. In the oldest extant hero tale, the *Epic of Gilgamesh,* episodes from around 2600 B.C.E. saluted an urban Mesopotamian civilization. The vintner Siduri urged Gilgamesh to feast among good company and good food as a way to enjoy life at its fullest. For Mesopotamians, around 2500 B.C.E., feasting was a communal experience, whether celebrating a cult or wedding or reverencing the spirit of the dead. For maximum demographic inclusion, hosts paid tribute to a king or dignitary and also fed the poor. In Turkey, generous hosts traditionally displayed their hospitality with the *dastarkhan* (great spread), a festive table topped with abundant and varied dishes to treat the guest of honor. At the other end of the Mediterranean, the Moroccan *diffa* (banquet) welcomed pilgrims from a journey to Mecca with cushioned divans and dishes of bean dip, lamb brains, meat tagines, and delicate salads served with fruit juice.

Records of ancient dining picture feasts in mural and verse. In Egypt around 1450 B.C.E., tomb art depicted grand wining and dining as a time for a varied menu and flowers to adorn guests. Royalty established its sophistication by staffing a well-run kitchen and coordinating dizzying arrays of appetizers and main courses. To create ambience, servants assisted diners in hand washing and offered fragrant unguents. In the Hittite tradition of ancient Anatolia (present-day Turkey), from 1460 to 1180 B.C.E., propitiation of gods at feasts, military thanksgivings, and state cult ceremonies included Hurrian or Mesopotamian blessings on royal brides and grooms, oaths of devotion, and chants accompanying libations and sacrifices of oxen on holy altars.

In India, conspicuous consumption of luxury foods contrasted with the dietetic concerns of the health conscious for Ayurvedic regimens, which date to 1500 B.C.E. The compilation of ecstatic Hindu banqueting verse in the Rig Veda resulted in a unique hymnal, the *Sama Veda* (*Chant Lore,* 1000 B.C.E.), a collection of 1,549 liturgical poems, table invocations to Indra, the lord of heaven, and feasting and tippling melodies. At the soma sacrifice, guests passed platters of rice and sour curds blended with barley and served with ghee (clarified butter). At the height of a ram sacrifice, cooks diced the meat and added flour before shaping the mix into meatballs. The sacred repast concluded with cakes made with butter and sugar or molasses and quaffs of soma, which songs declared nourishing, sparkling, and spiritually purifying.

Feasting as Fellowship

Unlike Hindu religious opportunities for dining, ancient Greek feasting, such as Alcinous's welcome to Odysseus in Phaeacia in Homer's *Odyssey* (ca. 800 B.C.E.), stressed fellowship in the prefix *syn-* (together)—as in *symposion* (drinking together) and *syssition* (dining together) with a *syndiepnos* (table companion). The concept of company in Crete and Sparta overrode other motivations for the simple hearth meal and for the generous spread, including the table topped with dishes contributed by community members. At major gatherings known as Dionysia, honoring cultivation of vines, and the Panathenaea, a grand celebration of the goddess Athena, citizens judged each other on the basis of public and private hospitality around the sacred fire. To valorize the idea of sharing food in a peaceful atmosphere, diners reverenced Demeter with gifts of grain and presented wine to Dionysus. Regard for the two deities of nature's bounty strengthened the social virtues of humility, altruism, and civility.

For Greek men during the classical era, the feast—whether for relaxation and serious discussions, the welcome of foreign envoys, or client promotion—extended an opportunity to accentuate male values. In Homer's *Iliad* (ca. 800 B.C.E.), grief for the death of Patroclus in battle took the form of a congenial man's meal of spit-roasted meat of a goat, ox, sheep, and swine. In soldierly style, the Greeks ate on the ground around the fireside without plates or utensils. They joined in postdinner athletic competitions, which ended with prizes—armaments, a tripod, a silver urn, and female slaves.

For some banquets, slaves delivered oral invitations. Neatly dressed guests removed their sandals and reclined on dining couches alone or in twos. While leaning on the left elbow, the diner selected finger foods from platters or scooped vegetable mélanges or meat stew with bread. Slaves removed individual tables and brought in new ones with the next course. Guests shared meat sacrificed and flame-broiled on the altar before sharing loving cups of watered wine, a gesture of restraint. Music and entremets (entertainment between courses) preceded *kottabos,* the game of flinging wine residue from a chalice toward a target. The feast concluded with welcome to *hetaerae,* sophisticated courtesans, often foreigners admired for their exotic looks, dress, and makeup.

Republican Rome imitated the Greek symposion and personalized it as a *convivium,* a private dinner party served at groups of three couches forming the *triclinium.* The aspiring aristocrat or nouveau riche cultivated their social superiors with status-defining hospitality. Both men and their wives or mistresses received invitations and, in some cases, a list of table topics to discuss at the event. Additional female company ranged from lute players and singers to stage performers, acrobats, and dancers. Wait staff extended welcome at the door and removed guests' sandals. Dinner began with a formal invocation to the gods. The service of from three to seven courses and the afterdinner drinking could last from mid-afternoon to early morning. Complex combinations of flavors and textures teased participants to guess the secret ingredient and prompted them to vie for employment of freelance cooks and pastry chefs.

The Orderly Table

Into the mid-600s, Arab notables dined on exotic or bizarre wild foods from Africa. They congratulated themselves that high birth and wealth allowed them to avoid the coarse, meager, and repulsive fare of Bedouins, their social inferiors, who survived on hunting and gathering. The Ghassanids of southern Arabia, the self-ordained "Sons of the Large Platter," competed with each other for service of the most arcane recipes, some of which travelers imported from Byzantium. Presentation of the best *huwwara* (white bread) with clarified butter, honey, and olives preceded boiled camel or goat cooked in sour milk, broiled mutton, or gazelle haunches, a male favorite for their proof of a successful hunt.

The dissemination of rice, sugar, and other food crops varied the Islamic diet from dates, milk, and the meat of camels, goats, and sheep to more varied dishes available in public markets and private homes. The elite favored banquet entrées of birds, fish, kid, and lamb and perfumed condiments gilded with saffron. Persian historiographer Firdawsi won world acclaim for his dynastic epic *Shahnameh* (*The Book of Kings,* ca. 1010), which balanced sober laws and moralizing with commentary on status dining, wine sharing, royal coronations, and Zoroastrian feasts that spread merriment throughout the Persian court. Feasters anticipated almond paste candies, pies and sweet biscuits, puddings, pistachio nuts, an after-dinner coffee flavored with cardamom pods, and an array of nonalcoholic fruit drinks pressed from blackberries, dates, grapes, pomegranates, and raisins and flavored with honey. Camphor, musk, and rosewater added beguiling scents.

According to Islamic courtly art and the travel memoir of Ibn Battuta, *Tuhfat al-Nuzzar fi Ghara'ib al-Amsar wa'Ajaib al'Asfar* (*On Curiosities of Cities and Wonders of Travel,* 1354), late-medieval Arab dining at At'izz followed a regimented social order. Two types of catering acknowledged hierarchy with an abundance of food to accommodate unexpected guests. Seating placed the sultan among advisers, sharifs, judges, and other guests, who ate from the primary dishes. The rest of the company—sheikhs, emirs, and military officers—chose from secondary servings. On the Night of the Bonfires each November, residents of Baghdad spread banquet tables along the Tigris River and drew the caliph's barge at the head of a boat procession. Dining, camp-side tea, and bonfires lasted all night.

In other cultures, placement of invitees impacted the political and social intent of upscale feasting. The Chinese seated their guests of honor with backs to the wall, thereby providing a commanding glimpse of other tables and ensuring safety from assassins. The organization of entrées from cold jellyfish noodles, lotus root, and thousand-year-old eggs preceded such hot dishes as dumplings, eels and prawns, mitten crabs, roast duck, and soups. Cups of tea cleansed the mouth between courses.

In Europe, the seating of guests above and below the salt indicated political and social relationships with the laureates at the head table. A sign of largesse, the procession of wait staff bearing a whole roast pig to the table made presentation of the entrée the height of the celebration. Service of meat slices on trenchers, thin layers of crustless bread, soaked up natural juices like present-day bread bowls. After waiters cleared the table, they distributed trenchers to the poor who clustered outside.

Displays of Plenty

The Renaissance set European event planners on the trail of the most glamorous table settings and unusual entrées matched with the appropriate aperitifs, wines, and cordials. In the 1450s, readers of the classics revived the ambience of the Roman villa in the *sala* (reception hall) and the *triclinium.* Colored jellies, parmesan cheese, and sausage replaced roast peacock and swan. Banquet literature recorded enticing scents of cinnamon, clove, and ginger and

the prominent positioning of marzipan table scenes, rosewater fountains, silvered swans, edible table favors, fruit cascades and pyramids, and tarts gilded with gold leaf. Amid the usual table greens, the era's sweets craze added rococo sugar sculptures and sugar ribbons and plaques, often perched on mirrors amid flickering tapers for maximum display.

To the French court of Henry II, Queen Catherine de Médici ferried north with her trousseau the basics of the Italian *banchetto,* the theatrical dining stage essential to the power-hungry Estes, Gonzagas, Sforzas, and Urbinos. She elevated the artichoke and asparagus as royal vegetables and introduced the gratin, a cheese-topped casserole toasted to a bubbly brown crust. Carvers added elegance to the slicing and plating of roast pork and veal, which bearers carried whole to the carving board. For a diversion, the knowledgeable chef presented oysters and shellfish; capons, guinea hens, partridges, pheasants, pigeons, or turkeys; or seafood, birds, and meats lighter in flavor and devoid of the heavy layers of fat in the medieval ox. Easier to manage on the recently introduced ceramic plate and faience dish, such wild fare posed in the well of a bordered expanse amid their natural juices.

A practical means of distributing solids with sauces, premodern tableware enabled guests to display delicate table manners and the flair of the new utensil, the Italian dinner fork. The restoration of Charles II to England's throne in 1660 reinstated the ritual gala, at which royalty and courtiers dined at public feast tables while their subjects watched in silence. The house-proud, after 1755, flaunted the permanent *salle à manger* (dining room).

In premodern Japan at feasts for aristocrats, shoguns, and high-ranking samurai, the appearance and significance of delicacies outweighed the importance of consumption. The *shikibocho* (knife ceremony) displayed skillful disjointing, filleting, and sectioning of fish, duck, and quail. Plates of ceremonial snacks provided artfully arranged fruits and vegetables shaped like flowers or in geometric designs for guests to admire and compliment as well as tidbits to carry home. Diners anticipated the *shikisankon,* a series of nine rounds of sake poured into thimble-sized cups and hoisted to friendship and courtesy. Between rounds, guests consumed snacks of abalone, dried chestnuts or squid, pickled apricots, or seaweed. Each serving bore symbolic value as tokens of military glory and prosperity. In the 1500s, restrained guests at wedding feasts pretended to devour these totemic foods, then tucked them discreetly into a pocket or kimono sleeve. The hosts concluded elaborate displays of food platters with thick tea and tea sweets, a final tray of chestnuts, rice cakes, and yams.

In Britain, the coronation of Edward VII in August 1902 ended an era of meal rituals and table splendor called *cuisine classique.* The onset of World War II decimated Victorian below-stairs kitchen staffs; a world depression terminated such opulence as fruit cornucopias shaped in ice. The technology of food preservation, refrigeration, and global delivery of exotic and out-of-season foods such as asparagus, citrus fruit, and strawberries sapped menus of their surprise. Restaurants further dampened enthusiasm for the state banquet by offering local dining in Cajun, Cantonese, Indian, Libyan, Malaysian, and Szechuan fare. Hollywood film and television convinced men and women that light dining and sensible portions could slim the body and extend youth and longevity.

On October 12–16, 1971, Reza Pahlavi, the shah of Iran, recalled the splendors of ancient Asia by hosting an elaborate international celebration of the 2,500th anniversary of the Persian Empire. Coordinated for ten years at a cost of $200 million, the event took place at Persepolis, the capital city since 550 B.C.E., and commemorated the historical link between the shah and Cyrus the Great. A vast tent city welcomed 600 dignitaries to a sumptuous menu, orchestrated by Chez Maxim's of Paris and served on Baccarat glassware and Limoges china, the result of the collaboration of 160 bakers, chefs, and waiters.

For the birthday of the queen, Farah Pahlavi, on October 14, waiters arranged a serpentine table to hold caviar-stuffed quail eggs, crayfish mousse, lamb with truffles, and foie gras–stuffed roast peacock, Iran's national bird. The banquet, highlighted by 25,000 bottles of wine, concluded with champagne sorbet, figs in raspberry cream, mocha coffee, and cognac. Dining extended more than five and one-half hours, a world record for modern times.

See also: Athenaeus; Egyptian Diet and Cuisine, Ancient; Greek Diet and Cuisine, Ancient; Japanese Diet and Cuisine; Luau; Médici, Catherine de'; Persian Diet and Cuisine; Roman Diet and Cuisine, Ancient.

Further Reading

Albala, Ken. *The Banquet: Dining in the Great Courts of Late Renaissance Europe.* Urbana: University of Illinois Press, 2007.

Rath, Eric C. *Food and Fantasy in Early Modern Japan.* Berkeley: University of California Press, 2010.

Strong, Roy C. *Feast: A History of Grand Eating.* London: Jonathan Cape, 2002.

Van Gelder, Geert Jan. *God's Banquet: Food in Classical Arabic Literature.* New York: Columbia University Press, 2000.

Fermented Foods

While extending the use of foods, fermentation enriches cuisine with varied flavors, hues, scents, and textures in alcohol, bread, cheese, pickles, sausage, vinegar, and wine. The chemical phenomenon that converts carbohydrates into acids or alcohols transforms staples in all parts of the diet—beans into miso and soy sauce, cassava into silage and Indonesian *tape*, cocoa pods into chocolate, corn into posole and smut, herbs into sarsaparilla, milk into curds and yogurt, peanuts into Javanese *oncom*, potatoes

into baker's yeast, rice into *arroz amarillo* (yellow rice), tea into *kombucha* and semi-fermented oolong, and vegetables into black bean sauce, breadfruit loaves, and cucumber and walnut pickles.

Historically, meat made unique alterations under enzymatic action: fish into *garum* (fish sauce) and Norwegian *rakfisk,* pork into chorizo and pepperoni, and shrimp into Indonesian *blachan* (shrimp paste). Alcoholic drinks derived from a wide range of ingredients—beer from barley or wheat and honey, brandy and cider from cherries or peaches and apples, Celtic mead and metheglyn from honey, koumiss from mare's milk, Macedonian *baza* beer from millet, *pulque* from agave and corn, rum from cane sugar and cassava, sake from rice, and vodka from potatoes.

The distinctive colors and tastes that evolved over time generated ethnic specialties as closely linked to cultures as Chinese tofu, Filipino mango and papaya pickles, German sauerkraut, Greek green olives, Hawaiian *poi,* Himalayan smoked yak, Indian ghee and *shrikhand* (sweetened sour cream), Irish whiskey, Italian capers and salami, Korean *kimchi* (pickled Chinese cabbage), and Nigerian *fufu.*

From as early as 10,000 B.C.E. in China, Libya, and the Near East, some four millennia before the invention of earthenware storage containers, food preparers altered and preserved natural resources through incidental biotransformation, such as the fermentation of cow's milk by Libyans in 9000 B.C.E. The Egyptians began baking flatbread in the ninth millennium B.C.E. In 1500 B.C.E., two millennia after they brewed the first barley beer, they leavened bread to produce a lighter, tastier crumb than flatbread. By mixing risen dough with new batches, bakers perpetuated the formation of sourdough from the action of carbon dioxide and ethanol from soured milk on flour and water. As risen loaves came into demand, bakers formed their own manufacturing guilds, which concealed each group's fermentation methods and kneading and rising secrets.

From bacteria, filamentous mold, lactic acid, and yeast, raw and cooked dishes acquired new qualities and improved food safety and nutrition, natural assets of preservation. Via inadvertent chemical changes in unpreserved dough, fruit juice, meat, and milk, clans learned that they could extend the shelf life of perishables while treating themselves to an aesthetic culinary experience. After the evolution of Babylonian beer in 7000 B.C.E., farmers enhanced revenues by making new beverages from dates and palm sap and by diverting malted grain to brewing 26 different beers. By 3000 B.C.E., the use of 40 percent of Babylonian cereal grains for beer introduced a new social problem, drunkenness and the attendant ills of alcoholism.

The First Wines

Wine grapes (*Vitis vinifera sylvestris*) originated in the Caucasus Mountains around 6000 B.C.E. Along the Tigris and Euphrates rivers, the Babylonians became the first to ferment the juice of wild vine fruits and to fill jars with wine. In 4500 B.C.E., vintages from the Macedonian uplands attained popularity, favorably compared to Chian wine (from the Greek island of Chios) as "soft and fair" and praised into the second century C.E. by Egyptian food writer Athenaeus of Naucratis. Digs in a cave on the Arpa River in Areni, Armenia, located a winery dating to 4100 B.C.E. that produced sacred beverages reserved for ritual. The site consisted of a yard-square clay basin where workers pressed domesticated grapes with their feet. Juice trickled into airless 15-gallon (57-liter) fermentation vats. From there, a dry red wine passed to storage jars bound for trade sites as distant as Anatolia, Palestine, and Syria.

By 3000 B.C.E., wineries flourished in China, Egypt, and Sumer. The *Epic of Gilgamesh* (ca. 2600 B.C.E.) includes the oldest surviving account of wineries, describing an urban Mesopotamian culture that valued fermented drink. In this work, a female vintner named Siduri urges Gilgamesh to treasure wine and merrymaking as two of the joys of mortal life. The Chinese evolved their own vintages after 2000 B.C.E., dubbing their product *hou jiu* (monkey wine) from the stacking of wild fruit by monkeys. The pre-Olmec of Mexico and the Nubians of Sudan developed their unique alcoholic beverages in 2000 and 1500 B.C.E. The Egyptians turned fermented beverages into taboo drinks for ordinary citizens by reserving wine for pharaohs, priests, and state officials. Wine jars in the tomb of King Tutankhamen, sealed in 1323 B.C.E., attested to the boy king's preference for red wine.

The Etruscans, Greeks, Romans, and Phoenicians dominated the commercial cultivation of vineyards and the exportation of beverages for dining and medicinal use. Around 800 B.C.E., Homer referred to fermentation methods, which concluded with the blending of the vintage with seawater. A century later, the techniques recurred in Hesiod's *Works and Days* (700 B.C.E.) with descriptions of air-drying grapes to temper the flavor, treading out juice, and storing it in terra-cotta jars. Settlers of Magna Graecia in Sicily and southern Italy in the fifth century B.C.E. named their colonial network "Enotria" (land of wine) for its success at the wine trade.

Essential to the technology governing enzyme action, the specialty jobs of wine pressing and coopering (wooden cask making or repairing) turned home fermentation into an international business. Into the Middle Ages, Catholicism allied with vintners in Corsica, Iberia, Italy, and Provence as a source of wine for the Eucharist.

Fermented Foods for the Road

Over centuries of adapting food preservation techniques, cooks learned to control fermentation to maintain a particular aroma, mouthfeel, or flavor, such as the taste of Chinese rice wine, first fermented around 7000 B.C.E., and the coagulation of *dahi* (sour milk) and the churning of butter in India around 6000 B.C.E. Nomads valued bio-enhanced foods as insurance against starvation or the waste of raw foods during migrations. The Egyptians advanced industrial by-products by turning soured wine into vinegar, one of their most popular commercially processed foods. In 2838 B.C.E., herbalist Shennong (Shen Nung), the "Father of Chinese Medicine and Pharmacology," added the preserved soybean to the curative foods described in his herbal handbook, thus introducing to Asian cuisine one of its most distinctive and versatile staples.

Food preservation enhanced the success of such military expeditions as Alexander the Great's march from Macedonia to the Indus River. For Greek and Roman seamen and soldiers, supply trains carried fermented green olives and sourdough biscuits along with beer and wine. Preserved rations ensured healthful food and beverages devoid of the types of bacteria and amoeba that caused muscle-sapping intestinal complaints. The Roman Emperor Tiberius chose sauerkraut to dispatch on marches to Germania and Parthia, where Roman legionaries frequently incurred dysentery. Present-day research concurs with Tiberius by confirming the value of lactic acid bacteria in the gut to promote friendly intestinal flora and to quell cholera and typhoid fever.

Bioengineered Foodstuffs

Other fermenting techniques dot the history of prepared dishes. Around 4000 B.C.E., Middle Eastern herders curdled milk in skin bags. By 3200 B.C.E., milk fermentation in Egypt anticipated the pickling of soft Greek feta cheese in 1184 B.C.E. and the popularity of koumiss, which became the staple drink in Asia. By 1500 B.C.E., the Babylonians and Chinese blended ground meat with salt, spice, and sugar and stuffed sausages for drying.

During the Zhou dynasty, publication of the Confucian ritual text *Zhouli* (Chou-li, Rites of Chou, compiled ca. 1116 B.C.E.) covered the transformation of meat and millet into *chiang,* a brined mash fermented in sealed jars for 13 weeks. Fermented with yellow aspergillus mold, chiang produced a salty flavor similar to soy sauce. During the Han dynasty (202 B.C.E.–220 C.E.), the fermentation of seasonal fish added a natural accompaniment to chiang as well as to pickled beets, cabbage, cucumbers, radishes, and turnips, which the Chinese preserved as condiments and as transportable rations for coolie laborers. In the first century C.E., the substitution of soybeans for meat and the addition of barley, rice, or wheat and select herbs individualized the appeal of chiang flavors.

History and art recorded the advances in commercial food fermentation, beginning in 800 B.C.E. with sausage making in Homer's *Odyssey* and covering commercial Roman bakeries in the second century B.C.E. By 500 B.C.E., the Chinese turned soybean mold into an antibiotic. In 54 B.C.E., Julius Caesar discovered the sharp savor of cheddar cheese manufactured in Britannia. He contributed another ingredient to antipasti in 48 B.C.E. with the introduction of sausage to the cuisine of Republican

Rome. The Emperor Probus reintroduced wine grapes to Alsatia in 277, two centuries after farmers gave up vineyards for wheat fields.

The chronology of fermented foods scrolled out a list of new taste sensations—Roquefort cheese in 1070, Parmesan cheese in 1200, Spanish sherry in 1430, California wines and Dutch Gouda cheese in 1697, Dom Pérignon champagne in 1698, and California sourdough in 1850. Until the Industrial Revolution, brining, drying, and fermentation remained the most essential food preservation methods. By the late 1700s, improved study through microscopy and application of gas laws turned the art of fermenting foods into a science.

See also: Beer; Bread; Cheese; Cider; Korean Diet and Cuisine; Manioc; Pickling; Sausage; Silk Road; Sourdough; Standish, Miles; Tofu; Vinegar; Wine; Yeast.

Further Reading

Farnworth, Edward R., ed. *Handbook of Fermented Functional Foods.* Boca Raton, FL: CRC, 2008.

Hutkins, Robert Wayne. *Microbiology and Technology of Fermented Foods.* Chicago: IFT, 2006.

Steinkraus, Keith H. *Industrialization of Indigenous Fermented Foods.* 2nd ed. New York: Marcel Dekker, 2004.

Fertile Crescent Diet and Food Trade

The cradle of civilization, the Fertile Crescent, a metaphoric name for Mesopotamia, bridged three continents—Africa, Asia, and Europe. Spreading over 193,000 square miles (500,000 square kilometers), the region flourished 10,000 years ago at a time when hunter-gatherers gave place to the world's first agrarians. Populated between the Anatolian highlanders of the Taurus Mountains to the north and the nomads of the Syrian Desert to the south and watered by the Tigris and Euphrates rivers, the verdant arc extended from the Mediterranean Sea to the Persian Gulf.

The environmentally blessed expanse encompassed the people of the Levant and Mesopotamia—present-day Iraq, Jordan, Kuwait, Lebanon, Palestine, and Syria and parts of Iran and Turkey. A felicitous climate furthered civilizations created by the Sumerians (2900–1730 B.C.E.), Akkadians (2334–2112 B.C.E.), Assyrians (2000–539 B.C.E.), Hittites (2000–1100 B.C.E.), Amorites (1900–1600 B.C.E.), and Babylonians (1800–1170 B.C.E.). Contributing to Mesopotamian prosperity, a dwindling population of cave-dwelling hunter-gatherers competed against the seminomadic settlers for territory.

The Fertile Crescent solved a major obstacle to human growth and health. The limited nutrition of staple crops left a mark on early peoples, who suffered anemia, blindness, stunting, and skeletal anomalies. In comparison to neolithic hunter-gatherers, a limited diet reduced average height of agrarians from 5' 9" to 5' 3" (1.75 to 1.6 meters) among males and from 5' 5" to 5' 0" (1.65 to 1.52 meters) among women.

Over time, diversification of agricultural crops and pasturage for cattle, goats, sheep, and swine underlay a unique cuisine for such emergent city centers as Abu Hureyra, Aleppo, Babylon, Catal Huyuk, Damascus, Jericho, Megiddo, Nineveh, Susa, and Uruk, the first trading center. Of the world's edible food plants, 32 grew along the crescent, offering a remarkably varied diet in contrast to the four food plants of sub-Saharan Africa and the absence of any agrarian sustenance in Australasia. A range of elevations spread harvests of annual plants from moist valleys into well-drained highlands. Before residents became farmers, they reaped wild grasses and developed a diet based on carbohydrates and leafy greens and herbs, which they supplemented with the meat acquired by hunting and fishing.

World's First Farmers

In the Neolithic era, after the settlement of Abu Hureyra in western Mesopotamia (Syria) in 11,050 B.C.E., a millennium of drought forced inhabitants to cultivate wild seeds, beginning with rye (*Secale cereale*). As a result of clustering around the most moist and productive fields, population density rose from one to 15 persons per square mile (less than one to 6 persons per square kilometer). To feed all inhabitants, protofarmers domesticated the eight self-pollinating, early-maturing founder crops—barley, bitter vetch, chickpeas, einkorn wheat, emmer wheat, flax, lentils, and peas.

- Flax served human needs from 30,000 B.C.E. A source of food dye and linseed oil, flax heads are 40 percent oil.

- Dating to 9800 B.C.E., emmer, a self-sowing hulled wheat, grew wild in Israel and on the West Bank of the Jordan River valley. From 7700 B.C.E., emmer flourished at Damascus, Syria.

- Lentils, a high-protein pod plant from the Levant, were a Stone Age food crop that entered the human diet in 9500 B.C.E.

- In 9000 B.C.E., wild einkorn, a more productive grain than emmer, introduced wheat cultivation in southeastern Turkey. Agrarianism rapidly replaced the more rigorous and risky hunter-gathering lifestyle.

- Syrians first cultivated barley in 8500 B.C.E. at Abu Hureyra as a nutritious cereal grain and a source of bread and beer. Around 1000 B.C.E., the biblical Israelites used the grain in temple sacrifices. Barley spread along the west-east axis of Eurasia south to Egypt, west to Carthage, and east through Iran to the Indus Valley.

- From 7500 B.C.E., cooks in the Jordan River valley and southeastern Turkey relied on the protein-rich chickpea for food and well-being.

- Bitter vetch, a prolific forage crop, required the leaching of bitter residues to make it palatable. From 7000 B.C.E., vetch served the lowest classes of people as a vegetable and curative and fed communities undergoing drought.

- From 6000 B.C.E., pea cultivation not only nourished farm families with its protein but also enriched garden plots with the plant's nitrogen-fixing roots.

To rid staples of toxins and indigestible hulls and to access maximum food value for adults, children, infants, and invalids, cooks learned to grind, soak, parboil, and rinse some grains and to roast and grate root crops. Grindstones introduced mineral particles to flour and weakened teeth by wearing down enamel and abrading root lines.

The Mediterranean diet had its beginnings in developments dating to 5000 B.C.E. The Akkadian myth *Atrahasis* (1700 B.C.E.) described the survival of humanity between the Tigris and Euphrates as dependent upon the ditching of land, a tedious and backbreaking job and the impetus to stooped posture and arthritic joint pain. Canals controlled flooding and watered rows of arugula, beans, coriander, cucumbers, cumin, eggplant, garlic, leeks, lettuce, and onions. Slaves and press gangs cultivated and harvested food crops that produced the highest yield and offered a lengthy shelf life. Metalwork introduced the ard plow and the reaping knife, two essentials of farming.

Unlike females in hunting societies, women of the Fertile Crescent gained status as food gatherers and preservers. Storage required the digging of cache pits and lining them with grass to preserve root crops. Domed mud sheds and ceramic vessels with fitted lids kept grain safe from weevils, locusts, and rats. Preparation involved abrading grains between rocks and fanning the chaff away from edible kernels. From rock tools evolved the mortar and pestle, essential culinary tools for reducing raw food to a palatable form.

World's First Grocers
Prosperity transformed human diet and behavior concerning private property and delayed consumption of foodstuffs. Men and women gathered at city gates to sell surplus anise seed, jerboas (rodents), jujubes, fish, turtles, and skins of wine and navigated the rivers to carry edible wares to nearby commercial centers. Sumerians achieved a 40 percent surplus of grain for brewing eight

varieties of barley beer, eight emmer beers, and three blended ales.

In addition to cultivating lush fields, farmers around 4000 B.C.E. added orchards to their food production by growing fruit and pistachio trees. Although shrubs, trees, and vines required up to three years to produce a harvest, they augmented a grain-based diet with apple, cherry, and pomegranate juice and puree, fresh and dried dates and figs, grapes and raisins, and olives. Fruits supplemented prehistoric peoples' diet with iron, fiber, potassium, and vitamins A, B, and C. From date palms, growers extracted sap to crystallize into jaggery (palm sugar), an iron-rich commodity easily stored. Merchants transported it to buyers in lumps for dissolving into a sweetener to balance salty, sour, and spicy dishes and for use as a tonic and treatment of anemia and coughs.

Among the Assyrians, dining well on a variety of courses denoted prestige and authority. The king's hunting parties stalked wild boar and banqueted on the kill, prepared by his phalanx of cooks and pastry chefs. With the near extinction of wild gazelles, a paleolithic herding culture added domesticated meat to the commoner's diet. Cuisine of the Fertile Crescent extended the menu with ducks, geese, onagers (donkeys), pigeons, sheep, and swine along with milk, cheese, and yogurt from aurochs (wild cattle) and goats. At Jericho, the world's oldest inhabited city, the forging and honing of flint-bladed axes and knives simplified slaughtering. Around 6500 B.C.E. at Catal Huyuk in Anatolia, meat consumption preceded bull worship and ritual slaughter. Priests distributed the meat as evidence of the divine grace of the bull-god.

Food and Change
In the world's first food production center, permanent settlements along silt-edged watercourses undergirded Southwest Asia's agrarian-pastoral economy. Chiefs superintended planting, harvesting, and food storage from 5500 B.C.E. For governance, Sumerians chose a *lugal* (leader) to manage water distribution and use. Distribution followed dynastic lines through the extended family.

By 2100 B.C.E., pharmacists prescribed dietary treatments compounded from herbs and honey that targeted specific diseases and organ complaints, such as stomach and digestive ills. Shops offered fresh produce, dried beans and onions, ale, and pastries to nonfarming specialists, specifically, bakers, basket makers, carpenters, millers, potters, and weavers. Recipes for meat, pigeon, and turnip broths accompanied more complicated preparations of roasted meat flavored with garlic and leeks and for pigeons simmered in fragrant gravy and baked *en croûte* (in a crust). At cyclical Mesopotamian festivals, such as the feeding of dead spirits at the monthly *kispu,* food hawkers advertised sweets and cool drinks in the streets.

Traders loaded sacks of barley and sesame seeds on donkeys for transport to metal-producing centers in Afghanistan and Anatolia. By 2000 B.C.E., wheeled carts drawn by horses sped foodstuffs to market faster than donkey- or ox-drawn sledges. Standardized measurements and balance-beam scales invented in Pakistan controlled commodity distribution and pricing. Simple arithmetic kept track of livestock. The abacus figured profit and loss; pictograms and cuneiform account tablets recorded income.

In studies of the Fertile Crescent, archaeologists and anthropologists have obtained detailed dietary information from bones, coprolites, and middens. Bas-relief and sculpture illustrated the brining, drying, oiling, and smoking of foods. From market contacts, farmers of the Fertile Crescent expanded diet and cuisine with new food crops—chestnuts, rhubarb, rice, and taro from Asia and, from Africa, millet, sorghum, and yams. During times of famine, tribes migrated to richer strongholds to barter for subsistence foods or applied the strategies of hunter-gatherers.

From the ability to feed more people with less effort, residents of the Fertile Crescent achieved a higher birthrate and population density within cramped mud brick villages. Surplus foodstuffs fed the priestly caste and provided city accountants with a basis for stockpiling, distribution, and taxation. As early as 2000 B.C.E., Assyrian worshippers honored the god Anu and goddess Ishtar with the nation's food wealth—the best dates, figs, and grapes; milk-raised calves and barley-fed mutton and lamb; dormice, ducks, geese, and turtledoves; and eggs from ducks and ostriches.

With the evolution of writing, the essentials of animal husbandry, plant cycles, and food growing and preservation passed through community learning centers to subsequent generations. The rise of capitalism and the foundation of a sedentary merchant class created concerns for riches accumulated from the sale of commodity crafts and foods, such as the kitchen stock of cloves found in a Syrian dig and dating to 1700 B.C.E. From a neophyte warrior class, in 1000 B.C.E., cities mustered standing armies and fought rival horse-mounted tribes for possession of property and stored goods. A diet rich in high-calorie carbohydrates and proteins kept soldiers vigorous and ready to defend the region's food-based affluence.

See also: Agriculture; Coprolites; Hunter-Gatherers; Irrigation; Middens; Poultry; Taro; Trade Routes; Vinegar.

Further Reading

Bellwood, Peter. *First Farmers: The Origins of Agricultural Societies.* Malden, MA: Blackwell, 2005.

Civitello, Linda. *Cuisine and Culture: A History of Food and People.* 3rd ed. Hoboken, NJ: John Wiley & Sons, 2011.

Diamond, Jared M. *Guns, Germs, and Steel: The Fates of Human Societies.* New York: W.W. Norton, 1999.

Kiple, Kenneth F. *A Movable Feast: Ten Millennia of Food Globalization.* New York: Cambridge University Press, 2007.

Film, Food in

The image of food preparation has permeated movie scenarios with the centrality of satisfying hunger. A key to the humor in the Ma and Pa Kettle films—*Ma and Pa Kettle* (1949), *Ma and Pa Kettle Back on the Farm* (1951), and *Ma and Pa Kettle at Home* (1954)—is the backwoods kitchen and cooking style of Ma, mother of 15. More serious food preparation scenes have permeated some of Hollywood's blockbusters, particularly the last farm-style meal as Okies depart from the dust bowl in *The Grapes of Wrath* (1940) and the Texas barbecue and freshly unwrapped steer's head that celebrate a ranch wedding in *Giant* (1956). Late-twentieth-century cinematic presentation of kitchens and meal service as found in *Mystic Pizza* (1988), *Fried Green Tomatoes* (1991), *The Road to Wellville* (1994), *Soul Food* (1997), and *Tea with Mussolini* (1999) expresses the gamut of humanistic themes and motifs—libido, spirituality, clan customs, and creativity as well as the cook's aspirations and virtues.

A natural vehicle for characterizing unity, cookery dominates Julie Dash's balletic *Daughters of the Dust* (1991), an Edwardian era dreamscape where residents ponder leaving Gullah society on the South Carolina coast and abandoning the family traditions that have strengthened their families since slave days. Similarly lyric, Paul Sylbert's *The Grass Harp* (1995), adapted from Truman Capote's autobiographical novel, depicts the repressed Dolly Talbo, who stirs up kitchen cures while feeding and rearing nephew Colin Fenwick. In both instances, the films ally skill at mixing ingredients with the ability to balance hunger and longing.

Asian Food Films

Asian cinema makes its own tradition-centered version of food films that parallel meals with relationships. *Tampopo* (1986), an episodic Japanese comedy, follows the antics of a restaurateur concocting a ramen dish. By juxtaposing scenes involving slurping spaghetti, ordering from a gourmet menu, rifling garbage, and allying food with sexual pleasure, the film extends food influence to multiple aspects of behavior. In the French Vietnamese *The Scent of Green Papaya* (1993), filmmaker Tran Anh Hung examines social disorder and the symbolic uplift of orderly seeds in the fruit. With classic Cinderella elements, the story epitomizes a girl's sexual awakening with her delight in cookery and the aromas and flavors of fresh fruits.

Eat Drink Man Woman (1994), Ang Lee's domestic comedy, pictures a Taipei chef witnessing his family's disintegration. Similar in setting and tutorial style to *Tortilla Soup* (2001), Lee's film dramatizes the control of three daughters through the widowed chef Chu's manipulation of diet and family guilt. Tangled in a skein of personal and career miseries, the girls fulfill filial duty while eluding Papa's control. During the preparation of 100 recipes, the cook readies his girls for self-sufficiency. In all three Asian films and in *Tortilla Soup,* the celebration of food reveals an essential element of life and love that, like a recipe missing an ingredient, requires deft adjustments for balance.

French Fare

An evocative food extravaganza, *Babette's Feast* (1987), a classic screen adaptation of a story by Danish fablist Isak Dinesen, won the Oscar for Best Foreign Film in 1988 for celebrating a shared dinner as a love feast. Dubbed in French and Danish, the ritual begins with the charity of a cook, an outsider on a small-hearted Norse island where desiccated salt fish supplies the daily meal. In thanks for hospitality, Babette blesses local people with a gourmet dinner observing their deceased founder's birthday. Like the biblical widow's mites, the purchase of foodstuffs and glassware consumes all of her 10,000 francs, the proceeds of a winning lottery ticket.

Played by Stephane Audran, Babette the cook flees fame as a Paris chef renowned for her original dishes and superb wine selection. In an archaic kitchen overlooking a bleak Nordic seascape, she chops, stirs, simmers, pensively samples, and adjusts a grand menu featuring crated sea turtle, clusters of grapes, and bottles of champagne and a fine Amontillado for her culinary innovations. The camera follows the heroine's hands as she trusses quail, stirs and samples turtle soup, and pours wine for each course. Beyond satisfying hunger, Babette restores diners to humility and forgiveness, traits they had banished as piety, petty complaints, and regret subsumed their better natures.

Filmmaker Gabriel Axel tinged the mounting joy with a controlling irony—to restore love to the sour Lutheran community, Babette sacrifices all she has for a "last supper," a sumptuous meal as fine as anything in Paris. For service, she instructs a country lad while remaining at the stove as she orchestrates a communal change of heart. To the quarreling, sniping elderly congregation, she plates her dishes as a gift that reconciles them to each other and as a token of thanks to her loving employers. Babette concludes that she is never poor because she always has her art.

Lasse Hallström's cinema fable *Chocolat* (2000), adapted by Robert Nelson Jones from the Joanne Harris novel of the same name, parallels *Babette's Feast* in depicting the conflict between spiritual aridity and sensual generosity. Protagonist Vianne Rocher, an itinerant chocolatier, sets up shop in a small-minded French village in the 1950s. Her generous samples of sweets and counseling to troubled people enrage the Comte de Reynaud, a self-appointed censor and moral director who condemns extravagance during Lent. In a predictable progression, Vianne squares off against the Comte at an Easter Sunday "Grand Festival du Chocolat," a communion in the Christian sense of selfless joy.

Within the obvious set-to between conventionality and joie de vivre lies Vianne's compensation for her family's rootlessness. In the rustic kitchen, she rules a confectionery domain where mincing block chocolate and creaming fillers and spreading icing and piping curlicues create window fantasies. Her candies grow so powerful that they redress loneliness, timidity, alienation, and sterility. The landlady quickly perceives the connection between lust and delectable chocolates and compares the refurbished patisserie to a Mexican brothel.

The rescue of people from coercion, similar to the motifs of *The Grass Harp* and *Fried Green Tomatoes,* rewards minor characters with bursts of creative expression, the preface to self-forgiveness. Vianne, a skilled rescuer, shields a victim, Josephine Muscat, a desperate abused wife of the village. Grasping at self-esteem, Josephine masters the flirty grace of the white-tipped Nipples of Venus, an example of the carnal goodies for sale in Vianne's patisserie. When Muscat stalks his errant wife, Vianne clouts him with a frying pan, the symbolic weapon of the master chef.

Food as Liberation

Just as movie cookery liberates, so it channels kitchen work into an outlet for frustration and untapped energies. *Like Water for Chocolate* (1992) applies magical realism to a mother-daughter standoff. In the microcosm of a rancho kitchen, the unloved, unappreciated Tita retreats to a surrogate mother, the peasant cook Nacha, who reanimates her while teaching daily lessons in slicing onions and kneading dough.

While Tita's mother marries off Rosaura, the favored daughter, to Tita's love, Pedro, the repressed kitchen maiden immerses herself in sensual recipes, an escape valve that saves Tita from implosion. Releasing sorrow and yearning, she infects guests with the emotions stirred into the raw ingredients, causing them to weep, laugh, vomit, and lust for their true loves. The birth of Rosaura's child imbues Tita with breast milk that nourishes the unhappy babe and enrages the inadequate mother, who recognizes that her marriage and motherhood truly belong to Tita.

A fairy tale built on pathos, humor, and magic, Tita's story releases her from the stern, repressed mother to a band of revolutionaries and an Anglo physician who offers Tita marriage and security. Still pulled to her first love, Tita opts for the grand emotional recipe, a brief night of love with her badly injured brother-in-law. Encased in food fable, Laura Esquivel's masterful hyperbole enlarges the circumscribed life of Tita, who possesses the womanly skills that even death cannot suppress.

Twenty-First-Century Releases

Subsequent cinema has retained the themes and vigor of cookery as a reputable effort, as in the Thanksgiving of black, Hispanic, Jewish, and Vietnamese families in *What's Cooking* (2000), the parody of fast-food chains in *Waiting . . .* (2005), the comedic debacle at a Passover seder in *When Do We Eat?* (2006), and teaching young city toughs to cook in *Pressure Cooker* (2008). A cartoon study of the career chef in Disney's *Ratatouille* (2007) illustrated the vicissitudes of training and the element of luck that boosts a food magician into a star. His vehicle, a pot of soup, stresses the importance of the basics to transcendent table experience.

The award-winning culinary comedy *Julie & Julia* (2009) saluted food diva Julia Child's influence on American cookery. A determined beginner, the young New York blogger Julia Powell, in the early 2000s, strives to complete 524 of Child's recipes in a year's time by adopting the outlook of her idol. Both mentor and imitator exude the bonhomie and fearlessness of the kitchen scholar who relieved ennui in post–World War II Europe by mastering French gastronomy. Essential to Child's presentations are her endearing efforts to turn dining into a communion of gourmands over a delicious repast.

Less pleasant, the perusal of feeding the drought-ridden Horn of Africa in *Beyond Borders* (2002) poses the fearful dynamics of food riots during famine in Ethiopia, Somalia, and Sudan. From an opposite perspective, the filming of *Under the Tuscan Sun* (2003) romanticizes the Italian kitchen with images of a lone American divorcée feeding workers at her rustic villa with platters of eggplant and peppers. Table generosity broadens the outlook of a newcomer looking for belonging among hardy peasants.

The insidious nature of anorexia nervosa among competitive ballerinas in *Black Swan* (2010) contrasts the generosity of *Under the Tuscan Sun* with self-punishment and excessive yearnings. Nina, the climber in a New York City ballet company, clutches bottled water, a period token of obsessive dietary concerns. Unlike the slow starvation of Irish immigrants in the Australian drama *Ned Kelly* (2003), Nina has choices. Like professional dancers who restrict daily diet to 1,200 calories, Nina rejects normal meals while ravaging her body with rehearsals and self-denial. The depiction of self-torment from competition and eating disorders reveals a period disability among starstruck, body-conscious youth.

See also: African Food Trade; Famine; Markets and Marketing; Trade Routes.

Further Reading

Bower, Anne L., ed. *Reel Food: Essays on Food and Film.* New York: Routledge, 2004.

Ferry, Jane. *Food in Film: A Culinary Performance of Communication.* New York: Routledge, 2003.

Keller, James R. *Food, Film, and Culture: A Genre Study.* Jefferson, NC: McFarland, 2006.

Tobias, Ruth. "Mealtime at the Movies: 15 Food Films." *World Literature Today* 83:1 (January/February 2009): 40–46.

Finger Food

Dishes and appetizers intended to be eaten out of the hand, finger foods include attractively shaped, ready-to-eat bites that require no knives, forks, spoons, or chopsticks. The selection of food by hand suits etiquette in England, where Cornish meat pies appeal to shoppers, and in Ethiopia and Mexico, where diners scoop a mouthful of tahini or guacamole with bread or tacos, rolled up for convenience, and eat without need of utensils. The simple presentation of finger food also refers to blinis, cocktail wienies, corn on the cob, curry puffs, date balls, ice cream cones, olives, pizza slices, rice balls, sandwiches, and tapas. Some finger foods—buffalo wings, chips, french fries, nuts, popcorn, chapatis, scones—are more suited to baskets than trays.

Before the popularization of flatware, meals among the Arabs, Aztecs, Incas, and Persians relied on finger foods, such as Arab *meze* and Aztec tacos. In the Agora from as early as 500 B.C.E., Athenians purchased *koulouri* (seeded barley buns), mainly for children. In Constantinople, Rome, and Smyrna, wait staff plated one-bite servings, the forerunner of Italian antipasti and Spanish *tapas,* to accommodate diners reclining at table and leaning on one elbow. In Baghdad, Syrian vendors sold triangular pies fried in sesame oil; Greek street sellers offered roasted chickpeas and souvlaki. In Japan, merchants opened hors d'oeuvres shops and sold baby bees and *yakitori* (beef, chicken, and seafood kebabs) to draw the after-theater crowd from Kabuki and Noh performances.

In the early Middle Ages, deep-fried stuffed figs piqued taste buds with their combination of flavors and mouthfeel. The poor made do with meaty knucklebones and ribs. After 1099 C.E., crusaders brought back to Europe sugared comfits and gingerbread, a savory addition to medieval meals that diners ate out of hand. Into the 1700s, peddlers in Western Europe sold finger foods at public squares, fairs, and weekly markets.

Gradually, street hawkers at mobile barrows and fixed stands drew buyers to the fragrance of cool drinks and hot snacks. Top sellers in Armenia specialized in cheese and custard pies, honey cakes, and baked carrots. By the 1800s, variety increased to include fried bonito, meatballs, pilaf, sesame desserts, and spanakopita (spinach pie). Strollers carried paper cones of roasted chickpeas, pistachios, and pumpkin and sunflower seeds for nibbling while shopping.

North Americans adopted tidbit foods from immigrants, including the Chinese dim sum and pupu platter, French palate pleasers, and Scandinavian smorgasbord. The Pueblo Indians anticipated the American flair for hors d'oeuvres with offerings of fry bread. In the 1950s, the growth of fast food and patio cookouts increased the eating from hand of buns and rolls with meaty fillings and of fish sticks and kebabs. Magazine and electronic ads pictured a relaxed atmosphere among people who selected choice bites and consumed them at a leisurely pace while carrying on vibrant conversations.

The distribution of finger foods accommodated attendees at brunches, cocktail parties, and receptions

With roots in the teahouse snacks that fed travelers along the Silk Road, dim sum—dumplings, buns, rolls, pastries, and other bite-size delicacies—became a Cantonese custom. Traditionally, dim sum is served from early morning to mid-afternoon. *(Eric Brissaud/Gamma-Rapho/Getty Images)*

with inventive combinations of ingredients. In the 1990s, the slang term *grazing* referred to sampling varied offerings. Caterers dispatched waiters with deli trays and salvers containing bruschetta, crudités, cupcakes, fruit and cheese cubes, julienned vegetables, miniature quiches, open-face canapés, oysters on the half shell, and tortillas, with some tidbits served atop cocktail napkins or paper doilies. Currently, at centralized buffets and snack tables, as appetite stimulants, attendees dip chips, chunks of bread, and crackers into cheese balls, fondue, hummus, pâté, salsa, or tapenade.

See also: Appetizers and Hors d'Oeuvres; Crackers; Grilling; Kebabs; Polynesian Diet and Cuisine; Snack Food; Street Food.

Further Reading

Civitello, Linda. *Cuisine and Culture: A History of Food and People.* 3rd ed. Hoboken, NJ: John Wiley & Sons, 2011.

Davidson, Alan. *The Oxford Companion to Food.* Ed. Jane Davidson, Tom Jaine, and Helen Saberi. New York: Oxford University Press, 2006.

Katz, Solomon H., and William Woys Weaver, eds. *Encyclopedia of Food and Culture.* New York: Charles Scribner's Sons, 2003.

Meyer, Arthur L., and Jon M. Vann. *The Appetizer Atlas: A World of Small Bites.* Hoboken, NJ: John Wiley & Sons, 2003.

Fish and Fishing

From prehistory, consumers have esteemed fish for its fragrance, mouthfeel, and taste and for its minerals and protein. From 100,000 B.C.E., waste from burbot, perch, pike, and trout in middens in Alaska, France, Greenland, Korea, and Peru attest to the centrality of finfish

to diet. One example, Hawaii, thrived on some 600 coastal species, including anchovy, barracuda, bonefish, flying fish, grouper, herring, milkfish, mullet, sole, and wrasse. The abundance of choices enlarged a vegetable diet with an inexpensive, wholesome meat that energized islanders.

Heavy catches contributed to the global economy, which traded in dried, salted, and smoked stock, such as the grunion nabbed by hand by California tribes. Around 3000 B.C.E., Babylonians creamed herring into a dried paste for flavoring stew. Across the Sahara Desert, North African nomads benefited from trading camels for surplus fish netted by shore tribes. The wanderers diversified a monotonous diet with dried fish, a finger food unharmed by extremes of aridity and heat.

Hunter-gatherers enlarged forest diets with marine food, such as the reef fish prized by Australian Aborigines. Native American digs among the remains of the Abenaki of Maine, the Ainu and Jomon of Japan, the Ertebolle of Jutland, the Huaca of the Andean highlands, and the Vedda of Sri Lanka revealed remains of the alewife, cod, ling, pike, salmon, tuna, and whitefish. The Inuit valued finfish dishes and sauced char and sculpin with fat from sea lions and whales. Mothers chewed fillets and tongue-fed the pulp into toddlers' mouths.

Among the Tikopia of southwestern Polynesia, marine food so bolstered tribal security that they designed calendars around fish runs. The early Maori based cuisine on grouper, jack, parrotfish, and yellow tang, a common reef fish. Wrapped in pandanus or ti bundles, ahi and swordfish roasted in earth ovens alongside tubers.

Tahitians marinated in lime juice *poisson cru,* raw lagoon parrotfish and ocean bream and snapper. At Tongareva in the Cook Islands, lagoons offered safe, reliable soldier fish and wrasse, which cooks prepared with algae and seaweed. Fresh species varied with the availability of streams, which numbered 15 on Tahiti and 111 in New Guinea, where cooks preferred bream, grunter, mullet, and perch. On Tonga, from around 1000 B.C.E., spear fishermen boiled their catch in pottery jars in herbed water. For ritual voyages by double-hulled canoe or outrigger back to Tahiti, mariners ate fresh supplies and netted or trolled for fresh snapper and tuna.

Fish in Asia and Europe

To the south of the Fertile Crescent, canals, fens, ponds, and rivers supplied 52 fish species. Netters and spear fishermen supplemented a grain and red-meat diet with carp, jack, and vorax, which enabled Babylonians to thrive in cities rather than on farms. Preservers dried, salted, and smoked each catch for the pantry and for trade with Caucasus and Himalayan mountain dwellers. Keys to freshness, the cleanliness of handlers and processors and the speed by which caravans reached markets ensured quality fish free of pathogens that could sicken consumers.

As customers of Phoenician boat traffic, Egyptians acquired protein from brined and dried imports, which doubled as currency. Locally, they relied on carp, catfish, mullet, and perch from the Nile River delta and the oasis at Faiyum as well as from tuna that coursed the Mediterranean Sea in season. Baskets filled with salt fish accompanied the Egyptian builder Kha to his Theban tomb around 1395 B.C.E. In reference to the convenience and nutrition of coastal fish, Homer's *Odyssey* (ca. 750 B.C.E.) declared marine food a blessing.

From 1200 to 333 B.C.E., the land-poor Phoenicians of Lebanon enjoyed a varied diet from imported bream and mullet and fermented *garum*, a fish-based condiment that supplied naval vessels. The Phoenicians exploited the marine market via coasters for short hauls to ports surrounded by reefs and shoals. Around 1000 B.C.E., shipwrights designed larger cargo carriers that transported sturgeon and trout along oceans and major water routes, primarily the Danube, Nile, and Rhone rivers.

At the height of Greek civilization, fishermen retrieved Mediterranean bass, bluefin, and hake with harpoons, *lamparos* (fish lights), lines, *madragues* (net mazes), seines, and tridents. Around 350 B.C.E., the Greco-Sicilian poet Archestratus praised the bonito, a mildly fatty relative of tuna, for its ease of grilling and baking in hot ash. His advice preceded fish saucing and stuffing recipes in the Roman cookbooks of Apicius and Athenaeus. Early Christians preferred fish to red meat because of the symbolism of the five loaves and two fish by which Jesus fed

Swedish fishermen clean and crate herring at a North Sea fishing village. From Scandinavia to East Asia and the coastal Americas, commercial fishing is an economic mainstay. Aquaculture, however, accounts for a growing percentage of global fish consumption. *(National Geographic/Getty Images)*

4,000 followers. By popularizing fish entrées, the catch of Jesus's fishermen apostles, Christ cults eroded classical Greek vegetarianism.

Until the first century of the Roman Empire, cooks followed the trend of cooking pond dorade and lupus, the subjects of frescoes, mosaics, and the poetic works of Ovid, Plutarch, and Oppian. The Roman encyclopedist Pliny the Elder surveyed pisciculture in depth. Of fish for the table and tavern service, he identified 1,000 types of marine food and extolled Italy for its seagoing fleets, which relied on Bavarian salt for preserving the catch. He admired fish heads over the rest of piscine meat and, for taste and texture, recommended hake, mackerel, mullet, rockfish, scarus, sturgeon, and wolffish.

In the Roman kitchen, chefs blended myrtle leaf, the emblem of Venus, goddess of passion, in mortars with coriander, grape must, lovage, and oregano to produce a sauce for moray eel or mullet. For satisfying flavor, Pliny singled out the anchovy that Apicius pickled in garum. Because of the significance of marine food to the Roman kitchen, Pliny complained of the price of imported lake barbel, chub, pike, and tench fermented by Lombards. By 301 C.E., sea fish cost almost twice as much as flatfish, mullet, and scarus, fad foods either raised in *piscinae* (fishponds) or wild caught.

In winter, commercial ice fishermen caught sturgeon from the Black Sea to store in icehouses for trade in Christian Byzantium. Salting extended the shelf life of coastal goods for the provisioning of armies, press gangs, and ships' galleys. Because Catholic prelates enforced by law numerous fast days, which included Wednesdays, Fridays, and Saturdays, nonmeat menus avoided cheese, eggs, and milk in favor of fresh fish, eels, and salted kippers, a small oily herring eaten pickled or smoked.

In the Middle Ages, monoculture in inland ponds and adjacent to the shore proved the commercial value of propagating a single fish species. From the first century C.E., Japanese pisciculture at Hokkaido yielded fresh water carp and salmon and saltwater bream and yellowtail. The focus on a single species enabled pond laborers to monitor health and vigor and to prevent disease and parasites. Itinerant Jewish merchants returned home with Chinese carp, which the Ashkenazim of southern Europe preferred for fish balls, patties, and stuffing with eggs and onions.

Around the Baltic Sea, formation of the Hanseatic League by Henry the Lion of Saxony at Lübeck in 1159 stabilized prices by evening out surpluses of grain and salt herrings. To ensure quality, in 1272, Edward I chartered a London fishmongers guild to protect freshness and to control pricing. Among member powers, the control of fishing in the Thames regulated the salmon catch, which the French were already growing in artificial tank environments to compete with wild stock.

During Lent in the Middle Ages, on meatless days, Benedictines ate eggs, frogs, smelts, and snails. Only lords

Recipe: Pollock Balls

Cut 1 pound of pollock into 1/2-inch cubes. In a food processor, pulse the cubes with two egg whites, 2 tablespoons of minced onion, 1 cup of dry bread crumbs, 1/2 cup of cornstarch, and black pepper and sea salt until thoroughly blended. Add three ice cubes and blend for three minutes. Squeeze the mixture into 1-inch balls. Deep-fry in oil or cook in boiling water for five minutes. Serve with a sprinkling of chopped coriander or parsley.

could buy cod, haddock, or halibut pie and salted herring as alternatives to poultry and red meat. As the focus of banquets, the carver artfully sliced whole stuffed carp and lampreys into "gobbets" (bites), a luxury unavailable to the poor.

The poor of Britain dined on poached monkfish or stargazy pie, a Cornish specialty that placed pilchards under a crust with their heads poking through to allow oils to moisten the vegetables below. Scandinavians relished cod or ling soaked in lye and slaked lime to produce lutefisk, a regional favorite served with bacon and potatoes. Danes and Germans panfried plaice, a common flatfish; Norwegians resorted to the strong-flavored pollock for mashing in a mortar and shaping into fish balls.

Resourceful cooks grilled pike in wine sauce and poached salmon in beer. For Muslims in Egypt and Syria, the grilling of whole anchovies satisfied tourists with handy snacks. Among the Roma, recipes for salmon in the 1300s sauced fish steaks with dandelion root and mushrooms. In China's first cookbook, Huou, Kublai Khan's chef, published the first marine recipe for carp salad. To marinate raw slivers, the cook made a dressing from basil, chives, ginger, knotgrass, and radishes, all stimulants to digestion. In 1375, Taillevent, Charles V's cook, advocated mustard for saucing cod.

Fishing in History

Overfishing in the Baltic Sea preceded a herring collapse in the 1400s. Coastal fleets sought schools in the Atlantic Ocean and North Sea. The superior organization of the Dutch placed them above German and Scandinavian fishermen for 200 years. Commercial traders profited from the technology of Willem Beukelszoon, a Zeeland fisherman, who altered dry salting methods by "gibbing" (pickling) herring in brine. The processed fish boosted the prominence of Dutch seafarers and colonizers of the New World.

Italian navigator John Cabot discovered Newfoundland on June 24, 1497, and proclaimed it a haven for drying and salting cod. Farther south and west, Basque fishermen launched 1,000 vessels on the St. Lawrence River to commercialize Atlantic species. Along the California coast, Mission Indians explained to Spanish evangelists the value of eulachon (candlefish), a source of dried food and oil used for cooking or as indoor lights. Along Lake Huron, Ottawa netters pulled in 100 whitefish at a time and supplied their families with pike and walleye and surplus fish for trade.

At Plymouth, Massachusetts, soldier Miles Standish welcomed Samoset on April 2, 1621, when the Wampanoag sagamore donated roasted herring to the starving English colony. Under Indian mentoring, the Pilgrims learned to fertilize corn by burying oily menhaden at its roots and to fatten cattle on fish offal. Over the next century, fish and fish cakes fed the enslaved and impoverished, such as finnan haddie, haddock smoked over peat and poached in milk for a Scots breakfast.

Native fishermen disdained the European sport of line fishing and chose instead jacklighting, canoe fishing by night with lanterns that drew fish to the surface. Indians demonstrated the harvesting from schools at deltas and harbors, where they set traps and weirs (brush fences). For herring egg dishes, the Tlingit thrust hemlock boughs into the seabed at spawning season and collected ova for herring egg salad. Along the Delaware River, the Mohawk and Mahican bartered fish and maple sugar with Dutch explorers, who introduced aborigines to tin kettles. Native cooks demonstrated to Europeans how to stone-boil a one-pot fish and seaweed soup in mocucks (woven boxes) or animal stomachs. For heat, preparers placed hot rocks in the fish broth with antler forks or branch tongs.

Fish in Commerce and Cuisine

Fish monopolized the royal European diet. At Hampton Court, the Tudor palace of Henry VIII, after 1529, fresh water bream and carp swam moats and ponds until removed for cleaning and cooking. A wet larder stored kippered herring in barrels of seaweed. After the death of King Edward VI in 1553, his half sister, Mary I, reverted to Catholic fast days to shield fishermen from bankruptcy. Tudor entrées continued to feature fish each Friday and Saturday. Chefs baked, boiled, fried, grilled, and poached cod, dace, ling, loach, and sturgeon. In the 1590s, when grain harvests lagged, rural families stretched stores of Russian or Scandinavian stockfish. Cooks ground cod, haddock, or hake bones; liver; and roe into *mortrews,* a pâté thickened with bread crumbs and eggs for shaping into dumplings or fritters.

Supplying fresh fish to the post-Renaissance table accommodated local foodways. In the 1600s, Czechs elevated carp to the focal Christmas dish; other central Europeans ranked poached catfish as a Yuletide delicacy. Germans, Scandinavians, and Ukrainians turned pickled herring or rollmops (herring fillets wrapped around pickles) into an all-purpose holiday dish for Christmas, Easter, and Midsummer.

Among the *boucaniers* (French pirates) of the Mississippi River delta, a secret life of outlawry in Louisiana swamps required ingenuity. To conceal their fires, the men pit-cooked bass, bream, catfish, crappie, and drum over fruitwood or hickory fires and flavored fillets with fruit and spice. In 1682, Russian Czar Peter the Great imported smoked pike, salmon, and sterlet from France as a meal refinement. In 1700, brisk Atlantic trade between Great Britain, the Caribbean, and the American ports of Charles Town, Boston, Newport, New York, and Philadelphia required guards to protect dried and pickled mackerel and spearfish from thievery.

In Portugal around 1750, monks diverted the Alcoa River through Alcobaca Monastery to supply the kitchen with fresh bass and mullet. Around 1774, Greenland's nomadic Eskimo marketed catches of cod and halibut to Scandinavians. Metalworkers in 1810 applied tin to iron containers to produce inexpensive canned cod and herring for sale to the laboring class. By 1850 along the Great Lakes, population growth supported the marketing of caviar, fish oil, and salmon.

In the late 1800s, table displays included sculpted ice surrounded by albacore tuna, barracuda, marlin, sailfish, sturgeon, swordfish, and wahoo, particularly for buffets and receptions. Because lake trout decreased at the rate of thousands of tons annually, state hatcheries targeted the species for restocking. In contrast to upscale cuisine, the middle class favored the lamprey and mullet in New England, perch and striped bass in the Hudson River valley, buffalo fish and carp in the Mississippi River basin, and pompano, red snapper, and shad as common chowder ingredients in Florida. Jewish cooks shaped carp into gefilte fish, a blend of fillets with matzoh meal and onion for poaching into savory nuggets. During the protracted Jim Crow era, black sharecroppers and poor whites relied on bottom feeders—carp, catfish, and suckers—for breakfast meat and fish fries. Cooking involved rolling fillets in cornmeal and seasoning with hot pepper and salt for "salt-'n'-pepper" entrées.

The International Council for the Exploration of the Sea, the oldest intergovernmental science organization, was formed in Copenhagen in 1902 to define fair catch for European fishing industries. Simultaneously, to meet American needs, the U.S. Bureau of Fisheries began propagating 1.5 billion food fish. Cod, flounder, pike, salmon, shad, trout, and whitefish yielded the most numerous fingerlings, which were added to depleted waters. In 1908, a price comparison established that fish cost from one-third to one-half less than beef, justification for the popularity of fish with middle- and lower-class consumers.

In the 1930s, canned fish ensured protein for families during the Great Depression. Mounting concern over rickets, a vitamin D deficiency that deformed children's skeletons, sent mothers to women's magazines for recipes supplementing the diet with deep-sea fish and Newfoundland cod liver oil, a mineral tonic mixed with orange juice. Before the iodizing of commercial salt, sea fish also prevented goiter. In a study of goitrous and nongoitrous areas of the United States, a chart of iodine-rich fish instructed the home cook on the dietary value of haddock and mackerel.

Another issue, the dwindling supply of marine edibles, beset nations with concerns for the future of the marine trade, notably, flounder from the Gulf of Mexico, which had declined statistically by 90 percent from preindustrial levels. The consequences of overfishing in the early 1900s killed off fresh water Russian species, reducing a source of wild foods for Siberians. In the mid-1900s, the Japanese, the world's top fishermen, exploited their coastline to satisfy appetites for fish, both raw and steamed. Because Americans continued to favor beef, chicken, and pork, the public accepted the philosophies of catch and release and no-kill zones, in which sport fishermen returned to the wild bass, cod, flathead, marlin, salmon, tarpon, and trout.

In the seven decades preceding the late 1960s, the global catch increased by 2,700 percent. For China, Russia, and the United States, sophisticated fishing methods—long-range navigation (loran), plane spotters, radar, and sonar—enabled factory ships to pull in huge catches for canning or freezing. Local regulations encouraged the rescue and release of bycatch, the species unintentionally ensnared in nets. The burbot disappeared from British waters. The Scandinavian fishing industry netted so many wild Atlantic salmon that ichthyologists began to worry about extinction. Similar short runs of Pacific salmon off British Columbia, California, Oregon, and Washington presaged a loss of sustainable fishing.

In 1973, the U.S. Endangered Species Act protected the habitats of imperiled fish from biocide, human exploitation, and poaching, especially North American halibut. The law came too late to save the extinct pupfish, but it did protect bluefish, chub, cod, eulachon, menhaden, shad, smelt, sturgeon, sucker, and wild salmon. Kenyan, Tanzanian, and Ugandan fishermen stopped harvesting Nile perch, the most seriously overharvested species in the region. In the late 1970s, to monitor home waters, nations began declaring offshore fishing grounds exclusive economic zones as far out as 200 miles (320 kilometers), including the declining hake runs off Argentina and Chile. Greenpeace red-listed the deepwater marlin, monkfish, ocean perch, shark, skate, sole, and swordfish as food and sport species vulnerable to destructive capture methods and pirate fishing.

Japanese American chefs in California popularized sushi and created a 1970s trend for California rolls, a blend of avocado and whitefish bound with mayonnaise and rolled in rice. Exacerbating the demand for marine food, the vogue of omega-3 fatty acids in the diet in the 1990s caused restaurants to popularize broiled salmon as entrées and salad toppings. Diners anticipated reductions in blood pressure, circulatory problems, hardening of the arteries, heart arrhythmia, rheumatoid arthritis, and triglycerides. Seafood processors ballyhooed oily anchovies, halibut, herring, mackerel, salmon, sardines, and tuna. To limit consumption of dioxin, heavy metals, and polychlorinated biphenyls (PCBs), the World Health Organization in 2006 established the International Fish Oil Standard, a sophisticated monitoring agency at the University of Guelph, Ontario.

The quality of pond-raised fish required additional federal scrutiny for spurious substitutions. In the early 2000s, the U.S. Department of Agriculture regulated 100 percent organic fish by outlawing genetic engineering of species, growth hormones, and irradiation. In processed cod cakes and fish sticks, the "organic" label indicated at least 95 percent organic fish or at least 70 percent pure fish blended with organic breading.

Late-twentieth-century health concerns refuted previous advocacy of fish in the diet. The promotion of marine meals in the early 1900s did not anticipate the outcry over fat-soluble pollutants and mercury or the banning from human consumption of endangered ahi, mackerel, orange roughy, shark, swordfish, and tilefish. High mercury adulteration of albacore and bluefin tuna threatened pregnant women. Another deterrent to fish in the diet, parasites such as roundworm infestation of wild salmon and cod worms, flukes, nematodes, sea lice, and tapeworm in ceviche, gravlax, sashimi, and sushi decelerated consumption of uncooked fad foods.

In the twenty-first century, fish remains prominent in national and regional cuisines throughout the world—Alaskan stink fish, Baja-Mex fish tacos and veracruzana ceviche and red snapper, Barbadian breakfasts of grilled flying fish with lime, Filipino kinilaw (cold cured fish) marinated in chili sauce, Hawaiian raw poke appetizers (sliced raw fish), Irish fish and dulse, New Zealand fish kebabs, Norman chowder, raw tuna for Japanese sushi, Scots haddock and chips, and Vietnamese fish ball soup and *nuoc mam* (fermented fish sauce), a fragrant dipping sauce. As finger food, consumers prefer cod, haddock, and plaice in English fish and chips, Japanese imitation crab sticks made from hake, Korean *eomuk* (pureed whitefish on a stick), and Russian blini with sturgeon roe and pickled herring.

Keeping pace with a world demand that tripled from the mid-1960s, aquaculture produced an estimated 45 million tonnes (50 million tons) of fish in 2004. Such innovations as the raising of salmon by Canadian, Chilean, New Zealand, Norwegian, Russian, Scots, South African, and Tasmanian fisheries and of grouper in ponds off the coast of India and the Middle East have broadened the definition of farming to include hydroponics. Additional culturing sites in China, France, Spain, and Turkey produce turbot, a flatfish that yields four white fillets for baking and poaching. Commercial operators have upgraded purity in propagated catfish and tilapia, sources of easily digested protein in comparison with mammalian meats. Food-deficit countries such as Ghana, Namibia, Nigeria, Senegal, and Thailand exploit anchovy, hake, and tuna marketing as a means of requiting national debt and relieving malnutrition.

See also: Aquaponics; Cod; Endangered Species; Lapérouse, Jean François Galaup; Poisonous Foods; Roman Diet and Cuisine, Ancient; Scandinavian Diet and Cuisine; Shellfish; Trade Routes; Tudor Diet and Cuisine; Whaling.

Further Reading

Abulafia, David. *The Great Sea: A Human History of the Mediterranean.* New York: Oxford University Press, 2011.

Fagan, Brian M. *Fish on Friday: Feasting, Fasting, and the Discovery of the New World.* New York: Basic Books, 2006.

Greenberg, Paul. *Four Fish: The Future of the Last Wild Food.* New York: Penguin, 2010.

Schwartz, Maurice L. *Encyclopedia of Coastal Science.* New York: Springer, 2005.

Tennant, S.G.B. *Wild at the Table: 275 Years of American Game & Fish Recipes.* Minocqua, WI: Willow Creek, 2004.

Food Network

Inaugurated in New York City on April 19, 1993, the Food Network began offering viewers a panoply of expert cookery and advice on heirloom and trendy ingredients, holiday and special occasion menus, food safety, and kitchen equipment. Every day begins at 5:45 A.M. with prepping dishes, purchasing flowers and ingredients, and staging sets to accommodate the guest chef of the day. Researchers outline the background of culinary history from salt to sea urchins. Web specialists post recipes from the day's lineup. The full effect of the Food Network is a revitalization of American cuisine.

Essential to daily shows, hands-on preparation illustrates for home cooks the intricacies of a vegetable chiffonade and the blending of egg mixtures in hot sauces, two deft touches on chef Sara Moulton's call-in show *Cooking Live* and sequel, *Sara's Secrets,* and trussing poultry, an on-camera skill aired on a classic episode from the Julia Child library. One of the network's most popular chefs, Emeril Lagasse, a cook of Massachusetts-Portuguese background and longtime host of *Emeril Live* and *Essence of Emeril,* injected humor and verve into his demonstrations, jolting recipes with generous amounts of garlic and spices.

Iron Chef America, the U.S. adaptation of a popular Japanese cooking show, is a flagship series on the Food Network. In each episode, a new challenger takes on one of the regular celebrity chefs in a cooking competition that features a theme ingredient. *(Jim Cooper/Associated Press)*

Other past programming established the unique approaches of network stars. For straightforward culinary training, Wolfgang Puck, the Austrian maven of fusion cuisine, tutored beginners on *Wolfgang Puck's Master Class.* Casual, easygoing Rachael Ray hosted *30 Minute Meals* and *$40 a Day,* seductive-voiced Ina Garten accentuated a low-key prep style on the *Barefoot Contessa,* and Mario Batali invigorated *Mario Eats Italy* and *Mario, Full Boil.* Graham Kerr, a puckish Londoner starring in *The Galloping Gourmet,* teased his fans into enjoying kitchen work as fun and relaxation. In 2004, the network exploited the wedding of Paula Deen, the exuberant doyenne of Southern cookery on *Paula's Home Cooking* and *Paula's Best Dishes.*

Viewers caught the fever in challenge events such as *Last Cake Standing, Bocuse d'Or,* and *Iron Chef America,* one of the network's longest-running series. For the latter, contestants, facing off in a kitchen stadium, receive a main ingredient to be used in the entire contest menu—Arctic char, asparagus, barracuda, beets, chilies, cranberries, even elk. Major winners have included Southwestern grilling specialist Bobby Flay and Greek and Mediterranean master chef Cat Masaharu Morimoto of Japan.

Additional flair derives from other celebrity foodies and chefs, such as TV meteorologist Al Roker, BBC broadcaster Nigella Lawson, potables adviser Kevin Brauch, low-calorie expert Juan-Carlos Cruz, and Chinese American restaurateur Ming Tsai. One jovial duo, Jennifer Paterson and Clarissa Dickson Wright, injected eccentricity into *Two Fat Ladies,* a four-season hit in the mid-1990s featuring British favorites—bubble and squeak (fried potatoes and vegetables), deviled kidneys, fish pie, and roast goose with prune stuffing. The two cooked with flippant unconcern for the healthy food movement and directed sassy salutes to cigarettes, cocktails, and fat calories from beef drippings, butter, lard, and unpasteurized whole milk.

Varied personalities have ensured idiosyncratic style to suit the demands of tailgate parties, New Year's Eve bashes, backpacking, and sedate banquets. Programmers boosted appeal with catchy series titles—*Aarti Party; Have Fork, Will Travel; Licence to Grill; Lighten Up!;* and *Sugar Rush.* Avoiding the cliché of uptight kitchen regimens presented with surgical precision, Food Network programmers win viewer approval and commercial advertisers with such innovations as *Cupcake Wars, The Great Food Truck Race,* and *Diners, Drive-Ins and Dives.*

See also: African Diet and Cuisine, Sub-Saharan; Famine; Maritime Trade Routes; Vegetarianism.

Further Reading

Darling, Jennifer, ed. *Food Network Kitchens Cookbook.* Des Moines, IA: Meredith, 2003.

Jackman, Ian. *Food Network Star.* New York: HarperCollins, 2011.

Schrager, Lee, and Julie Mautner. *Food Network South Beach Wine & Food Festival Cookbook.* New York: Clarkson Potter, 2010.

Stockton, Susan, and Jill Novatt, eds. *Food Network Favorites: Recipes from Our All-Star Chefs.* Des Moines, IA: Meredith, 2005.

Free-Range Foods

The liberation of farm animals from cages results in free-range dairy, eggs, meat, and poultry produced under humane standards of animal welfare. A compassionate philosophy of husbandry based on living in nature and feeding by browsing, free-range farming relies on an animal's natural instincts to feed itself rather than to rely on daily allotments of grain and water in a cage or barn. In exchange for unfettered movement in fresh air and sunshine, the animal, whether quadruped or poultry, tramples plants and hurries the return of green matter to the Earth as rain-absorbing humus. In anecdotal reports, food experts across the United States, Europe, China, and Pacific Rim declare that the symbiotic relationship between plant and animal yields stronger limbs and wings and tastier, higher-quality animal products.

All free-range livestock lives on green forage as opposed to corn, cottonseed, and soy meals bolstered with antibiotics and artificial additives, the typical feed on industrialized farms. Browsing herd animals—cattle, goats, horses, llamas, pigs, sheep—thrive on subdivided pasture and paddock rotation, a system similar in biological control to salmon and shrimp aquaculture. Swine such as those pastured in Australia eat better when they have access to fresh-flowing water and lanes to mud wallows to cool their skin. Lamb producers in New Zealand lower energy expenditures by pasturing rather than confining sheep in sheds. Grass-fed beef is less often exposed to herbicides and pesticides and is less likely to bear *Escherichia coli (E. coli)* contaminants than are penned and stalled cattle.

The logic of raising unfenced animals rests on traditional, benign methods of husbandry. By freeing birds to comb pastures for alfalfa, clover, insects and seeds to nest naturally, Austrian and British farmers reduce cannibalism and feather pecking and end the need to debeak chicks. Birds that spend their days outdoors occupy cleaner, drier houses at night. By ranging over the land, they promote an ecosystem that requires less labor, energy, and equipment for maintenance. Eggs from foraging hens contain thicker albumin, deeper orange yolks, lower cholesterol and fat, and more omega-3 fatty acids and vitamins A, B12, and E.

Opposition in the United States to free-range livestock derives from fears for neighboring properties and for potential losses to a $350 million natural beef industry and a $7 billion poultry industry that yields 78 billion eggs per year. Industrialized farmers claim that constant manuring of yards and pastures from up to 80 chickens per acre (200 per hectare) results in ammonia odors, dead grass, and muddy, polluted runoff. Another danger to the public, the availability of polychlorinated biphenyls (PCBs) to foraging livestock increases threats to packaged meats and milk. Producers who prefer yarding and feedlots to free range complain that competitors make unsubstantiated claims about nutrients in their eggs, milk, and meat and that they earn inflated prices by playing on the sympathies of animal rights defenders.

See also: Agribusiness; Aquaponics; Local Food Movement; Taboos, Food.

Further Reading

Bennett, Jacob M. *The Complete Guide to Grass-Fed Cattle: How to Raise Your Cattle on Natural Grass for Fun and Profit.* Ocala, FL: Atlantic, 2011.

Bowden, Jonny. *The 150 Healthiest Foods on Earth: The Surprising, Unbiased Truth About What You Should Eat and Why.* Gloucester, MA: Fair Winds, 2007.

McWilliams, James E. *Just Food: Where Locavores Get It Wrong and How We Can Truly Eat Responsibly.* New York: Little, Brown, 2009.

Ruechel, Julius. *Grass-Fed Cattle: How to Produce and Market Natural Beef.* North Adams, MA: Storey, 2006.

Freeze-Drying

The physical condensation of ice to a gas, freeze-drying (or lyophilizing) reduces the liquid in food and pharmaceuticals to retard spoilage and yield the highest-grade of dried processed comestibles. At Machu Picchu, in Peru, the Inca preserved potatoes by freezing them on slopes of the Andes Mountains. The low air pressure at high altitude allowed water to vaporize, leaving the tubers in a light, brittle state easily reconstituted with cooking liquids. Around 500 C.E., Japanese monks at a Buddhist temple on Mount Koya perfected a similar process of drying fresh *koya-dofu* (soy tofu).

Invented in 1890 and developed in Switzerland by Nestlé in 1938 to preserve coffee, modern lyophilization produced Nescafé as a means of saving surplus beans for the Brazilian Coffee Institute. Processing required vacuuming moisture at -45 degrees Fahrenheit (-43 degrees Celsius) before sealing coffee in cans to prevent rehydration and damage by oxygen. During World War II, Nestlé manufactured Nescafé as a standard military beverage. The reduction of liquid also preserved blood plasma and penicillin at room temperature over an extended period

for ease of handling and storage. With concepts created by Hungarian scientist Sándor Mihály in the 1960s, the Nestlé Company continued experimenting on the freeze-drying of foods.

Preservation Breakthroughs

Freezing and drying preserved instant soup, fruit juice powder, guacamole, royal jelly, seaweed, ready-to-eat meals, vacuum-dried fish fillets, and wheatgrass, a health food powder that removes heavy metals from the body. The dehydrated food retained more fiber and vitamin C than oven- or sun-dried produce and remained stable during transport. Food processors applied dehydration to açaí, apples, bananas, coconut, mangos, peaches, raspberries, and strawberries, such as the fruit added to muesli, and to basil, chives, ginger, parsley, and other common cooking herbs and spices. Lettuce and melons, however, proved the poorest candidates, for losing too much of their cell structure from rehydration and yielding a gritty texture.

Because of the reduction in heat damage caused by other methods of drying, early attempts at freeze-drying fresh meat, sausage, and seafood produced a higher-quality product and lower microbial content than did other preservation strategies. Dehydrated food cubes, liquids, and powders supplied John Glenn's Mercury-Atlas earth orbit on February 20, 1962. For subsequent Apollo missions, Whirlpool freeze-dried food into bite-size cubes and Neapolitan ice cream into bricks. Pureed foods and liquids sipped from tubes proved less appealing for their lack of mouthfeel.

For 14 years of shuttle missions to the International Space Station, the National Aeronautics and Space Administration (NASA) packed freeze-dried foods, such as broccoli, cauliflower, shrimp, snacks, and spinach at some 20 percent of their original weight. Pouches contained a valve for the injection of water before placement of each dish in a warmer. Meals reheated in ten minutes. Another plus for bulk control, the packaging served as a disposable eating dish, thus lightening loads for return trips. Limited entrées, however, caused menu fatigue.

Marketing

In the 1960s, food technologists predicted a wider application of freeze-drying to the marketplace. In 1966, two cryogenic engineers, James L. Mercer and Hachiro J. Togashi of San Francisco, pioneered hot water extraction and freeze-drying to Tasters Choice coffee, a Maxwell House product. Mercer's patents included freeze-dried green beans for the U.S. Army, domestic spices, and fresh fruit in See's chocolates. Because of the reduction in weight in the first freeze-dried items, meals for cyclists, expeditioners, mountain climbers, rescuers, and spelunkers were less bulky and more convenient for carrying in backpacks and emergency kits. The food became porous but, upon reconstitution, retained aroma, color, flavor, and texture as well as vitamins and minerals.

In 1968, during the Vietnam War, the 11-ounce (312-gram) Long Range Patrol (LRP, pronounced "lurp") ration for the U.S. Marine Corps included flexible packaging of beef hash, chicken stew, mutton, pork, sausage, shrimp, or squid to ensure consumption of 1,100 calories per day. Each lurp required 3 cups (0.71 liters) of water to reconstitute entrées, rice, and vegetables. By 2001, the military increased food value to 1,560 calories and offered 12 LRP menus, including scrambled eggs and bacon, spaghetti, teriyaki, and a western omelet. In Bozeman, Montana, AlpineAire experimented with high-energy sports and survival meals, including couscous, potato cheddar soup, gumbo, lentils, and split peas. However, apart from coffee processing and extreme military and outdoor needs, freeze-drying stalled because of increased efficiency in chilling and freezing foods.

Since 1970, Mountain House, a division of Oregon Freeze Dry, has offered a variety of zippered pouches of barbecue, beef stew, chicken and mashed potatoes, chili, lasagna, noodle and rice dishes, scrambled eggs and ham, seafood chowder, surimi, sweet and sour pork, and turkey tetrazzini. Vegetarian stock includes applesauce, avocado, blueberry cheesecake, corn and peas, cottage cheese, granola, macaroni and cheese, milk, mushrooms, onions, pasta primavera, pudding, whole eggs, and wild rice and mushrooms. Except for fruit and ice cream, food sealed in pouches lasts seven years and offers less enticement to prowling bears. For dieters, the prepackaged meals from Nutrisystem require minimal handling and the addition of water for rehydration.

Because durable enameled cans retain contents for up to 25 years, families store cases of freeze-dried meals for use in disasters. Survival kits are available for spans of from three to 90 days, including meals for dogs, ferrets, and fish. Customers demand quality preserved foods, such as Belgian and Dutch lactobacillus, cheese made from kefir cells, chicken nuggets, chocolate, Finnish cultured milk, freeze-dried Bolivian *chuño* (potatoes), green tea powder, Miyako brand miso from California and Japan, and malolactic and mesophilic bacteria for acidifying feta cheese and yogurt. A brisk business encourages companies to improve freeze-drying technology and to reduce the costs of food preparation and packaging.

One advance involves the coating of brittle foods with whey protein film to prevent bruising and crumbling. Another application, the centrifuging and dehydration of beta-carotene for insertion into capsules, reduces the size and weight of a nutraceutical absorbed in the small intestines. In India, Nigeria, and Pakistan, the addition of freeze-dried leaf plants and milk concentrates to children's meals combats anemia and kwashiorkor, an acute stage of malnutrition.

See also: Beef; Coffee; Inca Diet and Cuisine; Industrial Food Processing.

Further Reading
Barbosa-Cánovas, Gusatavo V., Enrique Ortega-Rivas, Pablo Juliano, and Hong Yan. *Food Powders: Physical Properties, Processing, and Functionality.* New York: Kluwer/Plenum, 2005.
Hui, Yiu H., et al., eds. *Food Drying Science and Technology: Microbiology, Chemistry, Applications.* Lancaster, PA: DEStech, 2008.
Ratti, Christina. "Hot Air and Freeze-Drying of High-Value Foods: A Review." *Journal of Food Engineering* 49:4 (September 2001): 311–319.
Singh, R.P., and D.R. Heldman. *Introduction to Food Engineering.* 3rd ed. New York: Academic Press, 2001.

French Diet and Cuisine

Evolved by a vigorous, food-oriented culture, French cuisine satisfies the passion of both earthy and urbane tastes. In the 400s, early medieval French fare tended toward brined and dried meats and vegetables and heavy seasonings for pies and hippocras, a dessert wine. The agricultural class relied heavily on grains. The elite raised carp and pike in ponds and kept poultry yards for pheasants and pigeons. Dolphin, peacock, and swan entrées came to the table dyed and gilded for display amid a crush of pitchers and platters.

Into the 800s, Charlemagne, king of the Franks, managed the French market economy by controlling food prices, funding food banks, and standardizing market weights and measures. He elevated respect for beans and chickpeas and dignified table behavior. For the sake of a healthy citizenry, he modeled abstemious consumption of roast meats and wine.

Taillevent, the fourteenth-century Norman-French compiler of France's earliest-known cookbook, de-emphasized late medieval spicing. His revamped recipes allowed chief ingredients to unleash natural flavors, the foundation of classical French cookery. By the late 1400s, guilds controlled commerce in fish and grain and provided catering and pastry at contract rates.

The Elegant Table
At the height of the Italian Renaissance, the arrival of Catherine de' Médici, bride of Henry II, from Florence to Paris turned dining into a sensory experience. She introduced refined touches to game and added to kitchen gardens artichokes, asparagus, broad beans, and peas. For her grand dinners, Italian cooks abandoned heavy medieval recipes in favor of aspic, ice cream, layered pasta, onion soup, seafood, sherbet, truffles, and turkey, a North American import. Tableware featured the fork, an innovation in place settings.

In the 1600s, Pierre La Varenne, chef to Queen Marie de' Médici, systemized the principles of French

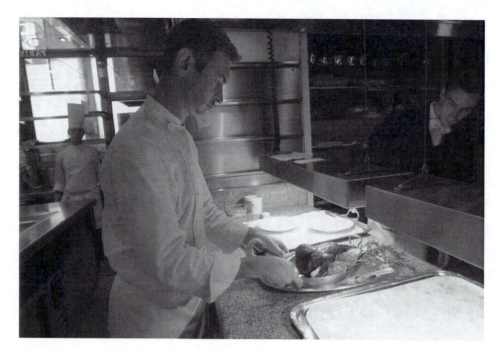

The head chef puts finishing touches on pressed duck, the specialty of the house at La Tour d'Argent in Paris. Claiming origins in 1582, Tour d'Argent is the oldest and most famous restaurant in the city. The ducks are farm-raised and numbered. *(Christophe Ena/Associated Press)*

gastronomy and popularized light pies and desserts. In place of heavy reliance on bread crumbs as thickeners, he exemplified to a generation of cooks the quick-stirring of roux (fried flour) as a basis for gravies and sauces. His rational examination of showy table fare foretokened the evolution of modern foodways and the rise in stature of the *saucier.*

In 1691, caterer François Massialot, author of *Le Cuisinier Roïal et Bourgeois (The Royal and Middle-Class Cook),* publicized the banquet and reception menus favored under Louis XIV. Among Massialot's innovations, the text listed crème brûlée, marinade, meringue, and ragout, all produced with specialized utensils. After the dissolution of the royal dynasty during the French Revolution, democratization produced a demand for restaurants, a concept uniquely French in its commercialization of catering to suit the nouveau riche.

In the early 1800s, chef Marie-Antoine Carême elevated French cuisine with the architectural *pièce montée* (mounted display), created to please the Emperor Napoleon and his entourage. Carême defined basic saucing under the headings *allemande* (cream and egg sauce), *béchamel* (white sauce), *espagnole* (brown sauce), and *velouté* (meat glaze). His contemporary during the early 1800s, food writer Jean Anthelme Brillat-Savarin, turned eating into an intellectual exercise in savoring exotic ingredients of the nation's postwar revival of grand cuisine.

Georges Auguste Escoffier, the "Father of Modern French Cuisine," polished the innovations of his predecessors by regimenting kitchen staff into specialists. After formulating the first à la carte menu and Russian style service of one course at a time, he introduced individualized plating by waiters, which French chef Félix Urbain Dubois popularized. In place of Carême's decorative ex-

tremes, Escoffier focused on taste rather than table decor. In some 5,000 recipes, he created innovations that included crêpes Suzette, pêche Melba, and soufflés. To the four basic sauces outlined by Carême, Escoffier added hollandaise (a thick dressing of butter, egg yolk, and lemon juice) and tomato sauce. His light touch guided heavy gravies toward flavorful dressings and garnishes and the hearty flavors of *coq au vin* (braised chicken with wine).

Modern Flair

From 1900 to the present, the French solidified their centuries-old reputation for fine dining. To direct the post–World War II boom in culinary tourism, Michelin Guides ranked, with a star code, comfortable and luxurious inns, restaurants, and regional entrées at reasonable cost. The handbooks directed amateur gourmets to the best in peasant dishes and high-end dining that paired entrées with suitable wines.

In the *Larousse Gastronomique* (1938), culinary encyclopedist Prosper Montagné clarified French techniques for smoothing a bisque, glazing a *galantine,* and injecting moisture into a *farci* (stuffing). His text described the provenance of regional specialties—Alps cheese, Alsatian sauerkraut and sausage, Bordeaux wines, calvados and *galettes* from Brittany, currants and mustard from Burgundy, Catalan snails, Gascon pâté, mushrooms from the Loire River valley, and herbs and honey from Provence. He explained how heritage cookery accommodated Algerian pilafs, American barbecue, Corsican chestnuts and citrus fruit, German sauerbraten, and Italian aperitifs to generate a sophisticated Continental fare.

In the 1960s and 1970s, nouvelle cuisine, pioneered by Paul Bocuse, replaced elaborate *haute cuisine française* (high French cookery) with short menus featuring uncomplicated free-form dishes devoid of formality. In place of sauceing, chefs flavored entrées with meat stock and reductions that suited the demands of health-conscious consumers. From the 1970s into the present, American kitchen maven Julia Child gave credibility to French gastronomy through cookbooks and television demonstrations of such kitchen skills as kneading dough for brioche and trussing a goose.

In recent times, *cuisine du terroir* (regional gastronomy) has replaced the undisciplined experimentation of nouvelle cuisine with respect for traditional country fare. Rustic dishes have advanced to prominence for their sensible combinations of herbs with fresh ingredients for such dishes as cassoulet and quiche. In 2010, UNESCO declared France the perpetuator of an "intangible cultural heritage" in fine eating.

See also: Boré, Jean Étienne de; Brillat-Savarin, Jean Anthelme; Carême, Marie-Antoine; Charlemagne; Child, Julia; Creole Diet and Cuisine; Cussy, Louis, Marquis de; Escoffier, Georges Auguste; La Varenne, Pierre; *Larousse Gastronomique*; Médici, Catherine de'; Nouvelle Cuisine; Sauces and Saucing; Taillevent.

Further Reading

Ferguson, Priscilla Parkhurst. *Accounting for Taste: The Triumph of French Cuisine.* Chicago: University of Chicago Press, 2004.

Gopnik, Adam. *The Table Comes First: Family, France, and the Meaning of Food.* New York: Alfred A. Knopf, 2011.

Schehr, Lawrence R., and Allen S. Weiss, eds. *French Food: On the Table, on the Page, and in French Culture.* New York: Routledge, 2001.

Scully, D. Eleanor, and Terence Scully. *Early French Cookery: Sources, History, Original Recipes, and Modern Adaptations.* Ann Arbor: University of Michigan Press, 2002.

Trubek, Amy B. *Haute Cuisine: How the French Invented the Culinary Profession.* Philadelphia: University of Pennsylvania Press, 2000.

French East India Company

The French East India Company (FEIC, La Compagnie Française des Indes Orientales) pursued vast colonial dreams but succeeded in the food trade only on the French islands of Mauritius and Réunion. Established in January 1664 by Finance Minister Jean-Baptiste Colbert, the French venture began at a disadvantage against the Dutch, English, Portuguese, and Spanish, who had established prominence in the Asian beverage and spice trade. The joint-stock endeavor replaced three forerunners—the Companie de Chine (China Company), Compagnie de Madagascar (Madagascar Company), and Companie d'Orient (Eastern Company)—with a single brokerage operating under a royal charter from King Louis XIV.

The FEIC issued stock worth £625,000 and commissioned a flagship, the armed frigate *Saint-Paul,* to set sail from Brest. Because of the hesitance of entrepreneurs to risk cash against established European commerce, Louis XIV became the major FEIC stockholder. Management fell to three competent traders: Director-General François Caron, a 30-year Dutch East India Company veteran hired by Colbert; Director Marcara Avanchintz, a Persian merchant from Armenia; and Admiral Pierre de la Haye, an ambassador heading a nine-ship fleet. Colbert directed writer François Charpentier to manage an advertising campaign to arouse the French from economic insularity, which enslaved the economy to foreign commerce. Charpentier published a pamphlet, "A Treatise Touching the East-Indian Trade" (1664), available in French and German, urging capitalists to invest in the import of cinnamon, coffee, cotton, and pepper.

During French colonial expansion, the FEIC built on the explorations of Admiral Paulmier de Gonneville in 1603. Authorized by France's Henry IV, the firm determined to exploit markets in the Indian and Pacific oceans. After introducing French commerce in West Africa in 1624, the French merchant marine created trading ports at Île de France (Mauritius) and Île Bourbon (Réunion), where settlers began arriving in 1665 to plant highly profitable coffee and sugarcane. The FEIC excelled at commerce in coffee, cotton, food dye, pepper, and sugar. Under Colbert's restrictions, warehouses stocked only top-quality goods from Guinea, India, the Levant, and Senegal.

One disaster, the wreckage of the *Taureau* on July 11, 1666, off Antongil Bay, Madagascar, cost the company a full load of rice; on November 1, 1681, the *Soleil d'Orient* disappeared with its hold filled with Siamese cotton and spices. Additional losses to attack, cyclone, the pirate La Buse (Olivier Le Vasseur), reefs, a slave mutiny, and yellow fever proved to nervous investors the hazards of the sea trade.

Brokerage centers at Surat and Masulipatam in 1668 and Pondicherry in 1673 based French merchants in India for the first time. Pondicherry grew into a major European stronghold. Attempts at building an additional outpost at Ceylon (Sri Lanka) and St. Thomas on the Coromandel coast in 1672 to market French beans, millet, and rice failed to dislodge the Dutch.

Because of financial instability in 1719, the FEIC reorganized four years later under the name Companie Perpétuelle des Indes. Officials opened a new outpost at Mahé in Malabar and operated 14 merchantmen out of India's southwestern shore. The annual sale of goods in 1735 reached 2,667 tons (2,419 metric tons) of coffee, opium, and tea, which swept England, France, and Holland as a mealtime fad.

By 1740, French colonies turned an annual profit of 250,000 livres on cacao, coffee, cotton, ginger, and rum. Quickly, however, the FEIC lost business clout to British merchants. In 1741, Robert Clive, governor-general of the

British East India Company, expelled the French from Indian trade and governance. After the FEIC sent Governor-General Joseph François Dupleix to colonize southern India for the Bourbon throne, he seized Madras and established a capital at Pondicherry in southeastern India. In 1751, local chiefs sided alternately with the French and British in a company conflict known as the Second Carnatic War. The superiority of the English navy and land forces decided the commercial fate of India. After the British captured Pondicherry, the FEIC dissolved in 1769.

During this period, the FEIC continued to cultivate Mauritius and Réunion as well as the Seychelles in 1750, when islanders exported surpluses of corn, rice, and wheat. The islands served as naval refueling stations and victualers (provisioners). Naval nutritional deficiencies decreased after ship surgeons insisted on stocking lemon juice as an antiscorbutic. Island agronomists planted test nurseries with 3,000 specimens of pepper vines, mountain rice, along with breadfruit, camphor, cinnamon, clove, cocoa, coconut, lychee, mango, and nutmeg stock that bio-pirate and environmentalist Pierre Poivre smuggled from Mocha and Timor.

In his travelogue, titled *Travels of a Philosopher: or, Observations on the Manners and Arts of Various Nations in Africa and Asia* (1770), Poivre described the rich flavor of Mauritian coffee, which workers gathered in dry weather when the beans reached perfection rather than harvest in the wet season like West Indian growers. An intellectual of the age of enlightenment, Poivre valued creativity. He credited Admiral Bertrand-François Mahé de la Bourdonnais, governor of Réunion, with furthering agricultural projects with cinnamon, cocoa, coffee, cotton, indigo, mulberry, pear trees, sugar, tea, and "Turkey corn" (*Dicentra formosa*), a tuber from the corydalis plant. La Bourdonnais also introduced manioc, which became a principal foodstuff for field slaves.

Poivre made significant strides in advancing the world's consumption of imported foods. He promoted the Malayan sago as a source of soft nourishment for an invalid diet and also recommended Vietnamese dates and saffron and Siamese fruits, particularly the banana, durian, gac fruit, mango, mangosteen, orange, and pineapple. Poivre regretted that, despite the natural food wealth of Siam, the people lived in misery under a despotic government that exported the highest grade of local food for profit. By his persistence in planting denuded ground in the French islands, Poivre succeeded in smashing the Dutch monopoly on clove and nutmeg.

See also: British East India Company; Dutch East India Company; French West India Company; Peppers.

Further Reading

Ray, Indrani, and Lakshmi Subramanian, eds. *French East India Company and the Trade of the Indian Ocean.* New Delhi, India: Munshiram Manoharlal, 1999.

Stephen, S. Jeyaseela. *The Indian Trade at the Asian Frontier.* New Delhi, India: Gyan, 2008.

Wellington, Donald C. *French East India Companies: An Historical Account and Record of Trade.* Lanham, MD: Hamilton, 2006.

French West India Company

In its short life (1664–1674), the French West India Company (FWIC, Compagnie des Indes Occidentales) capitalized on trade at 12 Caribbean islands. The region flourished from French pioneering, receiving some 150 freighters per year, most of them Dutch. In the absence of currency, shopkeepers accepted tobacco. To the dismay of Finance Minister Jean-Baptiste Colbert, only four of the merchantmen represented French brokers. In the name of King Louis XIV, Colbert founded the French West India Company and formulated a policy of *l'exclusif* to redirect profits to France.

Colbert intended to monopolize the island trade in coffee, cotton, ginger, hides, indigo, roucou cheese dye (*Bixa orellana,* or annatto), sugar, syrup, and tobacco and to turn the French colonies into a source of revenue. Investors planned to stem paganism by spreading Christianity while supplanting the Dutch, English, and Spanish at profiteering on Caribbean plantations. Colbert also maintained a personal interest in Martinique and St. Lucia, where he owned plantations.

From data gleaned from a survey of the West Indies by Admiral Bertrand d'Ogeron in 1656 and an inspection of Martinique the following year, the king on May 28, 1664, granted the FWIC the remains of the French African Company at Senegal and extended to Amerindians full French citizenship if they converted to Christianity. Encompassing territory from Cape Blanco, Senegal, to the Cape of Good Hope in South Africa for a period of four decades, the commission superintended land between the Amazon and Orinoco rivers in South America, all of Canada and Acadia, Newfoundland, and the French West Indies. The latter consisted of Grenada, the Grenadines, Guadaloupe, Hispaniola (Saint-Dominigue or Haiti), Marie Galante, Martinique, St. Barthélemy (St. Bart's), St. Christopher (St. Kitts), St. Croix, St. Lucia, Tobago, and Tortuga. (Because investments were international, possession of individual islands shifted erratically among Europeans.) The FWIC also absorbed the Cayenne Company, Company of New France, and Company of the Cape Verdes and Senegal. Only fishing rights remained free of government control.

Exports vs. Daily Food

Carib attacks, hurricanes, malaria, and tillage of the islands proved so devastating that few of the earliest settlers survived. To encourage immigration, the French abolished arbitrary duties and taxes and standardized currency,

Recipe: Grenadan Oil Down

Soak 1 pound of salt pork or ham and 1 pound of salt cod overnight in cold water. Bring to a boil and drain. Core and slice 3 pounds of cassava into 1/2-inch pieces. Stir-fry one chopped sweet onion and one chopped garlic clove in 1 tablespoon of vegetable oil. Slice one bunch of green onions and chop with 1/2 cup of chives, one celery rib, and two sprigs of thyme, and stir into the drained fish and meat. Add this and the cassava to the fried onion and garlic. Season with one whole habañero pepper and 3 to 4 cups of coconut milk. Simmer for one hour until the cassava absorbs the milk. Serve with glasses of citrus juice.

measures, and weights. The prohibition of trade with the Dutch on September 30, 1664, deprived islanders of necessities. The situation worsened as the French directed the planting of cash crops, labor-intensive work that prevented laborers from fishing and cultivating vegetable gardens. Instead of beef, chicken, and wheat, islanders subsisted on sea cow (manatee) and salt cod, lizards, pigs, yams, other vegetables, and cassava root, the main source of bread for workers and slaves. A standard dinner consisted of bacon, pea soup, and cassava bread or "oil down" (stew) flavored with hot pepper.

Deficiencies in FWIC finances prevented French expeditions from leaving Nantes. Parts of a convoy arrived at the Cape Verde Islands and Martinique in February 1665, when agents distributed clothing, salt beef, and wine from Anjou and Nantes. Subsequent surpluses of cod, vegetables, and wheat arrived from Canada. Settlers complained that the French failed to satisfy food needs in a timely manner and demanded the return of Dutch traders. The strongest opposition from peasants arose at Guadeloupe, Hispaniola, Martinique, and Tortuga, where sentiment favored commerce with the Dutch and Flemish. Nonetheless, aristocrats at Martinique celebrated the formation of the FWIC with feasting and toasts to the king.

Food Business

In a year's time, after the FWIC began building merchantmen, agents dispatched 60 ships from the ports of Bordeaux, La Rochelle, Nantes, and Rouen. Sales advanced from offices at Bordeaux, Dieppe, Havre, Honfleur, and St. Malo as well as from Texel, Holland. Refineries sprang up in France to turn raw sugar into cooking-grade sugar and syrup, sweeteners that replaced honey in French recipes.

In February 1665, the company appointed D'Ogeron governor of Tortuga and of French colonies in Hispaniola,

the major source of profits from sugar. Company officials planned to trade French bacon, biscuit, brandy, flour, Irish butter, livestock, olive oil, peas, and wine for Caribbean food and indigo, which FWIC brokers marketed in Baltic, Flemish, and French ports.

In summer and fall 1665, English corsairs captured five FWIC vessels and confiscated ginger, sugar, and tobacco. War with England in 1666 forced French captains to remain in port. Investors chafed at the expensive hiatus, which slowed the expulsion of Spanish colonists and inhibited agricultural expansion into cocoa, cotton, indigo, and tobacco. When islanders at St. Christopher threatened revolt, company agents formed a militia to put down the rebels.

In 1669, after a company reorganization, FWIC prospects improved at headquarters in Fort Royal, Martinique. Unaccustomed to the intense heat, white workers gradually bought themselves out of indenture and invested their money in African slaves. French commerce blossomed but not to the degree that Colbert had hoped. As the sugar trade burgeoned, investors wondered at the failure of commerce to produce profits. The reason—free trade—derived from the independent spirit of the islanders, who refused to maintain loyalty to the FWIC. They welcomed Dutch merchantmen to Petit Goave, Hispaniola, and drove out D'Ogeron, who retreated to Tortuga. Merchants also supplied dried beef, salt cod, staples, and wine to the cash-rich pirates at Tortuga.

In 1670, D'Ogeron returned to power under orders to capture or scuttle all Dutch merchantmen. At Port de Paix, Hispaniola, he rewarded islanders with a boatload of 50 female orphans, whom he auctioned for wives, but the irregular importation of food continued to dampen planters' enthusiasm for colonialism. Nantes profited from expeditions and dispatched 24 vessels in 1672. Within two years, the islands produced 6,000 tons (5,400 metric tons) of sugar, making France the prime merchant of granulated sweeteners to European kitchens.

In December 1674, Colbert abandoned his grandiose plan, abolished the company, and ceded control of trade to the crown and private companies. Nevertheless, by 1683, France was marketing 10,350 tons (9,400 metric tons) of sugar per year.

See also: French East India Company; Manioc.

Further Reading

Boucher, Philip P. *France and the American Tropics to 1700: Tropics of Discontent?* Baltimore: Johns Hopkins University Press, 2008.

Findlay, Ronald, and Kevin H. O'Rourke. *Power and Plenty: Trade, War, and the World Economy in the Second Millennium.* Princeton, NJ: Princeton University Press, 2009.

Pritchard, James S. *In Search of Empire: The French in the Americas, 1670–1730.* Cambridge, UK: Cambridge University Press, 2004.

Frézier, Amédée François (1682–1773)

Scots-French explorer, engineer, and spy Amédée François Frézier made culinary history by introducing Europeans to the Pacific Coast strawberry, an indigenous plant that flourishes from Alaska to Patagonia. Frézier's family crest, dating to 916 C.E., displayed three *fraises* (strawberries), a portent of his contribution to world fruit production and consumption.

Born at Chambéry, Savoy, to a law professor, Frézier chose not to follow his father's profession. After training in science and theology in Paris, he conducted postgraduate work in architecture and art in Italy. At age 18, he entered the French infantry as a lieutenant and compiled a treatise on fireworks. His knowledge of ordnance earned him a position in military engineering and intelligence at Saint-Malo.

Posted to Chile and Peru by King Louis XIV on January 7, 1712, to advance defensive fortification on the Pacific, Frézier charted watercourses of southwestern South America. From his observations, he plotted fort and harbor construction along the coast. Posing as a merchant skipper, he infiltrated Spanish installations at Concepción, Chile, and recorded troop strength, escape routes, and ordnance storage. He noted the apparent ease with which native provisioners grew artemisia, bay, balm, chamomile, endive, mint, sage, tansy, and turnips and how they specialized in dye plants as well as herbs for aromatherapy. He marveled at how the introduction of apples and pears after the Spanish conquest had so quickly produced fruit orchards. At Santiago, he appreciated the bounty of peaches at Carnival Time. He remarked on the daylily, the root of which Indians dried in an oven and ground into meal for making pastries.

Frézier's immersion in local biota pinpointed the beach, or coastal, strawberry (*Fragaria chiloensis*), a larger, firmer heart-shaped fruit than the tiny wild Alpine strawberries in Europe (*Fragaria vesca*). The Chilean variety produced an appealing fragrance and clusters of rosettes along stout 18-inch (46-centimeter) stolons that were three times the length of Alpine berry runners. Frézier was not the first European to investigate the indigenous coastal strawberry. Initially viewed by Spanish conquistador Francisco Pizarro at Cuzco, Peru, in 1550, the whitish-red berry, called the *frutilla* (little fruit), became a staple in the Chilean Huilliche and Mapuche diet.

Amerindian farmer's markets sold two dozen berries wrapped in a cabbage leaf for small change—half of one Spanish real. Shoppers tended to eat the fruit raw or dried or to cook it into a sauce for jam or a fruit roll-up. They compressed strawberry leaves into healing poultices to treat canker sores and styes or steeped leaves into a tea to combat diarrhea, gastric bleeding, or infant colic.

Frézier grew specimen plants and nurtured their ground-hugging creepers on the six-month return voyage from Concepción around Cape Horn to Marseilles. To satisfy the plants' need for constant moisture, he sacrificed his allotment of drinking water. Of the five surviving plants when he arrived in August 1714, he kept one for himself and sent another to naturalist Antoine de Jussieu to grow in the Jardin du Roi, the royal herbarium. For Frézier's scientific endeavors, statistics, and map corrections, the king awarded him 1,000 écus.

A sketch of Frézier's strawberry and his commentary in *Relation of the Voyage to the South Sea, Along the Coast of Chile and Perou, Made During the Years 1712, 1713, and 1714* reached print in 1714 and in English translation in 1717. During a posting to Hispaniola in 1719, he suffered from malaria. After constructing forts in Brittany and Germany and compiling a text on three-dimensional geometry, he retired at age 82 and devoted himself to hobby engineering, history, and travel.

Through Frézier's influence, a profitable berry business at Brest ranged from the Chilean varieties to similar salt-resistant hybrids. The fruit earned its place among other foods that prevent scurvy. In 1720, Dutch botanist Herman Boerhaave studied Frézier's discovery, which he passed to English horticulturist Philip Miller at Chelsea in 1727. Miller accidentally crossbred the Chilean berry with the North American *Fragaria virginiana*, which grew from Canada to Virginia. Propagation resulted in 1766 in the modern garden strawberry, *Fragaria ananassa*, which grew to plum size. Swedish naturalist Carolus Linnaeus boosted the popularity of the Chilean strawberry, which the French interplanted with the *Fragaria moschata* and *Fragaria virginiana* varieties at Cherbourg to yield fruit 7.5 inches (19 centimeters) in diameter. Thomas Jefferson, at his experimental gardens in Monticello, Virginia, scoured the market for the large-fruited Chilean plant stock but was unsuccessful. By 1882, berry farmers at Plougastel, France, marketed 1,500 tons (1,350 metric tons) of Frézier's Chilean berries.

Further Reading

Darrow, George M. *The Strawberry: History, Breeding and Physiology.* New York: Holt, Rinehart and Winston, 1966.

Gollner, Adam. *The Fruit Hunters: A Story of Nature, Adventure, Commerce, and Obsession.* New York: Simon & Schuster, 2008.

Kingsbury, Noel. *Hybrid: The History and Science of Plant Breeding.* Chicago: University of Chicago Press, 2009.

Fructarianism

An extreme pacifist subcategory of veganism, fructarianism limits the diet to fruit, nuts, and seeds—all foods that fall readily from the plant. The diet reflects the life source of early hominids, who were frugivores (those who eat fruit only). It gained popularity in the 1910s as a progressive solution to land use and human drudgery. A more inclusive form allowed chocolate, corn, cucumbers, eggplant, grain, honey, legumes, olive oil, pepper, pumpkins, sesame and sunflower seeds, sprouts, and tomatoes. Another version, liquidarianism or hydrorianism, excludes pulp and seeds and relies solely on alternating fasting with fruit juices.

The philosophy of a fruit diet derives from the first chapter of Genesis, which describes the plants grown in the Garden of Eden. Under Jainism, the purpose of grain and meat taboos is to avoid killing animals or plants. Strict fructarians believe that their role in nature is to subsist on the flesh that surrounds the seed and to spread the seed to new locations.

Advocates maintain that the rapid putrefaction of meat indicates a danger of gut poisons that slow-decaying fruits avoid. Another argument for fructarianism, the appeal to the senses engages eye, nose, hand, and mouth in appreciating the natural grace and appetite stimulation of berries and fruit. Because fruits are ready for immediate consumption, they involve no recipes or preparation to intervene between collection and enjoyment. Diners eat fruit skins as a benefit to the body. They consume edibles at room temperature, introducing no extremes of hot or cold to the alimentary system.

Nutritionists scrutinize the fruit diet for deficiencies in calcium, fat, iron, protein, vitamins B12 and D, and zinc. Its limitations may threaten the growth and maturation of children, whom social agencies may seize from parents who withhold more conventional foods. Critics of a strict fruit diet for children warn of anemia, malnutrition, and protein and vitamin deficiency. A lesser argument against an extreme diet, social isolation sets fruit consumers apart from those who eat a wider range of raw and cooked foods, including bread, meat, milk and dairy products, and sweets.

Fructarians respond that fruits, especially bananas, coconut, dried dates, and marmalades, are naturally sweet and that almonds and peanuts, nut butters, and nut milk provide sufficient carbohydrates, fats, minerals, and proteins to sustain health and longevity. Avocados and bananas gain respect for adding fat, protein, potassium, and amino acids to the diet.

Proponents of fructarianism list the advantages of individual varieties, claiming the value of strawberries to the joints and the anti-inflammatory qualities of blackberries, blueberries, and pineapples. They assert that fruits and nuts cause less colitis, diarrhea, hyperacidity, and indigestion than meats. Fructarians also state that apples and grapes, applesauce, apple tea, cider, grape juice and wine, and raisins satisfy while ridding the intestines and mucous membranes of microbes.

Fruit eaters contrast factories that process foods to the beauty, balance, and fragrance of fruit gardening. Fru-

givore eating habits reforest the earth with self-replicating bushes, trees, and vines and cleanse the air and land of pollutants.

Further Reading

Gollner, Adam. *The Fruit Hunters: A Story of Nature, Adventure, Commerce, and Obsession.* New York: Simon & Schuster, 2008.

Hak, Marriaine. "Extreme Diets." *Vegetarian Times* 315 (November 2003): 74–75.

Iacobbo, Karen, and Michael Iacobbo. *Vegetarian America: A History.* Westport, CT: Greenwood, 2004.

Vaughan, J.G., and Catherine Geissler. *The New Oxford Book of Food Plants.* New York: Oxford University Press, 2009.

Wood, Kate. *Eat Smart, Eat Raw.* Garden City Park, NY: Square One, 2006.

Fungi

Living in symbiosis with bacteria, flora, and fauna, some 70,000 types of fungi augment diet and cuisine as vegetables and as components of beer, bread, and cheese. Growing like plants, fungi reproduce from spores and feed on organic matter. Unlike true plants, the fungal fruit-body lacks chlorophyll, flowers and leaves, roots and stems, and seeds.

Examples—*Aspergillus,* baker's yeast, and Quorn—permeate gastronomy with specific flavors, textures, and improvements to recipes. *Aspergillus* forms the essence of sake and soy sauce; baker's yeast (*Saccharomyces cerevisiae*) releases gases that raise dough for dumplings and loaves.

The truffle is the most luxurious of edible fungi, sometimes referred to as the "diamond of the culinary world." The black truffles of France's Périgord region, among the most prized, grow in the shade of hazelnut and oak trees. *(Jean-Pierre Muller/AFP/Getty Images)*

As a "functional food," fungi benefit the body as bioactive promoters of wellness and reducers of disease. For a vegetarian regimen, Quorn, a trademark form of *Fusarium venenatum,* offers a healthful substitute for meat.

Edible mushrooms, such as button and portobello varieties, are a natural food dating to the hunter-gatherers from 200,000 to 10,000 B.C.E. Taoist priests treasured medicinal fungi, nutraceuticals such as the bamboo and *Trametes* mushrooms, for treating cancer, hepatitis, infection, immune system failure, and reproductive and respiratory ills. In the kitchen, mushrooms add complex aroma, flavor, and texture to cuisine. Gourmands favor costlier blue, Roquefort, and Stilton cheeses, enoki and porcini mushrooms, and truffles for their uniqueness.

Despite the ubiquity of fungi in cookery, a small percentage of mushrooms can cause hallucinations and severe intestinal and cardiac reactions leading to illness or even death. For some varieties, toxicity accumulates over time. Historically, ergotism from a rye fungus precipitated medieval and Renaissance era sorcery trials and persecutions of folk healers.

The appeal of chanterelle, cremini, king oyster, and morel mushrooms derives from their plump shapes and fresh, earthy scent. They require little handling or trimming and survive in the pantry in oil or vinegar as well as dried or frozen. They pair well in green salads and appetizers with capers, herbs, and olives. The caps and vertical slices hold hearty stuffings for a brief broiling or toasting. Sliced mushrooms in frittatas, gravy, pasta, pilaf, quiche, and soup complement the flavors of lemon and mustard as well as parsley and dill. Another common use, sautéed mushrooms enhance the aroma of vegetarian sandwiches.

See also: Beer; Bread; Cheese; Poisonous Foods; Wild Food.

Further Reading

Cheung, Peter C.K., ed. *Mushrooms as Functional Foods.* Hoboken, NJ: John Wiley & Sons, 2008.

Halpern, Georges M. *Healing Mushrooms.* Garden City Park, NY: Square One, 2007.

Lyle, Katie Letcher. *The Complete Guide to Edible Wild Plants, Mushrooms, Fruits, and Nuts.* Guilford, CT: Globe Pequot, 2004.

Schinharl, Cornelia, and Michael Brauner. *Mushrooms.* San Francisco: Silverback, 2006.

Spahr, David L. *Edible and Medicinal Mushrooms of New England and Eastern Canada.* Berkeley, CA: North Atlantic, 2009.

Fusion Cuisine

An innovative convergence of ingredients and cooking styles, fusion cuisine merges regional and national gastronomy to produce novel dishes that preserve individual traditions. The concept of eclectic cuisine flourishes in areas experiencing high immigration, particularly eastern Australia, Canada, Hawaii, and the Middle East. The best of fusion techniques dispels otherness with an auspicious union of strange and familiar ingredients, such as British Columbian game birds prepared low-fat style and complemented with wasabi.

In multicultural settings, adventurous gourmands try new flavors, much as Alexander the Great nibbled his way from Macedonia to the Indus River. Chefs prepare unfamiliar ingredients by established cooking styles and top the new with sauces and garnishes as identifiable as Nigerian peanut sauce and French meunière (brown butter sauce). Likewise, tourism brings disparate peoples together with unfamiliar cuisine, introducing Cantonese to British high tea, Scandinavians to Thai spring rolls, and restaurateurs worldwide to the American demand for Coca-Cola, hamburgers, and french fries.

Hybrids in History

Historically, the hybridizing of food traditions tends to follow political, religious, and military transitions. In the first century B.C.E., the posting of Roman legionaries throughout Africa, Asia Minor, and Europe tempted Italian men to try British barley beer, Iberian paella, and Arab desserts made from dates and figs. After 1096, the Crusades yielded a new height in cultural mixing by sending European adventurers to the Holy Lands for lengthy duty. In the hot Mediterranean environment, Muslim chefs cooled menus with melon dishes and pomegranate sorbets. From returning soldiers, European restaurants developed a culturally diverse offering of chilled fruit drinks and herbed eggplant. One introduction, spiced gingerbread iced British style and served with lemon curd, found its way into Christmas desserts, Easter fairs, and tea tables.

A Renaissance explosion of fusion menus followed the arrival of Christopher Columbus in the New World in September 1492. Global food choices doubled with the addition of barley bread, beef, cabbage, cheese, figs, lettuce, olives, pork, salted herring, and wine to Cuban and Haitian dishes and avocados, chili peppers, chocolate, corn, pecans, potatoes, tomatoes, and turkey to the traditional recipes of Italy and Ireland. Italians sauced their pasta with tomato gravy; the Irish added potatoes to nearly every meal. After the Spanish invasion of Mexico in 1519, Aztec cuisine accommodated dairy items and grains introduced by the Spanish and Portuguese. From the collision of forces grew a serendipity, post-Columbian Mesoamerican cuisine.

Voyages became the conduits of global foodway unions. The arrival of Asian Indians to the West Indies influenced curry experiments in the beef and seafood restaurants of Guyana, Jamaica, Tobago, and Trinidad. Likewise, immigration from the Black Sea and Baltic Sea after 1920 expanded markets and recipes in Russia. In a border accommodation, in 1945, Hispanic chefs altered Mexican cookery to suit the tastes of the American Southwest.

Texas restaurants referred to their menu selections as "Tex-Mex," the first named fusion cuisine. Along the eastern Mediterranean on May 14, 1948, the establishment of the state of Israel brought together Jews from multiple food traditions, including Moorish almond cakes and nougats from Iberia and chicken soup and cream and egg combinations from Eastern Europe.

Commercialized Fusions

The proliferation of fusion restaurants in the United States followed Chinese American chef Richard Chow Wing's Chinese-French improvisations in the 1960s in Hanford, California. His eclectic background as a U.S. Army cook for General George C. Marshall introduced Wing to varied entrées from China, Germany, Italy, Russia, and Switzerland. His restaurant, the Imperial Dynasty, fed Chinois flavors to famous actors, entrepreneurs, and politicians, including escargot with ginger root and Napa wines to Chiang Kai-shek and Madame Chiang.

California pioneered commercial food diversity with a wealth of fresh ingredients from field, ocean, and orchard. In 1971, chef Alice Louise Waters, educated in Corfu, London, Paris, and Turkey, orchestrated local organic ingredients at her award-winning Berkeley restaurant, Chez Panisse. Her lighthearted combinations wed wax beans to figs and prosciutto, lamb to black-eyed peas, and nectarines to bourbon-pecan ice cream.

In 1973, a parallel experiment in Lima, Peru, caused Nobuyuki Matsuhisa to formulate a traditional Japanese menu by trial and error with Peruvian market produce. From South American ingredients, he concocted a Japanese roll sauced with Peruvian ceviche, sashimi tacos with kelp salad, squid pasta, pumpkin chips with mustard miso, and a signature entrée, yellowtail with jalapeño pepper. His dishes pleased clientele at his restaurants in Argentina, Australia, the Bahamas, China, Dubai, Hong Kong, Hungary, Italy, Russia, and South Africa.

In the 1990s, *fusion cuisine* replaced *nouvelle cuisine* as the period food buzzword, with Florida rapidly gaining on California for the culinary melding of "Floribbean" food. In defiance of the terroir concept of cooking cheese, grain, vegetables, and wine grown in the same microclimate, audacious cooks expanded on trans-American and Eurasian menus. Austrian chef Wolfgang Puck, who apprenticed in Monaco and Paris, brought his styles to Spago in Los Angeles and Cut in Singapore. His menu at Spago featured his flair for mergers—Virginia striped bass with bok choy and shiitake mushrooms, New York steak with bordelaise sauce, American club sandwich with Italian aioli (garlic mayonnaise), and goulash with German *spätzel* (egg noodles). In the early 2000s, fusion cooks acquired a reputation for overreaching, a tendency to dismay diners with such bizarre juxtapositions as Mexican chutney and tandoori chicken with Turkish puff pastry, brought together as trendy curiosities.

See also: Columbus, Christopher; Huou; Israeli Diet and Cuisine; Mexican Diet and Cuisine; Sicilian Diet and Cuisine; Silk Road.

Further Reading

Baylor, Ronald H., ed. *Multicultural America: An Encyclopedia of the Newest Americans.* Santa Barbara, CA: ABC-Clio, 2011.

Davé, Shilpa, LeiLani Nishime, and Tasha G. Oren. *East Main Street: Asian American Popular Culture.* New York: New York University Press, 2005.

Hjalager, Anne-Mette, and Greg Richards, eds. *Tourism and Gastronomy.* New York: Routledge, 2002.

Reinfeld, Mark, and Bo Rinaldi. *Vegan Fusion World Cuisine.* New York: Beaufort, 2007.

Gama, Vasco da (ca. 1460–1524)

A long-distance Portuguese navigator and colonizer of East Africa and India, Vasco da Gama, the first European to reach India by sea, used food as a diplomatic tactic.

A native of the fishing village of Sines, Portugal, da Gama excelled at astronomy and mathematics. In 1492, King John II dispatched him to sea to protect Portuguese merchantmen from French seizure.

Duplicating the explorations of Bartolomeu Dias around the Cape of Good Hope to western India the previous decade, Admiral da Gama set out from Lisbon on July 8, 1497, under King Manuel I, to redirect the Arab-Venetian spice monopoly from the Silk Road to a sea route around Africa. Aboard the flagship *São Gabriel,* he led three other ships, including a supply vessel carrying flour, honey, lentils, onions, plums, salt beef and pork, sugar, and wine. His mission was the expansion of the Portuguese *cartaz* (trade monopoly) to African and Asian ports of call.

According to an anonymous chronicler in *Roteiro da Primeira Viagem de Vasco da Gama* (*Journal of the First Voyage of Vasco da Gama*), the route took da Gama's flotilla to Cape Verde for fresh fruit, vegetables, and water. Down Africa's western shore, he observed natives plying torches to smoke out bees before robbing the hive of honey.

In January 1498, da Gama noted in his crew swollen extremities, rank breath, and ulcerated gums extending over teeth—the symptoms of scurvy, a disease unknown to Iberians and caused by a deficiency of vitamin C. Beached at St. Helena Bay in South Africa in November, he remarked on natives who ate only herbs, gazelles, seals, and whales but made no connection between recovery from scurvy and the provisioning of his men with a variety of fruit. In exchange for trinkets, a tribesman at the Cape of Good Hope supplied the sailors with an ox for roasting, a treat to men overfed on salted meat. Da Gama arrived on the eastern side of South Africa, during Christmas 1497, and named the place Natal, the Portuguese term for Christ's birth. At Mozambique in March 1498, the Portuguese offered their limited trade goods and had to settle for pigeons, vegetables, and fruit, which also relieved scurvy.

Pirate and Legate

On the route north to Kenya, da Gama fired cannon on Mozambique in retort to Muslims who refused to fill his water tanks. The admiral stoked his anger against Muslims. As he sailed for Mombasa and Malindi, Kenya, he attacked and raided three Arab merchant ships for gold and silver.

He accepted from Indian Hindu sailors gifts of cloves, ginger, nutmeg, and pepper but puzzled over their rejection of beef. In token of gifts of fruit and sheep, da Gama invited the king of Malindi aboard the *São Gabriel* and served him conserves, marmalade, sweets, bottles of preserved almonds, and cured olives, the most pleasing of the dishes. The Indians rejected gold carafes of wine, with which they were not familiar. The repast concluded with ritual hand and mouth washing from heavy gilt basins and ewers. Because the vessels had served a king, da Gama indicated that no commoner could ever use them. The king accepted them as gifts. Upon the Portuguese departure on April 24, the king sent 12 compact water tanks sewed tight with coir (coconut husk fiber) and caulked with pitch.

Arriving at Calicut (Kozhikode, in southwest India) on May 20, 1498, Admiral da Gama found West Indian markets stocked with inexpensive citrus fruit, dates, melons, dairy products, rice, and palm wine. His chronicler remarked on nan, thin cakes of unleavened bread baked in ash.

The admiral revealed his Portuguese nationality, which aroused enmity in the competitive Arabs. He received from the king fruits resembling figs and melons and a container of betel nut, which his people chewed like gum for a soothing effect. Da Gama insulted the king by presenting paltry gifts—casks of honey, oil, and sugar—and by failing to pay harbor tolls and duties with gold, the usual exchange medium.

Food helped to break the cultural impasse. A gift of Portuguese wheat stirred the attention of the king, who asked for a ship's cook to explain the use of flour in making biscuits. In exchange, the king dispatched cauldrons of rice, roasted mutton and stuffed poultry, butter, coconuts, figs, nan, and sugar to the fleet. Da Gama won the king's trust by eating Indian food without exhibiting fear of poisoning and reciprocated with a gift of pear preserves and a silver-gilt fork. Because the king insisted that traders deal honestly with the Portuguese, the crew bartered for a small barrel full of spices worth more than 60 times the value of the Portuguese offerings.

Toward Empire

On the homeward route, da Gama lost 116 of his crew of 170 to scurvy and tuberculosis. In March 1499, he paused at Mossel Bay, South Africa, to salt enough anchovies, penguins, and seals to supply the crew with meat. He reached Lisbon in July 1499, having negotiated a commercial agreement to trade with India in cinnamon, cloves, gold, and pearls. King Manuel rewarded da Gama with a coin struck in his honor.

The navigator's piracy and ruthlessness on the second voyage established his reputation as a freebooter. He and his crew of 800 bombarded Calicut in 1502 and mutilated Hindu fishermen. At Madayi, he captured a shipload of 400 Muslim pilgrims, locked them in the hold, and observed men, women, and children through a porthole as he burned them to death. The cruel gesture displayed to Arabs that the Portuguese intended to control the sea route to Asian riches.

Da Gama's first two ventures set Portugal on the way toward empire through the Portuguese East India Company, which monopolized commerce in India's food products. He returned to Lisbon on November 10, 1503, with his ten merchantmen and five warships laden with Asian goods. At Cananor, he left a factor and warehouse to deal in coconuts, dried fish, honey, oil, rice, and sugar and dismayed the Muslim traders by ending their monopoly in pepper and drugs.

On a third voyage, in 1524, da Gama traveled under a new title, viceroy of India, and set a grand table for welcoming dignitaries. Before he died of malaria at Goa on December 24, 1524, he established a Portuguese cinnamon monopoly with Ceylon. From his introduction of Portugal to East Africa and India came ingredients of Portuguese cuisine—coriander, curry, ginger, pepper, yams, and sweet oranges, the basis of Iberian marmalade.

See also: Coconut; House of India; Maritime Trade Routes; Portuguese East India Company.

Further Reading

Ames, Glenn Joseph, ed. *Em Nome de Deus: The Journal of the First Voyage of Vasco da Gama to India, 1497–1499.* Boston: Brill, 2009.
———. *Vasco da Gama: Renaissance Crusader.* New York: Pearson/Longman, 2005.
Disney, Anthony, and Emily Booth, eds. *Vasco da Gama and the Linking of Europe and Asia.* New York: Oxford University Press, 2001.

Genetically Modified Food

By reordering the essential material that establishes the uniqueness of a plant or animal, technologists genetically modify ova and seeds. The Green Revolution, a post–World War II scientific initiative that boosted the world's agrarian yield, introduced manipulation of the very fount of nourishment.

From its inception, genetic modification (GM), a humanitarian bioproject, raised controversy among those who feared bioengineering and its effects on the world's food supply, human health, and the environment. Nonetheless, innovators, cognizant of the potential benefits, refused to be stymied by such objections. By 1973, the first GM bacteria proved the feasibility of engineering animal life. Subsequent improvements increased the size of wheat grains and lengthened the shelf life of melons and tomatoes. The first successes opened the way to enabling plants and animals to resist fungus, nematodes, and virus and to withstand drought, frost, and saline soil.

For centuries, hybridizing through traditional breeding processes upgraded the bulk and productivity of crops and animals. New in world history, the use of recombinant DNA by Bayer, DuPont, Monsanto, and Syngenta engineered rapid, controlled change. Poised for breakthroughs in biological restructuring, the world's food analysts proposed distributing hepatitis B vaccines in bananas and goat's milk and producing mature carp and salmon at 30 times the normal rate of growth. Coffee researchers scrambled to isolate the caffeine gene to produce a naturally decaffeinated transgenic coffee bean. Also on the prospectus for alteration were the nutrition and shelf stability of the most perishable produce—alfalfa, apples, bananas, canola, corn, cottonseed, papaya, soy, squash, strawberries, and tomatoes.

Opposition to Change

On the negative side, institutional and commercial cooks feared lawsuits from patrons who suffered ill effects from "Frankenfoods" on blood, kidneys, and liver and on the unborn. Their concerns rallied an all-star list of complainants against big business, big science, and designer foods: Bioengineering Action Network (BAN), Center for Food Safety, Council for Responsible Genetics, The Ecologist, Ending Destructive Genetic Engineering, Environmental Defense Fund, Food First!, Friends of the Earth, GE Food Alert, GE-FREE-LA, genetiX snowball, GeneWatch, Greenpeace USA, Grocery Manufacturers of America, Hexterminators, Mothers for Natural Law, Public Interest Research Groups, Rural Advancement Foundation International, A Seed, Seize the Day!, Sierra Club, Totnes Genetics Group, and Union of Concerned Scientists. Concern for the future of agriculture and nutrition

At a Monsanto Company research field in Brazil, two genetically engineered soybean plants, one designed to tolerate a company herbicide and the other to provide in-seed protection from insects, grow in adjacent rows. *(Bloomberg/Getty Images)*

spawned defiance on both sides of the issue and fueled the Campaign to Label Genetically Engineered Food and to remove altered food from school lunch programs.

In the United States on September 22, 2000, Kraft Foods, a subsidiary of Philip Morris, recalled $10 million worth of tortillas, snack chips, and taco shells from the shelves of Albertson's, Food Lion, Kroger, IGA, Safeway, and Walmart stores. The summons resulted after a consumer group, Genetically Engineered Food Alert, warned that Mexican bakers used corn adulterated with Cry9C, a protein that kills corn borers. According to the U.S. Food and Drug Administration (FDA), the grain, marketed under the name StarLink by Aventis CropScience of Raleigh, North Carolina, violated federal law, which prohibited any food contaminant that had not received FDA approval.

Ecofeminist Vandana Shiva of the Research Foundation for Science, Technology, and Natural Resource Policy in the Himalayan foothills of India put a humanistic spin on the worth of genetic modification. She maintained that peasant women were more trustworthy than scientists looking to claim a higher yield. In her book *Stolen Harvest: The Hijacking of the Global Food Supply* (2000), Shiva pointed out that miracle seeds and chemical fertilizers introduced into the subcontinent in the 1960s injured the economy, destroying traditional farms and making crop growers dependent on expensive chemicals. She also questioned the motives of multinational firms that patented India's neem tree and basmati rice. She blamed chemical companies for monopolizing food by "[appropriating] the indigenous agricultural products that are in the hands of the women of those nations and claim them as their exclusive inventions."

In the Philippines, Neth Daño, executive director of the Southeast Asia Regional Institute for Community Education, substantiated Shiva's claims with her own backlash against GM foods. In harmony with the Network Opposed to Genetically Modified Organisms (NO GMOs), she began urging the public in 1998 to stop the sale of bioengineered foods in the island chain, where Monsanto began trials of altered corn two years later.

A compatriot in Rio Grande do Sul, Brazil, Maria José Guazzelli of Centro Ecológico, warned farmers and government authorities that programs involving genetic alteration of foodstuffs had been in operation for two decades. In her opinion, the result might be biological pollutants that could destroy existing food diversity. The immediate benefit of her campaign promoted purer foods from Brazil to compete in the world market against suspect GM goods from the United States. By mid-2001, however, Brazil teetered toward allowing genetically altered seed, which its black market distributed.

Pro-GM forces looked beyond local qualms to an attainable upgrade in human survivability in oppressed locales, a reason for the United Nations' support of the biotech industry. Altruists and moralists in support of GM declared that abandoning biotechnology at this stage of the world's development would condemn overpopulated regions to certain death from famine and malnutrition. Addressing the impact that genetically altered seed can have on lifeways, Kenyan agronomist Florence Wambugu explained the need for herbicide-resistant crops currently overrun with witchweed (*Striga asiatica*), a parasitic plant that strangles corn roots:

> We could liberate so many people if our crops were resistant to herbicides that we could then spray on the surrounding weeds. Weeding enslaves Africans; it keeps children from school.

Rather than allow more millions in India and China to atrophy from malnutrition, the fearful demanded immediate fortified riziculture among the world's have-nots. As of 2000, 25 percent of American cornfields produced altered grain; in supermarkets, 70 percent of processed foods contained transgenic corn and soybeans. In January 2000, 130 concerned nations inked the Cartagena Protocol on Biosafety, forcing exporters to request permission to ship altered seeds and to label them accordingly.

Families may have the last word on what foods they buy and serve to their children. As of 2001, shoppers could buy GM beets, canola, corn, peanuts, peppers, potatoes, soybeans, sunflowers, and tomatoes. To halt their sale and use, protests, food alerts, Internet blitzes, and marches of homemakers and parents of infants and toddlers in strollers induced such food processors as Frito-Lay, Gerber, Kellogg, McDonald's, and Nestlé to abandon modified ingredients and maneuvered the European Union into imposing a moratorium on GM seeds.

Prospects

Despite public and media outcry, critics of futuristic foods failed to squelch the enthusiasm of biotechnologists. The announcement in 2001 of the world's first tomato that can grow in salty water offered a potential solution to a pressing agrarian problem. According to Eduardo Blumwald of the University of California at Davis, the plant could flourish in China, the Indian subcontinent, and the western United States to produce fruit that suffers no alteration in taste. The breakthrough could lead to more hybrid food plants that grow in salt-damaged cropland. In the future, by shifting the delivery of nutrients from emergency workers to home shoppers, food engi-

neers hoped to significantly reduce world hunger among 3 billion rice-dependent people.

In 2003, AquaBounty Farms of Waltham, Massachusetts, predicted the sale of the first chinook salmon raised on growth hormones that enabled it to grow to 8 pounds (3.6 kilograms) in 18 months. To end anemia in some 2 billion people, biochemist Peter Beyer enhanced Golden Rice with the beta-carotene from daffodils and the *Erwinia uredovora* bacterium, which bolstered the diet with iron; this enhancement also prevented child blindness from related vitamin A deficiency. Meanwhile, British and Japanese scientists pondered similar enrichment of beans, cassava, corn, tomatoes, and wheat, all staples with the potential to curtail malnutrition. In 2006, the engineering of swine with omega-3 fatty acids and with phosphorus-absorbing genes increased nutritional value, while lowering the phosphorus content of pig wastes. Envious growers in have-not nations complained that foodstuffs of the industrialized world dominated research to the detriment of indigenous cowpeas, millet, and teff.

By 2011, grocers were stocking GM apples, bananas, beets, kiwi, lettuce, strawberries, sugarcane, and zucchini as well as flounder, tilapia, and trout, both fresh and in processed foods. The Chinese announced a herd of transgenic dairy cows that produced milk as nutritious as human breast milk. Canadian and U.S. produce carried no warning, but GM foods in Australia, the European Union, Japan, and Malaysia bore labels indicating genetic alteration. At the same time, an increasing number of packaged foods featured non-GM ingredients.

Proponents continue to battle for modification to relieve malnutrition and to augment profitability for world farms. Opponents claim that the outcrossing of unnatural seeds by wind, bees, and birds is already compromising crops grown from pure seed. In August 2011, anti-GM vandals destroyed GM wheat warehoused for distribution to victims of famine in Somalia. The face-off between forces for and against transgenic food brought into focus the reality of hunger and the race to produce enough food for all.

See also: Biopiracy; Ecofeminism; Hormones in Food; Industrial Food Processing; Seed Trade.

Further Reading

"Can Biotech Food Cure World Hunger?" *The New York Times,* October 26, 2009.

Freedman, Jeri. *Genetically Modified Food: How Biotechnology Is Changing What We Eat.* New York: Rosen, 2009.

Henningfeld, Diane Andrews, ed. *Genetically Modified Food.* Detroit, MI: Greenhaven, 2009.

Rees, Andy. *Genetically Modified Food: A Short Guide for the Confused.* Ann Arbor, MI: Pluto, 2006.

Skancke, Jennifer L., ed. *Genetically Modified Food.* Detroit, MI: Greenhaven, 2009.

Gourmet Cuisine

The cultural epitome of fine food and beverage, gourmet cuisine satisfies refined consumers with the best in dining while enhancing social status. Gourmet cuisine, which got its start in the 1700s with the rise of commercial eateries, received its first clarification by food critic Grimod de la Reynière, who published a guide to Paris restaurants in 1803 and throughout the Napoleonic era. The term applies to sophisticated fad foods, such as raspberry blini and *gâteau chocolat au rhum,* esteemed for their rarity and price, as well as to food admired by discriminating arbiters of taste at raw juice shops and sushi bars. As a show of savoir faire, gourmets attend wine and cheese tastings in search of a delicious find or order Grand Marnier soufflé, roast guinea fowl, or anything flambé served with freshly ground pepper.

In 1941, Earle R. MacAusland's *Gourmet: The Magazine of Good Living,* forerunner of *Bon Appétit, Food & Wine,* and *Saveur,* published up-to-the-minute commentary on restaurants for educated readers, offering taste thrills and recipes by Elizabeth David and Jane Grigson. After the rationing and shortages of World War II, color photos pictured the good life as a porterhouse or T-bone steak. Gourmands upped the appeal by demanding Chateaubriand, carved at the table by an expert and plated with high drama. European favorites permeated menus with bouillabaisse, brioche, *coquilles St. Jacques,* and *pollo alla cacciatora.* Cooking schools and articles by M.F.K. Fisher taught neophyte gourmets how to debone a quail and hand-dip chocolates.

In the 1950s, gourmet food co-ops formed among foodies who welcomed imported exotica or wild fare and experimented with innovative ways of cooking favorites, such as chocolate fondue and plank-grilled salmon with wild rice. Over the next decades, affluent families generated enough cash to fund dining out and shopping at specialty stores for items recommended by food mavens James Beard and Julia Child or advertised under such toney brand names as Godiva, Häagen-Dazs, King Arthur Flour, and Yoplait. In the 1970s, gourmet cuisine abandoned cultic French crepes and beurre blanc for Chinese egg rolls, pad thai, and Japanese dishes stir-fried in a wok from enoki mushrooms, snow peas, and tofu. Details added panache, as with veal in pink peppercorn sauce. The shift from chafing dishes, Bundt pans, and electric skillets required re-equipping kitchens with Chinese cleavers and bamboo tongs and skewers from Williams-Sonoma.

The emergence of California cuisine and Tex-Mex introduced to 1980s yuppies a new vocabulary, including Cuisinart food processors, Jelly Belly jelly beans, mano and metate, *pico de gallo,* skirt steak, and whole bean coffee ground and prepared in a Krups machine. Pantry items followed the trends, with Hunt-Wesson's Blue Plate Foods, Orville Redenbacher's popcorn, and Paul Newman's dressings and marinara. The cognoscenti stocked goat cheese and kefir, frisée and hearts of palm, mesclun lettuce, and mesquite for savory grilling.

Televised demonstrations spoke casually of crème fraîche, panko crumbs, roasted peppers, squash blossoms, and sun-dried tomatoes in garlic oil as though they were everyday purchases. Chef Craig Claiborne redefined the term *gourmet* with his recipes, which featured haute cuisine without the guilt; Graham Kerr deglamorized the concept with his television show *The Galloping Gourmet.*

A shift away from red meat and to farmer's markets sent gourmet locavores in search of the modish heirloom potatoes served at Chez Panisse in Berkeley, California, and the wood-fired pizzas popularized by the Austrian-born California chef and restaurateur Wolfgang Puck. The desire to stay current quickly discarded pretentious recipes involving espresso powder, honey mustard, pineapple chutney, and pomegranate juice but popularized bok choy, cage-laid eggs, champagne grapes, couscous, orzo pasta, and Vietnamese coriander. At the same time that *gourmet* began to disappear from restaurant names, teens made their own splash in the early twenty-first century by gravitating toward veganism. Internet shopping simplified the updating of the domestic kitchen with the latest implements and ingredients necessary to gourmet cuisine.

See also: Beard, James; Child, Julia; David, Elizabeth; Exotic Food Clubs; Nouvelle Cuisine; Travel Food.

Further Reading

Inglis, David, and Debra Gimlin. *The Globalization of Food.* New York: Berg, 2009.

Johnston, Josée, and Shyon Baumann. *Foodies: Democracy and Distinction in the Gourmet Foodscape.* New York: Routledge, 2010.

Lovegren, Sylvia. *Fashionable Food: Seven Decades of Food Fads.* Chicago: University of Chicago Press, 2005.

Reichl, Ruth, ed. *The Gourmet Cookbook.* New York: Houghton Mifflin, 2004.

Greek Diet and Cuisine, Ancient

From 6000 B.C.E., the ancient Greeks allied notions of food and nourishment with concepts of godhood and piety. Because the goddess Demeter bestowed bread and Dionysus provided grapes for wine, Greeks honored food through ritual, hymns, and sacred dance.

The Mediterranean triad—grain, grapes, and olives—got its start in 3000 B.C.E. with the importation of wine making from Asia. Unlike other oenophiles of the Mediterranean world, the Greeks preferred sweet drinks made from overripe grapes or raisins. To shield the vintage from oxidation, vintners produced retsina, a resinated drink that mainland Greeks took on their travels to the Crimea, Cyprus, Dalmatia, France, Italy, Lesbos, Rhodes, and Sicily.

Around 2000 B.C.E., the orchardists of Crete first cultivated the olive tree. Its culture passed to the mainland in 1700 B.C.E. Within four centuries, the olive and its oil became dietary staples. Growers spread hides under the trees and beat the limbs with sticks to dislodge the fruit. After air-drying the olives, preservers salted and pressed them into clay jars for curing. The presentation of olive oil marked special occasions, notably as a prize for the winning charioteer.

Because of the sanctity of the olive grove and its basis of the mainland economy, farmers gave insufficient acreage to barley and wheat. Athenians had to import some 70 percent of their grain from as far away as Syria and the Black Sea and from Greek colonies in Ionia, Magna Graecia, Massalia, North Africa, Spain, Syracusa, and Thrace. Historians surmise that the interruption of the Peloponnesian grain trade caused the rift with Troy in 1200 B.C.E. that poets romanticized as the Trojan War.

As dramatized in Homer's *Iliad* (ca. 800 B.C.E.), wearied soldiers partook of a Pramnian wine posset blended with barley and honey and topped with grated goat cheese. The hero Achilles took the time to prepare baskets of bread, roasted mutton, and wine for the elderly Trojan King Priam, who humbled himself to beg for the corpse of Prince Hector. In the *Odyssey* (ca. 750 B.C.E.), Homer omitted fish from the classical diet and pictured grain as the source of human marrow. The farmer-poet Hesiod considered grain a holy gift from Demeter to Greek heroes. In *Works and Days* (700 B.C.E.), he linked emmer wheat with *bíos* (life) and testified to the centrality of *maza* (barley) porridge or biscuit, which dominated 70 percent of dietary intake. To spread welcome at table, hosts distributed biscuits and flatbread in wicker baskets.

In the wake of Alexander's forays into Asia that preceded the Hellenistic era, the unleavened baked goods of the classical era changed to loaves and rolls. By importing Egyptian knowledge of leavening in the fourth century B.C.E., Greek bakers learned to make risen loaves.

Flavoring the Menu

An adjunct to wheat, honey provided a natural sweetener, dietary aid, funerary gift, and medicine for dressing wounds, a purpose it shared with butter. Beekeepers fed their hives with the flowers of sage, an herb treasured for its curative powers. With top-quality honey from Mount Hymettus, east of Athens, cooks made meat sauces, wine sweeteners, and cakes and pastries. For salads of beet greens, cabbage, and lettuce, cooks blended a traditional dressing, *oximeli,* an emulsion of honey with vinegar. In worship of Demeter, all Athenians, regardless of station, processed to Eleusis each August to offer honeyed loaves at the Celebration of the Bread, an agrarian ritual.

Bakers contributed flavor to specialty breads and entrées with caraway, coriander, fennel, garlic, *garós* (fish sauce), mint, and rosemary. From Sumer, the Greeks imported thyme, an aphrodisiac; from Crete they imported saffron, a royal herb. Herbs also combined well with lemon juice and sea salt to add subtlety to lamb and vegetable stews. Farther north in Boeotia and Thessaly, more fertile land provided a more varied diet than that of Athens and Sparta. The addition of Cypriot capers to the Greek diet provided savory tight buds for pickling with onions to serve as appetizers or chopped toppings to add zing to rural dinners of beans and peas and cups of goat's milk.

The Greek Table

From prehistory, daily meals fit significant movements of the sun: a light meal at *áriston* (first light), a hot meal at *deipnon* (midday), and a large dinner at *vesperna* (sundown). Kitchenware consisted of iron spits and simple clay hearth cauldrons, domes for baking bread rings, and jars for carrying water from the community well. Cooks ground herbs and forcemeat with salt in mortars and sizzled calamari and small fish on clay *plaki* (griddles). From plain beginnings, the Greeks developed cookery to an art. They invented chef's techniques such as dusting bowls and loaf pans with poppy and sesame seeds and stuffing dough and songbirds with pureed meat and herbed vegetables.

A full menu began with hors d'oeuvres as ordinary as olives and stuffed grape leaves and as unusual as cicadas and grasshoppers, sea urchins, and hyacinth bulbs. The main course of roasted meat included organ meats boiled into a pudding. The anticipated dessert course

An amphora dating to the late sixth century B.C.E. depicts Dionysus, the Greek god of wine, the grape harvest, and revelry. Wine, olive oil, and barley provided ancient Greece with dietary staples and economic mainstays. *(Dea/G. Dagli Orti/De Agostini/Getty Images)*

Recipe: Marinated Hyacinth Bulbs

Soak 1 pound of hyacinth bulbs in water for one hour. Trim the top of each bulb, dry the outer covering, and core the bottom. Parboil in water and drain. Simmer in 1 cup of fresh water and 1 tablespoon each of sea salt and red wine vinegar for 45 minutes and drain thoroughly. Pack bulbs in glass containers and cover with vinegar. Serve the bulbs over lentil soup or with other appetizers seasoned with olive oil and snipped chives.

ranged from cookies and sweet rolls to fruit fritters and custard. In "Banquet" (ca. 450 B.C.E.), the poet Philoxenos described a specialty, cheesecake, made with curdled milk and honey. After-dinner wine service accompanied dishes of fruit and nuts and small honey cakes.

After Alexander the Great's penetration of the Middle East, Persia, and India in 323 B.C.E., most Greeks ridiculed as Persian degeneracy the Theban importation of fads in unprecedented food preparation. Cooks from the Sicilian colonies earned gibes for their dainty spread of multiple delicacies. To provision the pantry, growers in Hellenistic Greece added to pear and plum orchards new tree fruits—apricots, carob, citron, jujube, and pistachios. Market dealers traded Greek oils and wines for asafetida, cardamom, cassia, cinnamon, cloves, fenugreek, ginger, myrrh, nutmeg, and pepper as well as rice from the East. Hearty Macedonian gorging encouraged wild game in Greek menus and open-faced sandwiches made from flatbread topped with meat slices.

Foodways

Greek food service affected all life events, including births and funerals. On departure to the military, *epheboi* (young recruits) packed their own grain rations, which they supplemented on the march with dried fish or meat and salted relishes. Spartans underfed young boys to encourage guile in stealing food. Men's clubs and academic gatherings held monthly dinner meetings. Theatergoers took intermissions from all-day performances by buying snacks and drinks from vendors.

Women lived more constrained lives. Matrons dined at home. Adult women ate together, apart from men and children. Before reclining on dining couches, devout females began the meal with drops of wine in tribute to the gods. For weddings, Greek ritual began with the wedding party banqueting with the bride's family. The mother of the bride extolled Hestia, goddess of the hearth and regeneration, as the heart and shield of the home. The bride presented the groom her own flatbread, evidence of her

kitchen skill. She carried a wreath of marjoram, a symbol of contentment, and encircled the groom's household fire to avert evil and sanctify her role as wife and mother. Guests tossed dried figs and nuts as a blessing from nature on monogamy.

The Greeks judged the moral probity of citizens by their avoidance of waste and their generous dinner invitations to strangers. Aristophanes' stage comedies ridiculed poor urbanites and soldiers as eaters of onions, *palafi* (fig cakes), and plain flatbread, while elevating the wealthy for a diet including fish, a food for the elite.

Each god accepted a particular sacrificial meat, always from a herd animal. The chef supervised distinctive occasions in the sanctuaries at Delphi and the Poseideia feasts at Delos. On the holy island of Delos, the Magnesians held the franchise for supplying the necessities of hospitality during annual sacrifices. The banquet servers at the Temple of Apollo tested new recipes and rare delicacies and adopted innovations for teaching to apprentices. Strict regulations controlled the age and condition of the selected beast and its slaughter, cooking, and distribution of the meat. The smoke from altar fires bore the smell of roasted flesh to the gods. Vegetarians risked their position in society by refusing to take part.

Food Philosophy

For the sake of health and wellness, Greek physicians associated proper diet with exercise, bathing, and hygiene as keys to survival and the cure for anemia and sickness. In the sixth century B.C.E., the Pythagorean cult invented dietetics, a science that Herodicus of Selymbria, the father of sports medicine, advanced for the athlete's training table before the Olympic Games. As interest in diet expanded, treatises commented on the daily needs of ordinary people. Hippocrates' *De Medicina Vetere* (*On Ancient Medicine,* ca. 390 B.C.E.) recommended pure drinking water and a balance of food textures—solids, emulsions, and liquids.

Around 450 B.C.E., culinary work advanced to a profession. The slave cook managed a range of recipes for the home kitchen. Large households augmented daily cookery with the work of specialists, who concocted beverages, jam, and pastry. Cooks and caterers from around the known world vied for elite positions. Their names attached to signature dishes: Agis of Rhodes with grilled fish, Aphthonetos with sausage, Eusthenes with lentils, Lamprias of Sparta with brown sauce made from a roux, and Nereus of Chios with steamed eel. Chariades of Athens refurbished the traditional Greek *thríon,* fig leaves stuffed with bacon, cheese, eggs, and milk, by serving it with an egg white omelette. Moschion opened Athens's first lunchroom. Ariston topped others in the elegance of his dinner planning.

Undergirding the concept of the bountiful table, the myths of Dionysus pictured him wandering the Earth in disguise to test human generosity. To welcome pilgrims at sacred sites, publicans operated *xenodocheia* (inns) and served group meals at banquet halls. For political reasons, Cimon of Athens maintained open house for Greeks and foreign visitors and stocked bath and clothing items and tableware to incorporate the visitor into household fellowship. Both host and guest kept the peace and exchanged handshakes, vows of nonviolence, and ritual gifts as prefaces to friendship, the Greeks' most treasured form of human relationships. As warnings to the unwary, drama, myths, and stories illustrated the dangers of preying on guests or hosts, notably, Menelaus's proper welcome to Paris, the Trojan prince, who abducted Menelaus's wife, Helen of Troy. Homer's *Odyssey* turned boorish behavior into motivation for mass slaughter after the wandering ruler returned and found his wife beset by wooers who lounged about his court and demanded hospitality. In fealty to the laws of Zeus, the private host extended hospitality in emulation of public banquets honoring visiting dignitaries.

The Greek Way

As trends shifted toward ostentation, conservatives defended the plain fare of their ancestors. Plato scorned Sicilian habits of heavy saucing and accused colonial Greeks of gluttony and sexual excess. Greco-Syracusan poet Archestratus's *Hedypatheia* (*Life of Luxury,* ca. 350 B.C.E.) advocated a guest list limited to five people and the service of the freshest fish and vegetables in bitesized pieces for casual picking up in one hand or scooping up with bread. Drawing on food experiences in 50 ports, he valued geese, pig's womb, and unsauced rabbit for entrées and pitied the poor for having no more variety than beans and chickpeas, apples, and dried figs. His unadorned recipes called for herbs and cheese sauce only to rejuvenate a poor choice of fish or one eaten out of season.

Greek table customs separated dining from the *symposion* (drinking), a subject that Athenaeus of Naucratis covered in his 15-volume *Deipnosophistae* (*The Banquet Philosophers,* ca. 190 C.E.). The sharing of food at a banquet emulated the gods of Mount Olympus, who consumed ambrosia and nectar while enjoying table talk and music. After the removal of platters from service, servants passed the *krater* (wine bowl) and pitchers of water for mixing wine with one-fourth to one-half water. During the drinking, diners continued to pass small plates of bar food, varying from nuts and olives to grasshoppers and peas.

Inebriates lost status by imbibing the sacred wine of Dionysus to excess and by behaving in an uncivilized public display, which sober Greeks linked with insanity. As a mark of civility and social order, according to the descriptions of Aristotle, Plato, and Theophrastus, dignified citizens observed manners suited to family and friends as well as to the *xénos* (visitor).

See also: Cereal; Grilling; Poisonous Foods; Poultry; Religion and Food; Theophrastus; Trading Vessels; Veganism; Vegetarianism; Wine; Yeast.

Further Reading

Adamson, Melitta Weiss, ed. *Regional Cuisines of Medieval Europe: A Book of Essays.* New York: Routledge, 2002.

Fraser, Evan D.G., and Andrew Rimas. *Empires of Food: Feast, Famine, and the Rise and Fall of Civilizations.* New York: Simon & Schuster, 2010.

Kaufman, Cathy K. *Cooking in Ancient Civilizations.* Westport, CT: Greenwood, 2006.

Martin, Thomas R. *Ancient Greece: From Prehistoric to Hellenistic Times.* New Haven, CT: Yale University Press, 2000.

Greenhouse Horticulture

An artificial means of trapping the sun's heat in the atmosphere of a transparent structure, greenhouse horticulture extends the growing season. Farming under glass forces the propagation of warm weather vegetables and fruits in cold climes from a free energy source.

The Romans introduced the forerunner of the glasshouse, or greenhouse, and heated grapevines and peach trees with bronze hot water pipes and flues that channeled heat from rotting manure. In 30 C.E., Tiberius demanded Armenian gherkins for his meals. Palace gardeners accommodated him by planting seeds in wheelbarrows to place in the sun or by growing vines under sheets of mica or oiled canvas.

In the decades preceding the Italian Renaissance, planters of the first indoor gardens grew tropical exotica and curative plants brought by voyagers from global travels. The concept of frost-free ecosystems appealed to growers in Sicily, the Vatican, Belgium, and the British Isles. In North Africa, the American tropics, China, and Japan, cool houses equipped with automatic misters protected temperate vegetables and fruits from dry winds, dust storms, and sun scorch. Experimenters advanced the notion of producing vegetables out of season by controlling ventilation to facilitate pollination and discourage pests. French botanist Jules Charles de L'Ecluse provided Leiden, Holland, with a greenhouse in 1599 to grow herbs and tamarind, which yielded pulp for a medicinal beverage to treat malaria and scurvy.

Luxuries under Glass

The French and Germans applied hothouse horticulture to lemons, oranges, and pineapples, which they grew in orangeries and pineries. Visitors to the French royal palace at Versailles admired the massive berry and fruit garden of Louis XIV. To nurture the 350 orange trees of Prince Friedrich V at Heidelberg Castle, in 1619, French engineer Salomon de Caus constructed a shelter with a demountable roof and wooden shutters over four furnaces. Because of low solar radiation, English apothecaries in Chelsea emulated the Heidelburg greenhouse in 1684 with a garden of curative bay leaves and myrtle berries under an opaque roof. To protect seedlings from frost, workers heaped embers in a floor pit.

Improvements to glass and angling techniques resulted in model greenhouses and herbaria in London, Munich, and New York. In Enoshima, Japan, Samuel Cocking planted a botanical garden displaying 165 species. In Boston, Huguenot refugee Andrew Faneuil established a fruit garden in 1737, a forerunner of George Washington's pineapple garden under glass at Mount Vernon and of Tudor Place, constructed for Thomas and Martha Custis Peter in Georgetown, a neighborhood of Washington, D.C., in 1805.

Steam heat reduced the complexities of heating with coal and wood furnaces. One successful glass-and-iron experiment at Kew Gardens outside London began in 1849. The conservatories housed a range of foodstuffs from leeks and turnips to chestnut trees and fruit groves. In 1850, the Dutch began growing grapes under glass in Westland. The addition of under-floor furnaces and mechanical window closing increased productivity of a luxury table grape variety. By 1855, professional greenhouse engineer Frederic A. Lord of Buffalo, New York, erected curvilinear lean-tos and sunrooms to suit individual sites and enhance professional truck gardening.

More Garden in a Smaller Space

Greenhouse horticulture bore new meaning in urban spaces. In 1915, Gilbert Ellis Bailey invented the concept of vertical farming in skyscraper greenhouses that stacked artificial ecosystems on multiple floors. By increasing the productivity of acreage, hermetically sealed gardens promised food for urban areas. Bailey envisioned delivery of fresh goods to neighborhoods without the cost and delay of overland or rail transportation. The invention of polyvinyl chloride in 1920 reduced the weight and construction cost of innovative structures, some erected atop tall buildings. The concept of maximizing food growth in limited areas appealed to small nations, particularly Holland and Israel.

Growers in Central America, Colombia, Kenya, and Mexico adopted greenhouse gardening as a source of exports. In the United States and Canada, the tomato dominated greenhouse horticulture, by which growers could schedule fruiting and packing and negotiate sale of their produce in advance of planting. In Pittsburgh in 1926, the H.J. Heinz Company selected tomato seeds to grow in greenhouses for its ketchup recipe. The company farmed out plants to contractors who grew the seedlings to maturity and returned ripe fruit high in viscosity, solids, and pectin.

Post–World War II competition in the vegetable and fruit market forced northwestern Europeans to devise new ways to challenge the influx of foods from the Mediterranean. By the 1950s, hybrid cultivars, drip irrigation, recirculated water, acrylic tunnels, and plastic film for home quonset huts increased possibilities for the hobby gardener and university research centers. In addition, biothermal systems reduced the cost of heating by redirecting the methane exuded by decomposing garbage, manure, and vegetable waste. Enclosed ecosystems profited from sequential plantings, which offered restaurants a year-round supply of salad greens and summer vegetables. In Newfoundland, proponents of the local food movement began promoting the economy by harvesting fresh greenhouse produce to sell at farmer's markets and to inns and restaurants.

Small businesses fed the home gardener's need for vegetable transplants, notably asparagus crowns, onion sets, and broccoli, cabbage, cucumber, melon, pepper, and tomato plants. In the 1970s, Tokyo greenhouses yielded marketable cucumbers, eggplant, grapes, oranges, pears, peppers, and tomatoes. In the mid-1980s, Japan led the world in greenhouse use, at 67,499 acres (27,337 hectares), as contrasted with 42,000 acres (17,000 hectares) in Italy and 32,420 acres (13,130 hectares) in China.

High-Tech Greenhouses

In 1999, ecologist Dickson Despommier at Columbia University expanded on the seasonless garden by allying hydroponics and aeroponics. His variants of in-ground planting yielded beans, corn, herbs, lettuce, and potatoes via the Genesis system, a soilless root enclosure misted with water and nutrients. Trellises relieved root structures of the weight of leaves and fruit. The National Aeronautics and Space Administration (NASA) developed the concept as a cost-efficient means of growing disease-free produce in the low gravity of space stations.

Late in the twentieth century, the geodesic dome altered the boxy glasshouses of the past with latticing that evenly distributed thinner surfaces. In one model, the Plexiglas and aluminum Climatron in the Missouri Botanical Gardens of St. Louis, gardeners tend 400 plant varieties, including bananas, cacao, cassava, chicle, coffee, palms, pineapple trees, rice, and vanilla. The world's largest greenhouse, the Eden Project, opened in Cornwall, England, in 2000. In a complex of plastic domes, engineers reproduced global climate zones.

Complementing the hops, lavender, medicinal plants, sunflowers, and tea of the outdoor garden, the Mediterranean biome produces grapes and olives. Desert and tropical sectors replicate the food-growing atmosphere of the hottest climes.

See also: Agriculture; Local Food Movement; Plant Disease and Prevention; Restaurants.

Further Reading

Hanan, Joe J. *Greenhouses: Advanced Technology for Protected Horticulture.* Boca Raton, FL: CRC, 1997.

Sonneveld, Cees, and Wim Voogt. *Plant Nutrition of Greenhouse Crops.* New York: Springer, 2009.

Van Straten, Gerrit, E.J. van Henten, L.G. van Willigenburg, and R.J.C. van Ooteghem. *Optimal Control of Greenhouse Cultivation.* Boca Raton, FL: CRC, 2011.

Grilling

The history of grilling parallels the control of fire, a crude method of exposing raw foods to flame that remains a culinary favorite to the present day. After 498,000 B.C.E., humans advanced methods of bringing food and flame together immediately after the hunt. The human direction of heat and light broadened activities to after-dark cookery, which extended the usability of raw game. To enhance the reach and grasp of human fingers, inventors shaped the long fork and tongs. Fire cookery provided hunter-gatherers with additional calories from easily chewed meals to sustain humankind during the initial stages of settled life. The circular nature of cooking fires and the gratifying nature of grilled food loosened tongues for chants, songfests, and storytelling, elements of natural human loquacity.

Mongol horsemen embraced grilling techniques because they required simple equipment for turning gamy venison into a palatable meal. Fireside cookery involved elemental methods of transferring flame to meat, beginning with the heating of stones to stuff into carcasses and insert external cookery into inner tissues. Condiments began with bags of salt granules for rubbing on haunches and organ meats and developed into dry rubs and spice pastes creamed from individualized blends of wild herb fronds, leaves, and roots and lubricated by sizzling animal fat.

The union of sensual pleasures—sound, fragrance, browning of ingredients, and the resulting taste and texture—endorsed a cooking method that spread south as far as Burma, Cambodia, Laos, Thailand, and Vietnam. To the west in India, the use of the tandoor, a large clay jar, adapted from Arab cookery. Each required long hooks for suspending meat, which contrasted the horizontal gridiron cooking common farther north. For fish, the preparer placed a gridiron over the mouth of the tandoor.

Grate and Gridiron

From 2000 B.C.E., the biblical Hebrews placed gridirons over coals for heating cereal paste into flatbread. Homer speaks at length about ritual beasts, which sacrificers grilled on bronze tripods, a standard prize for athletic prowess. In the post-Homeric era in Egypt and Greece, the sea bream that came to the table with split peas and red lentil soup received its tasty crust and juicy, nutritious meat from live-fire grilling on a footed grate. In *De Diaeta* (*On Diet,* ca. 410 B.C.E.), the physician Hippocrates of Cos, known as the "Father of Medicine," described beneficial cookery as the dehydration of wet foods, such as anchovies, eggplant or turnip slices, sardines, and smelts, by grilling and roasting. Around 350 B.C.E., the Sicilian poet Archestratus added his own praise of grilling by discussing how easily he prepared bonito, a popular fish among the Turks, who flavored it with clove and oregano.

The Romans adopted Greek grilling styles, which antiquarians have analyzed at Paestum and Pompeii and at Roman enclaves in Britannia and North Africa. For small-portion grilling, such as dormice and songbirds, they selected a special grate. Slaves raised birds in home pigeoncotes and prepared them for cooking by plucking, gutting, halving, and flattening with a mallet. After grilling, the bird required a roll in chopped parsley or thyme to flavor the succulent skin. Apicius's *De Re Coquinaria* (*On Cookery,* ca. 35 C.E.) applauded the era's open-fire innovations, including gridirons for shipboard cookery and the home grilling of beans to prevent intestinal fermentation and gas.

Medieval cookery required the maneuvering of heavy boar and deer over fireplace grates for carving and service to aristocrats and clergy. In the early sixth century, the Empress Theodora supervised the kitchen of the Emperor Justinian the Great, in which chefs from Greece, India, Persia, and Syria presented a three-course fare, beginning with lightly grilled appetizers. The menu featured Byzantine comfort food—grilled sea bass and sturgeon—and added griddle bread and a dessert. Wood fires began in winter with olive wood and in summer with orchard and vineyard prunings. Aromatic herb blends in water simmered in a pan nestled in the coals. Bubbling liquids generated a flavorful mist to flavor and tenderize meats and to lure diners to the final moments of meal preparation.

In Japan around 710 C.E., Zen Buddhist vegetarians based their diet on seasonal produce and nonmeat grills, specifically tofu, which released the meatlike tang known as umami. The Japanese developed *yakitori* grilling, a partial cooking of bite-size *momo* (chicken, beef, or fish pieces) interrupted by brushing with marinade or plunging bamboo skewers into an earthenware jar of sauce. The cook finished the tidbits with a deep char to deepen a glossy brown crust and the sensuous aroma of double caramelization. Tending the grill required constant shifting of portions beween hotter and cooler sections of the rack to protect foods from overcooking.

In the 900s C.E., Scots grilled dulse, a red alga known as sea lettuce. In Baghdad, Syrian chefs grilled red meat kebabs and spitted whole lamb with a garlic marinade over a low charcoal flame. Jordanian and Lebanese cooks raised *masgouf,* a butterflied carp, over an upright grill, which burned out the fish fat. In 1071, eastern Turks abandoned more complicated recipes for intense meat flavors—freshly slaughtered lamb roasted or grilled over hot coals. Along the Silk Road at Xi'an in central China, Arab and Bactrian merchants introduced Turkish-style skewering and grilling methods to Chinese cuisine. In Beijing's streets in the 1100s, vendors grilled lamb and mutton in the open air. Shoppers strolled while nibbling the fragrant meat wrapped in wheat pancakes.

Ögödei Khan's Mongol invasion of Korea in spring 1231 brought soldiers who grilled their suppers over campfires and flavored the meat with black pepper. In the 1300s, Mongol nomads added to Chinese menus *kao* cuisine, meat threaded on iron rods and charcoal grilled. On tabletop grates, diners joined in casual roasting of morsels to individual tastes in doneness. Farther east, Japanese recipes named grilled curd as a popular tofu recipe. In 1375, Taillevent, the Norman French master of late medieval cuisine, described how grillers soaked brochettes to inject woody flavors into the meat. He favored dorade, eel, salmon, shad, sole, and tench, which cook in 20 minutes over a low fire.

New World

The Western Hemisphere astounded European voyagers with evidence of grilled human flesh. In December 1492, Christopher Columbus witnessed West Indian Arawak and Carib pitmasters barbecuing arms, legs, and organ meats on a green wood rack, a source of aromatic vapor. During slow cooking, clouds of smoke warded off insects and halted decay by dehydrating tissues. On Hispaniola, grillers blistered peppers over a rack and hustled into place whole cow and pig carcasses, which butchers split for maximum exposure to heat and smoke. Pacific Coast tribes grilled their most common foods—acorn bread, quail, rabbit, seafood, and venison. When the Californios adapted native cookery to their own use, a favorite dish, *frazada,* involved the rapid salting and heating of the meat covering beef ribs, which they lopped off and devoured almost raw.

In Central America and southeastern Mexico, the Maya preferred iguana and turkey on the gridiron. According to Spanish conquistadors, Mexican grillers in the 1500s specified mesquite coals for flavoring *barbacoa* (barbecue) and *carnitas* (roast meats). Simultaneously, they heated corn-on-a-stick, a finger food grilled by the pre-Hispanic Aztec. Argentines mounted a *parrilla,* a wooden framework that accommodated tongue, tripe, and whole carcasses over radiant heat. The portable frame suited impromptu fiestas and religious celebrations, whether over an outdoor fire or a stone pit.

The Modern Era

Upon her arrival in France in 1533, Catherine de' Médici introduced Italian recipes for grilled songbirds, a delicacy unknown to northwestern Europeans. Because of her example, chefs rid high Renaissance menus of unwieldy meat joints and substituted a medieval Venetian treat, individually sized *ucelli*—small blackbirds, larks, thrushes, teal, and warblers—sauced in light broths and herbs. To ready fish or poultry for rapid heating, butchers butterflied the carcass, a gutting and flattening that simplified the arrangement of a Cornish hen or filet of sole on a gridiron

or the threading of a duck on an iron rod. The geometrics of an iron grill branded a finished bird or fish with a lattice pattern blackened into the skin.

From the seventeenth century, grilling history evinced a flair for the unusual. Elizabethans sliced and scored sheer carbonadoes of mutton shoulder for quick scorching on the grill and dressing with garlic, onions, and vinegar. Brazilians devoured grilled devils on horseback—dates or pitted prunes stuffed with green mango chutney and wrapped in bacon. Indonesians added savor to grilled lamb with cashew and ginger sauce. South African cooks grilled bananas for chopping into relish. Australian Aborigines survived on a found diet of crocodiles, snakes, and witchetties, a large white grub easily grilled into bite-size snacks. In this same era, Ottoman travelers to Erzurum, in eastern Turkey, filled pitas with lamb carved from a *cag kebabi,* a horizontal spit that impaled carcasses for grilling and basting with onion sauce.

West Indian barbecue popularized the metal rack, trendy equipment erected over a charcoal or wood fire for low temperature grilling of Jamaican jerk snapper drenched in pineapple juice and enlivened with a sluice of allspice, cayenne, and hot pepper sauce. Atlantic Coast grillers focused on rustic goods—braised apples with cheddar cheese and maple syrup. In the North American wild, a grill simplified the cooking of dressed squirrel. Cajun cooks favored marinating and grilling for crawfish, shrimp, and tasso (pork shoulder), a fatty cut that developed taste from a sugary salt cure and hot smoking with cayenne pepper, cinnamon, garlic, and paprika. Tidbits of grilled tasso offered its complex flavor to gumbo, jambalaya, and red beans and rice.

On the American frontier, wranglers preferred beef brisket as well as beef, goat, pork, and venison for grilling. Developing skills from colonial hearth cuisine, chuck wagon "cookies" suspended heavy lidded pans and gridirons over campfires at variable heights, depending on the tenderness of the meat, the butchery style, and the method of readying it for consumption. The finishing touch, the sauce, gave the griller leeway to select from Alabama white sauce, Asian five-spice rub, Carolina vinegar-and-tomato sauce, Creole rub, Jamaican jerk, Kansas City sweet sauce, Lebanese and Memphis dry rub, Louisiana hot sauce, Mexican chili rub, Provençal paste, and red wine marinade. The most popular along the Rio Grande, Texas mop sauce, a thin brown gravy spiced with local ingredients—ancho powder, beef drippings, beer, chili, cumin, dry mustard, green pepper, and onion—penetrated the meat and replenished moisture.

During the Victorian era, the middle-class English emulated the royal family's togetherness at "heavy breakfast," sometimes called a "British breakfast." Housewives and their cook staffs spread the sideboard with an Ulster fry-up grilled on a buttered long-handled gridiron or an iron rack greased with suet. The morning menu offered grilled, self-serve black pudding and oatcakes, mushrooms and tomatoes, kidneys or kippers, link sausage or mutton chops, liver or rashers of streaky bacon, and marmalade and mustard for dressings.

A handy kitchen gadget, the hinged gridiron held together tender morsels of mushrooms and sprats, small oily fish. A hollowed gridiron offered grooves for directing fat and gravy back toward the handle to prevent drippings from leaching out into the fire and causing a smoky blaze. Less affluent cooks grilled their morning oysters or herring snacks over a plain four-bar gridiron, a common metal kitchen device that Alexis Soyer characterized in *A Shilling Cookery for the People* (1854).

In the 1890s, French chef Auguste Escoffier, the "Father of French Haute Cuisine," ranked the *rôtisseur* above the *grillardin,* the preparer of grills and roasts, but Escoffier's dictum ignored the global diaspora that brought ethnic grill cookery to new venues. Before World War II, food maven Elizabeth David, a British expatriate, sampled Nile-side specialties—quail kebabs and charcoal-grilled pigeon, quick-cook meats that retained natural meatiness. Her promotion of sidewalk café gastronomy preceded the American adoption of Japanese *yakitori,* a postwar favorite.

The Contemporary Griller

James Beard's *Cook It Outdoors* (1942) introduced camp cooking and grilling as one of the most appetizing methods of preparing meat. He considered grilling serious cuisine based on scientific principles, such as completing the roasting of chicken hearts on all four sides, the quick charring of flank steak for sandwiches, or the crisping of cocktail franks for dressing with mustard and sour cream. His philosophy proved prophetic of the postwar boom in urbanism.

With city life came backyard grilling, boating, camping, and picnicking on hamburgers and hot dogs. George A. Stephen, a Chicago welder who manufactured harbor buoys, caught the attention of home barbecuers with the Weber kettle grill, a lidded half buoy on legs. First marketed in 1952, the spherical container for a rack suspended over charcoal offered the backyard chef more control of heat and smoke and a lid that prevented ash from blowing into the meat.

Cycles of grilling trends in the 1900s illustrated the method's versatility, even extending to popcorn. One of the innovations in heating, charcoal briquettes, was the brainchild of automotive mogul Henry Ford, who, in 1921, recycled the wood scrap from a car factory. In the 1950s, Australians and New Zealanders gave up formal English meat service and embraced barbecuing for special occasions by grilling game or skewered chicken, lamb, and sausages. In the 1960s, food faddists created a demand for technologically advanced barbecue grills, a departure from the common small cast iron Japanese hibachi and flimsy wire and sheet metal braziers. In Little Rock, Arkansas, Melton Lancaster and William G. Wepfer reengineered the charcoal grill to accommodate natural gas as fuel for the fire.

In the post–World War II era, after the arrival of Cuban émigrés, Floridians popularized the pressed Cuban sandwich, a grilled Swiss cheese and ham with mustard and pickles on sweet *pan cubano* (Cuban yeast bread). Mexican cuisine made use of the opuntia *nopales* (cactus paddles) pickled or deep-fried with chili and cumin as accompaniments to a grilled ratatouille. From Austin and Houston, Texas, in 1973, the standard Tex-Mex entrée menu showcased fajitas, a sizzling plate of marinated skirt steak with grilled peppers and onions. Korean restaurants offered table barbecuing of short ribs over a small grill. The Taiwanese grilled corn on a skewer and embellished it with cayenne, garlic, onions, and soy sauce. Late in the twentieth century, grilled quesadillas boosted lunch choices from ho-hum chef's salads to an enticing grilled cheese sandwich served with charred corn on the cob, jalapeños, and lime quarters.

See also: Barbecue; Beard, James; Caribbean Diet and Cuisine; Kebabs; Nouvelle Cuisine.

Further Reading

Denker, Joel. *The World on a Plate: A Tour Through the History of America's Ethnic Cuisine.* Lincoln: University of Nebraska Press, 2007.

Heine, Peter. *Food Culture in the Near East, Middle East, and North Africa.* Westport, CT: Greenwood, 2004.

Ono, Tadashi, and Harris Salat. *The Japanese Grill: From Classic Yakitori to Steak, Seafood, and Vegetables.* New York: Random House, 2011.

Symons, Michael. *A History of Cooks and Cooking.* Urbana: University of Illinois Press, 2000.

Trang, Corinne. *The Asian Grill: Great Recipes, Bold Flavors.* San Francisco: Chronicle, 2006.

Gruel

See Pulses

Guar

An annual legume, guar remains in demand for producing a high-viscosity gum that stabilizes processed foods. Known as the cluster bean, or *Cyamopsis tetragonolobus,* the high-protein guar bean is a forage crop for livestock. A green manure grown in Africa, Australia, China, northwestern India, and Pakistan and in Arizona, Kansas, New Mexico, Oklahoma, and Texas, the plant supplements depleted fields.

By husking, milling, and gelling the nearly tasteless endosperm in water, processors reduce powdered beans into a digestible, odorless guar gum. The colloid solidifies cream cheese and cold cuts and emulsifies and suspends solids in ice cream and sherbet to prevent crystal growth and ingredient settling. Food producers value the mucilage for suspending starch in liquid and for ameliorating the effects of freezing and thawing.

Because guar gum has eight times the thickening agency of cornstarch, it binds liquids and retains moisture in baked goods to extend shelf life. The versatile powder volumizes barbecue sauce, cereal, dough, dry soup, icing, instant oatmeal and pudding, ketchup, pastry filling, popsicles, orange juice and fruit ades, pet food, relish, salad dressings and marinades, sports drinks, and whipped cream. Aficionados sprinkle guar on berry pie fillings and whisk it into pan juices to make gravy. In gluten-free recipes, the powder thickens with soluble fiber granola and smoothies as well as bread, piecrust, and pizza dough. In milk and yogurt, like the action of pectin in jelly, guar gum maintains homogeneity.

In 1983, British biochemists created a high-fiber, low-starch bread. Sold in Holland, Scandinavia, and the United States as Wasa Crispbread, the formulation controlled appetite and cholesterol while emulating the mouthfeel and satisfying quality of ordinary bread. Five years later, weight-reducing compounds touted guar powder as a breakthrough in dieting.

After millennia of use in central Asian pharmacopoeia, guar has established its worth to alternative and complementary Western medicine. The bean serves the human diet as a table vegetable, a treatment for childhood enteritis, and a control of irritable bowel syndrome and obesity. It also is an ingredient in some diabetes drugs.

See also: Dairy Food; Ice Cream; Ketchup.

Further Reading

Barceloux, Donald G. *Medical Toxicology of Natural Substances: Foods, Fungi, Medicinal Herbs, Plants, and Venomous Animals.* Hoboken, NJ: John Wiley & Sons, 2008.

Biliardis, Costas G., and Marta S. Izydorczyk. *Functional Food Carbohydrates.* Boca Raton, FL: Taylor & Francis, 2007.

Carpender, Dana. *1000 Low-Carb Recipes: Hundreds of Delicious Recipes from Dinner to Dessert.* Gloucester, MA: Fair Winds, 2010.

Driskell, Judy Anne, and Ira Wolinsky, eds. *Energy-Yielding Macronutrients and Energy Metabolism in Sports Nutrition.* Boca Raton, FL: CRC, 2000.

Hui, Yiu H., ed. *Handbook of Food Science, Technology, and Engineering.* Boca Raton, FL: Taylor & Francis, 2006.

Halal

According to Muslim law, food choice and preparation divides ingredients into two distinct categories, *halal* (permissible) and *haraam* (forbidden). From the beginning of the faith, the devout followed godly proscriptions contained in the Koran, the sacred work compiled by followers of the prophet Muhammad in 652 C.E. For the sake of unity, Muhammad encouraged piety and cultural conformity.

As instructed by scripture, Islam's early followers avoided selling or consuming alcohol, amphibians, birds of prey, blood, carrion, insects, sacrifices from foreign altars, and some cheeses and gelatins. Like Jews, Muslims rejected pork, which the Koran excluded from the table as an unclean meat. In one doctrinal difference of opinion, Shi'ite Muslims rejected shellfish, which Sunnis considered edible. In dire situations, starving people received forgiveness for eating forbidden food.

For details and clarification, readers of the Koran studied the *hadiths,* the Prophet's pronouncements concerning everyday behavior. Ritual slaughter of healthy beasts by a Muslim butcher began with an invocation to Allah. A quick slice of the throat avoided suffering. Scripture grudgingly allowed the meat of predatory animals, snakes, and eels as *makrooh* (unwholesome but allowed). To prevent contamination, the faithful avoided eating from kitchens that produced both permissible and unlawful dishes, such as blood sausages or carnivorous bushmeat.

Muhammad was wary of cheese and grapes but advocated the daily consumption of dates. To the Muslim cook, he dictated that food should be thoroughly cooked, kept covered, and cooled before serving. He advised diners to eat only when seated and to leave the table without filling the stomach. He also instructed his followers to walk after eating, a therapeutic aid to digestion.

Shopping for foodstuffs among imported goods extended approval to meats slaughtered and dressed by Christians and Jews. The removal of blood from meat required soaking in vinegar. To ensure cleanliness, the cook heated meats to full doneness to prevent the appearance of blood. Cooks replaced wine in recipes with vinegar and sour fruit juice and continued the tradition of sautéing raisins to remove the risk of fermentation. They cleverly circumvented the injunction against drinking alcohol by first boiling it. Because coffee, opium, tea, and tobacco were vegetable stimulants, they fell into the category of halal.

In the 1920s, the Nation of Islam, led by African-American preacher Elijah Muhammad, reinterpreted injunctions to the advantage of sect food businesses in inner cities, including Steak-n-Take and Whiting H.&G. Simplifying questions of dining out for Muslim travelers, caterers and restaurants posted certificates of cleanliness and obedience to holy injunctions.

In the early twenty-first century, African-American Sunnis adapted standard halal fare to accommodate Southern soul food—black-eyed peas, collard greens, fried chicken, kebabs, macaroni and cheese, and okra. U.S. Muslim immigrants from Africa, Bosnia, and India contributed to the diversification of the halal diet. Some devout diners compromised by observing halal cookery and marketing, which is increasingly available (see image on page 270), but eating out at fast-food chains. Advocates for American Muslims published guidance on combating diabetes, high blood pressure, and obesity by avoiding foods high in fat, salt, and sugar, the hazardous cuisine associated with slavery.

See also: African Food Trade; Alcoholic Beverages.

Further Reading

Campo, Juan Eduardo. *Encyclopedia of Islam.* New York: Facts on File, 2009.

Hayes, Dayle, and Rachel Laudan, eds. *Food and Nutrition.* New York: Marshall Cavendish, 2009.

Nasir, Kamaludeen Mohamed, Alexius A. Pereira, and Bryan S. Turner. *Muslims in Singapore: Piety, Politics, and Policies.* New York: Taylor & Francis, 2009.

Riaz, Mian N., and Muhammad M. Chaudry. *Halal Food Production.* Boca Raton, FL: CRC, 2004.

Schneller, Thomas. *Meat: Identification, Fabrication, Utilization.* Clifton Park, NJ: Delmar, 2009.

Hanna, Gordie C. (1903–1993)

A hero to produce growers, agronomy professor Gordie Consyntine "Jack" Hanna developed a tomato that could survive mechanical picking, thereby revolutionizing the industry.

As Arab peoples emigrate in growing numbers, halal foods, or those deemed permissible under Islamic law, have become increasingly available in the West. For meat to be halal, slaughterers must bleed and process carcasses according to a prescribed method. *(Elise Hardy/Gamma-Rapho/Getty Images)*

A native of Quannah, Texas, Hanna was born on July 1, 1903. From 1929 to 1933, he worked in crop research at the Ryer Island Field Station. He advanced to lecturer in olericulture (truck crops grown for city markets) and issued numerous monographs, beginning with *Asparagus Production in California* (1935) and *Crown-Grading Experiments with Asparagus* (1940).

The need for faster, less invasive, mechanical tomato handling derived in 1941 from a wartime dearth of migrant Mexican field labor. After the University of California at Davis invented a tomato-picking machine, the device disappointed the agricultural engineering department with its rough handling of delicate fruit.

In 1942, on staff in the Vegetable Crops Department at Davis, Hanna began hybridizing a small, high-yielding tomato with a firmer skin and more fibrous pulp, an elongated crossbreed of the Gem and San Marzano varieties known as Red Top. He walked his test fields selecting cultivars of 2,000 varieties to toss into Hutchison Drive adjacent to the campus to observe their durability for transport by truck. An initial problem with susceptibility to fusarium and verticillium wilt made colleagues believe that Hanna chased a faulty ideal. He proved them wrong with the VF145 A & B, two resilient varieties of the block-

shaped tomato that would remain on conveyor belts during sorting and packing.

Hanna's hybrid accommodated picking at the peak of ripeness for cooking and peeling. It held an intense red hue suited to ketchup and pasta sauce. In 1951, he retired from teaching and joined Petoseed, one of the world's largest vegetable seed companies. Because of its rapid and simultaneous setting of fruit, the VF145 tomato became available from the Castle Seed Company. With dependable traits, it succeeded in the products of Campbell's, Heinz, Pizza Hut, and Unilever.

In 1961, Hanna and agricultural engineers Coby Lorenzen and Istvan J. Sluka refined a method of picking tomatoes that required nine patents. The machine plucked the entire plant and deposited its fruit on conveyor belts for sorting and culling. Made by Blackwelder Manufacturing, the machine reduced harvest time by nearly 50 percent and increased California's tomato crop from 7 percent of the state's acreage to 85 percent.

Hanna and Lorenzen published their findings in January 1962 in *Agricultural Engineering*. Within three years of the demise of the Bracero Program—a federal contract laborer program for Mexicans from 1942 to 1965—more than 80 percent of U.S. tomatoes derived from machine harvesting. Mechanization put the small grower out of business and reduced planting in the Midwest, where picking machines balked at crossing boggy fields or topping hills. By 1970, no commercial grower picked tomatoes by hand. Farmers ceased hiring *braceros* and employed local women to stand on the picker machine platforms.

Hanna's improvements shifted tomato growing and its profits to California. The reduction in farm labor dropped prices by half and increased agrarian yield in a $3 billion industry. Hanna, Lorenzen, and Sluka shared the 1976 John Scott Award from the city of Philadelphia for improving human comfort and welfare. In 1981, Hanna and Lorenzen won the Cyrus Hall McCormick Medal. Hanna continued aiding farmers by improving strains of broccoli, cabbage, and sweet potatoes, as well as disease-resistant asparagus.

See also: Hybridization.

Further Reading

Janick, Jules, and Robert E. Paull, eds. *The Encyclopedia of Fruit and Nuts.* Cambridge, MA: CABI, 2006.
Jones, Carl M., Charles M. Rick, Dawn Adams, Judy Jernstedt, and Roger T. Chetelat. "Genealogy and Fine Mapping of Obscuravenosa." *American Journal of Botany* 94:6 (June 2007): 935–947.

Hardtack

See Biscuit

Haute Cuisine

A product of the early 1800s, haute cuisine introduced the European elite to fine dining, professional service, and elaborate tableware in upscale hotels and restaurants. Shortly after the emergence of the upper class following the French Revolution of 1789, Marie-Antoine Carême, a chef to British, French, and Russian royalty, refined European gastronomy with the best of exotic ingredients from around the world. The wealthy looked to him to create status dishes to enhance their prominence at receptions and state dinners in grand halls and châteaus.

Because sumptuous food spectacle became a measure of social class, Carême catered to poseurs and social climbers as well as the truly genteel. To heighten gustatory expectations, he named his recipes for aristocrats and devised dramatic presentations that intermingled aroma, taste, and texture with visual effects, notably stuffed peacock, saumon à la Neptune on a pedestal, and candied fruits suspended from limbs. At his death in 1833, his five-volume encyclopedia for food professionals, *L'Art de la Cuisine Française* (*The Art of French Cuisine,* 1833–1834), remained unfinished. Subsequent cookbooks and cooking journals extended his codification of the best in dining.

Because of Carême's influence on Continental cooks, the French maintained an intimidating presence in gastronomy and a reputation for unequaled taste and table style at such classic restaurants as the Grand Véfour, the oldest in Paris. Americans boasted their own showcase recipes at Chicago's Palmer House and Delmonico's and the Waldorf-Astoria Hotel in New York City. Piquing the interest of the American nouveau riche in the Gilded Age, the cultural commentary of Henry James for *Atlantic Monthly,* the *Nation,* and the *New York Tribune* in such vignettes as "Occasional Paris" (1883) and "An International Episode" (1892) began the rush of North American imitators of refined fare.

In 1890, French chef Auguste Escoffier, the "Father of French Cuisine," brought Gallic flair to the Savoy Hotel, newly opened in London. His discipline of the kitchen brigade generated order and dignity in the preparation and presentation of hearty dishes sauced with a distinctive béchamel or velouté. His phalanx of kitchen officers specialized on separate courses—the *garde manger* over cold food, the *entremetier* over soup and vegetables, the *rôtisseur* over grills and roasts, the *saucier* over sauces and *fumets* (scented additives), and the *pâtissier* over pastry.

With the aid of hotelier César Ritz, Escoffier quickly turned English nobles into aficionados of haute cuisine. The Michelin Guides increased the notoriety of luxury hotels in 1900 by listing the toniest service, which was available at exorbitant prices. Escoffier further standardized the artistic menu by publishing *Le Guide Culinaire* (1903), a touchstone of Gallic food philosophy.

The posh style of cookery depends on formality and artistic form. From the folding of napkins and the curling of butter to service of the finest postdinner Mocha coffee, haute cuisine calls for attention to detail. Menus favor cassis aperitifs (predinner drinks) and foie gras (goose liver) and snail appetizers preceding citrus sorbet to clear the palate. The height of haute cuisine resides in heavily garnished and sauced beef, fish, and poultry.

Recipe: Salmis of Pheasant

Roast a pheasant to slightly rare and dismember. Skin and trim pieces. Reheat meat in a covered pan with clear drippings and 1/2 teaspoon of burned brandy. Pound the carcass and trimmings and simmer in 1 pint of red wine, three chopped shallots, and 1/2 teaspoon of peppercorns. Simmer bones and skin with 1/2 cup of brown sauce made from beef stock, vegetables, bay leaf, butter, and flour. Sieve and filter the sauce twice. Add butter to the sauce and marinate the bird pieces. Top with sliced mushrooms and truffles.

Notable meats involve ox cheek, frogs' legs, dolphin and porpoise, and veal tongue served with the appropriate garnishes and wines. Lengthy meals conclude with mousses, pastries, and soufflés, petits fours, a cheese tray, and a dessert wine and cognac.

See also: Carême, Marie-Antoine; Dairy Food; *Larousse Gastronomique*; Marshall, Agnes; Poultry; Restaurants; Tofu.

Further Reading

Ferguson, Priscilla Parkhurst. *Accounting for Taste: The Triumph of French Cuisine.* Chicago: University of Chicago Press, 2004.

McGee, Harold. *On Food and Cooking: The Science and Lore of the Kitchen.* New York: Simon & Schuster, 2004.

Schehr, Lawrence R., and Allen S. Weiss, eds. *French Food: On the Table, On the Page, and in French Culture.* New York: Routledge, 2001.

Trubek, Amy B. *Haute Cuisine: How the French Invented the Culinary Profession.* Philadelphia: University of Pennsylvania Press, 2000.

Health Foods
See Curative Foods

Hearth Cookery

A technique from earliest times, hearth cookery provides a flexible means of applying heat to raw foods, including boiling, stir-frying, and ash baking. Both indoors and outside, fire keeping begins at ground level with flaming fuel and heat radiating from coals. Stone Age cooks developed sophistication with types of fuel—camel dung, charcoal, peat, pith, pine bark, dried seaweed—to determine which produced the most reliable and controllable fire. In North America, they supplemented the best hardwoods, hickory and oak, with more readily available woods, such as ash, beech, birch, fruitwood, locust, and maple.

Fireside cookery dominated Lapp camps, Bedouin tents, Mongolian yurts, Celtic raised hearthstones, and Sicilian cave sites, creating a sense of unity and hospitality for clans. The early Romans, Chinese, and Pueblo Indians halted from serving hearth meals to feed a bite to the household gods, deities they shared with Greeks, who named their home goddess Hestia, or "hearth." In Malaysia, the term *hearth* also meant "extended family," a personal and historic reference to the spread of Pacific Island food customs from Fiji, Samoa, and Tonga throughout the region.

In addition to cooking foods, the hearth warmed bodies and enabled hunters to dry hides for clothing and blankets. The Japanese *kotatsu* was a wood frame over a sunken hearth in the floor. From the 1300s, families huddled at the edge and warmed their feet on the pot filled with charcoal that they had used to cook their dinner. A quilt covering the frame and hearth kept the heat from dissipating. For the Irish, tunnels called "shores" circulated air under slate floors. Sliding wood baffles increased or reduced the flow of outside air feeding hearth fires. Back wall "keeping holes" served as storage niches for drying vegetables and fruit and for warding off dampness in the salt box.

Children required reminders of hot handles and popping coals; adults were treated for burns and scalds if they got too close to the open flame or boiling liquids. The concern for burns caused housewives to become adept at stirring up salves as treatment for the second-greatest cause of death after childbirth. Thus, gendered chores inclined women toward child care, hearth management, cookery, and healing—the four areas of expertise expected of females. In 1845, New Brunswick pioneer Frances Beavan declared that colonial prosperity relied on women's hearth skills.

Fire Keeping

Fire builders sorted burnables into pinecones, branches, and splits and chips of wood for a quick, hot blaze and placed limbs and backlogs atop fire dogs (andirons) for the slow production of hot coals. They experimented with varied equipment by roasting fish on slabs of aromatic wood, heating stones to boil soups or porridges in the paunches of animals, roasting tasty bits in shells or on forked sticks, sauteing garlic in an iron wok, baking dough on convex stones, and fashioning clay pots to perch on brick or stone tripods to hold boiling meats and one-pot stews. Above the hearth, rising heat dried and cured preserved goods—strings of beans and peppers, bags of chestnuts and peanuts, braided onions, loops of pemmican, bunches of herbs, and round slices of pumpkin and winter squash. On plantations, slave cabins as crude as those at Boone Hall Plantation outside Charleston, South Carolina, contained small versions of residential fireplaces called half rounds, a brick semicircle on a dirt floor that lacked the chimneys and iron equipment of the main house.

Each stage of hearth tending impacted family well-being, even the removal of ash, an essential in soap making and fertilizing a vegetable bed in the colonial era. For Canadian Mennonites, the heating of traditional apple butter and spiced cider and the scalding of milk for soft cheese required control of fires by avoiding the burning of pine, poplar, willow, and other quick-burning softwoods. Several small fires aided the cook in controlling heat for the delicate tasks of coddling eggs and congealing a custard. For extra light while doing meticulous handwork, such as sausage making and potting jam, housekeepers kept pine knots soaking in turpentine, which burst into a bright flare.

Daily, the homemaker kept water heating for utilitarian uses—washing dishes, scrubbing hearthstones, rinsing seafood, and dressing game. Grueling labor strained the back with constant stooping and lifting. At bedtime on the frontier, a layer of coals under a soil and brush mattress kept bodies cozy, even in snowy weather. Cooks used leather thongs to bind haunches of meat and truss birds to keep the meat from falling from the bone into the fire. Experience with broth, herbs, oil, and salt encouraged new flavorings and the formulation of eighteenth-century recipes, which they shared by word of mouth.

Sophisticated Cookery

More complex kitchen methods required the rotation of pots for even cooking inside and the elevation of wood racks for smoking, drying, and barbecuing. Hearth tenders learned to rely on the senses—the smell of roasting venison, the sound of frying catfish, the feel of coal-baked sweet potatoes, the appearance of bubbles in maple syrup and glaze on strawberry fruit leather. The skilled cook enhanced the simple one-pot method by setting colanders on top of soup for steaming a dish of mashed turnips or by topping the stew pot with a flat lid for baking drop biscuits to accompany the meal. Jugging, a parallel of the bamboo steamer and the bain-marie, began with the suspension of a smaller container by a thong from the handle of a cauldron to cook a second dish in the heat radiating from the main dish. Thus, the cook could steam dumplings Cantonese style or complete a shore dinner of roasted potatoes and corn with clams steamed in seaweed.

One of the first advances involved the elevation of the hearth above floor level to provide a ledge for preparing pots of food and to ease the hardships of reaching down to a fireplace to move containers nearer or farther from the blaze.

The arrival of Europeans in the Western Hemisphere in the late fifteenth century introduced native peoples to ironwork, a major advance over clay for the sturdiness of containers and their handles and trivets. English and Spanish cooks introduced Indians to griddles, Dutch ovens, drip pans, long-handled tongs, spiders, rotating spits, and closed kettles, all advances over native kitchen gear. A clockwork or clock jack saved labor by turning spits with a regulated system of weights and pulleys.

Seventeenth-century engineering of the flue and brick or stone chimney rid the hearth of smoke and soot. The creation of the hob and inglenook, a built-in shelf and offset from the fireplace, allowed the user to vary temperatures and hold pots of tea and hasty pudding at a low temperature until their service at table. Blacksmiths made the cook's work easier and more exacting by supplying a variety of iron attachments and niceties, from pokers, ember shovels, and prongs used to hold roasting ears or yams to griddles for baking oatcakes and wafer irons for toasting sweet crackers and waffles. A salamander, a disc on a long handle, radiated heat directly above apple slump and twice-baked potatoes for browning. Nails

on and below the mantel kept utensils at hand. The handiest technology, the damper, allowed the cook to control the airflow up the chimney and to feed or starve the fire of oxygen, depending on need.

Cranes attached by S hooks to a pivot or pot chain swung the boiling food nearer or farther from the fire. Lug poles installed in the chimney secured iron trammels and adjustable hooks for raising and lowering frying pans. Reflecting ovens called "tin kitchens" extended hearth cookery to the outside of the fire and made use of radiant heat for baking muffins and pigeon pie. Some hearth ovens contained rotisseries for pheasant and duck roasting. The ovens produced moister meat with a savory caramelized crust basted in natural juices. Alongside the hearth, stores of emery rock, pumice, or sand provided the scouring grit to remove burned-on food. By the 1840s, cast-iron cookstoves began replacing hearth work in all but the most isolated coves and backwoods, including the sheep camps of Australia.

The hearth remains a feature on tours of historic sites at Grasshopper Pueblo, Arizona; Henry VIII's home at Hampton Court in London; and Monticello and Williamsburg, Virginia. At Old Salem, the Moravian stronghold of North Carolina, visitors can observe the use of a brick and soapstone wall bake oven capped with a roof. Masons insulated the baking chamber and equipped it with fireplace and smoke hood. A rear and bottom exhaust rerouted smoke to the oven top in a design the Amish dubbed a "squirrel tail." To test temperatures, users cast a handful of cornmeal on the stone floor and calculated, by the feel of heat on the hand and arm and how long the cornmeal took to burst into flame, before they slid in loaves and pans of cookies on a wood peel.

Beyond the two-and-a-half-story main building at Mount Vernon, Virginia, George and Martha Washington's kitchen served the nation's first couple as a culinary command post. A slate-floored room with modest fireplace at one end, it offered triangular niches at each side of the chimney for keeping dishes warm and suspended copper molds and brass warming pans and ladles. The cooking area itself broadened inward from a brick hearth. An iron bar topped the fire chamber; pots and kettles clustered at the hearth attest to the constant use of embers and the adjacent bake oven, which is bricked into the wall at right. The hearth regularly turned out fare for 240 residents plus guests.

See also: Cantonese Diet and Cuisine; Literature, Food in; Medieval Diet and Cuisine; Pennsylvania Dutch Diet and Cuisine; Roman Diet and Cuisine, Ancient; Tudor Diet and Cuisine.

Further Reading

Lucas, Fiona. *Hearth and Home: Women and the Art of Open-Hearth Cooking.* Toronto: J. Lorimer, 2006.

McLean, Alice L. *Cooking in America, 1840–1945.* Westport, CT: Greenwood, 2006.

Rubel, William. *The Magic of Fire: Hearth Cooking.* Berkeley, CA: Ten Speed, 2002.

———. "Thanksgiving by the Hearth." *Vegetarian Times* 315 (November 2003): 48–55.

Smith, Andrew F., ed. *The Oxford Companion to American Food and Drink.* New York: Oxford University Press, 2007.

Heirloom Plants

A revolt against industrialized monoculture and a shrinking gene pool, the heirloom plant movement introduces to the food chain a wide variety of native fruits, grains, and vegetables that once graced the human table. The term *heirloom* derives from the historic and sentimental value of organic foods treasured by a family or clan, such as the Mortgage Lifter tomato, Jerusalem artichokes, Hubbard squash, and Amish Moon & Stars watermelon. Specific to a place and climate—the German Chocolate tomatoes of Texas and the German Johnson tomatoes of North Carolina, for example—these crops establish their value simply by surviving.

By cultivating the hundreds of Peruvian potato cultivars, the Bergamot orange, and the Judean date palm, the Ark of Taste, Seed Savers Exchange, and other seed-saving endeavors return to use rugged, disease-resistant crops and aromas and flavors of the past. Venturesome gardeners return to their land cranberry beans, flint corn, pawpaws, persimmons, and satsumas, vintage foods that ancient peoples enjoyed.

Instead of patented varieties propagated for their suitability to mechanical harvesting and global shipping, heirloom growers sample foods displaying a variety of genetic makeups, such as cardoons, birch syrup, Harrison cider apples, Meyer lemons, and Brandywine, Green Zebra, and Cherokee Purple tomatoes. A parallel effort returns to use beekeeping amid rhododendron and rosemary for heirloom honey and raising heritage breeds of cattle, sheep, and goats for traditional sausages and cheeses.

The years immediately following World War II mark the rise of industrial agriculture. With it came intense hybridizing that modified open plant and seed stock to produce bioengineered commercial varieties that replaced Austria's vineyard peach and the Chilean white strawberry. Consequently, while richer nations now limit themselves to select plants, preindustrial countries retain

A retail outlet in Petaluma, California, offers a variety of heirloom seeds, handed down by tribe and family members to grow native, nonhybrid plants and vegetables. Heritage horticulture is part of the explosion of interest in locally grown organic foods. *(Ben Margot/Associated Press)*

the most food variety, such as nutritionally rich Chinese black rice and the red rice of Bhutan, both marketed by Lotus Foods in El Cerrito, California. The company aims to sustain global farming by isolated growers who preserve traditional heirloom seeds and cultivation methods, such as the production of *kaipen,* a dried algae produced in northern Laos. Nutritionists support the revival of heirloom foods for their antioxidants and for their impact on reducing poverty in agrarian cultures.

Throughout Europe since the 1970s, the regimented list of commercial foods insists on distinct varieties that are uniform and stable rather than such insect- and wind-pollinated plants as Tuscan dinosaur kale and French blonde peas. Rules limit the sale of Dutch white beets, German Hori onions, Kentish cobnuts, Portuguese Ermelo's oranges, Spanish Denia raisins and Ganxet beans, and other heirloom produce. Over time, fewer people raise the meaty San Marzano plum tomatoes integral to pasta sauces and the Long Horn okra that remains tender to the length of 8 inches (20 centimeters). In the United States, a similar winnowing out of food types in the late 1990s reduced the 1900 list of vegetables in the Department of Agriculture catalogs by 97 percent.

In defiance of such regulation, botanists have established heirloom arboretums and seedbanks, cold storage facilities such as the Svalbard Global Seed Vault in Spitsbergen, Norway, and the Millennium Seed Bank Project in West Sussex, England. Preservers select, type, and store ancient cultivars for the sake of biodiversity. The concept also preserves dormant varieties of the past as a hedge against catastrophic war, epidemic, or natural disaster. Seeds that degrade from dry storage, such as avocado, cocoa, lychee, and mango, require constant replacement to save them from extinction.

See also: Agribusiness; Commodity Regulation; Heritage Foods; Kitchen Gardening; Local Food Movement; Monoculture; Seed Trade.

Further Reading

Barrett, Judy. *What Makes Heirloom Plants So Great?: Old-Fashioned Treasures to Grow, Eat, and Admire.* College Station: Texas A&M University Press, 2010.

Coulter, Lynn. *Gardening with Heirloom Seeds.* Chapel Hill: University of North Carolina Press, 2008.

Duram, Leslie A., ed. *Encyclopedia of Organic, Sustainable, and Local Food.* Santa Barbara, CA: ABC-Clio, 2010.

Thorness, Bill. *Edible Heirlooms: Heritage Vegetables for the Maritime Garden.* Seattle, WA: Skipstone, 2009.

Herbs

The boost to flavor, scent, and texture from herbs elevates mere cookery to an art. From prehistory, cooks have associated herbs with taste as well as health and longevity.

Classical Greeks and Romans took herbs seriously and elevated verbena to a sacred realm. In the third century B.C.E., the poet Theocritus, a Greek colonial living in Syracusa, Sicily, wrote verse on the good life, which he equated with rural produce. In his *Idylls* (ca. 270 B.C.E.), Theocritus pictured himself garlanded and sipping on aged wine by the hearth while waiting for the cook to finish preparing his beans. Meanwhile, he reclined near fleabane and asphodel mingled with wild celery. The image reflects comfort in the texture and fragrance of green herbs, which rid the house of vermin and cleansed the air.

The basics of a kitchen herb garden called for a variety of greens and culinary plants for cooking, home needs, brewing, and curing meat. The term *herb* remained so valuable to cookery that it characterized vegetables (pot herbs), salad greens (sallet herbs), flavoring (sweet herbs), and simples, compounds of healing herbs for teas and compresses. By the seventeenth century, the drift toward enlightened medicine ended dependence on herbs for cures. Instead of dosing growers with plants, humanist and kitchen gardener John Evelyn, author of *Acetaria: A Discourse of Sallets* (1699), characterized the bud, flower, seed, leaf, stalk, and root of 73 salad plants and determined whether to blanch, chop, pickle, steam, or steep each for the table.

One rebel went to the extreme to refute late Renaissance medicine. American president Thomas Jefferson, an influential disprover of previous regimens, refused to believe unverifiable claims. He used his mint and hyssop for cooking and aromatics. At Monticello, his Virginia manor, he chose herb tea as a curative over the practice of bleeding, which he considered a sham and endangerment of the body. For his family's table and health, he grew rue and tansy, balm for fevers, and thyme for stomachache.

Around 1800, the importation to England and the Americas of the Chinese herb boat—also called a ship grinder, ship mill, sow & pig mill, or go-devil—applied the technology of the mano and metate to crushing herbs. A boat-shaped wood base set on bootjack legs accommodated a cast-iron wheel pierced by a pair of dowel-shaped wood handles. By leaning forward and rolling the wheel back and forth in the groove of the trough, the user could rapidly extract juice and reduce leaves, roots, and woody stems to fragments. The Chinese powered the Asian original with their feet.

The first successful New World kitchen herb business began at the Shaker commune in New Lebanon, New York. From tentative kitchen gardens, the industry grew to 50 acres (20 hectares) of physic gardening, which produced aconite, belladonna, burdock, conium, dock, horehound, hyoscyamus, lettuce, marjoram, poppy, sage, summer savory, taraxacum, and valerian. In addition to 200 local varieties, growers introduced about 40 varieties from the Southwest and Europe.

To build their stock, Shaker herbalists gathered wild catnip, dandelion, pennyroyal, peppermint, sarsaparilla, snakeroot, spearmint, wintergreen, and witch hazel from the wild outside their property. By 1861, the commune bottled, corked, and labeled extracts in glass vials. Workers shaped wintergreen lozenges, sewed moth-repelling herbs in bags, pressed leaves, and pulverized roots, totaling 7,000 pounds (3,200 kilograms) annually. The success of New Lebanon's herb business encouraged parallel endeavors at Shaker communes in Canterbury, New Hampshire; Enfield, Connecticut; Harvard, Massachusetts; New Gloucester, Maine; Union Village, Ohio; and Watervliet, New York.

The gender-neutral Shaker industry put all hands to work at the herb trade, including children, who learned herbalism from adults. Sisters worked at picking and drying purslane and sweet marjoram, soaking juniper berries, trimming sarsparilla roots, and culling lobelia flowers and leaves. They cut bugleweed for bitters, racked burdock and sage near the hearth, washed vials and pasted labels, and measured catnip powder into paper envelopes. In their kitchens, they concocted lotions, rosewater, and ointment. Within a span of 15 years, they dressed and prepared 37.5 tons (34 metric tons) of herbs for pharmaceutical use.

While preindustrial cultures continue to treat disease with belladonna and wormwood elixir, in the mid-1800s, industrial pharmacists such as Wallace Abbott, Friedrich Bayer, Eli Lilly, and Charles Pfizer edged out traditional herb gardening and plant infusions over 20 percent of the world. In the early twenty-first-century, however, clinical trials revisited traditional herbal cures and found that they contained a surprising number of anti-inflammatories, antioxidants, and phytochemicals, including salicin from willow bark for fever, capsaicin from chili peppers for arthritis, and echinacea from purple coneflower for boosting the immune system. Seriously ill patients sought Latino botánicas, Ayurvedic gurus, and Cherokee and Navajo shamans for advice on treating cancer, diabetes, and vascular ills. Abandoning belief in magical properties, seekers turned to alternative and complementary healers and herbalists, who based dosages on experience rather than controlled laboratory analysis.

Currently, medical journals acknowledge aloe for simple burns, blackberry and cranberry juice for treating urinary tract infection, and valerian for insomnia. Health journals boost the popularity of chamomile, cumin, lemongrass, oregano, Saint-John's-wort, saw palmetto, and turmeric for a variety of ills, from depression to dyspepsia and prostate engorgement. Along the Amazon River and into sub-Saharan Africa, India, and northern Siberia, ethnobotanists and biochemists comb the cultural wilds for food enhancers, such as black cohosh, crocus, hoodia, lavender, and medicinal fungi, that lower incidence of Alzheimer's disease, bipolarism, high blood pressure, menopausal complaints, and obesity. Herb markets dispense age-old Chinese curatives—*dong quai* (angelica), *mahuang*

(ephedra), salvia, and spurge (euphorbia)—all applicable to a host of ills. In August 2011, reports on the potency of coriander seed oil against microbes including *Escherichia coli* (*E. coli*), MRSA, salmonella, and staphylococcus raised possibilities for a harmless control of food bacteria by a natural product.

See also: Apicius; Culpeper, Nicholas; Curative Foods; Physic Gardening; Seacole, Mary Jane; Appendix: Herbal Foods and Uses.

Further Reading

Kitchen Cures: Homemade Remedies for Your Health. New York: Reader's Digest, 2011.

Mitchem, Stephanie Y. *African American Folk Healing.* New York: New York University Press, 2007.

Tucker, Arthur O., and Thomas DeBaggio. *The Encyclopedia of Herbs: A Comprehensive Reference to Herbs of Flavor and Fragrance.* Portland, OR: Timber, 2009.

Wilkins, John M., and Shaun Hill. *Food in the Ancient World.* Malden, MA: Wiley-Blackwell, 2006.

Heritage Foods

The term *heritage foods* implies an authentic regimen of cooking and eating for a particular population. The binding nature of place anchors heritage foods to a region and its produce, from high mountain goats and geoduck to prickly pear fruit and dried dates. Great Lakes Indians turned buffalo meat into a cottage industry of jerky and pemmican, two trail foods valued by expeditioners. Lao cooks localize *pahdek* (fish sauce) as an accompaniment to rice and bland entrées.

Traditional foods—Mexican salsas, Indian curry and dal, and Iberian paella—identify and preserve a people and provide staying power to culture. The binaries of a people and their foods create instant recognition of Barbadian flying fish, French wines, Japanese sushi, Norwegian herring, and Russian borscht. Enhanced by farmer's markets and locavores, ancestral dishes gain new devotees in the younger generation while nurturing pride in origin. By participating in the agrarian cycle—as by picking wild bilberries and stirring sorghum into molasses—youths learn the rhythms of their ancestors and experience the demands of feeding a family.

The reality of food migration implies a major shift in regional fare at least once a century. For example, the cuisine touted in elite eighteenth-century European cookbooks gave place to the national diets that arose from peasant staples and paralleled the fervor of modern nationhood. In place of imported haute cuisine, Poles reclaimed sausage; Jamaicans celebrated the pepper pot. In the American colonies, clam chowder and Christmas ambrosia marked high points in comfort food, the specialties that foster unity and fellowship.

European immigrants who settled the North American West evolved heritage dishes from fishing, foraging, and hunting. Coexistence resulted in mingling with first peoples, who already knew how to gather and dry blueberries and pine nuts, and to collect fiddlehead ferns for vegetables, and process birch and maple syrup for sweeteners. As farmers acclimated to new lands, butter and local honeys gained distinct taste and consistency from pasture clover and the lavender and lemon balm in herb beds.

Visual evidence of Moroccan tagine, Scots haggis, and Turkish figs certifies culinary history at the same time that it nurtures classic food legends, such as the West African source of okra in New Orleans gumbo and the lengthy list of potato dishes on Irish menus. The demand for historic food experiences bolsters heirloom seed marketing, the viability of small, specialty farms and artisanal bakeries, and higher sales of farmstead cheeses and niche jams and sausages. Fairgoers jam Heritage Food Day booths to taste genuine local treasures, the chicken pies, beef satay, and Caribbean boil-downs that date to the kitchens of regional founders.

An incentive to local cooks, heritage foods provide proof of cultural longevity, a tangible, edible evidence of such classic foodways as English ale and Kenyan bushmeat. The agritourist market injects among local diners outsiders who expect authenticity, from Minnesota wild rice and Mexican pineapples to Australian wallaby. Visitors to northern China look for venues serving Mongolian koumiss and hot pot, much as new arrivals to Tahiti anticipate menus featuring coconut-flavored mahimahi (dolphinfish).

The educated traveler knows that ancestral dishes offer better flavor, freshness, quality, and variety than the processed foods that industrial agriculture offers the standard grocery chain. Heirloom foods generally come to market unwaxed and undyed. Because of their suitability of soil and climate, they require less chemical nourishment, antibiotics, and pesticides. Another plus for heritage foods is the renewed stocking and low-volume husbandry of rare or endangered species—limbertwig apples, Buckeye chickens, Bourbon Red turkeys, and Southwestern Simmental cattle—and such custom crossbreeds as the beefalo.

See also: African Diet and Cuisine, Sub-Saharan; Dairy Food; Idiocuisine; National Dishes; Pemmican; Regional Cuisine; Seed Trade.

Further Reading

Bendrick, Lou. *Eat Where You Live.* Seattle, WA: Skipstone, 2008.

Duncan, Dorothy. *Nothing More Comforting: Canada's Heritage Food.* Tonawanda, NY: Dundurn, 2003.

Misiura, Shashi. *Heritage Marketing.* Burlington, MA: Elsevier, 2006.

Snell, Ala Hogan, and Lisa Castle. *A Taste of Heritage: Crow Indian Recipes and Herbal Medicines.* Lincoln: University of Nebraska Press, 2006.

Wilk, Richard R., ed. *Fast Food/Slow Food: The Cultural Economy of the Global Food System.* Lanham, MD: Altamira, 2006.

Herodotus (ca. 484–ca. 425 B.C.E.)

The Greek "Father of History," Herodotus of Halicarnassus introduced readers to the dietary manipulations and idiosyncrasies of the peoples he visited. He grew up on Samos and learned the Ionian dialect and Mediterranean lore. His family appears to have joined a cabal against a local tyrant and to have infused the boy with libertarianism. One of his anecdotes lauded the Samians for feeding honey cakes topped with sesame seed to 300 boys whom the Corinthians had marked for starvation.

Herodotus traveled the Crimea, Middle East, India, and Africa and compiled legends and observations for a systematic history. His accounts of civic and military strategy frequently expressed the dangers of losing control of city stockpiles or army supply trains. Among his conclusions, he stated that food choices by agriculturalists marked the height of civilization, while pagans far from centers of learning, such as the Padaeans of India, ate like savages and cannibals.

Herodotus's masterwork, *The Histories* (ca. 428 B.C.E.), described unique aspects of the known world, including the grain produced on land watered annually by the Nile overflow. He admired the health of Egyptians and noted their love of barley beer, imported Greek wines, and millet breads. By reporting on the Persians under Cyrus, Cambyses, Darius, and Xerxes, Herodotus drew conclusions about the luxuries and wrongheadedness of Athens's most virulent enemy. The withdrawal of Xerxes' army from Greece forced soldiers to eat bark, grass, and leaves, a source of epidemic dysentery. Upon arriving in Egypt at Abydos, the forces died in alarming numbers from stuffing themselves with food and from undergoing a change of water, a violation of Hippocratic dietary regimen.

The historian filled in details of food history, including the use of wood tuns to transport Armenian wine, the absence of figs in Babylonia, and the scheduling of athletic contests at Atys (present-day Turkey) to distract citizens from an 18-year famine. His survey of the builders of King Cheops's pyramid noted expenditures for bread, garlic, leeks, onions, and radishes. Far from the meat-centered diet of Greece, Herodotus observed Hindus existing on a vegetarian diet. To audience applause, he read his astounding mélange of stories at the Olympic Games. Banished from Halicarnassus for taking part in a rebellion, he died at Thurii, a Greek colony in southern Italy on the Tarentine Gulf, around age 59.

In place of predictable narrative, Herodotus permeated his storytelling with digressions on oddities, such as the Egyptian priest's love of goose meat and avoidance of fish, the use of swine to thresh grain, and the presentation of a mock cadaver and coffin at banquets to remind diners of their mortality. He seemed fascinated by the Egyptian loaves made from lotus heads and papyrus roots and by the offering to Isis of a bullock stuffed with bread and honey, figs, raisins, and frankincense and myrrh, his only detailed recipe. He covered extreme foods, such as Harpagus's cannibal feasting on his own son, whom the Mede tyrant Astyages surreptitiously served boiled and roasted. *The Histories* marveled that one tribe on an island in the Araxes (Danube River) lived entirely on roots.

Herodotus made value judgments about human diet, such as the Thracian fondness for drunkenness, war, and pillage and the soft Persian diet that yielded soft soldiers. He admired the Babylonian diet of honey, palm fruit, sesame oil, and wine and extolled both the Babylonians and Arabs for refraining from meals until they had washed themselves. Herodotus made an example of the Spartan self-restraint of Pausanias, the general who rejected the sumptuous spread in Commander Mardonios's tent as a sinful example of Persian hubris and vanity.

Herodotus also stressed the political cost of violating local foodways. The Persians flouted the custom of watering table wine at a feast for the Massagetae (Iranians), whom the Persians defeated by deflecting them from war to gorging themselves. When Persian legates to Macedonia insisted that women join them at dinner, young males disguised themselves as girls and slew the ambassadors with daggers. Some of the tales led critics to call Herodotus the "Father of Lies"; later historians called him the "Father of Comparative Anthropology."

Further Reading

Baragwanath, Emily. *Motivation and Narrative in Herodotus.* New York: Oxford University Press, 2008.

Finch, Caleb E. "Herodotus on Diet and Longevity: How the Persians Fed on Dung and Lived to 80, While the Tall, Handsome Ethiopians Ate Boiled Meat and Lived Beyond 120." *Journal of Aging, Humanities, and the Arts* 3:2 (2009): 86–96.

Herodotus. *The Landmark Herodotus: The Histories.* Ed. Robert B. Strassler and Andrea L. Purvis. New York: Anchor, 2009.

Thomas, Rosalind. *Herodotus in Context: Ethnography, Science, and the Art of Persuasion.* New York: Cambridge University Press, 2000.

Hiatt, Jesse (1826–1898)

The cultivator of the Red Delicious apple, fruit grafter Jesse Hiatt propagated one of the world's preferred health foods, an icon of American agriculture.

A native Quaker of Randolph County, Indiana, Hiatt learned grafting and pruning from his father, William Hiatt. Jesse farmed until his parents' deaths and then migrated to Mill, Indiana. Upon settling in East Peru, Iowa, in 1856, he, his wife, Rebecca Jane Pearson Hiatt of Ohio, and their ten children occupied a two-room log cabin and operated a flour mill. After traveling southwest by wagon with his brother Aaron to buy tree stock in Oskaloosa, Jesse Hiatt hybridized an apple orchard of Hiatt Blacks and Hiatt Sweets.

In October 1872, two rows of Hiatt's apple seedlings, Yellow Bellflowers and Winesaps, produced a mutation called a "sport" or "sucker." For two years, he cut back the shoots. In the third year, he allowed the loner to grow. A decade later, the scion yielded its first fruit, an American original he named the Hawkeye. Into the 1880s, Hiatt advertised his uniquely sweet, long-bodied apple at Iowa fairs. A heavy producer, Hawkeyes yielded 750 boxes per acre, as opposed to other strains that yielded only 200 boxes.

In 1893, Hiatt sent four Hawkeye apples to a fruit show in Louisiana, Missouri, to compete against the popular Ben Davis, a rugged commercial apple. The judge, U.S. chief pomologist Henry Elian Van Deman, awarded first prize to the Hawkeye. Clarence McCall Stark acquired rights to the apple and, in 1895, marketed it for Stark Brothers Nursery as the "Delicious." To introduce its uniqueness, Stark gave bundles of ten free saplings in orders to apple propagators. After acquiring a Yellow Delicious in 1914, Stark renamed Hiatt's hybrid the "Red Delicious."

By 1922, for appearance, flavor, postfrost flowering, and integrity in storage, the Red Delicious apple sold 8 million trees. Iowans honored Hiatt's mutation by fencing in the original tree, which survived until an ice storm toppled it in 1940. A granite monument honors the spot. By the early 1940s, the fragrant, strawberry-red apple revolutionized the American fruit industry. It introduced a profitable family farm product by generating more income than any other apple.

Orchards rewarded growers with a strong-limbed tree resistant to fire blight that adapted to most soils and required little pruning. Subsequent offshoots—the Starking, Richard, Starkrimson, Redspur, and Royal Red—earned awards for taste and texture in the United States and throughout the world. By the 1980s, 70 percent of Washington State dessert apples were Red Delicious. Although harvested between August and October, high-tech chillers and atmospheric controls made the apples available year-round.

Because further tinkering with color, shape, firmness, and juiciness reduced taste, subsequent crops of 300 variants of Delicious apples sold poorly. While health advocates lauded apples for reducing cancer of the colon and lungs and for lowering cholesterol, buyers rejected later strains for mealy pulp and thick, bitter skin made chewier by waxing. In the late 1990s, the apple industry foundered, requiring government aid.

In 2003, as the Cameo, Fuji, Gala, and Granny Smith gained favor, only 37 percent of Washington State farmers grew the Red Delicious. Desperate orchardists in New York and Wisconsin turned to heritage strains and organic fruit. As of spring 2011, only 10 percent of Washington State acreage grew the Red Delicious.

Further Reading

Calhoun, Creighton Lee. *Old Southern Apples: A Comprehensive History and Description of Varieties for Collectors, Growers, and Fruit Enthusiasts*. White River Junction, VT: Chelsea Green, 2010.

Egan, Timothy. "'Perfect' Apple Pushed Growers into Debt." *The New York Times*, November 4, 2000.

Higgins, Adrian. "Why the Red Delicious No Longer Is." *Washington Post*, August 5, 2005.

Holiday Dishes and Festival Foods

Celebratory meals and holiday dishes commemorate life and reclaim national pride or group identity. A barbecue may honor a regional celebration such as Juneteenth or Australia Day every January 26. The spicing of red snapper commemorates Southern heritage on Martin Luther King Day every January 15 since 1983. Shared cake and punch at weddings, births, bar mitzvahs, graduations, and funerals foster personal regard for beliefs and ethnic identity, as with fiesta dishes for July 24, Simón Bolívar Day in Bolivia, Colombia, Ecuador, Panama, and Venezuela. In one instance, Heiva I Tahiti, spit-roasting a pig acknowledges the end of French colonialism in the Windward Islands on June 14, 1985.

Banquets and food fairs enhance community values, such as cupcakes in the colors of the French flag for Bastille Day, piki corn for a Hopi kachina initiation dance, hot *syllabub* for a Welsh winter solstice festival, a crab boil-up at the end of a Newfoundland fishing expedition, and Eastern Orthodox Easter eggs in Armenia. Commemorative banquets acknowledge survivors of epidemics, invasions, and wars, notably chocolate coins and jam-filled Hanukkah doughnuts that have honored Hasmonaean strongman Judas Maccabees since 160 B.C.E. and D-Day banquets that have reunited Allied soldiers and members of the French Resistance every June 6 since 1945.

The selection and preparation of food and drink for holiday occasions join celebrants worldwide in the enjoyment of festal foods. Specific ingredients connect to seasons of the year, especially meats served fresh during fall slaughtering and fruits and vegetables connected with garden harvests, such as Kwanzaa. Wild clover honey, plover eggs, walnuts, and strawberries stress the control of natural cycles over human sustenance. Sources link specific dates to religion, culture, and food lore. The following list includes some of the most notable.

January 1: The Greek *vasilopitta* (New Year's cake), flavored with lemon rind and anise seed, bears the new year inscribed in the crust. The baker inserts a good luck coin in a slit; the finder enjoys 12 months of prosperity.

In Ireland, traditionally, a wife serves the year's first raisin bread to her husband. He takes one bite each for Father, Son, and Holy Spirit, then hurls the leftover piece to defy famine. The ritual ends with a prayer that no family member may suffer hunger. The wife gathers the pieces to serve guests.

In the American South, cabbage and rice for New Year's Day ensures riches. For health, families eat field peas with hog jowl and collard greens. A lavish outlay for the family reunion fills trestle tables with corn pudding, squash casserole, and sweet potato pie, traditional New World fare that Native Americans cooked for millennia.

From the 1700s, French confectioners molded vanilla, cinnamon, orange, lemon, and rose bonbons and sold them in *bonbonnières* (holiday boxes). French woodsmen taught the Sioux of St. Paul, Minnesota, recipes for New Year's cakes.

January 6: On Epiphany at the Feast of Kings commemorating the arrival of the Magi to the Christ Child, the French pastry chef decorates a *galette du roi* (king's cake), a regal dessert derived from the Roman Saturnalia and containing a token identifying the year's Twelfth Night king, who reigns for a day.

In colonial Cahokia, Illinois, Frenchmen enticed their sweethearts to make pancakes on Epiphany night. To supply the kitchen, the men processed in costume on New Year's Eve to panhandle sugar, maple syrup, and ratafia, an almond-flavored fruit liqueur.

January 7: In Kyoto, Japan, the eating of seven-grass rice gruel began under the Emperor Daigo in 897. Cooks soft-boil rice blended with wild celery, shepherd's purse, turnip, and daikon radish.

January 25: In Scotland, the preparation of haggis on Burns' Night commemorates plowman poet Robert Burns, born in Ayrshire in 1759. To accompany whiskey, cooks grind heart, liver, lung, oatmeal, onion, spices, and suet for tying into sheep stomachs. They boil the bundle for three hours to serve with clapshot, a purée of "tatties and neeps" (potatoes and swedes).

February 1: The Irish and Welsh celebrate St. Brigid of Kildare, an enslaved native of fifth-century Croghan and the patron of dairiers. For the hungry, she miraculously

A family in northeast China gathers at the table to welcome the new year. A celebratory meal and traditional festive dishes commemorate religious, civic, and folk holidays among people everywhere. *(Reza/Getty Images)*

produced milk and butter. A feast honors her with spreads of dairy foods, raisin bread, and colcannon, a mix of onions, cabbage, and potatoes.

February 2: In midwinter, Candlemas delights people worldwide as Pancake Day. Cooks make fritters, pancakes, doughnuts, and biscuits to commemorate the purification of the Virgin Mary, who presented the infant Jesus at the temple of Jerusalem according to Jewish law.

February 14: On St. Valentine's Day in the 1600s, Englishwomen gathered at 11 P.M. to bake a "dumb cake" from salt and wheat and barley flour. Taking turns rolling the dough, they pricked their initials on the surface and baked the cake in silence. At midnight, they awaited their true love.

March 1: To welcome spring, the Romansh of Engadine, in western Switzerland, observe Chalandamarz, a children's festival derived from the old Roman New Year on the first day of March. They prepare such folk delicacies as cream-drenched chestnuts, caramels, fruit and nut breads, and tarts.

March 17: Throughout the Catholic world, the Irish reverence Patrick, Ireland's patron saint, who died on March 17, 493 C.E. Bakers shape cakes in the form of shamrocks and tint both confections and beer green, a symbol of promise.

March 19: Italians indulge in fritters, cream puffs, and *bigne,* a fried doughnut, at the Feast of St. Joseph. In Sicily, bakers fill dough with chocolate, pistachios, and sugar as votive offerings to the saint, who protects them from famine.

March 20: On Persian New Year's Eve, Iranian cooks shape egg noodles, a stringy peasant dish first mentioned in Arab cookbooks in the 1200s. The threads, added to bean soup, symbolize the reins of life as well as the unraveling of knotty problems and life's tangled paths. The noodles also bless the bonds that unite a family.

April 1: On April Fool's Day, French confectioners shape chocolates into the *poisson d'avril* (April fish) in recognition of Pisces and the vernal equinox.

May 1: From early Celtic times, Scots made bannock cake to celebrate Beltane, a Wiccan holiday. Each loaf had nine knobs. Ritual required participants to tear off and toss the knobs over their shoulders and dedicate the bread to the god of livestock. Herdsmen lit the Beltane fire and whipped eggs into milk, cream or butter, and oatmeal to dress the bannocks.

Shrove Tuesday Eve: On Collop Monday in England, Christians cut bacon collops, or pieces, to salt and hang during Lent. Before the meatless period begins, Cornish observers make pea soup; the Irish gorge on meat, pancakes, eggs, and dairy goods.

Shrove Tuesday: The day before Lent, Fastens-Een begins with a Scots carnival, a bonanza of fried foods, pancakes, roast meats, and serpentine cakes. The tradition dates to the Roman Saturnalia, when cooks embellished baked swans, peacocks, herons, or pheasants as food spectacles.

Lent: Among Christians, abstinence preceding Easter calls for fish, lentil, cheese, and bean dishes as alternatives to meat. A more stringent apostolic meal also rejects eggs and dairy items during Lent.

Mothering Sunday: On the fourth Sunday in Lent, English cooks around Bristol make mothering buns, an iced yeast bun topped with decorative candies and served at breakfast.

Palm Sunday: On the Sunday preceding Easter, French bakers honor the arrival of Jesus on a donkey at Jerusalem by making animal cookies.

Good Friday: Bakers at Old Chelsea Bun House in Jews' Row, London, advertise hot cross buns for breakfast. The custom echoes Babylonian offerings to the goddess Astarte and combines the traditions of Jewish Passover cakes and the Eucharist.

Holy Saturday: A Russian Orthodox ritual meal of savory and sweet treats remains spread until Easter Monday. To symbolize the Trinity (Father, Son, and Holy Ghost), food preparers fill Easter baskets with ham, sausage, and roast veal. A sweet cheese molded in a tall pyramid becomes a crown when decked with raisins and cherries to suggest majesty and resurrection.

Easter: Globally, the egg symbolizes rebirth and regeneration. On Easter eve, German housewives wrap eggs in patterned cloth and hide them for children who await the Easter hare. Cooks throughout Christendom shape treats like rabbits and hens.

Russians carve a block of butter into a reclining lamb and add tinfoil horns. Celebrants exchange eggs and exult "Christ is risen," a phrase abbreviated on baking molds. On the same date, Zoroastrians boil eggs as New Year's gifts.

June 11: In 1871, Hawaii's King Kamehameha V decreed June 11 as a holiday recognizing his grandfather, Kamehameha I, the patriarch and unifier of the Hawaiian islands in 1810. Hawaiians celebrate with parades and a luau, a native feast.

June 24: In Prado and Madrid, Spain, cooks fry fritters in the public square on St. John the Baptist Day or Midsummer Day. Latvian housewives make cheese and light solstice bonfires.

Early August: In Gallup, New Mexico, a Pueblo festival involves fry bread and piki cakes to accompany corn and hoop dances, drumming, and chant.

August 24: Swedish briners age herring in barrels until August 24, St. Bartholomew's Day, when cooks serve it with sour milk or cream, cheese, bread, and onions.

September 29: In July 1588, after the defeat of the Spanish Armada, Queen Elizabeth I proclaimed roast goose an annual Michaelmas dish.

Harvest: Among the Seneca of New York, a traditional harvest feast called for cauldrons of succotash, dog meat, and cabbage. The day concluded with a corn dance in thanks for a successful garden.

October 21: In Majorca, observers of St. Ursula Day and the Feast of the Virgins make sugared pastries or fritters to serve with wine to the young men who serenade girls with guitar solos.

October 31: British families roast nuts on the night preceding All Saint's Day. The nuts that glow steadily predict constant love; those that burst into flame foreshadow a brief romance.

November 1: On All Saints' Day, Czechs consume soul cakes with cold milk to cool souls in Purgatory.

November 11: In Anglo-Saxon times, Martinmas welcomed winter. After animal slaughter, "pig cheer" provisioned the pantry and smokehouse.

Thanksgiving: The American Thanksgiving commemorates the first Christian harvest festival. After the Battle of Gettysburg on July 3–4, 1863, President Abraham Lincoln declared August 6 a day of national gratitude. Subsequent presidents emulated his example on the last Thursday of November, a national holiday associated with expanded tables—featuring turkey—to treat family and guests.

December 4: At the Tsubaki Grand Shrine in Mie, Japan, and its sister religious site at the Tsubaki American Shrine in Stockton, California, part of a ritual calendar of events schedules a Shinto ceremony, *Mochi-tsuki,* the ritual making of *mochi* (rice cakes).

December 13: Swedish children deliver a festal breakfast to adults on St. Lucia Day, which honors the Roman virgin's martyrdom in 304 C.E. The oldest girl prepares a tray of coffee and sweet St. Lucia buns pocked with raisins for a pre-Christmas breakfast.

December 17: Ancient Rome feasted and celebrated the height of December. To honor Saturn and mark the beginning of the agricultural calendar, citizens and slaves acknowledged Saturnalia with banquets and cries of "Io,

Saturnalia!" Disapproving of the pagan source but applauding the egalitarian motives, Christians converted the citywide indulgence into Christmas, a pious celebration of the birth of Christ.

December 24: For Yule feasts, Europeans seek the best foodstuffs. In Italy, a flat circle of sweetened focaccia serves throughout the season. Russians place a samovar for tea along with varieties of fish and cakes and a blessed wafer to be divided among guests.

As described in Laura Ingalls Wilder's *Little House on the Prairie* series, frontier Kansans anticipated holiday baking. Ma Ingalls kneaded salt-rising and rye 'n' Injun breads and made Swedish crackers and beans seasoned with molasses and salt pork.

December 25: The Dutch celebrate Christmas with gingerbread. For the annual wassail bowl, which accompanies a feast, punch preparers dissolve spices in boiling water and add wine, sugar, and a frothy egg yolk topping. Bakers distribute wheat biscuits spiced with cinnamon as a sandwich cookie with almond paste in the center.

Medieval English cooks prepared a boar's head with crisp, brown skin. They garnished the beast with mustard, wreathed it in bay leaf and rosemary, and secured a lemon in its mouth as a Norman symbol of abundance. Wait staff processed around the table with the centerpiece lifted on a platter.

In Toledo, Spain, where Arab confectioners introduced marzipan in 700 C.E., the *mozarabes* (Christians under Muslim rule) shaped almond paste into holiday figures and glazed them with colored sugar-water. Convent kitchens began their own candy-making fund-raisers with ancient recipes and food dyeing techniques.

Victorian Christmas celebrations called for prunes and raisins for punch, puddings, porridge, and plum cake. In Charles Dickens's *A Christmas Carol* (1843), the emblematic Cratchits, surviving in penury on "fifteen 'bob' a week," manage a festive roast goose, applesauce, potatoes, sage and onion dressing, and gravy, with a dessert of flaming, brandy-soaked pudding. The story so fixed itself in the English-speaking world that re-creations in art, drama, song, and film elevated the Cratchits' holiday into a folk sacrament.

December 26: First celebrated in 1966, the U.S. observance of Kwanzaa from December 26 to January 1 commemorates the seven principles of blackness with candles and a first fruits table. Guests share a loving cup and feast on fresh fruits and vegetables prepared in West African style.

December 31: After the Catholic Church banned Christmas celebrations in 1649, Scots compensated with a huge New Year's Eve event, which they named Hogmanay for the Anglo-Saxon "Holy Month." The traditional bash featured oatcakes, cheese, black buns, and a Highland stir-up of oatmeal, honey, cream, and Scotch whiskey.

Among Orthodox Christians in Greece, the celebration of St. Basil's Day (January 1) begins the night before with the baking of brioche into a yeasty loaf-upon-loaf crowned in almonds and walnuts. After the head of house cuts the cake, diners look for a foil-wrapped good-luck coin inside.

Memorable ingredients—mincemeat pies and plum pudding with sherry for Christmas in England, wheat pudding on March 20–21 for Persian Norouz on the vernal equinox, corn dishes on May 1 for the Zuñi Green Corn Dance, and rice pudding for the Hindu Diwali (festival of lights)—respect traditions dating into the past. Examples incorporate special items—strawberries in cream for Swedish Midsummer, fried carp for Czech Christmas Eve dinner, matzoh cake for Jewish Passover, *mikigaq* (fermented whale meat) for the Inuit dead whale requiem on December 10, roasted chestnuts and stollen (sweet loaves) in Germany and panettone (fruitcake) in Italy for Christmas, and abalone soup for Vietnamese New Year. The consumption of four-leaf-clover cookies and green beer on March 17, St. Patrick's Day, brings out the Irish in people worldwide.

In prehistory, Koreans celebrated the winter solstice each December 21 with red bean porridge and rice balls. Since the rise of Judaism, Sukkot, a harvest festival, has called for stuffed eggplant or zucchini as a symbol of satiety. From the fifth century C.E., Old Norse Seto-speakers of Estonia honored the warrior class with picnics at barrow graves. After the seventh century, Muslims in Somalia celebrated Eid al-Fitr, the end of the Ramadan fast, with beef turnovers. On Malta, since the eleventh century, New Year's celebrants have eaten grapes to ensure wellness throughout the year; the Chinese observe the same occasion by boiling long noodles and steaming fish whole to promote longevity.

The Christianization of nations replaced pagan cuisine with ritual dishes, such as the sweet rolls and chocolate consumed on the Mexican Día de los Muertos (Day of the Dead), a replacement for the Aztec Miccailhuitontli, which honored deceased children. Russians introduced cakes with domed tops in imitation of Orthodox cathedrals. The African diaspora inspired Kwanzaa, a midwinter festival of harvest foods that restores ties to primal West African roots. In Mexico, as early as 1798, Catholic cooks prepared waterbug eggs as a garnish for shrimp *revoltijo* to serve on Christmas Eve and Maundy Thursday.

Whatever the holiday, food represents the nourishment of human hopes and faiths. Since September 18, 1810, Chilean cooks have celebrated independence from Spain with empanadas, turnovers filled with meat or fruit and raisins. In 1950, worshippers in Sri Lanka formalized Vesak, the observance of Buddha's birth in May or June.

Cooks kept the occasion with green mango curry. Malaysians fried rice vermicelli, which they flavored with bean sprouts and mustard.

See also: Chocolate; Customs, Food; Dal; Moravian Diet and Cuisine; Religion and Food; Silk Road.

Further Reading

Cornell, Karl A. *Holiday Cooking Around the World.* Minneapolis, MN: Lerner, 2002.

Hall, Colin Michael, and Liz Sharples. *Food and Wine Festivals and Events Around the World: Development, Management.* Burlington, MA: Elsevier, 2008.

Schmidt, Arno, and Paul Fieldhouse. *The World Religions Cookbook.* Westport, CT: Greenwood, 2007.

Thompson, Jennifer Trainer. *The Joy of Family Traditions: A Season-by-Season Companion of 400 Celebrations and Activities.* Berkeley, CA: Ten Speed, 2008.

Honey

An organic sugar and natural curative, honey holds a unique place in culinary history for its viscous consistency and sweet flavor. Spanish cave paintings in Bicor attest to the collection of wild honey in 13,000 B.C.E. Egyptian undertakers preserved corpses in beeswax and honey as early as 3300 B.C.E. Mourners supplied the dead with honey to nourish the spirit in the afterlife and ensure immortality. The first organized beekeeping began in clay pipes in 2400 B.C.E. throughout Lower Egypt, where papyri recorded 900 remedies concocted from honey.

In 2100 B.C.E., Mesopotamians paid a dear price—one silver shekel for 2 liters (about 2.1 quarts) of honey—and offered honeycombs as emoluments to officials and gifts to the gods. Cooks in classical Greece and Italy relied on honey as the standard sweetener and imported the best variety, thyme honey, from Attica, the Greek Isles, and Sicily. One simple dish began with the curdling of milk with fermented honey, a forerunner of honeyed yogurt. Another steeped stuffed fig leaves in honey. Sauces balanced honey with vinegar for topping fish, poultry, roast game, and salad greens. Epaenetes, a late-Hellenist food writer, described a honey stuffing made with cheese, onions, organ meats, and vinegar. Because kitchen demand exceeded supply, farmers profited from beekeeping.

Roman cookery echoed the honey-centered dishes of Greece. One specialty dish, *libum* (cheesecake), ended with the soaking of warm buns in fresh honey. Around 45 C.E., Apicius's recipes relied on honey for flavoring fish, meat, and vegetable cookery and for making mead and desserts. Homemakers cooked gruel in honey, preserved fruit and meat in honeyed liquids, and served diners *mulsum,* a fresh blend of wine with honey, or *conditum,* an aged mulsum spiced with laurel, pepper, and saffron.

Middle Ages and Early Modern Era

At the collapse of the Roman Empire in 476 C.E., Christian convents and monasteries took over the beekeeping once pursued by farmers. Monks and abbesses preserved bee colonies to supply churches with wax for pure-scented candles and with honey and propolis (honey resin) for refectories and hospices. Scandinavian prelates fermented wine from honey and spiced their drinks into hippocras, hydromel, and metheglin, a honeyed apple cider flavored with cinnamon.

Archaeologists in northern Israel have unearthed remnants of a 3,000-year-old beekeeping industry, including the oldest intact beehives ever found. Documentary evidence of organized apiculture dates to about 2400 B.C.E. *(Amihai Mazar/Hebrew University of Jerusalem/Associated Press)*

Simultaneous with Christian food history, evidence from the Mayan, Hebrew, Buddhist, Islamic, Norse, Celtic, and Hindu cultures depicted honey as a skin treatment, health food, aphrodisiac, fertility enhancer, and gift of the gods. Practitioners of Ayurvedic medicine ranked honey high among foods that balanced organ activity. In the *Compendium of Materia Medica* (1578), Li Shih Chen, a Chinese apothecary, prescribed honeyed food and drinks as analgesics. Later Chinese medical texts extolled honey for "benefiting vital energy" and boosting the healing power of hundreds of herbs. Nutritionists recognized that honey, like alcohol, was a rare food that energized the body by going directly into the bloodstream; Japanese gastronomes prized honey and bee larvae, sold together in open-air markets. In North America, Canadian first peoples served wild strawberry puree in honey, a treatment for sore throat and inflamed tonsils. Plains Indians recommended cooking beans with honey, the forerunner of American baked beans.

Industry

Art elevated the bee as a metaphor for organized urban centers and honey as a symbol of civilized industry. British colonial activity, beginning in Virginia in 1622, spread the European bee (*Apis mellifera*) and beekeeping techniques to the Americas, Australia, New Zealand, and Tasmania. The seventeenth-century cook turned spiced rye cake into honeyed *pain d'épice* (gingerbread), a delicacy and energy food favored in multiple cuisines, from France, Germany, Norway, Poland, and Switzerland to the Middle East. Across Europe, hosts warmed guests by the fireside with mulled wine, a honeyed and spiced wine heated with a fire poker plunged into each tankard.

By the 1800s, the honeybee spread west in North America, distributed in part by Mormons settling Utah and by apiarist L.I. Langworth, who practiced scientific apiculture in Los Angeles. Hive managers set up colonies with hive frames, smokers, and honey extractors, the tools of commercial apiculture. Villagers from the Catskills to the Sierra Madres promoted local honey for its unique flavor and crystallized candies for their nutritive value.

Throughout the abolitionist era, U.S. boycotts of slave-produced foods ruled out molasses. In 1839, to promote free-labor honey as a substitute, reformer and poet Elizabeth Margaret Chandler of Tecumseh, Michigan, published a honey tea cake recipe in the antislavery newspaper *Genius of Universal Emancipation*. During the Civil War, women's groups issued the recipe in fund-raising cookbooks to aid the Sanitary Commission in opening and equipping rehabilitation centers for the wounded.

The availability of cane sugar in the mid-1800s generated the first substantial competition with honey for condiments and confections. During World War I, German medical teams monopolized supplies of honey for sanitizing wounds. Sugar rationing during World War II increased demand for natural sweeteners, including honey, birch sugar, and maple syrup. A postwar glut of sugar in the 1950s reduced the price of honey and forced many professional beekeepers out of business. The industry continued to thrive among smallholders, however, as illustrated by the success of organic honeys from the Hawaiian Islands.

Currently, beekeepers market products based on terroir, the complex influence of geography, climate, and temperature. Aficionados reject blended stock and seek monofloral sources made from the nectar of acacia, clover, heather, honeysuckle, lime, orange blossoms, or sourwood. Choice honeys offer rich aftertaste—fruity savor from blackberry or blueberry honey, floral tones from white sage honey, malt from buckwheat honey, and citrus from saw palmetto honey. Artisans pair monofloral honeys with other foods, such as nutty chestnut honey with Gorgonzola or Parmesan cheese. To prevent allergies, buyers prefer raw, in-the-comb, unfiltered, and unpasteurized honey containing pollen that lessens eye, nose, and lung sensitivities.

Since late 2006, colony collapse, a biotic catastrophe to hives from pathogens, monocultural farming, or pesticides, concerns European and North American farmers. In 2011, honey packagers who rely on the honeybee for pollination and hive and honey generation feared for the survival of the planet's colonies and for future pollination of fruits, tree nuts, and vegetables.

See also: Adulterated Food; Apicius; London Virginia Company; Sicilian Diet and Cuisine; Sugar and Sweeteners; Theophrastus.

Further Reading

Altman, Nathaniel. *The Honey Prescription: The Amazing Power of Honey as Medicine.* Rochester, VT: Healing Arts, 2010.

Marchese, C. Marina. *Honeybee: Lessons from an Accidental Beekeeper.* New York: Black Dog and Levanthal, 2011.

Readicker-Henderson, E., ed. *A Short History of the Honey Bee: Humans, Flowers, and Bees in the Eternal Chase for Honey.* Portland, OR: Timber, 2009.

Rosenbaum, Stephanie. *Honey: From Flower to Table.* San Francisco: Chronicle, 2002.

Hormones in Food

The steroid hormones that control development, growth, and reproduction in animals cause consumer concern when they infiltrate human meals. With the artificial enhancers—estradiol, melengestrol acetate, progesterone, testosterone, trenbolone acetate, zeranol—synthesized in the 1950s, livestockers inject some 80 percent of young animals with unnatural hormones or add steroids to their feed. The additives cause injection lesions but make animal young achieve adult size 20 percent faster at a growth rate of up to 3 pounds (1.4 kilograms) per week. Speedy maturation limits the amount of stall-feeding necessary before slaughter. The injections increase profitability by boosting feed efficiency with less food and by reducing fat marbling in meat.

Similarly, dairy cows and goats treated with bovine pituitary extract give 15 percent more milk over an extended lactation period, thus reducing the need for large herds and their impact on the environment. The treatment stresses the cow, which incurs an increase of milking time from eight to 12 weeks. In addition, hormones increase risk of calf deformity, increased twinning, and smaller offspring as well as internal bleeding, mastitis, ovarian cysts, retained placenta, and hoof disease and sores causing lameness. Because the ailments require treatment, antibiotics increase additives in milk and dairy products.

Consumers question the unmonitored drugs in dairy foods and meat. Synthetic steroids such as diethylstilbestrol (DES) increase cancer risk from uncontrolled cell division in the breast, colon, prostate, and testes. Since 1950, incidence of breast cancer has risen 55 percent. More alarming are the 120 percent increase in testicular cancer and 190 percent rise in prostate cancer. DES also causes child breast enlargement, early onset of puberty, and vaginal cancer in daughters of mothers treated with DES during pregnancy.

In the late 1970s, U.S. Food and Drug Administration inspectors banned time-release DES pellets from ear implants in cattle and sheep, but not from use in poultry and swine. The European Union (EU) concluded that growth hormones have carcinogenic, developmental, genotoxic, and neurobiological effects on human consumers. The EU issued a ban on synthetic hormones in 1989, and a decade later, Canada halted the treatment of beef cattle with growth enhancers. Additional rejections of hormones in beef occurred in Australia, Japan, and New Zealand.

Since 1993, the addition of Monsanto's genetically modified bovine growth hormones (BGH) to dairy cattle has spread to 30 percent of U.S. cattle. The intervention in natural cycles raises milk production by some 25 percent but causes alarm in farmers, consumers, and scientists. More objectionable to the public, the injection of 90 percent of calves raised for veal with the hormones meant for adult cattle leaves uncalculated the amount of growth drugs that remain in the meat.

Until veterinary authorities evolve exact testing measures for food additives, the medical community fears for the safety of children, pregnant women, and the unborn. A 2007 study raised the issue of low sperm count in men whose mothers ate meat treated with potent sex hormones. Generating alarm for the environment, pollution of watersheds by hormone-bearing cow feces has resulted in freakish gender and reproductive changes in wild fish, causing lower fish sperm count. Consumers avoid ingestion of synthetic steroids by purchasing only hormone-free and organic beef and milk, but their choices boost the price of

food without guaranteeing better quality. Spurring caution were reports from Shanghai, China, in 2005 that 330 consumers died from eating pork tainted with clenbuterol, a weight-loss steroid that had been banned since the 1990s.

Further muddling the issues of synthetic food additives, the media charges that organic farmers generate propaganda to spread myths about growth hormones and their effects on human health. Animal rights advocates respond that organic animal husbandry produces healthier animals needing neither antibiotics nor hormones and meat containing more omega-3 fatty acids. In answer to the consumer's quandary, some medical authorities advocate cutting back on meat and dairy to limit the amount of synthetic animal nutrients in the body.

A model of biotechnology in pisciculture, raisers of AquAdvantage Salmon at AquaBounty Technologies, a land-based facility in Waltham, Massachusetts, apply growth boosters to produce fish twice as large as wild Atlantic salmon. The control of biological processes through gene and protein analysis results in sterile all-female fish requiring 10 percent less feed and enhances disease resistance while shortening the growth period by more than 200 days. The end product outweighs wild salmon by 4.4 pounds (almost 2 kilograms).

Medical authorities fear that low concentrations of hormones over time may damage the human consumer and contaminate groundwater; however, tests, both industry funded and independent, are inconclusive. In July 2011, company officials declared transgenic fish biologically and chemically indistinguishable from native species and promoted more fish farming to prevent the possible extinction of major food species by 2050.

See also: Animal Husbandry; Beef; Exotic Food Clubs; Organic Foods; Pork; World Trade.

Further Reading

Duram, Leslie A., ed. *Encyclopedia of Organic, Sustainable, and Local Food.* Santa Barbara, CA: ABC-Clio, 2010.

Mitchell, Deborah. *Safe Foods: The A-to-Z Guide to the Most Wholesome Foods for You and Your Family.* New York: Signet, 2004.

Redman, Nina. *Food Safety: A Reference Handbook.* Santa Barbara, CA: ABC-Clio, 2007.

Shore, Laurence S., and Amy Pruden, eds. *Hormones and Pharmaceuticals Generated by Concentrated Animal Feeding Operations: Transport in Water and Soil.* New York: Springer, 2009.

Horses

A controversial topic in world food analysis, horse meat, or *viande chevaline,* suits the tastes of diners in Asia, Europe, and South America but repulses potential consumers in Australia, Canada, Ireland, and the United States. Taboos derive from beliefs that indiscriminate horse slaughter wastes a dignified sport and work animal. Jews and Hindus condemn the consumption of horse meat; Muslims prohibit the eating of donkeys and respect a social taboo against horse consumption.

Much sentimentality caused by equine consumption arises from gratitude. The ass, burro, donkey, horse, mule, and pony enabled nomads to achieve a settled life. In Kazakhstan and the Ukraine about 4500 B.C.E., herders gentled the horse, a major contribution to streamlined labor and a source of gelatin, glue, hair, leather, meat, and milk.

Around 550 C.E., farmers modernized soil preparation with the invention of the horseshoe and halters for draft horses and the moldboard plow for inverting weedy clods and exposing the roots to the sun. A heavier metal-faced plow crafted around 600 C.E. improved yield and fostered a population spurt. The arrival of the dog and horse in the Western Hemisphere after 1492 presented methods of pulling plows and travois and introduced native Americans to a new source of jerky.

As a food, horse meat offers a low-calorie source of iron and protein. Hippocrates, a Greek physician in the fifth century B.C.E., considered the flesh tender, digestible, and more palatable than beef. Horse meat contains less fat than deer or rabbit and more protein than kid, lamb, pork, or venison. However, slaughtering horses raises ethical and religious questions about their designation as dietary staples.

Horse Meat in History

Historically, the Arabs, Koreans, Russians, and Sumatrans were long-term horse meat fanciers. The Chinese preferred the flesh of white horses. Their physicians prescribed horse meat to reduce fever and the horse brain and mare's milk for treating scurvy, but they discarded the liver as toxic. Huns and Tartars treated horse sores by placing salted jerky under their saddles. Mongols treasured koumiss, fermented mare's milk, as a daily refreshment high in vitamin C. Persians celebrated birthdays by roasting whole asses and horses. Sarmatians and Thessalians made cheese from mare's milk and ate horse meat raw.

The pagan Teutons regarded horse consumption as an honor to the god Odin. In response to Germanic idolatry, Pope Gregory III in 732 C.E. issued a ban to St. Boniface, a missionary to Germany, on hippophagy, or the eating of horses, which the church valued as companions and as mounts for cavalry under assault by an Islamic army. After 741, Pope Zachary upheld the interdict and equated horse eating with the consumption of beavers, crows, rabbits, storks, and other unclean animals.

At the Second Council of Nicaea in 787, Bishop Gregory of Ostia denounced hippophagy. In 1000, when Icelanders accepted Christianity, at the direction of Catholic priests, the islanders forfeited horse dishes from their tables and stopped exposing unwanted babies in the wild. The pairing of the two practices captured the revulsion Christians felt for wanton slaughter.

While socially taboo or legally prohibited in the United States and elsewhere, the consumption of horse meat persists in parts of Asia, Latin America, and Europe. This butcher shop in Paris specializes in *chevaline*. (Christophe Simon/AFP/Getty Images)

From the late Middle Ages to the nineteenth century, horse meat traditionally relieved famine, such as the loss of Christian army rations during the Crusades in July 1149 after Turks burned provisions and the starvation accompanying the British naval siege of Copenhagen from August 16 to September 5, 1807. To save money, Danes served prisoners boiled, roasted, and salted chevaline as well as horse sausage. Spaniards ate the horses killed during bullfights. Ottoman Turks rated horse meat on par with the meat of antelopes and camels. Italians made a delicacy of sun-dried horse jerky; Belgians at Ghent manufactured horse bologna. The English supported an under-the-counter business in horse meat, which fed the underclass.

The French developed a fondness for chevaline. Rather than waste the flesh of the dead animals, they marketed horse meat. After French soldiers developed a taste for equine flesh during Napoleon's retreat from Moscow in late 1812, French ministers questioned the origin of anti-hippophagy. A French culinary commission established in

1825 examined the difference between beef and chevaline and determined that horse meat cost little. Army surgeons asserted that horse meat strengthened the body during convalescence from wounds.

Conflicting Opinions

On two sides of the English Channel, consumers differed in their response to hippophagy. In the 1860s, a Paris restaurant advertised steaks and *consommé de cheval* (horse broth). In 1864, the Société d'Acclimation distributed chevaline free to the poor. As an enticement to French gastronomy, an English society promoting hippophagy held a banquet for 150 on February 6, 1868, at the Langham Hotel in London. The menu featured boiled withers, "Sole in Rocinante Oil," "Roast Pegasus," stuffed horse, jellied hooves, and "Sorbets against Prejudice." During the Prussian siege of Paris from September 19, 1870, to January 28, 1871, horse slaughter took the place of beef butchery. A fad for chevaline, donkey, and mule dishes increased French equine consumption. In 1875, French promoters of chevaline judged the time to be right for opening a specialty butcher shop in London. The meat market failed in four months.

The slaughter of war horses during World War I provided meat for troops, who dismembered fallen army mounts and cooked the joints in the field. A similar recycling of horse carcasses during World War II fed hungry German soldiers stationed on the Russian front and the poor in cities, where rationing forbade meat distribution on meatless Mondays and Tuesdays. In postwar Japan, starving citizens survived on deliveries of American horse meat. In 1949, film director Georges Franju protested horse slaughter in the French documentary *Blood of the Beasts*. Nonetheless, French meat dealers continued to profit from chevaline, especially the white meat of colts, which doctors recommended for the treatment of cardiac illness.

Despite claims that horse meat augments the world's food resources, more than 500 agencies protest horse slaughter in the United States as a form of cannibalism. In 2008, the Department of Agriculture compiled photos of maimed and tortured animals, many of them retired racehorses. After their transport to Texas, the Beltex and Dallas Crown abattoirs rendered 1,000 animals per week. Improper handling and the absence of feed and water stressed animals as they moved from auction to feedlot to slaughter. As meat in foreign lands, the haunches require testing for antibiotics, pesticides, and sulfonamides. One advantage to imported horsemeat, it remained unaffected by bovine spongiform encephalopathy (mad cow disease).

Presently, horse meat supplies protein at the rate of 2 pounds (900 grams) a year per person in Italy, where restaurant cooks value donkey and horse flesh for its sweetness and low fat content. Additional horse butchery in Argentina, Austria, Germany, Holland, Iceland, Kazakhstan, Malta, Mongolia, Polynesia, Quebec, Romania, Serbia, Slovenia, Spain, Sweden, and Switzerland contributes roasts and salted and smoked sandwich meat. The cuts are often menu features on Lufthansa airlines.

Horse slaughter in the United States earmarks the grass-fed Western burro and mustang, wild residents of the frontier since the early 1500s. Dealers earn $700–$900 per animal for meat that contains no artificial foods, chemicals, or drugs. Slaughter results in the export of 90 percent of the meat to feed feral cats in zoos and for human consumption, primarily in Belgium, Canada, France, Japan, and Mexico.

See also: Agriculture; Animal Husbandry; Eliot, Jared; Sanitation; Trade Routes; Vegetarianism.

Further Reading

Civitello, Linda. *Cuisine and Culture: A History of Food and People.* 3rd ed. Hoboken, NJ: John Wiley & Sons, 2011.

Gratzer, Walter Bruno. *Terrors of the Table: The Curious History of Nutrition.* New York: Oxford University Press, 2005.

McIlwraith, C. Wayne, and Bernard E. Rollin. *Equine Welfare.* Ames, IA: Wiley-Blackwell, 2011.

Toussaint-Samat, Maguelonne. *A History of Food.* Hoboken, NJ: Wiley-Blackwell, 2009.

Hot Pots

An economical source of cold weather comfort food, the northern Chinese or Mongolian hot pot heats broth for poaching or simmering individual choices of meat, seafood, and vegetables. A cozy, clannish form of on-site preparation, the heating of sliced foods and dried chrysanthemums and the dipping of scalded bits in sauce illustrate the communalism in Asian lifestyles. Variants include charcoal-fired brass, ceramic, porcelain, or steel tureens and the Korean stone pot carved from solid rock. Current heating styles replace charcoal with flaming alcohol, gas, and electric hotplates.

The use of a central cooker dates to the Zhou era around 2000 B.C.E., when ritual cookery in a three-legged cauldron drew participants around an open fire. The first identifiable variety, the mutton *huo guo* (hot pot) of northern nomads, influenced cookery in the early tenth century. A colorful legend describes how Mongol warriors boiled lamb and mutton dumplings in their helmets rather than load their horses with heavy cauldrons. Japanese adapters named the cooking method "Genghis Khan cuisine" for its Mongol origins.

Communal firepot cuisine spread quickly through China. Around 220 C.E., five-section copper or iron hot pots extended the variety of liquids in one meal. In the Yuan dynasty after 1280, the Mongol invaders replaced Chinese cuisine with their own. In the Yangtze River basin in the fourteenth century, Chongqing fishermen popularized regional flavors in hot pots, which drew diners to small restaurants and street stalls. By 1650, imperial chefs served meals firepot style to Qing rulers and to the shoguns of Edo, the capital of Japan. When mainland Chinese migrated to Taiwan in 1949, they brought Cantonese *shacha* hot pot cookery as a form of family togetherness, an ancestral trait.

The endless combinations encourage the consumption of seasonal ingredients, especially fresh lettuce. In southern China, seafood lovers favor carp heads, crab, clam, jellyfish, mussels, sea cucumber, and squid. Simple nonmeat choices—bean noodles, dumplings, kelp, quail eggs, seaweed rolls, tofu, water chestnuts, and wontons—encourage the participation of vegetarians. Produce ranges from leafy bok choy and napa cabbage and green and mung beans to delicate enoki mushrooms, ginger and shallot slices, coriander and lime leaves, and bland potatoes and taro. The final dousing in sauce invites individuality in the choices of chili, chopped coriander or garlic, hoisin or soy sauce, and sesame oil and vinegar.

Currently, Chinese steamboats feature sections for the heating of chicken stock, milk broth, red chili, and herbed or salted water. To secure morsels, diners use chopsticks or a strainer. Szechuan style hot pot applies hot pepper oil to broth for spicing eels, goose intestines, and beef and pork blood, brain, intestines, marrow, and tripe. Mandarin aristocrats prefer thin slices of frozen mutton for cooking in mushroom and shrimp soup and eating with bean curd, pancakes, and sesame butter. The Manchurian hot pot contains sauerkraut to produce an acidic pucker. Hong Kong cooks shape fish balls and meatballs around a surprise center, such as mango. Hiroshima cuisine merges the Japanese love of oysters with miso for a balanced taste devoid of fishiness.

See also: Beef; Cantonese Diet and Cuisine; Szechuan Diet and Cuisine.

Further Reading

MacVeigh, Jeremy. *International Cuisine.* Clifton Park, NY: Delmar Cengage Learning, 2009.

Ono, Tadashi, and Harris Salat. *Japanese Hot Pots: Comforting One-Pot Meals.* Berkeley, CA: Ten Speed, 2009.

Waldron, S.A., C.G. Brown, J.W. Longworth, and C.G. Zhang. *China's Livestock Revolution: Agribusiness and Policy Developments in the Sheep Meat Industry.* Cambridge, MA: CABI, 2007.

Zibart, Eve. *The Ethnic Food Lover's Companion.* Birmingham, AL: Menasha Ridge, 2001.

House of India

A Portuguese joint-stock company, the Casa da India (House of India) managed a bonanza in the world food trade. From 1481 to the early 1500s, the small European country dominated commerce in spices and pepper, the world's most common flavoring. Because pepper became more valuable than gold, it served as currency. Organized in 1443 as the Company of Guinea, originally called Casa da Guiné (House of Guinea), the House of India employed merchant sailors who ventured south down the western coast of Africa, ostensibly spreading Catholicism.

Established on Portugal's southern tip at Lagos by Prince Henry the Navigator, the company focused on transporting sugarcane from the Madeira Islands by caravel. By bartering with English liqueur, marketers succeeded in crushing the monopoly in "sweet salt" that Venetians managed from Crete and Cyprus. Planters, led by merchant Bartolomeo Marchionni, extended their cultivation of sugarcane to the Canary Islands and the Cape Verde Islands.

At Henry's death in 1460, King Afonso V moved the royal trading syndicate to Lisbon. Renamed the Casa da Mina (House of Mina), it received West African shipping from Fort St. George at Elmina, Ghana. Under regulation by the economic officials, the Portuguese merchant fleet imported fish, grain, kola, and salt as well as slaves. Pepper (*Piper nigrum*), which the Portuguese honored as *fume dos olhos* (the light of the eyes), outsold the other foodstuffs.

The Portuguese flourished at trade, earning a profit of 260 percent. A royal agent, Fernao Gomes, initiated exclusive trade in guinea pepper, a sacred Nigerian digestive and flavoring for beer and sausage known as "grains of paradise." For a pungent deterrent to household odor and sickness, homemakers made pomanders out of oranges pierced and permeated with cardamom, cinnamon, cloves, nutmeg, and pepper. Guinea pepper became a European fad, but it eventually faded as Asian black pepper regained prominence in cuisine and the spicing of ale.

After the Ottoman Turks closed caravan routes from India to Baghdad and Aleppo in the late 1490s, under King Manuel I, the Portuguese inaugurated a third boost to the maritime food trade. On July 8, 1497, Admiral Vasco da Gama commanded two carracks, a caravel, and a supply ship on an expedition to the Indian Ocean. His exploration introduced the "golden route" around the African Cape of Good Hope up the East African trading cities from Sofala, Portugal, to Ethiopia and east to Calcutta and Goa, India. In wresting pepper and spice concessions from Muslim importers, Portuguese traders destroyed the monopolies held by Arabs, Italians, and Turks.

From Calcutta, Da Gama's fleet of 13 vessels carried 1,700 tons (1,550 metric tons) of spice, more than Venetian competitors sold in one year. To the dismay of Egyptian and Venetian wholesalers, the price of high-quality Kanara pepper from Malabar fell by 20 percent worldwide. To handle the logistics of unloading carracks in Lisbon and sorting and distributing goods, the House of Mina evolved into two divisions, the House of India and the Casa da India e da Guiné (House of India and Guinea).

After merchantmen inaugurated a route to India and back up the Tejo River to the Ribeira Palace in central Lisbon, under King Manuel I, commercial operations generated 65 percent of his nation's revenue. At the royal compound, the firm built and outfitted vessels, hired cartographers and sea captains, trained its food agents, recorded duties and income, and oversaw contractual agreements. For Manuel's rule over luxury foods, the French dubbed him the "spice king" and "the grocer." He depended on the naval expertise of Pedro Alvares Cabral, discoverer of Brazil; Francisco de Almeida, India's first colonial viceroy and trade negotiator; and Admiral Afonso de Albuquerque, who advanced Portugal to a global sea power in the Indian Ocean and Persian Gulf.

Late in 1500, Portugal's armadas faced the animosities of Arabia, Bijapur, Calcutta, Egypt, Gujarat, the Ottoman Turks, and Venice, a combined force dominated by Muslims. By building trading forts along the commercial routes, Portugal had little to fear from itinerant privateers, who operated without land bases.

By 1503, the House of India had established its pepper empire and dominated trade licensing and pepper distribution throughout Flanders, France, Hungary, and Germany. Agents bought pepper in India for 3 ducats per hundredweight and sold it in Lisbon for 22 ducats. Navigators discovered a new cinnamon source at Ceylon (Sri Lanka) in 1505, when cinnamon brought nearly seven times its initial cost.

A year later, through decisive military intervention, Portugal began a climb from dominating 25 percent of Asian trade to controlling half the Asian food market in cinnamon, cloves, and pepper. Shippers transported goods from warehouses at Anjediva Island, Cannanore, Cochin, and Quilon, a source of pepper, ginger, and cashew nuts, an additive to Chinese, Indian, and Thai sauces, stews, and desserts. From the viny environs of Iddicki, Kerala, Portuguese agents collected bagfuls of the world's darkest and most aromatic peppercorns, known in the trades as "black gold."

The Portuguese advanced in 1511 to control the spice harvest in Ceylon and Malabar, India. In addition to merchandising salt fish, the House of India outsold Venetian sugar at Antwerp, Flanders, and Bristol, England. By 1515, the House of India was as wealthy as the nation's Catholic Church. However, aggressive moves by the Dutch, English, and Venetians began dislodging Portugal from command of international trade.

During the next two decades, the Portuguese faltered at commerce because they owned no plantations, lacked control of intra-Asian trade and overland routes, and lacked the sophisticated finances to transport specie from Portugal. The company remained in business until its bankruptcy in 1560, when the Levant (southeastern Turkey, Syria, and Lebanon) reactivated its vigorous commerce.

See also: Abreu, António de, and Francisco Serrao; British East India Company.

Further Reading

Pearson, Michael Naylor. *The Indian Ocean.* London: Routledge, 2003.
Prange, Sebastian R. "Where the Pepper Grows." *Saudi Aramco World* 59:1 (January/February 2008): 10–17.
Rodrigues, Jorge Nascimento, and Tessaleno C. Devezas. *Pioneers of Globalization: Why the Portuguese Surprised the World.* Lisbon, Portunal: Centro Atlantico, 2007.

Hudson's Bay Company

The world's oldest merchandiser, the Hudson's Bay Company has dealt in trade goods and foodstuffs since its chartering on May 5, 1670. Originated as a fur clearinghouse, the corporation derived from cartographer and explorer Pierre-Esprit Radisson, a friend of the Iroquois and pelt trader among the Cree, Northern Algonquin, Ojibwa, and Ottawa along Lake Michigan and Lake Superior. Disgruntled by the high-handedness of the French fur licensers, he joined his brother-in-law, Médard Chouart des Groseilliers, in a venture that brought two ships from England to Hudson's Bay under the sponsorship of Sir George Carteret, Prince Rupert of Bohemia, and his cousin, King Charles II.

On June 5, 1668, Radisson, the royally favored entrepreneur, sailed the *Nonsuch* past the St. Lawrence River and approached the trading zone via Hudson's Bay in north-central Canada, a northerly route that reduced the cost of exporting beaver pelts and, to a lesser extent, the fur of lynx, marten, mink, muskrat, otter, and sable. A total of 19 stockholders profited from a monopoly over Rupert's Land, a vast, partially charted territory bisected by numerous streams emptying into Hudson's Bay, covering an expanse larger than Europe.

At Charles Fort on the Rupert River delta, the firm introduced Amerindians and the Métis nation, a literate and multilingual mixed-blood people also called les Canadiennes, to a limited role in a market economy. Natives earned profits primarily on commercial sales of cured or smoked buffalo tongue and pemmican, a native pack supply and Canada's first instant food. Introduction of Europeans to this high-energy, low-volume source of fat and protein enabled explorers, settlers, and the military to abandon heavy stores of bread, porridge, and salt meat and, thus unencumbered, to push farther north and west toward the North Pole, Yukon, and Russian Alaska.

In October 1754, explorer Anthony Henday added the Blackfoot of modern-day Edmonton, Alberta, to the company alliance with indigenous pemmican traders.

The business cycle ranged over five months as ships made trades and completed the loop to and from England, where the first 27 lots of furs went on sale at Garraway's Coffee House at Cornhill in east-central London, an auction site for coffee, sugar, tea, textiles, and sea salvage. In 1780 at Witney, Oxfordshire, Thomas Empson expanded the range of trade goods by weaving durable "point" blankets, which Indians bought for two and a half points, or pelts. Profits from pelts advanced from $1 million in 1780 to $6 million in 1800, when the company supplied furriers in London, New York City, and Paris.

Bicultural Business

Based at Fort Nelson, Manitoba, the Hudson's Bay Company fielded more exports than imports, set pricing, and generated its own banks, currency, provisioning storehouses, and maritime fleet. To ensure a working relationship with tribes, until a policy shift in 1806, Hudson's Bay employees typically married Indian woman, who secured a steady supply of food staples and medicinal plants and introduced the men to Amerindian food preservation and diet.

The Hudson's Bay Company spread its control of trade among the nomadic Cree, Eskimo, Ojibwa, and Slave along depots at the ports of the Red and Saskatchewan rivers and into Ontario and Quebec. The company flourished unchallenged until competition from Simon McTavish's North West Fur Company emerged in Montreal in 1783.

Depot managers consisted mainly of Englishmen and Scots with European wives living in log houses. In exchange for exotic European goods—bacon, blankets, buttons and needles, calico, copper kettles, guns, iron chisels, salt beef and pork, sugar, tea, tobacco, and twine—local Indians provided beadwork, birch syrup, dried and cured pike, moccasins, and the meat of buffalo, caribou, deer, moose, and wild sheep. Between 1801 and 1808, their trade in pemmican alone rose by more than 400 percent. Factors (agency merchandizers) introduced incoming Canadian missionaries and European consumers to pemmican, a reliable Amerindian trail food supplied by the Assiniboine, trading partners of the Cree. Traders, canoe expeditioners, and ox-carters consumed pemmican raw, broiled over a buffalo chip fire, or as a basis of stew.

During the mercantile period of colonization, the Hudson's Bay Company seized the Yukon River and dominated trade with the Athabascan of Chilkoot Pass. Famine among settlers proved so serious on January 8, 1814, that Governor Miles Macdonnell at Fort Douglas issued the Pemmican Proclamation, restricting the Métis from exporting trail meat from the colony along the Red River to their outlet in St. Paul, Minnesota. At La Souris, Manitoba, Sheriff John Spencer impounded 18 tons (16.3 metric tons) of contraband pemmican from the North West Company, which supplied its 219 canoes with 29 tons (26.3 metric tons) annually.

On June 19, 1816, resisting the restriction of their trade, the Métis rallied under the slogan le commerce est libre (free trade), attacked the fort, and seized the pemmican stores. They continued marketing the pemmican to the North West Company, which sold the trail food as far east as France, Great Britain, Switzerland, and the United States.

Expansion to the Northwest

After winning the Pemmican War against its rival, the Hudson's Bay firm expanded its southern routes into present-day Michigan, North Dakota, and Wisconsin and its eastern outreach to Holland, Russia, and Scandinavia. Commodities trade succeeded on a par with the East India Company at global interchange of cod, lumber, minerals, and wheat. The Convention of 1818 established the southern boundaries of the Canadian territory and limited the rights of American fishermen to catch, dry, and cure fish from the coasts of Labrador and Newfoundland. In 1821, the Hudson's Bay Company spanned the continent after it merged with the North West Company and reestablished its monopoly. Voyageurs—Métis transporters of goods between whites and Indians—and coureurs de bois—free agents who ignored French state and church laws—based their speed on canoes and pemmican. The demand for trail meat usually outpaced supply.

Company scouts set up trade with the Chinook of the Willamette Valley in Washington Territory in 1825, built a Pacific headquarters at Fort Vancouver, and pushed south in 1827 to Idaho, Oregon, Nevada, and California in search of new territory to exploit. The erection of Fort Langley in British Columbia in 1827 added dried salmon to Hudson's Bay Company trade offerings. Colonel Christopher "Kit" Carson, a company agent, pressed into Blackfoot territory on the Yellowstone River.

The Hudson's Bay Company appears to have made its cash on Rupert's Land at an ideal time. The coming of the Canadian Pacific Railway, the Imperial military, and more prairie pioneers pushed the dispossessed hunter-gatherers farther west toward an unfamiliar new life in agriculture. From 1826, the demand for meat rose from 1,923 buffalo tongues every five years to a height of 25,657 in 1845. In an average year, the Hudson's Bay Company sold meat from 17,000 buffalo. Buyers preferred the flesh of cows above that of bulls, thus hastening the depletion of nomadic herds. In 1843, the Puget Sound Agricultural Company, a company subsidiary, profited from trade in fruits and vegetables, dairy, beef, and pork as far west as Alaska, Hawaii, and Tokyo.

The Post-Buffalo Market

Anticipating shifts in animal populations, company officials at Fort Edmonton tried hybridizing the beefalo in 1844, a failed crossbreeding scheme involving cattle and buffalo. Trade continued to flourish in Saskatchewan in

1846, where Indians sold 1,100 bags or about 50 tons (45 metric tons) of pemmican.

By 1850, the Hudson's Bay Company had begun its retreat from the north-central United States by yielding trading rights along the Columbia River. In 1857, the Canadian Dominion purchased Hudson's Bay Company territory for £300,000 plus trading-post acreage and 6.6 million acres (2.7 million hectares) around Lake Winnipeg and the North Saskatchewan River. In the 1860s, the Métis subdued their Cree competitors and dominated the pemmican trade to the Hudson's Bay Company. While the Indians lost stature and control of trade routes to the railroad, tariffs protecting the white-owned company from John Jacob Astor's American Fur Company sustained British profits. In 1871, prices reflected the tastes of Canadian Indians for domestic meat:

Commodity	Price per Pound
beef	17¢
buffalo	15¢
pemmican	11¢
pork	25¢

According to the newspaper *Les Métis* in 1877, trade in buffalo hides at Red River reached 74,000 buffalo robes, but declining prices forced brokers to broaden their product line to dried and fresh meat and pemmican. Loss of the buffalo reduced the Métis to starvation and begging.

At the near extinction of the buffalo, prices shifted erratically, with pemmican rising in value by 1,150 percent and dried meat by 400 percent. Missionaries and pioneers paid 25¢ per pound for pemmican. Eastern Indian traders shifted commodities to cured or smoked deer tongue, deer-meat pemmican, fish, moose, rabbits, soft and hard game fat, and wild rice, while Western tribes used Winchester rifles to decimate the remaining buffalo herds.

After gold rushes shifted exchanges from trade to cash, the Hudson's Bay fur depots developed into a retail department store chain and mail-order business, beginning in Winnipeg in 1881. As Canada began to face deer and moose shortages, woodsmen protested the uncontrolled slaughter of wild birds, fish, and game and proposed restricting hunting to limited seasons. Differences of opinion about hunting rights destabilized the multicultural society and diminished the Hudson's Bay Company to a historical relic. Winnipeg's old-timers formed the Winnipeg Game Preservation League in 1882 and looked back on the early days of the Hudson's Bay Company as a halcyon era of hunting excursions.

The twentieth century brought new challenges to New World food traders. The Hudson's Bay Company prospered from the sale of candy, canned salmon, coffee, liquor, tea, and tobacco and sidelines in gas, oil, and In-

uit art. During World War I, while Norway supplied the Allies with fish, the Hudson's Bay Company distributed frozen meat, wheat, and armaments to Belgium and France via the 300 ships of the company's steamship line.

By 1920, the commissioning of an icebreaker introduced company agents to the eastern Arctic at Inukjuak, Quebec, for trade in arctic fox fur, fossilized mammoth tusks, walrus teeth, whale blubber and oil, whalebone, and salt fish. The establishment of trading posts among the Inuit expanded their knowledge of steel traps, munitions, and European foods—beans, flour, lard, rolled oats, and whiskey and brandy. The Hudson's Bay Company yielded to animal rights protests in 1991 by ceasing to deal in animal fur.

See also: Buffalo; Dried Food; Middens; Pemmican; Supermarkets.

Further Reading

Bryce, George. *The Remarkable History of the Hudson's Bay Company*. Reprint. New York: B. Franklin, 1968.
Morrison, Jean F. *Superior Rendezvous-Place: Fort William in the Canadian Fur Trade*. Toronto: Natural Heritage, 2007.
Rich, E.E. *The History of the Hudson's Bay Company, 1670–1870*. London: Hudson's Bay Record Society, 1958–1959.

Hunter-Gatherers

A mobile society of omnivores subsisting on foraging and stalking, prehistoric hunter-gatherers scoured the wild for food for immediate consumption. Hunting-and-gathering societies began in eastern Africa with the first hominids, *Australopithecus afarensis,* a race of primate fructivores, or fruit eaters, that lived up to 4 million years ago. An opportunistic strategy of human life during 99 percent of human history, the scavenging of foodstuffs demanded intense social activity and provided short-term gains for *Homo sapiens* from 200,000 to 10,000 B.C.E. By the end of the period, historians estimate the Earth's population at 4 million.

Nomadic groups gravitated toward the best sources of food—lakes, river estuaries, seashores, and valleys. To sustain life, hunter-gatherers acquired few possessions and stayed on the move. They ranged about their environs in search of birds and eggs, fish, fruit, grass seeds, honey, insects, mollusks, mushrooms, nuts, reptiles, rodents, seaweed, small game, and wild plant varieties. Partially devoured beast kill offered a shortcut to hunting. Residing in an egalitarian cooperative, each member carried the same status and the same responsibility for finding food. Only advanced age added prestige to the individual.

At Abu Hureyra, settled in western Mesopotamia (Syria) in 9500 B.C.E., archaeobotanists have identified 150 high-fiber, high-protein plants and tubers valued as food, including chickpeas, gazelle and donkey meat, hackberries, lentils, and pistachios. Mothers bore children at 48-month intervals, a spacing that prevented too many infants and toddlers for nomadic families to carry.

To prepare barley, rye, and wheat for adult use, girls and women ground the husks off grain with saddle querns (concave grinding stones) over a period of several hours before each meal. Squatting to rotate the grinder caused widespread deformities of the big toe, cartilage erosion in the knees, and disk damage to the last vertebra. Before weavers invented the sieve or potters shaped containers for soaking grain, powdered rock from the quern eroded teeth. Mineral grit that lodged next to molars caused gum infection. The shift from rough grains to porridge allowed mothers to wean infants sooner and to substitute pap and gruel for breastfeeding. The shift to cooked cereals shortened the span between births, introduced sticky carbohydrates to teeth, and increased incidence of dental caries.

Neolithic bands adapted readily to temperate zones as well as to the extremes of the tropics and tundra. Individuals mentally cataloged an extensive observation of flora and fauna within the food web as well as sources of salt. The keenest hunter-gatherers knew the hibernation and migratory patterns of animals and birds and the seasonal efficiency of scouting the most propitious climes, such as groves of bananas and pineapples among the Tupi and Guaraní of Brazil.

Attitudes concerning nature tended toward wonder and magic, the ineffable source of subsistence and offspring. People lived in the present with little thought of guilt, regret, and shame and little anxiety about an afterlife. They cultivated a low standard of living, observed straightforward traditions forbidding food waste, and sacrificed privacy and individuality to a communal mentality. Hunter-gatherers developed sturdy frames—an average of 5′ 9″ (1.75 meters) for men and 5′ 5″ (1.65 meters) for women in Greece and Turkey—but tended to die young because of accidents (falls, drowning, and crushing injuries), attacks by fierce animals, or snakebite.

Non-Acquisitive Wealth

Hunter-gatherers of the past and present made no attempt to control nature. They collected only what they could carry and limited their wants, craft items, food stocks, and garments.

Alaskan Eskimo, hunters of bowhead whales, seals, and walrus, thrived on a diet of 50 percent fat, 35 percent protein, and 15 percent carbohydrate. The Kalaallit of Greenland consumed meals of 96 percent meat from fish and sea mammals; the most prominent meat eaters, the semi-nomadic Nunamiut Inupiat of Anaktuvuk Pass, Alaska, ate caribou and only 1 percent berries.

In contrast, the Hadza of north-central Tanzania and the aborigines of Australia and Papua New Guinea preferred a diet dominated by honey and vegetable matter.

The Hadza favored baobab fruit, ekwa tubers, and marula nuts as well as bee larvae, buffalo, dikdik, eland, jackal, tortoise, and warthog. A gendered taboo forced females to choose congolobe berries over meat, while the males opted for meat over berries.

Because of the overhunting of game in the Kalahari Desert, the !Kung in Botswana, Namibia, and South Africa currently consume only 33 percent meat and 67 percent plant food—88 percent of which consists of mongongo nuts, oily kernels that gatherers collect from elephant dung. The proportion of meat and plant foods for the Gwi San bush people of Botswana in the central Kalahari tended toward only one-quarter animal food. When game was plentiful, hunter-gatherers gorged on high-energy meat, a dining pattern common to the Kalahari bush people and to North American buffalo hunters.

Control of fire from 498,000 B.C.E. increased the palatability of food plants and released more nutrients into human metabolism. Homo sapiens further adapted cookery in 18,000 B.C.E. with the first use of grinding stones to separate husks from digestible tissues of nuts and grains. Females interspersed daily tasks of hauling water and combustibles, cracking nuts, and cooking with visiting, sewing, and entertaining. Networks of children assumed responsibility from age five for gathering ground-level foodstuffs, such as acorns, cactus fruit, crustaceans, grubs, quail eggs, and shellfish at low tide. In the least promising environment, men worked no more than four hours per day to feed their families and rarely encountered dental problems, malnutrition, or starvation. During downtime for male hunters, they conversed, copulated, dined, educated the young, and danced and shared leftovers with pet dogs. Such tribes owned no slaves, gave little thought to storing food for the future, and abstained from raiding and war. When conquered, they adapted poorly to a European-style work ethic.

The Casteless Society

After the extinction of giant animals—the bison in North America, dodo in Mauritius, giant lemur in Madagascar, moa in New Zealand, and nene in Hawaii—meat eaters concentrated on antelope, coyote, deer, elk, and raccoon. Migratory tribes followed cyclical routes to seasonal hunting camps and shore sites. From the Great Plains of North America to Chile, tribes of 50–100 members broke into hunting bands of 10–30 to scout more abundant game.

Living in rock shelters or portable tents, families pursued gendered tasks—men hunted; women and children dug roots and gathered fruit, plants, and seafood. Both genders fished. Men typically introduced youths to the dangers of hunting and turned puberty rituals into extensive training sessions in weaponry, slaughter, and evisceration and disjointing of the kill.

An ample kill of beaver, bison, mammoths, mastodons, musk ox, or reindeer allowed low-density communities to enjoy periods of leisure and the safety and warmth of shelters, a boon to pregnant and lactating women and to their infants and toddlers. Relatively low levels of toil allowed women to breastfeed their children for three to four years. Lactation suppressed ovulation and lowered the birthrate, thus lessening competition for available foods within the clan.

Until the evolution of agriculture around 8500 B.C.E., lives depended on day-to-day flexibility and the sharing of muscle and organ meats and the marrow from cracked bones. Before the age of greed and pillage that accompanied agriculture, hunter-gatherers welcomed outsiders. In contrast with later peoples, the protein intake and hardy lifestyle predisposed Neanderthals to robust muscles, a larger brain and greater cerebral activity, and sophisticated cuisine and cooking tools.

See also: Amerindian Diet; Animal Husbandry; Cannibalism; Fertile Crescent Diet and Food Trade; Grilling; Lapérouse, Jean François Galaup; Paleolithic Diet; Polo, Marco; Polynesian Diet and Cuisine; Shellfish; Soft Drinks and Juices; Swiddens; Wild Food.

Further Reading

Freedman, Paul H. *Food: The History of Taste.* Berkeley: University of California Press, 2007.

Hewlett, Barry S., and Michael E. Lamb, eds. *Hunter-Gatherer Childhoods: Evolutionary, Developmental, & Cultural Perspectives.* New Brunswick, NJ: Aldine de Gruyter, 2005.

Milton, Katharine. "Hunter-Gatherer Diets—A Different Perspective." *American Journal of Clinical Nutrition* 71 (2000): 665–667.

Ungar, Peter S., ed. *Evolution of the Human Diet: The Known, the Unknown, and the Unknowable.* New York: Oxford University Press, 2006.

Huou (fl. 1270–1330)

After the birth of the Yuan dynasty in 1260, Huou (Hu Szu-hui), the chef of Kublai Khan's imperial kitchen, became medieval China's first native gastronome and an originator of fusion cuisine. At the Forbidden City, a bastion of wealth and power at Dadu (Beijing), Huou inserted food knowledge of Turkish origin and Islamic dietary advice. He lived during a period of discovery, including the development of macaroni and ice cream and of charcoal- and oil-fired cook stoves and flowing water to the kitchen. As a master chef, he cooked for a luxury-loving emperor, an obese gourmand who subjugated the southern Sung. Each recipe had a medicinal property intended to prevent sickness and extend longevity from such ingredients as bottle gourd and cardamom.

Information about Huou is available mainly through inference about the khan's kitchen demands on his dietary physician, who replaced hunter-gatherer fare from Mongolia with subtle, cosmopolitan cookery. According to legend, the khan invaded Moscow at age 23 and returned with a recipe for steak tartare, raw minced beef or horsemeat seasoned with capers that honored the bold Tartars (Mongols). Although open to new dishes, he also insisted that his staff preserve Mongol cuisine and pay no heed to the scriptural food demands of China's Muslims.

Huou's era saw the politicizing of menus after 1271, when the defeated Chinese Tang dynasty rejected lamb as a protest to northern insurgents. Kublai Khan intended to turn Dadu into a world cultural and trading hub with a blended Mongo-Turko-Chinese cuisine. Wracked by alcoholism and gout in his 80s, he demanded fine ingredients and wines from Baghdad, Kashmir, and Manchuria. Huou turned the food delivered via the Silk Road to the Dadu palace into such specialties as carp cakes with asafetida and eggplant with orange-flavored lamb stuffing.

To assuage the humiliation of his failed invasion of Japan in spring 1281 and his grief over the deaths of his favorite wife, Chabi, in 1281 and their second son, Crown Prince Zhenjin, in 1285, the khan demanded a constant supply of food and koumiss (fermented milk) from the 10,000 imperial white mares. As a warning about dissipation to the 69-year-old emperor, Huou followed the Tao by endorsing moderation in food, alcoholic consumption, and sexual pleasure.

Although Kublai Khan dressed in the Chinese fashion, he dined regally at the palace on kid and lamb dishes, a Mongol specialty, until his death in 1294. In the royal kitchen, Huou's staff barbecued meat and distilled rice wine. Under the direction of Egyptian specialists, the sous-chefs refined sugarcane into crystals for confections. Workers slew four or five sheep daily and boiled them in huge vats for the khan's pleasure and diet therapy.

From service to the mid-thirteenth-century khan, Huou recorded pantry tastes and feasts honoring the Celestial Throne. His three-volume survey, *Yin-shan Zheng-yao (Proper and Essential Things for the Emperor's Food and Drink,* 1330), China's first cookbook, compiled court details. The text features 236 recipes for vegetarian soups in sheep stock and *congees* (watered gruel) of donkey's head and fox and such delicacies as pomegranate baklava and lightly sauteed spinach sprinkled with sesame seeds. Grape vintages, according to the book, have the power to relieve worries and improve digestion, but overindulgence can kill. In a scholarly preface, Yu Chi, a court official, proposes that diners aim for a harmony of yin and yang and that they conserve their strength to lengthen their days.

The Empress Babusha approved Huou's cookbook and had it engraved on woodblocks for dissemination. The text, the first record of food boiling, warned of unsafe combinations, notably eggs with turtle and sugar with shrimp. It featured line drawings of the wolf and the crab, a Mongol fad food. At Shandu (Xanadu) in

Inner Mongolia, the location of the bamboo and marble summer palaces of the khan, Venetian adventurer Marco Polo, a contemporary of Huou, corroborated the trend toward crustaceans by describing crabs for sale in specialty shops.

See also: Polo, Marco.

Further Reading

Akasoy, Anna, Charles Burnett, and Ronit Yoeli-Tlalim, eds. *Islam and Tibet: Interactions Along the Musk Routes.* Burlington, VT: Ashgate, 2010.

Buell, Paul D., and Eugene N. Anderson. *A Soup for the Qan: Chinese Dietary Medicine of the Mongol Era as Seen in Hu Szu-Hui's Yin-shan Cheng-yao.* New York: Kegan Paul International, 2000.

Craughwell, Thomas J. *The Rise and Fall of the Second Largest Empire in History: How Genghis Khan's Mongols Almost Conquered the World.* Beverly, MA: Fair Winds, 2010.

Laudan, Rachel. "Review: *A Soup for the Qan.*" *Journal of World History* 14:4 (December 2003): 563–566.

Hybridization

Hybridization of food sources, which dates to paleoagricultural techniques, altered global thinking about farming and the sustainability of life on the planet. In plants and animals, natural interbreeding continues food species as well as diversity, as in the cases of bread wheat (*Triticum aestivum*), Haas avocados, Indian mustard, navel oranges, sweet bananas, and wild grapes. From as early as 13,000 B.C.E., neolithic farmers altered the natural habits of fruit and grain, beginning with Chinese and Indian strains of rice. Nomads spread their stock across similar terrain, breeding barley, beets, oats, and einkorn and emmer wheat in the Mediterranean and maize, manioc, millet, plantain, rice, sorghum, soybeans, and sweet potatoes in the savannas. In the tropics, the lowlands produced coconut, the highlands the potato, and the forest sugarcane.

The manipulation of crop and livestock species facilitated enormous genetic modification, as in lysine in corn, iron-rich broad beans, oversized greengage plums, and vitamin A in rice. In one of the greatest achievements, around 3000 B.C.E., the Anasazi hybridized maize from teosinte, a wild Mesoamerican grass, and evolved corn varieties suited to a hot, dry climate.

German botanist Joseph Gottlieb Kölreuter reported the first artificial hybridization in 1761 through artificial pollination. A century later followed the field research of William James Beal, Charles Darwin, and Gregor Mendel.

Modified Plants at Work

Hybridizing passed from the laboratory to the farm by 1875, when U.S. farmers were testing crossbred oats. By such transgenic means, human plant growers expanded food production to 5 billion tons (4.5 billion metric tons) per year and foresaw such health benefits as bananas that protected children from enteritis. However, the benefits lasted for only one generation of bananas and required ongoing genetic upgrading.

The success of new food species is obvious in the beetle-resistant Bt (*Bacillus thuringiensis*) potato and the long-lived Flavr Savr tomato, but less so with the loganberry and the triticale, a cross between rye and wheat used in Europe as a livestock feed grain. In the early 1900s, the British navy purchased the early fruiting loganberry, a cross between blackberry and raspberry, which became a valuable source of vitamin C that prevented scurvy in sailors.

The grapefruit originated naturally in the Barbadian or Jamaican wild from the pomelo and sweet orange. The blended citrus species entered scientific notation in 1837 and passed to subtropical Florida. The grapefruit thrived as a commercial crop in Orange County in 1870 for shipment to New York City and Philadelphia.

Grapefruit became a culinary success in 1929 with the patenting of the Ruby Red, followed in 2007 by the Rio Red, a Texas specialty. Nutritionists recommended aromatic fruit for lowering cholesterol, burning body fat, slowing aging, and adding antioxidants to the diet. When crossed with the tangerine in 1897, grapefruit generated another popular hybrid, the uniquely flavored Minneola tangelo, or honeybell, a popular winter gift item and table fruit.

Genetic Modification

Genetic engineering applies high-tech methods to the refinement of genes. Laboratory manipulation improves the commercial and nutritional value of plants by increasing domestication of wild species, antibiotic resistance to fungus and pathogens, and the viability of crops near brackish water, an advance that boosts the value of coastal land for farming such grains as Yecoro wheat, a moderately salt-tolerant variety. From 1903 to 1904, American plant geneticist George Harrison Shull invigorated hybrid corn to yield predictable results. More detailed data on corn DNA emerged from the later work of cytogeneticist Marcus Morton Rhoades, a generator of higher corn yields.

In 1925, Italian agronomist Nazareno Strampelli directed *La battaglia del grano* (The Battle of the Grain), a national effort under dictator Benito Mussolini to make Italy self-sufficient. On heavily subsidized *latifundia* (plantations), Strampelli's early-ripening dwarf wheat, hybridized from the Japanese Akagomughi strain and inoculated to resist smut, doubled the yield by 1939; Italy exported seed to Sonora, Mexico, that shortened the growing season and enhanced yield and disease tolerance. Pasta makers today continue to purchase Strampelli's Senatore Cappelli variety of durum wheat. The work of Orville A. Vogel with Norin 10 wheat in 1948 introduced a valuable addition to grain cultivation in the Pacific Northwest, Mexico, and Russia.

Building on Vogel's developments, American microbiologist Norman Ernest Borlaug, the "Father of the Green Revolution," decreased food shortages in India, Mexico, and Pakistan by researching advances in barley, maize, sorghum, and triticale. His major breakthrough, semi-dwarf wheat, resisted stem rust and adapted to lowlands and highlands, thus doubling the annual yield. Grown on shorter, thicker stalks, the larger seed heads thrived in 1963, when Borlaug's wheat accounted for 95 percent of Mexico's harvest. The success altered the nation from an importer to an exporter of wheat.

A similar rescue mission underwritten by the U.S. Department of Agriculture applied Borlaug's expertise in the mid-1960s to wartime famine in India and Pakistan, brought on in part by rice stunt and annual monsoon rains. The crop, particularly in the Punjab, swamped the region's labor force and transportation and storage facilities.

Through Borlaug's theory of intensive monoculture (growing a single crop), both India and Pakistan supplied their nation's demand for food. The application of hybrid short-stalk wheat achieved similar successes in Africa, Central America, and the Middle East. Borlaug's genetic tinkering also influenced rice cultivation throughout Asia. In 1970, cereal crops increased their yield by 10 percent. For ending decades of chronic undernourishment and for slowing deforestation and wildlife extinction worldwide, Borlaug received the 1970 Nobel Peace Prize. In 1984, he came out of retirement to introduce his methods in famine-plagued Ethiopia. Within a decade, Ethiopians achieved nearly a one-third increase in grain productivity.

Looking five decades ahead, Borlaug predicted that agriculture would have to double yields by 2050. After saving more than 1 billion people from hunger through grain hybridization, he targeted Africa, Brazil, and former Soviet Russia as still in need of bioengineering of sustainable crops and a reduced dependence on herbicide use, for example, by introducing Bt toxins in peanuts to protect them from European corn borers. In opposition to high-cost organic farming, he advised researchers to boost the protein quality of corn and to continue transgenic plant manipulation through recombinant DNA techniques, chromosome engineering, and improved fertilizer efficiency. He predicted heightened resistance to rust to supply enough barley, corn, rape, rice, sorghum, soybeans, sugar beets, and wheat to meet global food needs.

In recent years, consumers leery of genetically modified (GM) foods assaulted the media and government agencies with outrage against "frankenfood," a Gothic term suggesting an oversized monster raging out of control. Anti-GM forces in Canada and the United States protested processed foods that incorporated such altered ingredients without warning the public. The outcry in Europe forced the European Union to declare a moratorium on the sale of GM seeds. In October 2011, BASF sought approval for Fortuna, a GM potato that resists blight, the source of the Irish Potato Famine in the 1840s. The following month, Monsanto informed Pakistanis of the benefits of GM corn in an attempt to alleviate doubts about the safety of genetically modified foods.

See also: Blueberries; Burbank, Luther; Frézier, Amédée François; Genetically Modified Food; Hanna, Gordie C.; Heirloom Plants; Hiatt, Jesse; Ketchup; Livingston, A.W.

Further Reading

Borlaug, Norman E. "Ending World Hunger: The Promise of Biotechnology and the Threat of Antiscience Zealotry." *Plant Physiology* 124 (October 2000): 487–490.

Cullather, Nick. *The Hungry World: America's Cold War Battle Against Poverty in Asia.* Cambridge, MA: Harvard University Press, 2010.

Entis, Phyllis. *Food Safety: Old Habits, New Perspectives.* Washington, DC: ASM, 2007.

Morgan, Sally. *Superfoods: Genetic Modification of Foods.* Portsmouth, NH: Heinemann, 2003.

Hydroponics
See Aquaponics

Ibn Battuta
(1304–ca. 1378)

An Arab theologian and traveler over three continents for 30 years, Abu Abdullah Mohammed Ibn Battuta perused the customs and food consumption of disparate peoples and seagoing crews. His account of the Middle East, North Africa, and central Asia is the most comprehensive of the Middle Ages.

An Islamic academic born of Berber stock in Tangier, Morocco, Ibn Battuta left home on June 14, 1325, and traveled the world by land and water before publishing a memoir, *Tuhfat al-Nuzzar fi Ghara'ib al-Amsar wa'Ajaib al'Asfar (On Curiosities of Cities and Wonders of Travel,* 1354). Along the way, he observed the importance of diet and food to Muslims, who welcomed a fellow believer with gifts and feasting.

As he passed through Tunis, he encountered the typical urban food trade—citrus fruit, dates, dried and smoked fish, kebabs, pastries, sherbet, spices, and wines and water mixed with fruit juice. He avoided the limited fare of small towns in favor of the cosmopolitan menus in metropolises. Alexandria's wealth staggered his imagination with its immense bazaar, offering goods from Africa, India, and Malaysia.

From the opulent Nile port in spring 1326, he cruised upriver to Cairo, where Iraqi and Syrian refugees clogged the city. Because of the absence of kitchens and pantries for the homeless, the outsiders fueled a brisk business in street food. Buyers consumed their purchases amid sweaty throngs and the dung of camels and donkeys.

Devotion to Islam motivated the Moroccan's itinerary, which varied and shifted because of local wars. After fasting for Ramadan in Damascus, Syria, he set out on a hajj (annual Muslim pilgrimage) and an obligatory stop in Mecca, Arabia, the cradle of Islam. In obedience to the Koran's call for charity, Mamluk authorities provided dray animals, food, skins of fresh water, and medicine for poor Muslim pilgrims. Travelers packed combustibles and cooked along the way in copper cauldrons. Grocers raised food prices to bilk rich pilgrims of their funds.

Ibn Battuta reached Mecca on October 26, 1326. Inside the Great Mosque, he observed, pilgrims could eat and sleep but not cook. At Tabriz, in northwestern Iran, he admired a world-class food bazaar selling multinational goods and dined heartily on bread, meat, rice, and

sweets. The stopover established his love of fine dining, which he satisfied along the Silk Road, Eurasia's chief trade route.

Middle East and Africa

On November 17, 1326, Ibn Battuta continued moving east and south. He joined a caravan through Persia and journeyed by night in a litter before boarding a lateen-sailed sloop in Mesopotamia from Basra, Iraq. The boat moved along the Ubulla canal toward the Tigris River. Overhanging the route, fruit orchards and palm trees shaded the passage. Inland at Kufa, Iraq, citizens offered bread, dates and fruit, fish, and milk. At 'Aydhab, Sudan, on the African side of the Red Sea, he observed the exquisite trade goods of the Silk Road, which brought sugar to Muslim kitchens. Beja islanders on Awakin had to collect or import potable water and lived on a diet of gazelle, goat, ostrich, and wild ass along with butter, milk, and millet. Unfortunately for his appetite, heat and brackish water soured his stomach. By the end of his first year on the road, he had covered 4,000 miles (6,400 kilometers).

The route took Ibn Battuta into the Indian Ocean to Somalia on Africa's eastern horn. On the Gulf of Aden, he avoided Zeila, where the air around the meat market carried the stench of slaughtered camels and fish. Farther south in Mogadishu, the voyager observed street fare, mostly bananas and seafood, sold by Arabic, Bantu, and Swahili speakers. When local dignitaries learned that the visitor was an Islamic scholar, he received welcoming servings of areca nuts, betel leaves, and a carafe of rosewater, a skin emollient, sweetener, and air freshener that he shared with the ship's captain. Among students of religion, the traveler entered the home of Sheikh Abu Bakr for three days of hearty dining on rice steeped in ghee and topped with chicken, fish, meat, and vegetables. Accompanying the dinner, dishes of bananas in milk, curry, pickled chilies, and lemons over mango and milk increased his pleasure in sour dishes, which local people served with a bland base. He commented on the gluttony of his hosts, who were obese.

Eastern Europe and the Levant

The Moroccan preferred wealth to poverty. After days of sumptuous treatment at the island of Kilwa (off present-day Tanzania) on the East African coast, Ibn Battuta disdained the peasant life in mud and wattle huts and their coarse meals. He admired Sultan Abu al-Muzaffar Hasan for sitting and eating with humble people. Hospitality gifts poured in to Ibn Battuta, ranging from clarified butter and sacks of grain and rice to a bull. When he moved on in May 1332, he found the ruler of the Golden Horde, Khan Ozbeg, a new convert to Islam, camped north of the Azov Sea in the Ukraine. The khan's massive entourage included portable bazaars, kitchens, mosques, and 300 wagonloads of clothing and food. In July, Ibn Battuta separated from the khan at Astrakhan, Russia, on the Volga River delta to escort Bayalun, Ozbeg's pregnant wife, to Byzantium for the birth of their child. For the trip, Ozbeg supplied 5,000 cavalry, 500 bodyguards, 400 wagons, and a personal staff of 220.

In Byzantium, Ibn Battuta visited street markets and viewed the wonders of Hellenism and the onslaught of Christianity in defiance of the advance of Islam. In Anatolia in 1333, he found the food delicious and remarkably sanitary. Fraternities of young men called him brother and treated him hospitably at bountiful feasts.

At the beach town of Azak, he noted the coarseness of the emir's table service for the rich. Despite being aristocrats, they ate boiled horsemeat and mutton, macaroni, and millet porridge and washed it down with millet beer and koumiss, the Mongolian staple beverage fermented from mare's milk. Affronted by the violation to the Koran, he learned that Mongol Muslims allegedly drank alcoholic koumiss for medicinal purposes. During Eid al-Fitr, an annual movable feast ending Ramadan's fasting, Ibn Battuta observed the khan staggeringly drunk at afternoon prayers. Among the Uzbeks, the Emir Timur dazzled the newcomer with a wealth of fruit served in Iraqi glassware on gold-embroidered silk tablecloths.

Hindus and Muslims in India

Traveling with commercial camel trains, Ibn Battuta returned to Mecca. He reached India in early spring 1333 and accepted appointment as Delhi's hospice administrator, a post he held for eight years. Court life suited the Moroccan, who gloried in royal functions and dinners, horse dancing, and an elephant salute from uplifted trunks. At the palace of Sultan Mohammad bin Tughlaq at Delhi, a staff of 460 included a hierarchy of chefs and waiters. Table service of gold and silver bowls and ewers by attractive maidens involved ladling food from copper trays onto plates. Each wife served her husband by superintending his place setting and washing his hands. Royal dinners ended with distribution of sweets and buttermilk or curds. A gesture of hospitality, gifts of betel leaves for after-dinner chewing cleansed the breath and acknowledged the nobility of the guest. A similar passing of betel leaves and rosewater ended Muslim funerals.

Outnumbered by infidels, the Moroccan surveyed Hindu abstinence from meat and alcohol. Religious tenets limited meals of the devout to rice, sesame oil, and vegetables and forbade wine. Strict separation from Mus-

lims disallowed Islamic visitors and prevented Muslims from handling Hindu dishes and utensils. Ibn Battuta described the gathering of wild grain, which the poor beat in a wood mortar until the white kernel separated from the husk. Cooking kernels in buffalo's milk turned the grain into a stew for baking. He approved the Hindu diet of barley, lentils, millet, mung beans, and rice but sampled taboo foods. He relished a breakfast of peas and enjoyed chapati bread fried in ghee, meat kebabs, minced meat with nuts and onions, and damson plums and admired the use of fruit—coconut, grapes, mangoes, oranges, and pomegranates—in refreshing desserts. A surprising processed fruit, dried watermelon became a lucrative export from Delhi to Mecca.

In summer 1335, a calamitous seven-year famine began killing thousands of North Indians. Survivors resorted to meals of animal pelts, spoiled meat, and human remains. The Moroccan donated his own foodstuffs to save the stricken and ordered grain transported to Delhi to feed the poor. Culture shock overcame him when he saw violations of Koranic abstinence from alcohol.

On August 2, 1341, Ibn Battuta traveled from Calicut by junk, which offered stewards and room service. At Sudkawan (present-day Chittagong), he found a port so stocked with farm produce that he listed prices of cotton, meat, poultry, oil, rice, and sugar.

On July 22, 1342, Ibn Battuta set out on an official visit to China. Shipwreck off the Malabar coast of India forced him to the Maldive Islands, where he remained for 18 months at Mahal. He served the islands in the official capacity as judge before moving west to Ceylon in August 1344. During his sojourn, he took four wives and joked that he subsisted on coconuts, a known aphrodisiac.

Later Travels

Subsequent voyages took Ibn Battuta to Beijing, China, and south to Sumatra and back to Calicut. Before embarking, the crew stored two elephant loads of rice, ten sheep, two buffalo cows, and four pounds of julep, a common Arab antidote to stomach upset. At sea, he protected his health by eating lemons, an antiscorbutic valued by mariners. Galley supplies of pickled ginger, lemons, mangoes, and pepper arrived in earthen storage jars distributed from the trading port of Martaban on the Gulf of Burma. In addition to pickles, the crew ate dried ginger, perhaps as an antidote to seasickness, and grew vegetables in wood tubs, possibly a source of bean sprouts or greens.

At Baghdad in January 1348, Ibn Battuta initiated another pilgrimage to Mecca. On returning to Damascus in July 1348, he observed the onset of the Black Death. To combat bubonic plague, Argun Shah, the governor of Syria, encouraged people to avoid eating at public markets. He charged polluted air with infecting the populace and recommended meals of fruit and pickled onions and baths in rosewater and vinegar. For buboes, physicians urged the sick to coat them in egg yolk and to sprinkle bed linens with flower petals.

Ibn Battuta returned home to Morocco in November 1349 but determined to visit Africa. By caravan, he crossed the Sahara in fall 1351. Along the route to Taghaza in northern Mali, he found salt miners living on bitter water, camel haunches, and sacks of dates. Bags of salt and spices served as common currency for the purchase of food and lodging. Farther south, he mused on the subsistence of West African communities on millet porridge and milk and on the availability of water and fresh honey in rotted baobab trunks. He found verdant areas rich in apple, apricot, peach, and plum orchards and gardens producing peanuts, an ingredient of fried cakes and a source of cooking oil. At Walata, he examined the planting of watermelons in shady date groves.

A visit to Mali's capital—probably Niani—on June 28, 1353, left the traveler bedridden for eight weeks from eating undercooked or tainted yams. An emetic of anise and sugar did nothing to rouse him. Upon his recovery, the sultan sent beef fried in shea butter, bread, and a gourd of yogurt, a humble repast that insulted the Moroccan. In retort to poor hospitality, Ibn Battuta recorded that many Malians ate asses, dogs, and vultures. An encounter with a Berber included a meal of cow's milk, spitted goat, and roast mutton.

At age 49, the traveler returned home to become a judge at Fez. At the prompting of Morocco's Sultan Abu Inan Marini, Ibn Battuta began dictating the *Rihla* (*Travels*) in 1354. The travelogue, completed on December 9, 1355, was the work of redactor Ibn Juzayy. It earned the name "gastronomical atlas of the Orient."

See also: Breakfast; Currency, Food as; Kebabs; Medieval Diet and Cuisine; Nuts and Seeds; Silk Road.

Further Reading

Dunn, Ross E. *The Adventures of Ibn Battuta: A Muslim Traveler of the 14th Century.* Berkeley: University of California Press, 2005.

Fleming, Fergus. *Off the Map: Tales of Endurance and Exploration.* New York: Grove, 2004.

Hamdun, Said, Noel King, and Ross E. Dunn. *Ibn Battuta in Black Africa.* Princeton, NJ: Wiener, 2005.

Waines, David. *The Odyssey of Ibn Battuta: Uncommon Tales of a Medieval Adventurer.* Chicago: University of Chicago Press, 2010.

Ice

Frozen water, the planet's most abundant solid and most efficient food preservative, chills food and drink to add variety and texture to cuisine and refreshments. In the ancient world, a store of ice in ice caves or icehouses distinguished the dining of royalty and aristocrats. For their signature sorbets, Persian ice masters beginning in 1700 B.C.E. packed frozen chunks in ice sheds or in subterranean caches amid insulating ash, clay, goat hair, lime, sand, or sawdust and a topping of straw.

Similar systems of harvesting and insulating ice and snow served the Chinese along the Yangtze River around 1100 B.C.E. and the Inca in the Andes Mountains. Alexander the Great in 332 B.C.E. served ice in summer fruit ades to Macedonian soldiers. At Petra in Jordan, he had 30 trenches filled with snow and topped with oak limbs to preserve his impromptu chilling technology. At Constantinople, a similar method of storing ice blocks in holes—sprinkling them with water and covering them with shore rushes—kept ice on hand into summer, when beverage sellers sold iced sweets on public streets.

Athenian chefs and the Roman Emperor Nero dispatched servants with ice carts and sledges before dawn to transport blocks from frozen slopes for cooling evening meals and drinks. Street vendors lined their wine counters with snow and turned the cold crystals into honeyed drinks incorporating fruit puree and wines. The ancient Greek physician Galen of Pergamum recommended snow as a method of keeping fish from putrefying by establishing a barrier against oxygen and against the dehydration of natural juices.

Table Art

Medieval cooks applied ice to specific tasks, such as the immediate chilling of new beans or peas in fourteenth-century France to halt cooking and retain crispness. Culinary displays in Asia and Europe involved exhibitions of complex ice sculptures for banquets. Shapes such as pensive Buddhas and filigreed lanterns became conspicuous symbols of wealth when rendered as transparent objects that rapidly degraded into water. The planes and surfaces reflected flickering candlelight and stimulated conversation among diners.

In the Renaissance, manor houses, especially in Naples, sported conical or domed ice mounds or north-facing wells set in cool glades near springs. To add steam to baking, Italian pizzerias began adding ice cubes to the oven floor before baking focaccia or pizza. Peasants pressed snow into frozen blocks, which remained solid in *dogana della neve* (snow warehouses) into summer months for use in beverages and confections.

Late Renaissance food service required a *garde manger* (food keeper), a chilling room or cold cellar for storing sculpted butter, carved vegetables and fruits, chilled soups, cold cuts, fruit ices, game, hors d'oeuvres, molded salads and terrines, and patés. Dessert specialists prepared snow desserts with wire whisks, which fluffed and separated the ice crystals.

After 1573 at the court of Henry III of France, wine service by the royal *bottigliere* (cellar master) required a dollop of ice or snow in each glass. The chilling of brandy into a table liqueur in Paris preceded the sale of lemonade as a medical restorative. Joining other European doctors, however, Laurent Joubert, physician to Catherine de' Médici, warned that too much cold in food could upset a delicate physical balance, causing painful postdinner headaches or apoplexy.

Business

In the seventeenth century, ice sales introduced a lucrative trade. Natural surface freezing of lakes and streams created ready supplies, as with the Thames in England and Walden Pond in Massachusetts Bay Colony, though the British never developed the taste for chilled foods equivalent to that of North America. In this innovative era, showy table displays included ice sculptures surrounded by fish, shellfish, and sorbets, particularly for buffets, brunches, and wedding receptions. Popular shapes ranged from birds, fish, and flowers to fanciful arches, flames, palaces, water spouts, and waves.

In the early 1800s, entrepreneurs shipped Norwegian ice to Great Britain and blocks from Silver Lake in Rochester, New York, to the American South and the West Indies. In the coldest parts of January and February, employees used augers and ice saws for cutting, ice tongs and pike poles for stacking, and pulleys and conveyor systems to load supplies on wagons and into factories.

Ice chunks helped prevent spoilage at abattoirs, breweries, creameries, curing plants, dairies, drugstores, meat markets, and packinghouses. Hospitals along the Hudson River incorporated ice into treatments for swelling and pain. Sellers of ice touted its value in the slogan "nature's gift to everybody."

Health

During a yellow fever outbreak in August 1805, Frederic Tudor of Boston shipped the first load of ice, 130 tons (118 metric tons), to Caribbean hospitals. Within two years, he increased his shipment to 240 tons (218 metric tons) to Havana, Cuba, and acquired a monopoly on the ice trade to the West Indies. His success in the ice business in Calcutta, India, the island of Martinique, and Rio de Janeiro, Brazil, as well as in Southern U.S. cities—New Orleans, Savannah, and Charleston—earned him the nickname "Ice King."

Although inventor Nathaniel Wyeth designed an insulated ice storage shed in 1825 at Cambridge, Massachusetts, the health conscious began demanding greater oversight of water sources and storage sanitation. Cutting into Massachusetts vendors' trade, Maine ice operators sawed exceptionally pure blocks from the spring-fed Kennebec River and deposited them directly into ships' holds. In 1844, Chicago Mayor Alson Smith Sherman peddled ice to city dwellers. The trade developed into a major employer of tens of thousands of ice workers and distributors.

The use of domestic ice in the United States increased in the mid-1800s, after companies began delivery by horse and wagon to home ice chests, wooden boxes that held block ice. The business surged during the Civil War and peaked in 1870, when it reached an annual profit of $267,000, mostly from sales in Atlantic Coast cities. Gustav Franklin Swift, Chicago's meatpacking mogul, upgraded the ice bunker insulation of railcars, patented in November 1867 by J.B. Sutherland of Detroit, and enabled Swift & Company to ship freshly butchered beef to distant states. At points along the route, ice shovelers refreshed each car by topping off food mounds. The shipping of meat rather than livestock turned a seasonal business into a year-round bonanza for farmers and packers.

For the sake of public health, Pennsylvania and New England ice harvesters obeyed laws against taking blocks from such polluted sources as the Schuylkill River. Too late, French ice harvesters at Rennes in 1899 discovered that champagne served with ice polluted by sewage in the Vilaine River spread typhoid fever to an entire military regiment.

Commercial Freezers

From the 1870s, commercial chilling introduced to coastal communities large-scale preservation of halibut, salmon, and shellfish, a deviation from the high-sodium content of salted fish and meats. The Gitga'at people of Hartley Bay, British Columbia, also packed seaweed in ice after the drying season passed. Poultry farmers discovered that they could lengthen the shelf life of eggs by storing them in icehouses.

At the 1893 World's Columbian Exposition in Chicago, artificial ice manufactured with ammonia coils won an award for engineers at the Frick Company of Waynesboro, Pennsylvania. North American ice merchants on the Pacific Coast began shipping to Hawaii, Hong Kong, and the Philippines in 1898, when meatpackers introduced Oceania to American tastes in beef and game. A broadened choice of meat suppliers enabled cooks to refine their recipes to exact standards of flavor and texture.

Because chemical softening rid water of magnesia and sulphates of lime, the food-saving quality of pure commercial ice spread from Britain to Australasia and New Zealand, two shippers of lamb and mutton, and to Argentina, a competitive global source of beef. Steamers supplying U.S. troops in Manila during the Spanish-American War maintained cold storage and ice plants for the use of provisioners and hospital staff.

The growth of ice making in South Africa at Cape Colony and Transvaal decreased the price of meat, which previously had spoiled in hot weather. By 1899, builders began erecting ice plants in the Orange Free State in South Africa and Singapore, in Hawaiian clipper ships and Nova Scotian fishing fleets, and at malt liquor breweries in Cuba and Puerto Rico.

According to reports in the *Cold Storage and Ice Trade Journal,* when demand exceeded supply in March 1906, New England's ice harvesters looked toward Michigan, Ohio, and Wisconsin and as far south as Missouri to supplement sources. Supplies sold to homemakers and bar-keeps at 15¢ per hundred pounds (45 kilograms). Ice blocks in refrigerated railcars preserved cheese, fruit, meat, and vegetables for cross-country transport. One Missouri farmer made a profitable ice cake by directing a stream of spring water into a wood box measuring 20 feet (6.1 meters) on each side and drilling out pieces for sale.

Modern Ice Making

By 1915, the creation of a small ice compartment in Frigidaires allowed homemakers to insert their own metal ice trays for freezing. The invention of the ice cube maker made it possible to keep ice year-round. All in all, ice had become a necessity, not a luxury. While sellers of natural ice supplied grocers' freezers and railcars, ice generators crystallized and dispensed pure bag ice as flakes, blocks, and cubes for use in boating, camping, fishing, and picnicking.

Today, flake ice suits the needs of fishermen and fish restaurants because of its delicate surface, which chills without denting flesh. Gourmet ice makers spray water upward to produce layered freezing that is free of air bubbles and clouding by carbonate of lime or other impurities. Hawaiians value shaved ice for cooling treats in a variety of flavors, a recipe similar to the Filipino dessert halo-halo, a mix of shaved ice with evaporated milk, fruit, and sweet beans.

See also: Escoffier, Georges Auguste; Fish and Fishing; Maritime Trade Routes; Shellfish.

Further Reading

Belasco, Warren James, and Roger Horowitz, eds. *Food Chains: From Farmyard to Shopping Cart.* Philadelphia: University of Pennsylvania Press, 2009.

Gosnell, Mariana. *Ice: The Nature, the History, and the Uses of an Astonishing Substance.* Chicago: University of Chicago Press, 2007.

Marling, Karal Ann. *Ice: Great Moments in the History of Hard, Cold Water.* St. Paul, MN: Borealis, 2008.

Parrish, Christopher C., Nancy J. Turner, and Shirley M. Solberg, eds. *Resetting the Kitchen Table: Food Security, Culture, Health and Resilience in Coastal Communities.* New York: Nova Science, 2008.

Ice Cream

A sweet frozen dessert marketed by the dairy industry, ice cream is a versatile basis for cake and fruit or syrup and a popular side dressing for choux pastry, pie, and Yule log cakes. When served in cones and sandwiches or on a stick, ice cream appeals to children and to attendees at parks and sports events. Favorite flavors tend toward chocolate, strawberry, and vanilla with international variants—Chinese mung bean, Greek fig, Italian tortoni (almond and maraschino cherry desserts), Japanese green tea and red beans, and Turkish *salep* (orchid tubers).

History

The history of ice cream began around 2000 B.C.E. with snow, the basis for Chinese snow cream treats. Simultaneously, Mongol horsemen carried cream in animal intestines. While traveling the Gobi in frigid weather, they agitated the cream while it froze. Around 400 B.C.E., Persians invented *faloodeh,* a chilled sorbet of thin vermicelli blended with lime and saffron, sweetened with honey and rose syrup, and topped with pistachio nuts. In 335 B.C.E., Alexander the Great developed a liking for snow blended with nectar. In China from 200 B.C.E., cooks mixed rice with frozen milk for an early sherbet. They chilled containers with saltpeter and snow, which lowered the freezing point. Under the Emperor Nero, after 54 C.E., gala Roman dinners ended with gelato, a honey- and snow-based dessert and forerunner of Renaissance ice cream.

In the decline of the Byzantine Empire, Asians developed iced desserts to a height of enjoyment. Arabs carried their expertise west after the armada of 200 ships under Caliph Uthman ibn Affan of Damascus invaded Sicily in 652 C.E. In Baghdad, Damascus, Cairo—wherever Arab cuisine flourished in the 900s C.E.—chefs stirred up dairy desserts and added the scent of rosewater, the sweetness of cane sugar, and the texture of fruit and nuts. To the east after the birth of the Yuan dynasty in 1260, Huou, Kublai Khan's imperial chef, became late-medieval China's first native gastronome and an originator of ice cream recipes. After 1526, in Delhi, Indian dessert makers treated Mughal aristocrats to iced fruit custard.

Along with Renaissance ideals, European applications of iced dairy treats moved north from Florence to Paris, St. Petersburg, and Vienna. In 1533, Catherine de' Médici, the Florentine bride of Henry II of France, arranged continental menus that concluded with "cream ice," granitas, profiteroles (cream puffs), sherbet, and zabaglione (egg custard). Neapolitan scientist Giambattista della Porta discovered a secret of freezing in 1589, when he mixed ice and salt as a rapid cooling agent. French chemist and food writer Nicolas Lémery of Rouen, the royal apothecary of Louis XIV, published the first French ice milk recipe in *Recueil de Curiositéz Rare et Nouvelles de Plus Admirables Effets de la Nature* (A Selection of Rare and Innovative Curiosities of the Most Wondrous Phenomena of Nature, 1674).

Farther east, ice cream maintained its cachet at the courts of Catherine the Great of Russia and Gustaf III of Sweden. After 1682, Peter the Great of Russia promoted flaky pastries, champagne, and decadent chocolates and ice cream for dessert, a treat reserved for the imperial table because of the high cost of refrigeration. The imperial delight in iced desserts remained in vogue after the coronation of the Emperor Alexander II in 1856. In Vienna on October 1, 1716, journalist Lady Mary Wortley Montagu observed Austrian plutocrats displaying dishes

Baked Alaska—ice cream on a bed of sponge cake and covered with meringue, heated in the oven to create a hard shell—commemorates the U.S. purchase of Alaska on March 30, 1867. However, National Baked Alaska Day is February 1. *(Larry Crowe/ Associated Press)*

of ice cream at elegant Kolhmarkt stalls as privileges of wealth.

Following the popularity of dairy drinks in coffee-houses and milk bars in the mid-1700s, sweet French dessert cheeses and festive custard and berry ice cream in London cookbooks migrated to the North American colonies. Pure vanilla remained popular as a flavoring at the Philip Lenzi confectionery, America's first ice cream parlor. After opening in 1774 on Dock Street in New York City, three years later, the London-born caterer advertised his frozen cream desserts and water ices in the May 12 edition of the *New York Gazette.* In 1789, Thomas Jefferson, the U.S. envoy to France, brought home to Monticello an 18-step recipe for ice cream in pastry shells and enough vanilla beans to enrich the filling.

Presidential cravings for ice cream enticed George Washington to install "cream machines for ice" at Mount Vernon. Dolley Madison introduced ice cream desserts at James Madison's second inaugural feast in 1813 as a state dish. Jefferson's cousin, Mary Randolph, issued a dessert collection in *The Virginia House-Wife: or Methodical Cook* (1824), the first American anthology to feature ice cream and sherbet. The hand-operated churn with a two-spatula dasher and crank, which New York inventor Nancy M. Johnson patented in 1843, scraped ice crystals from the barrel and broke up air pockets. The device made frozen desserts available to the householder in 20 minutes.

Technology democratized ice cream. In the 1860s, a decade after the opening of the first ice cream factory in Baltimore in 1851, the dessert became a by-product of American breweries. In 1863, before President Abraham Lincoln's formal recognition of Thanksgiving, the Second Wisconsin Volunteers at Arlington, Virginia, indulged

in a lavish menu of turkey rounded out with ice cream and sparkling Catawba wine. Post–Civil War innovations yielded confectioner William A. Breyer's recipe for ice cream, which limited ingredients to cream, milk, sugar, and vanilla.

Dairy desserts, sundaes, and ice cream sodas continued to mark historic events. To honor U.S. Secretary of State William Henry Seward's purchase of Alaska on March 30, 1867, Charles Ranhofer, a French chef at Delmonico's Restaurant on William Street in Lower Manhattan, invented baked Alaska, a sponge cake dessert topped with ice cream and meringue and broiled to create a hard shell. In 1875, during the reformation of American Judaism, Isaac Mayer Wise shocked orthodox guests by serving nonkosher food—seafood and ice cream to follow meat.

At the Philadelphia Centennial International Exhibition of 1876, the first world's fair in the United States, American visitors viewed a range of culinary advances, including Boston silversmith James Walker Tufts's ice cream arctic soda fountain. With less grandeur, vendors on bicycles or pushing carts targeted children in the North Atlantic states and in England. Italian sellers crying *O, che poco* (Oh, how little [it costs]) confused English speakers, who referred to ice cream as "hokey-pokey." In *Miss Beecher's Domestic Receipt-Book* (1846), Catharine Esther Beecher, forerunner of the home economics movement, declared ice cream a boon to treatment of fevers.

In 1885, English kitchen entrepreneur Agnes Marshall published *Ices Plain and Fancy: The Book of Ices,* followed in 1894 by *Fancy Ices,* both illustrated with line drawings and recipes for bombes, glaces, parfaits, and *tartufos,* balls of ice cream iced in chocolate. Her instant freezing of cream with liquid nitrogen into geometric shapes and miniature monuments astonished diners and produced a rush to buy her name brand of ice cream freezers and molds for ices made from jam and liqueur syrup. Marshall's lace paper doilies and ice cups simplified serving and cleaning dishes of such specialties as *crème panachée,* her version of an ice cream cake made from ingredients with contrasting colors, flavors, or textures. She also turned ground almonds into the ice cream cone, which she called "cornet à la crème."

Period recipes specified coconut oil for flavoring ice cream and creamy yellow dyes made from lemon-flavored citral or yellow-orange annatto. In 1912, California horticulturist Luther Burbank hybridized a spineless prickly pear, which yielded pulp for Southwestern ice cream and sorbet. By husking, milling, and gelling guar beans in water, ice cream processors produced a digestible, odorless guar gum that emulsified and suspended solids in ice cream and sherbet to prevent crystal growth and ingredient settling. Ice cream makers also used the gluten found in carrageenan and kelp.

Food producers valued vegetable mucilage for suspending starch in liquid and for ameliorating the effects of freezing and thawing. By 1920, the stability of frozen ice cream made possible chocolate-covered Eskimo Pies and the Good Humor Bar on a stick, which uniformed distributors sold from vans while beguiling neighborhoods with calliope music. Rocky Road, introduced in 1929 in Oakland, California, contained enough viscosity to hold marshmallow and walnut pieces suspended in Edy's ice cream. In 1934, *Popular Mechanics* magazine proposed that health food makers add cod liver oil to ice cream and milkshakes to halt the effects of malnutrition in poor children.

Rationing in the 1940s limited America's top novelty food, including Thomas Carvellus's Carvel frozen custard, sold from a truck in Hartsdale, New York. As wheat supplies dried up during World War II, ice cream vendors improvised a new cone-making flour from crushed, sweetened popcorn. Creameries dispensed Dixie Cups and substituted coconut and cottonseed oil in the mix for rationed butterfat.

Food writer Elizabeth David summarized the style and flair of regional cookery in *Italian Food* (1954), which applauded the taste of Neapolitan and Sicilian ice cream fanciers. Her validation of luxury iced desserts predicted the late-twentieth-century rush toward gourmet ice creams, such as Godiva and Starbucks, which feature greater proportions of chocolate and cream.

Recent Developments

From the early twentieth century, packagers of ready-to-eat foods added potato and rice flour, oat fiber, and soybeans as the standard thickeners that gave sensuous mouthfeel to ice cream. Caramel concentrate, a traditional food dye, offered an intense brown hue to chocolate ice cream. To combine the top flavors in a single product, dairiers invented choc-van-straw, or Neapolitan ice cream, a trio of popular tastes. Apollo astronauts enjoyed Neapolitan ice cream in freeze-dried bricks. By the 1970s, Australia and New Zealand competed with the Northern Hemisphere in marketing dairy desserts. Simultaneously, frozen yogurt, first marketed in Boston in 1978, further restructured the ice cream market.

The Baskin-Robbins and Howard Johnson chains faced competition from Dairy Queen and Tastee Freez, distributors of soft-serve desserts puffed with air. High butterfat content made Ben & Jerry's and Häagen-Dazs premium ice creams more flavorful and spiked sales of Cherry Garcia, Chocolate Chip Cookie Dough, and Super Fudge Chunk, among other flavors.

Despite warnings from the healthy food movement, recipes worldwide—Argentine *helado,* Filipino halo-halo, Hawaiian shaved ice, Italian gelato, Korean *pathingsu,* Malaysian *ais kacang*—retain the original concept of a fruity iced sweet. In the Azores and China, chefs add sugar to pureed taro for ice cream and pie filling. A favorite Arctic dessert, *agutak,* or "Eskimo ice cream," blends the flavor of whipped fat or tallow with blueberries, cloudberries, cranberries, crowberries, or salmonberries. Raw foodists make sundaes from frozen raw milk and Thai coconut. Globally, ice cream fanciers enjoy more than 1,000 flavors, including apple gingersnap, Christmas ale, cinnamon cocoa, cranberry crisp, and matzoh crunch.

See also: Additives, Food; Guar; Ice; Marshall, Agnes; Taro; Trans Fat.

Further Reading

Gosnell, Mariana. *Ice: The Nature, the History, and the Uses of an Astonishing Substance.* Chicago: University of Chicago Press, 2007.

Powell, Marilyn. *Ice Cream: The Delicious History.* New York: Penguin, 2009.

Quinzio, Jeri. *Of Sugar and Snow: A History of Ice Cream Making.* Berkeley: University of California Press, 2009.

Idiocuisine

A current interest of anthropologists and sociologists, idiocuisine reflects agrarian and kitchen conditions and market sources and their influence on traditional family eating habits. Essential to daily sustenance are the ingredients and recipes indigenous to the household and its forebears. From clan preferences grow the true idiocuisine, the foods that families prefer for everyday consumption and for holidays and feasts. In each instance, the exigencies of rationing, conquest, and war threaten the familiar, such as the near extinction of the buffalo and laws against whaling and collecting sea turtle eggs.

The familiarity of idiocuisine forces clan foodways to evolve over time. In frontier days, European newcomers to North America incorporated the New World flavors of avocados, blueberries, buffalo meat, pecans, and persimmons in their heritage recipes. The substitutions of cranberries for English currants in fruit leather, collards for spinach in spanakopita, and corn bread for Italian wheat loaves and French baguettes turned relocation into a culinary challenge. Further skewing established patterns of eating, mixed marriages introduced both members of a culture to considerable adaptation, such as the Indian wife's addition of jerky and pemmican to the white frontiersman's diet and the black homemaker's blend of callaloo and black-eyed peas into the everyday meals of her biracial children.

Historically, diasporas forced compromise into familiar eating styles and acceptance of available commodities. Newcomers ventured from ethnic bruschetta, nan with kebabs, pita pockets, tacos, and wraps to Americanized sandwiches and heroes. During the stress of acculturation, kitchen innovations heightened the positive aspects of life made different by conditions and locale. In major adaptations—such as the replacement of European wild sage honey and beet sugar with molasses and of Turkish dates and figs with dried wild plums—the immigrant's idiocuisine remained in a state of recipe shift and kitchen experimentation.

Refugees and migrants brought pervasive culture change to their new homelands, as did Filipinos in Hawaii, Mexicans in Texas, Nigerians in Canada, Pakistanis in England, Parsis in India, and Portuguese in Mozambique. New Englanders augmented barley- and wheat-based recipes with cornmeal, thus inventing the johnnycake. Similarly, New Orleans Creole cookery found ways of blending the West African okra pod with *filé* (dried sassafras leaves) and of turning French nougat and walnut recipes into pecan-based pralines. While newcomers to the Mississippi River delta fused words and concepts into a New World patois, cooks made similar shifts in their daily coffee by blending it with chicory for a taste indigenous to southern Louisiana.

As gastronomy moved in another direction, toward homogenization—exemplified by British-style curries in India and boxed Italian gnocchi and pasta rather than homemade—regional food gradually lost its idiosyncrasies and became an endangered species. Celebrity chefs advanced idiocuisine into culinary exhibitionism by extending novelties to traditional recipes, an improvisation attuned to showy tour-de-force entrees and snacks, such as stuffed squash blossoms, mango salsa, piki (blue cornmeal) chips, and jalapeño poppers, rather than stable regional specialties.

Fortunately for purists, travelers and academic chefs in the 2000s began shifting pop food culture away from indiscriminate snacking, overprocessed foods, and drive-through fill-ups toward authentic ingredients and cookery. Adventurers turned to *Bon Appetit, Cuisine,* and *Saveur* magazines for data on holistic nourishment at patterned meals, a revolution that restored authenticity to idiocuisine. Patronage of local food markets brought free-range chickens and eggs and artisanal beers, cheese, and sausage into regional use, supplying the home pantry once more with the aromas and flavors of memory.

See also: Fusion Cuisine; Heritage Foods; Local Food Movement; Nouvelle Cuisine; Regional Cuisine.

Further Reading

Cooke, Philip, and Luciana Lazzeretti. *Creative Cities, Cultural Clusters and Local Economic Development.* Northampton, MA: Edward Elgar, 2008.

Deaux, Kay. *To Be an Immigrant.* New York: Russell Sage, 2009.

Dixon, Jane. *The Changing Chicken: Chooks, Cooks and Culinary Culture.* Sydney, Australia: University of New South Wales Press, 2002.

Howell, Jim. "On Waikaia Plains Station—Developing a Cuisine of Stewardship." *In Practice* 124 (March/April 2009): 8–11.

Parrish, Christopher C., Nancy J. Turner, and Shirley M. Solberg, eds. *Resetting the Kitchen Table: Food Security, Culture, Health and Resilience in Coastal Communities.* New York: Nova Science, 2008.

Immigrant Diet and Cuisine

An exercise in adaptation, the diet and cookery of immigrants and refugees make immediate shifts away from heritage recipes to the availability of ingredients and cooking techniques in a new locale. Native cuisine arouses fierce loyalties, as with the Italian midday meal of macaroni with oil and the Irish consumption of cabbage, corned beef, and soda bread on St. Patrick's Day. Shoppers maintain centuries-old habits, particularly buying potatoes or rice by the bushel and purchasing peppers and tomatoes several times per week to ensure freshness.

Over time, compromise produced Chinese, Italian, Mexican, Taiwanese, and West Indian foodways that accommodated American and Canadian tastes. Similarly, newcomers from Jamaica, South Africa, and Sri Lanka in England reconfigured dining styles and entrées to suit the colder climate and agricultural produce of Great Britain. To appeal to shoppers, grocery chains began stocking dal and quinoa; specialty shops introduced sashimi and tamales.

When Spanish immigrants settled at Nootka Sound in western Vancouver, British Columbia, in the 1790s, they fertilized gardens with fish offal and seaweed and planted kitchen gardens plus orchards and pastures. Fenced-in vegetable patches produced angelica, artichokes, barley, beets, cabbage, carrots, celery, chickpeas, eggplant, lettuce, onions, parsnips, peppers, potatoes, and rape, all suited to North American rainfall and snowy winters. Spanning the next two centuries, cabbage, potatoes, and turnips remained prominent in local cuisine alongside imported flour, salt beef, sugar, and tea.

Upon reaching Ellis Island, new arrivals to the United States abandoned the limited choices of beans, cabbage, gefilte fish, and peas in their shipboard stashes for free meals from the Department of Immigration. Children indulged for the first time in bread and butter and coffee with milk and sugar, treats that had the power to plump up bony frames. The height of dining hall largesse, the Thanksgiving banquet introduced immigrants to cranberry sauce, sweet potatoes, and turkey. Jubilant women placed celery sprigs in their lapels while children peeled mandarins and savored them section by section.

Cooks established home kitchens, some with open hearths, and spent about 40 percent of family incomes on food, compared with native-born budgets of 33 percent. In ethnic neighborhoods, women tsk-tsked over produce in handcarts. Tenement kitchens echoed with the sounds of cabbage chopping and garlic mashing and the smell of spaetzel grated into boiling stock. Housewives proudly shared their expert meatballs and tamales at potluck dinners and parties.

Americanization required adaptation to the new and strange, such as chewing gum and popcorn. For sustenance, Greeks, Italians, and Syrians lived by the lowest nutritional standards, as compared with German Jews and Slavs. At ghetto restaurants, immigrants indulged in cheap fare served by wait staff, the first strangers that newcomers had seen serving meals. Children learned to pass bowls rather than grab from a central platter or pot. The simple act of receiving plated entrées and hot coffee poured into cups rather than mugs conferred dignity and respectability on a people who had fled persecution and serfdom.

Social workers explained the mysteries of the double boiler and introduced such unfamiliar foods as the grapefruit. Home economics classes coaxed girls away from overcooking nutrients out of cabbage and greens. Those immigrants who found jobs in American restaurants and home kitchens gained new perceptions of holiday specialties, such as fruitcake, champagne, and eggnog for Christmas rather than Old World *baba*, *lebkuchen*, and *syllabub*.

The dramatic shift in immigrant diet altered the demographics of disease, primarily dental caries, diabetes, and heart disease. Accustomed to the peasant fare of Cambodia and Vietnam, children of the "boat people" in the 1970s found potato chips and cola drinks more palatable and varied than Old Country snacks. Laotians, who traditionally chopped small portions of meat and added it sparingly to rice dishes, increased the proportion of chicken and beef in their diet, thereby reducing intake of fish and vegetables. Ethnic mothers suspected school cafeterias of circumventing the female's control of nutrition and of demeaning ethnic meals as inferior.

Female householders who spoke little English or recognized no writing in the standard alphabet made more haphazard grocery choices in gathering the ingredients for shaping German Jewish blintzes and strudel, Chinese dumplings, or Italian cheese-and-tomato *pizzarelli* (fried cakes). Also unsettling to nuclear family solidarity, the interruptions of electronic media in industrialized countries lured children away from the communal table and respect for their elders. Traditional gatherings, such as Muslim enclaves celebrating Ramadan and Eid al-Fitr, increased the likelihood that such ritual foods as nut cookies and samosas (stuffed pastries) continued to hold a place of reverence.

Currently, immigrants contribute to the social fabric by offering diversity primarily in food preferences and gustatory celebrations. Worldwide, the consumption of frankfurters and hamburgers with mustard and relish betokens the spread of German peasant cuisine to fairs and sports events. In Canada, the government endorses unity in citizenship and patriotism and the uniqueness of cultural tradition, a change of pace from the ordinary. Tolerance for differences makes cosmopolitan cities such as Montreal, Quebec, Toronto, and Vancouver havens of ethnic restaurants and dining experiences.

See also: Fusion Cuisine; Idiocuisine; North American Diet and Cuisine; Polynesian Diet and Cuisine; Regional Cuisine; Sicilian Diet and Cuisine.

Further Reading

Burrell, Kathy, and Panikos Panayi. *Histories and Memories: Migrants and Their History in Britain.* London: I.B. Tauris, 2006.

Deaux, Kay. *To Be an Immigrant.* New York: Russell Sage, 2009.

Levine, Susan. *School Lunch Politics: The Surprising History of America's Favorite Welfare Program.* Princeton, NJ: Princeton University Press, 2010.

Parrish, Christopher C., Nancy J. Turner, and Shirley M. Solberg, eds. *Resetting the Kitchen Table: Food Security, Culture, Health and Resilience in Coastal Communities.* New York: Nova Science, 2008.

Ziegelman, Jane. *97 Orchard: An Edible History of Five Immigrant Families in One New York Tenement.* New York: Smithsonian/HarperCollins, 2010.

Inca Diet and Cuisine

One of the marvels of Amerindian sustenance, the Inca diet contained an astonishingly varied diet dominated by amaranth, corn, lima beans, peppers, tomatoes, and tubers called "earth nuts." A nation of master farmers that thrived in the fifteenth and early sixteenth centuries, the Inca introduced seeds and plants from neighboring tribes and accessed raised garden plots with llama paths and stone irrigation canals. A unique field account system relied on a knotted string called a quipu and a nature-based method of weather prediction.

Beginning in 200 B.C.E., a potato-rich cuisine fed 12 million subjects of the largest empire of the Bronze Age, stretching from Pasto, Colombia, down the western coast of South America to Santiago, Chile. A Spanish explorer and historian from Madrid, Pedro Cieza de León, compiled an 8,000-page eyewitness account of Pacific Coast life that introduced Europeans to the Inca diet and cookery. An adventurer from his early teens, he joined expeditions to Colombia, Panama, and the West Indies and discovered that the Inca cultivated 70 separate crops, more species of foods than other parts of the world. The potato became the only Inca staple to reach immediate global popularity.

In 1548, Cieza de León settled at Lima, Peru, and began chronicling New World events from the Gulf of Darien to La Plata. His four-part *Chronicles of Peru*, composed in Latin in the early colonial era, reached print piecemeal, concluding in 1979 with the discovery of a missing section in the Vatican library. In addition to chronologies of the Spanish conquest of Peru and subsequent epidemics that killed 80 percent of the Inca, his text details the consumption of two meals a day, one at sunrise and the second shortly before sunset. Cooks completed preparations in clay pots inserted into holes in the stove. Diners sat or squatted on the ground.

The historian introduced Europeans to salt collection on the Consota River; to Peruvian fauna, particularly the llama; and to native vegetables and cuisine based on guava, lima and red beans, *oca* (yams), pepper, potato, pumpkin, quinoa, and squash. Cooks served beans in oil and vinegar and flavored grain soups with birds, frogs, larvae, pink peppercorns, snails, or worms. They boiled quinoa kernels into a grain base, similar to rice, and served it with *ají* peppers and leaves and wild bitter herbs. In one startling encounter, the Spaniards killed a giant

snake, discovering in its gut an undigested deer. They retrieved the deer and cooked the venison for dinner.

Staples

In the first volume of his chronicles, Cieza de León observed the harvesting of palm hearts from palm groves and recorded the variety of uses for coconut in the manufacture of cream, lard, milk, and lamp oil. In terraced highland gardens, he cataloged root crops (*camote, maca, oca,* potato, *ulluco,* and yuca), pigs and tapirs, fish, and an abundance of birds and turkeys. The preservation of ulluco produced a powdered antidote for stomach ills and labor pains. The sweet potato served as a vegetable for frying, roasting, or stewing or as a fruit cooked into preserves.

By alternately sunning and freezing potatoes over a five-day period and trampling them under foot, farmers dehydrated the tubers into *chuño,* which natives steamed and used to thicken broth. They also dried salt meat into *charqui,* the original jerky. When llamas ended their service as beasts of burden, cooks sliced their meat into strips for drying and tenderized it by pounding it between stones. Drying promoted a long shelf life in stone silos and warehouses and portability for travel. The Spanish turned chuño to commercial advantage by shipping the freeze-dried potatoes to Potosí, Bolivia, to feed the press gangs who worked the silver mines.

The chronicler continued down the South American coast along the central Andes and described the foodstuffs of the Huari near Lake Titicaca and the predominance of quinoa in pantries at the seaport city of Collao. Along the coast, fish drying provided the Inca military with their main staple. In the Chacama Valley of northwestern Peru, farmers grew sugarcane to make into sugar and conserves.

At Cartagena, the historian observed a wake for the chief. During the ritual, mourners gathered to drink *chicha,* a ritual corn beer flavored with goldberries and fermented in jars buried in the ground. Survivors amassed platters for a feast, jugs of chicha, and women and servants to bury alive with the mummied corpse.

At Puna Island, off the coast of Ecuador, residents fed on birds, corn, and yuca; at Huanca to the southwest, dogs were a delicacy. At Guayaquil and Puna, herbalists treated pestilence with sarsaparilla and a diet of "delicate meats." The historian ranked the sarsaparilla root as the world's best and most useful herb and root.

Cieza de León described common foods of Peru as well as temple gardens and the reciprocity by which royalty repaid laborers with elegant feasts in sumptuous plazas. In the Andes, forest-dwelling Quechua sowed corn and gourds, dug root crops, and cultivated orchards of avocado, cocoa, custard apples, eggfruit, *pacay* (ice cream bean), and passion fruit. To extend gardening inland to Cuzco, Indians spread loam from the Andes over barren soil, which, thus enriched, produced two crops of corn and potatoes per year. In addition to vegetables, the Inca

Recipe: Azul Potatoes in Spiced Tomatoes

Boil ten *azul* or blue potatoes (*Solanum ajanhuiri*) for 20–30 minutes. Cool, peel, and slice the potatoes and arrange the slices on a platter. Heat 1/4 cup vegetable oil. Saute two *aji* peppers, one garlic clove, and one chopped white onion. Add six pureed tomatoes and flavor with pepper and salt, 1 cup of chopped cilantro, and a small bunch of chives or green onions, chopped. Simmer for five minutes and dress the potatoes with the spiced tomato mixture and a sprinkling of vinegar.

of Cuzco chewed coca, an herb that empowered workers even when they were tired, hungry, or suffering pain. In irrigated fields fertilized with guano from the bird islands and sardine heads, they produced ají peppers, corn, cotton, gourds, sweet potatoes, and yucas.

The assembly of citizens for a banquet required no plates or bowls. Diners consumed fruits, roasted meat, and tubers with their hands. At a display of Peruvian cuisine, the historian marveled at a dinner of roasted llama, which he deemed the best meat he had ever eaten.

Corn and Its Accompaniments

Meticulous corn planting so dominated Peruvian agriculture that the Inca arranged the calendar around the stages of corn sowing, ripening, and harvest. They ate corn roasted, boiled, popped, or ground into meal for dumplings to add to stews or for shaping into dough for tortillas. Corn coordinated well with other foods, including fried guinea pig, nuts, and seafood and seaweed. Runners hurried fresh fish and oysters from the seacoast to the royal kitchen of the emperor, Sayri Túpac. One flavoring, the *pepino*, a striped cucumber, Cieza de León found sweet but indigestible.

Peruvians also domesticated ducks for feathers and meat, which they disjointed and carved with copper knives. They reserved the roasting and stewing of alpaca, fish, guinea pig, and llama meat for special occasions. To protect the people from years of famine, rulers controlled the hunting of wild game and stockpiled up to a seven-year supply of food in storehouses, such as the ones the historian viewed in the Xayanca Valley of northwestern Peru. The state guaranteed citizen subsistence by maintaining a network of food distribution to even out shortfalls with surpluses from other regions.

In the second volume, Cieza de León admired the moral integrity of the Inca, who suppressed cannibalistic hunter-gathers and outlawed their "abominable sin" of eating the flesh of sacrificed men and children. During the Inca propitiation of the creator god, worshippers preceded the harvest festival with fasting, abstained from meat and salt, and consumed a 12-day diet of only water and chicha, served during morning hours. Holy virgin brewers fermented the sacred beverage and poured it from silver carafes into gold chalices. Chosen victims drank heartily of chicha before priests strangled and canonized them. The culminating late-morning banquet at Cuzco involved the slaughter of doves, guinea pigs, white llamas, and sheep and the anointing of idols and the portals of temples with animal blood. Augurs read the entrails of the sacrificed animals for portents. At a ritual garden, they erected gold corn stalks among gold dirt clods, replicas of indigenous vegetable plots.

See also: Amerindian Diet; Peppers; Pit Cookery; Potatoes; Religion and Food; Salt; Trade Routes.

Further Reading

Bray, Tamara L. *The Archaeology and Politics of Food and Feasting in Early States and Empires.* New York: Kluwer Academic, 2003.

Crosby, Alfred W. *The Columbian Exchange: Biological and Cultural Consequences of 1492.* Westport, CT: Greenwood, 2003.

MacQuarrie, Kim. *The Last Days of the Incas.* New York: Simon & Schuster, 2008.

Somervill, Barbara A. *Empire of the Incas.* New York: Chelsea House, 2009.

Indian Diet and Cuisine

Over five millennia, India evolved a cuisine unique in its application of herbs and spices and in taboos surrounding meat consumption. Around 1700 B.C.E., scripture in the Vedas championed balanced combinations of dairy foods, grain, honey, meat, fruit, and vegetables. The Asian concept of the body in balance, derived from China, depicted eating as a form of self-medication, with foods and herbs that cured indigestion, lethargy, and impotence.

Parallel to the carnivorous diet, vegetarianism gained advocates, primarily from Aryan Hindus, who denounced animal butchery and the waste of dairy herds. Hindu jurisprudence criminalized the consumption of animal flesh and replaced meat burning on altars with gifts of milk. In place of animal sacrifice, peasants worshipped at altars with gifts of flowers, fruit, incense, oil, and vegetables. In Jharkhand, the stress on meatless entrées elevated the importance of sweet potatoes, Indian beans, pumpkin, bamboo shoots, chutney, and fruit. In contrast, Kerala developed a vegetable-based diet that allowed fish and poultry, edibles preferred by Christians and Muslims.

By 800 B.C.E., a moral handbook, the Baudhayana Sutra, stressed the ascetics of portion control from unadorned dishes of barley, dairy products, oil cake, and rice. The Mahabharata (ca. 200 B.C.E.), the Indian epic, further condemned beast butchery and promised vegetarians longevity and a sound memory for their purity of heart. After 320 C.E., the Gupta Empire in northern India introduced a golden age of religion, philosophy, and Ayurvedic medicine, which promoted tea and cooking spices, a bold introduction of appetite stimulants to a bland Indian diet. In the 1400s, Timur's invasion of Kashmir created a fusion cuisine of Indian and Persian elements that featured lamb and rice.

In the 1500s, the Indian renaissance evolved the Mughlai cuisine, a further elevation of taste and aroma in pungent kebabs, meatballs, rice and egg dishes, cardamom-flavored pudding, chili stews, and pilaf (rice simmered in broth). A model, chicken tikka masala, curried chicken in a masala sauce, defined the age. The iconic recipe passed to Bangladesh and Pakistan; British colonials adopted the spicy chicken as representative of colonial Indian

Traditional Chettinad cuisine, from a region in southern India, features spicy, aromatic nonvegetarian dishes such as curry and biryani with chicken, lamb, or fish (no beef or pork). Popular spices include star aniseed, red chilies, tamarind, cardamom, fennel, and cloves. *(India Today Group/ Getty Images)*

cookery. In Pondicherry, French colonials influenced Indian recipes for tandoori potatoes, coconut curry, baked mung beans, and stuffed cabbage. In the Himalayas, the Sikkimese diet featured northwestern grains—millet, buckwheat, barley, soybeans, and wheat, a contrast to Bengali entrées of lentils and greens cooked with shad, mullet, catfish, or bass.

Distinctive regional foods exploited local ingredients, including fruit and seafood in Andamanese cuisine and coconut and tamarind in Hyderabad cookery. Telugu cuisine centered table staples on rice and lentils; Assamese specialties favored dried fish and pickled vegetables. Bihar chefs built a local reputation for flatbread, fish with mustard, and dairy buttermilk, ghee, and yogurt. On the coast, Goa cooks sweetened seafood platters with rice steeped in coconut milk, an element of the seafood dishes of Lakshadweep. Manipur localized pantry staples with chili peppers and leafy vegetables from kitchen gardens and domestic fish from ponds.

See also: Chutney; Curry; Dal; Gama, Vasco da; Pit Cookery; Portuguese East India Company; Silk Road; Spices; Vegetarianism.

Further Reading

Banerji, Chitrita. *Eating India: An Odyssey into the Food and Culture of the Land of Spices.* New York: Bloomsbury, 2007.

Chapman, Pat. *India: Food & Cooking: The Ultimate Book on Indian Cuisine.* London: New Holland, 2007.

Hughes, Martin, Sheema Mookherjee, and Richard Delacy. *World Food: India.* Oakland, CA: Lonely Planet, 2001.

Madavan, Vijay. *Cooking the Indian Way.* Minneapolis, MN: Lerner, 2002.

Monroe, Jo. *Star of India: The Spicy Adventures of Curry.* Chichester, UK: John Wiley & Sons, 2005.

Indonesian Diet and Cuisine

Over five major land masses and 6,000 smaller islands, Indonesian menus feature local ingredients and the influence of colonial and commercial domination by Asians and Europeans. Nature blessed the region with cloves, galangal, and 600 bird species, as well as bananas, rambutan and jackfruit for juices, and coconuts, an all-purpose ingredient. Nutmeg, native to the Banda Islands, developed into one of the world's costliest comestibles. Gourmet peppers—Sumatran *lampong* and *sarawak* from Borneo—heighten the taste sensations of hot, spicy stews.

In New Guinea, Malaysians domesticated sugarcane around 8000 B.C.E. and passed the plant to traders from northern India. After 3000 B.C.E., island hunter-gatherers added wild rice to edibles. Sustenance depended on the addition of chayote, greens, beans, sago palms, breadfruit, and taro. Growers domesticated rice in 2300 B.C.E. The sowing of wheat from China and India produced noodles, steamed buns, and loaves. Along with mustard, ginger, cabbage, and jasmine tea, Indonesian cooks adopted Chinese stir-frying. After 1050 B.C.E., Chinese rice varieties thrived in Malaya as a grain and a stem steamed like bamboo shoots.

Waves of insurgents influenced heritage recipes. Curry, black pepper, lemongrass, shallots, cinnamon, candlenut, cumin, cardamom, fennel, coriander, onions, cucumbers, mangos, eggplant, and tamarind came from

India in 300 C.E. in exchange for extra-hot long pepper (*Piper longum*), an Indonesian staple that merchants in India passed to buyers in Poland, Russia, and the Ottoman Empire. Simultaneous with Chinese contributions of marbled eggs, garlic, ginger, and scallions and Hindu vegetarianism in the 600s, Arabs introduced yogurt and kebabs during the spread of Islam. After 900, Laos contributed sticky rice, an essential for puddings and desserts.

At the end of the Middle Ages, Muslims imported lamb cookery. The arrival of Portuguese navigators in 1512 revealed to Europe the treasure of the Maluku islands in cubeb, cloves, and nutmeg. By the 1600s, Dutch traders adopted Indonesian grated nutmeg rind for spicing beans, brussel sprouts, cauliflower, cider, turnips, eggnog, pudding, sausage, and wine. From the Dutch, Indonesians experienced their first barbecue, bread and pastries, cheese, and pancakes. Spanish adventurers traded for Indonesian spices with African yams and New World potatoes, cassava, corn, chili peppers, and sweet potatoes. Imported peanuts provided cooking oil and formed the basis of meat sauces and marinades. In European style, Indonesians drank coffee and tea with sugar.

Regional dishes exhibit the creativity of island cooks in combining fresh ingredients, particularly bok choy, yard-long beans, and bean sprouts with rice and goat meat. The Javanese specialize in beef and noodle soup, rice balls, corn, and shrimp paste. Balinese restaurants feature spiced duck and minced meat on a stick. Sumatrans celebrate events with roast dog, buffalo, or pork boiled in blood and vinegar and served with mung beans, durian sauce, or sago dumplings. A meatier cuisine in Sulawesi, Papua, and the Maluku islands bases meals on poultry, roast boar, and seafood as well as red snapper and tuna. Families center wedding dinners on pork in the style of the Hawaiian luau.

In the twenty-first century, Indonesian restaurants and pushcarts advertise national dishes—fried rice with chili and soy sauce, cucumber and bitter melon salad with peanut sauce, *satay* (skewered goat, beef, or tofu), and mutton or offal *soto* (soup), a national dish. Rice, the basis for innovative gastronomy, absorbs coconut milk and lemon juice and undergirds wine and desserts. Curry spices and indigenous *sambals* (chili-based sauces) enliven vegetable stir-fries. Chinese enclaves and the non-Muslims of Bali, Maluku, and Papua feast on lard-fried carp and grilled pork, which Islamic law forbids.

See also: Lapérouse, Jean François Galaup; National Dishes; Portuguese Diet and Cuisine; Rice; Spices; Vanilla.

Further Reading

Cornell, Kari A., and Merry Anwar. *Cooking the Indonesian Way.* Minneapolis, MN: Lerner, 2004.

Forshee, Jill. *Culture and Customs of Indonesia.* Westport, CT: Greenwood, 2006.

Taylor, Jean Gelman. *Indonesia: Peoples and Histories.* New Haven, CT: Yale University Press, 2004.

Industrial Food Processing

The alteration of raw ingredients into marketable food for cooking or serving out of the package involves industrial food processors in intimate nutritional influence on human health. From Neolithic times, hunter-gatherers devoted most of their waking hours to food security. To extend the shelf life of potential famine supplies, they slaughtered fish and mammals, dried herbs and berries, smoked meats, and salted goods, limiting their cuisine to the foodstuffs at hand. To vary their diet, clans had to migrate closer to lakes and seashores and to abundant hunting and foraging grounds.

The evolution of agriculture in Neolithic Syria in 12,000 B.C.E. introduced grain to the diet along with the toil of threshing, milling, stirring porridge, and baking, the rudiments of processing food for storage and distribution. Ready-to-eat meals—Cornish pasty, flatbread, haggis, jerky, pemmican, roasted corn—fed journeymen and soldiers who had no opportunity to build a cookfire. The growth of cities added to the tables of the elite labor-intensive baklava in Istanbul, beer at Ur, sun-dried vegetables in Cairo, *garum* in Rome, *kimchi* at the Korean royal court in Seoul, couscous in Jerusalem, tea in Edo, soba noodles in Tokyo, and coffee in Aden, Yemen.

With urbanization came greater body height and longer life spans, two benefits of enriched processed foods. Offsetting the benefits, slavery and servitude diverted kitchen tasks to the lowest social echelon, the one least likely to enjoy such complex dishes as macaroni, sorbet, and hot chocolate.

Factory Food

The Industrial Revolution and steam engines augmented the choices of pantry items and travel fare that relieved the cook of peeling, chopping, and stirring and the artisan of hand-kneading dough for pasta, grinding corn on a mano and metate (grinding stone), milling wheat on a saddle quern, and pressing olives for oil and grapes for wine. After Nicolas Appert introduced vacuum canning in 1809, cooks superintending mobile kitchens and ships' galleys broke the tedium of meals prepared only from salt pork, dried beans and fruit, biscuit, tea, and flour. Tinned tomatoes and tuna received processing in rural agrarian enclaves and along global shores, increasing jobs for women and the unskilled. By 1818, the British navy became a regular customer of tinned food. In 1824, Ezra Draggett and Thomas Kensett increased canning possibilities in glass, which reduced the potential of lead poisoning from metal cans.

Discoveries and improvements marked the remainder of the 1800s. Gail Borden's production of canned milk in 1856 and the invention of pasteurization in France in 1862 enlarged the pantry even more with stable, safe milk and other dairy products. Tear strips and key winds simplified the opening of canned goods. Grape juice, beer, and liquor processing and ice plants tended to function best near sources of water. Oat milling, which earned higher profits when situated close to grain fields, required warehousing and distribution by wagon and canal boat.

The twentieth century brought food commodification to new heights with tanker-delivered baby food, canned soup, freeze-dried coffee, fruit concentrates, milk, sliced Hawaiian pineapple, and preservatives that kept bread fresh for days. Factory handling of bread and meat made the greatest shift from neighborhood bakeries and butcher shops to anonymous food handlers. Dried foods—bread mix, cereal, milk, rice, instant tea—allowed rescuers to ferry sustenance to areas plagued by epidemic, famine, flood, and siege.

Canned and frozen foods such as green beans and sliced mushrooms came to the table in uniform bites and consistent quality. To boost merchandise appeal, factories developed artificial aromas, colorants, flavorings, sweeteners, and synthetic vitamins that enhanced boxed pudding, citrus fruit, and such bottled toppings as maraschino cherries and walnuts. Additives generated concerns for allergies, which caused serious reactions from monosodium glutamate, nut residue, and red dyes.

Convenience food boosted cuisine to a new era of rapid satisfaction of hunger and a decentralization of meals in family life. In 1951, as the television set began to consume home "together" time, Swanson sold 10 million frozen chicken pot pies in its first year of distribution. The next year brought frozen fish sticks and Birds Eye frozen peas, both marketed to harried moms. The philosophy of "quick and easy" accepted into the modern idiom french fries, Nescafé, Cheez Whiz, Tang, Green Giant, Sweet'N Low, and Butterball Turkey.

Pop-top cans, TV dinners, Reddi-Wip aerosol whipped cream, microwave egg rolls and popcorn, surimi (simulated crab sticks), boiling pouches, pressure extrusion of cereals, and boxed diet meals further aided the working homemaker by shortening preparation time and simplifying cleanup. Internet sales made available exotic herbs and spices as well as vacuum-packed mutton and salmon.

Cost cutting with the use of hydrogenated vegetable oils and high fructose corn syrup caused concern for rising incidence of coronary and vascular disease, diabetes, and obesity. Less publicized alterations, such as the use of pectin to homogenize fruit juice, begged the question of processing for the sake of commerce rather than food for health.

Food Standards

The cleanliness of agroprocessing factories historically generated scandal and class-action suits against careless and dishonest processors, notably, the Chicago meatpackers targeted by Upton Sinclair's exposé *The Jungle* (1906). As the proliferation of highway systems and supermarkets simplified suburban shopping, U.S. scrutiny increased on food handling and distribution with the addition of regulations and frequent inspections, especially of imported prepackaged fish, meats, and tea from Argentina, China, Japan, and New Zealand. In 1949, the U.S. Food and Drug Administration (FDA) initiated government oversight of processed food with a guidebook, "Procedures for the Appraisal of the Toxicity of Chemicals in Food," compiled by Arnold J. Lehman, the "Father of American Toxicology."

In 1963, irradiation first sterilized dried produce to kill vermin and halt sprouting. The following year, the FDA banned sodium cyclamate, a diet sweetener and known carcinogen, originally used in candy and juices formulated for diabetics. In 1976, the banning of Red No. 2 coloring reminded consumers of the many ways that additives impact diet, especially among children. For the remainder of the century, commercial food producers advertised concern for nutrients and fiber in products, the dangers of salt and sugar in baby food, and control of caffeine, cholesterol, fat, and sodium. In 1980, *Food Processing* magazine foresaw a shift in industrial focus on profits to nutrition and accurate labeling. A countermove to limit solid waste in 1991 resulted in tough laws in Germany against overpackaged processed foods.

The twenty-first century turned the tide on ready acceptance of industrialized foods. Although bottled water outsold carbonated drinks, shoppers increased purchases of organic food by 95 percent and launched a campaign against genetically modified corn in Kraft snack chips, taco shells, and tortillas. In 2000, U.S. meat inspectors applied the Hazard Analysis and Critical Control Point (HACCP) law to meat testing by abandoning sight and smell as criteria in favor of scientific measures of pathogens. The media abetted grassroots efforts to upgrade the global diet by publicizing the investigation and punishment of malfeasance in the food industry.

In September 2008, the sickening of 300,000 Chinese babies on impure milk powder resulted in six deaths and 300 extended hospitalizations. The cause, melamine in the milk powder, caused serious harm to kidneys. For the role of the Sanlu Group in the scandal, two people received death sentences and one life imprisonment, the most serious punishments of negligent food industrialists in modern history.

See also: Biscuit; Canning; Crackers; Curry; Freeze-Drying; Guar; Ice Cream; Ketchup; Liebig, Justus von; Pickling; Pork; Seaweed; Soft Drinks and Juices; Sugar and Sweeteners; Vanilla; Vinegar; Yeast.

Further Reading

Blay-Palmer, Alison. *Food Fears: From Industrial to Sustainable Food Systems.* Burlington, VT: Ashgate, 2008.

Graedel, T.E., and Jennifer A. Howard-Grenville. *Greening the Industrial Facility: Perspectives, Approaches, and Tools.* New York: Springer, 2005.

Lelieveld, H.L.M., et al., eds. *Hygiene in Food Processing.* Boca Raton, FL: CRC, 2003.

Richardson, Philip S., ed. *Thermal Technologies in Food Processing.* Boca Raton, FL: CRC, 2001.

Insects

Cultures differ in their acceptance of entomophagy or insectivory, the consumption of insects for food, which flourishes in 80 percent of the global population. The eating of some 1,000 varieties of "mini-livestock"—insect eggs, larvae, cicadas, and moths—dates to Paleolithic diets, when hunter-gatherers depended on available staples. History attests to the consumption of termites and weevils in Angola, caterpillars in the Congo, and wild bee pupae in Altamira, Spain, after 30,000 B.C.E.

According to historian Bernardino de Sahagún's *Historia General de las Cosas de Nueva España* (*General History of the Things of New Spain,* 1558), a multivolume overview of Aztec life, Montezuma II valued insect eggs, which he imported for feasts at Tenochtitlán. The Aztec prized the *meocuili* (maguey worm), which fed off the agave plant. Cooks fried the larvae to a crisp on comal bakestones or packed them into leaf pouches to roast over embers and serve as condiments.

In 1885, Vincent M. Holt issued *Why Not Eat Insects?,* a monograph proposing the eating of slugs and wireworms as a solution to potential starvation in the British working class. He stressed that insects are clean and palatable because they are particular about their diet. His open-mindedness toward available famine food validated Navajo regard for crickets and grasshoppers and Thai and Chinese consumption of fried scorpions as street food in Bangkok and Beijing. Readers vilified Holt's menus because the choice of insects as a respite from a meat crisis disturbed Westerners and violated Jewish kosher laws, which characterized insects as *treif* (inedible).

In the twenty-first century, changing attitudes toward arthropods value them as sources of fats, minerals, and protein, a given in Botswana, Cambodia, Colombia, Ghana, Japan, Malawi, Mexico, Mozambique, Papua New Guinea, South Africa, and Zimbabwe. Raised in small confines, agave worms, cockroaches, crickets, silkworms, and termites are naturally renewable, a fact that ensures food security in the Congo and the village of Tulancalco, an insectivore community in Hidalgo, Mexico. Insects reproduce rapidly and make efficient use of food. They exude less methane and nitrous oxide than cattle and require no antibiotics and less growing space to yield nutritious meals. In China and India, farmers raise fish, pigs, and poultry on cost-effective insect diets comprised of houseflies, mealworms, and silkworms.

The experience of insectivores tends to be positive, especially when they prepare insects with additives and cook them alive, such as baby bee appetizers in Japan. In Quito, Ecuador, diners cook white beetles with pork and vegetables, but eat lemon ants live for their vivid flavor. Mexicans add insects to salsa and marinades and choose aromatic larvae for tucking into tacos. In Mexico City, vendors continue to sell the Aztec insect taco, toasted waterbugs, fried worms, green sauce with ant eggs, mosquito egg patties, and guacamole topped with dry-roasted grasshoppers. Other delicacies range from chinch bugs, red ant and waterbug eggs, and toasted locusts to wasps and larvae served over cactus or turkey cake.

Insects contribute to global biodiversity. In Australia, the witchetty grub and ants are filling, thirst-quenching field food. Sardinians consider the larvae that permeate *casu marzu* (sheep cheese) a delicacy. In the tropics, the economic appeal increases because insects grow larger in humid climates. The Tukanoan Indians of the northwest Amazon receive 26 percent of their protein from a cuisine featuring 20 types of insects. For malnourished children in Laos, crickets, locusts, and wasps increase calcium intake in a population suffering from a high incidence of lactose-intolerance. In southern Africa, growers turn the mopane worm into a cash crop. The markets of Oceania feature insects as pantry staples.

See also: Australian Diet and Cuisine; Coprolites; Curing; Kosher Food; Lapérouse, Jean François Galaup; South American Diet and Cuisine.

Further Reading

Carrington, Damian. "Insects Could Be the Key to Meeting Food Needs of Growing Global Population." *The Guardian* (London), August 1, 2010.

Gullan, P.J., and P.S. Cranston. *The Insects: An Outline of Entomology.* Hoboken, NJ: Wiley-Blackwell, 2010.

Morris, Brian. *Insects and Human Life.* New York: Berg, 2004.

Inspection and Safety, Food

As interest in world cuisine increases demand for new tastes, scrutiny of global commodities requires the inspection and testing of domestic and imported foods. Situations range from refrigeration failures at convention facilities and orange juice transport by unsanitary tanker trucks to Chinese flour adulterated with benzoyl peroxide and pork contaminated by swine flu at filthy feeding stations. Voluntary compliance with the European Food Safety Authority and World Health Organization standards attests to the business ethics of companies that process and distribute food, especially during droughts, typhoons, and other climate-related crises. However, noncompliance raises doubts about chemical pollutants in food from Belgium, Bulgaria, and Great Britain; bacterial contamination in goods from Portugal and Russia; and toxic raw ingredients from Finland, New Zealand, and Turkey.

In the United States, mandatory assessments by 15 federal agencies enforce codes stipulating date and coverage of inspection—for example, examination of leafy vegetables by the Animal and Plant Health Inspection Service and lab tests for waterborne microbes overseen by the Environmental Protection Agency. Subsequent to an outbreak of *Escherichia coli* (*E. coli*) in 1993, the labeling of stockyard feed by the National Marine Fisheries Service and slaughtering at meat-processing plants follow the regimen of the Pathogen Reduction and Hazard Analysis and Critical Control Point system. At U.S. military installations, soldiers trained for the U.S. Army Veterinary Corps sample goods procured as field rations, particularly high-risk staples such as raw ground turkey. Overseers of the complex monitoring network ensure that food processors cannot conceal questionable goods in sketchy paper trails or depend on end-stage irradiation to negate a host of possible infractions in sanitation.

The U.S. Department of Agriculture tests soil for heavy metals and follows edibles from planting to harvest. Field sanitarians document the sources of potentially hazardous foods arriving at national borders, enforcing the Federal Meat Inspection Act at abattoirs and maintaining on-site survey of eggs, meat, poultry, and seafood. Examples include discoveries in late April 2011 of clenbuterol, a performance-enhancing drug, in pork from Hunan, China, and ink and wax in noodle dough made in Changsha, China. In Chongqing, China, on September 15, 2011, inspectors found melamine in the milk powder used in chocolate candy, ice cream, and pastry. The criminal adulteration boosted the protein content of watered milk, thus allowing the manufacturer to save money on dairy ingredients.

Within states, county and city inspectors as well as private-sector auditors at food-processing plants such as Kellogg's and Sara Lee scrutinize environments, ingredients, and work habits. Surprise annual evaluation of cleanliness and food storage in bars and restaurants applies regional codes to dishwashing and ice makers. Agents record observations of bare hands in raw chocolate chip cookie dough, misbranded or unlabeled spaghetti sauce storage containers, and cross-contamination of sinks from mixed use with shrimp and beef liver. Surveillance of the internal workings of machinery affects the operation of bone cutters, bottle washers, homogenizers, meat mincers, and taco-making machines. Inspectors insist on apple and pepper washing with noncarcinogenic citric distillates, undeviating storage temperatures in iced tea dispensers, sterilization of salad prep tables and soup ladles, discarding of outdated pie filling and potato salad, and ridding worker environments of ceiling mold and flying insects.

Tourism depends on the safety of food and drink. During unusually heavy human traffic at British forts, Mexican street fairs, and agricultural shows in Australia, food handlers require a license guaranteeing worker health.

Agents take samples of bread dough, peanut butter, pistachios, and raw hamburger for laboratory evaluation of fecal contamination and parasites. The most common risk factor involves inadequate cooling and storage of cold foods, which accounts for 92 percent of infractions.

At the 2008 Olympic Games in China, inspection vans moved quickly to troubled spots and congested food venues to analyze air and water and to monitor contagion among chefs and servers. To inform the public, Chinese authorities issued a media blitz at bus and train stations and on television informing consumers of the dangers of chemical additives that boost company profits, such as sodium nitrite to speed the ripening of vegetables.

Also in 2008, the U.S. Government Accountability Office demanded greater protection from *E. coli,* salmonella, and food-borne illness by the Food and Drug Administration (FDA). The primary threat arose from the influx of polluted fruits and vegetables from Central

A lab technician at the seafood inspection station in Mississippi examines a specimen from the Gulf of Mexico after the Deepwater Horizon oil spill in 2010. The FDA has primary responsibility for U.S. food safety; NOAA oversees fisheries management. *(Patrick Semansky/Associated Press)*

America, which consumers can eat unwashed and un-cooked. The highway joining Nogales, Mexico, with Arizona carries hundreds of trucks daily bearing tomatoes to northern consumers, who have steadily increased consumption of fresh comestibles. Imports stagger the underfunded FDA, which lacks the inspectors and scientists to ensure the American diet of wholesome food by swabbing meats and baked goods for adulterants and by surveying kitchen ventilators and the cleanliness of salad bars, walk-in coolers, and grocery produce sprayers.

A similar concern for deaths from listeria in 2008 prompted the Canadian Food Inspection Agency to spend an extra $100 million for agent training and lab technology. Among the faults located in 2011, traces of diarrhetic shellfish poisoning marred the edibility of mussels. In China, the Administration of Quality Supervision, Inspection, and Quarantine issued recalls of foreign goods from Denmark, Japan, New Zealand, and the United States. Rejected supplies failed to comply with local standards of bacteria levels and tainted ingredients, including the thawing and freezing of susceptible pizzas and TV dinners.

See also: Commodity Regulation; Disease, Food-Borne; Fast Food; Halal; Kosher Food; Packaging; Sanitation.

Further Reading

Bakker, Henk. *Food Security in Africa and Asia: Strategies for Small-Scale Agricultural Development.* Cambridge, MA: CABI, 2011.

Brown, Amy C. *Understanding Food: Principles and Preparation.* Belmont, CA: Wadsworth, 2011.

Ford, Andrea. "The Holes in America's Food-Safety Net." *Time* (September 30, 2008).

Hefnawy, Magdy. *Advances in Food Protection: Focus on Food Safety and Defense.* New York: Springer, 2011.

Nielsen, S. Suzanne. *Food Analysis.* New York: Springer, 2010.

International Food Aid

Global food gifts to the impoverished and to victims of famine and natural disasters derive input from an array of humanitarian and religious organizations and altruistic individuals and corporations. Food sharing has produced one of the landmarks of civilization. The issue of food justice compels industrialized nations to examine the plight of developing countries and to defend human worth and dignity. The growth of the present altruistic community dates to the founding of the Red Cross in Switzerland in 1863; the Salvation Army in 1865; Caritas International, a Roman Catholic relief agency, in 1897; and the Red Crescent in 1919, following massive displaced persons and refugee movements after World War I.

In guaranteeing food as a fundamental human right, multilateral response after World War II directed one-third of urgent assistance to Asia and sub-Saharan Africa.

The bulk of staples included barley, corn, millet, rice, and sorghum in 85 percent of shipments. The remainder consisted of 8 percent beans and peas, 4 percent vegetable oil, and 3 percent biscuits, canned fish and meat, dried dates, ghee, milk products, salt, sugar, and vitamin and mineral premix. Warehousing in anticipation of need required a preponderance of freeze-dried and dry food in vacuum-packed bars, which lowered shipping weight and simplified distribution of uncooked supplies. Although some foods were unfamiliar to people preferring a cuisine of roots and tubers, short-term supply ensured rehydration and stabilization of nutrients and body weight.

Subsequent emergencies involved CARE in relieving famine in Lima, Peru, in 1970 after an earthquake and the Salvadoran Ecumenical Association in aid to El Salvador during the mass killings and displacement in 1981. In more recent history, the European Union and International Monetary Fund stemmed hunger in Soviet Russia in 1991 and Iraq in 2003, when economic sanctions halted trade. Muslim Hands, an Islamic antipoverty charity, joined world givers in 1993 to stem human misery in the Balkans by shipping food and medicine to war-torn Bosnia. In 2007, the International Fellowship of Christians and Jews sent packets of fish and meat, fruit and juice, grains and vegetables, and sugar to Moscow's poor. More philanthropy involved Egyptian wheat shipments to the Gaza Strip in 2008 and the International Red Cross's aid to flood-deluged North Koreans in mid-August 2011.

The global rescue efforts achieved unity and synchrony in 1960, when U.S. politician George McGovern proposed a consortium of civilian-led food aid programs organized by the United Nations (UN). On a three-year trial basis, the World Food Programme (WFP) coordinated 36 nations in saving refugees and catastrophe survivors from hunger. The governing board resolved to raise nutritional levels among the most vulnerable, including children and the feeble and disabled. The ultimate WFP goal lay in building ongoing food banks and assisting the poor in controlling their own food security. Facilitators, headquartered in Dubai, established a record of emergency response within 48 hours, a feat that directed media attention to the war on acute and chronic hunger. From 1985 to 2000, global cereal donations rose 25 percent, from 12 million tons (10.9 million metric tons) to 15 million tons (13.6 million metric tons).

Because civil strife, economic stagnation, and looting in sub-Saharan Africa endangered feeding efforts, the region dominated international humanitarian aid from the mid-1970s. In the mid-2000s, the WFP engaged guards in armored vehicles to ensure delivery to the hungry in Chad, Ethiopia, Guinea, Ivory Coast, Kenya, Lebanon, Liberia, Myanmar, Sierra Leone, Somalia, Sudan, and Uganda. In 2004, the WFP, joined by logistical teams from Indonesia and the Chinese Red Cross, delivered food to 1.3 million left helpless after a tsunami struck Aceh, Sumatra.

A UN airlift delivers much-needed food relief during the Angolan civil war in the mid-1990s. Hundreds of thousands of internally displaced Angolans depended on UN food aid for survival. Civil conflict often makes distribution difficult. *(Scott Peterson/Getty Images)*

Although surrounded by peacekeepers, the WFP staff lost 14 employees to snipers over three years in East Africa. To boost local economies, the outreach bought corn and sorghum from regional sources, thus reducing both effort and risk by shortening the distance from warehouses to feeding camps and aid stations. Distributors prevented theft by administering "wet feedings," the dispersal of cooked porridge rather than raw grain. Agents furthered aid to the vulnerable by funding rural work-for-food programs, school lunches, and take-home packets, an incentive for parents to seek education for their children, particularly girls.

In August 2011, with food crises extending from northeast Africa to Swaziland, the World Bank committed to a $500 million donation. The WFP dispatched 900 tons (816 metric tons) of energy biscuits to Ethiopians and Somali fleeing an East African famine on the Kenyan border, where 2.4 million received meals. Amid fragile refugees beset by drought, hunger, and guerrilla sabotage, airlifts to Mogadishu pushed through al-Qaeda and al-Shabaab forces to reach victims, 80 percent of whom were female. Aid workers joined agents from UNICEF (the United Nations Children's Fund) and the UN Food and Agriculture Organization to halt a daily death rate on the Horn of Africa of 13 out of 10,000 children under age five.

A tumble in world economies and food hoarding in Russia and Vietnam diminished the stock of dried milk, corn, wheat, and rice that donations could buy. Oxfam, a British humanitarian organization, predicted that food insecurity would hamper the rescue of East Africans into 2050.

See also: Airlifts, Food; Famine; Famine Relief; Malnutrition.

Further Reading

Barrett, Christopher Brendan, and Daniel G. Maxwell. *Food Aid After Fifty Years: Recasting Its Role.* New York: Routledge, 2005.

Clay, Edward J., and Olav Stokke, eds. *Food Aid and Human Security.* Portland, OR: Frank Cass, 2000.

Shaw, D. John. *The UN World Food Programme and the Development of Food Aid.* Basingstoke, UK: Palgrave, 2001.

Southgate, Douglas Dewitt, Douglas H. Graham, and Luther G. Tweeten. *The World Food Economy.* Malden, MA: Blackwell, 2007.

World Food Programme. *Hunger and Markets.* Sterling, VA: Earthscan, 2009.

Irrigation

The artificial watering of soil and vegetation increases the success of dryland farming in areas incurring inadequate rainfall and humidity. A regular distribution of water prevents soil compaction, suppresses dust, and rinses fields free of debris and accumulated salts. Efficient water diversion from bores and rivers in Australia, for example, feeds the nation and provides cereal grain, fruit juice, meat, milk, nuts, sugar, and wine for profitable exports. By contrast, according to hydrologists, too little irrigation and overcultivation of fragile drylands result in desertification, the cause of declining grain fields and famine north of Africa's Sahel and in pastoral Chile and India.

Historically, balanced water systems have advanced civilization. From 3100 to 539 B.C.E., Mesopotamians developed sophisticated catchments and surface watercourses through fertile wheat fields and date palm orchards. Simultaneously, Peruvian Indians of the Andes Mountains terraced land to dam snowmelt and directed it through canals to pepper and potato fields. Similar methods distributed rainfall to agriculture and pasturage in China, Harappan India, and Syria. Southeast Asians watered rice paddies with a "walking pump" (treadle system), a labor-intensive method. Argentines preferred a furrow system, which regulated flow through shallow channels.

Concentrated irrigation efforts have also raised nutritional standards. After 1800 B.C.E., Egyptian growers relied on the oasis at Faiyum to preserve Nile floodwaters for borderstrip watering, a system similar to beans, corn, and squash farming by the Anasazi, the ancient Pueblo Indians of North America's Great Basin. By 600 B.C.E., Armenia and Egypt supported viticulture (the cultivation of grapes) with irrigation canals. Engineering advances around 500 B.C.E. brought the *shaduf* (dip bucket) in use in Egypt, the *noria* (water wheel) in North Africa, and hydraulic engineering in China. In Sri Lanka in 300 B.C.E., the Sinhalese initiated water storage in a hammered granite tank and invented the valve pit, a sluice network regulated by a dam and 25-mile (40-kilometer) canal.

In the next century, Roman *latifundia* (plantations) distributed to vineyards and orchards rainwater stored in cisterns or supplies pumped from aqueducts, springs, and wells. Roman methods of hydrology increased food production throughout the empire, particularly in Iberia and Tunisia. Advanced hydrology relieved the Romans of complete dependence on Egyptian grain, a source of chronic international military and diplomatic crises.

Engineers focused technology on the best use of labor and water. In 100 C.E., ox-powered chain pumps in China rotated circular discs in tubes to maneuver water to higher levels for watering palace gardens and vegetable plots. In medieval Iberia, the *huertas* (irrigated districts) of Murcia and Valencia codified laws to stabilize water use and prevent conflict. As the consumption of meat replaced the former cereal-dominant diet, Korean scientist Jang Yeong-sil's invention of the rain gauge and water gauge in 1441 enabled farmers to compute the best allotment of stored water by erecting a calibrated stone column in the reservoir.

The exacting dispersal of supplies enabled orchardists to grow citrus fruit in Israel and vintners to establish grapes in California's Napa and San Joaquin valleys and Australia's Murray-Darling basin. By 2000, irrigation reached a height in northern India and Pakistan and furthered crop growing and animal husbandry with networks covering 68 percent of Asian farmland, 17 percent in North America, and 9 percent in Europe.

In an era when food growers compete with cities and industry for water, the efficiency of motor-driven pumps in China, India, Libya, Oman, and the central and southwestern United States threatens watersheds by removing enough water to destroy aquifers. Aquifer subsidence compresses clay and silt, causing permanent loss of groundwater recharge, a situation in the Ogallala Aquifer that plagues northern Texas. Over a decade in Tamil Nadu, India, extraction of groundwater from collector wells dropped the water table by 98 feet (30 meters). In China and Pakistan, inadequate drainage and waterlogging upped salinity 20 percent on irrigated acreage.

Growers and livestock managers support fields and pasture with more efficient drip lines, trickle streams, pivoting or rotary sprayers, and computerized pressure or rolling sprinklers, which avoid waste from evaporation and misdirected flow. The combination of in-ground microirrigation with plastic mulch, desalinated water and wastewater distribution, and liquid fertilizers formulates equitable use of strapped water systems. In Burkina Faso, Kenya, and Sudan, the harvesting of runoff for irrigating corn, peanuts, sorghum, and yams in a subsequent season triples yields. The direction of water from three lakes and 13 rivers in Malawi intensifies cropping, resulting in a tomato yield to support a local cannery. More complex subirrigation lifts seepage to the top of the water table or to the surface of high-tech greenhouses, such as Tokyo's seasonless growing complex.

See also: African Food Trade; Agriculture; Aquaponics; Plant Disease and Prevention; Water.

Further Reading

Cech, Thomas V. *Principles of Water Resources: History, Development, Management, and Policy.* Hoboken, NJ: John Wiley & Sons, 2010.

De Villiers, Marq. *Water: The Fate of Our Most Precious Resource.* Boston: Houghton Mifflin, 2001.

Shiva, Vandana. *Water Wars: Privatization, Pollution and Profit.* Cambridge, MA: South End, 2002.

Solomon, Steven. *Water: The Epic Struggle for Wealth, Power, and Civilization.* New York: Harper Perennial, 2011.

Israeli Diet and Cuisine

A Jewish fusion cuisine, Israel's diet coordinates Middle Eastern staples with Ashkenazic, Mizrahi, and Sephardic kosher traditions. Heritage foods from the early Israelite culture in 1200 B.C.E. centered on barley bread and dairy items from goats and sheep to accompany dates and figs, beet greens, whole fish and spit-roasted game, olives and olive oil, and honeyed or acetic wine. From Constantinople's Topkapi Palace and the table of Suleiman the Magnificent from 1520 to 1566, Ottoman influence introduced baklava, butter cookies, and bulgur pilaf, a Jerusalem specialty made with long-grain rice. Ordinary Turks fed on more mundane dishes—crusted gratins and stuffed vegetables and pastries.

More than any other socioeconomic element, Israeli cuisine made the most change over time yet maintained kosher taboos. By the 1870s, Jerusalem supported a lively public food market. Modernization altered domestic tradition in 1875 with Berman's Bakery, Palestine's first, which a Lithuanian couple from Reisen, Kreshe Berman and Todrus HaLevi Berman, opened in Jerusalem's Old City. While Todrus studied scripture, Kreshe enhanced her kitchen business by selling Christmas honey cakes and black bread to Christian pilgrims.

In 1881, influxes of Polish and Russian Jews brought recipes for artichokes, chickpeas, eggplant, pepper, and zucchini. The Bermans and their sons, Eliyahu and Yehoshua, contributed to home baking needs in 1886 by opening a flour mill. In 1934, the nation received its first homemade ale from the Palestine Brewery, which was built with French backing.

Rituals specified either fasting for Yom Kippur or individual foods for holidays—apples, radishes, fava beans and spinach, almonds, cherry compote, and cheese blintzes or cheesecake for Shavuot and herbs and meat dumplings with challah and knot pastries on Rosh Hashanah. On Tisha B'av, eggs and lentils represented mourning. Couscous preceding honey and fruit turnovers with wine symbolized Purim. At the height of the year, bitter herbs and horseradish, sponge cake, macaroons, and unleavened bread captured the themes of Passover seders. Hanukkah called for sour cream on latkes (potato pancakes) and jelly doughnuts. Medieval refinements added gingerbread, lentil pancakes, ragout, salads, and tarts. To prevent work on the Sabbath, beef, fish, and poultry slow-cooked the night before with barley, beans, and potatoes.

The birth of a Jewish state on May 14, 1948, nationalized a people and their myriad cultures from the Balkans, central Europe, Iberia, India, North Africa, North America, and Russia. As 1 million transients and Holocaust survivors crowded into Israel over the next decade, rationing required clever masking and simulation, notably, *ptitim* (toasted pasta) in place of rice, at the request of Prime Minister David Ben-Gurion, and turkey kebabs and schnitzel to replace lamb and veal. For Israel Independence Day, mallow leaves commemorate the siege of Jerusalem, when citizens picked *hubeza* (mallow) in the fields as makeshift greens. By 1958, the nation began patronizing its first supermarket.

Over the decades, foreign influences have permeated Israeli traditions. Immigrant adaptations have featured identifiable contributions to the national cuisine:

Falafel—mashed chickpea balls deep-fried and served in a pita pocket with chopped salad or pickled vegetables and tahini (sesame) sauce—is iconic Israeli street fare and popular throughout the Middle East. *(Larry Crowe/Associated Press)*

Heritage	Dishes
Algerian	argan nuts and oil; plums
Arabic	fried falafel balls with sour pickles; halvah; meatballs
Austrian	Wiener schnitzel with parsley potatoes; sugar cake; strudel
Bulgarian	brined *quark* (white cheese); cucumber soup
Central Asian	chopped seedless cucumber and plum tomatoes in vinegar; halvah pastries
Czech	barley beer; coffee cake
Dutch	pickled herring with onion; corn; butter cookies
Ethiopian	pancake bread
Georgian	nut candy; phyllo pastry; vegetable stew
German	sauerbraten; kugel; cabbage soup
Greek	*galakto* pastry; mackerel cooked in tomato and onion sauce
Hungarian	paprika dishes; sweetened curd cheese
Indian	mango pickles; dal and rice; fried bananas
Iranian	chickpea dumplings; omelets; chicken with pomegranate
Iraqi	laffa bread; crisp rice; cardamom cookies; turnips with date honey
Kurdish	semolina dumplings in soup; date cookies
Lebanese	*baba ghanoush* (mashed eggplant with tahini); dry-rubbed grilled lamb
Moroccan	couscous; dolma; fried cauliflower; tagines; tomatoes and pepper in garlic and chili pepper
Polish	noodles; *matzoh ball soup*; bagels
Portuguese	tzimmes (cooked vegetables and raisins); raisin syrup
Romanian	*ikra* (carp roe) with oil; calf's foot jelly with boiled eggs and mustard cream
Russian	borscht; gefilte fish; dark bread; vodka
Salonikan	*borek* (fried pastries); white bean soup; whole carp
Slovak	*bryndza* cheese; pierogi
Spanish	flounder fried in olive oil; semolina cake; puff pastry
Syrian	red lentils with bulgur
Transylvanian	green bean soup; cheese dumplings
Tunisian	liver and spinach sausage; offal in tomato paste; tuna and potato sandwich
Turkish	red pepper relish; hummus with pita; *leben* (sour cream); wheat berry pudding
Ukrainian	bagels; *babkas* (yeast cakes) with sweet filling
Yemenite	marrow soup; grilled meat with pita bread; falafel

Recipe: Israeli Salad

Dice six Roma tomatoes, six pickling cucumbers, one yellow bell pepper, and one red onion. Coat this mixture with a whisked dressing made of 6 tablespoons of olive oil, 4 tablespoons of lemon juice, 2 tablespoons of chopped parsley, 1 tablespoon each of chopped dill and mint, and pepper and sea salt to taste.

Israeli farmers, meanwhile, developed coastal agrarianism to grow and export apricots, avocados, Jaffa oranges, loquats, and prickly pear. Kibbutzim supplied the key herbs—cumin and *zaatar,* an herbal mix with sesame and salt—and the basics of a vegetarian diet, such as soy schnitzel with mushroom gravy and orange and almond pilaf. From citrus groves near the Mediterranean shore to pomegranates and figs of the uplands and cherries and grapes of the Golan Heights, the subtropics of the Sea of Galilee rounded out the fruit fare with bananas, kiwis, and mangoes.

Bolstered on cottage or labneh cheese and eggs for breakfast and a heavy lunch, diners choose *mezes* with tahini (sesame paste) dip or the "kibbutz dinner," a light spread of cheese and yogurt, vegetables with sour cream, eggs and olives, smoked herring and bread, and orange juice or coffee. Schoolchildren snack on chicken noodle soup and hummus on pita with fresh fruit desserts and drinks. For fast food, many snackers rely on falafel, or fried chickpea croquettes, a national craze typically eaten in a pita pocket with raw or pickled vegetables and a tahini sauce. To please American and European tourists, cosmopolitan restaurants feature a unique haute cuisine served with Israeli salads and local wines.

See also: Caravans; Crusaders' Diet and Cuisine; Kosher Food; Monoculture; Olives and Olive Oil.

Further Reading

Helstosky, Carol. *Food Culture in the Mediterranean.* Westport, CT: Greenwood, 2009.

Marks, Gil. *Encyclopedia of Jewish Food.* Hoboken, NJ: John Wiley & Sons, 2010.

Nathan, Joan. *The Foods of Israel Today.* New York: Alfred A. Knopf, 2001.

Reuveni, Gideon, and Nils H. Roemer. *Longing, Belonging, and the Making of Jewish Consumer Culture.* Boston: Brill, 2010.

Italian Diet and Cuisine

A source of dining pleasure worldwide, Italian food demonstrates the innovations possible from a variety of

An Italian chef prepares *linguine pomodori e melanzane* (narrow, flat pasta with tomato sauce and eggplant). Pasta, tomatoes, and olive oil define central and southern Italian cooking; pasta comes in literally hundreds of varieties. *(Bloomberg/Getty Images)*

fresh ingredients prepared simply. Italy's cooks have given the world Parma ham, Reggiano cheese, olive oil, balsamic vinegar, gelato, and regional olive oil. Since Roman times, surrounded by stable diets in Greece, Crete, Sicily, and the Levant, Italy has incorporated whole grains, lemons, almonds, grilled fish, and legumes into a healthful cuisine. The Roman preference for barley bread, greens, and pulses undergirded rural foodways that valued fresh vegetables and risotto balanced with capers, eggs, polenta, pasta, tuna, anchovies, peaches, pecorino cheese with basil, and *panna cotta* (milk custard).

Peasant cooks established the family table with platters of eggplant, crusty loaves, broiled calamari and fish, and pitchers of red wine preceding *macedonia di frutta* (fruit salad). Antipasti trays showcased salami, *gamberoni* (jumbo shrimp), artichokes, and carpaccio, aged beef sliced thin. Children and adults ate slowly, valuing the time for sociability and enjoyment of aromas and tex-

tures of white bean soup, grilled lamb, steamed mussels, and marinated peppers. Food processors enhanced the appeal of Italian produce by packaging unusual pasta shapes, bottling pears and peppers, and preserving lemons in salt.

In the Renaissance, regional Italian fare reached a height of table appeal. In the Piedmont, frittatas (omelets) and truffles vied with pesto sauce, fish and mussel soup, grilled radicchio, sardines, osso buco (veal bone), and *fonduta* (melted cheese) for popularity. Desserts ranged from *torrone* (nougat) in Cremona to holiday *panettone* (fruitcake) in Milan. Down the Apennines, Umbrian suckling pig, Florentine lasagna and minestrone, and Marche dried cod exhibited the variety and flexibility of central Italian menus. To the south, Campanians developed mozzarella from buffalo's milk, and Apulia offered stuffed cuttlefish, oysters Tarantino, and herbed goat and lamb.

After World War II, a host of cookbooks presented to the world the precepts of the Mediterranean diet, a collection of robust recipes for chicken cacciatore, veal scaloppine, gnocchi with pancetta (dumplings and bacon), and fig and port wine sauce over pork. Glossaries differentiated between bolognese (meat) and carbonara (egg and cheese) sauce and *grissini* (breadsticks) and focaccia (yeast bread). Coffee shops added cappuccino and espresso with amaretto to beverage lists. Alerts to exploitations of national standards exposed the American creation of pseudo-Italian pepperoni pizza, buttered *crostini*, and fettuccini Alfredo, a cream-and-cheese diet buster.

In the 2000s, to prevent high cholesterol and cardiac disease, nutritional reexamination of healthful foodways extolled Italian cuisine for stressing small portions and avoiding cola drinks and between-meal snacks. Cooking classes instructed chefs on boiling pasta *al dente* (firm), preparing herbed bread, limiting alcohol consumption, and lessening the amount of meat and seafood in main courses. Nutritionists reintroduced diners to pasta primavera (a vegetarian pasta dish),

Recipe: Amalfi Citrus-Tomato Pizza

Slice three plum tomatoes thinly and drain on paper towels. On an unbaked pizza crust, spread the slices evenly. Top with the zest from two lemons. In a food processor, crumble 4 ounces of mozzarella with one stalk of fresh thyme and two stalks of basil. Sprinkle the cheese and herbs on top of the pizza. Bake for ten minutes at 450 degrees Fahrenheit. Serve with lemon wedges.

ricotta desserts, bread salad with tomatoes and cucumbers, and noodles with beans, a satisfying Tuscan main dish more healthful than Americanized spaghetti and meatballs.

See also: Fish and Fishing; Médici, Catherine de'; Mediterranean Diet and Cuisine; Olives and Olive Oil; Pasta; Roman Diet and Cuisine, Ancient.

Further Reading

Capatti, Alberto, and Massimo Montanari. *Italian Cuisine: A Cultural History.* Trans. Aine O'Healy. New York: Columbia University Press, 2003.

Mariani, John F. *How Italian Food Conquered the World.* Foreword by Lidia Bastianich. New York: Palgrave Macmillan, 2011.

Matalas, Antonia-Leda, et al., eds. *The Mediterranean Diet: Constituents and Health Promotion.* Boca Raton, FL: CRC, 2000.

Jacobean Diet and Cuisine

During the rule of James I of England, who was simultaneously James VI of Scotland, the king pleasured himself at table while fighting threats to human well-being and longevity. When he came to power in England in 1603—the beginning of the Jacobean era, which lasted until his death in 1625—the typical upscale Briton lived to age 35. Peasants survived only 25 years on average, in part because of high infant mortality, bouts of scurvy, and epidemics of plague and typhus. Food shortages worsened chances for a long, healthy life, as did coshering, the paying of landlords in food-rents of cattle and grain.

In this era, playwright William Shakespeare dramatized the discriminate palate of Jacobean England. As images of distaste, he called to mind dry biscuit and stale cheese and criticized overdone roast and greasy entrées, the fault of lax kitchen staff. He fancied mustard, nutmeg, pepper, and saffron as well as sauces to complement and enhance flavors, such as the raisin-laced warden pie the shepherds anticipate in *The Winter's Tale* (1610–1611) to celebrate the annual sheep shearing.

As indicated by the witches' brew in *Macbeth* (ca. 1603–1606) and the title figure's hallucination before dinner guests, the English audience viewed Scotland as an exotic, menacing locale. Lady Macbeth's reference to breast feeding and slaying her infant alludes to suspicions of Scots and their barbarity. The discussion of regicide while King Duncan is at supper and Lady Macbeth's choice of an evening posset (spiced milk punch) for drugging guards implies a Scots contempt for hospitality and outright scorn for the divine right of kings.

Agricultural failures and a burgeoning population kept the isolated poor in Cumbria south of Hadrian's Wall on the edge of famine, a topic in Shakespeare's *Coriolanus* (ca. 1605–1609) and *Pericles* (ca. 1606–1608). In the latter, court gluttony among the degenerate of Tarsus contrasts with pervasive starvation among the humble, a motif that returns in *Timon of Athens* (ca. 1606–1608). The English table fare of aristocrats favored beef and game with white bread, while relegating salt cod, boiled vegetables, and coarse oat or rye bread to the lower classes. Fruit reached the tables of the wealthy in pastry, syrup, and tarts. Meanwhile, the poorest Britons simmered vegetables into a mush thickened with grain. Scarcity increased food crimes and pantry thefts as well as infanticide.

The King's Table

In a golden era of cuisine, James I deepened social disparities and economic strain through extravagance. He employed a French cook for himself and kept four Stuart households, his own and those of Queen Anne, Prince Henry, and Prince Charles. The total food expenditures rose to £80,000 annually.

Earls gladly wore the king's livery while slicing meat for his table. James's staff made a show of seating him at a carved armchair and of removing crystal decanters and silver from lavish cupboards. The display of platters on buffets and sideboards exhibited entrées as visual treats. Heavy framed mirrors lit by ensconced candles doubled the show.

During James's 23-year reign, the palace pantry stocked exotic trade goods, from Middle Eastern dates and olives to almonds, ginger, pepper, and sugar, and the royal diner enjoyed baked eel, boar brawn (jellied loaf), liver pudding, mince pie, and poached salmon. Roast goose, a holiday favorite, was featured in the Yule season from November 1 to Twelfth Night on January 6. In 1616, the king urged landowners to honor the season by remaining at their manors over Christmas to dispense food and drink to their tenants.

In Scots style, James refused pork in favor of game. His courtiers and hangers-on dodged obligatory meatless Wednesdays, Fridays, and Saturdays by dropping coins in the charity box to pay for exemptions.

During a state dinner at the Merchant Taylors' hall in London on July 16, 1607, James I feasted in a separate room on special dishes and imported fruit. Safe from the boorish or potential assassins, he and Prince Henry observed through a window the Lord Mayor and aldermen in scarlet robes and the after-dinner entertainment written by Ben Jonson, the court dramatist.

Typically, after a meat course and its complement, the poultry course, the court retired to a less formal locale, such as a privy chamber or gazebo, to enjoy sweetmeats. Favorites of the era ranged from marchpane (sugar and almond desserts) and sweet biscuits to light suckets (preserved fruit) and fresh fruit. A sugar sculpture set the tone of the last course, which wait staff served on thin dessert plates. Dances and masques rounded out the evening.

James's lack of information about silkworms caused him to order the planting of 10,000 mulberry trees on 4 acres (1.6 hectares). Although the worms refused the leaves, jam makers turned mulberries to profit. Such condiments followed homesteaders to the New World and brightened the unvarying meals of the Plymouth and Virginia settlers.

Setting an Example

The king took exception to drunkenness and depravity and to the fad of tobacco consumption as both a drug and a recreation replacing the dessert course of a banquet. The growing of tobacco had begun in England after 1573, when privateer Francis Drake brought seed from the Americas. Sir Walter Raleigh promoted the fad of smoking and snuff. Doctors claimed the leaves cured cancer, gonorrhea, halitosis, intestinal parasites, tetanus, and toothache. One treatment for asthma and cough involved powdering the leaves with chamomile, coltsfoot, lavender, rosemary, thyme, and wood betony for ingestion. Farmers also valued tobacco as a sheep dip and pesticide.

In 1604, James I issued *A Counterblaste to Tobacco,* a treatise denouncing smokers and tobacconists. He rejected the notion that tobacco's "stinking suffumigation" protected Native Americans from plague. Rather than adopt the barbarous pagan practices of taking snuff and spitting phlegm, he advocated a holistic "physic" (cathartic) that balanced the anatomical humors, a prevailing concept of wellness in his day. The pamphlet added to the king's tirade a castigation of drunkards for "their swinelike diet," which tended to shorten life, and of diners who sullied the atmosphere at table by lighting up a malodorous weed to "infect the aire." To stem pollutants, James I increased taxes from tuppence per pound to 6 shillings and 10 pence.

The king attempted to standardize medicinal dosages in April 1618 by issuing the *Pharmacopoeia Londinensis.* In support of the Society of Apothecaries, the text prescribed the dispensing of spices and chemicals. The decree represented a larger program of regulating foreign and home commerce in corn, pepper, and other edible commodities in standard measures and weights.

See also: Cookbooks; Grilling; Honey; Pastry.

Further Reading

Caton, Mary Anne, ed. *Fooles and Fricassees: Food in Shakespeare's England.* Washington, DC: Folger Shakespeare Library, 2000.

Fitzpatrick, Joan. *Food in Shakespeare: Early Modern Dietaries and the Plays.* Burlington, VT: Ashgate, 2007.

———, ed. *Renaissance Food from Rabelais to Shakespeare: Culinary Readings and Culinary Histories.* Burlington, VT: Ashgate, 2010.

Spencer, Colin. *British Food: An Extraordinary Thousand Years of History.* New York: Columbia University Press, 2002.

Japanese Diet and Cuisine

The focus of Japanese gastronomy harmonizes rice and tofu with small amounts of fish, meat, and vegetables for a healthful diet that controls coronary disease and obesity and lengthens life. Cooks arrange dishes on small bowls and plates for eye appeal to encourage consumption of fat-free broth and fruit, which produce a meal that is some 800 calories lower than the standard Western diet. The average Japanese diner eats little dairy food or spice but consumes six times more rice than Americans, a daily allotment that includes every meal.

Ancient Fare

From 14,000 B.C.E., Japanese hunter-gatherers collected acorns and chestnuts and prized the foxnut, the seedpod of a water lily. As agrarianism altered food interests, protofarmers in 4000 B.C.E. cultivated buckwheat. In Hokkaido, Japan, the Ainu abandoned raw food in preference for roasted and skewered pieces of badger, fox, salmon, sea anemones, and wolf. From pounded ubayuri lily bulbs, they shaped flat dumplings, a prototype of the soba, somen, and udon noodle.

By the Iron Age and the invention of heat-proof, leak-proof cookware, filling winter miso soups softened rootstock of carrot, *gobo* (burdock), and leeks. In Hokkaido, processors boiled *kombu,* nori, and *wakame* in iron kettles filled with fresh water before drying fronds on bamboo racks. After nighttime ocean forays by lantern light for cuttlefish and squid, fishing families dried the meat for barter or sale.

After 400 B.C.E., Japanese growers planted taro tubers in paddies as a pantry staple. The vegetable anchored the diet until Asian immigrants initiated the cultivation of short-grain rice in terraced paddies in the late Jomon period (ca. 300 B.C.E.), establishing Japan's culinary identity. Rice contributed to a rapid population spurt. In addition to supplying the family table with a staple cereal and the makings of filled rice balls and fried rice, homemakers introduced rice *congee* (gruel) to infants before advancing to adult foods—bonito flakes, miso (soy paste), and sea tangle (kelp), a food high in minerals.

Before 200 B.C.E., the fermentation of rice with kojii yeast yielded a holy drink, sake (or saki), a religious gift to the *kami* (nature gods) and cultural token of hospitality. Sake makers supplied the imperial household, monasteries, and Shinto temples and shrines. Diners anticipated the *shikisankon,* a series of nine rounds of sake poured into thimble-sized cups and raised them in toasts to guests. At weddings, the couple sipped sake as symbols of the home.

From Meat Dishes to Vegetarianism

In the first century C.E., island herders bred oxen and brought Wagyu cattle from the Korean Peninsula to supply marbled beef alongside venison and wild boar. Cooks sliced meat into thin bites for addition to stir-fried vegetables and soups. Monastery and temple cooks may have been the original distributors of bean curd, the prime source of protein in Japanese cuisine. Around 500 C.E., Buddhist monks at Mount Koya perfected a process of drying fresh *koya-dofu* (soy tofu), a protein-rich curd formed of cooked soybeans and bittern extracted from sea salt. The progressive censure of butchers and meats resulted in the first antimeat edict in 675, when the Emperor Temmu forbade the consumption of cattle, dogs, horses, poultry, and simians. Only pond fish, whale meat, and wild birds survived as menu items.

After the 600s, the Japanese grocer acquired imported stocks of Chinese cotton, pepper, sesame, wheat, and yellow beans. The introduction of tea offered both a refreshing stimulant and an altar gift for reverencing ancestors. Around 710 C.E., tofu makers developed industrial processing. The acceptance of tofu coincided with the Zen Buddhist vegetarian diet, which banned the meat of horses and oxen and encouraged seasonal produce and nonmeat grills, kebabs, and soups.

During the Nara era of the eighth century C.E., the Japanese cultivated their national staple, rice, along with barley, beans, millet, and sorghum. Vinegar makers widened their niche of the grocery market by supplying samurai with a daily drink. Cooks popularized soured rice wine as a standard table flavoring. Meatless meals waned in daily observance. Under the Emperor Daigo, the consumption of seven-grass rice gruel began in Kyoto in the early 900s, when table settings added spoons to chopsticks. Servers dished up soft-boiled rice blended with daikon radish, shepherd's purse, turnip, and wild celery. Wild celery remained a winter staple and a traditional delicacy on New Year's Eve.

In about 1100, during five centuries of isolationism from imported foods, the Japanese domesticated quail as a source of attractive entrées and tiny eggs that developed into a luxury finger food available at street stalls. The Japanese tea cult in 1190 took hold of customs and enforced coded courtesies and refinements as a civilizing agent. To draw noble Heian theatergoers from Kabuki and Noh performances, gourmet vendors opened hors d'oeuvre shops and sold baby bees and *yakitori* (chicken, beef, or seafood kebabs).

Housing styles reflected the importance of food storage to the average family. In the miso room, an unheated outer closet, farm wives protected dried sardines and shiitake mushrooms in lidded hampers, flour in stoppered bamboo cylinders, and tofu in conical baskets. They fermented pickles and soy sauce, a slurry of wheat, soybeans, rice yeast, and salt cured in flat-bottomed wood barrels. For thickening broth and ladling into noodle broth or stew, they blended condiments from barley, rice yeast, salt, and soybeans.

From the 1300s, the typical Kyushu housewife prepared meals at a stove in a dirt-floored lean-to. The *ko-*

A Japanese sushi chef shapes oblong mounds of vinegary rice (*shari*), topped with slices of salmon, tuna, and other seafood to create *nigirizushi*. Some are bound with narrow strips of seaweed (*nori*). *(Shizuo Kambayashi/Associated Press)*

tatsu, a wood frame over a sunken floor hearth, enabled cooks to keep dishes warm. Families crouched at the edge and warmed their feet on the cook pot filled with charcoal. A quilt covering frame and hearth kept feet snug and tea at drinking temperature.

In contrast to peasant cuisine, aristocrats, shoguns, and high-ranking samurai during the Kamakura era consumed delicacies on banquet tables as evidence of privilege. Ceremonial snacks of fruits and vegetables shaped like flowers or geometric designs appealed to the eye. Between sake rounds, guests celebrated prosperity by nibbling abalone, dried chestnuts or squid, pickled apricots, and seaweed. The gathering ended with baroque food service of thick tea and confections consisting of chestnuts, *mochi* (rice cakes), and yams.

Shifting Tastes

During the Renaissance, food writers summarized innovations, including the baking of hard crackers as a naval staple, the steeping of turmeric tea, and the special drying of the abalone catch for home dining. Around 1550, Portuguese Jesuits introduced tempura, or batter-fried shrimp and vegetables. In the late 1500s, as a complement to tea drinking, dried tofu accompanied the beverage service. Advanced tofu menus featured curds topped with chili sauce, dried shrimp, onion, or soy for breakfast. For healing, Japanese prowled open-air markets in search of curative bee larvae and honey. For celebrating, they claimed a Persian liquor, *shochu,* a barley drink containing 25 percent alcohol.

In the early 1600s, Dutch and Portuguese trading vessels penetrated Dejima, a port in southern Japan, bringing corn from Peru, curry and sugar from India, and spices from Malaysia. Aquaculture elevated seaweed from shore wild food of ten species into a coastal industry of 21 strains of algae, which form 10 percent of the Japanese diet. The cultivation of nori (*Prophyra bangiaceae*), a red algae, occurred by accident in the early 1600s in Shinagawa outside Tokyo, where the shogun Ieyasu Tokugawa discovered seaweed growing on the fence around his fish farm. Cooks used seaweed to encircle and preserve sushi, flavor noodles and tempura, and texturize soup.

At Edo, the capital of Japan, imperial chefs in the mid-seventeenth century served meals firepot style with cups of mirin, a sweet sake that suppressed fishy odors. Called "Genghis Khan cuisine" for its Mongol origins, *shabu-shabu,* the individual simmering of thin slices of meat, seafood, and vegetables in hot broth, revived the peasant concept of sitting at a round table and consuming fresh food in a convivial atmosphere.

During the eighteenth century, while rural folk continued pounding rice in mortar and pestle, monks collected recipes in cookbooks to promote vegetarianism. Ornate food preparation promoted urban kitchen artistry with the sweet potato, a new arrival. Espaliering gave outlets to dwarfing specialists who engineered miniature fruit orchards. Japanese soyfood makers abandoned the coarser Chinese recipes to create soft, white curd cheese prized for its delicacy. The first soy curd cookbook, *Book of Tofu* (1782), cataloged 230 dishes.

Late-nineteenth-century technology generated a demand for milled grain and rice powder, an ingredient in cake and noodles. By 1900, the Japanese were harvesting enough sea vegetables from their 18,000-mile (29,000-kilometer) coastline to generate a $2 million industry. To make the fronds appeal to food shoppers, Hokkaido processors boiled them in iron kettles filled with fresh water and green dye before drying them on bamboo racks.

During the 1940s, imperial militarism ended refined dining by stressing the patriotism of feeding soldiers. As meat supplies dwindled and citizens reverted to a rice and vegetable cuisine, the Japanese high command substituted tofu in army rations. In defeat, the Japanese family subsisted on famine food and grew kitchen gardens. American suppliers stocked warehouses with horse meat.

Despite generosity from the victors, in May 1946, allotments of butter and sugar in Tokyo averaged half of official ration allowances, with rice consumption declining to two-thirds its previous level. Hunger forced citizens to forage for wild food much as the prehistoric Ainu had done. The Japanese government began a propaganda campaign urging consumption of nutritious unrefined rice or blends of rice and barley.

The end of hard times brought a hunger for expansive cookery and varied flavors, especially American-style bread. Cooking once more without scrimping or substituting, Japanese women shopped for the best ingredients they could afford, such as Alaskan king crab, eel, herring, mackerel, octopus, pollock and salmon roe, sardines, sea urchins, and tuna. The demand for fish boosted Japan's consumption to 10 percent of the world's catch. Salad bar ingredients featured indigenous bean sprouts in Japanese *goi gia.*

The popularity of sushi in the 1970s reclaimed a healthful combination of raw fish and rice, a traditional pairing. The Japanese version of nouvelle cuisine elevated fine mousses and puréed fruits and vegetables as bases for revamped dishes, such as tempura. The health food movement promoted edamame beans as alternatives to meat and green tea as a source of antioxidants.

See also: Poisonous Foods; Rationing; Rice; Sanitation; Seaman's Diet and Cuisine; Seaweed; Shellfish; Tea Ceremony; Tofu.

Further Reading

Aoyama, Tomoko. *Reading Food in Modern Japanese Literature.* Honolulu: University of Hawaii Press, 2008.

Ono, Tadashi, and Harris Salat. *Japanese Hot Pots: Comforting One-Pot Meals.* Berkeley, CA: Ten Speed, 2009.

Rath, Eric C. *Food and Fantasy in Early Modern Japan.* Berkeley: University of California Press, 2010.

Tsuji, Shizuo. *Japanese Cooking, a Simple Art.* New York: Kodansha International, 2006.

Jefferson, Thomas (1743–1826)

One of America's first famous horticulturists, Thomas Jefferson, a founding father, author of the Declaration of Independence, and epicurean U.S. president, cultivated 500 varieties in an experimental vegetable garden, orchard, and vineyard. As chief executive, he hired a French chef, Honoré Julien, to serve distinguished guests the first spring produce and promoted commercial gardening for the citizenry by sharing his seeds with farmers. He also shared seed with naturalist William Bartram and presidents George Washington and James Madison.

Beginning in 1770 at Monticello, his hilltop manor in eastern Virginia, Jefferson applied slave labor to an

80- by 1,000-foot (24- by 300-meter) terraced expanse surrounded by a 10-foot (3-meter) paling fence to keep out rabbits. Overlooked by a modest viewing tower, the terrace faced south and absorbed heat radiated from stone retaining walls.

Jefferson's holdings extended to 300 fruit trees and 24 strains of European grapes. He began the sowing year in February with biweekly seeding of head lettuce, which continued until September. He interplanted with corn salad, endive, Pisan sorrel, and spinach. His employee, Jeremiah Goodman, added a second lettuce bed adjacent to the stable to accommodate up to 19 strains. A consultant advised arranging cedar or pine branches between rows and overlaying with dry straw to defeat frost.

Jefferson's garden yielded rows of Chilean strawberries, currants, Marseilles figs, gooseberries, and raspberries and a vineyard and 8-acre (3.2-hectare) orchard. From 1794 to 1814, with the aid of head gardener Wormley Hughes and overseer Edmund Bacon, along with slaves Abram, Davy, and Shepherd, Jefferson's herb planting yielded 16 varieties. He believed that heavy manuring strengthened feeble plants against insect attack and reserved cool evenings for work in the rows. In friendly competition with his neighbors, he attempted to harvest the first English peas of spring, even after arthritis stiffened his joints.

Jefferson loved rare and imported edibles, which he served with French Bordeaux wines. He stripped his garden of the mundane and insipid to accommodate such novelties as black salsify, scarlet runner beans, and serpentine cucumbers. His black-eyed peas, broccoli, and squash came from France, his peppers from Mexico, radicchio from Italy, and beans and garlic from Tuscany. On return from his ministry at the court of Louis XVI in France, he imported macaroni, Parmesan cheese, and raisins. Explorers Lewis and Clark brought him beans and salsify from their trek up the Missouri River to Oregon. From Bernard McMahon, a Philadelphia horticultural writer, Jefferson acquired Egyptian onion and Sugarloaf cabbage.

Monticello's beds juxtaposed Arikara beans, cauliflower, and celery alongside Brown Dutch and Spotted Aleppo lettuce and Chinese melon. His native American favorites ranged from hot chocolate, Jerusalem artichokes, lima beans, peanuts, potatoes, and tuckahoe to chokecherries, persimmons, and wild grapes and plums. Jefferson admired the globe artichoke and recorded the tending of asparagus crowns and sweet potatoes from the end of his second term on March 4, 1809, to 1826. His curative herbs include senna, valerian, gentian, cohosh, spurge nettle, lobelia, three kinds of mallow, three kinds of snakeroot, and stramonium, a source of asthma treatments. In 1824, he published in the May 21 issue of *American Farmer* his "General Gardening Calendar," a month-by-month guide to kitchen gardening gleaned from his meticulous notes on sowing, harvest, and seed preservation.

For aesthetics, Jefferson grouped eggplant and okra by color, blanched sea kale heads, and grew rhubarb for desserts and cherry trees for shade along the grassy walkways. He added orach and nasturtiums to his salad plants and relegated meat entrées to the position of condiments for vegetables. His cooks, Eda and Fanny, made boiled lettuce, gumbo, johnnycake, ketchup, and sweet potato pone and whipped up a salad dressing from sesame oil and tarragon vinegar, sieved egg yolks, mustard, salt, and sugar. His detailed recipes cover precise proportions for making coffee and the amount of salt for curing ham.

See also: Beans and Legumes; Heirloom Plants; Herbs; Ice Cream; Ketchup; Randolph, Mary; Vanilla.

Further Reading

Fowler, Damon Lee. *Dining at Monticello: In Good Taste and Abundance.* Chapel Hill: University of North Carolina Press, 2005.

Hailman, John. *Thomas Jefferson on Wine.* Jackson: University Press of Mississippi, 2006.

Jefferson, Thomas. *Thomas Jefferson's Garden Book.* Ed. Edwin Morris Betts. Chapel Hill: University of North Carolina Press, 2002.

Loewer, H. Peter. *Jefferson's Garden.* Mechanicsburg, PA: Stackpole, 2004.

Jerky

Jerky, a preserved survival meat, exemplifies one of the world's first processed foods. In prehistory, the concept of air- and fire-drying flavorful meat suited the needs of both paleo-Amerindians and Phoenicians. Models of Egyptian honeyed or salt jerky survived in the tombs of pharaohs Amenhotep II and Thutmose III; tomb scenes of Thunefer at Thebes depict the processing of duck or ostrich meat. In the 1500s, the Spanish recorded eyewitness accounts of the Inca of Peru trimming bone, fat, and gristle from beef, deer, elk, horse, and llama muscle and reducing moisture to produce dense, lightweight meals. After salting, Inca processors sun- and wind-dried or freeze-dried the rumps and shanks into *charqui,* the Quechuan name for the original jerky.

As did chicle, chocolate, tomatoes, and other New World commodities, jerky intrigued newcomers. Preparers in Argentina, Brazil, Chile, Peru, and Uruguay sliced the meat into strips for sun-drying and tenderized it by pounding it between stones. Dehydration promoted portability for nomadic travel and slave food, and a long shelf life in stone silos and loft bags free from fungus and rot.

Highly competitive South American jerky processors sold dried meat to all comers, who valued its adaptability. In imitation, Spanish sailors converted Pacific island goats into *carne seca* (dried meat) to stock their galleys for long voyages. In reference to the English colonies in *The*

Generall Historie of Virginia (1624), Captain John Smith became the first author to refer to beef preservation in the West Indies as "meat jerking."

Farther north, Great Lakes Ojibwa turned bear and buffalo haunches into a cottage industry of jerky and pemmican, two trail foods valued by Sioux warriors, Ohio River valley fur traders, expeditioners, and pioneers. Buffalo hunters rack-dried enough jerky for clan provisions and trade. Packing jerky with mint discouraged vermin during caching. The preparers sliced cured fat, suspended from the smoke hole of a lodge, and used slabs like bread for jerky sandwiches.

In fall 1766, British navigator Captain James Cook described provisions he purchased in Rio de Janeiro, Brazil. At the rate of 7 pence for 4 pounds (1.8 kilograms), he could buy fresh or jerked beef for his sailors. Brazilians cured the meat with salt and dried it in the shade until they could debone it. After slicing thin strips, they sold it as jerky, which remained fresh at sea. A similar system of curing meat by South African Afrikaners or Boers resulted in biltong, hard, dry strips of eland, elephant, kudu, ostrich, oxen, or fish marinated in coriander, herbs, pepper, salt, sugar, and vinegar.

In the late 1800s, legends of the wily Apache war leader Geronimo describe how he bested white pursuers through the *lava malpais* (badlands), a deadly expanse of black chunks of lava spewed from a volcano and sparsely blanketed in soil. After the U.S. Cavalry foundered on the jagged edges, Geronimo recovered their dead horses and dried the meat into jerky to feed his starving people.

Pacific jerky appealed to less desperate diners. Hawaiian cattle ranching shifted entrées from traditional island fare toward beef and broiled beef jerky, which they called *pipikaula,* a traditional luau dish. In this same period, Aussie trekkers favored jerky, as did plainsmen, pioneers, wranglers, explorers, and miners who dried long strips of meat on forked sticks in the sun or over a smoky fire.

Today, beef, turkey, and other meat and fish jerky sell well as energy snacks for their low fat, high protein content. Curing and drying reduce tissue moisture by as much as 80 percent. Processors add a variety of sweeteners and flavorings—brown sugar, chili pepper, corn syrup, garlic, liquid hickory or mesquite smoke, maple syrup, onions, and teriyaki sauce.

Specialty shops in Hong Kong and Macau feature fresh sliced jerky, a parallel of the beef jerky sticks and shredded lean meat sold to U.S. backpackers and packed on NASA spaceflights and in gift boxes to American soldiers in the Mideast. Other forms of the global meat snack market include the defatted beef and horse *bresaola* and *slinzega* of Lombardy, wind-dried Armenian and Turkish *pastirma,* donkey or horse *coppiette* in Rome, French beef *brési,* spiced *quant'a* in Ethiopia, Chinese and Malaysian beef *bakkwa,* Swiss beef *bindenfleisch,* and the Spanish beef *cecina* of León and tuna *mojama* of Phoenician ancestry.

See also: African Diet and Cuisine, Sub-Saharan; Caribbean Diet and Cuisine; Dried Food; Inca Diet and Cuisine; Pemmican; Travel Food.

Further Reading

Aberle, Elton David, John C. Forrest, David E. Gerrard, and Edward W. Mills. *Principles of Meat Science.* Dubuque, IA: Kendall/Hunt, 2001.

Black, Rick. *Deer Burger Cookbook: Recipes for Using Ground Venison in Soups, Stews, Chilis, Casseroles, Jerkies, and Sausages.* Mechanicsburg, PA: Stackpole, 2006.

Keoke, Emory Dean, and Kay Marie Porterfield. *American Indian Contributions to the World: 15,000 Years of Inventions and Innovations.* New York: Checkmark, 2003.

Tarantino, Jim. *Marinades, Rubs, Brines, Cures, and Glazes.* New York: Random House, 2006.

Jiménez de Quesada, Gonzalo (ca. 1499–1579)

Córdoban attorney and explorer Gonzalo Jiménez de Quesada introduced Iberia to the Colombian potato, which became a staple throughout Europe and provided a safeguard against famine.

In search of El Dorado, the fabled city of gold in North America, Quesada assumed the post of chief colonial magistrate of St. Marta. In April 1536, he led an expedition of 900 men to the Colombian interior along the Magdalena River into the Andean highlands. More than 82 of the troops died en route from hunger, fever, and snakebite.

After killing Chief Zipa, the Spaniards routed the Chibcha, a nation of mountain traders in cloth, crafts, food, and salt. Upon the approach of the Spanish, the Chibcha fled the Valle de la Grita, abandoning stocks of beans, corn, and potatoes to the insurgents. The region, a fertile plateau east of the Cordillera Mountains, fed starving soldiers on corn and blue potatoes. Although Quesada's travelogue is lost, historians cite a comment that the potato plant grew 24 inches (61 centimeters) high and produced floury, egg-sized roots in blue, red, white, and yellow.

Early in 1537 at Sorocotá, Juan de Castellanos, a cavalryman and epic poet, recorded in his notes for *Historia del Nuevo Reino de Granada* (*History of the New Kingdom of Spain,* 1886) the Chibchan diet and cuisine. He noted the variety of food and drink—bread made from various roots, a drink called *chicha,* and plantains, a common starchy vegetable, which local cooks usually fried. He detailed how natives made and used clay pots for boiling saltwater. After the moisture evaporated, the salt maker broke the exterior to release a solid salt cake. In addition to the saltworks, Castellanos surveyed tuber culture at high altitudes and compiled the first European comments on the potato. He described it as a Chibchan delicacy that Spanish soldiers liked.

After subduing the Chibcha, Quesada founded Santa Fe de Bogotá, the capital of Nueva Granada (New Spain). In addition to bags of emeralds and gold, he returned to Spain in 1550 with the potato, which he touted for its nutritional value. The tuber sold for a high price to locals, who grew it as an ornamental. Initially, the Spanish compared the plant to the mushroom, called it *tartuffo* (truffle), and fed it to livestock.

Because of the resilience of the potato over long storage, however, ships' provisioners purchased it from the port of Cartagena to feed to the Spanish navy. Cooks prepared the potato as boiled tubers and added it to cakes, flour, and fritters. The potato surprised the military hierarchy by protecting crews from scurvy. By 1585, the potato flourished in the fields of northwestern Europe, where it proved cheaper to grow than rice or wheat.

Because the potato could remain in the ground longer than grain could last in the field, farms were less vulnerable to marauders and more resilient against cyclical crop shortfalls during war and weather disasters. As a food, potatoes adapted to kitchen invention and required no milling or grinding. Across Europe, from Ireland southeast to the Balkans, throughout the Industrial Revolution, governments promoted potato growing as an economical source of food for factory laborers and miners and as a backup against starvation.

See also: Barbecue; Famine; Potatoes.

Further Reading

Graham, R. Cunninghame. *The Conquest of New Granada: Being the Life of Gonzalo Jiménez de Quesada.* Reprint, 1922. Boston: Longwood, 1978.

Reader, John. *Potato: A History of the Propitious Esculent.* New Haven, CT: Yale University Press, 2009.

Kebabs

Historically, in North Africa and Asia, meats and vegetables braised or roasted on a stick offered a convenient method of moving aromatic dishes briskly to the table for eating without utensils. From the 1600s B.C.E., Greek artisans crafted sets of skewers for slow-roasting meat over fire. Recipes from classical Greece mentioned *obeliskos*—skewered shrimp brushed with honey for roasting over embers, a forerunner of the Greek gyro.

Spitted meat became the standard for meal preparation along the Silk Road from China to the Middle East. For convenience, nomadic Turkish Tartars and the Bakhtiari of southern Iran cooked lamb cubes as kebabs, which they varied with chunks of eggplant, mushrooms, and onions. The Ainu of Hokkaido, Japan, abandoned raw food in preference for roasted and skewered pieces of badger, fox, salmon, sea anemone, and wolf.

Persian cooks made use of limited fuel by cooking meats in small chunks, a kitchen trick they borrowed from soldiers who fire-roasted their dinner on the tip of a sword. Bazaar dining introduced food on a stick with onion kebabs, slices of whole roasted sheep and mutton, and pickled cauliflower and cucumber sticks wrapped in bread. Preparers flavored entrées with cinnamon, garlic, lemon and lime, nuts, onions, parsley, pomegranate seeds, raisins and prunes, and saffron.

In the 900s C.E., in the Muslim city of Baghdad, cooks stoked charcoal to a low flame for simmering red meat kebabs and spitted whole lamb spiced with garlic. Arab and Bactrian merchants traveling the Silk Road to Xi'an in central China contributed Turkish-style grilled and skewered meats to regional cuisine. Ceylonese and Indian traders brought their own version, kebabs with nan.

Mid-medieval cuisine varied the mix of spitted food service. Armenian poetry of the 1100s pictures feasts of heavily spiced lamb kebabs as a symbol of joy and satiety. Italian favorites consisted of fish or seafood threaded on iron rods. Japanese recipes identified various forms of tofu skewered in kebabs. In Beijing's streets, shoppers munched on skewers of lamb or mutton grilled in the open air and wrapped in wheat pancakes.

In the 1300s, Mongol nomads taught the Chinese *kao* cuisine, toasting meat on skewers over charcoal grills. By placing individual grills on tables, cooks offered informal diners the opportunity to roast morsels to the desired

amount of doneness. Ibn Battuta, a Moroccan traveler, discovered kebab cookery in Delhi in 1334. He relished a breakfast of *mash* (peas) and enjoyed meat kebabs with thin slabs of chapati (bread) fried in ghee.

Kebabs in history involved skewered meat in violent and serene settings. In 1504, a Shi'ite warlord, Shah Ismael I, conqueror of Tabriz, Iran, spitted his captives and fed human kebabs to his followers as a test of loyalty. Suleiman I, the sultan of the Ottoman Empire from 1520 to 1566, hunted stag for relaxation and devoured the heart of his kill after his companions roasted the meat kebab style. In seventeenth-century Istanbul, spitted game liver served drinkers as the meat of choice for an evening's debauch.

Tudor England produced a British version of kebabs with game birds skewered on spits and basted with herbed drippings as they roasted on andirons by the fire. After buffalo hunts on the North American plains, children waited their turn for roasted chunks of small intestines wrapped on skewers. In the same era, Ottoman travelers to Erzurum, in eastern Turkey, enjoyed pitas and slices of meat from a *cag kebabi,* a horizontal spit that impaled lamb for grilling and basting with onion.

In early-nineteenth-century France, Marie-Antoine Carême's set of decorative cooking swords skewered delicacies from shrimp to whole fish, an element of the era's baroque cuisine. Late in the era, Haci Iskender, a northwestern Turk from Bursa, invented the Iskender kebab, a vertical spit that rotates meat over a flame for cooking and slicing in thin strips. His name survived in the Iskender Kebab, a Turkish specialty common to public venues.

After World War II, the Jewish diaspora to the new state of Israel required rationing. To feed 1 million transients and Holocaust survivors, Prime Minister David Ben-Gurion proposed schnitzel and turkey kebabs to replace lamb and veal. Cooks in Botswana, Lesotho, Namibia, South Africa, Zambia, and Zimbabwe developed the *braai,* a barbecue over a gas or wood flame of Dutch-style *boerewors* (sausages), rock lobster, and skewered *sosaties,* the Afrikaans terms for spiced kebabs. Diners enjoyed their meat with cornmeal mush, *chakalaka* (hot sauce), and chutney.

In the 1950s, Middle Eastern immigrants influenced Australians to balance the standard roast-and-potato menu to include lamb kebabs. Australians and New Zealanders embraced barbecuing for special occasions by grilling game or skewered chicken or lamb and sausages.

A Palestinian street vendor in the West Bank sells grilled kebabs during the holy month of Ramadan, when devout Muslims fast from dawn to dusk. Marinated meat on skewers is pervasive in the Middle East. *(Muhammed Muheisen/Associated Press)*

Among hearty herbed and curried finger foods, British snack trays displayed shrimp satay and Turkish fish and lamb shish kebab served with a national condiment, cucumbers in yogurt. The growth of Caribbean and North American fast food and patio cookouts increased the eating from hands of buns with meaty fillings and of fish, fruit, meat, and vegetable kebabs, a staple of finger food.

The urge to experiment and personalize has produced myriad kebab variants in modern cuisine. Egyptian, Lebanese, Pakistani, and Turkish immigrants cook bar, street, and van specialties in Central and Eastern Europe, Iberia, Ireland, Korea, and Scandinavia. Wedding receptions and afternoon teas frequently accompanied small cakes with fruit kebabs, a colorful presentation of grapes, kiwi slices, pineapple chunks, and strawberries. In the 1980s, an example of the nouvelle cuisine at the Papiamento Restaurant on Aruba listed chicken and shrimp kebabs cooked on the traditional island coal pot. U.S. fairgoers jam food booths to taste genuine regional treasures, with chicken pies sharing tables with Malaysian *satay* beef, Arabic shawarma, Greek pork gyros, and Mexican fajitas. A visual treat, Azerbaijani doner kebabs require a rotating vertical spit that cooks chicken or lamb over a flame or electric broiler for service as street food with eggplant, peppers, pilaf, and tomatoes and a wrapping of taboon bread.

Variations of spitted meats—chicken breast, meatball, sausage, sirloin, and swordfish—please consumers in bazaar diners and kebab houses worldwide. Middle Eastern and North African cubes of shark, trout, or tuna require wrapping in grape leaves, perhaps with chunks of cheese, for fitting onto a skewer. Cajun brochettes begin with threading chunks of tasso (pork shoulder) on sticks. Other locales offer gourmet groups authentic street food, a stroller's choice of Filipino eel and frog's legs, Korean *eomuk* (pureed whitefish on a stick), or fried Chinese beetle larva or crickets on a skewer. The Taiwanese favor grilled corn on a skewer topped with cayenne, garlic, onions, and soy sauce. Indian turmeric, grown in the tropics, colors Sumatran *satay padang,* a skewered beef topped with a deep yellow sauce.

See also: Arab Diet and Cuisine; Finger Food; Grilling; Shellfish; Sicilian Diet and Cuisine; Street Food; Tofu.

Further Reading

Davidson, Alan. *The Oxford Companion to Food.* Ed. Jane Davidson, Tom Jaine, and Helen Saberi. New York: Oxford University Press, 2006.

Denker, Joel. *The World on a Plate: A Tour Through the History of America's Ethnic Cuisine.* Lincoln: University of Nebraska Press, 2007.

Heine, Peter. *Food Culture in the Near East, Middle East, and North Africa.* Westport, CT: Greenwood, 2004.

Singer, Amy, ed. *Starting with Food: Culinary Approaches to Ottoman History.* Princeton, NJ: Markus Weiner, 2010.

Ketchup

A mass-market tomato food enhancer, ketchup defines the American and English taste in salty-sweet, zesty chutney. Derived from *koe-chiap,* a seventh-century C.E. Cantonese fish sauce, the word *ketchup* refers to a condiment based in the 1690s on pickled anchovies or oyster brine mixed with beans, mushrooms, and walnuts. The appeal of a tangy dipping sauce spread to East India, Malaysia, and Singapore.

By the 1700s, British and Dutch explorers and colonial administrators introduced both ketchup and soy sauce to Europe, where cooks made their own gravy substitutes and marinades by replacing soybeans with kidney beans or mushrooms. Nineteenth-century convenience foods inspired industrialists to market condiments, including creamy horseradish, HP sauce (brown sauce), and tomato ketchup. Innovative ketchup recipes named anchovies, cucumbers, gooseberries and other berries, herring, kidney beans, lemon peel, liver, and pome fruit as fundamental ingredients.

American Ketchup

From the Regency period into the mid-Victorian age, the rage for ketchup appeared in the writings of Lord Byron, Jane Austen, Charles Dickens, and Rudyard Kipling. In 1800, U.S. ketchup followed Old World recipes. Imitators used a variety of ingredients, including chestnuts, curry, mussels, oysters, and walnuts until New England cooks settled on tomatoes for the dominant flavor and coloring. Farmers acquired seeds for tomatoes from sailors traveling between Maine and the Caribbean or Mexico. Innkeepers served the tart, ruddy sauce on codfish cakes.

At Monticello, Virginia, Thomas Jefferson's cooks Eda and Fanny made batches of ketchup in iron kettles and stored the sauce in stone crocks. In the undercroft kitchen, they stemmed and seeded the red globes before squeezing out pulp and boiling it with salt. The all-day job required straining the slurry and adding allspice, cinnamon, cloves, ginger, mace, nutmeg, pepper, and white vinegar before the final boiling and bottling. The yield for 100 tomatoes was five bottles. Jefferson's cousin, Mary Randolph, included the recipe in *The Virginia House-Wife* (1824), the first documentation of American foodways.

In 1837, Jonas Yerkes, a Pennsylvania farmer, became the first U.S. commercializer of ketchup by recycling green tomatoes and cores and skins from canneries into a chutney sold in pint and quart glass decanters. The Thurber Company, a New York grocer, bought Yerkes's business. Although the sauce quickly gained popularity, in the treatise *Lectures on the Science of Human Life* (1839), reformer Sylvester Graham called for a ban on cinnamon, ketchup, and mustard as enervators of the body and precipitators of dyspepsia and exhaustion. Activists agreed with Graham based on unsanitary warehousing of tomato scraps in holding tanks and the enhancement of redness with coal tar.

The development of a suitable tomato for ketchup began in the greenhouse. In 1870, a self-taught hybridizer of heritage cultivars, seedsman Alexander Wilmers Livingston of Reynoldsburg, Ohio, developed the Paragon tomato, a uniform, fleshy fruit and profitable food crop. His hybridization techniques yielded 31 additional tomato varieties, which he categorized by canners, hothouse varieties, and fruit for reducing into a sauce or marinade.

The Heinz Phenomenon

The F&J Heinz Company, a horseradish bottler that operated out of a two-story farmhouse in Sharpsburg, Pennsylvania, produced tomato ketchup in 1876. Heinz ketchup contained salt and vinegar plus allspice, black and white pepper, brown and cane sugar, cayenne, celery seeds, cinnamon, cloves, garlic, ginger, horseradish, mace, mustard seeds, and slippery elm bark. To guarantee customers a wholesome product rather than tomatoes adulterated with turnips or cellulose, the company distributed ketchup in glass bottles. Sealing began with cork, a dip in hot wax, and crowning with foil.

At the Centennial International Exhibition of 1876, the first world's fair in the United States, Americans examined displays of Heinz's tomato ketchup. The company pioneered advertisements that contributed images of wholesome food and wellness. By buying tomatoes at their peak and offering consistent quality, Heinz was able to undercut the price of competitors. In the first year, the company grossed $44,474 for its national brand. Heinz profited by shipping 46-gallon (174-liter) tuns of ketchup, America's national sauce, to Australia, Canada, China, Great Britain, Japan, New Zealand, South Africa, and South America.

Into the early twentieth century, for binding and texture, packagers of ready-to-eat tomato condiments added potato and rice flour, oat fiber, and soybean products, standard thickeners that gave authentic mouthfeel. Bottlers volumized ketchup with guar gum, which had eight times the thickening agency of cornstarch. The ban on sodium benzoate by the 1906 Pure Food and Drug Act inspired Heinz to reformulate the recipe to include other preservatives.

In Pittsburgh, Pennsylvania, in 1926, the H.J. Heinz Company selected tomato seeds to grow in greenhouses for its ketchup recipe. The company farmed out plants to contractors who grew the seedlings to maturity from June to August. At harvest, suppliers gathered ripe fruit high in pectin, solids, and texture. In 1942, Gordie C. Hanna, a specialist in olericulture (truck crops) at the University of California at Davis, began hybridizing a small, high-yielding tomato with a firmer skin and more fibrous pulp, an elongated crossbreed of Gem and San Marzano known as Red Top. The crossbreed exhibited an intense ruby hue suited to ketchup and pasta sauce.

The Reagan administration created a stir in 1981 over the reclassification of ketchup as a vegetable in federally subsidized meals. The identification of a condiment as a major part of the diet allowed school cafeterias to reduce nonmeat offerings. So much ridicule erupted in the media that the U.S. Department of Agriculture abandoned the shift of ketchup from salt- and sugar-laden dressing to vegetable.

By the twenty-first century, ketchup remained in demand at the International Space Station, where laminated retort pouches retained sterility. After salsa outsold ketchup as a condiment, Heinz attempted a resurgence in 2000 by dyeing the red sauce blue and green; it ended the experiment in 2006. Further variations included hot and spicy ketchup, introduced in 2002, and, in 2011, a ketchup made with balsamic vinegar.

See also: Condiments; Guar; Hanna, Gordie C.; Livingston, A.W.; Randolph, Mary; Sauces and Saucing.

Further Reading

Foster, Debbie, and Jack Kennedy. *H.J. Heinz Company.* Charleston, SC: Arcadia, 2006.

Hartley, Paul. *The Heinz Tomato Ketchup Cookbook.* Berkeley, CA: Ten Speed, 2008.

La Boone, John A. *Around the World of Food: Adventures in Culinary History.* New York: iUniverse, 2006.

Skrabec, Quentin R. *H.J. Heinz: A Biography.* Jefferson, NC: McFarland, 2009.

Smith, Andrew F. *The Tomato in America: Early History, Culture, and Cookery.* Urbana: University of Illinois Press, 2001.

Kitchen Gardening

The planting of berries and fruit, herbs, and vegetables alongside a residence gives visual evidence of respect for fresh ingredients. The first kitchen gardeners grew radishes adjacent to the huts of Egyptian commoners and cabbages, mustard, and onions within the internal *hortus* (garden) of the Roman villa. Formalized in the Middle Ages as abbey and cottage plots, culinary gardening became a convenience for the cook and healer. Seeding and growing involved the full natural cycle, initiated with trench digging as deep as 36 inches (91 centimeters), which encouraged deep rooting of dal and other pulses in Indian house gardens.

In Renaissance Europe, the layout of the *jardin potager* (soup garden) advanced to aesthetic interplantings of aromatic and edible flowers in parterres. Large culinary plots

held dwarf trees, shrubs, and vines as well as kidney and runner beans and tomatoes introduced from the New World. Designers structured plots in geometric shapes permeated with walkways and surrounded by heat-retaining walls, which shielded tender currants from frost and melons from thieves. During early morning perusals, cooks clipped dewy borage and nasturtium blossoms for garnishing, chives and lavender for fragrance, chamomile and gooseberries for restorative beverages, and coriander, mint, and rosemary for savory meat dressings.

Royal Kitchen Beds

In Tudor England, Hampton Court Palace, a Thames-side estate in East Molesey, Surrey, a model of food growing featured orderly walled beds built by chief minister Thomas Wolsey, archbishop of York. For serving guests in the 45 apartments, the kitchen garden produced chicory, endive, fennel, mallow, purslane, rocket, and smallage (wild celery). After Henry VIII purchased Hampton Court in Middlesex, his kitchen bed layout, which abutted the orchard, influenced visitors from Germany with its arrangement of herbs and mints, which he shared with growers about the realm.

At Versailles in the mid-1600s, the *Potager du Roi* (king's kitchen garden) of Louis XIV displayed 44 complex mazes, weeded and harvested daily. His master grower, Jean-Baptiste de la Quintinye, fostered diversity by grafting fruit to foreign stock and by seeding hardy cauliflower, chard, and kale in forcing frames to lengthen the growing season. He trained dewberry vines and cucumbers on trellises and anchored multiple cultivars close together, thus assisting natural hybridization. Quintinye's use of sun-heated walls simulated a microclimate, a basis of preseason cultivation of fruits, tender pea pods, and young salad greens that influenced colonial gardening. Settlers of Canada emulated the cozy clustering of kitchen beds within hedges and fences.

The idea of a royal kitchen garden came into favor in 1672 with the Kensington palace beds that supplied the table of William III and his coruler, Queen Mary II. In 1844, Queen Victoria cultivated plants and vines at Frogmore Gardens, where a greenhouse and hothouse supplied the royal family in London and at Windsor Castle. Head gardener Owen Thomas chose from harvested melons and strawberries and sent flats of fruit to the royal green produce room. In Russia, the aristocratic appetite for the freshest vegetables led diners to devour garden legumes raw. The imperial admiration for fresh produce instilled pity in the elite for serfs, who tended small kitchen beds as sources of sustenance.

Local Gardening

Industrialization in the mid-nineteenth century produced a flight from agrarianism in Europe and North America. At the same time, changing attitudes toward fresh produce brought a mass swing toward vegetarianism and a diverse diet. Heirloom and hybrid vegetable seeds and tubers abounded, many from California, the kitchen garden of America. Locavores promoted the functional backyard plot as a source of organic produce and a savings on fuel, both for food transportation and for mowing lawns.

At the height of world colonization, friendships with other growers, such as Philadelphia botanists John and William Bartram, furthered discussion of recipes for clover honey, horehound, and rue in cough syrups, lotions, and veterinary salves. The thinning of carrots, leeks, lemongrass, and onions preceded the sharing of extras or sales at farmer's markets. Trades from one kitchen to another involved dividing asparagus crowns and disseminating seeds and rootstock, such as dill, garlic, Jerusalem artichoke, rhubarb, sorrel, and thyme. Seasonal chores concluded with adding stalks and leaves to the compost pile and adding seaweed and manure from the stables to help break down detritus into friable mulch, tasks assumed by the Jesuits on the islands off Macao and the English and Irish settlers of New Zealand and southern Australia.

Sustainable living influenced residential design throughout history, particularly Asian kitchen gardening of the Japanese pea and wild perennials and some 20 Chinese varieties of edamame and green vegetable soybeans. Among the Pueblo of the American Great Basin and black smallholders on Barbados, the reciprocity of herb drying and cooking illustrated the centrality of homegrown food to women, who superintended the planting of gourds and the air-drying of beans.

On the North American frontier, the home plot commanded daily attention and constant replanting of herb and salad crops convenient to the kitchen and storage lean-to. Lacking fresh produce markets and dry goods stores, frontier women such as Ory Baxter, in Marjorie Kinnan Rawlings's historical novel *The Yearling* (1938), excelled at plowing and seeding. For advice, they turned to almanacs and well-thumbed copies of Bernard McMahon's *The American Gardener's Calendar* (1804), a manual that remained the home culinary standard for over half a century. By involving children in weeding and picking, parents turned produce growing into training in the work ethic and in dietary wisdom.

Gardening in Hard Times

During the economic depression of 1893, kitchen gardening in Michigan helped restore dignity and spirit to

Suburban neighbors work together in a community victory garden during World War II. Local groups transformed vacant lots, city parks, and open spaces across America into gardens that produced up to 40 percent of the nation's vegetables and fruits. *(Associated Press)*

the unemployed. In Detroit, Mayor Hazen Stuart Pingree helped 1,000 families sustain themselves by planting home gardens. The city provided implements and seed. Reach-in plots and raised potato patches suited the abilities of the disabled and the elderly. Within one season, participants harvested beans, pumpkins, and squash and 40,000 bushels of potatoes. His concept of self-help thrived in Boston, Chicago, Denver, Duluth, Minneapolis, New York, and Seattle.

During the great conflicts of the twentieth century, American, Australian, Canadian, and European families tended war gardens, called liberty or victory gardens, a patriotic project to supplement rationed foodstuffs with homegrown produce. By 1918, Americans tilled 5,285,000 kitchen gardens that grew around 2,643 tons (2,398 metric tons) of food valued at $350 million. Chopping and hoeing gave growers a respite from fear and worry about hunger. The effort empowered noncombatants with opportunities to support the military and to uplift their own vitality and hope.

Throughout World War II, families revived depression relief plots in backyards, city parks, and vacant space. Right up to the front door, Irish families planted potatoes in available space. London apartment dwellers turned a bomb crater into crop space. Some 20 million Americans harvested tons of food from yards and rooftops, which publicity agents dubbed "vitamin factories." The U.S. total contributed 40 percent of fresh goods that fed the nation while lowering prices of commercially grown produce and ensuring the diet of soldiers.

American farm agents opened neighborhood canneries as a hands-on teaching experience for homemakers in canning and drying the harvests of their kitchen plots. Posters applauded savings on fuel and proclaimed, "Every war garden a munitions plant." Australians recycled green waste as feed for chickens, a part of the nation's "Dig for Victory" concept. By selling surplus chickens, eggs, and vegetables, community collectives, called "garden armies," raised funds for the Red Cross, Salvation Army, and YWCA (Young Women's Christian Association).

The U.S. Department of Agriculture issued garden handbooks and produced a 20-minute film of a model victory garden planted by the Holder family in northern Maryland. At the White House, first lady Eleanor Roosevelt set the example of kitchen gardening, which citizens emulated in public vegetable plots in Boston, Minneapolis, New York, and San Francisco. A similar example in Hyde Park, London, piqued enthusiasm among beginning gardeners and cooperatives.

The concept of growing ingredients of a healthful diet to fight obesity returned to prominence in March 2009, when first lady Michelle Obama tilled and spaded a patch on the White House lawn. The media applauded her for introducing young growers to fresh food that rewarded them with flavor and nutrition. Agrarian experts extended the range of edible gardening possibilities from backyard homesteading to containers on balconies, patios, and windowsills.

See also: Espaliering; Greenhouse Horticulture; Herbs; Jefferson, Thomas; Physic Gardening; Travel Food.

Further Reading

Campbell, Susan. *A History of Kitchen Gardening.* London: Frances Lincoln, 2005.

Forsyth, Holly Kerr. *The Constant Gardener: A Botanical Bible.* Carlton, Victoria, Australia: Miegunyah, 2007.

Helphand, Kenneth. *Defiant Gardens: Making Gardens in Wartime.* San Antonio, TX: Trinity University Press, 2006.

Liebreich, Karen, Jutta Wagner, and Annette Wendland. *The Family Kitchen Garden.* London: Frances Lincoln, 2009.

Kitchen Lore

The oral history of food selection and cooking elevates age-old beliefs into mythic science. The holistic approach to where and how plants grow and the phases of the moon that govern their nutritional and medicinal strengths anchors the diet of preliterate cultures worldwide. According to Romanian religious historian Mircea Eliade, the emergence of agrarian lifestyles involved protofarmers in the "oneness of organic life." The cycle of seasons, when compared with human lives, governed the ability of annual plants to provide nourishment and to resurrect themselves from death through the magic of regenerated vines and seeds, the sources of Greek worship of Dionysus and Demeter.

Unsubstantiated by science, dietary beliefs gained credence because of their longevity and mystery. Preliterate cultures maintained a primal reverence for agave, cassava, eggs, honey, milk, and soybeans. Religious significance attached to such natural occurrences as the fermentation of Persian wine into a religious intoxicant, the comfort the grieving received from eggplants, and the appearance of corn smut, spongy galls that the Aztec valued as a delicacy. A blend of animism and culinary skill endowed foods with transcendent strengths—algae with the mystic resurgence of the sea, basil with restoring human fertility, ginseng and pepper with revitalization of libido, green tea and piñon nuts for boosting the immune system, salt and smoke with the ability to extend the edibility of fish and meat, and turmeric with sensual pleasures and spiritual fulfillment.

Early Diet Guides

Medieval food commentary favored subjective conclusions, such as the refutations of Galen and Hippocrates's advice on meats proffered in the verse narrative *Regimen Sanitatis Salernitanum* (*Code of Health of the School of Salernum,* ca. 1099), possibly written advice to Robert Curthose, eldest son of William the Conqueror, on the way home following the First Crusade. Hierarchies of roast joints and poached whole fish also arranged the order in which diners should ingest courses, beginning with meat and rounding out meals with bread and coffee. Additional advice specified cures for warts and worms and the types of cider, hypocras, or perry that complemented the dominant humors, bilious, melancholy, phlegmatic, and sanguine. Such specious debate over diet and nutrition illustrated the faulty logic that circulated before empirical science replaced anecdotal evidence with research.

Much kitchen lore featured a time element. According to the anonymous treatise *Provençal Dietetic* (ca. 1290), the seasons placed demands on human digestion. Spring was the right time for lettuce, goat's milk, and chicken, quail, and partridge eggs. Summer was more suited to squash and cucumber, apples, and veal or kid dressed in verjuice or vinegar. Fall brought to the table ripe figs and grapes, chicken, mutton, and game birds cooked in saffron or ginger. Winter was the only time to consume capons and roast chicken, large game, roast meats, and spitted pork and for cracknels retrieved from the larding process.

Merchandising of fresh goods required seasonal calendars such as the anonymous *Le Grant Kalendrier des Bergiers* (*The Great Shepherds' Calendar*, 1491), a moralistic treatise printed by Guiot Marchant in Paris in 1493. Based on astrology, these timetables cataloged when individual items reached their peak of flavor and ripeness and when their qualities complemented body humors. A regimen protecting the body from digestive ill forbade summer brussels sprouts and lettuce, fall lamb, winter chard, and spring boar, root crops, stag, and sweets.

In the late 1960s, Eliot Wigginton, a teacher at Rabun's Gap, Georgia, coordinated research among his high school students of the ancestral lore of Appalachian mountaineers, many of British lineage. Their efforts produced a magazine and, in 1972, *The Foxfire Book,* the first of 11 compendia of photos and interviews. The books summarized planting and harvesting by astrological signs and by beliefs about spring tonics from birch bark, cress, morels, nettles, spicebush, and wild garlic and onions. Two favorite salad greens, mustard and pokeweed, allegedly purified the blood. As a healthful drink and basis for candy and jelly, sassafras earned veneration for thinning the blood and strengthening the heart. By drinking the tonic in March, people ensured a year without depression or sickness.

The Curative Diet

Even in the current age, food lore persists as an amalgam of pseudoscience and hope. Curative legends continue to connect red wine with sustaining the vascular system and the Mediterranean diet of cereals, fish, and olive oil with rescuing victims of Alzheimer's disease from mental oblivion. Introductions to Asian cookery emphasize the Ayurvedic combination of rice with dal, the Mongolian and Turk reverence for koumiss (fermented mare's milk) as a cure-all, and the Chinese balance of cold and hot ingredients to preserve *qi* (energy).

A subset of cookbooks and nutritional manuals, self-help kitchen guides introduce trendy food lore. Individual titles proclaim grapefruits for burning fat, garlic and olive oil as miracle medicines, and fish and nuts as brain stimulants. True believers in kitchen lore look to food for prolonging life, the ultimate benefit. The plethora of life extenders is said to include acai, amaranth, buckwheat, goji berries, and zinc-rich almonds, grains, and pumpkin and sunflower seeds. Extreme kitchen handbooks recommend a retreat from animal products through veganism.

See also: Art, Food in; Customs, Food; Film, Food in; Literature, Food in; Taboos, Food; Veganism.

Further Reading

Grotto, David W. *101 Foods That Could Save Your Life!* New York: Bantam, 2011.

McGee, Harold. *On Food and Cooking: The Science and Lore of the Kitchen.* New York: Simon & Schuster, 2004.

McNamee, Gregory. *Movable Feasts: The History, Science, and Lore of Food.* Westport, CT: Praeger, 2007.

Patrick-Goudreau, Colleen. *Vegan's Daily Companion.* Beverly, MA: Quarry, 2011.

Shi, John, Chi-Tang Ho, and Fereidoon Shahidi, eds. *Functional Foods of the East.* Boca Raton, FL: CRC, 2011.

Korean Diet and Cuisine

Based on traditional combinations of fish and meat and vegetables with rice, the Korean diet features the crisp bite of fermented condiments. Developing from simple hunter-gatherer cuisine from 8000 B.C.E., regional cookery depended on available viands, such as burdock, kelp and laver, lotus root, mugwort, mushrooms, scallops, seabird eggs, and silkworm larvae. After 6000 B.C.E., forest dwellers made culinary use of acorns and chestnuts, arrowroot, and turnips. The cuisine acquired an agrarian flair in 1500 B.C.E. from Manchurian immigrants, who introduced the growing and eating of barley, legumes, millet, rice, sorghum, and wheat.

Korean cooks acquired sophisticated means of diversifying taste. Kitchen techniques involved the air-drying of cuttlefish and sardines, the curing of mung and red beans, and the steeping of barley into tea. After 18 B.C.E., cooks of the Baekje realm in southwestern Korea embellished recipes for *kimchi,* a piquant appetite stimulant pickled in brine. Lactobacilli fermented the mix of shredded cucumber, garlic, mustard leaf, napa cabbage, onions, and radishes into versatile digestives. The mix developed zest from curing underground in traditional flat-topped earthenware jars. Communities judged female cookery primarily from the zing of household kimchi.

A shopkeeper in Seoul, South Korea, packs a container with *kimchi*, the national dish. A mix of pungent fermented vegetables (mostly cabbage), kimchi complements almost every meal. Koreans consume some 40 pounds (18 kilograms) per person each year. *(Lee Jin-man/Associated Press)*

Outside Influences

Waves of insurgency impacted Korean gastronomy with unique kitchen methods and flavors. After 300 C.E., Buddhist, Confucian, and Taoist foodways replaced traditional cooking with wholesome grain and vegetarian entrées and ceremonial tea service. An elevation of regional vegetable growers as the nourishers of civilization accompanied a mounting disgust for butchers and meat handlers. By the 900s, Chinese gastronomy dominated the peninsula, promoting hot soups as winter warm-ups and sources of fiber and vitamins.

Ögödei Khan's Mongol invasion in spring 1231 introduced *mandu* (dumpling) and glass-noodle making, grilling, and black pepper as the major condiment. The promotion of agrarianism resulted in early Renaissance manuals, notably *Nongsa Jikseol (Practical Farming, 1429)*, a treatise on grains compiled by state ministers Byeon Hyo-mun and Jeong Cho and translated into Japanese. While the commoner's meal reflected seasonal fare, court dinner tables dramatized a diversity enjoyed only by the privileged, including baby clams, beef brisket, matsutake mushrooms, panfish, ring pheasant, rock tripe, sea bream, and winter melon.

The elite dined five times a day, eating light spreads in the afternoon and before retiring. They began with *miemsang* (breakfast), a serving of *juk* (soupy rice porridge) with additions of abalone, mushrooms, pine nuts, or sesame. Side dishes of oysters fortified the main dish. Main meals in the morning and early evening consisted of heavy casseroles, soups, and stews.

Key to banquet menus, procurements of ancestral bean sprouts and fern shoots, liquor and wine, octopus, pancakes, quail eggs, rice cakes, and sea cucumbers as well as curative herbs and *wakame* (seaweed) kept phalanxes of female cooks occupied. For appetizers, guests wrapped pancakes around strips of bamboo shoot, bellflower root, carrot, mushroom, onion, pine nuts, and shrimp. The final dish, a glutinous rice kneaded with chestnuts, cinnamon, honey, jujubes, pine nuts, soy paste, and sugar, honored guests at birthdays and weddings. Persimmon punch concluded the repast with a gingery, sweet drink high in vitamin C.

Commerce with Europeans, Filipinos, and Okinawans introduced isolated Korean consumers to foods from the Western Hemisphere. In addition to adding corn, squash, sweet potatoes, and tomatoes to recipes, cooks discovered the fiery tang that chili pepper sauce gave to kimchi. By the 1860s, Korean ports welcomed traders from Europe and the United States. Shippers sold upscale grocers liquor from China and spices from Japan.

A 35-year occupation by the Japanese, beginning in 1910, forced Korean smallholders into agribusiness. While earning profits by exporting rice, local farmers grew small kitchen plots of barley and millet for their own pantries. Hard times during the division of the peninsula into North Korea and South Korea in 1948 and during the Korean War in 1950 reduced peasants to subsistence eating to stave off starvation. From U.S. Army supply, cooks acquired canned ham, hot dogs, sausage, and Spam to flavor with chilies and kimchi for a one-pot ragout called *budae jjigae* (army base stew). American cheese and baked beans plus macaroni, soybeans, and tofu turned the dish into an unpredictable catchall.

Self-Sufficiency

A period of prosperity in the 1960s fostered scientific agriculture and the shucking off of Chinese influence. Industrialists profited from food processing, notably the factory canning of kimchi in 1966 for global export. As fish and meat consumption rose and rice eating declined, Koreans realized the health benefits from decreased dietary carbohydrates and salt and more milk products. Families ate more sesame oil, squid jerky, and soft tofu and consumed 400 tons (360 metric tons) of kimchi annually.

Farm experimentation produced new fruits—bananas, kiwi, oranges—to add to Asian pears and strawberries. Restaurants offered table barbecuing of short ribs over a small grill and settings of spoons and thin metal chopsticks for the selection of noodles from soups and bean curds and julienned carrots and celery from salads. Simultaneous with coastal progress, North Koreans suffered a nationwide famine in 1997 that claimed nearly 2 million citizens.

Recipe: Beef Soup

Slice 2 pounds of lean beef into bite-size pieces. Boil with one-half of a *mangchi* (Korean radish) in 4 gallons of water. Simmer for one hour. Remove solids and skim fat from the liquid. Slice the beef and radish into paper-thin sections and return them to the broth with five garlic cloves. Bring the mixture to a boil. Add one large green onion sliced into rings and 4 ounces of egg noodles with black pepper and sea salt to taste. Serve after the noodles soften.

In October 2011, weather crises from flooding and typhoons ruined crops and elevated the prices of staples. The World Food Programme estimated that one-third of preschoolers suffered skin infection and stunted development from malnutrition. According to observations by Mercy Corps, Samaritan's Purse, and World Vision, more than 6 million North Koreans, including pregnant and lactating women, required food aid.

See also: Fermented Foods; Hot Pots; Middens; Pickling; Sausage; Travel Food; Vinegar.

Further Reading

Ling, Kong Foong. *The Food of Asia.* North Clarendon, VT: Tuttle, 2002.

Pettid, Michael J. *Korean Cuisine: An Illustrated History.* London: Reaktion, 2008.

Price, David Clive, and Masano Kawana. *The Food of Korea: Authentic Recipes from the Land of Morning Calm.* North Clarendon, VT: Tuttle, 2002.

Seth, Michael J. *A History of Korea: From Antiquity to the Present.* Lanham, MD: Rowman & Littlefield, 2011.

Kosher Food

Obedience to *kashruth,* Torah dietary law, obligates Jews to follow detailed regimens for food selection and cleanliness. The laws originated in the Bible (Leviticus 11:1–47), during an era when the Israelites kept themselves apart from the Canaanite idol worshippers and child sacrificers who surrounded them. The observant ate ruminants with split hooves—cows, goats, sheep—and meat and roe from finny fish, especially, bass, cod, flounder, halibut, herring, mackerel, trout, and salmon. Jews avoided *treif,* foodstuffs unfit for consumption, including amphibians, camels, carrion eaters, eels, rabbits, shellfish, turtles, and whales. Pigs received a serious injunction because of their propensity for trichinosis infestation.

In the classical era and the Middle Ages, infections from blood and the connection between shellfish and cholera and typhoid fever explained the need for rabbinic inspection of markets to prevent contamination of kosher fish. Jewish butchers followed the specifics of humane slaughter, which required a quick slice to the carotid artery, esophagus, jugular vein, and trachea. Animal death preceded the immediate draining of blood with a kosher salt solution.

Relying on word of mouth, devout Jewish housewives patronized a network of abattoirs, bakeries, delis, fish

Orthodox Jewish rabbis inspect slaughtered chickens at a Jerusalem processing plant. To earn the kosher label, food preparation must follow strict dietary laws. For commercial foods, an inspector certifies the process, equipment, and facilities. *(Paula Bronstein/Getty Images)*

markets, picklers, and wineries governed by respect for scriptural food and sanitation regulations. At home, inspection of grains spared diners from consuming weevils. Orthodox Jews prohibited the mixing of meat and milk in cooking and required separate utensils and vessels for preparing each, as well as separate sets of dishes, kitchen linens, and cutlery. Meticulous observance demanded replacing tablecloths with clean ones between courses as well as hand washing.

Because of the peripatetic history of Judaism, Ashkenazi and Sephardic Jews adapted their foodways through historical culinary borrowing and acquired traditional menus featuring bagels, blintzes, chicken soup, chopped liver, knishes, and matzoh ball soup. In the tenth century, French and Italian clans moved into the Rhine River valley, where scholarly rabbis pondered unavoidable infractions in idiocuisine, the diet and table customs of individual families. During the religious persecutions of the eleventh and twelfth centuries, roasted pig fattened on chestnuts tested the faith of Sephardic Jews who pretended to convert to Catholicism by eating nonkosher foods. Jewish merchants reverted to pragmatism, shuttling through their shops bacon and ham, along with exotic marzipan, nuts, spices, and sugar.

Over the succeeding centuries, distinctly religious communities arose in Germany, Poland, and Russia. Each displayed religious adherence to kosher meals and table spirituality as forms of nonassimilation. After the discovery of the Western Hemisphere, the potato became a favorite, with latkes assuming importance at Hanukkah. In contrast to European Jewry, modern Israeli cuisine made the most changes over time because of mass immigration, yet the nation maintained kosher taboos, including sifting flour to remove insects.

Early twentieth-century Reform Judaism abandoned kosher rules, which tended to isolate Jews within mainstream society, particularly from community events, hospitals, and commercial diners, cafeterias, fast-food eateries, and restaurants. The 15 to 20 percent of U.S. Jews who observed kosher regulations found adequate choices under the company names Del Monte, Green Giant, Hebrew National, La Briute, Lender's, Manischewitz, Maxwell House, and Smuckers, all of which followed the example of Procter & Gamble, which began marketing kosher Crisco in 1912.

Obeying the precepts of the Orthodox Union's Kosher Certification Service, set up in 1935, the obedient avoid carmine dye, chewing gum, gelatin, marshmallows, microwave popcorn, nondairy creamer containing caseinate, yeast, and yogurt. They even purchase kosher food for family pets. Cooks examine artichokes, asparagus, berries, broccoli, brussels sprouts, cauliflower, and leafy vegetables for insect infestation. For travel, serious kosher diners purchase self-heating meals and certified salami and smoked fish.

See also: Cookbooks; Farm Subsidies and Government Agricultural Programs; Poultry; Sauces and Saucing.

Further Reading

Bennett, Todd D. *Kosher.* Herkimer, NY: Shema Yisrael, 2005.

Blech, Zushe Yosef. *Kosher Food Production.* Ames, IA: Wiley-Blackwell, 2008.

Eidlitz, Eliezer. *Is It Kosher?: Encyclopedia of Kosher Foods, Facts and Fallacies.* Nanuet, NY: Feldheim, 2004.

Fishkoff, Sue. *Kosher Nation.* New York: Random House, 2010.

Garfunkel, Trudy. *Kosher for Everybody: The Complete Guide to Understanding, Shopping, Cooking, and Eating the Kosher Way.* San Francisco: Jossey-Bass, 2004.

La Varenne, Pierre (1615–1678)

A rejuvenator of food writing and French cuisine, François Pierre La Varenne redirected national gastronomy from Italian influence and ushered native cookery into the modern age. A native Burgundian, he relished the clean smells and savors of bay leaf, chervil, parsley, sage, tarragon, and thyme. He studied kitchen work in boyhood and climbed the career ladder from pot boy to king's cloak bearer. Trained in the household of Queen Marie de' Médici, consort of Henry IV of France, La Varenne served for a decade in Chalon-sur-Saône as personal chef of the Marquis of Uxelles.

In his thirties, La Varenne adopted his unexplained pen name and revolutionized the medieval rules for gastronomy in original cookbooks. He abandoned the heavy Arabic spicing introduced during the Crusades and concentrated on cooking fresh artichoke hearts, asparagus, cauliflower, cucumber, and peas. His menus featured fresh fish and meats roasted in their natural juices as well as salads and fruit drinks, which he summarized in 1650 in *Le Confiturier François* (*The Preserves Maker*).

In *Le Cuisinier François* (*The French Cook*, 1651), La Varenne systemized the principles of regional fare. Beginning with stocks, his text presented clear recipe ingredients and temperatures, cross-references, and alphabetic indexing. Avoiding issues of dietetics and health foods, he wrote strictly about *haut goût* (full flavor). He codified methods of creating béchamel sauce, bisque, bouillon, coulis (puree), a rudimentary hollandaise from creamery butter, and a Barbe Robert (brown mustard sauce) for topping duck, eggs, fried fish, and roast hare. His detailed instruction covers the bundling of herbs into a *bouquet garni* (garnished bouquet) for accentuating reductions, soups, and stock.

La Varenne followed with an overview of pastry in *Le Pâtissier François* (*The French Pastry Maker*, 1653) and an omnibus edition of all three of his compilations, which suited a range of needs in army camps and the kitchens of beginning cooks. He appealed to the amateur by speaking in first person of his own culinary experiences. His precise vocabulary standardized gastronomic terms, including *au naturel* (unsauced), *boeuf à la mode* (pot roast), *oeufs à la neige* (floating island pudding), *poissons au bleu* (rare fish), and ragout.

To rescue dishes from the heavy animal fats that disguised natural flavors, La Varenne stressed butter as a clean fat. He popularized roux, a versatile fried-flour basis for gravies and sauces that replaced the medieval dependence on bread crumbs. He validated Renaissance sweet-and-sour toppings and originated duxelles sauce and a meatless *poivrade* (pepper sauce) from citrus peel, onion, pepper, salt, and vinegar. His menus banished exotica—pheasant, swan, and whale—and concentrated on cuts of meat, poultry, and salmon subtly sauced with capers and herbs.

The chef married well, to the eldest daughter of the Count de Tessé, a military hero. Renowned and wealthy, La Varenne retired to Dijon. At age 63, he died of a four-day fever. Significantly, his texts were the first French cookbooks translated into English. Still in print in 1815, his kitchen tutorials thrived in 30 editions, translations, and pirated versions. His philosophy of light, flavorful cuisine influenced Georges Auguste Escoffier and Julia Child.

See also: Bouillon; French Diet and Cuisine; Pan-European Diet and Cuisine; Sauces and Saucing.

Further Reading

Albala, Ken. *Food in Early Modern Europe*. Westport, CT: Greenwood, 2003.

DeJean, Joan. *The Essence of Style: How the French Invented High Fashion, Fine Food, Chic Cafés, Style, Sophistication, and Glamour*. New York: Free Press, 2005.

Freedman, Paul H. *Food: The History of Taste*. Berkeley: University of California Press, 2007.

La Varenne, François Pierre de. *The French Cook*. Lewes, UK: Southover, 2001.

Language, Food

Fortunately for culinary history, worthy individuals have applied themselves to the collection and recording of gastronomic terminology. In 1900 B.C.E., a Mesopotamian scholar compiled a bilingual Sumerian-Akkadian dictionary on 24 stone tablets. Written in cuneiform script, the text named 800 table items, including 300 types of bread, 100 soups, and 20 cheeses. Additional details from kitchen deliveries at Ur characterized ducks, fresh water fish, geese, lambs, pigeons, and piglets. These lists glimpse the sophistication of the Mesopotamian, leading culinary historians to conclude that the region enjoyed a diverse menu.

Medieval wordsmiths of the quality of Alpharabius and John of Garland compiled words that explained one culture to another. One literary antiquarian, Thomas Wright, a Quaker scholar of Trinity College, Cambridge, compiled the *History of Domestic Manners and Sentiments in England during the Middle Ages* (1862), which cataloged the Anglo-Saxon terms for common objects: *bolla* (bowl), *crocca* (crock), and *disc* (dish). Wright's contribution prefaced the massive effort begun in 1879 by Sir James Murray, who headed a scholarly compilation of the *Oxford English Dictionary* (OED), also called the *New English Dictionary* (1928), a definitive historical dictionary of the English language in 12 volumes, with a one-volume supplement.

French Influence

After the arrival of Christianity to the British Isles in 597 C.E., English acquired more pantry terms (beet, lentil, lobster, millet, mussel, oyster, and radish) plus plant and herbal terms (aloe, balsam, fennel, hyssop, mallow, pine, rue, and savory). From Scandinavian invaders, the language picked up bull, calf, egg, and steak. The greatest influx of new thoughts and terms arrived with William the Conqueror after the Battle of Hastings in 1066, when Norman invaders brought with them dining styles—collation, dinner, feast, mess, repast, and supper. Specifics enhanced the language with types of fish (bream, mackerel, perch, salmon, sardine, sole, and sturgeon) and types of meat (beef, chine, haunch, loin, mutton, pork, sausage, tripe, veal, and venison).

A rush of Norman vocabulary to the table named meaty dishes (brawn for boar meat and gravy), grain dishes (gruel and pottage), and birds (fowl, partridge, pheasant, pigeon, poultry, pullet, and quail). The baker named his breads biscuit, pastry, and toast; the greengrocer identified plant foods as almond, cherry, date, endive, fig, fruit, grape, lemon, lettuce, orange, peach, and raisin. Shopkeepers dispensed condiments (mustard and vinegar), herbs and spices (cinnamon, marjoram, and nutmeg), and sweets (confection, jelly, tart, and treacle). Also from Normandy came names of basic kitchen techniques, such as blanch, boil, force, fry, grate, mince, roast, scald, stew, quarter, and table vessels, including the basin, cauldron, cruet, goblet, plate, platter, and saucer.

Linguistic Mixing

The intricacies of word introduction extended beyond wars and power shifts to less dramatic borrowings, as with the Teutonic ale, bread, milk, and salt; the low German gherkin; and the Dutch cookie, cranberry, and cruller. Still expanding and redefining itself, the language picked up from the French aperitif, Camembert, consommé, chocolate, and tomato and from Spanish and Portuguese anchovy, apricot, banana, cocoa, marmalade, potato, rusk,

sarsaparilla, and yam. From Mexico came avocado and chili; from the West Indies, barbecue and maize. High German added noodle, pretzel, and sauerkraut. Peruvian Quechua speakers coined jerky; Brazil provided cayenne and tapioca. India supplied curry, mango, punch, and toddy. Africa offered food terms from a variety of the continent's languages: *kaffe*/coffee (Ethiopian), *kingombo*/gumbo (Tshiluba), *nguba*/goober (Bantu), *nyami*/yam (Fulani), and *okuru*/okra (Igbo). Additional driblets came from the Chinese (chop suey), Dutch (coleslaw), Magyar (goulash), Maori (kiwi), Mongolians (koumiss), Persians (pilaf), Turkish (sherbet), Yiddish (nosh), and the English, who named the sandwich after an earl.

North American English offered native vocabulary—hickory, hominy, pecan, pemmican, pone, squash, succotash, terrapin—and the lusty American dialect terms apple butter, hoecake, and popcorn. Subsequent tradings, either directly with foreign cultures or indirectly through American English, produced the Japanese hibachi and sashimi, Polynesian *poi* and taro, Brazilian manioc, Scandinavian smorgasbord, Turkish shish kebab, and Chinese chow mein, dim sum, kumquat, lychee, tea, and wok.

Century by century, the power and expressiveness of English burgeoned with marzipan, melon, mushroom, and pineapple in the 1500s, and with caviar, macaroni, omelette, and scone in the 1600s. By 1700, English welcomed muffin, paté, salmagundi, and yogurt. The 1800s added béchamel (white sauce), hors d'oeuvre, ice cream, kipper, meringue, soufflé, and spaghetti. The twentieth century exploded with methods (food processor, microwave, and taqueria) and fast foods (crepe, hamburger, pizza, and tostados).

Unique Terms

The *Oxford English Dictionary* (OED) enlightens twenty-first-century readers on food and dining history long in the English-speaking past, such as the derivation of *lady* from the Saxon *hlaefdige* (loaf kneader) and *lord* from *hlaefward* (loaf keeper). One example, the posset, puzzles a generation unfamiliar with the combination of spirits with hot milk to produce a substantial hearthside drink for entertaining as well as a bedtime remedy for chills and colds. Another, the kickshaw, which Joseph Addison mentioned in 1709 in the *Tatler,* is an anglicized version of the French *quelque chose* (something), an offhand term denoting a little dish of sweetmeats, dainties, or trifles cooked up for company. English food expert Hannah Glasse, author of *The Art of Cookery Made Plain and Easy: Excelling Any Thing of the Kind Ever Yet Published* (1747), applied kickshaw to a fruit pie eaten out of the hand.

The *OED* also accounts for eponyms, such as *negus,* a flavored wine named for eighteen-century Colonel Francis Negus, and *graham flour,* bearing the name of nineteenth-century food faddist and reformer Sylvester Graham. One cook who made the pages of the *OED* was Sally Lunn, an Englishwoman of the late 1700s who created a warm, crumbly yeast bread bearing her name. As a culinary business, she hawked her bread in the streets of Bath, a fashionable spa.

The *OED* preserves a variety of categories of culinary vocabulary along with shades of meaning, alternate spellings, and either an exact derivation, a surmise, or a blank.

Word	Original Meaning	Language of Origin
avocado	testicle	Nahuatl
baxter	baker	Old English
brake	kneading machine	Dutch
brewer	ale maker	Old English from Indo-European root
butter	cow	Scythian
candy	sugar	Sanskrit
cayman	water spirit	Arawakan
chowder	boil	French
coconut	skull	Portuguese
hominy	treated food	Algonquin
ketchup	fish sauce	Cantonese
mayonnaise	capital of Minorca	French
midden	dung hill	Danish
must	fresh	Latin
orange	orange tree	Arabic from Sanskrit
peel	baker's shovel	Latin
sashimi	pierce the flesh	Japanese
tart	bread	Late Latin
toddy	palmyra palm	Hindi
whiskey	water of life	Old Irish

See also: Literature, Food in; Pennsylvania Dutch Diet and Cuisine; Tea.

Further Reading

Durkin, Philip. *The Oxford Guide to Etymology.* New York: Oxford University Press, 2009.

Katz, Solomon H., and William Woys Weaver, eds. *Encyclopedia of Food and Culture.* New York: Charles Scribner's Sons, 2003.

Skeat, Walter William. *A Concise Etymological Dictionary of the English Language.* New York: Cosimo, 2005.

Toussaint-Samat, Maguelonne. *A History of Food.* Hoboken, NJ: Wiley-Blackwell, 2009.

Lapérouse, Jean François Galaup (1741–ca. 1788)

A forerunner of French colonialists, sea captain and explorer Jean François de Galaup, Count de Lapérouse (or La Pérouse), acquainted the Western world with the native foods and diet of Pacific Coast aborigines. By refraining from military intervention in aboriginal life, he and his staff composed valuable observations of island and coastal lifestyles from Tierra del Fuego to New Zealand, where natives ate uncooked herbs and meat to symbolize the elements of the wild.

Born at Albi in south-central France on August 23, 1741, to the Galaup clan, Lapérouse added his family's holdings at La Pérouse to his name as a patronym and reduced the name to one word. After study at Albi's Jesuit monastery school, he completed naval training at Brest in 1756 and, as a midshipman, made a first voyage to supply the French fort at Louisbourg, Nova Scotia.

A subsequent delivery of goods to the French placed him in danger of British shore patrols. At age 18, he survived two battle wounds and a year's imprisonment until his exchange. Courage in additional Atlantic and Arctic naval battles, waged to disrupt British fishing off Newfoundland, boosted his rank to commodore.

During the age of enlightenment, at age 44, Lapérouse led a humanitarian fact-finding expedition circumnavigating the globe, following the path of the British navigator and explorer Captain James Cook, whom a Hawaiian warrior murdered in 1779. To compete with the British for world wealth, King Louis XVI in 1785 instructed Lapérouse to establish trade routes to new markets and to redraw maps of sea-lanes based on sightings of island clusters and shorelines. In addition, the crew searched for unidentified atolls that dotted a flawed Spanish chart, while an academic coterie collected forage plants, fruits, and vegetables to propagate in France.

In exchange for new flora, under royal instruction, scientists carried the seeds of beets, cabbages, carrots, corn, and pumpkins to enrich the diet of Pacific nations. From the Société d'Histoire Naturelle de Paris, Lapérouse received instructions on the types of foodstuffs to collect and methods of packaging and cataloguing seeds with Chinese characters as well as common and Linnaean binomial classifications. The botanists marked mysterious biota *inconnu* (unknown) and left to experts a formal identification. Among his missions, Lapérouse compiled reports on agriculture, fur trading, native nutrition and health, and Pacific whaling.

The Sailor's Diet

Aboard the 500-ton (450-metric-ton) *La Boussole* on August 1, 1785, Commander Lapérouse preceded Captain Leuriot de Langle in *l'Astrolabe* on the combination business and scientific mission to uncharted Pacific territory. To supply a diverse company of sailors and specialists, Lapérouse stocked the two ships with cows, hens, pigs, sheep, and hay as well as sacks of beans, cabbages, flour, fruit, greens, and potatoes. He also filled the pantry with dried fruit, molasses, and malt and spruce essence, all scurvy preventatives.

On Lapérouse's departure, agronomist Jean-Nicolas Collignon, supervisor of the king's gardens, loaded cuttings, roots, and seeds for dispersal of European flora about the Pacific to benefit natives with a more varied choice of nutritious foods. He selected apple and pear kernels and the pits and stones of almond, apricot, cherry, currant, gooseberry, grape, melon, peach, and plum. He also loaded artichokes, celery, chervil, grain, peppers, and root crops—beets, carrots, garlic, onions, parsnips, potatoes, radishes, and turnips. Aboard *La Boussole*, the gardener assembled for distribution a miniature forest of chestnut and fig cuttings, grapevines, quince bushes, and stone fruit and olive trees.

The 220 crewmen survived scurvy by adopting Captain Cook's antiscorbutic diet. One of Lapérouse's provisioners stocked up on chocolate, lemon concentrate, and 100 tablets of antiscorbutic broth of sauerkraut. At the first sign of nutritional deficiency, the captain secured flour, meat, wheat, and fresh vegetables, including white beans, a dried legume that stored well at sea. West of Morocco at Madeira, he laid in stores of candied lemons, Malmsey wine, and rum. His mariners gladly went ashore to collect celery, onions, and sorrel along streams in the coves and caught cod, flying fish, herring, plaice, salmon, and trout to cook with herbs. In his journals, Lapérouse singled out fresh produce as a basic health need of shipmen and added that he kept salt pork and sea biscuit locked up from the mess cook to serve in emergencies. His comments about the weakening of mariners' strength indicate his concern for the crew's well-being and efficiency.

Pacific Landfalls

The route took the 220 expeditioners west around Cape Horn to Concepción Bay, Chile. In January 1786, Collignon brought European hybrid potatoes back to their New World origin and exchanged them with Chileans for bananas and a variety of vegetables and for the seeds of cotton, lemons, and oranges. He also gathered three types of artemisia, nightshade, starwort, and yarrow for use in beverages, medicines, and salads. The crew sampled Pacific shellfish—abalone, turban snail, and whelk—before sailing northwest in March. Crucial to the survey of valuable flora, the staff's insistence on scholarly notes and drawings resulted in corrections of botanist Louis Feuillée's compendium *Histoire des Plantes Médicinales* (*History of Medicinal Plants*, 1714–1725).

On April 9, 1786, the two ships reached Easter Island, where Lapérouse offered stockmen European goats, pigs, and sheep and seeds for agricultural cultivation. Dr. Rollin, the *Boussole*'s chief surgeon, outlined a limited island diet of bananas, chicken, fish, seaweed, sugarcane, sweet potatoes, and yams. To increase dietary variety, Collignon sowed gardens with vegetable seeds and planted orchards with European stock.

To the northwest at the Sandwich Islands (present-day Hawaiian Islands) on May 29, 1786, Lapérouse became the first outsider to survey Maui. While harsh weather kept the two ships offshore, sailors, reduced to one bottle of water per day, looked out on gushing waterfalls and banana trees. According to Dr. Rollin at Keone'o'io Bay, Hawaiian traders approached the ships in 200 canoes loaded with gifts of bananas, coconuts, pigs, and vegetables. While Lapérouse traded with islanders for calabashes, Rollin observed serious human health problems, notably elephantiasis, leprosy, psoriasis, and venereal disease, as well as swine afflicted with tubercles that rendered the pork inedible.

During exploration of the Canadian coast from the Yukon as far south as British Columbia, at Alaska on June 23, 1786, the expeditioners encountered the Tlingit. In contrast to the ill health of Hawaiians, the robustness of the Tlingit appeared to derive from meals of salmon and trout balanced with food plants—chicory and wild celery—and woods fruit, particularly elderberries, gooseberries, raspberries, and strawberries. From the profusion of pelts from bear, beaver, ermine, fox, lynx, marmot, marten, otter, seal, and squirrel, Lapérouse deduced that meat protein dominated the aboriginal diet. As an antidote to scurvy from a deficiency of vitamin C, the Indians added mimulus and sorrel to their meat soups.

The captain predicted that a harsh winter would reduce the shore people of Lituya Bay to inactivity and near starvation. Thus, hunger would leave them vulnerable to an excess of alcoholic beverages and quarrels over gambling.

Mission Indians

Continuing south, the captain docked at Monterey, California, on September 14, 1786, and perused the tribes domesticated by Franciscan missionaries dispatched to Alta California by Father Junípero Serra of Majorca. Because of transportation problems from the warehouses at San Blas, the missions endured late shipments and rotted or spoiled goods. Lapérouse considered the region a likely place to donate seeds from Paris and bags of Chilean potatoes.

The generosity of the Indians impressed the visitors. The aborigines fleshed out the mission's diet of milk and pea gruel with fresh deer and elk. Monterey Bay supplied the natives with salmon, smelt, and trout as well as abalone, clams, ducks, geese, mussels, seals, sea otters, and whales. In a land of "inexpressible fertility," Lapérouse admired the hunter-gatherers for avoiding the rigors of plowing and planting wheat. He observed the importance of shared food to native life, including acorns, berries, bulbs, dried venison, greens, pine nuts, and seeds. His list of common staples strayed to grasshoppers, mice, songbirds, and squirrels—foodstuffs that Europeans classed as inedibles or vermin.

In defiance of the Franciscans' low opinion of Mission Indians, Lapérouse describes gathered tribes as energetic and adept at food preparation. Women commandeered the caching, drying, shelling, and cooking of acorns, the chief carbohydrate. Intense cleaning concluded with eight

Recipe: Tuolumne Acorn Stew

Dry and peel black oak or tan oak acorns. Rinse the nutmeat repeatedly with spring water, draining through a filter until all bitterness is leached out. Allow the nutmeat to dry and grind it in a mortar with pestle. Simmer 2 pounds of venison or venison jerky with marrow bones in 1 quart of water until the meat separates. Remove the meat and chop fine. To the broth, stir in 1 cup ground acorn meal. Return chopped venison to the broth. Simmer and stir until the mixture thickens and turns creamy white, flecked with yellow. Flavor with chopped nasturtium petals, peppers, or wild celery, garlic, or onions. Season with pepper and sea salt.

to ten hours of leaching and draining through cedar boughs to remove tannic toxicity and bitterness. Female workers followed by pounding and sifting the gluten-free acorn flour. Lapérouse's journal refers to the beauty and sophistication of their acorn soup preparations, which required stone boiling, the dropping of heated stones into mixtures to heat them.

He refers to ritualized reciprocity as a form of group security. His comments note that Spanish missionaries appealed to natives by sharing exotic European food, such as cow's milk and boiled barley gruel, an Indian favorite they called atole. Native women tried to reproduce the technique of roasting grain. In place of clay and metal pots, they used bark baskets set over small fire pits.

The Western Pacific

In September 1786, Lapérouse stocked his ships' stores with milk, mission chickens, and vegetables and set sail from California west toward southern China. On January 3, 1787, he arrived at the Portuguese colony at Macao to trade Alaskan furs in a Cantonese market already glutted with otter pelts. During the brief layover, Collignon shipped two tin boxes of plant matter and seeds to André Thouin, head gardener of the Jardin des Plantes in Paris. Thouin was particularly eager to acquire breadfruit saplings for transplant to Isle de France (present-day St. Bart's) and other French colonies as a vegetable ensuring human survival. On February 28, 1787, Lapérouse crossed the South China Sea and approached Manila Bay, where he mailed home to France the first installment of his observations, *Voyage de La Pérouse Autour du Monde* (*Lapérouse's Voyage Around the World,* 1797).

In May, Lapérouse sailed north up the East China Sea to Korea and Japan. Among eastern Asians, he observed the common pattern of eating from wood bowls with "little sticks," his term for chopsticks. Because of

their shared dining habits, he deduced that East Asians claimed a common origin.

From the Ainu, Japanese aborigines, he acquired maps of Sakhalin, Hokkaido, and the Kuril Islands. Lapérouse's French crew enjoyed regular shore meals of salmon, which they paid for with gifts of alcohol and tobacco. The commander determined to buy little dried or smoked meat, lest he cause the Ainu to starve during winter. The men observed the local use of angelica, dried yellow lily roots, and wild garlic and onions as vegetable flavorings for the meat-heavy Ainu diet. Lapérouse discovered that the shore people ate only the head, spine, and tail of fish and reserved the flanks to smoke or dry and sell once a year to the Manchus who ruled China. The beaching of whales set the people to digging trenches and sinking tubs to collect oil from the rotting carcasses. Because of the dominance of seafood preparation and the garnering of fish oil in animal stomachs and bladders, a fishy stench permeated Ainu kitchens and sleeping quarters.

From Japan to Russia and Samoa

After sailing north through the Bering Strait to Kamchatka, Russia, Lapérouse examined the limited fare of Cossacks and Russians. He found officers growing little patches of potatoes and turnips, an adaptable pair of vegetables for a rough terrain. Hunter-gatherers added cloudberries, cranberries, crowberries, raspberries, whortleberries, and wild garlic to a diet dominated by dried and raw salmon and trout. Favorites included a garlic beverage or sweet herb brandy, loaves of rye bread, and putrified salmon that had been buried in the ground.

Because Russian ports iced over in winter, the commander on October 7, 1787, sent interpreter and diplomat Jean Baptiste Barthélemy de Lesseps overland by sleigh, horseback, and carriage through Siberia to the French court with letters, charts, and reports. Ironically, de Lesseps saved valuable data from the doomed expedition, which never returned home.

Because the French expedition failed to locate a northwest passage to Hudson's Bay, Canada, royal instructions redirected Lapérouse southeast to New South Wales, Australia, via Samoa and Tonga. In view of lean larders, he rejoiced with his men in the catching of eight bonito and later, a curlew and two sharks, as a relief from monotonous shipboard cookery. To make the curlew edible, the ship's cook stewed it in wine into a salmi, a highly flavored ragout of roast bird and mushrooms.

Upon arrival at Samoa on December 6, 1787, the expedition welcomed trade in coconuts for glass beads and iron items. For each food plant the botanists sampled, Samoans collected one bead. At the Tonga Islands, traders in rickety pirogues bartered for axes, iron, and nails with bananas and coconuts, but no meat. Lapérouse wrote in his journal that islanders lived well off a "pleasant variety" of bananas, breadfruit, chickens, coconut, dogs, guavas, oranges, and pigs.

At Botany Bay, Australia, on January 24, 1788, Lapérouse felt at home among fellow Europeans on the far side of the globe. During a six-week layover, he built a stockade and observatory and dug and built two longboats. In the spirit of agricultural exchange, he seeded an experimental vegetable garden, which was still in use a decade later, when British soldiers tended the rows. Lapérouse received British hospitality and dispatched letters and journals to France in care of the HMS *Sirius*.

Lapérouse's two frigates set out for the Solomon Islands on March 10, 1788, and disappeared in June. The ships wrecked in the New Hebrides at Vanikoro, where cannibals savaged the survivors. The combined knowledge of the expedition's intellectuals—botanists, cartographers, engineers, geographers, linguists, mathematicians, naturalists, physicians, plant illustrators, and ships' surgeons—disappeared with the crew. Letters, dispatches, and journals, the historical survivors of the altruistic food exchange, reached Louis XVI on October 17, 1788, and preserved details of the French survey of unknown people and their cuisine.

See also: Cook, James.

Further Reading

Dunmore, John. *Where Fate Beckons: The Life of Jean-François de la Pérouse.* Fairbanks: University of Alaska Press, 2007.

Rigby, Nigel, Pieter van der Merwe, and Glyndwr Williams. *Pioneers of the Pacific: Voyages of Exploration, 1787–1810.* Anchorage: University of Alaska Press, 2005.

Williams, Roger L. *French Botany in the Enlightenment: The Ill-fated Voyages of La Pérouse and His Rescuers.* Dordrecht, Holland: Kluwer, 2003.

Larousse Gastronomique

An encyclopedia of food and French cooking history and techniques, the *Larousse Gastronomique* extended into the 1900s the haute cuisine of the previous century. The work of compiler and food expert Prosper Montagné, the 1938 edition exhibited the quality training and experience that he received in hotel restaurants in Brussels, Monte Carlo, Paris, and San Remo. He gave demonstrations at Le Cordon Bleu and wrote about food and tourism for *L'Art Culinaire* and *Revue Culinaire.*

In 1885, Montagné's practical knowledge of dietetics, etiquette, taste, temperature, and appearance convinced him at age 20 to abandon the baroque pastries garnished with congealed mutton fat, silver ornaments, and wax flowers. He recognized the flawed objectives in the architectural *pièce montée* (mounted display) that turned ingredients into decor rather than edibles. After some persuasion, Georges Auguste Escoffier, the "Father of

Modern French Cuisine," agreed that table panache did not guarantee delicious food.

The privations of World War I further convinced France's top chefs of the centrality of seasonality, simplicity, and taste to the *fonds de cuisine* (basics of cooking). On field tours of army kitchens in 1917, Montagné tasted ragouts and soups and chided camp cooks for wasting peapods and the tops of carrots, radishes, and turnips as sources of flavor. He stressed the value of fresh fruits and vegetables at the height of flavor.

In 1.3 million words written in longhand from 1933 to 1937, Montagné took a scholarly approach to culinary history, which he entrusted to former writing partner Philéas Gilbert, editor of *L'Art Culinaire*. Escoffier provided a preface and noted Montagné's liberal use of recipes and text from Escoffier's monumental text *Le Guide Culinaire* (1903), a comprehensive compilation of over 5,000 recipes.

Montagné's entries clarified cooking terms and advanced techniques—bisque, farci, fraisage, *galantine,* marmite—and provided biographies of chefs and commentary on the purchase and storage of foodstuffs for 8,500 recipes. His minutia of beer making and meat curing and the effects of poisonous mushrooms challenged the specialty works of his day. Illustrations included 2,000 drawings and maps and 16 color plates. For his professional vision and historical perspective, Montagné received a Legion of Honor award.

Larousse Gastronomique first appeared in American and British English in 1961 under the editorship of Nina Froud of London and Charlotte Turgeon of Massachusetts. The editors reapportioned metric measures of ingredients and juggled terms, such as *courgette,* into the American *squash* and British *marrow.* The edition maintained the oddities of Montagné's version, which described cooking eggs in sherry and marinating young camel's feet in vinaigrette.

A second edition of *Larousse Gastronomique,* edited by Jennifer Harvey Land and issued in 1988, reflected culinary advances with 900 color photos and 70 black-and-white illustrations. It preceded a longer updated version in 2001 and an abridged edition in 2003. To maintain the work's reputation as the ultimate reference source on cookery, editor Patrice Maubourguet assembled a consulting staff to ensure the authenticity of such details as butchering poultry and employing rare kitchen tools. The 2001 text and its 1,350 pages and 400 photographs reflect an appreciation of the evolution of a diverse global cuisine.

The 2001 index lists 45 biographies of chefs and 64 comments on cafés and restaurants, 59 percent of which operated at Paris locations. The 106 entries on wines cover regional vintages from the Balkans, Georgia, Hungary, Lebanon, New Zealand, and South Africa. Familiar foodstuffs include the less-known eddo, lapwing, *potimarron,* and prickly pear. A catalog of some 3,500 recipes incorporates world favorites, from dolmas, fiddlehead fern, Kurdish lamb, Mikado salad, and tabbouleh to

American barbecue, cranberry sauce, and jambalaya. In a critique of the finished product, chef Sheila Lukins declared, "*Larousse* sets the standard."

See also: Cookbooks; French Diet and Cuisine; Haute Cuisine.

Further Reading

Kurlansky, Mark, ed. *Choice Cuts: A Savory Selection of Food Writing from Around the World and Throughout History.* New York: Penguin, 2002.

Montagné, Prosper. *Larousse Gastronomique: The World's Greatest Culinary Encyclopedia.* Ed. Jennifer Harvey Lang. 3rd ed. New York: Clarkson Potter, 2001.

Prince, Rose. "The French Cooking Bible Is Back—and Bigger Than Ever." *The Telegraph* (London), October 20, 2009.

Robuchon, Joel. *New Concise Larousse Gastronomique: The World's Greatest Cookery Encyclopedia.* London: Hamlyn, 2007.

Las Casas, Bartolomé de (ca. 1484–1566)

A Dominican priest and chronicler of Spanish history, Bartolomé de Las Casas surveyed and defended the lifestyle of Indians from Cuba to Peru.

A native of Seville, Las Casas sailed at age 18 to Hispaniola with the 30-ship fleet of the tyrannical Nicolás de Ovando. Upon their arrival at Santo Domingo in 1502, Indians greeted the Spanish with gifts of bread, cooked vegetables, and fish, a harbinger of the purpose of native bondage to feed their enslavers. Las Casas immediately noted that the Spaniards consumed ten times the normal Indian diet.

On Hispaniola (present-day Dominican Republic), the forced labor of some two million shackled aborigines to mine gold and transport it on their backs drew farmers away from fields of *aji* (chili pepper), cassava, garlic, and sweet potatoes. The Indians survived on beans and herbs or starved in corrals as punishment for finding no ores. When laborers died in neck chains, the Spanish lopped off their heads to save the trouble of unlocking them. The women, left to till the fields, produced too little breast milk to keep their infants alive. Sailors carried young girls to their ships to debauch, leaving them to die of hunger and thirst and their remains to be tossed into the sea. According to Las Casas, depopulation from disease and mistreatment reached 90 percent, further depressing food production. While the Spaniards went hungry, the bondsmen died by the thousands from starvation.

During the Ovando expedition, the Spanish initiated the planting of sugarcane through arduous peon cultivation. Las Casas bought slaves, planted crops at his encomienda (plantation) in Cibao in north-central Hispaniola, and fought in Spain's wars against the Taíno. At age 26, he became the first Roman Catholic priest ordained in the New World. He anticipated that he could cultivate highly profitable crops of cloves, ginger, and black pepper on his land. For his atrocities to bondsmen, however, Dominican friars charged enslavers with genocide and denied Las Casas confession for starving his laborers and working them to exhaustion and early death.

In 1513, Las Casas joined in the conquest of Cuba and the massacres of the Ciboney and Guanahatabey. He accepted a second encomienda at Cienfuegos in north-central Cuba and a post as chaplain. Echoing in his ears were the pleas of islanders, "*hambre, hambre*" (hungry, hungry). Lack of Christian charity caused Indians to reject evangelism and despise Catholicism.

From Exploiter to Defender

A conversion to nonviolence in 1514 ended Las Casas's role as an exploiter and enslaver. He evangelized colonists to cease abusing aborigines. Aboard the *Santa María de Socorro,* he repatriated to Spain to dissuade King Ferdinand II of Aragon from imperialism by warning him that Europeans were killing off natives of the Americas. Among the priest's complaints was a list of taxes on 500 Peruvian families in Arequipa: 2,000 baskets of peppers, 1,000 bushels of corn, 1,000 hens, 850 bushels of wheat, 180 sheep, 60 baskets of coca, 40 wolf pelts, and 30 pigs, plus fish, tallow, and voluntary field labor for the Spanish planter.

Las Casas's insightful denunciation of imperialism in *Memorial de Remedios para Las Indias* (*A Treatise on the Remedies for the Indies,* 1516) and *Brevísima relación de la destrucción de las Indias* (*A Short Account of the Devastation of the Indies,* 1542) followed his urging of Holy Roman Emperor Charles V to revoke the privileges of absentee landlords and to abjure Indian press gang agriculture and replace it with black African slavery.

Apostle to the Indians

Las Casas accepted residency in the New World as bishop of Chiapas, Mexico, and protector of Indians. He blamed Christopher Columbus for initiating an Indian tribute system, by which farm drudges fed greedy Spanish colonists. From a scheme of temporary provisioning begun in 1496 grew a permanent bondage of first peoples to their European masters.

Ovando institutionalized the system in December 1503, when he received from Queen Isabella a plan to build plantations in the West Indies. Armed Spaniards robbed the granaries of corn and put Indians to the sword; butcher shops sold the human remains as dog food. In particular, Las Casas resented the enslavement of pearl divers, who lived on cod and corn bread while diving repeatedly in search of oysters and dying of diarrhea, exposure to cold, and lung hemorrhage. In Guatemala, he taught Mayans about Christianity through songs rather than starvation or coercion. As a human rights advocate, he devoted a half century to arguing with Spanish overlords that they could profit more humanely from domination of Central America and the West Indies by treating aborigines as human equals.

The core of Las Casas's arguments in favor of peaceful conversion lay in establishing that Indians maintained civilized, orderly lives. For their knowledge of astronomy, medicine, and writing, in his *Apologética historia sumaria* (ca. 1559), he equated Aztec and Inca pagans with the Greeks and Romans of classical times. In defense of the native diet, he extolled peanuts as more delicious than any Spanish snack and compared them to beans, chickpeas, and peas. For agricultural industry, he commended Hispaniolan sugar mills and admired the Maya of Yucatán for the abundance of their beeswax, honey, and fruit. He praised the Caribbean capsicum, both the long red pepper and the spherical cherry pepper, which became so indispensable to Aztec cookery that cooks featured them in most entrées.

His description of the Taíno mounded fields outlined the swidden system of burning brush to fertilize the soil and the hoeing of hillocks. Laborers pierced each mound with digging sticks to receive cuttings of cassava, which bread makers dried and cooked into loaves on clay griddles. He demeaned Spanish snobbery for rejecting cassava, maize, and yams as kitchen staples and for lamenting the absence of barley, figs and grapes, olives, and wheat, which were unknown in Mesoamerica. In 1542, Las Casas's efforts resulted in the adoption of "New Laws," which ostensibly freed Indians from enslavement and made them Spanish subjects.

See also: Aztec Diet and Cuisine; Cod; Díaz, Bernal.

Further Reading

Castro, Daniel. *Another Face of Empire: Bartolomé de Las Casas, Indigenous Rights, and Ecclesiastical Imperialism.* Durham, NC: Duke University Press, 2007.

Staller, John E., and Michael Carrasco, eds. *Pre-Columbian Foodways: Interdisciplinary Approaches to Food, Culture, and Markets in Ancient Mesoamerica.* New York: Springer, 2010.

Vickery, Paul S. *Bartolomé de Las Casas: Great Prophet of the Americas.* New York: Paulist, 2006.

Liebig, Justus von (1803–1873)

To ease problems of feeding infants and convalescents, German Baron Justus von Liebig, the nineteenth-century founder of physiological chemistry, created foods for the undernourished and emulated breast milk.

A working-class native of Darmstadt, Liebig was the son of Maria Caroline Moser, the Swabian manager of a hardware store, and Johann George Liebig, a dyer and salter. Liebig observed the devastation of 1816, when a volcanic eruption in Indonesia caused decreases in global temperature and widespread food shortages in the Northern Hemisphere, which shaped his career in agricultural chemistry. After apprenticing to a druggist for ten months, he studied at the universities of Bonn and Erlangen. In Paris at age 19 under a grant, he received mentoring from a variety of experts—zoologist Georges Cuvier, physicist Joseph Louis Gay-Lussac, and naturalist Alexander von Humboldt.

In his classroom at the University of Giessen, Liebig introduced the laboratory method of pedagogy. In 1828, he perused French sugar refining and imported foreign methods to Hesse. He continued his eclectic study of food processing in England and Scotland and, in 1840, analyzed the nutrients that passed from the soil into the human digestive tract. From his study of the nitrogen cycle, he improvised nitrogen fertilizer and described his findings in *Chemistry in Its Applications to Agriculture* (1840), one of his 15 textbooks.

After proving that chemistry is the same in living and inorganic substances, Liebig boiled meat into soluble and insoluble constituents and discovered the value of *extractum carnis* (meat juices) to consumptives and patients convalescing from intestinal ills. He made his first batch in 1848 to treat a friend's child recuperating from typhus in Liverpool. At the height of the Industrial Revolution, he foresaw the application of beef extract for Europe's "potato-eaters," factory workers who could not afford meat. For his genius and altruism, he accepted an appointment to chair the German Academy of Sciences in Halle in 1852.

Liebig quantified the value of creatinine and albumin in meat and classified edibles by their makeup of carbohydrates, fats, and oils. He began analyzing coca leaves and mineral waters and manufacturing Extract of Malt, a nutritious food more palatable to children than cod liver oil. In 1865, his Liebig Extract of Meat packagers at Fray Bentos, Uruguay, Buenos Aires, Brazil, and Melbourne, Australia, marketed a beef extract later called Oxo.

The reduction of an entire ox to its essence resulted in eight tins selling for 96 shillings. Reconstituted at the rate of 1 teaspoon per cup of water, the powder made 1,000 bowls of soup, a boon to expeditioners Roald Amundsen, Isabella Lucy Bird, Robert Falcon Scott, Ernest Henry Shackleton, and Henry Morton Stanley. Nursing pioneer Florence Nightingale recommended Oxo for use in hospitals, military kitchens, nurseries and orphanages, prisons, ships' galleys, and workhouses. Within a half century, Oxo and Fray Bentos Corned Beef turned a huge profit and created extra income from the recycling of hides, manure, and tallow.

In the mid-1860s, Liebig's experimentation turned to kitchen essentials, including the best way to steep coffee to preserve both flavor and aroma. In 1865, to create synthetic mother's milk, he began with proportional blends of carbohydrates, fats, and protein in a farinaceous food called Liebig's Soluble Food for Babies. For extra strength to infants failing to thrive, he increased the concentration to twice that of human milk and tested outcomes at Munich's Maternity Hospital and at a British foundling home at Bethnal Green, in northeastern London. Historians have called his introduction of artificial milk the world's largest uncontrolled experiment on humans.

In 1867, Liebig's Registered Concentrated Milk Company in London shipped *Kindersuppe* (artificial mother's milk) to American and European markets at 6 pence per quart. He followed the liquid version with a powder of dried cow's milk, malt and wheat flour, and potassium bicarbonate for reconstitution with milk and water. A eulogy in *The Lancet,* a weekly medical journal published in London, honored the reliever of misery in the poor, sick, and wounded. A letter to another scientific periodical from London, the *Medical Times and Gazette,* in 1877 proclaimed the formulation "a panacea to little children from birth, and in every rank of society."

Sociologists rebutted the praise and charged Liebig with encouraging the separation of mother and child. Nonetheless, Henri Nestlé, a Swiss food processor, employed Liebig's research in baby food. German food processor Carl Heinrich Knorr and Swiss food experimenter Julius Maggi used the biochemist's outcomes to make precooked powdered soups.

See also: Baby Food and Infant Feeding; Dried Food; Markets and Marketing.

Further Reading

Brock, William H. *Justus von Liebig: The Chemical Gatekeeper.* New York: Cambridge University Press, 2002.

Coff, Christian. *The Taste for Ethics: An Ethic of Food Consumption.* New York: Springer, 2006.

Fairlie, Simon. *Meat: A Benign Extravagance.* White River Junction, VT: Chelsea Green, 2010.

Lesch, John E. *The German Chemical Industry in the Twentieth Century.* New York: Springer, 2000.

Shephard, Sue. *Pickled, Potted, and Canned: How the Art and Science of Food Preserving Changed the World.* New York: Simon & Schuster, 2000.

Lind, James (1716–1794)

The concern of Scots physician James Lind for diet and pure drinking water consumed by the Royal Navy improved military well-being, earning him the nickname "Pioneer of Clinical Trials."

Born on October 4, 1716, in Edinburgh, Lind earned a medical degree from Edinburgh University and became a naval surgeon at age 23. He entered practice during an era of heavy food shipments by the British East India Company, which required regular military escorts. During this era, ships at sea longer than one month incurred a high incidence of scurvy, evidenced in achy joints, putrid gums, spotty skin, and weakness.

Lind was appalled by the incidence of scurvy during Commodore George Anson's 1740 round-the-world voyage, during which half of 2,000 crewmen died, 996 of scurvy and four of battle wounds. While assigned to the HMS *Salisbury* in 1747, Lind initiated the Salisbury Experiment, a test of antiscorbutics on twelve sailors through dietary supplements to galley meals of gruel, mutton broth, pudding, and barley with raisins. Lind divided his five control groups into those dosed with lemon and orange juice, herbal barley water with tamarind pulp, vinegar, cider, and seawater.

After only six days of the 14-day study, Lind determined that scurvy—a nutritional disorder first recorded by Hippocrates and described during the Crusades—resulted from a deficiency of vitamin C, or ascorbic acid, a fact that the Chinese had remedied in the fifth century C.E. by supplying sailors with ginger. Lind proposed that he could curb the disease by a similar dietary shift—adding fresh fruits and vegetables to galley meals, particularly dishes and beverages containing citrus fruits and juice. By supplementing a diet dominated by biscuit, dried meat, and salt, he promoted the formation of collagen and tissue synthesis to cure anemia and heal swollen gums, loose teeth, subcutaneous bleeding, and blood-stiffened knees and elbows.

Lind's study had a greater effect on naval provisioning than any other commentary on suitable foods for seagoing crews. He followed it with *On the Most Effectual Means of Preserving the Health of Seamen* (1757), which recommended limited alcohol intake and an upgraded diet as antidotes to stomach upset and seasonal fevers. He named as beneficial foods fresh beef and broth with greens as well as bitter herbs, fish soup seasoned with lime juice, and Indian curries.

In 1758, Lind joined the staff of Portsmouth's Haslar Hospital, treating men of the Royal Navy. From the study of thousands of cases of dysentery, scurvy, and typhus, he began improving shipboard conditions to prevent diminished service, crippling, and death of sailors. He proposed a method of preserving citrus fruit juice in a ship's galley and improved life on ships by advocating delousing and better ventilation below deck. He also invented a system of distillation of seawater for drinking.

After publishing *An Essay on Diseases Incidental to Europeans in Hot Climates* (1768), the world's first handbook on tropical medicine, Lind proposed the stationing of hospital ships in tropical ports. For his concern for the health and hygiene of sailors, he earned the title "Father of Naval Medicine." In 1772, the third edition of Lind's treatise explained the German method of making *zoorkool,* a brineless sauerkraut preserved under a heavy weight, which released its juices.

For nearly 40 years, the Royal Navy remained apathetic to Lind's success with improved diet. At the insistence of Sir Gilbert Blane, naval physician and personal doctor of the prince regent, naval administration altered galley practice in 1795, when the addition of citrus fruit to daily fare virtually obliterated scurvy. The effect immediately improved naval morale and effectiveness. For his clinical study, Lind earned a double knighthood.

When the navy purchasing department began supplying ships with limes from the British West Indies rather than lemons from the Mediterranean, Americans dubbed British sailors "limeys" and their ships "lime-juicers." The Merchant Shipping Act of 1854 applied similar dietary standards for the British merchant marine.

Further Reading

Dear, I.C.B., and Peter Kemp, eds. *The Oxford Companion to Ships and the Sea.* 2nd ed. New York: Oxford University Press, 2005.

Gratzler, Walter Bruno. *Terrors of the Table: The Curious History of Nutrition.* New York: Oxford University Press, 2005.

Merrill, Ray M. *Introduction to Epidemiology.* Sudbury, MA: Jones and Bartlett, 2010.

Linnaeus, Carolus (1707–1778)

Swedish ethnographer and naturalist Carolus Linnaeus, the "Father of Biological Taxonomy" and "Prince of Botanists," systemized the Latinate classification of organisms into a model of the natural order of the universe.

Born Carl von Linné on May 23, 1707, in the peasant community of Stenbrohult in southeastern Sweden, he studied plants and animals from childhood and observed farming and rural food consumption. His father home-schooled him and spoke Latin with his youngest child as a basis for future scholarship. After a year in medical school, Linnaeus entered the University of Uppsala in 1728 to study botany and dietetics and made a field trip to the Sami of Lapland (northern Norway, Finland, and Sweden, and the Kola Peninsula of Russia), where he survived on dried fish and reindeer cheese but missed "spoon food." He concluded that, even without bread, a meat-centered diet is good for health. He recommended sitting lower at the table, cooling food before consuming it, and wearing loose garments, all of which eased the Sami digestion.

Travel enlarged Linnaeus's interests in food. In Dalarna, Sweden, and London, he sampled local foods and developed an appreciation of pure water as a beverage. While attaining advanced study in syphilis treatment in Holland, he published *Systema Naturae* (1735), a classification of living things by genus and species. After three years of practicing medicine, he accepted a staff position at Uppsala in 1741 and selected students to conduct field study on world voyages.

Linnaeus's views on food illustrate his application of botanic principles to bolster diet. He considered bread the noblest food. To strengthen Swedish women, he promoted consumption of chocolate, then sold in drugstores in a mix of ground cocoa, ambergris, cinnamon, sugar, and vanilla. He initiated the description of the food chain, and, in 1753, became the first Swedish civilian to receive a knighthood. Five years later, he issued the tenth edition of his book on nomenclature. In his writings, he urged agriculturists to study the life stages of insects as a means of protecting crops from infestation.

In 1757, Linnaeus turned his attention to causes of famine and informed King Adolf Fredrik of the risks of widespread hunger among commoners. Among his list of 30 edible wild plants, his notes contained suggestions of famine food from arum root and pine bark. His dissertation *De Pane Diaetetico* (*On Bread in the Diet,* 1757) examined the types of biscuits, buns, cakes, flatbread, loaves, pies, and tarts preferred by Swedes. His observations on class differences contrasted the use of wheat by the wealthy and barley and oats by the poor and of the blending of bran, peas, and vetch into soft dough as extenders. His catalog of bread sources listed South African fish bread, American slave bread (corn bread), German potato bread, and millet and sorghum from France and Italy.

Linnaeus detailed classic and foreign bread recipes from Africa, America, and India and the style of milling and storing edible grains to avoid grit and mold in the diet, two sources of gastric complaint. To improve the moisture and flavor of bread, he recommended the addition of currants, egg, and sugar. By choosing the right bread, he believed that consumers could avoid dropsy, flatulence, indigestion, and intestinal disease.

To refine Swedish cuisine, Linneus promoted a natural diet and listed as unnecessary cinnamon, coffee, liquor, nutmeg, raisins, sugar, tea, and wine. In their place, he valued fresh fruit as the best food for the hands and mouth and dry rusks as stimulants to digestion through chewing and salivation. For flavorings, he selected aniseed, coriander, cumin, fennel, and saffron, which improved health and stimulated lactation in breast-feeding mothers.

Linnaeus attempted to add crops to Swedish farms to make the nation less dependent on imports. In 1764, Antoine Nicholas Duchesne initiated an eight-year correspondence with Linnaeus, a series of 107 letters on the unisexual and bisexual nature of plant varieties. After 1766, Linnaeus boosted the popularity of the Chilean strawberry, which the French interplanted with the *Fragaria moschata* and *Fragaria virginiana* varieties at Cherbourg to yield fruit 7 1/2 inches (19 centimeters) in diameter. In 1783, Sir James Edward Smith founded London's Linnaean Society by creating a library of the botanist's specimen collections and writings.

See also: Chocolate; Famine; Frézier, Amédée François.

Further Reading

Blunt, Wilfrid. *Linnaeus: The Compleat Naturalist.* London: Frances Lincoln, 2004.

Ford, Brian J. "The Microscope of Linnaeus and His Blind Spot." *The Microscope* 57:2 (2009): 65–72.

Koerner, Lisbet. *Linnaeus: Nature and Nation.* Cambridge, MA: Harvard University Press, 2001.

Literature, Food in

Because of their contributions to human energy and group activities, food and dining anchor countless scenes and themes in world literature. Like a polite servant, the labor that precedes eating often remains shadowed in the background with only brief, but significant exertions visible to the viewer.

In Book VII of Homer's *Odyssey* (ca. 850 B.C.E.), the epicist glides gracefully past humble domestics as the shipwrecked hero Odysseus enters King Alcinous's palace. Homer honors the 50 royal cook staff for hand milling grain for a throng, a massive chore replicated around the world. As the guest, Odysseus sits idle at the hearth anticipating the arrival of a maid with basin and pitcher for predinner hand washing. The housekeeper who makes cleanliness and food available to royal guests passes him bread, a universal token of bounty and welcome.

Homer stresses the gendering of lives, with men providing wild game, while women remain home waiting to spread a table and serve a meal. Upon Odysseus's returning to his hearth in Ithaca after a 20-year absence, Homer prefaces the homecoming with a rush of staff set a-scurry by Eurycleia, the aged housekeeper. She demands sweeping, table scouring, and the fetching of water to fill wine bowls and cups. Recognizing the words of the king's top servant, 20 women set about preliminary cleaning while the men perform the hearth work by splitting firewood and choosing "three fat porkers" for slaughter, elements of Mediterranean hospitality that permeate the anonymous *Homeric Hymns* (ca. 650 B.C.E.) and stage drama and comedy of the classical period.

Hesiod, the homebody Boeotian poet living some two generations after Homer, wrote less lyrical verse on toil and toiler. Of the hardscrabble farm life in *Works and Days* (ca. 800 B.C.E.), he makes no embellishment or refinement of scarred hands and sweaty brows. Rather, he focuses on the motions of cooks at lifting away heavy lids from jars and opening fresh wine bottles. His poems speak in pictorial flashes of the good servant and the satisfactions of small pleasures in a pantry chock-full of abundance, proof of the farmer's household economy. The farmer's enemies—animals, drought, insects, spoilage—threaten the table with a persistent onslaught. The plaint of the beggar Perses accomplishes nothing, for Hesiod, like Aesop's scold in the fable "The Ant and the Grasshopper" (ca. 31 C.E.), has no pity for the slothful.

Feasts

Traditionally, satiric feast literature, such as the *Satyricon* (ca. 60 C.E.) of Roman novelist Petronius Arbiter, focused on the excesses of gluttons, snobs, and social climbers. Rather than eat for sustenance, spoiled diners assessed menus according to the inclusion of out-of-season fruits and vegetables, exotic sweetbreads, and unprecedented blends of flavors and stuffings. Petronius details table perversities: semihatched peafowl eggs, a hare with wings, and a tray of dishes representing the 12 signs of the zodiac—a ram's head, a bull's testicles and kidneys, wineskins spouting fish sauce into a moat, and the uterus and teats of a virgin sow. At the peak of Trimalchio's feast, the host presents the royal cupbearer and the elegant carving of whole beasts, two emblems of excess that swamped the Roman Empire.

The fall of empires recurs in table scenarios, including the boastful warrior feast in the anonymous epic *Beowulf* (800 C.E.), gluttony and waste during the Qing Empire in Cao Xueqin's (Tsao Hsueh-Chin's) classic Chinese novel *Dream of the Red Chamber* (1791), and the declining Napoleonic regime in Ivan Krylov's Russian fables and William Makepeace Thackeray's *Vanity Fair* (1848). In the final year of the Russian Empire, Muscovite social reformer Alexander Pushkin caricatured the class-conscious posturing of Russian czars Nicholas I and Alexander II. Pushkin's ridicule of the imperial court's banqueting extremes targeted prelates and royalty for alienating citizens and for belittling the peasantry. The unfinished narrative poem *Peter the Great's Feast* (1837) mocks the monarchy's extravagance by implying a lack of dignity in carnivalesque festivities, an insult to Russian culture and husbandry. The parody pictures ordinary citizens as naively expecting only good from the enlightened autocrat.

Hardship

In American literature, food lore has imbued nonfiction and memoir with a fresh appreciation of food getting and meal preparation. In 1903, Southwestern essayist and poet Mary Hunter Austin immortalized the work of Comanche, Mojave, Navajo, Papago, Paiute, Shoshone, and Ute in *The Land of Little Rain,* a lyric study of common toil. The day's survival in Death Valley depends on finding drinkable water. Nomadism demands careful selection of mesquite beans and flour that are unlikely to ferment on the trail. The appeal of supplies turns a crow into a robber capable of stealing bacon and whole potatoes and of competing with human scavengers for berries, chuckwallas (lizards), and turtles. Of fireside labors, Austin surmises that cooking is a form of artistry, just like the weaving of bowls to hold grain and watertight baskets for stew pots.

One of the most graphic descriptions of food service during World War I came from German novelist Erich Maria Remarque's *All Quiet on the Western Front* (1928), a gritty pacifist novel. Refusing to romanticize the soldier's meal, he pictures food as a focus of young infantrymen. Miles from the western front, both rookies and veterans dream of bellies filled with beef and green beans. During good times, the protagonist, Paul Baumer, receives jars of jam from his mother, who denies herself a full plate while treating her son to a taste of home. The jovial camp cook ladles ample stew to precede coffee, simple pleasures that raise spirits and humanize trench warfare.

In lieu of military supplies, Remarque honors the guile of the forager. Men scout out game or fish or liberate a goose from a farmyard. Against the backdrop of aerial bombing and sporadic rattle of machine-gun fire, they pluck, gut, and cook their bird in the middle of the night in amiable communion over the lucky find. The shared job of basting the bird becomes a unifying and assuaging moment. Paul and his fatherly sergeant carry leftovers to a buddy locked in the stockade, a gift that elevates comaraderie through shared food. The good times set into perspective a hideous war and the uncertainty of staying alive on a ravaged landscape.

Repetitive Chores

In 1936, virtuoso American author James Agee paired with photographer Walker Evans for a survey of sharecroppers and migrant farm families in Alabama. The two produced *Let Us Now Praise Famous Men* (1951), a lyric tribute to the bottom rung of the laboring class. For all of its poesy, Agee's scrutiny refuses to flinch from the poverty that reduces the family to the simplest, sparest of mealtime amenities. Text and photos admire the graceful, repetitive "motions, progressions, routines and retracings" of the cook as she sifts flour through a window screen and mixes in lard, salt, soda, and water for biscuits. As though witnessing a fine choreography, Agee and Evans study thin arms and hands and bare feet as the meal maker slices salt pork into a black skillet, breaks eggs, puts chairs to table, and sets out condiments—sorghum, butter, sugar, salt, pepper. The text dramatizes the seriousness of filling the belly before a full day of fieldwork.

Earlier in the twentieth century, Southern authors memorialized the black domestic, the slave/servant who labored as cook, waiter, and surrogate parent across Dixie. In William Faulkner's stream-of-consciousness novel *The Sound and the Fury* (1929), Dilsey the cook becomes the matriarchal bulwark of the gentrified Compsons of Jefferson, Mississippi. Faithful to her employers, even on a holiday, she enters the kitchen on Easter morning, stirs fire in embers, and begins rolling out biscuits on a breadboard. Her rising song overtakes a troubled spirit, causing her to set down the sifter, lift her apron hem, and wipe her hands before shouldering thankless chores.

Food escalates in importance in Margaret Mitchell's *Gone with the Wind* (1936) after Abraham Lincoln frees the slaves and armies rob plantations. Ironically, it is the strength and loyalty of Mammy, the O'Hara family housekeeper, that enable a newly widowed Scarlett O'Hara Hamilton to face feeding an extended family on her gleanings of neighboring farms. Mitchell ennobles two

cook pots, one containing vegetable stew and the other, simmering apples, a meal for nine people that was "hardly enough for two." Like the biblical Ruth scavenging in alien corn, Scarlett continues grubbing up sparse grain and root crops to supply Mammy's larder. In the American West, Fred Gipson, Texas-born author of *Old Yeller* (1956), inadvertently epitomized the work of the wilderness householder. In a *bildungsroman* of 14-year-old Travis Coates, Papa enumerates the unending food chores—cutting wood for the stove, milking cows, and tending pigs. Overall, he reminds Travis of the corn patch, the source of the winter's bread corn. Mama Coates, the unnamed *materfamilias,* rises to a female version of frontier heroism in her role as head of household and mistress of the kitchen. To feed her children on milk, greens, and roots, she tends dairy cows, gathers watercress, and treks "clear over to the Salt Licks" to dig up desert tubers. The image of Mama mastering a blending of corn bread and flour gravy, roasting venison, frying catfish, stewing squirrels, and boiling blackeyed peas suggests the resolve of settlers of the Texas outback to eat well despite hardships.

A new frontier in space influenced the food writing of fantasists Ray Bradbury and Arthur C. Clarke. In Bradbury's *The Martian Chronicles* (1950), a distribution of a matchbox of food pills, defrosted meals from flying icicles, and food tins from a spaceship reduces sustenance to a chore similar to maintenance on mechanical equipment. In *2001: A Space Odyssey* (1968) and *The Fountains of Paradise* (1979), Clarke depicts a similar futuristic feeding of explorers in tubes of prepared food and compressed nutritional tablets, the ultimate in processed meals. The functional nature of satisfying hunger strips mealtime of camaraderie and cultural memory. Bradbury restores the primitive yearning for campfire eating in *Fahrenheit 451* (1953), in which book salvers gather in the wilderness to share wisdom from the past. To Montag, the protagonist, the dissemination of poetry, scripture, and history reminds him of spiritual food from a tree grafted with a dozen species of fruit and yielding leaves to heal nations.

See also: Darwin, Charles; Díaz, Bernal; Ibn Battuta; Polo, Marco; Religion and Food.

Further Reading

Albala, Ken. *Food in Early Modern Europe.* Westport, CT: Greenwood, 2003.

Appelbaum, Robert. *Aguecheek's Beef, Belch's Hiccup, and Other Gastronomic Interjections: Literature, Culture, and Food among the Early Moderns.* Chicago: University of Chicago Press, 2006.

Cary, Nancy, ed. *Hunger and Thirst: Food Literature.* San Diego, CA: San Diego City Works, 2008.

LeBesco, Kathleen, and Peter Naccarato, eds. *Edible Ideologies: Representing Food and Meaning.* Albany: State University of New York Press, 2008.

Livingston, A.W. (1821–1898)

A self-taught hybridizer of heritage cultivars, Alexander Wilmer Livingston in 1870 developed the Paragon tomato, a profitable original food crop.

A seedsman from Reynoldsburg, Ohio, Livingston was born on October 14, 1821, near a stagecoach stop on the National Road to the frontier, where he saw his first wild tomatoes at age ten. Watery and sour, they were ribbed on the outside and hollow at center. After a sketchy education, at age 21 he worked for a local seed grower at the rate of $8 per month. By 1856, he owned the inventory of the Buckeye Garden Seed Company, which he propagated on his own 70 acres (28 hectares) and on 113 leased acres (46 hectares).

Livingston's trial-and-error method called for planting a field in one variety. Instead of stockpiling the best-seeded fruit, he selected plants with the most promising output. After five years of his reproducing a highly variable parent, the Paragon variety, a "sport" or chance cultivar, emerged unexpectedly, as did the subsequent Perfect and Dwarf Stone varieties. At a time when food processors mass-produced peeled tomatoes in cans, the Hummer and the Paragon varieties earned regard for flawless skin and exceptional taste that suited both canners and shippers. Because the Paragon tomato produced shoots that yielded a late field-crop fruit, it soon rivaled the potato in popularity. Seeds sold for 2¢ each, a price suited to the pocketbooks of farmers.

In 1875, the owner and his 25-year-old son Robert launched A.W. Livingston's Sons, a commercial packet seed company advertising "true blue" vegetable seeds in catalogs and the media to hobby growers and retail outlets. His simple instructions explained the sowing of cabbage, corn, field peas, Hubbard squash, lima beans, muskmelon, onion, parsnip, and turnip seeds before setting plants in the garden. In 1876, testimonials poured in.

Relocated to Columbus, Ohio, Livingston promoted the tomato as a focal agrarian moneymaker. The following year, he sold 4,400 boxes of seeds and advised farmers to plant half their acreage in tomatoes. His specific hybridization produced the heirloom Magnus and Ox-heart varieties, the flat-bottomed Perfection, the heavy-bearing Beauty, the meaty Favorite and Lorillard, and the Royal Red, bred for canning whole and remaining solid after cooking. The Potato-Leaf tomato thrived in clay soil and responded to pruning; garden-proud growers liked bragging about the size of the fruit on the New Stone tomato. The Aristocrat and Ignotum varieties grew well in greenhouses, a quality that won the grower cash prizes from the Iowa State Agricultural Society.

An altruist and volunteer teacher at the Ohio Penitentiary, Alex Livingston determined to satisfy the needs of market gardeners and food preservers. After moving to Des Moines, Iowa, in 1880, he studied exhibits at fairs across the country and contributed articles on state-by-state climate and soil variance to *Station Bulletin,* a publication of the New Hampshire Agricultural Experiment Stations.

To achieve a more uniform, flavorful tomato variety, Livingston cross-pollinated plants that yielded smooth-surfaced, soft-core globes. In 1882, he produced the Golden Queen, a medium-sized yellow fruit ideal for slicing. Simultaneously, he developed two sturdy potatoes, the Banner and the Seneca Beauty. His hybridization techniques produced 31 varieties of tomatoes, which he categorized by canners, hothouse varieties, and fruit for ketchup and preserves. In addition, he sold nine types of celery, the Cannon Ball watermelon, and the Evergreen cucumber.

The grower described his stock in *Livingston and the Tomato* (1893), an autobiography and collection of 60 recipes. He particularly recommended the fruit for feeding invalids. For kitchen versatility, he listed recipes for baking, frying, reducing to butter, roasting, stewing, and making into custard, pie, and soup or serving with macaroni. The text remained a farm standard long after his death, on November 11, 1898. By 1901, his sons, Josiah and Robert Livingston, were selling 6.5 tons (5.9 metric tons) of tomato seed annually. Of the 40 tomato varieties introduced by 1910, one-third were Livingston's superior crossbreeds.

A disastrous fire on April 1, 1919, destroyed a Livingston warehouse. Representatives from McCullough's Sons Seed Company in Cincinnati intervened and filled orders to keep the firm in business. Seed savers and collectors have since located documented organic plants, thus reintroducing home gardeners and commercial growers to the mammoth Buckeye State (14.6 inches [37 centimeters] in circumference), the late-keeping Dwarf Aristocrat, the prolific Gold Ball, and the rot-proof Rose Peach, Livingston's most profitable specialty strains of tomatoes.

Recipe: Uncooked Tomato Pickle

In his recipe collection, A.W. Livingston recommends: "Cut one peck of green tomatoes in quarter-inch slices, sprinkle over them one cup of salt, and let them stand 24 hours. Then drain very dry. Slice 12 small onions thin. Mix one small bottle of prepared mustard, two tablespoonfuls of ground cloves, one tablespoonful of ground pepper, and one of allspice. Then into the jar in which the pickle is to be kept, put alternate layers of tomato, spice, and onions until all is packed. Cover with cold vinegar and let them stand until the tomato looks quite clear, when they are ready for use."

His hometown of Reynoldsburg earned the name "Home of the Tomato."

See also: Ketchup.

Further Reading

Smith, Andrew F. *The Tomato in America: Early History, Culture, and Cookery.* Urbana: University of Illinois Press, 2001.

Vaccariello, Linda. "The Perfect Tomato." *Cincinnati Magazine* (July 2001): 58–59, 125–126.

Weaver, William Woys. *Encyclopedia of Food and Culture.* New York: Charles Scribner's Sons, 2003.

Local Food Movement

Begun in the early 2000s, the local food movement encourages consumers to subsist on area harvests of flora and fauna, ideally from within a distance of no more than 100 miles (160 kilometers) or so. Worldwide, local shopping extends a marketing system that dates to the Middle Ages, before monoculture turned rural farming into big business.

Throughout Central America, mobile vendors bring diverse crops to crossroads and villages. At Arles, France, the weekly market introduces natives and tourists to baskets and other local handicrafts as well as area grains and flour, cider, mushrooms, stone fruit jams, and whole fresh fish. Australian shoppers in centralized locations embrace farmhouse cheese, jerky, soda bread, and warrigal greens. In Newfoundland, fresh fish and greenhouse produce draw buyers to produce stands and inns and restaurants, thereby channeling jobs and money into the local economy.

In the United States, in the decade following 1997, farm-to-consumer sales rose by more than 200 percent and increased the amount of local fruits and vegetables purchased for school cafeterias and soup kitchens. Grassroots actions by locavores and ecofeminists reclaimed the farmer's market and popularized heirloom varieties from gleaning programs, roadside stands, neighborhood abattoirs and apiaries, bread co-ops, and pick-your-own farms and orchards, which first flourished in the 1930s and 1940s. At the same time, gardeners found seeds, seedlings, and tubers for growing at home. The Slow Food movement spawned a parallel resurgence in artisanal sausage, goat cheese and milk, herbs, nuts, wild berries, syrup, and free-range chickens and eggs.

In 2002, Helen Clifton, a spokesperson for local foods among the Gitga'at nation at Hartley Bay, British

Food vendors set up a booth at a locally grown, organic produce market in the Bedford-Stuyvesant neighborhood of Brooklyn, New York. A growing number of community gardens and special programs bring fresh local foods to the inner city. *(Chris Hondros/Getty Images)*

Columbia, regretted that family gardening had declined from the 1950s along with food storage of surpluses for lean times. The displacement of native peoples to reservations limited access to traditional plant and animal habitats and to the division of labor by which families harvested and preserved staples from the food web. Children reared on food stamps and government handouts lost contact with an age-old diet. Knowledge and experience of growing, preparing, and preserving food dwindled as the older generation died out. Clifton feared that junk food, boxed macaroni and cheese, bologna, and hamburgers would supplant local produce, seafood, and shellfish at the family table. She urged elders to instruct the younger generation on the availability of a healthful, natural diet on the Pacific shore.

Currently, consumption of regional produce is gaining vocal converts and advocates as vigorous as Helen Clifton. Teachers use street markets as lessons for the young on where food comes from, how it gets to the table, and why processed foods and beverages exacerbate obesity. Under the influence of enthusiasm for tradition, young U.S. homemakers in New England, the Great Lakes, Arizona, California, and the Pacific Northwest promote ancestral dishes and pride in homegrown foodstuffs, such as heirloom tomatoes, homemade wines, and live geese and rabbits raised for the table. Holiday sales connect consumers with those producing Thanksgiving and Christmas poultry and eggs for dyeing at Easter, Halloween pumpkins, and favorite foods for All Souls' Day altars.

In competition with overprocessed, salted, smoked, and dried foods, locavores stress the freshness of seasonal commodities. Face-to-face commerce with growers ensures low overhead of direct-to-consumer sales, which encourage bartering and involve no sales tax. By shortening the supply chain, local commerce improves food security and sanitation. Regional produce requires less transportation, preservation, and packaging and shorter distribution time from producer to buyer. In 2011, in a new twist on locavorism, "invasivores" crusaded for eating invasive species, especially fennel and field mustard in San Francisco, Canada geese and Japanese knotweed in New York, frog's legs and kudzu jelly in the Carolinas, nopales in New Mexico, and lionfish caught off the Florida Keys.

See also: Agriculture; Australian Diet and Cuisine; Child, Julia; Ecofeminism; Heritage Foods; Polynesian Diet and Cuisine; Sicilian Diet and Cuisine; Slow Food; Vegetarianism.

Further Reading

Cobb, Tanya Denckla. *Reclaiming Our Food: How the Grassroots Food Movement Is Changing the Way We Eat.* North Adams, MA: Storey, 2011.
Duram, Leslie A. *Encyclopedia of Organic, Sustainable, and Local Food.* Santa Barbara, CA: ABC-Clio, 2010.
Halweil, Brian. *Home Grown: The Case for Local Food in a Global Market.* Ed. Thomas Prough. Washington, DC: Worldwatch Institute, 2002.
Ryder, Tracy, and Carole Topalian. *Edible: A Celebration of Local Foods.* Hoboken, NJ: John Wiley & Sons, 2010.

London Virginia Company

The London Virginia Company (also called the Virginia Company of London) harvested New World medicinal and food plants to sell in England. It established an English colony north of the Cape Fear River, stretching north to coastal and inland Canada and east to Bermuda.

Chartered by King James I of England on October 26, 1606, the firm promoted an agrarian economy the following December, to be tended by 144 male volunteers. The settlers, made up of volunteers unfamiliar with farming, hunting, and prospecting, lost 40 workers en route. The rest arrived at Cape Henry on the Chesapeake Bay (present-day Virginia Beach, Virginia) on April 26, 1607.

After three weeks of attacks by Algonquin Indians, the arrivals began raising palisades for a triangular fort on Jamestown Island, a deep but swampy port in tidewater Virginia. Hindering community spirit, more native forays by the Paspahegh Indians, the icy winter of 1607–1608, a town fire, dysentery, malaria, and typhus and ill health from poor nutrition, mosquitoes, and brackish water contributed to squabbling and dissension among the English. Pocahontas, the 13-year-old daughter of Chief Powhatan, visited the fort in January 1608, bringing corn and fish every four or five days. The arrival of Admiral Christopher Newport in September 1608 aboard the supply ship *John and Francis* halted the disgruntled colonists before they deserted the bay.

Because of the deft leadership of Captain John Smith, London profiteers boosted investment. In February 1608, he built a trading alliance with Powhatan by swapping blue beads, copper, and iron for beans, corn, squash, and venison. Settlers, indentured to the company for seven years, immediately began producing glass and potash, stockpiling pitch and tar, making beer and wine, cutting cedar posts and walnut wainscoting, digging iron ore, planting corn, collecting clams and mussels, and salting cod, hake, and fish roe. They also harvested two native commodities, sassafras roots and the roots of the vining smilax, called greenbriar, the nation's first forest exports. The English had first received the sassafras root from Mexico in 1536 and compounded it into a licorice-sweet root beer and candy flavoring and into a tonic, oil, powder, or tea to treat eczema, impotence, inflammation, migraine, psoriasis, rheumatism, and syphilis.

English merchant John Frampton translated a Spanish text, Spanish physician and botanist Nicolas Bautista Monardes's *Historia medicinal de las cosas que se traen de*

Recipe: Sassafras Tea

For sassafras tea, hot or cold, collect four young sassafras roots, each about 6 inches long. Remove the bark and wash the inner part. Chop the roots into small pieces and drop into a gallon of boiling water. After cooking for 20 minutes, strain and serve the tea with honey.

nuestras Indias Occidentales, into *Joyfull newes out of the newe founde worlde* (1577), which extolled sassafras as a wonder drug. Doctors so prized sassafras as an Amerindian panacea for arthritis, catarrh, dysentery, ophthalmia, scurvy, and typhus that the market flourished from a "sassafras rush." In 1602, demand boosted the price to £336 per ton. The root had other uses as a smoke, pesticide, and flavoring for liqueurs.

Rescued by Tobacco

From September 1609 to the following May, the "starving time" beset Jamestown, forcing survivors to resort to cannibalism. The arrival of the supply ships *Deliverance* and *Patience* from Bermuda on May 23, 1610, found the sick and malnourished colony reduced from 214 to 60 members and in the process of abandoning the town.

When investors learned of the near collapse of the colony, the London Virginia Company faced £1,000 in debt and complex litigation. Stockholders countered bad publicity with a vigorous propaganda campaign consisting of broadsides, pamphlets, and 27 books advocating pro-Christian proselytizing of Amerindians and hyping pro-English patriotism, tobacco, and capitalism.

Businessman John Rolfe arrived on June 10, 1610, with contraband seeds from Trinidad of a tastier variety of tobacco (*Nicotiana varina*) than wild Virginia strains (*Nicotiana rustica*). In 1612, at Varina Farms up the James River from Jamestown, Rolfe settled and planted the area's first cash crop, which sold for 3 shillings per pound and challenged the dominance of Spanish tobacco. After wedding his garden-savvy wife Pocahontas two years later, Rolfe began promoting commercial tobacco as the company's staple, a trendy smoke. With Sir Walter Raleigh popularizing pipe smoking, 7,000 tobacco shops flourished around greater London and provided excise taxes for the crown amounting to 12 pence per pound.

By late March 1618, the "great migration" boosted the Jamestown populace from 400 to 4,500. The importation of 20 black captives by the Dutch in 1619 introduced agrarian slavery to the New World. Virginia farmers spent their early profits on imported English wives, whose passage cost 150 pounds (68 kilograms) of top-leaf to-bacco each. Called Orinoco tobacco, the crop grew even in the streets and sold well in China, France, Korea, Russia, Spain, and Sweden as a recreational smoke, snuff, a hallucinogen, and a controversial cure for arthritis, epilepsy, and nervous disorders.

New World Economy

By 1620, with the tobacco market from Virginia having grown to 20 tons (18 metric tons) per year, a glut on the sassafras market reduced profits from $140 to $56 per pound. Sir Walter Raleigh, who held the patent on sassafras medicinals, complained of an infringement by explorer Bartholomew Gosnold, who had sailed Cape Cod in 1602 in search of the famed root. Jamestown's trade continued in hazelnuts and in medicinal plants—dittany, fustic (smoketree), ginseng, honey, ipecac, jimsonweed, linseed oil, rapeseed oil, saffron, Virginia snakeroot, sumac, and wax. Physicians and apothecaries arrived at the colony in 1621 to practice their professions and to compound drugs and flavorings from New World flora that ethnographer Thomas Harriot had recommended in his *Briefe and True Report of the New Found Land of Virginia* (1588).

On January 13, 1622, the Jamestown treasurer, John Pory, reported abundant pasturage, deer, turkeys, and wild fruit—five kinds of grapes, cherries, gooseberries, huckleberries, plums, raspberries, and strawberries. He anticipated selling wine as a commodity and received a request for 30 tons (27 metric tons) of sassafras on the return to England of the *Abigail.*

In 1624, the crown rescinded the stockholders' charter, dissolved the London Virginia Company, and made Jamestown a royal settlement. Land values along the Tobacco Coast exploded, creating a demand for property in England's first permanent New World colony. By 1630, planters ventured 30 miles (18 kilometers) up the James River to clear more ground. In 1638, Jamestown advanced to both a burgeoning trading center and North America's first slave market. For a century after the issuance of Nicholas Culpeper's *The English Physitian* (1652), the English continued to demand drugs made from New World plants, including ipecac, rhubarb, sarsaparilla, tobacco, and wild cherry bark.

See also: Cod.

Further Reading

Carbone, Elisa. *Blood on the River: James Town, 1607.* New York: Penguin, 2007.

Craven, Wesley Frank. *The Virginia Company of London, 1606–1624.* Charlottesville: University Press of Virginia, 1957.

Kupperman, Karen Ordahl. *The Jamestown Project.* Cambridge, MA: Harvard University Press, 2007.

Varey, Simon. *Searching for the Secrets of Nature: The Life and Works of Dr. Francisco Hernández.* Stanford, CA: Stanford University Press, 2000.

Luau

From Hawaii to Samoa and Tonga to the Maori of New Zealand, Polynesians developed the luau, a feast or a community celebration of prosperity. The occasion, first reported by Captain James Cook in the 1780s, honored visits from raconteur Robert Louis Stevenson and Prince Alfred of England as well as the launching of a new canoe on Tonga or a military victory, notably, the Tahitian homage to July 14, Bastille Day.

King Kamehameha II introduced the custom on Maui in early November 1819 by abandoning royal privilege. He abolished the separation of genders at banquets and sat on the floor alongside female guests sharing delicacies that taboos once denied to commoners. Kamehameha III hosted the largest luau on July 31, 1847, inviting 10,000 guests to his estate at Nuuanu Valley. His staff served 4,945 fish, 4,000 taro plants, 2,245 coconuts, and 241 hogs.

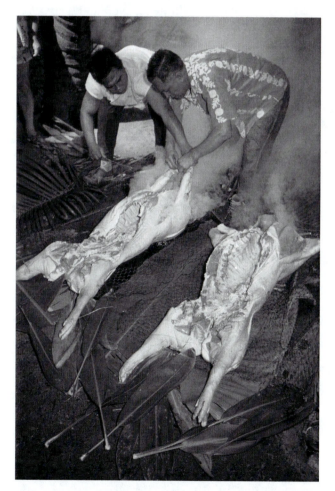

The cooks at a traditional Hawaiian luau place hot stones inside pig carcasses (*kalua*) before wrapping them in banana leaves for cooking in a sand pit (*imu*). Rubbed with herbs and covered to keep in moisture, the meat cooks underground for six or seven hours. *(B. Anthony Stewart/ National Geographic/Getty Images)*

The term *luau,* referring to a spread of indigenous foods—an appetizer of poke (sliced raw tuna or octopus and seaweed) preceding platters of chicken and taro greens baked in coconut milk—first appeared in print in 1856. Diners feasted at place settings of fern fronds and ti leaves. They ate with their fingers rather than utensils. The highest compliment to the host involved loud sucking of greasy fingers.

Hosts cooked in a ground oven known in Hawaiian as an *imu,* in Tongan as an *umu,* and in Maori as a *hangi,* a sand and hot rock pit steamer used to cook *kalua* (whole) pigs, bananas, breadfruit, sweet potatoes, chicken, and flying fish in red Hawaiian salt and banana leaves heaped with damp burlap bags. The dish of note—kalua, a pig roasted whole—was typically the event feature for its smoky aroma and savor. Islanders developed in-ground cookery to tenderize wild pig and to kill trichinella, a serious parasite. Chefs served the meat shredded in drippings along with sea snails, *inamona* (*kukui* nut relish), and *haupia,* a coconut milk pudding. Alternate desserts included *faikakai* (baked breadfruit with sugar) or *kulolo* (taro pudding).

For festivals or rituals, communities built the pit oven as the center of attention, a tradition re-created by Samoan chefs in Chicago at the World's Columbian Exposition of 1893 and on Oahu in 1945 for sailors returning from Okinawa's battlefields. Tourism encouraged the arrangement of grand shore or poolside luaus punctuated with chanting, hula, gourd drumming, and fire sword exhibitions or a Maori *haka* (warrior) dance. Chef Sam Choy, formerly of New York's Waldorf-Astoria Hotel, developed the Pacific Rim cuisine at a chain of Hawaiian restaurants and on American Airlines.

Currently, hotels in the Pacific as well as Disneyland and Sea World emulate the luau by staging the stuffing of a pig with hot stones and roasting it in the ground. Because of health restrictions, however, the staff serves kitchen-cooked pork and salty butterfish with rice. Side dishes range from *lomi-lomi* (diced salmon salad) with *poi,* a cream of baked taro corms, to imported blends of onion and tomato with wasabi (Japanese horseradish) and kalua turkey, all washed down with Samoan kava or Hawaiian mai tais. Such an evening may involve pineapple bowling with a coconut or honeydew used as the ball.

See also: Beef; Holiday Dishes and Festival Foods; Jerky; Pit Cookery; Polynesian Diet and Cuisine; Religion and Food; Taro.

Further Reading

Choy, Sam, and the Makaha Sons. *A Hawaiian Luau.* Honolulu: Mutual, 2003.

Imada, Adria L. "The Army Learns to Luau: Imperial Hospitality and Military Photography in Hawaii." *Contemporary Pacific* 20:2 (September 22, 2008): 329–362.

Lal, Brij V., and Kate Fortune. *The Pacific Islands: An Encyclopedia.* Honolulu: University of Hawai'i Press, 2000.

O'Connor, Kaori. *The Hawaiian Luau: A Cultural Biography, with Recipes.* New York: Kegan Paul International, 2008.

Lunch

Lunch receives erratic commentary throughout history, leading culinary historians to believe that cultures varied widely in the emphasis and time spent on a midday meal. After 3100 B.C.E., the Egyptians soaked bread in water to ferment *bouza* (beer), a nutritious drink that children packed for a school break. The cosmopolitan atmosphere of Imperial Rome included an "anytime" lunch at a street cookshop, where diners sat under a tarp to enjoy fried fish, olives, or a dish of stew with wine in the shade.

The New World set unique standards for a midday meal. In pre-Columbian Peru, cooks baked manioc in earth ovens alongside pork and roasted corn, three hearty foods for lunch. In contrast to a heavy lunch, Spanish conquerors admired the Aztec tortilla, which paired well with cheese, guacamole, and salsa, the typical choices of field hands and school pupils.

In the sixteenth century, open kitchens and travelers' lodgings offered early afternoon fritters, pasties (meat pies), sliced beef or mutton, soups, and turnovers. With less flair, pubs dispensed ale and a cold snack of cheese and meat. At manor houses, the privileged class received hot fish or meat served with wine. Throughout the 1700s, central European farm laborers paused at noon for ale and bread, a monotonous fortification of the body meant to last until the late-afternoon meal. Colonial Americans tended toward a meat sandwich, corn bread, raisins, fruit pie, and cider.

The Midday Meal and Business

The rise of the industrial class in the British Isles in the 1830s created a need for a portable lunch, which factory workers satisfied with tin pails filled at home with leftovers or by purchasing boiled eggs and sandwiches from lunch counters. In 1850, nutritional research addressed the need of schoolchildren for a wholesome hot meal, the impetus for the building of on-site cafeterias and formal boarding school dining rooms. In 1853, to rid New York City of young vagrants, the Children's Aid Society, under the aegis of Methodist reformer Charles Loring Brace, served America's first free school lunch at the rate of 5¢ each, underwritten by donors. Disabled children arrived at school and returned home via the society's wagon.

In the mid-1800s, lunch added family concerns to mealtime traditions. British gentry emulated the spread of filling entrées served to the family of Queen Victoria and Prince Albert. Australians developed their own version of the English shepherd's pie, a lamb dish topped with mashed potatoes. After electricity and gas increased the intimacy of the American dining room, rural families gravitated from heavy midday eating toward a substantial evening meal.

For urbanites, Walter Scott of Providence, Rhode Island, invented the lunch cart. In 1872, his horse-drawn freight wagon dispensed boiled eggs, egg or ham sandwiches on homemade bread, apple or huckleberry pie, and coffee. He capitalized on second- and third-shift constables, construction workers, journalists, and laborers, whose lunchtime varied from other consumers by eight hours. His competitors altered the lunch menu to include hot dogs, thus changing the name of their service to *dog carts.*

In the southwestern United States, the 1800s saw a flurry of Tex-Mex chili cafés offering spicy one-dish Frito pies in Oklahoma, Kansas, New Mexico, and Texas. In San Francisco, barkeeps offered free lunch to "49ers," mostly male gold miners who claimed no culinary skills and kept no kitchens. In 1872, New Orleans saloons started advertising a free lunch with the purchase of one drink. Two years later, female temperance volunteers opposed the poorly disguised lure to drinkers. Despite the gender backlash, by 1894, some 60,000 Chicago bar patrons per day received lunch from 3,000 city saloons.

Women devised their own lunchtime havens by opening tearooms, a pleasant diversion and source of female income. Menus featured fresh-brewed tea with sandwiches, pastries, puddings, scones, and tarts. At the Brown Palace in Denver, Colorado, harp music accompanied genteel sandwiches and cookie plates served with clotted cream and black tea or fruit blends, including blackberry and peach.

Global Styles

For garment districts, sweatshop workers relied on finger food—mashed potato or sauerkraut knishes (turnovers)—from coal-burning Ukrainian food carts. At the train station in Topeka, Kansas, in 1876, the Atchison, Topeka, and Santa Fe Railway initiated a chain of 47 Harvey House luncheonettes. Under British manager Fred Harvey, the eateries advertised quality menus and a genteel atmosphere appealing to ladies.

British Asia produced the word *tiffin* to describe a noontime bag or box lunch of chapatis (flatbread), curry, dal (lentils), *dosas* (crepes), or *idlis* (cakes), all suitable foods for schoolchildren, soldiers, and workers. For the elite European, in 1877, the Simplon-Orient Express began serving lunch from a restaurant car. The menu featured partridge and Turkish coffee, a rich fare outdistanced in April 1912 aboard the RMS *Titanic* by a choice of anchovies, brill, herring, ox tongue, or sardines.

For blue-collar Americans, from 1906 to 1961, the Worcester Lunch Car Company dispatched 651 custom-made railcars as wheeled diners from New England as far west as Flint, Michigan, and south to Key West, Florida. Like the Orient Express, the lunch car made its own statement about class and dining with a flashy stainless steel interior and seating on padded stools at the counter. Short-order meals ranged from chili, sandwiches, and stew to "sinkers" (doughnuts) and coffee, all priced on the menu board. Local specialties included Pennsylvania pierogis and Georgia catfish filets with cheese grits.

School Lunch

During World War I, the physical status of draftees alarmed nutritionists. Mothers agreed with scientists that urban schoolchildren should receive balanced noon meals. Schools dispensed simple entrées at a cost of 5¢ to 8¢. To a heavy allotment of bread, the addition of cocoa and milk with crackers allegedly boosted pupils' concentration and retention. Teachers superintended dining and modeled courtesy, hygiene, and table manners.

During the Great Depression, U.S. school lunches gained support from the Federal Surplus Commodities law passed on August 24, 1935. Secretary of Agriculture Henry Wallace bought surplus dairy products, pork, and wheat for use in free cafeteria meals. Between 1937 and 1939, the school districts participating in the allotment rose by 267 percent, from 3,839 to 14,075. By 1942, surplus commodities nourished 6.2 million pupils per year. For rural children bringing cold food from home, Wisconsin developed the "pint jar method," a hot water bath on the classroom stove. At the suggestion of nurse Mabel S. Stevenson, children could set glass jars of chili, cocoa, pasta, soup, and stew in the bath to maintain heat until lunchtime.

On June 4, 1946, President Harry S. Truman launched the National School Lunch Program, a uniquely popular welfare program designed to feed school pupils in all states, Guam, Puerto Rico, and the Virgin Islands. Eligibility studies revealed that children who ate no lunch had substandard reading scores. The program became the single most vital source of nutrients to poor children, invigorating 60 percent with free noon meals. Funds subsidized cafeteria pantries with new taste sensations for some children—bulgur wheat, grits, soy protein, sprouts, and yogurt, all worthy additions to the home diet.

The cost-effective feeding system rapidly replaced sack lunches. The leading demand for free lunches occurred in urban areas: Chicago, 80 percent; Atlanta, 79 percent; and New York City, 72 percent. The national effort boosted the nutrition of school-age children while supplying growers with government contracts for eggs, meat, and milk. A similar program in Jamaica, the Philippines, and Venezuela offered school cooks milk and Nutribuns, a cheap, fortified wheat roll that ensures vitamins and minerals for growing children.

During the 1960s War on Poverty, while nonwhite students from A&T College demanded service at Wool-

worth's lunch counter in Greensboro, North Carolina, school cafeterias became battlegrounds as well. Nutritionists and children's welfare advocates fought to expand free and reduced-price meals and debated commercialization via cold sandwiches and snacks purchased from vending machines. Child nutritionists protested junk food and soft drinks consumed in lieu of tax-supported plate lunches and a daily allowance of milk.

In 1972, Congress amended the National School Lunch Act and the Child Nutrition Act of 1966 to allow vending machines to compete with subsidized cafeteria food. Dealers enticed school boards to sign exclusive contracts for machines dispensing candy, chips, and cola. Even with competition from child favorites, in 1990, the U.S. federal lunch program served 24.6 million students.

Contemporary Practices

Child feeding remains prominent in the noontime logic of Japan. Mothers fill *bentos* (convenience lunches) with nori-wrapped rice balls, rolled eggs, and pickled daikon radish wrapped in bamboo leaves to accompany fish or meat.

Disposable polystyrene boxes of lunch and chopsticks sold at convenience stores, take-out franchises, and train depots accommodate workers in Hawaii, India, Korea, the Philippines, South Africa, Taiwan, and Vietnam with sushi and tempura (deep-fried entrées) and salt-and-vinegar–cured apricots, gooseberries, plums, or tamarinds for dessert. From the sharing of field lunch kits at Hawaiian pineapple and sugar plantations came the islands' plate lunch, a portable venue offering dishes of adobo (stew), barbecued ribs, beef teriyaki, fried chicken, miso butterfish, and noodle soup. Workplace buffets serve similar hot entrées and soups in Finland and Sweden and jerk pork in Jamaica and St. Croix. In Cuba, El Salvador, Nicaragua, and Panama, a common lunch dish, *gallo pinto* (spotted rooster) or *Moros y Cristianos* (Moors and Christians), pairs black beans and rice for frying in coconut oil. Cooks who lack meat to add to the mix disguise the absence by stirring in shredded coconut.

In Brazil, Colombia, Guatemala, and Santo Domingo, office workers suspend business for a two- or three-hour lunch, a substantial break for soup, a meat and rice dish, and flan, followed by a relaxed chat over coffee and pastry. Similarly, in southern France, business associates size up their clients during a 90-minute lunch. Singapore's bankers and office workers retreat to a hawker center (open-air food court) in Chinatown or downtown for a look at the entrées offered by 20 food stalls. American salad bars offer diet-conscious diners a lunch featuring pasta salad, a re-creation of potato salad with pasta, vegetables, and vinaigrette.

In Africa and the Middle East, especially during hot days, Muslim males dine apart from women. South African men eat from a common bowl with a spoon or fingers rather than utensils. In Chad, cooking requires a single fire on the ground in the middle of three rocks for the preparation of millet and sorghum gruel served with broiled perch. Diners take two hours to consume noontime stew with rice, fruit juice, yogurt, and tea. After lunch, they dawdle a bit over Arabic coffee.

In contrast to the gender-separate style of Muslims, Jewish cooks spread Sunday tables with a lunch of chicken noodle soup, roast fish, and challah bread eaten with the entire extended family. The Ecuadorian *plato típico,* a heavy, starchy meal, supplies the traditional *almuerzo,* a sit-down lunch at noon for the whole family. The substantial meal symbolizes familial durability, a cultural cornerstone shared by diners in Bengal, Finland, Germany, Guadeloupe, Hungary, Iberia, and Sweden.

Other cultures—English, Danes, Nova Scotians, Scots—prefer a light repast of a baked potato, bread and cheese, fried clam sandwich, or a protein spread, such as pâté or peanut butter. French Caribbean lunches in St. Bart's and Thai lunch counters tend toward spring rolls and chopped vegetables in rice salad seasoned with vinaigrette. American light fare leans toward grilled cheese sandwiches and tacos as well as fast-food burgers and pizza consumed with cola.

See also: Cooking Schools; Fast Food; Mustard; Pan-European Diet and Cuisine; South American Diet and Cuisine; Street Food.

Further Reading

Gannon, Martin J., and Rajnandini Pillai. *Understanding Global Cultures.* Thousand Oaks, CA: Sage, 2010.
Gunderson, Gordon W. *The National School Lunch Program: Background and Development.* New York: Nova Science, 2003.
Gutman, Richard J.S. *The Worcester Lunch Car Company.* Charleston, SC: Arcadia, 2004.
Levine, Susan. *School Lunch Politics: The Surprising History of America's Favorite Welfare Program.* Princeton, NJ: Princeton University Press, 2010.